The Direct Marketing Guide

Volume 1

The Direct Marketing Guide

Published by

The Institute of Direct Marketing
1 Park Road, Teddington, Middlesex TW11 0AR

Tel: +44 (0) 181-977 5705
Fax: +44 (0) 181-943 2535

The IDM has made every effort to ensure that all information contained in The Direct Marketing Guide is as accurate and as up-to-date as possible. However, readers will appreciate that the data is only as recent as its availability, compilation and printing schedules will allow, and is subject to change during the natural course of events. If critical, please check.

ISBN 0 9518692 6 4

Typeset by Adjuvant (PWP) Limited, Hampton, Middlesex and printed and bound in Great Britain by Mail Marketing (Bristol) Limited.

Foreword

The future success of direct marketing rests on the responsibility shown by the industry itself. Good marketers learn to adapt to an ever-changing market. With that in mind, education and training are a lifeblood to grow expertise.

"The Practitioner's Guide to Direct Marketing" was launched in 1992 to address the gap for a comprehensive reference tool. The new 1998 edition, now called "The Direct Marketing Guide", is an essential tool for every marketer's desk. With over 70% of the Guide containing new material, it spotlights best practice and the latest technology and new media available. Marketers are guided through highly practical tips, checklists and case histories, enabling businesses to avoid making expensive mistakes.

"The Direct Marketing Guide" produced by The Institute of Direct Marketing (IDM), fully supports individuals making or influencing media choices in the advertising and marketing process. Over 40 industry specialists have contributed to the Guide, providing expert advice and commentary.

Consumers demand their direct communications to be relevant and dynamic. Even the most skilful direct marketing users must be relentless in their pursuit of new and better ways of communicating, so that their work stands out from competitors'.

Whatever the skill level, the Guide helps those with limited resources and experience as well as providing state-of-the-art thinking and inspiration for those who are already highly skilled in direct marketing.

The direct marketing industry works hard to raise standards and communicate best practice. For its part, Royal Mail is committed to support industry training and offer expert advice on the direct mail advertising medium.

Use this ultimate reference tool to your advantage. We look forward to your success.

John Tew
Director and General Manager
Royal Mail

Preface

Building on success

When IDM's forerunner, The Direct Marketing Centre, conceived the first edition of this Guide, it had no idea how it would be received.

A smaller organisation than it is today, it could not afford the research and testing advocated by its own educators. Instead, it had to rely on the gut-feel of a handful of practitioners who'd spent their lives direct marketing newspapers, magazines and book series.

Those battle-scarred gurus knew that the concept had to satisfy a genuine market need. It had to offer multiple benefits just like any other successful mail order product. And it had to be British to the core, unlike most of the competitive offerings.

The result was "The Practitioner's Guide to Direct Marketing", launched in 1992 and designed to appeal to direct marketers on **four** much-needed levels: as a comprehensive reference work; as a do-it-yourself instruction manual; as a modular training course; and as a teach-yourself textbook. On all counts it was an immediate success.

Thousands of copies found their way onto direct marketers' desks all over the world. Organisations of every shape and size snapped up copies. Royal Mail, who co-founded its production, used it as a sales aid. Colleges and universities based their emerging direct marketing programmes on its contents. Hundreds of students gained their Diplomas with its help. And new businesses made it their marketing text of first choice.

Inevitably, the 800-page first edition, now dog-eared with use in most cases, passed its sell-by date as new technology and new techniques entered the direct marketer's armoury. It was time to start again – and this time IDM researched it thoroughly.

Who had bought the first edition? Not much to fix there. Everyone in the business was represented: agencies, bureaux, printers and researchers were using it to train their burgeoning staffs. Direct marketing organisations bought it for its operational checklists and ready-reference capability. Traditional marketers from spheres as diverse as agriculture and heavy engineering looked to it to open their minds to the "new" discipline. 20% of the buyers were directors. 30% of the users admitted to being students on the threshold of a lucrative career.

So could it be better? Yes! was the unanimous response – and there was almost unanimous agreement on what improvements should be made. More of the same was the consensus, but with **many more case studies, examples, and illustrations**. A more efficient index was a frequent request – and a glossary of terms would be invaluable, said a large percentage of respondents. Not surprisingly, six years on, there were calls for more on the techniques and technology that barely existed when the first edition went to print.

This, the second edition now called simply "The Direct Marketing Guide" (you don't have to be a practitioner to make it work for you), has it all. The product of old-fashioned gut-feel and practical experience, coupled to state-of-the-art customer feedback, it has been updated to take account of the many developments in direct marketing that have evolved in recent years.

To demonstrate that this last claim is no lazy puff, here is a selection of the new topics included in these three volumes:

> new industry usage statistics – retail and fmcg applications – 9-page planning case study – new chapter on loyalty and retention programmes – 9 market research studies – new testing methodology – profit and loss calculations – data modelling and mining – new software packages – new advice on profiling and segmentation – direct response TV and radio – the Internet – new case studies on exporting by direct mail – expanded section on creativity with numerous examples – new personalisation equipment – revised price guidelines – more on telephone – a complete listing of Royal Mail services – update on the Data Protection Act – new comprehensive 670-word index – new over 45-page glossary.

Once again, IDM would like to thank all the experts who lent their precious time, and gave their knowledge, for education and the greater good of the industry. To the 18 first-time contributors, a renewed apology for stripping out some of the jargon and expanding on their explanations; please remember many readers will not yet have embraced our quirky industry – some will not use English as their first language. And a special thank you to Royal Mail for once more helping to make the project viable.

We estimate that some 70% of this edition is entirely new. Our mission, however, is decidedly not new – best summed up in this reprise from the original:

> During production we had many discussions about the positioning we should adopt for our new product. One school argued strongly that we should concentrate on the financial savings and additional profit you could anticipate as the result of equipping each of your staff with a personal copy. Another school argued for a platform based on making life easier, speeding the processes, reducing errors and generally raising standards – the professional approach.
>
> Finally we chose a platform based upon knowledge and power. If knowledge is power – and surely it is the ultimate power – then you have in your hands a very powerful instrument indeed.
>
> Be sure to use it every day.

This is a book to be **used**. If its over 1,200 pages are not well-thumbed, and its spines not groaning from exertion when the contents are next due for revision, then one of us is doing something wrong. If it's us, be sure to let us know.

Bryan Halsey
Editor

Acknowledgements

A word from The IDM

Over the last five years a copy of The Practitioner's Guide to Direct Marketing has never been more than four feet away from my desk and it is now somewhat dog-eared with notes scribbled in the margin. I've lost count of the number of times I have used it to answer questions, check practical details, help callers to The IDM, spark ideas and develop content for our course programmes. So perhaps you can appreciate my enthusiasm for this 2nd edition!

But you need more than enthusiasm to develop and produce a work of this range and depth, and it is with thanks and appreciation that I'm pleased to acknowledge the contributions of the following companies and individuals:

- ✔ Royal Mail, which played a key role in sponsoring the development of the Guide.
- ✔ Bryan Halsey, our editor, who allowed his golf handicap to take second place whilst he edited the specialist contributions from all our authors and consultants.
- ✔ To those same authors and consultants who patiently allowed us to pick their brains, craft their words and edit ruthlessly.
- ✔ To Glen Greenhill whose creative input resulted in the cover and page layout, and to Anne Cowlin who DTP'd every word.
- ✔ Finally, to The Mail Marketing Group, who supported our print and production process and ensured it was delivered to those for whom it was created – you.

With so many people and so much detail involved, we couldn't have achieved it without our dedicated and cheerful Project Manager, Emma Reed. She has been Bryan's right hand woman, enthused and supported contributors and offered a calm channel of communication for all parties. Her ideas, attention to detail and hard work have ensured that all those associated with the Guide can be proud of it. *Everyone* has asked me to thank her.

Bryan Halsey writes that an updated edition was essential because every aspect of direct marketing is evolving so rapidly. Predictions are that this will continue. So please, use the reply card in Volume One to give us your feedback. We'd like to include **your** ideas in our next edition.

Caroline Robertson
Programme Director

Explanation of icons used throughout this Guide

Case study or example

Checklist

Definition

Further reading

Money saver

Quotation

Remember

Tip

Warning

Contents

Volume 1

Chapter 1.1

How marketing went direct

This chapter includes:

- How the computer changed everything
- New method, old principle
- The advent of automated decision-making
- Reasons for mass marketing's decline
- The consumer, an individual once more
- Business buyers face more choice
- So what is direct marketing?
- Usage and acceptance statistics
- Where now? Examples of database potential

New idea? New industry? Neither, says Graeme McCorkell, we're talking new technology. A new method, not a new principle – and the computer made the difference. The direct marketer's ability to master information technology's potential allows us to talk once more to customers as individuals, just as Victorian shopkeepers did a century ago, knowing each customer's personal likes and dislikes and responding in ways, and at times, which suit them.

In this opening chapter of what is predominantly a practical guide, McCorkell sets the scene with a succinct review of the discipline's unstoppable history; its uses, benefits, and essential differences. You'll also find some statistics that demonstrate its growing popularity and acceptance (no doubt these will be surpassed by the time we go to press, such is direct marketing's phenomenal acceleration), plus a selection of thought-provoking case studies.

In conclusion, the author restates the case for more professionalism in our handling of the powerful tools we have at our disposal.

New in this edition. The latest definition of direct marketing; latest available statistics from The Henley Centre; new hypothetical studies showing how the database can be used in retailing, business-to-business, and packaged goods applications.

Graeme McCorkell, Author and Consultant

Graeme began his marketing career as a fast-moving consumer goods specialist. Then, in 1962, he found himself landed with his first mail order client. He quickly discovered that direct response was more interesting – if somewhat more nerve-wracking – than less measurable TV awareness campaigns. In 1970 he became a full-time direct marketing consultant working for McCann Erickson, Encyclopaedia Britannica and American Express.

In 1976, with two partners, he formed the direct marketing agency McCorkell, Sidaway & Wright (MSW) which grew to a payroll of over a hundred and numbered among its clients the AA, Abbey National, Encyclopaedia Britannica, GUS, IBM, Renault, Sun Alliance and TSB. In 1987, having sold out to the US direct group Rapp & Collins, he returned to full-time consultancy. Since then his ideas for marketing cars, credit, magazines and mail order have travelled around the world – not always with his permission!

More recently Graeme has chaired the Institute of Direct Marketing, lectured in the UK, US, France, Germany, Switzerland and Australia, been database consultant to a leading advertising agency, and authored two industry standard textbooks: "Advertising That Pulls Response" (McGraw-Hill) and "Direct and Database Marketing" (IDM). When not working he can be found walking in his beloved Shropshire where he has returned to live.

Chapter 1.1

How marketing went direct

How the computer changed everything

Growing out of direct distribution by mail order companies, magazine publishers and book clubs, "direct marketing" has become a blanket term for all kinds of targeted and accountable marketing activity whose aim is to **begin and foster enduring relationships between seller and end-user**.

Reasons for its growth and popularity among businesses are not hard to find. More and more companies came to recognise that their success depends on sharpening their focus on customer needs. This alone might have been enough. Then came the growing awareness that **profit depends more on the loyalty of established customers than on constantly trying to acquire new ones**. The proliferation of choice available to customers, which continues to create hard-to-reach niche markets and sows the seeds of brand promiscuity, might have been what tipped the scales.

Yet the enormous growth in direct marketing was fuelled more by what the computer made possible than by any external marketing influence. Without the technology to identify and recognise the potential value of each individual customer, the mere desire to do so would not have been enough. Marketing people rightly became entranced with the possibilities. It soon became clear that no company without a sophisticated end-user database could hope to compete successfully with one that had such a facility. Not only would its ability to communicate with its customers be restricted, but its management information would be impoverished.

No company without a sophisticated end-user database can hope to compete successfully with one that has such a facility.

New method, old principle

In the 1930s, sample surveys of consumer behaviour and opinions gained ground, allowing marketing decisions to be increasingly **informed by fact**. By the 1950s, most packaged consumer goods markets were covered by retail audits and consumer panel research on a continuous basis. In the same decade, Dr Ernest Dichter pioneered qualitative research into the underlying attitudes that determined and explained consumer behaviour.

We can see, therefore, that the use of one-to-one marketing databases to provide management with information to aid decisions is **not a departure in principle** from what has gone before. What is new is the ability to substitute measurements about the behaviour of a complete customer universe – and of all the individuals within it – for old-style research amongst a small, often biased sample of customers. What is also new is the ability to select individual customers and groups who behave in a particular way and accord them different treatment from customers and groups who behave differently.

And now . . . automated decision-making

We have now entered the age of automated marketing decision systems in which the timing and content of a communication to an individual customer can be driven not by a manager, but triggered by a recorded change in the customer's circumstances or behaviour. In many cases this change is noted mathematically by dynamic scoring software. Thus, a single decision to mail or telephone a large group of customers all at one time is being replaced by thousands, even millions, of decisions to **mail or telephone individual customers at the right time**. That is, the right time for each individual customer – with, of course, the right message.

Far from diminishing the role of the manager, such advances are enhancing it. An automated decision system must be designed to fit a manager's specification. Its possibilities are almost endless, restricted only by the manager's imagination and the imaginations of his advisers.

Reasons for mass marketing's demise

For the benefit of new students it might be as well if we recap quickly on the reasons for the decline of mass marketing:

- ✗ **The service based economy.** The products consumers buy today are almost all functional, reliable, affordable, and increasingly alike. Consumers look, therefore, for distinction in refinements and added value service.

- ✗ **A new social order.** Old social structures have been dismantled as people of all ages strive to express their individuality through their lifestyles, which in turn influence their choice of products and suppliers.

- ✗ **The heterogeneous society.** Today nobody is "typical". The nuclear family is now a minority group. Long ago it became impossible to target families using mass media without reaching more non-family readers or viewers.

- ✗ **Home owning, isolation and security.** More and more people own their homes and consequently spend more time within their four walls. Excursions are made almost exclusively by car – with an inevitable effect on what and how things are bought.

- ✗ **The age of experiment.** Paradoxically, people are travelling further and mixing more with other cultures. This influences the food they eat, the way they dress, even the design of their homes and gardens. Result: hundreds of new niche markets where none existed before.

- ✗ **Easier ways to pay.** The growth of cashless transactions has made possible scientific data-collection and targeting on a hitherto unimaginable scale – as well as helping customers to pay.

- ✗ **Redistribution of income.** Despite political claims and counter-claims, most consumers today have more money to spend than in previous generations. What they haven't saved they are more easily able to borrow.

- ✗ **The shift to distributor power.** Economic power in modern business continues to shift in the direction of distributors and service providers, the organisations most able to capture and benefit from customer information.

Diners Club	1950
Visa	1958
American Express	1958
Barclaycard	1966
Access	1972
Store cards, eg M&S	1985
Club cards, eg Tesco, Sainsbury's	1995

- ✗ **The splintering of media audiences.** VCRs, cable, satellite and digital TV, coupled to falling viewing figures, mean smaller niche audiences. Similar fragmentation is affecting the printed media, while the Internet has begun to distract audience attention. This splintering has been on-going since the early '80s.

> Since 1980 our advertising expenditure has grown more than 100%, but our media weight has declined by 25% ... to achieve the same weight as in 1980 must take £10 million a year more now.
>
> – Eric Nicoli, MD, UB Brands, 1988

- ✗ **The weakening of brand loyalty.** Increasing choice and awareness have led to a loss of what might be termed old-fashioned brand loyalty; today loyalty has to be earned and nurtured, a function for which direct marketing is ideally suited.

Let's summarise

For a host of reasons all undeniable, none stoppable, the consumer has become once more an INDIVIDUAL. Targeted marketing will INEVITABLY continue to replace mass marketing, in the process becoming more LONG-TERM in its orientation. One day most if not all marketing will be DIRECT marketing.

Business buyers face more choice

Business buyers, too, now have to select from an ever-expanding inventory of alternatives, the differences often becoming extremely subtle, while the time available to make increasingly complex decisions has diminished. **As a result, buyers have become intolerant of poorly directed and presented information and demand relevant information in a form that can be absorbed quickly.** They do not want to spend half an hour dragging out of a salesperson information which they could have got in five minutes from a printed communication, over the telephone, or via the Internet.

Not surprisingly, many of the new and especially successful exponents of direct and database marketing are to be found among business-to-business users as other contributors to this Guide will demonstrate.

So what IS direct marketing?

Faced with so much evidence for its success, is it necessary for us to define direct marketing? Well, yes, it is. Without a definition it is impossible to determine what is and what is not direct marketing. And if we cannot do that, then how can we measure its progress? And if we didn't want to measure its progress, we wouldn't be direct marketers.

But defining direct marketing presents a number of difficulties. Each new book, each new training course, tends to turn up yet another definition – with frequently yet another alternative title. Let us look, therefore, at some of these descriptions as they not only help to describe what we do – they also show how direct marketing has developed and where it's headed.

Direct response advertising. The original term firmly rooted in response to advertising, chiefly press advertising. Solely concerned with the acquisition of customers with no suggestions of retention or loyalty building.

Direct mail marketing. Emphasised the medium at the expense of the goals, but showed the growing importance of what we now call the personal media.

Direct marketing. Coined in 1961 by one of the industry's foremost gurus, Lester Wunderman. But his interpretation concentrated on "direct" as a method of distribution rather than as a means of gathering and using information.

Data-driven marketing. Introduced by pundits to emphasise the empirical basis of modern direct marketing. Unfortunately all marketing was by then driven by data of some sort.

Database marketing. A term that survives as a synonym for direct marketing, pointing up its foundation in individual customer data; a term which may well displace "direct" before the next edition of this Guide.

Relationship/loyalty marketing. Reflecting the fact that the thrust of direct marketing activity has turned to retention of hard-won customers but tends to exclude the important process of acquiring suitable customers in the first place.

Direct marketing. Has outlived all of its rivals to date, partly for reasons of establishment and partly, one suspects, because of its connotations of pro-activity and dynamism.

And how should we define it?

Many attempts have been made to define "Direct Marketing", most of them failing to embrace all the diverse activities carried out under its umbrella. The Institute of Direct Marketing itself unashamedly revises its favoured version periodically, which is now as follows:

Direct Marketing produces or uses data from interactions with customers or prospects in order to target marketing activity, generate continuing business and maintain control over marketing expenditure.

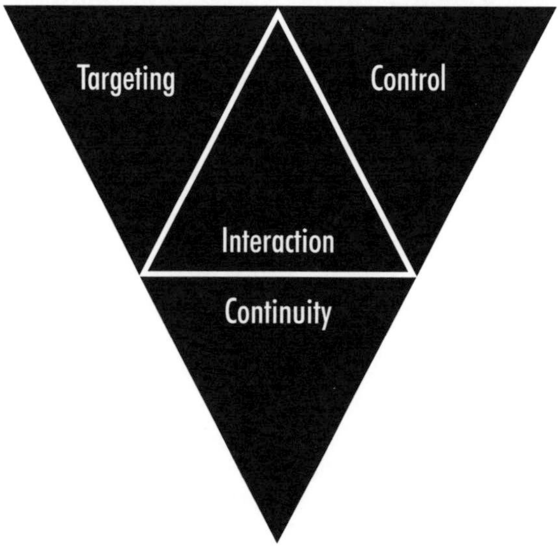

The cornerstones of direct marketing are, therefore, targeting, interaction, continuity and control (TICC), themes which we shall return to throughout this Guide.

Targeting – who will be interested?

Interaction – how did they respond before?

Control – what was the return on the investment?

Continuity – how can we further the relationship?

The beauty of the foregoing is that it encompasses the marketing activity of any organisation, large or small, which maintains on a PC or mainframe computer a list of customers together with details of their past transactions and other information, in order to drive future customer transactions.

So how successful is direct marketing?

There are three ways of measuring growth, usage and acceptance of direct marketing:

- ✔ Expenditure
- ✔ Usage and users
- ✔ Acceptance and attitudes

Expenditure – who spends what?

Attempts to quantify expenditure on direct marketing are bedevilled by the problems of definition as we have mentioned. What is and what is not direct marketing? Does every advertisement that includes a method of contacting the advertiser qualify? If so, do we include classified advertisements? Do we include product packs with advice lines? And how do we quantify and account for what is spent on the management of customer information systems that may be used for a number of purposes? How to rate call centres that deal with service calls as well as marketing calls? And should the cost of staff as well as direct costs be included?

For example, our definition should not include the advertising of a manufacturer who merely offers a brochure and a list of stockists; but if some effort were made to discover the results of sending out brochures and to improve the efficiency of the advertising or fulfilment as a result, it surely should be included.

The problem is that direct marketing is a **qualitative** description. It is not possible to quantify it accurately or easily in the way we can quantify expenditure on TV advertising or direct mail. Even if we could, what direct marketing costs is less important than what it achieves.

The UK expenditure on direct communications

The 1997 DMA Census of the UK Direct Marketing Industry concluded that a total of £6,192 million was spent on direct marketing communications in 1996, approximately 55% in personally addressed and 45% in non-personal media.

Direct marketing expenditure by type of medium – 1996

Medium	Expenditure (£ million)	Share of total	Source
Personal media			
Direct Mail *	1,489	24.05	Royal Mail
Telemarketing *	1,305	21.07	BT/Marketing Magazine
Database marketing	602	9.72	DMA/Henley Centre
Contract magazines	26	0.42	DMA
Sub-total	**3,422**	**55.26**	
Non-personal media			
Door-to-door	264.0	4.26	AHD
Inserts	249.5	4.03	News International
Press display †	624.0	10.08	DMA Monitor
Magazine display †	519.0	8.38	DMA Monitor
Regional display †	346.0	5.59	DMA
Television	551.0	8.9	Channel 4/Laser
Radio	100.0	1.61	R.A.B.
Cinema	3.0	0.05	Rank Screen
Outdoor/transport	51.0	0.82	Maiden Outdoor/ London Transport
New media	63.0	1.02	DMA
Sub-total	**2,770.5**	**44.74**	
All DM communications ‡	**6,192.5**	**100.00**	

* Includes figures for catalogues

† Display advertising only, ie not including classified, reader offers, etc

‡ Omits costs of data management

Source: DMA 1997 Census of Direct Marketing

NB: The above table was derived from aggregated estimates provided by various sources for individual media and is no better than a reasonable assumption. It is not possible to show trend data since no previous estimate is entirely comparable. The totals will almost certainly have increased since 1996.

Users and usage – 277 million responses

The second best measure of direct's growth and popularity is its usage by businesses and consumers alike.

Figures for business usage are notoriously difficult to compile, but today almost every business uses direct marketing (or its techniques) in some form or other. Very soon it will be used by virtually every business.

In 1995, in the United States, some 19 million people (almost 8% of the workforce) were estimated to be employed as a result of direct marketing. That number is expected to grow to 23 million (9.7%) by the year 2000.

In some UK industries, insurance for example, direct activity, once a small segment of the market, now represents the mainstream. Catalogue activity has for many years accounted for as much as 10% of all non-food/non-petrol retailing expenditure, and still continues to grow. And, in the US, even food catalogues proliferate, serving a wide variety of "tastes", literally.

Who responds to direct marketing?

A study by The Henley Centre conducted in 1995 found that 83% of UK adults participated as advertising or market research respondents in the previous twelve months. Over 277 million responses were received in all, the large majority being straightforward enquiries or orders for commercial goods and services – the first stage in developing an on-going relationship.

The table below shows how UK consumers related to the main types of direct activities:

How UK adults participated in direct activities (1995)

Activity	% adults participating	Average number of participations
Filled in application for goods or services	48	2.33
Completed questionnaire for money-off coupons or on guarantee form	41	3.02
Participated in market research	54	1.62
Phoned about goods or services	39	3.25
Responded to advertisement	45	2.91

Source: The Henley Centre, 1995

These results suggest that the proportion of the population responding to advertisements, applying direct for goods or services, and/or telephoning their enquiries is already significant, approaching almost 50% in some situations.

Acceptance and attitudes – 80% say "Try me"

The usage figures compiled by The Henley Centre (above) tell their own story. In the same study, The Henley Centre concluded that 80% of the population could be described as pragmatists, people who would be willing to provide personal data in exchange for a clear benefit or the promise of such a benefit. And most of us know from our own experience that Tesco and Safeway shoppers show no resistance to carrying "identity cards" when the benefits are clear.

Direct marketing appears to offer a better fit for the more thoughtful, canny market of the 1990s than it did for the expansive '80s. Now, as suspicion about computer-held personal data fades, the portents for the future appear excellent.

What about business attitudes?

In the first edition of this Practitioner's Guide we suggested there were **three prerequisites** for the continued growth of direct marketing. They were:

✔ Universal acceptance of direct marketing as a legitimate and logical marketing activity.

✔ Widespread knowledge of its precise functions and how these dovetail with other marketing activities.

✔ Availability of sufficient direct marketing physical resources and professional skills.

Since that time, progress has been made on all three fronts but there are still battles to win. Inevitably there is a time lag between the occurrence of a practical possibility, its widespread realisation, and eventual application.

For example, direct marketing practitioners foresaw the use of direct marketing in the automotive industry and, linked to EPOS, in retailing, some years before car makers and retailers seized on the opportunities IT development had dropped in their laps. Even today the potential is not being fully realised.

The easiest time to get managers to accept change is when it is forced upon them by the actions of more far-sighted competitors, the situation which now prevails in most markets. **The 1990s have seen direct marketing move to the forefront of senior marketers' thinking in many of the largest companies.** These managers have been swept along by the tide of technology and the gale force wind from above demanding faster and more assured returns on marketing investments.

Conventional advertising gets a bad press

Advertising investments that are not directly accountable have had a bad press in the 1990s. Meanwhile, loyalty marketing and customer service have enjoyed a very good press. Perhaps one of the most devastating comments on traditional thinking appeared in 1991 in the Harvard Business Review:

> Advertising serves no useful purpose. The new marketing requires a feedback loop; it is this that is missing from the monologue of advertising but is built into the dialogue of marketing.
>
> – Regis McKenna, HBR, 1991

That conclusion is so important, we ought to find room to repeat it. Try rewriting it in your own words, it will help you to remember it.

> Advertising serves no useful purpose. The new marketing requires a feedback loop; it is this that is missing from the monologue of advertising but is built into the dialogue of marketing.
>
> – Regis McKenna, HBR, 1991

Database companies come out on top

In the Marketing Council Survey of 373 senior marketers (1995), **increased customer focus was considered to be the most critical factor in ensuring future success**, being mentioned by 59% of respondents. The other most frequent mentions were of **creativity** (34%) and **quality** (21%).

In the same survey, respondents were asked which companies they most admired for their **historical** reputation in marketing. Perhaps not surprisingly, the four most admired companies were Procter & Gamble, Unilever, Coca Cola and Mars.

Asked which companies they most admired for their **present-day** reputations in marketing, they rated Virgin, British Airways, Tesco and Direct Line as the top four.

Historically, all the top-rated companies were packaged goods manufacturers, big TV spenders and heavy sales promotion users. **The new top four are all primarily service companies and all maintain customer databases.** Historically, no direct marketing company or financial service company appeared in the top twenty. Tesco leapfrogged Marks & Spencer and Sainsbury following the introduction of the Tesco Clubcard.

In the DMA's Dataculture study by The Henley Centre, 87% of respondents **believed a marketing database was critical to future success** and 69% **said their customers would be happy to volunteer personal information** in exchange for better service – rather less than the percentage suggested by customers themselves, as we saw earlier. Are business people lagging behind customers?

The users of direct and database marketing

By the mid-1990s direct marketing was a well-established method of trading for a large number of organisations. Without making any value judgements we can legitimately classify applications into three broad categories:

1. **Stand alone**, ie organisations that have virtually no other means of transacting business other than direct communications and direct distribution.

   Examples: the major catalogue and office supplies companies; telephone-based financial services organisations, eg First Direct and Direct Line.

2. **Integrated**, ie where organisations have alternative ways of transacting business but use their databases to make direct offers and/or support other activities. These are frequently organisations whose databases were originally built as a by-product of another activity such as accounting control.

   Examples: the traditional banks and building societies; travel and tourist businesses; motor manufacturers; the Automobile Association; almost all business-to-business users.

3. **Peripheral**, increasingly used by organisations who cannot readily capture data on all their individual customers.

   Examples: some retailers (a few have recently switched to a more integrated approach, eg Tesco); some packaged goods manufacturers, eg Pedigree Petfoods and Kraft General Foods.

In the three hypothetical cases, commencing on the facing page, we show how more use could be made of an individual customer database in three different scenarios: retail, business-to-business, and packaged goods. We can see how readily the database could be integrated into every sphere of the companies' businesses.

Where now?

Encouraging as the new uses and the changes in attitude are, there is still some distance to go before a genuine understanding of individual customer focus and its implications for one-to-one relationship marketing is achieved. **There is a world of difference between a loyalty promotion and the adoption of a zero-defections customer strategy.** The former is artificial, external and easily replicable by competition. The latter involves internal reorganisation, the abandonment of departmental objectives and a commitment to continuous improvement of the product-service package.

While it can be argued that there is scope for direct marketing to develop independently of the adoption of true customer focus, **development will be quicker and more assured with the recognition that the behaviour of individual customers can be tracked and influenced with the aid of modern information technology**. It is this recognition that leads to the database becoming the central marketing information resource. Only when the database is seen in this light will personal marketing communications take precedence.

Meanwhile, it is clear that **interest in interactive marketing continues to grow apace**. Marketers are becoming increasingly fascinated by its possibilities. The Internet has provoked much comment and interest. Telephone-based customer service, as exemplified by First Direct and Direct Line, has established a strong reputation for accessibility, service quality, customer satisfaction and effectiveness in establishing committed customer relationships.

Future marketing will be based on individual customer focus. There can be no retreat from what has come about through technological advance. There will be no return to the wasteful mass marketing methods of the past.

Are you sure you're not making these mistakes?

As direct marketers we must still strive to introduce the concept of total quality into **everything** we do. Direct marketing works when it recognises the customer's individuality and accords to that customer the recognition he or she deserves. **If our file selection is wrong so that our messages are inaccurately directed, we are not only wasting money, we are wasting someone else's time.** If our data is inaccurate, we cause further irritation by making unwarrantable assumptions about the recipient of our message. What could be more unflattering than to exhibit our ignorance of the customer's circumstances in such an unmistakable fashion?

Retailing applications

Modern stores employ EPOS or EFTPOS (electronic point-of-sale) terminals, giving the customer an itemised printout of the transaction. The terminals form part of an information loop that provides accounting and stock-control data. All that is usually missing is the identity of the shopper. The missing link to the customer can be joined by means of a membership scheme ...

An obvious advantage is the ability to poll customers on added-value services, changes of opening hours and levels of satisfaction with various aspects of the shopping package. Involving customers in the planning and enhancement of service and range leads to greater customer commitment and this is closely related to loyalty ...

A less obvious motivation for collecting individual customer data is that the store which knows who its customers are also knows who its customers are not. This is because the locations of customers can be plotted, so arriving at a clear definition of the catchment area ... It does not take a marketing genius to work out that it is more efficient to employ sales promotion and other techniques to entice identified non-customers from the primary catchment area than to make offers to the world at large. Making offers to the world at large means that most of them will be redeemed by regular customers ...

High-spending customers can be profiled. For example, families may spend more than single occupants. People within prosperous postcodes may spend more. This information can be derived from the transactional histories of regular shoppers. Now it becomes possible to target similar people within each catchment area segment.

The customer's 'phone number may be selected and dialled automatically, a screen showing the telemarketer who he or she is about to talk to and why the computer thinks the customer has defected. The computer may even advise the telemarketer what offer to make, according to the customer's previous value.

The technology to permit relationship marketing of this level of sophistication has been in place for years. You, the reader, may find it extraordinary that a store whose customers may spend £2,500 a year each with it doesn't collect and use such information assiduously ... The same customers may spend one-tenth of this amount with a mail order company. Yet this company will use automated decision systems to drive mailed or telephone messages to defecting customers. The difference in attitude is surely explained by history and habit. People find it hard to stop doing what used to be so successful for so many years. Now the wastage inherent in mass marketing methods is no longer acceptable.

Extracted and abridged from
"Direct and Database Marketing", Graeme McCorkell (IDM)

Business-to-business applications

It is sometimes overlooked that the purchasing power of businesses varies enormously. One company may have several thousand times the purchasing power of another ... If ever there has been such a being as an "average" consumer, there has never been an average business customer ...

In most markets it is practical to capture the identities of the companies that account for 80% or more of the market in value terms. If the business marketer supplies these large companies direct, it is possible to maintain a full transactional history for each customer, estimate the share of the customer's purchases that is leaking to competitors, and identify up-trading or cross-selling opportunities. It is also possible to target those large companies that are providing no business, even estimating their potential value in advance.

It all appears delightfully simple. Unfortunately it is not. The first complication may be internal. We may be negotiating sales through more than one channel. We may have more than one technical sales team with different teams specialising in different product lines. They may be dealing with different departments of the same client company. We may also maintain an inbound telemarketing department that takes orders for lower value items and, perhaps, an outbound team that sells such items over the telephone. Some customers may mail, fax or deliver orders electronically.

All of these sales channels are in a position to collect customer data and, if they have free access to the marketing database, to corrupt data by replacing correct information with erroneous information. Maintaining the integrity of customer information and clear rules of customer contact requires good management.

Externally, the complications are even greater. Large companies have their own ways of doing business and these ways may be as numerous as the names on the customer file. In-depth customer knowledge is essential. Furthermore, many purchasing decisions are not made by a single individual.

We may depend on our sales or telemarketing teams to collect the names and job titles of the real decision-makers. This means we must give them rights of access, though not necessarily direct access, to the database. We need a quality control procedure to ensure they don't enter incorrect information ...

We may also want to communicate with decision influencers and end-users in the client company. Business marketing is becoming increasingly collaborative and we may wish to consult end-users on how we can improve the product or the service support. It is a major task to identify these people but, if the company's business is worth hundreds of thousands of pounds, it is a task worth undertaking ...

We need what Regis McKenna, in "Relationship Marketing" (1991), describes as a feedback loop so that we can see how the business relationship is developing.

Extracted and abridged from
"Direct and Database Marketing", Graeme McCorkell (IDM)

Packaged goods applications

If heavy users could be identified, if repeat-purchasing could be stimulated and if cross-selling opportunities could be exploited, the high cost of one-to-one file building and contact could be clawed back.

The tobacco and drinks industries were influenced by the fear of an advertising ban. They saw the longer-term future of direct marketing as an alternative to conventional media advertising ...

Others, for example Pedigree Petfoods, became interested because they saw their media costs rising, while coverage and frequency fell ...

Finally, some smaller or newer manufacturers saw direct marketing as an alternative channel of distribution. They were shut out by the large corporations which had sewn up the available shelf space. One successful pioneer was Giorgio of Beverly Hills, using scent-strip inserts in magazines to sample their fragrance. Readers of the inserts could order direct ...

Consumer information and communications can be used to undertake selective sales promotion, to target competitive brand users, to reinforce brand values, to sell direct, to provide superior product information and advice, and to establish and strengthen relationships with users. They can also be used to cross-sell, introducing users of one brand to others from the same stable. Everything depends upon the gearing that can be obtained on the initial expense of data gathering and the subsequent expense of one-to-one communications ...

If customer values are sufficiently high, the investment can readily be justified. If not, it may be justified by spreading the investment across a portfolio of brands ...

It is impossible for the fmcg manufacturer who does not sell direct to maintain a transactional database of all the end-users ...

The best the fmcg company can do is maintain a transactional record of a sample of data-captured customers. One method is to have these identified as a subset on a consumer panel sample. This allows the fmcg manufacturer to follow the direct marketing discipline of control. By tracking the behaviour of a sample of customers, the behaviour of other like-minded and similarly treated customers may be inferred ...

Consumer names may also be collected through advertising, from telephone advice lines, from recommend-a-friend offers and other media. Multi-media sourcing is most often employed because it is extremely difficult to collect data about enough consumers through any one mechanism ...

Extracted and abridged from
"Direct and Database Marketing", Graeme McCorkell (IDM)

The adoption of industry standards of ethical behaviour is the easy part of this process. **The hard part is ensuring our messages are relevant and that our service to prospects and customers is impeccable.** It is not the ethical lapses of the occasional get-rich-quick entrepreneur that threaten the future of direct marketing; it is the mundane failures to spell recipients' names correctly, to deliver products and brochures on time and to avoid offering credit to 17-year-olds. These are what cause most irritation and adverse comment.

Direct marketing is about treating consumers or business prospects as real individuals, not as Mr and Mrs Average. It cannot work if it is driven by inaccurate data or slipshod production. Recipients do not make allowances for our mistakes. They see our assumed knowledge as a pretence.

The more dazzling the array of statistical, data processing and production techniques available to us, the more skill is required to apply them intelligently and with care. **The more precise our targeting technique, the greater the penalty when it goes wrong.**

This Guide is dedicated to helping practitioners of the new marketing, that is direct marketing, to practise their craft efficiently and effectively. Happy reading!

Food for thought

To close this introduction we highlight the Toyota company: a quotation from Womack Jones & Roos from their report "The Machine That Changed The World":

> Toyota was determined never to lose a former buyer ... it could minimise the chance of this happening by using its consumer database to predict what Toyota buyers would want next ...
>
> ... Unlike mass-producers who conduct evaluation clinics and other survey research on randomly selected buyers ... Toyota went directly to its existing customers in planning new products ... established customers were treated as members of the Toyota family.
>
> – Womack Jones & Roos: "The Machine That Changed The World"

Chapter 1.2

Planning your direct marketing strategy

This chapter includes:

- **The 9 major benefits of a good strategic plan**
- **Structure of a marketing plan, with model**
- **The creative contribution to planning**
- **Analysing your current situation**
- **Analysing customer's needs and wants**
- **Planning your business objectives**
- **The 7 sub-objectives for improving profitability**
- **Objectives, strategies and tactics – how they differ**
- **11-page financial services case study**

Many learned textbooks have been written around the subject of marketing planning, although some sceptics still insist that strategic planning is no more than commonsense: a simple matching of opportunities to resources – as if it were that easy! Direct marketing, however, is no longer merely a tactical tool to be used sporadically without regard for its broad long-term potential. Its strategic potential is now beyond question and its application requires skilful management – as several authors in this Guide will demonstrate.

In this chapter, Derek Holder and Tony Watson talk you through a typical direct marketing plan, beginning with the questions you must ask about your own organisation: your current market position, your products and services, your customers, your financial track record, and your resources. Once you know **where you are**, you'll be better placed to say **where you want to be**, and – this is where the strategy comes in – **how you propose to get there**.

For newcomers to marketing, Holder and Watson provide an impeccable lesson. But who among us, even though we may call ourselves old hands, can fail to benefit from having such an easy-to-follow route map close at hand?

New in this edition. A nine-page detailed study of how a leading financial services organisation drew up a strategic plan to increase its share of a niche market.

Derek Holder, Managing Director, Institute of Direct Marketing

Derek graduated from Manchester University (BSc) before taking marketing posts with British Airways and Ford. He then became Marketing Manager of McGraw-Hill, the publishers, and subsequently of The Reader's Digest Association.

In 1980 he was appointed Senior Lecturer and then Principal Lecturer of the Kingston Business School (now part of Kingston University), before founding the organisation now known as the Institute of Direct Marketing in 1987. In 1997 he was invested as Professor of Direct Marketing, Kingston University, the first such post in the UK.

As Principal and Managing Director of the Institute, Derek has developed numerous courses, seminars, in-company training schemes, and undergraduate and postgraduate programmes in direct marketing, and is personally responsible for creating the hugely successful Diploma in Direct Marketing, the world's first professional qualification in the discipline.

He still finds time to train many of the thousands of students and marketing professionals who attend the Institute's courses each year. His commitment to the professionalism of direct marketing extends to his growing family of staff, to whom he provides great inspiration and leadership and for whom he still finds time to act as mentor and guardian.

Professor Derek Holder M IDM
Managing Director
The Institute of Direct Marketing
1 Park Road
Teddington
Middlesex TW11 0AR
Tel: 0181-977 5705

Tony Watson, Managing Director, Lowe Direct

Tony graduated from Manchester University and, after a year in Italy, joined MacMillan Publishers to help promote their non-fiction titles. In New York, as Marketing Manager for the "New Grove Dictionary of Music" ($2,000 per set), he was introduced to direct marketing. Back in the UK he held senior marketing positions for MacMillan and McGraw-Hill before making his move to the agency scene.

After seven years with DDM, a Top 5 direct marketing agency, he joined Option One Direct as Client Services Director, where his accounts included the launch of First Direct. In 1991 he became Managing Director and the agency was relaunched as CGT Direct which, by 1995, had joined direct marketing's Top 10 agencies, with the GM Card, National Savings, RAC and The Daily Telegraph among his clients.

In 1996, with three partners, he co-founded Lowe Direct in association with The Lowe Group. His clients at Lowe include Lloyds/TSB, Orange, RAC and The Times/Sunday Times.

Tony lives with his family in an Oxfordshire village. Besides work, his interests are chiefly fine wines and most genres of jazz and blues.

Tony Watson
Managing Partner
Lowe Direct
Bowater House
68–114 Knightsbridge
London
SW1X 7LT
E-mail: enquire@lowedirect.co.uk
Tel: 0171-589 0800

Chapter 1.2

Planning your direct marketing strategy

The case for long-term planning

In this chapter we look at the strategic planning process already adopted by many businesses. However, included here are the specific nuances of direct marketing, showing how to prepare for an integrated direct marketing plan incorporating all facets of marketing.

Strategic planning is the managerial process by which a business changes and develops the most profitable fit between its direct marketing operations and its changing business opportunities.

> When it comes to the marketing concept today a solid wall often seems to divide the word and the deed. In spite of the best intentions of many able people, the effective implementation of the marketing concept has generally eluded them.
>
> – Theodore Levitt

In reality one often finds little or no planning. This is often caused by top management pressure to execute existing programmes or because line staff are overloaded with other areas of work. Sometimes the personnel preparing the plans are not qualified in the process and lack the overall knowledge of all the contributing functions of the business.

Planning as applied to direct marketing has two pursuits:

- ✔ Long-range planning (LRP)
- ✔ Strategic marketing planning (SMP)

The actual processes of long-range and strategic marketing planning – the phases, sequences, skills and tools employed – are very similar. The differences between them are related to the personnel, the issues, the documentation and the work produced.

Long-range planning covers a timespan of typically 2–5 years, in some instances 10–15 years. The personnel are board members, managing directors and senior personnel, eg marketing directors. They are responsible for the mission statement and assessing a company's competitive position in terms of its strengths and weaknesses. The issues tend to be topics like acquisitions and mergers, new corporate structures, and capital requirements.

Strategic marketing planning follows from the objectives established in the LRP process. SMP is normally concerned with yearly planning and involves line management. It is their task to choose appropriate market targets, establish objectives and strategies, and develop action plans and budgets that will direct and control the year's marketing effort.

In this chapter we concentrate on **strategic** marketing plans.

What constitutes a good direct marketing plan?

A good plan is not simply a list of ideas, summary notes from meetings, or sets of recommendations. Planning is not simply about problem-solving, forecasting or making decisions – all of which are day-to-day management functions.

A good direct marketing plan should be a written, comprehensive and detailed document. It should be prepared by direct marketing professionals and specify the directions of the operation for the following year.

Projects should be evaluated, start and completion dates set, costs and priorities assigned. All activities should be related to revenue and profit. The plan will attempt to target the company's future efforts and simulate all aspects of a business on paper.

Benefits of a good strategic plan

A **good** strategic plan will provide a structure in which its objectives can be achieved. It will optimise revenue and profits in line with the LRP, and is the key to maximising profits and growth.

A **good** plan will allow for organisation efficacy and will detail the priority of activities. It will also take advantage of new market opportunities.

"A good plan, once created," according to Richard Shaver, President of Response Imperatives (USA), "has significant and various uses." Top management can use it to gain a more thorough understanding of why requested funding should be approved and how next year's operations relate to their long-range planning. They can also assess line performance more accurately. Line managers, departmental personnel, and vendors can use it to develop superior tactical work as well as to control implementation, timing and costs, and to improve quality.

In summary, a good strategic marketing plan delivers nine major benefits to a company:

	The 9 major benefits of a good strategic marketing plan
1	Forces three-dimensional thinking
2	Allows specialists to perceive inter-functional relationships otherwise missed
3	Generates an extraordinary enthusiasm that improves tactical creativity
4	Allocates resources to impact on the most profitable potential
5	Creates benchmarks for future decisions
6	Improves staff quality-control and deadline performance
7	Elicits improved vendor performance
8	Enables faster roll-outs of successful programmes and faster shut-off of failures
9	Saves substantial top and middle management time and stress during implementation stages

A good strategic marketing plan will be effective not only in terms of its intentions, but also in its presentation. Here are the six qualities common to all good SMPs:

	The 6 qualities of a good strategic marketing plan
1	Easy to understand
2	Precise but detailed, to avoid confusion
3	Adaptable to change
4	Realistic in application
5	Covers all significant market factors
6	Clearly identifies responsibilities

The importance of an executive summary

Despite the best efforts to keep SMPs simple, in companies with many products, operating in many markets and with many types of customer, plans inevitably become complex. The result is that many people who should read the plan do not. If they do, they may not remember its details. A good management summary ensures that the dominant themes of the plan are expressed forcibly and clearly. No-one then has the excuse that they do not know where the company is heading. You might be surprised to know how often this is given as an excuse.

A good summary is a vital aid to understanding company direction. It is also a very helpful attachment to briefs to agencies and other suppliers (subject to confidentiality).

The summary should not, by its nature, go into much detail. It should concentrate on objectives, main target markets, opportunities and threats, key strategies and timings.

Typical structure of a marketing plan

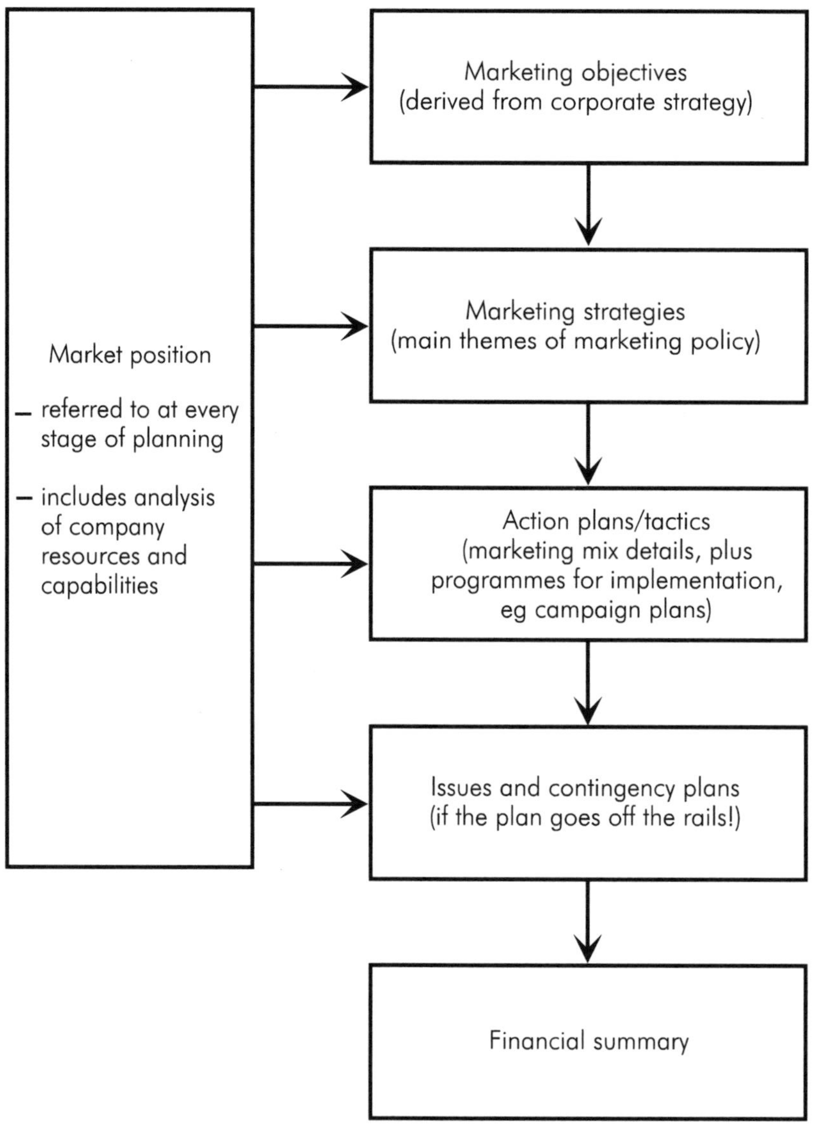

Managing the process – getting the right "mix"

In many organisations, planners (thinkers, creatives) are distinct from line managers (administrators, "doers"). Yet both are fundamental to effective planning.

Planners, like consultants, can maintain an overview of the company and its marketplace. Line managers ensure the practicability of the plan.

Good planning is a combination of quantitative and qualitative factors, combined with logical and psychological thinking. Planning often requires vision and three-dimensional thinking.

Why creativity is essential to planning

Many researchers have shown that "creative" people – or those who occupy the creative role in a team – bring specific benefits to the planning process as a result of their particular attributes:

Creative/planning/shaping people should be employed to:

- ✔ Construct networks by forming associations between people for the exchange of ideas, perceptions, and encouragement.
- ✔ Challenge assumptions and question what others automatically accept as true.
- ✔ Use chance to take advantage of the unexpected and be ready at all times to recognise accidents.
- ✔ See new ways by transforming the familiar into the strange and seeing the commonplace with new perceptions.
- ✔ Recognise patterns by focusing on significant similarities or differences in phenomena, events, or ideas.
- ✔ Make connections and bring together seemingly unrelated events, objects, or ideas.
- ✔ Take risks by daring to try new ways with no guarantee of the outcome.

A strategic marketing planning team should challenge assumptions, recognise new patterns, make lateral leaps and see connections across a business. This will create bold fresh strategic thinking. As Albert Einstein once remarked: "When I examined myself, and my methods of thought, I came to the conclusion that the gift of fantasy has meant more to me than my talent for absorbing positive knowledge."

The ideal direct marketing planning team

The need for creativity plus line management clearly affects the composition of a planning group and, within any direct marketing planning team, the following functional expertise should be included:

- ✔ Direct marketing strategic planning, coupled with the analytic knowledge of customer acquisition, retention and lifetime values.
- ✔ Media knowledge across all media from television to door-to-door.
- ✔ Creative expertise with familiarity with all media.
- ✔ Production talent to be abreast of the latest techniques and processes.
- ✔ Systems specialists who understand database marketing.
- ✔ Manufacturing and fulfilment to ensure customer satisfaction and service.

The planning process itself

When writing a direct marketing plan, the sequence is the same as for any planning process. It should comprise:

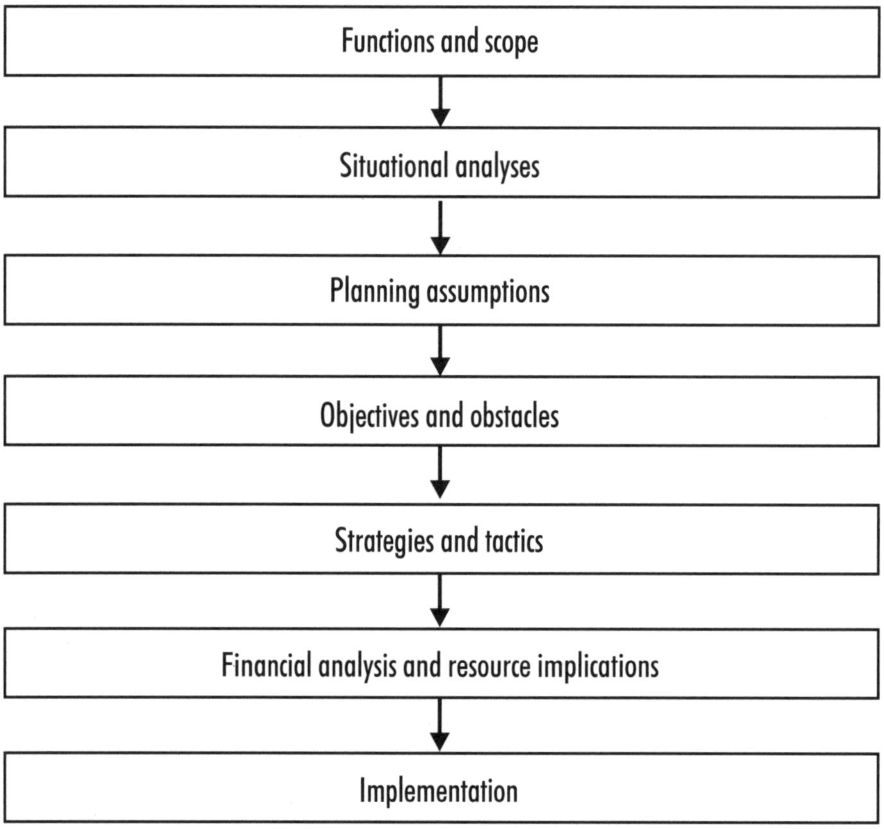

The process can be shown diagrammatically as on the facing page.

As can be seen from the diagram, the planning process begins with a painstaking assessment of the status quo: a description of the company, its functions and scope, followed by a two-part analysis of its present situation. The first part relates to the company and its customers, the second part to the company's competitors and **their** customers.

We now look at each of the planning steps in turn, concentrating on the most important stage of all – the up-front situational analyses.

Functions and scope – what business are we in?

By Functions and Scope we mean "What business are we in?" This is the company's overall goal or mission. A clear understanding of a company's products or services and target audiences is essential at the outset. Clarifying its methods of distribution and evaluating its products or services against the competition are vital. It is important at this stage to isolate points of difference from the competition in all marketing areas, whether these be product features or marketing techniques. **A business must be able to express its fundamental aim in words.**

A strategic planning model

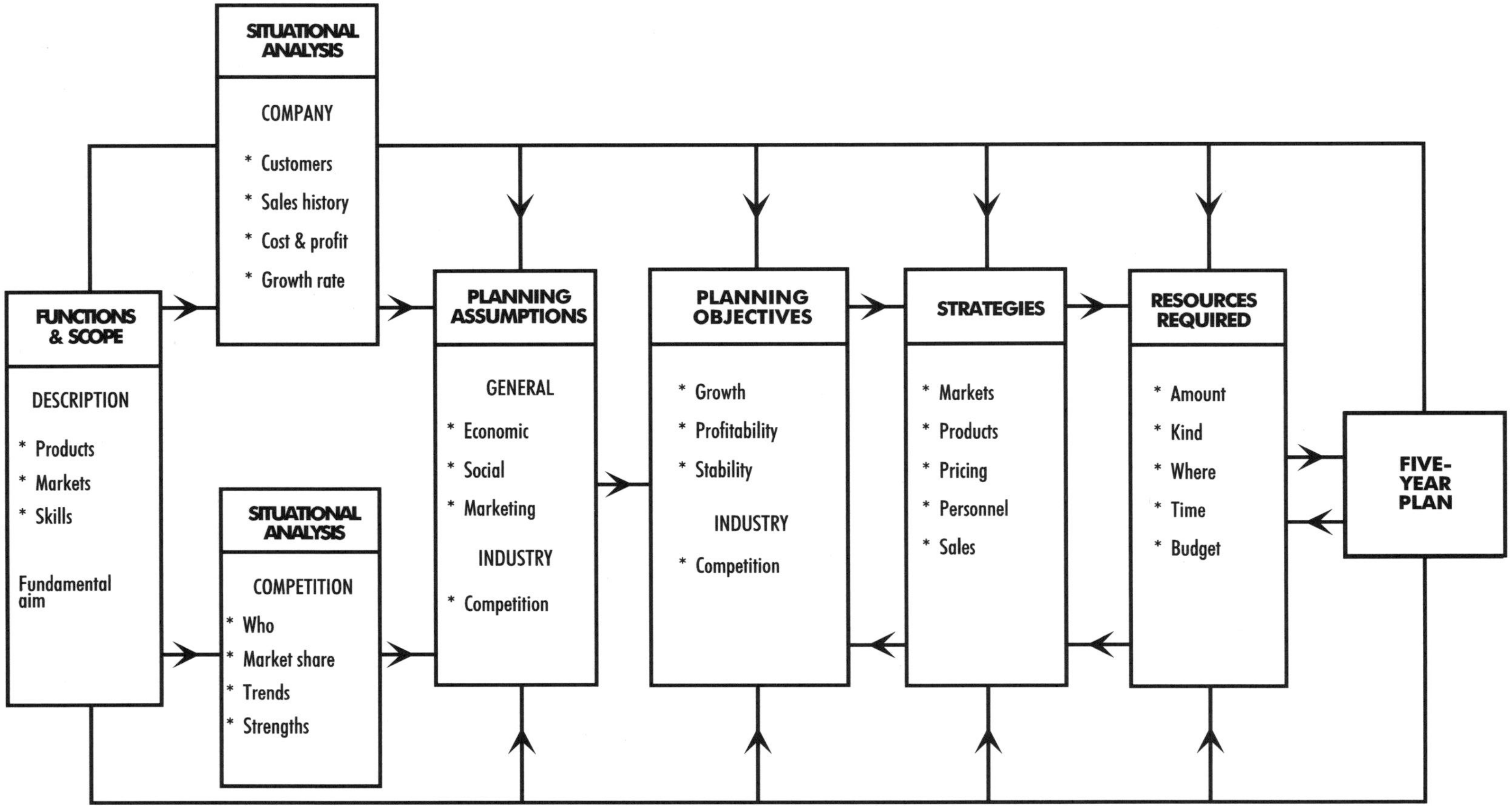

Situational analysis – where are we now?

Situational Analysis is the most critical and lengthy aspect of the planning process. An old analogy states "95% of a barrister's time is preparation, only 5% is spent in court." Achieving a crystal-clear picture of where a company is in relation to its past, its competitors, its marketplace and its target market is essential to planning.

Once achieved, the rest of the process is relatively straightforward. As much profit can be lost in this phase of planning as in any other area. **A misplaced assumption here can lead to a chain of mispositioned objectives, strategies and action plans.**

Of course, in "real life" there will not be "perfect" information. Whilst additional research may reduce uncertainty in decision-making, the pressures of cost and time may mean it is not feasible. The real skill is to differentiate between information and data. Data tends to be an amorphous mass of facts, which only careful editing can turn into useful marketing information.

Because situational analysis is so vital, let us now look more closely at what it is and how we do it. Let us look at it in two parts:

- ✔ Reviewing the company
- ✔ Reviewing the competitive environment

Reviewing the company

The first part of any situational analysis is to review the **organisation**. The following broad areas should be considered:

- ✔ Preliminary market position
- ✔ Products/services
- ✔ Customers
- ✔ Financial performance
- ✔ Resource levels

Preliminary marketing position statement

The starting point for any situational analysis is the Preliminary Marketing Position Statement. For this all potential sources of information must be examined. With probing, significant information may be located in the most unlikely areas.

Sources of information might include:

- ✔ Customers' feedback (enquiries, complaints, statistics)
- ✔ Previous enquirers (conversions to sales, near misses)
- ✔ Past or lapsed customers (attrition rates/trends)
- ✔ Existing research reports

- ✔ Statistical analysis reports
- ✔ Customer databases
- ✔ Media owners (data, reports, "gossip")
- ✔ List brokers (data including relevant experience)
- ✔ Awards entries, case histories
- ✔ Government reports and surveys
- ✔ Trade association reports
- ✔ Competitive data
- ✔ Experienced company employees (especially those with relevant experience of other organisations)
- ✔ Complementary product information
- ✔ Library research
- ✔ Consumer organisation reports

The important point here is that this information must be distilled down to essential facts. Statistical information should be expressed incrementally as well as absolutely. At the end of this exercise you will have a preliminary view of the current market position of the company.

What do we supply?

The next step is the Product/Services Review, an important part of your situational analysis whereby you define your products or services. Define only what they are and what they do. At this point you are not trying to isolate consumer benefits.

You can then consider a customer "needs and wants" analysis. **It is vital to examine needs and wants at the strategic stage, however self-evident they may be.** At one end of the spectrum it may be commonsense, but at the same time it can point to new needs among extant customers as well as to completely new customer types.

A thorough product analysis leads directly to benefit evaluation, customer profile identification, market segmentation and creative platforms.

It is useful to distinguish between needs and wants to determine which your products and services already satisfy or **could** satisfy. As you develop a picture of the levels of satisfaction your products and services provide, customer characteristics become clear. Indicators may include social/economic discriminators such as age, sex, income, occupation or marital status, and they may also include lifestyle characteristics. Both demographic and lifestyle characteristics will help pinpoint individual customer profiles.

Let us, therefore, remind ourselves of the eight basic needs and wants common to all purchasers and purchases:

What every customer needs and wants		
1	Save money	"Special pre-publication price, only £19.99"
2	Make money	"Earn £20,000 a year in your spare time"
3	Win praise	"Your employees will thank you"
4	Improve self	"Speak a new language in 3 months"
5	Save time/effort	"Weeds and feeds in one operation"
6	Impress others	"Be the first to own a satellite dish"
7	Help children/family	"Give your children a head start"
8	Have fun	"Watch TV while travelling to work"

Form a firm view on the ranking of satisfactions delivered by your product or service. You can then apply the six basic human instincts:

1. Self-preservation
2. Love
3. Gain
4. Duty
5. Pride
6. Self-indulgence

Have we a unique selling proposition?

A benefit is what a prospect thinks about before buying. All your product features should be expressed in concise benefit statements. Each identified need and want can be stated in terms of benefits. This process should also be carried out in terms of your competitors.

If, during this process, you can identify a unique selling proposition (USP) above the competition, this will have an immense impact on your final strategy. Rank the benefits and compare them against the profiles of potential consumers already identified. Increasingly unique benefits today are in the areas of service rather than product alone. For more on propositions, see Chapter 6.2.

Who are our customers?

A key aspect of the situational analysis is to develop a customer/prospect profile – to see your company and its products from your customer's perspective.

Here the key issues are:

? Who are the customers?

? How do they buy?

? What do they consider value?

? What needs do your products/services satisfy?

? Who are not customers and why?

? Which customers are most "at risk" and why?

? Would customers go to a competitor?

? What would it take to tempt them to go to a competitor?

Profit maximisation necessitates accurately defining customer profiles, selecting segments of the total customer base with similar characteristics, and communicating effectively with them to maximise sales during the customers' lifetimes.

The accumulation, retention, maintenance and retrievability of customer profiles and transactional histories are at the heart of profitability in direct marketing. Direct marketing is concerned with individual customer histories, and profiling is critical to direct marketing activities. See also Chapter 3.5.

The key profiling tools are:

✔ Customer supplied data

✔ Transactional data (customer behaviour)

✔ Demographics/geodemographics

✔ Psychographics

✔ Lifestyle data

Transactional information gives an accurate record of response and is a key discriminator. The best profiles are of those customers who have purchased recently, buy frequently, have a high monetary value and buy a variety of products. When you review mailing lists it is useful to compare a profile of prospects against profiles of your customers. The higher the correlation between prospect and customer profile, the more likely the list will be to produce a satisfactory response. Never overlook data which customers will often supply willingly.

Demographics, psychographics and lifestyle analysis are discussed at length elsewhere in this Guide. One of the key issues in segmentation and profiling is the ability to score customer records against their performance. Here standard statistical techniques such as factor or regression analysis are employed. Resultant information forms a vital component of the situational analysis. See also Chapters 3.6 and 3.7.

The customer's buying process

Whatever your marketplace, customers pass through a series of stages which influence their pre-purchase decisions.

The five steps most typically identified are:

✔ Recognition of a need, eg "We're running out of space"

✔ Evaluation of the solution, eg "Our furniture wastes space"

✔ Recommendation of the product, eg "Built-in units are the answer"

✔ Selection of the brand, eg "XYZ fits the bill"

✔ Approval of the decision, eg "The Board has agreed"

It is sufficient here to recognise that how customers buy is vital to effective communication and will affect the message delivered. In business-to-business marketing there may be multiple influences within the decision-making unit (DMU) which affect the ultimate decision. Recognition of these stages and influences is vital when developing a communications strategy.

Note from the two pyramid charts on the facing page how stages in the customer's buying process – from "Unaware" to "Re-purchase" – are closely paralleled by the advertising measures, from general awareness and prospecting advertising to cultivating loyalty and lifetime value through direct communications.

The critical issue in examining the buying process is to quantify and address the influences at every step. You are now in a position to compare the customer profiles with the buying influences and begin to identify market segments within the profile groups. **Remember: customer segments must be reachable by a cost-effective means.** Isolating a segment which cannot be located through existing media options presents an insurmountable challenge and will invalidate key parts of the plan, whereas isolating segments which can be reached through new media may well give the plan a new direction.

Where are we now – in numerical terms?

In any marketing plan, as part of the situational analysis, it is important to review areas which can be measured and monitored in statistical and financial terms. These include typically:

? Sales turnover and profitability

? Product analysis including unit-costing and volumes

? Media effectiveness

? Market performance/share/trends, etc

? Distribution channel efficiency

? Financial indicators

? Promotion and advertising budget effectiveness

Stages in the customer's buying process

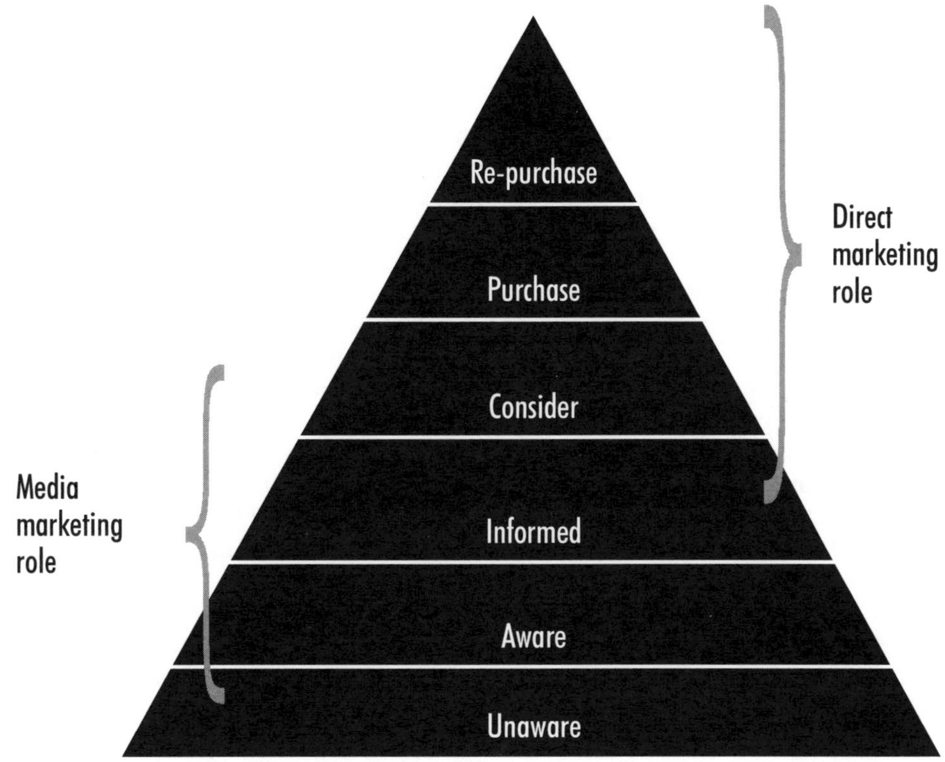

Advertising measures affecting the buying process

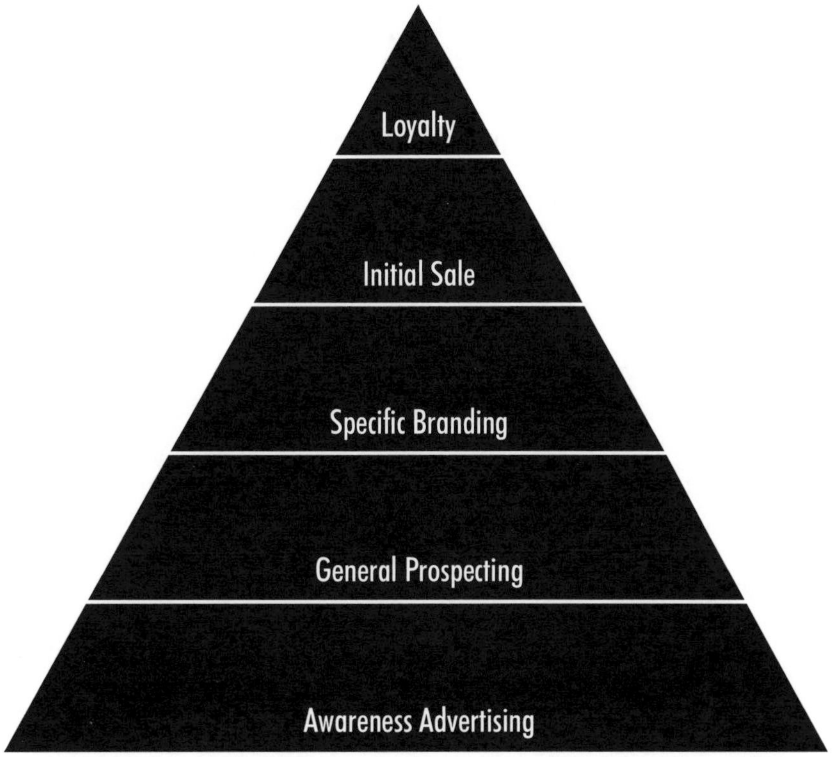

Whilst accounts, sales and profitability are relatively easily assembled, in-depth probing may be required to assess the advertising, media and distribution channels' true contribution. This may require different measures such as store traffic, call and conversion rates of salesforces, lifetime values of customers, and so on.

Experienced direct marketers always employ the following three critical financial measures:

1. Customer acquisition and break-even costs
It is imperative to know how much allowable marketing cost can be spent to acquire a customer and to acquire customers at the lowest possible allowable cost, as dealt with by other authors/consultants in this Guide. See also Chapters 1.3, 2.4 and 2.5.

2. Attrition curves
It is important to analyse the attrition curve of customers. That is to say the number of customers lost on a per annum basis. Every company will suffer losses through either natural attrition (eg death, re-location) or poor customer service (which may not show up until the retention phase).

3. Lifetime values (LTV)
Identifying the lifetime value of customers is fundamental in arriving at budgets for acquisition cost. For further information see Chapters 2.4, 2.5 and 2.6.

It is easier for large financial services organisations to calculate lifetime values, but even small marketers can easily examine their records to see how frequently and how much customers spend with them over a given period. On a larger scale a packaged goods manufacturer, on an individual household basis, could compute the LTV for that household over a number of brands.

It is, of course, relatively simple for organisations with a sophisticated transactional database to be programmed to compute the LTV figures – one more advantage of having a proper database.

Profit potential of established and future products

Obviously, when considering entering an existing market with a new product, or a new market with an existing product, you need a view as to its profit potential. This will guide future business planning and execution in both the short and long term.

Resource allocation

The resources and assets of a company must be deployed to produce long-term customer loyalty and satisfaction. Thus only profitable businesses can service their existing customers and maintain growth. There is little point producing more business if it cannot be serviced adequately. In order to understand a business's resource position the following areas should be reviewed:

? Database capability (storage capacity and processing speed)

? Distribution channels (how effectively do they move products to the market?)

? Fulfilment – from receipt of order to shipment and customer service procedures

? Capital available to fund expansion

? Staff expertise/quality in functional areas/training methods

? Quality of products and/or services

? Expectations associated with the company's reputation and name

Central to any direct marketing-oriented company will be the database's potential for providing management with the necessary reporting and controls to monitor and guide the business.

So far you have been looking only at your own company without regard for your competitors. You have a clearer idea of your organisation, its strengths, weaknesses and intentions. But it is a common mistake of many companies to look this far and no farther. The fact is your prosperity will be influenced in the not-so-long term more by activities and factors outside your control, not least of all those controlled by your competitors ....

Who are our competitors?

In monitoring the competition it is important first to determine with whom you are in competition. On a generic level you may be competing in a recreational market, on the specific level in different forms of leisure activity, and on a base level brand versus brand. It is vital to monitor market share movements and market trends and to gain knowledge of competitors' specific strengths and weaknesses.

Monitoring the competition takes place on three levels:

1. What is the state of the industry as a whole?
First you must determine where your industry is in its stages of evolution. This will help determine your objectives and resulting strategies. For example, is the business as a whole in a growth stage or has the industry entered maturity? Research here can be used to predict future trends as well.

2. How do we compare with industry trends?
The next stage is to assess the company's performance against industry trends – including customer base, annual turnover, cost per sale, attrition rates, etc. One of your chief aims is to confirm whether the company is performing above or below the industry average.

3. How do we compare with the competition?
As most direct marketers also communicate via public media, eg press or inserts, it is possible to monitor much competitive activity. You can gauge their level of expenditure on customer acquisition and compare positioning, creative treatments and offers. In this way new tests can be identified which, if not repeated, will indicate their lack of success, direct marketing being dependent on measurable response. See Chapter 4.1.

Equally by using professional researchers, and by buying competitive products, you can gain knowledge of competitive retention programmes, welcome procedures, service levels, etc. Being on a competitor's database permits you valuable insights into their strategies so that you can hone your attacks accordingly. This is made possible by direct marketing's dependence on customer information and database marketing.

The summary – now we know where we are

Situational analysis is an exhaustive process, but if conducted thoroughly and performed well, it has the following benefits:

- ✔ Identifies the wants and needs satisfied by our products/services.
- ✔ Determines customer profiles which can be converted into market segments and new markets.
- ✔ Identifies the distinctive attractions and failings the business has for its customers.
- ✔ Identifies emerging market segments, unsatisfied needs and competitive gaps.
- ✔ Audits the communication mix and distribution channels.
- ✔ Assesses the company's real ability to service its customers.

A summary of your complete situational analysis is an exact statement of where you are, a prerequisite of planning.

Planning assumptions – making the most of change

Returning to the planning process chart on page 1.2-9, we must now take account of Planning Assumptions.

Before setting objectives for the business it is important to bear in mind the environment in which the company is operating, which may have short- and long-term implications for the business. Environmental change, coupled with the situational analysis, may identify areas for a company to gain competitive advantage.

In order to forecast the market environment in which you will be operating over the period of the plan, you should concentrate on the market factors that have a real influence on your business and over which you have little or no control. This involves documenting and analysing economic conditions and social trends as they pertain to your business. Whilst the first attempt may be time-consuming, you will find it relatively simple to update this in future years.

Changes and trends in the marketplace that should be heeded include:

- ✔ Economic changes (eg unemployment, inflation, Gross National Product)
- ✔ Social changes (eg leisure trends, shopping patterns, home entertainment)
- ✔ Demographic movements (eg age and population distribution, household composition)
- ✔ Technological trends (eg PCs/CD-ROM/Internet, cable TV, EPOS/EFTPOS)
- ✔ Changes in government policy/legislation (eg tax, data protection, industrial deregulation)

Planning business objectives – where do we want to be?

Planning business objectives is a crucial stage in any planning process. Having reviewed your current market position thoroughly, both internally and externally, it is now time to point the company in a specific direction. An objective is the target a business strives to achieve. Without objectives the company will be aimless. With objectives, the subsequent strategic plans will focus a company's efforts to achieve those objectives.

Objectives should be broad enough to maximise the identified opportunities but narrow enough to ensure that the company's resources can be realistically deployed to achieve them. Objectives are the measure against which a company's performance can be monitored and form a statement of where a company wants to be at an agreed time in the future.

Objectives should be aspirational, moving the company forward to an ideal state. They should also be realistic and soundly based.

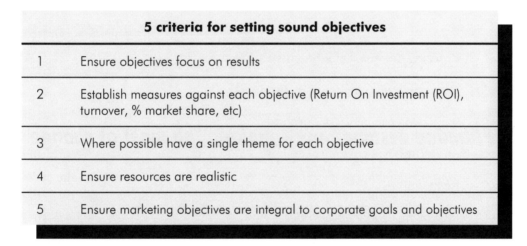

5 criteria for setting sound objectives

1	Ensure objectives focus on results
2	Establish measures against each objective (Return On Investment (ROI), turnover, % market share, etc)
3	Where possible have a single theme for each objective
4	Ensure resources are realistic
5	Ensure marketing objectives are integral to corporate goals and objectives

All objectives should be measurable – but not all are financial. For example: increasing market awareness is not a financial objective, but can be measured by recall or research.

So, first separate the financial objectives and rank them in terms of their contribution to the year's financial performance, **and** in terms of long-term or lifetime value. Then do the same for non-financial objectives.

Most organisations typically try to achieve these three major objectives:

✔ Faster growth in market share

✔ Improved profitability

✔ Maximum net cash flow

Growing market share – a popular option

Clearly, increasing sales volume within a category ought to grow your market share. It is a typical option for companies who live or die by market share, such as fast-moving consumer goods companies. For many direct marketing companies, especially in mail order, market share may be less important than turnover increases, increasing customer cross-selling, upgrading customers to more frequent purchases, growth of the customer base, encouraging higher average order values, and so on.

Quite often this means a period of heavy investment, with profitability expected to be maximised in the long run.

Improving profitability – every organisation's goal

Improving profitability is an objective common to virtually all organisations, including charities, and so-called non-profit organisations. Profit is **the** measure of efficiency and success.

The chart below identifies seven sub-objectives by which improved profitability is usually achieved. At their core is either expanding volume or increasing efficiency.

They are:

- ✔ Entering new market segments
- ✔ Converting non-users to buy products
- ✔ Increasing frequency of purchase
- ✔ Attracting rival customers to buy
- ✔ Reducing costs
- ✔ Improving product/price offer
- ✔ Improving sales mix/margins, etc

In summary, a good marketing planning objective is one that is simultaneously Specific, Measurable, Aspirational, Realistic, Timed – in other words **SMART**.

The 7 sub-objectives for improving profitability

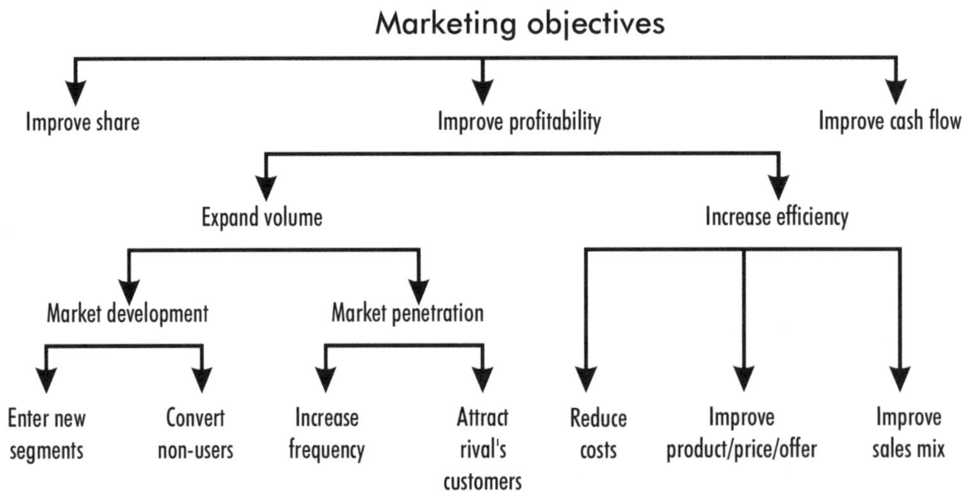

Strategy – how are we going to get there?

Having determined where you wish to go, it is time to determine how you plan to get there. We call this evaluating strategy options.

Each objective should have a corresponding strategy to achieve it where a number of strategies may contribute to meeting a specific objective. At this point you may have identified various obstacles which could block your objectives. One purpose of the strategy will be to overcome these obstacles.

There may well be alternative means for reaching your objectives, as we have seen. You could attempt to achieve profit objectives by entering new market segments or increasing penetration in existing segments. Any candidate strategy needs to be assessed against these major themes:

- ✔ Product/service offer
- ✔ Target market
- ✔ Marketplace and competition
- ✔ Current distribution channels
- ✔ Media plans and mix
- ✔ Financial situation
- ✔ Internal operational capabilities

If you are developing strategic plans, the checklist on the following page sets out a list of key business areas you could consider in relation to how they can best help you achieve your objectives.

Remember: whatever combinations are appropriate for your plan, you should **keep to brief top-line statements**. As soon as you delve into implementation details, eg campaign timings and list details, you will be delving into tactics, which should not be the aim at this stage in the planning process.

Jim Kobs in his article "Marketing Strategies for Maximum Growth" identified seven key questions direct marketers should ask when developing objectives and matching strategies.

The 7 key questions for setting objectives

1	Is it more important to build sales or profits?
2	How heavily should you invest in new customer acquisition?
3	Can present customers be profitably contacted more often with existing products or services?
4	Should a company try to grow the product category or penetrate the market deeper?
5	How should you position and price your product or service?
6	Can media or distribution channels be expanded?
7	Should you add new products, launch new businesses or develop new markets?

Developing your key business strategies

Product Strategy	?	How could you change your product/service to make it more appealing?
	?	What if you extended or reduced your product range?
R&D Strategy	?	What other needs/wants could you develop new products for?
	?	What new uses for existing products can you identify?
Pricing Strategy	?	What would happen if you shifted from mid-range to discount, or premium to mid-range?
	?	What if you increase or decrease the profit-per-unit?
Competitive Strategy	?	How might your competitors react to your actions?
	?	How will actions they might take affect you and how will you respond?
Positioning Strategy	?	What would happen if you altered the "personality" your product projects?
	?	How might it affect things if you move from, say, down-market to mid-market?
Branding Strategy	?	How would altering the values your product represents affect things?
	?	What if you shifted the image of the customer your product conveys?
Offer Strategy	?	What would be the effect of adding value or incentivising purchase?
	?	Can you add another, complementary, product to yours to form a stronger package?
Target Market Strategy	?	Are there other segments who would find your proposition attractive?
	?	Can you reach your customers' franchise more effectively or more efficiently?
Marketing Information Strategy	?	How would knowing more about your target audience help and how can you obtain this information?
	?	Would better knowledge of competitor plans be useful and how can you monitor this?
	?	How can you know more about the factors shaping your market environment both now and in the future?
Communication Strategy	?	Do you make optimum use of what you know in order to reach and influence the behaviour of your target market?
	?	Could your message be crafted more clearly and/or delivered with more impact potency?
Acquisition Strategy	?	What if you changed the allowable cost for customer recruitment?
	?	What if you broadened or changed the media channels you employ to recruit customers?
Customer Relationship Strategy	?	What might be the effect of changing the nature, extent or frequency of contact with customers?
	?	Could you develop new ways and employ new methods/channels for contacting customers?
Customer Service Strategy	?	How might changing your sales and/or aftersales handling take things forward?
	?	If you cut costs would quality necessarily suffer?
Database Strategy	?	How would increasing the amount or type or recency of customer data affect things?
	?	Can you improve the link between transaction/accounting data and customer profile data?
Sales Channel Strategy	?	What would be the effect of adding new sales channels or closing existing ones?
	?	What if you altered the mix of business between different channels?

Remember when developing strategies, to take into account the likely strategies of competitors too. Strategies which do not consider potential competitive responses and build in contingencies are more at risk of failure.

Tactics – what exactly are we going to do?

Tactics have been defined as "**the manoeuvring of the specific resources of the company within a framework defined by the overall strategy**". Sometimes referred to as Action Plans, this part of the planning process spells out the precise details for actioning the plan. Responsibilities are nominated, budgets are set and timings agreed.

Campaign execution will fall down if the strategies have not been clearly developed, leading to sub-standard tactical development. A mispositioned creative strategy or a weak media analysis are common mistakes.

A very important aspect of the action phase is to put in place controls to monitor progress, plan for errors and document all actions. "True communication occurs when what the customer hears is what the speaker said." This is why clear, concise, briefing instructions are vital to accommodate all parties involved in the implementation phase.

Action plans should specify:

- ✔ Products or services to be offered
- ✔ Pricing and payment terms
- ✔ Offers to the market segments
- ✔ Promise
- ✔ Positioning (generic or by segment)
- ✔ Production cost
- ✔ Creative treatment (copy, graphic approaches, component specifications)
- ✔ Timings
- ✔ Fulfilment and return handling
- ✔ Payment processing

Action plans will determine the resources required for their execution. They will determine not only the amount but also the quality of resource required, where it is to be found and the available budget for its provision. Resources may include external suppliers such as research agencies, advertising agencies, list and media owners, printers, mailing houses and computer bureaux. Internally there will be marketing staff and management services (systems/IT, credit scoring, inventory, customer service, legal, operations and finance).

Include tests in action plans

Direct marketing action plans should also include any tests of media, timing, offer, format, and creative execution. Remember tests must have clear objectives to deliver profit or develop the product. Testing represents a sizeable investment of budget. Limit sample sizes to sufficient minimum quantities, so that the majority of the customer base can be contacted with the most proven and profitable control packages. This is another means of maximising revenue. See Testing, Chapter 2.3.

Whose responsibility?

The responsibility for campaign control is a vital function. The role is to plan, control, monitor and analyse. It requires strong organisational ability, attention to detail, and the competence to motivate and control internal and external suppliers. Each stage needs double checking as information from many levels must be coordinated. Being able to stand back and review the picture and having foresight into possible problem areas is vital. Every one of Murphy's Laws of Management applies to this area.

It is also important to be able to project the future and question decisions, if in doubt. Anyone who masters this area will be in a much stronger position to develop **workable** strategic plans.

Statistical and financial analysis

The final stage of the direct marketing process is to prepare to analyse the results. The typical direct marketing results analysis may include the following:

✔ Response totals

✔ Cost per enquiry

✔ Conversion percentage

✔ Cost-per-order

✔ Average order values

✔ Test results by cell

✔ Repeat order values

✔ Renewal ratios

✔ Returns

Ultimately you will be measuring the ROI (Return On Investment) which is a critical financial analysis. The style of analysis will be determined by the objectives. In the pre-planning for results, the business analyst follows these steps:

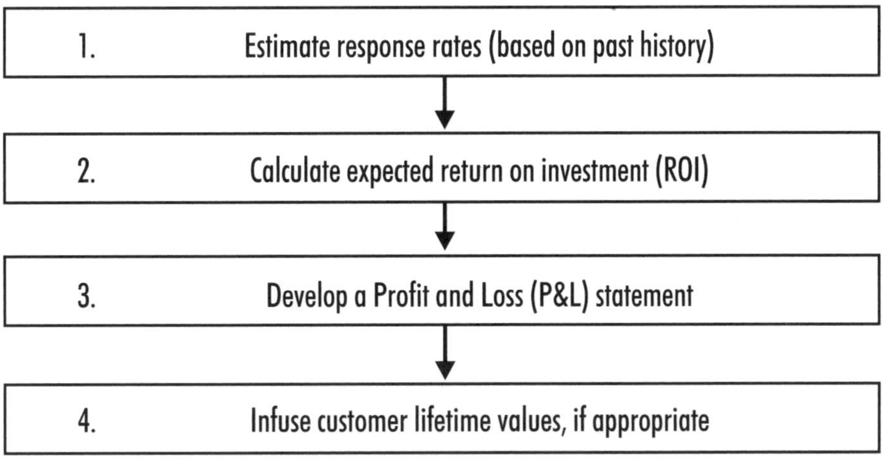

1. Estimate response rates (based on past history)
2. Calculate expected return on investment (ROI)
3. Develop a Profit and Loss (P&L) statement
4. Infuse customer lifetime values, if appropriate

Once actioned the plan will be monitored and the process should become a self-fulfilling cycle. See Profit and Loss, Chapter 2.5.

Objectives, strategies and tactics – the essential differences

To summarise the stages of the strategic marketing plan, remember the difference between objectives, strategies, and tactics – as depicted schematically below.

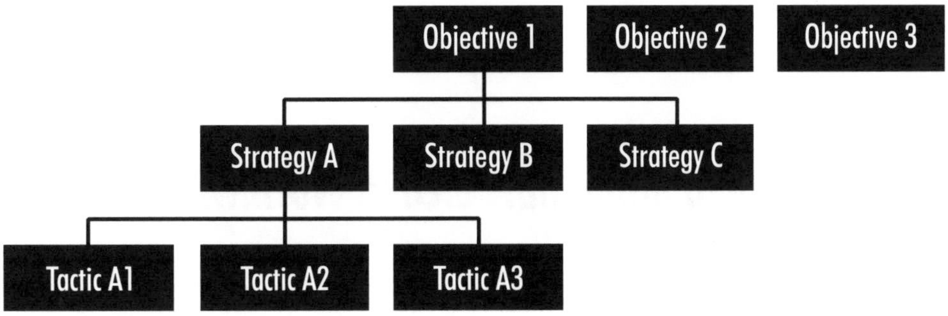

Objectives describe destinations (where are we going?). Usually they are stated in revenue and profit terms. There can be multiple objectives.

Strategies set out the route which has been chosen, or the means for achieving the objective (how do we get there?). Each objective will have an identifiable strategy, although some strategies may contribute to meeting more than one objective.

Strategies are:

✔ Theoretical

✔ Descriptive

✔ General

✔ Guidelines

Tactics, action plans, or campaigns constitute the vehicle for getting to the destination, the precise plan. They form the detailed execution of the strategy.

Tactics are:

✔ Operational

✔ Specific

✔ Detailed

> Planning is about making it happen.
>
> – John Harvey Jones, Consultant, former Chairman, ICI

This chapter has been predominantly concerned with strategic marketing planning. Unfortunately some companies who should know better still lack strategic plans, or see them as an annual ritual without serious intent. If your direct marketing plan is too detailed, confused over terminology, not integrated into the marketing strategy, or lacks the support of line management, it is doomed to mediocrity.

A good plan – by carefully reviewing the strengths, weaknesses, opportunities and threats, and by assessing the company's history, internal resources, competition and environment – will identify the key issues and opportunities confronting your business.

Whilst it is tempting for any manager to formulate and retain the planning process in his head – the strength and weakness of many an entrepreneur – a staged, written planning process such as that described here, that can be shared by **all** the members of the team, is essential for long-term success in this complex business of direct marketing.

A case study in planning: CIGNA Worldwide Insurance (1991)

To complete this chapter, in response to your requests following publication of the first edition of this Guide, we include a comprehensive case study in planning direct marketing, showing how the theory may be applied in practice.

The product is "Firstcover", children's injury insurance.

These case notes have been approved by Tony Watson, Managing Director, Lowe Direct.

CIGNA case study

I. Functions and scope: What business are we in?

CIGNA Worldwide is a global financial player in the insurance business. Specifically, it concentrates on property and casualty insurance with a particular strength in the marine and personal sectors. The latter focus on health and accident insurance.

Within the UK, CIGNA tended to operate "behind the scenes" relying upon brokers and other intermediaries as sales channels. It had a long-established global relationship with American Express and ran employee schemes sponsored by large employers such as Ford and Barclays Bank.

Taking the personal accident insurance sector, CIGNA was a leading player in the UK market and, within this, had become a principal insurer of children in independent schools.

2. Situational analysis: Where are we now?

In relation to the past:

- *had become, via a major broker, market leader in insuring children at private schools against accident or injury;*
- *had attempted in recent years, with little real success, to develop the market for this type of insurance amongst parents of children at state schools.*

In relation to the competition:

- *competitors' products were typically low cost and low margin representing generally very basic propositions offering limited cover, no added-value services and only available on a per-child basis;*
- *Municipal Mutual (a small specialist competitor) had secured deals with major Local Education Authorities to offer their product through state schools, while major composite insurers who were in the market (eg Norwich Union) tended to be preoccupied with other major categories (eg launching Norwich Union Healthcare).*

In relation to the market:

- *awareness of children's injury insurance, as a sector, was very low as was public awareness of CIGNA;*
- *there was a growing public awareness of accidents to children through TV programmes like "That's Life" and fundraising work by Jimmy Savile for Stoke Mandeville hospital, yet only about 5% of children were covered – mostly those in private education;*
- *most parents believed their children were covered somehow for accidents at school and were often very disturbed to discover that this was not the case.*

CIGNA case study (cont'd)

In relation to the target market:

- *approximately 12 million children aged 0 to 15, distributed in around 6.5 million households;*
- *all insurance industry experience showed that ABC1 socio-economic groups had a higher propensity to buy insurance products;*
- *allowing for those in private education, Cigna could safely project some 2.5 million ABC1 households with 0- to 15-year-old children in state education.*

3. Planning assumptions: What changes can we make the most of?

Economic climate:

- *whilst the recession had led to a reduction in disposable income, the anticipated upturn in 1992/93 was likely to allow ABC1s, in particular, to increase discretionary purchases.*

Social changes:

- *public awareness of accidents to children was expected to continue to grow;*
- *children's rights, generally, would be brought increasingly to public attention via media coverage.*

Demographic movements:

- *despite a slight slowing in the birth rate, two other factors were on the increase:*

  (a) women in employment (11 million in 1990)

  (b) one-parent families (17% of families in 1990).

4. Planning business objectives: Where do we want to be?

Cigna wanted to ***increase*** *the following factors:*

- *the market for children's injury insurance beyond the core of children in private education;*
- *their methods of distribution beyond their established broker/ intermediary route;*

CIGNA case study (cont'd)

- *the UK profile of CIGNA amongst the general public to assist with*
  - *the launch of their new children's injury insurance product,*
  - *the launch of any future consumer products,*
  - *the sales of existing CIGNA products, albeit via intermediaries;*
- *the profile of CIGNA amongst intermediaries.*

They also wanted to ***maintain*** *market leadership of the children's accident insurance market.*

5. Evaluating strategic options: How are we going to get there?

Three routes were presented for consideration and the third option selected.

1. *Step up efforts to develop the market amongst parents of state school children via brokers.*

- *past experience showed only modest penetration;*
- *distribution channels remain limited;*
- *did little to boost public profile of children's injury insurance or CIGNA.*

2. *Develop schools/LEAs as a commercial channel of distribution.*

- *competitive strength of Municipal Mutual;*
- *difficult to monitor and control, plus some evidence of resistance to commercialism from school/local government culture;*
- *provided only limited boost to public profile.*

3. *Develop direct sales operation using broadscale media targeting the product directly to parents.*

- *increased market for children's injury insurance;*
- *added a major new distribution channel;*
- *raised CIGNA's profile with the general public, plus knock-on effect with brokers.*

CIGNA case study (cont'd)

6. Major strategic themes

In mapping out the strategic marketing plan, four major themes were identified as follows: ***marketing information****,* ***product****,* ***communication*** *and* ***test marketing****.*

Marketing information strategy

Research requirements fell broadly under four headings:

- *how should the product be configured to attract the state school parent?*
- *how could this target audience be motivated to purchase a new type of insurance?*
- *how best could Cigna obtain active support from schools and teachers?*
- *what communication platforms would prove most productive?*

Product strategy

Given the rather basic nature of competing products, an added-value strategy offered most in terms of:

- *providing real product differentiation;*
- *creating a more comprehensive product proposition;*
- *helping to justify the higher price which CIGNA felt essential to warrant creating this new market at all.*

Communication strategy

Whilst the product would be sold directly to parents, the role of the school (and teachers) as a means to help distribute the marketing message was identified as key to helping to provide credibility. So, in broad terms, the communication strategy would seek to complement the direct approach to parents with the use of schools as a medium.

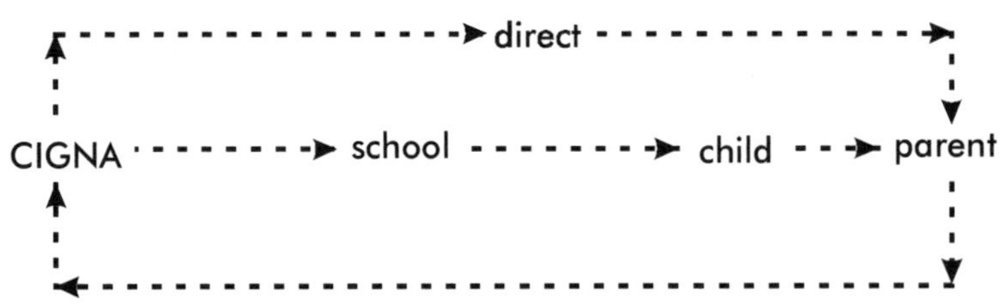

Test marketing strategy

As a new product launch into a new insurance sector, CIGNA recognised that success was far from guaranteed. But if a product or marketing initiative fails it's important to know why it has failed and not be left saying: "I wonder if it would have worked if we'd done such and such." Equally, though, there is always a cost attached to testing and finding things out, so the need for learning has to be balanced with fiscal responsibility.

CIGNA case study (cont'd)

The key issue to be addressed within the test was: "Do we have evidence that we can recruit customers at an acceptable marketing cost ***and*** *in sufficient volume to achieve the critical mass required for a full-scale launch?"*

How could Cigna MAXIMISE LEARNING and LIMIT FINANCIAL EXPOSURE, whilst gaining sufficient RELIABLE EVIDENCE FOR ROLL-OUT?

7. Resource requirements: What will we need in order to get there?

Four main resource areas were identified as follows: marketing, response handling, sales/administration and financial.

Marketing

- *a major programme of research on target market, product and creative platform;*
- *an agency or agencies to assist with direct response advertising and PR;*
- *an internal team to develop and market the product in detail.*

Response handling

- *a bureau (initially) to receive and fulfil 'phone and postal enquiries;*
- *a mechanism to follow up non-converting enquirers.*

Sales/administration

- *a number of systems and staff to take care of accounting, policy generation, claims handling, customer service, renewals and the customer database.*

Financial

- *a detailed test marketing budget to cover the first phase;*
- *first- and second-year provisional budgets and income projections.*

Tactics – what exactly are we going to do?

Action plans were developed for six main areas of endeavour, as follows: ***product development****,* ***media selection****,* ***regional testing****,* ***schools activity****,* ***response and conversion****, and* ***creative platform.***

Product development

A two-part research project was undertaken to help refine the product proposition as:

- *two levels of cover (at different premium levels) to chose from;*
- *a family rate for two or more children;*
- *cover applied to injuries received anywhere/anytime (school, home, UK, abroad);*

CIGNA case study (cont'd)

- *free counselling service to help cope with trauma of serious injury (ie claims-handling staff were counsellors);*
- *cash to cover expenses or lost wages if parent accompanies child on extended hospital stay;*
- *free home nursing if child requires post-hospital treatment.*

The main message was carried by the pack for schools (left) and a brochure for parents (right).

Media selection

The following media mix was selected in order to satisfy a number of requirements from the communication campaign:

- *awareness/image building*
- *response generating*
- *provision for regional variations for testing*
- *ability to use individually and in combination.*

TV	*Awareness building*
Radio	↑
Posters	
Press	
Inserts	
Direct mail	↓
Door-to-door	*Response generating*

CIGNA case study (cont'd)

Regional testing

Region	1	2	3
Public	TV Press Direct mail	Press Direct mail	Direct mail
Schools	Direct mail	Direct mail	Direct mail

In order to measure the productivity of media channels both individually and in combination, the matrix above was devised with response and awareness tracking mechanisms in place within the three regions.

Schools activity

Three clear stages of activity were devised to win support from schools, and head teachers in particular.

(a) Warm up – a mailing to head teachers offered free teaching materials relevant to safety, a newly devised Topic within the National Curriculum for which materials were somewhat "thin on the ground".

(b) Teaching materials – despatch of teachers' pack for use in classroom and beyond, as schools and ABC1 parents were keen on parental involvement. These materials were branded to CIGNA as the sponsor.

(c) Involving parents – teaching materials included a parental involvement guide, again branded to CIGNA and incorporating an application form.

Response and conversion

A carefully coordinated system was devised to manage the flow of leads (see chart on following page).

CIGNA case study (cont'd)

How will we handle responses and concessions?

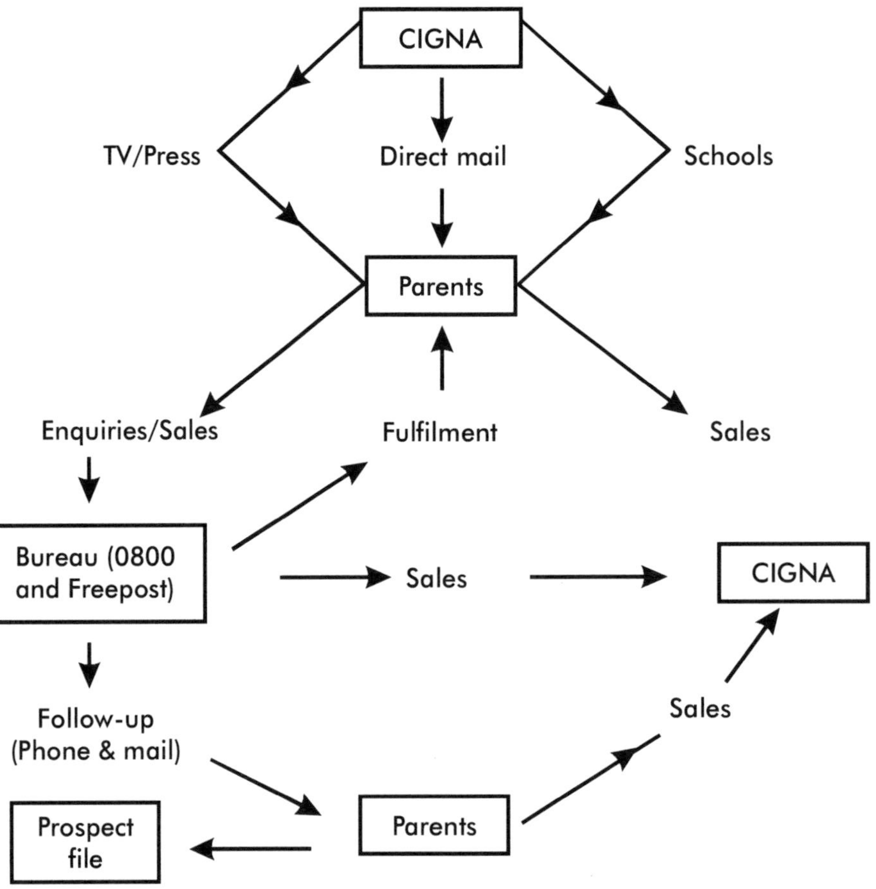

Creative platform

There were three major aspects to developing the creative positioning and establishing a persuasive creative platform for CIGNA and its new product.

(a) *Brand name*

- *since this is the first insurance a child is likely to have Firstcover seemed an appropriate name;*
- *a distinctive logo was devised which "grows up" from childlike scrawl for the "F" to a more mature typeface for "cover".*

(b) *Strapline*

- *CIGNA operates in the personal insurance sector, so an appropriate line is ... "Covering those precious to you".*

CIGNA case study (cont'd)

(c) *Tone of voice and imagery*

- *a further two-part research project indicated clearly that parents were most influenced by scenes of "kids being kids" juxtaposed with a hint of everyday dangers and some of the more disturbing facts about coping with children's injuries;*
- *this type of approach helped to create an awareness of the need for Firstcover;*
- *a degree of guilt was also harnessed as a motivator by drawing parallels between children as "items" and other, more everyday sectors that are readily accepted to be insured (eg car and home contents);*
- *the imagery and actual actors/models used in TV and print media were the same to provide continuity to the visual message;*
- *this integration was extended to the activity undertaken via schools in that the teaching materials were about "safety first" which was turned around within the materials to "first safety" and led smoothly into the product branding ... "Firstcover".*

Creative implementation

Examples of some of the creative materials used in this campaign are featured on the following double-page spread.

How the CIGNA planning became a campaign:

Press and TV advertising built awareness and generated immediate response

Every week nearly 200 children are ...

... seriously injured in accidents.

Firstcover Children's Injury Insurance

Call CIGNA free 0800 444 233

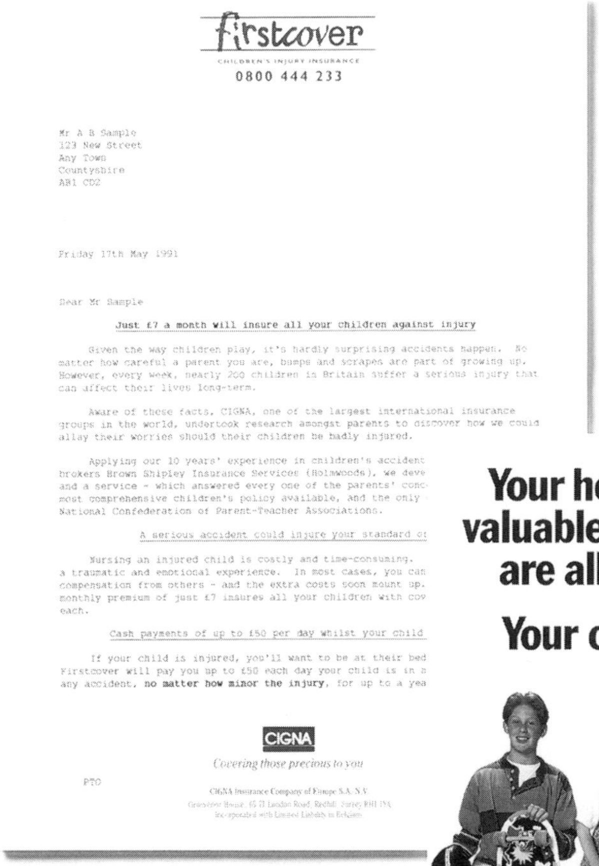

firstcover

CHILDREN'S INJURY INSURANCE

0800 444 233

Mr A B Sample
123 New Street
Any Town
Countyshire
AB1 CD2

Friday 17th May 1991

Dear Mr Sample

Just £7 a month will insure all your children against injury

Given the way children play, it's hardly surprising accidents happen. No matter how careful a parent you are, bumps and scrapes are part of growing up. However, every week, nearly 200 children in Britain suffer a serious injury that can affect their lives long-term.

Aware of these facts, CIGNA, one of the largest international insurance groups in the world, undertook research amongst parents to discover how we could allay their worries should their children be badly injured.

Applying our 10 years' experience in children's accident
brokers Brown Shipley Insurance Services (Holmwoods), we deve
and a service - which answered every one of the parents' conc
most comprehensive children's policy available, and the only
National Confederation of Parent-Teacher Associations.

A serious accident could injure your standard o

Nursing an injured child is costly and time-consuming.
a traumatic and emotional experience. In most cases, you can
compensation from others - and the extra costs soon mount up.
monthly premium of just £7 insures all your children with cov
each.

Cash payments of up to £50 per day whilst your child

If your child is injured, you'll want to be at their bed
Firstcover will pay you up to £50 each day your child is in a
any accident, **no matter how minor the injury**, for up to a yea

CIGNA

Covering those precious to you

PTO

CIGNA Insurance Company of Europe S.A.-N.V.

Incorporated with Limited Liability in Belgium

Direct mail produced response, allowed regional variations and facilitated testing

Chapter 1.3

Acquiring new customers: Starting the relationship

This chapter includes:

- Long- and short-term objectives
- Why prospects do and don't respond
- Elements of a successful acquisition programme:
  - product/offer
  - price
  - incentives
  - targeting
  - timing
  - allowable costs
- Acquisition media, flowchart
- Acquisition media, relative strengths and weaknesses

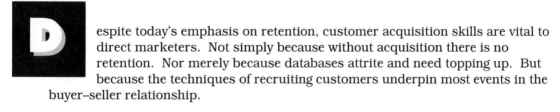

Despite today's emphasis on retention, customer acquisition skills are vital to direct marketers. Not simply because without acquisition there is no retention. Nor merely because databases attrite and need topping up. But because the techniques of recruiting customers underpin most events in the buyer–seller relationship.

For example, the ultimate purpose of retaining customers is that they should purchase occasionally! And to persuade them to respond, we fall back on the methods direct marketers have evolved for winning new business: analysis, testing, media planning, creativity, and so on.

Writing a brief chapter on acquisition isn't easy. Almost all the topics you'd like to develop are covered more fully by specialist authors further down the line. Recognising this dilemma, Lesley Godwin has provided us with a first-class overview of the stages involved, referring readers to later sections as appropriate. (We have subsequently added in the chapter references to aid your study.)

New in this edition. Most of the examples, and much of the advice.

Lesley Godwin, Marketing Director, Readers Union

Lesley started her career in direct marketing when she joined Which?, the Consumer's Association magazine, as a marketing assistant after a background in banking and IT. At CA she gained experience in all areas of direct marketing, taking on roles involving print and production, media buying, market research, creative, advertising and economic evaluation. She worked through various job titles including Direct Marketing Manager and Marketing Development Manager before becoming Marketing Director.

She was responsible for the sales of all the magazines in the Which? stable – selling over a million copies a month, plus a range of book titles including the famous "Good Food Guide". She also launched the Which? On-line service and Affinity credit card.

Which? has pioneered many of the customer acquisition techniques referred to throughout this Guide, and is especially noted for its extremely successful multi-component mailings (twelve pieces at the last count). Which? was also in the forefront of adopting the direct debit payment procedure for direct marketing.

Lesley is a member of the Board of the Direct Marketing Association (Deputy Chair and Chair of the Executive Committee 1995/96) and ex-member of the Board of the Telephone Preference Service. She also sits on the CAP Sales Promotion and Direct Response Panel – an advisory panel to the ASA – and she has just started a new venture as Marketing Director for Readers Union.

Lesley Godwin M IDM
Marketing Director
Readers Union
Brunel House, Forde Close
Newton Abbott
Devon TQ12 2DW
E-mail: lesley.godwin@virgin.net
Tel: 01626-323200

Chapter 1.3

Acquiring new customers: Starting the relationship

The need to acquire new customers

When the growth of direct marketing was at its height in the 1970s and '80s, direct marketers focused on advertising for new customers. Not much time or effort was spent on retaining them. Then, when businesses realised it was much cheaper to retain an existing customer than to acquire a new one, the focus quite rightly moved to investment in databases. The aim was to understand customers better, track their behaviour, predict their lifetime value and develop programmes designed to retain them longer.

However, in the midst of this shift towards customer retention, the basic need to acquire new customers must be re-emphasised. **The fact is: all organisations need to do both – to acquire customers and to retain them.**

To grow a business, you must either attract more customers – or make more profit from those you have. Even if you are fortunate and start with a customer list, perhaps derived from a non-marketing source, you cannot expect to keep all of those customers. An average renewal rate is around 75%. That means for every 1,000 customers you start with, you may need 250 new recruits each year just to keep your customer base constant. **However good your retention programme, you will lose customers.** Reasons, often beyond your control, include:

✗ Some will literally die or move away.

✗ Some will grow out of your market: their lifestyle or interests will change and they will stray from your product area.

✗ Some will change their financial circumstances; retire or lose their jobs.

✗ Some will move part or all of their custom to your competitors.

In business-to-business, similar attrition occurs due, for example, to movements of key personnel, technological change, mergers, takeovers, etc.

Although new customers are often very expensive to recruit, they can also be very profitable. It is crucial to look at the long-term value of a customer in order to set affordable acquisition costs. But remember: **the most profitable period in a customer's life is usually shortly after their recruitment**.

Setting objectives for customer recruitment

Before considering how to acquire new customers, you should first set down your objectives in numerical terms.

Your business strategy should determine what your main objectives are. Do you need:

? **Volume sales –** you may have a large quantity of time-sensitive products on your hands or you may need to increase membership of an organisation, or circulation of a magazine; or the costs of your product may reduce considerably at a volume which you would like to exceed.

? **Income –** do you need short-term income, or is your strategy to invest now for longer-term gain?

In practice, your objectives are likely to be:

either

✓ To achieve maximum sales within a given expenditure

or

✓ To achieve maximum sales at a given cost per sale.

Setting overall budgets

How to set budgets and estimate response and profitability are the subjects of separate sections of this Guide. However, there are some important points worth introducing at the outset.

If you are starting your operation from scratch, first conduct market research to refine the product/offer and identify the target market. You can then set up programmes to test a range of media and customer profiles. Concentrate on those profiles that most closely match your expectations: if your research says your product appeals most to BC1 males 18–30 years, target your media and copy to this group. But also test "around the edges" to see how wide the appeal is.

Your test programme will help you to estimate response rates, conversion and profitability before designing your next set of tests and/or the programme itself.

Your next step will be to determine the size of the budget on the basis of the affordable cost-per-sale. This will depend on how risky your move into direct marketing is, the size of the market for your product, and your timescale, ie how quickly you want to establish the profitability of the available media before "rolling-out".

Some customers will be much easier and cheaper to acquire than others. **Your initial campaign, therefore, should seek to acquire the lowest-cost sales first.** Generally speaking, the cost of acquiring customers depends on their status as prospects and the methods used to recruit them, as the following pyramid shows:

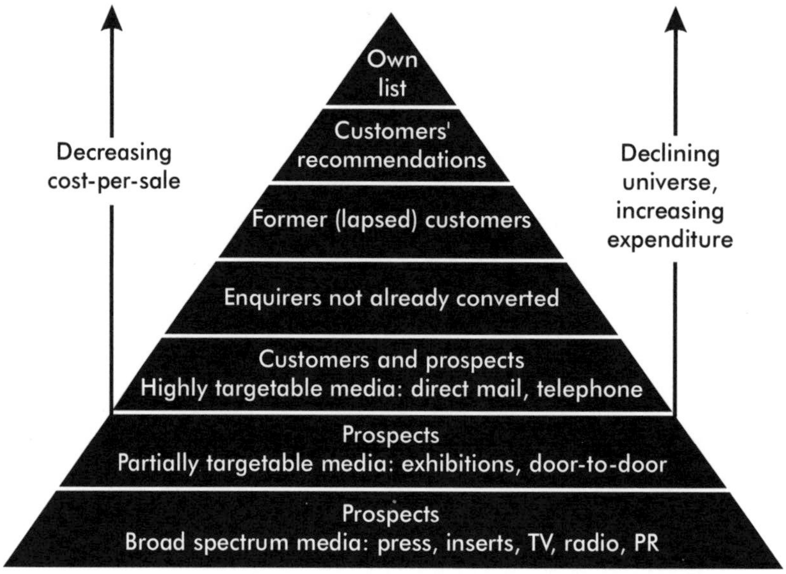

The pyramid indicates that the highest costs-per-sale are those prospects who cluster in large numbers towards the base. However difficult it may be to turn these into customers, they are where the volume lies. **Unless your business objectives can be met from the smaller numbers at the top of the pyramid, your test programmes should include working the lower levels of the pyramid, ie higher volume less-targeted media.**

Testing large volume/higher cost-per-sale media will help you to establish what proportion of the total universe can be economically promoted; the likely volume of sales; and the level of promotion investment required. These are all key to your long-term business strategy.

The allowable cost of recruiting a customer

To establish an allowable cost-per-sale we must understand the economics of the business. This stage is discussed in some detail in later sections of this Guide (see Chapters 2.4 to 2.6), and so again a few words of introduction.

Short term or long term?

How you determine your allowable-cost-per sale will depend on whether your objective is short-term or long-term gain.

If you are looking at the short term, then the profitability from the initial sale should be used.

If you are starting up and have little data on lifetime value, then again the profitability from the initial sale should be used – unless future incremental business is crucial to your business, in which case use industry guidance on expected lifetime value until your monitoring determines a more accurate figure.

If you have experience of future sales, and you are looking at the longer term, then take the future value into account.

Lifetime value – how important?

The importance of lifetime value cannot be emphasised enough. However, for **some** businesses and **some** products, the most significant profit is in the initial sale, while the theoretical increased profit over time is so small as to be insignificant.

Don't use lifetime value to set allowable cost-per-sale unless you are confident of the figures. The further out your theoretical lifetime horizon, the less robust your calculations. And remember: a proportion (probably a large one) of your customers will buy from you only once, so your lifetime value calculation has to be an average, taking into account those who will not stay with you.

That last point is worth re-stating as it is often misunderstood.

The lifetime value of a customer must be an average for ALL customers recruited at one time, not your expectation for each individual customer. It must take into account all those customers who buy little or nothing following their initial purchase.

Below are two examples showing different approaches to long-term value:

He who waits ...

A catalogue attracts customers with an initial offer of a single product, its objective being to sell them more from future catalogues. The advertiser expects the majority of its profit to come from incremental sales and does not look to breakeven on the initial promotion.

Covering their costs

A subscription magazine knows that the ultimate value of its customers depends on the length of time they subscribe. Nevertheless, the advertiser expects to make a profitable contribution from the initial promotion. There may also be incremental income from cross-selling other products or trading up to a higher level of service – if significant these should also be taken into account. The total profit derived from a new influx of subscribers depends upon their ***average*** *renewal rate.*

Calculating allowable costs-per-sale

Another important element discussed elsewhere but worth introducing here is **costs**.

When arriving at an allowable cost-per-sale, estimate anticipated response and hence revenue, then deduct promotion costs, product costs, fulfilment costs, and the minimum acceptable profit. Any costs that you allocate at this stage should be costs that are only incurred when you carry out the promotion and make sales.

Fixed overheads, ie costs that would exist whether or not you carry out the activity, should be excluded from the calculation. So, for instance, the fixed costs of setting up a process to produce a product should be excluded if you are producing the product anyway.

Marginal costs are the costs of producing a product after the fixed set-up costs have been recouped, ie the cost of running on "extra" quantities.

Marginal costing is an extremely difficult and important subject; different organisations adopt their own conventions for defining and allocating them. For a fuller discussion on costs, please refer to Chapter 2.5.

An important point to remember is:

Investment in direct marketing is usually just that – a decision to spend so much now in order to receive more later. By including fixed costs, you could prevent yourself from making profitable investment decisions. (There are, of course, occasions when it is right to consider fixed and start-up costs, eg when deciding whether to produce a product in the first place.)

The barriers to buying direct

The biggest hurdle direct marketers and their customers face is the perceived risk of buying "at a distance". This, of course, is most pronounced at the time of the first purchase, ie during the customer acquisition phase.

To quote Graeme McCorkell:

> People respond to advertisements only when the immediate gain in responding exceeds the risk or cost of responding by an acceptable margin ... and it appears easy to respond.
> – Graeme McCorkell, "Advertising That Pulls Response"

This is an important difference between direct marketing and other marketing disciplines and we should explore it more fully. It will help us to understand the requirements of direct marketing creativity later in this Guide.

Obviously, reasons for non-response include those causing a no-sale in any other situation, ie wrong product, wrong price, wrong audience, etc. But with direct marketing there are additional obstacles resulting entirely from the remoteness between seller and buyer, for example:

✘ Prospects may not be able to see or handle the product, or sample the service, until after it has been ordered.

✘ Prospects cannot easily assess the personality/integrity of the seller or the seller's organisation.

✘ Prospects may not be able to interpret the literature. Questions thus remain unanswered, which is highly destructive.

✘ There may be fears in relation to payment: Will the cheque arrive? Will I be able to sort out my account in the event of a query? Shall I be able to secure a refund if the goods are returned?

✘ There may be worries about delivery. When will the goods arrive? Will I be at home to receive them?

✘ There may be concerns about data protection and privacy.

✘ There may be specific fears about becoming involved, eg will a sales person turn up at the door uninvited? Will I be pursued for further orders/donations?

All of the above negative perceptions must be overcome before a prospect becomes a first-time buyer. A large part of direct marketing communication is directed towards overcoming objections.

Why prospects DO respond

Fortunately, to counter the negative associations, direct marketing offers prospects several distinct advantages, many unique to the discipline.

Prospects may choose to deal with a direct marketing organisation in order to:

✔ Acquire a **unique product**, one not readily available from conventional outlets.

✔ Acquire an everyday product in a **unique configuration**, eg with additional or different accessories.

✔ Acquire a product at a **lower price** or with **better payment terms** or **incentives**.

✔ Enjoy **better guarantees**, eg pay nothing if not satisfied.

✔ Enjoy a **wider product selection**, eg from a catalogue.

✔ Shop without consuming valued leisure time, without car parking hassle, with an option to try out goods at home, etc.

✔ Preserve **privacy**; **avoid embarrassment**.

✔ Be **better informed**: direct marketing offers are normally accompanied by more expansive information than is available from other channels.

✔ Enjoy an **on-going dialogue**: many prospects enjoy "belonging", whether to a club or a less clearly defined fraternity; they enjoy receiving correspondence and engaging in feedback.

Thus the communications task facing direct marketers at the recruitment stage – and at later stages in the customer dialogue – is to overcome negative associations whilst stressing the positive benefits of the direct route.

How people respond

We've talked about why prospects respond. Now is a good opportunity to consider **how** and **when** they respond.

The graphic below, based on research by a large London advertising agency, demonstrates who sees financial ads, who reads them, and who acts on them. How individuals react depends on their stage in the buying cycle, ie where they sit in the "target" below:

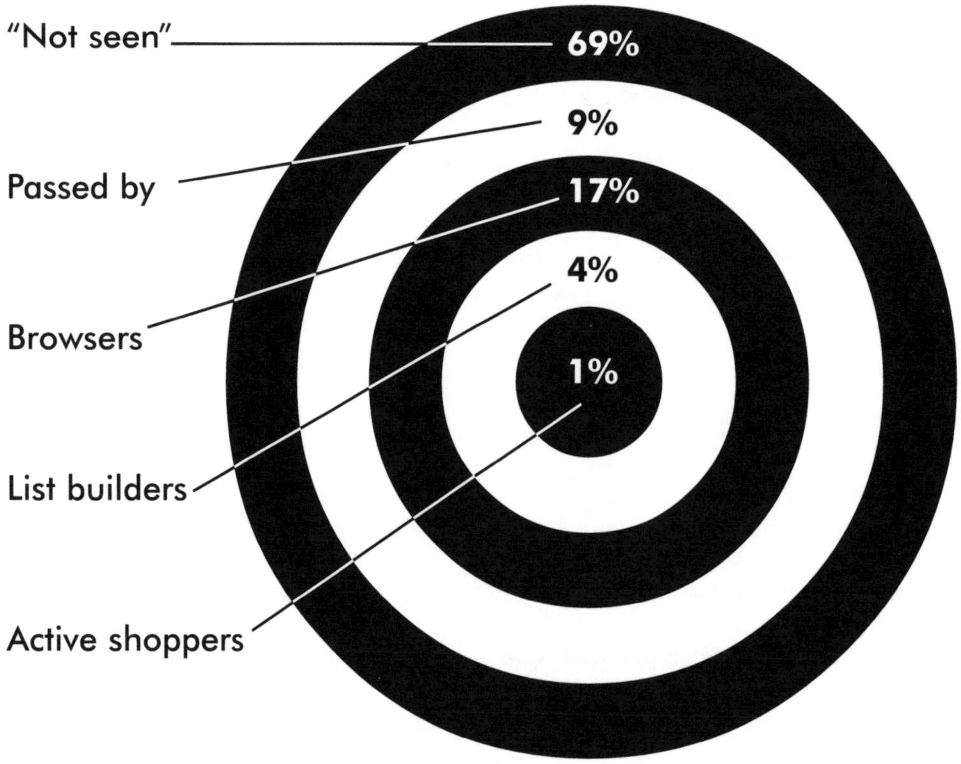

Source: Lowe Howard-Spink (1990)

Lowe Howard-Spink's research suggests:

✘ 69% do not notice financial ads in their newspaper.

✘ 9% notice but have no prior interest and move on.

? 17% browse financial ads with no **active** reason or interest.

✔ 4% are actively collecting information.

✔ 1% are in a buying frame of mind.

Thus, if you were running an enquiry ad, your realistic target would be the 4% information gatherers. If you were expecting a firmer commitment your target shrinks to 1%.

Any attempt to force this interest among the "outer ring" would not only be wasteful; it would probably divert attention from (and even alienate) true prospects. The 17% browsers may simply not yet be ready to act, but could perhaps be pursued, with a strong offer to respond **now**.

Direct sale or 2-stage enquiry generation?

Depending on a number of factors, some of which we have noted already, prospects become customers by either of two routes:

Direct (one-stage) sales. The prospect orders as the result of a single direct approach by printed ad, DRTV, radio, etc.

Enquiry generation (two-stage) lead. Prospects identify themselves by making a request for additional information, product sample, etc.

You may occasionally have the option of either route. More likely, however, your choice will be dictated by the key criteria summarised in the table below:

Direct sale	Enquiry
High-price products may allow high costs of one-stage direct sales but there are other more important considerations.	Price sensitive products are better suited to enquiry than sale (price may be omitted from initial communication).
Simple product with clearcut benefits and strong offer, may be easily demonstrated in print, on TV, etc.	Complex product/offer better explained at follow-up stage; requires more space/time than available in ad, TV commercial, etc.
Resultant database will grow more slowly but comprise proven buyers.	Larger database of enquirers who can be followed-up on several occasions, by 'phone, mail, personal call, etc.
More suited to short-term profitability.	Better suited to long-term prospect development.
More susceptible to response attrition as campaign progresses – less even flow of orders.	More consistent and predictable over longer campaign duration.

The elements of a successful acquisition programme

The elements of a successful acquisition programme are the success factors referred to throughout this Guide, namely:

- ✔ Product
- ✔ Price
- ✔ Offer
- ✔ Target/targeting method
- ✔ Media
- ✔ Creative (including response mechanism)
- ✔ Timing
- ✔ Fulfilment
- ✔ Data capture

These elements are frequently inextricably linked so it is **the whole** which the customer finds desirable. Especially closely linked are product, price, and offer; in combination these can be tuned to suit the available media, market, and economics.

But let us first look at them singly:

The right product – the first essential

The product is usually the most important element of the mix. It has to be right for selling at a distance.

- ? Does it have a unique benefit?
- ? Is it only available direct, or is it in the shops?
- ? Is it a niche product that is difficult to find in other outlets?
- ? Can it be successfully described in promotion material?
- ? Can it be satisfactorily delivered by carrier?
- ? Does it carry sufficient margins to support direct promotion/distribution?

To be successfully sold and distributed by direct marketing, a product will need at least some of these attributes. (Not all products promoted direct are actually delivered direct, although the diversity of products sold **and** distributed in this way is increasing.)

One example of changing the product to improve its direct appeal, frequently used by experienced direct marketers, is "bundling", ie putting a number of products together or adding some element to create a unique package, eg attachments for a vacuum cleaner, or an annual guide to a subscription magazine. Bundling may also enable you to increase the price without proportionately dropping the response, thereby improving profit margin.

Box clever

A standard toolbox was sold by direct marketing for many years after the advertiser hit upon the idea of filling it with a thousand nuts, bolts, screws, washers, etc – an example of an everyday product made unique by "bundling". It became an irresistible offer to DIY freaks which could not be purchased anywhere else.

The right price – and how it is presented

A low-priced product may not have a high enough profit margin to cover the cost of setting up a direct marketing campaign. Apart from simply trying to increase volume sales to cover the campaign cost, it may be possible to change the profitability in other ways.

A product may be sold more effectively by **changing its presentation**, eg from de-luxe to standard, or vice-versa.

Some marketers, for example, produce an **economy version** of a product for mail order sales, intending to offer a higher specification later (this is particularly viable with inbound telephone ordering where the upgrade can be offered immediately). Or a low-cost product could be sold as a **loss-leader** to generate names for future promotions. In effect it is acting as a filter, delivering a list of qualified prospects.

The method of payment can also be altered to form a different offer. For a subscription or continuity product, the commitment can be changed to reduce the perceived price (6 months' subscription instead of a year; 40 weeks instead of 52). Instalment billing linked to direct debit or credit card can be offered, so that the advertised price can be "only £10 per month for 4 months" rather than "£40".

The Which? way

Many publishers now offer subscriptions by direct debit rather than full payment by cheque or cash. Although this leads to a lower initial response, it has two main advantages. The subscriber does not have to be "renewed" every year, thus improving retention. Equally important, the ease and cheapness of applying for direct debit or credit card payment mean the price can be broken into smaller units.

Whereas it would not be feasible to have a renewal programme every 3 months for a cash subscriber, it is a strong proposition to offer a quarterly subscription to a magazine. ***Thus an annual subscription of £50 can be expressed as a quarterly subscription of £12.50.*** *The customer benefits as the commitment is less; the advertiser benefits because the perceived price is lower and response rates higher.*

Examples include Which? (Consumers' Association) who offer split payments, free trial and direct debit; and RSPB whose offer is similar but without split payments.

A thousand-and-one acquisition strategies ... how 9 marketers recruit new customers

On this and the next double-page spread we show examples of communications based on some of the acquisition strategies discussed in this chapter.

Press ad inserts

Grattan: multi-offer insert generates catalogue enquiries

Compton & Woodhouse: one-stage offer, first in a continuity series

Prevention: incentivised two-stage enquiry generator

FT: simple one-stage proposition

Source: John Watson, WWAV Rapp Collins, 15.10.97
J White, Financial Times, 15.10.97

Direct mail

TSB TRUSTCARD

TRUSTCARD

Head Office
Trustcard House
Gloucester Place
Brighton BN1 4BE

Our Ref: CI23

Mr Setty
113 117 Faringdon Road
LONDON EC1

A FREE GIFT WITH OUR COMPLIMENTS
IF YOU REPLY WITHIN 7 DAYS
If you accept this nomination and return the enclosed application form within 7 days, we will present you with this elegant Trustcard Travel Alarm Clock, once your application is approved and your card issued. Please see enclosed leaflet.
TRUSTCARD
Alarm Card

Dear Mr Setty,

TSB letter: incentive is conditional on firm order and acceptance

Here's how your £15 will help. Day or night, lifeboat crews are ready to go to sea, whatever the weather.

£15 keeps a lifeboat at sea for 20 minutes.

...the support of loved ones who wait behind and the help of supporters around the country. We rely entirely on voluntary contributions. Just £15 covers the cost of keeping a lifeboat at sea for 20 minutes.

Royal National
Lifeboat
Institution
0800 200 150
A Registered Charity

The number is 0800 200 150. We're waiting by the phones. Thank you.

RNLI seeks donation as first stage in an on-going dialogue

Radio

SFX: Footsteps coming closer. Loud knocking. Man gently calls "Ellie. Is that you Ellie?"

VO: Thankfully the NSPCC found Ellie in time. But for all the thousands of abused and abandoned children we've protected, countless more need our help this Christmas.
Please call us now on 0800 28 20 28 and give us what you can.
Your £15 could help fund our NSPCC Child Protection Helpline, which anyone can call if they fear a child is at risk. Your £15 could help us counsel a child suffering from the agony of emotional cruelty. And your £15 could help pay for the first vital visit to a child whose life may be in danger.

NSPCC uses radio to request donations, a one-stage strategy

Source: *John Watson, WWAV Rapp Collins, 15.10.97*

Video

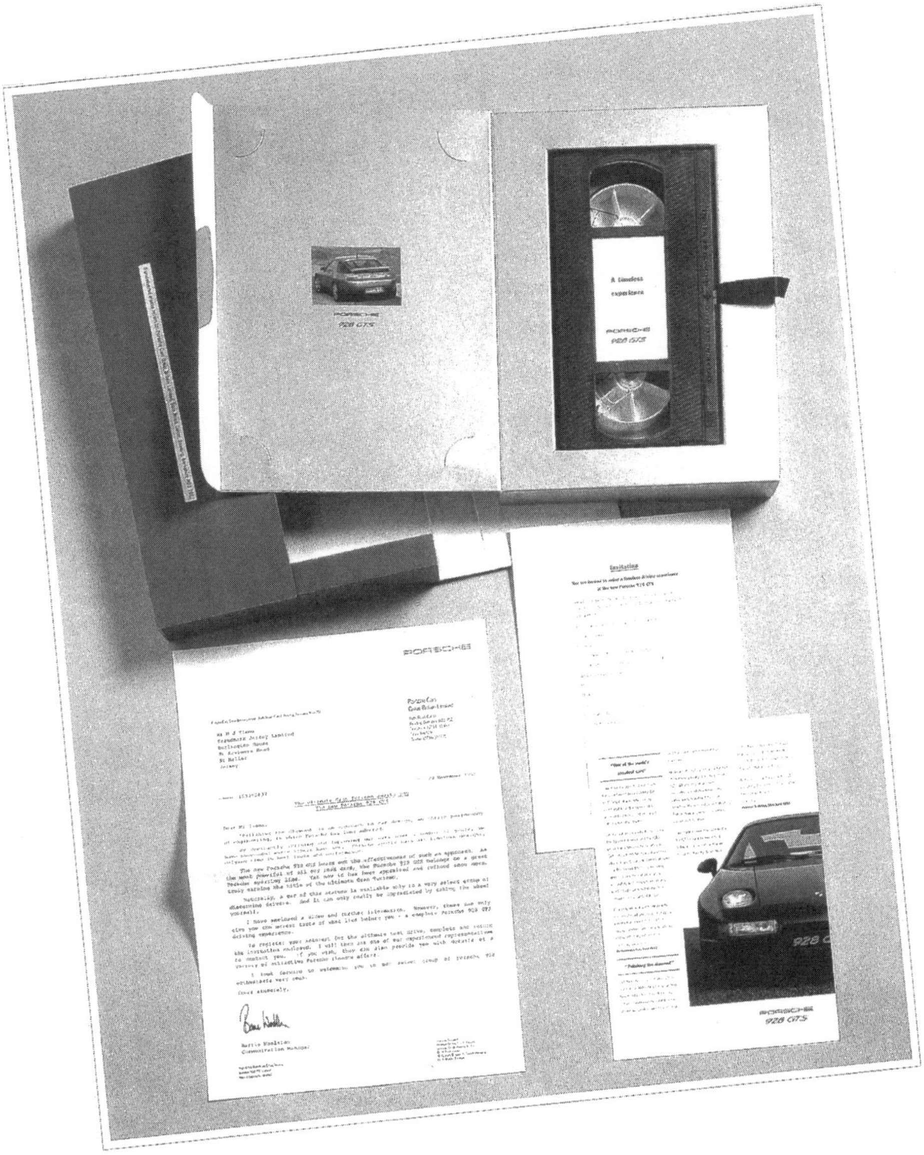

Porsche: with the "928" retailing at over £60,000, higher allowable selling costs are both inevitable and viable. This video is enclosed in a direct mail-pack; the second stage in a multi-stage programme.

Source: John Watson, WWAV Rapp Collins, 15.10.97

Consumers Association: this direct mail acquisition pack contains no fewer than nine separate components. It is extremely effective because there is a lot to read, a lot to do, a lot to gain – and nothing to lose.

Source: Illustration supplied by Marketing Department of Which? , 26.1.98

Free trials, on-approval and money-back guarantees

We have already noted some typical reasons for prospects **not** to respond. Usually these amount to fear in some form. Offers designed to alleviate fear and reassure the prospect include the following:

✔ **Sample product**, eg send for a sample of the product before committing to a purchase. Example: Which?

✔ **On-approval**, eg try the product at home for 10 days; return undamaged if not satisfied. Example: Bullworker.

✔ **Money-back guarantee**: if at any time you are not satisfied, return the product for a full refund. A strategy often used to pioneer new concepts.

✔ **Free trial**, eg try the product free for 30 days before you start to pay for it. Example: Linguaphone.

✔ **Invoice**: send no money now, we will invoice you later. Example: Institute of Direct Marketing training courses.

All the above offers will lift initial response with some loss of final, paid sales. Asking for cash with the order (CWO) will bring in fewer orders than "Invoice me" (sending an invoice with the goods), but the latter's higher response will often more than make up for bad debts.

Premia, incentives, and other inducements

However good your product, an added incentive to purchase will almost always be effective. It will help to overcome the inertia which otherwise characterises the direct response process.

Incentives, other than those we have already discussed above, include:

✔ Premia (gifts)

✔ Prize draw or competition entry

✔ Discounts (as opposed to price reductions)

The extra costs of premia and gifts should be offset by an increased response. The cost of the premium you can afford will depend on the price of the product and the level of risk. If you are offering goods on approval or free trial, you may make the premium available only on payment. If the premium is available whether or not orderers keep and pay for the product, you can obviously afford less per orderer than if you make the premium conditional upon payment.

Generally speaking, more generous offers produce better returns even after the cost of the premium has been taken into account. The table opposite, demonstrating the effect of low-cost premia, appeared in the first edition of this Guide and is just as valid today:

How a mail order direct seller benefits from premia

	Without incentive		With incentive	
Mailing quantity	400,000		400,000	
Orders received	24,000	(6%)	28,000	(7%)
Selling price	£12.95		£12.95	
Total revenue	£310,800		£362,600	
Extra revenue			£51,800	
Less premium (@ 50p each)			£14,000	
	Net extra revenue		£37,800	

This is an example of an "everybody wins" situation. The advertiser sells more and makes more profit; the purchaser receives an extra item free.

How many premia? If one premium works for you, try two! Alternatively, try offering a choice of premia. Some advertisers have evolved their acquisition campaigns to the point where they offer a wide choice of premia **plus** the opportunity to receive more than one. (Example: Grattan)

Successful marketers offer premia strategically to achieve specific objectives, eg for higher order values, for orders from specific ranges of goods, etc. "Early Bird" or "speed" premia are offered for response within a reasonable but short period of time.

What makes a good premium?

The ideal premium has a high perceived value and low actual cost. Information is often a very effective premium, eg booklets, brochures, videos, surveys. "Hard" premia (calculators, watches) will give higher response but at a higher cost. Beware, however, of mechanical and electrical premia because of their notorious failure rate.

Choosing the right premium is important. An editorial premium with an editorial product – more of the same – will normally be very effective, as will any other premium linked to the product (eg a tape measure with a DIY product). If the product and the marketing have wide appeal, the premium must also have wide appeal.

After a premium has been used for customer acquisition, make sure you change it when cross-promoting those same customers with different offers. People want only so many calculators or luggage sets!

Beware of "premium grabbers" – not all response is good! Track conversion rates carefully when using premia – you may find your conversion rates deteriorate as more people take advantage of your generosity. Ensure you retain data on people who trial your products regularly without buying; if possible, suppress them from future offers.

And business-to-business? Yes, premia are equally effective in most business markets. However, **a premium should be offered to generate an enquiry and not a purchase. Above all, it must be clear that it is a premium and not a bribe.** Some companies expressly forbid their staff to receive valuable premia and it is unwise to compromise them in any way. Whatever you do, make sure you do it openly.

If marketing overseas, remember in some countries it is illegal to offer gifts to incentivise purchase to consumers as well as to businesses. There are several other regulations applying to premia. See Chapters 5.2 and 8.1.

Discounts – powerful but dangerous

The most powerful incentive of all is often a lower price, or, more precisely, a **reduced** price. However, discounts are also the most expensive incentive: a discount of £5 means £5 less profit for you **unless the discount is linked to an increased order, in which case it may pay for itself much as a premium**.

Many catalogue advertisers successfully use volume discounts to increase profitability per sale, for instance:

- ✔ Buy 2, get 1 free
- ✔ Postage & packing free on orders over £20
- ✔ 5% discount on orders over £10, 10% discount on orders over £20, etc

Discounts can be counter-productive when used with quality products. A premium product should sell on its excellence – the marketing will stress its benefits and quality and the price may not be very visible. A discount in these circumstances can cheapen the product and needlessly draw attention to the price.

Prize draws and competitions

The distinction between draws, competitions, contests and games is so important in law that they are dealt with more fully in the legislative chapter of this Guide (see Chapter 8.1).

To introduce them very briefly here:

A **prize draw** calls for no skill on the part of participants and **must not** be conditional on the purchase of a product, ticket or anything else. Lucky numbers may be pre-drawn or post-drawn, ie before or after entry. In the case of pre-drawn numbers, nobody should know the identity of the prospect holding the winning number until the winner claims. The number will normally be drawn by computer.

Competitions (contests) are games of skill where there must be a clear application of skill and judgement (judged by a panel of experts). These can be linked to purchase; entries may be charged for.

Prize draws are best used in direct mail and inserts, where pre-drawn numbers can be printed on documents. Although prize draws normally involve pre-issued numbers this is not a requirement, and it is possible to offer prize draw entry through space and broadcast media. Contests are often preferred in more public media, and where the advertiser wishes to make entry conditional on purchase.

Prize draws are the most popular form of participatory incentive and can sometimes lift initial response by 100% or more. A draw can run for a number of months, even years, so amortising its costs over a number of promotions. The terms of entry should be made clear to entrants.

The most popular prizes are cash! But a prize draw can be run with a relatively small prize, or by offering products as prizes. The cost could also be reduced if you set up a venture with a company to provide the prizes in exchange for the promotion your advertising will give them.

As you might expect with such powerful incentives, prize draws normally boost initial response at the expense of poorer "back-end" performance. If you use prize draws or contests, take good legal advice and ensure you set them up correctly. See Chapter 8.1.

Acquisition media: If it works, use it

Almost every medium in the media repository can be used for new customer acquisition, with varying degrees of efficiency.

Better than simply listing recruitment media, we re-introduce here two charts that appeared in the first edition – both are still very much current.

The flowchart overleaf was compiled in the US by Messrs Baier, Hoke and Stone. It not only sets out virtually all available recruitment media, it also demonstrates their roles and inter-relationships in the media mix. These esteemed gentlemen will not object to our adding in the Internet.

Use this chart as a checklist. Have you considered **all** the media opportunities and strategies shown? You could do worse than look at the chart afresh at the start of each campaign.

The second chart (on page 1.3-21) is another time-honoured appraisal of the recruitment media, presenting a broad assessment of the relative strengths and weaknesses of each.

This chart is of little value to practitioners, but forms an extremely useful starting point for students. It has been updated to reflect the growing importance of DRTV, the potential of radio, and the arrival of the Internet.

For a fuller discourse on recruitment media, how they are used, advantages and disadvantages, please turn to Chapters 4.1 to 4.7.

Direct marketing flowchart

Martin Baier, Henry R Hoke Jr, Robert Stone

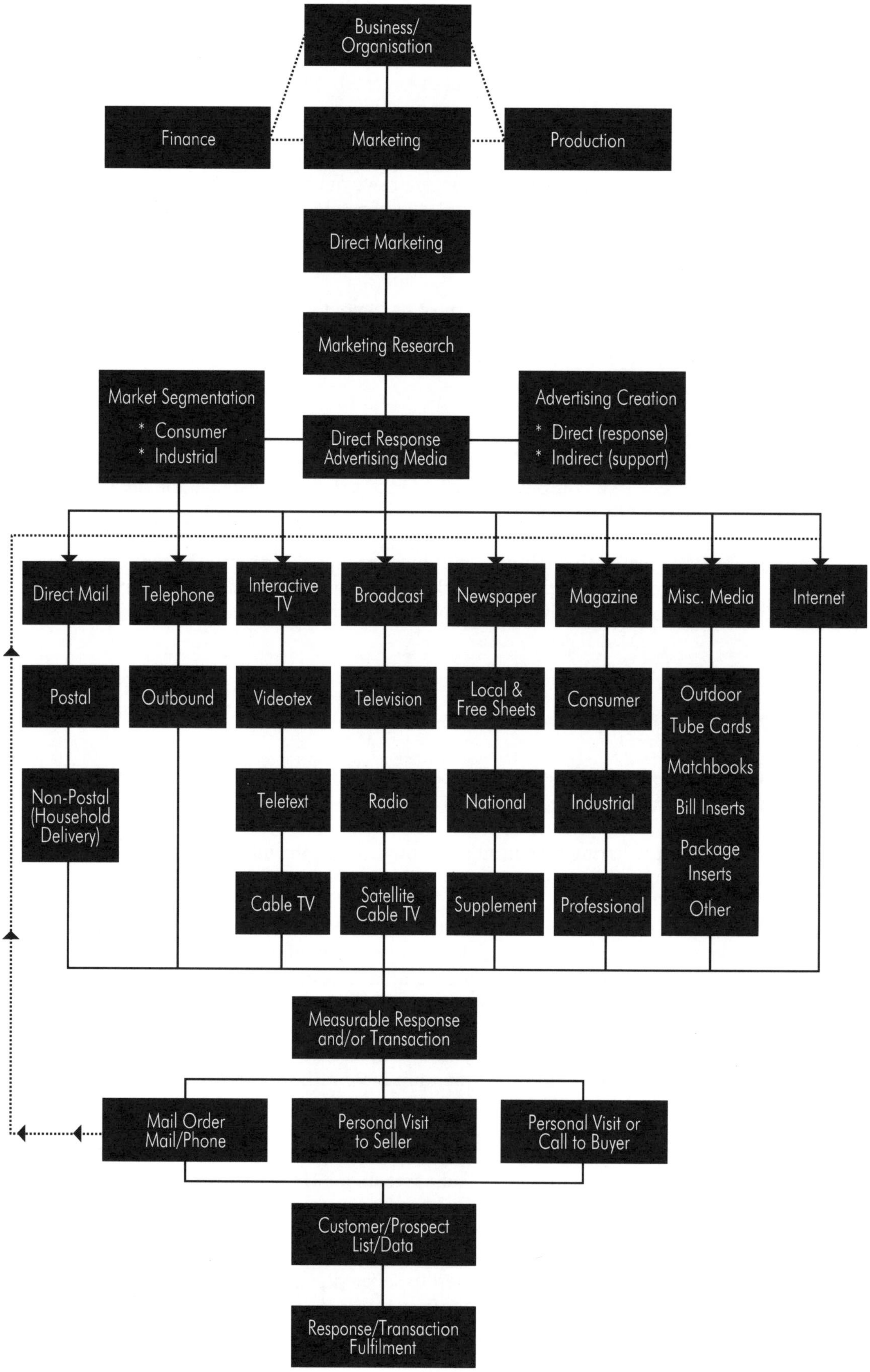

Media strengths and weaknesses: A very broad assessment

Medium	Applications	Targeting	Testing	Cost (per contact)	Speed		Response	
					Mount (average)	Response (cumulative)	Percent	Volume
Direct Mail	All. Weakest on recruitment of cold prospects, especially where no suitable list available.	V. good	V. good	V. high *	Slow (3–4 months)	Medium	High	Medium
Inserts (with newspapers & magazines)	Lead generation; direct sales, especially continuity offers and non cash-with-order sales.	Good & improving	V. good	Low–medium *	Medium (3 months)	Fast	Medium–low	High
Press: Newspapers	Lead generation; direct sales; general awareness; support for other direct activities; store traffic.	Medium to poor	Medium	V. low	Fast	Fast	Low (1 month)	High
Press: Magazines	Lead generation; direct sales; general awareness.	Medium	Low	Medium *	Medium	Slow	Medium	Medium
Posters	Awareness; store traffic boost; direct response negligible.	Poor	Nil	V. low	Slow	Slow	Nil	Nil
Door-to-door	Lead generation; sales promotion; store traffic; support.	Medium–	Good medium	Low– (3–4 months)	Medium	Fast	Medium	High
Direct Response TV	Lead generation (high-ticket items); direct sales; support for other direct activities.	Medium	Improving	Low	Fast (3 months)	Fast	Low	Medium
Radio	Awareness; store and event traffic boost; lead generation; support for other response media.	Medium	V. good	Low	Fast (1–2 months)	Medium	V. low	Improving, medium
Telephone	Order taking; re-order; renewals; follow-up; feedback and dialogue.	V. good	V. good	V. high	Fast	Slow	High	Low
PR	Awareness; direct enquiries.	Medium (as press)	Nil	Variable	Fast	Slow	Low	Low
Internet	All. Best for information dissemination. Very early days.	Low	Difficult	Low	Fast	Slow	Medium	Medium

* Business media averagely cost about 25% more than consumer equivalents due to shorter print-runs.

IMPORTANT – integrated media

It will not always be evident in the chapters on specific media that multi-media campaigns are increasingly used to maximise response. Look out for examples of support media, eg Book Club Associates' use of TV to boost response to its door-to-door campaign, and Reader's Digest's use of TV to lift its direct mail responses. The strength of the Internet is likely to be its role in supplying information (much as mail and 'phone) in response to enquiries generated by other media.

Acquisition media: Some rules of thumb

The most effective and efficient media are also:

- ✔ The most expensive (per thousand audience)
- ✔ The most intrusive and personal
- ✔ The least liked
- ✔ The most selective
- ✔ The so-called "below-the-line" media

The biggest volume media are also:

- ✔ The least expensive (per thousand audience)
- ✔ The least intrusive; the most public
- ✔ The most liked
- ✔ The least selective
- ✔ The so-called "above-the-line" media

Targeting – selecting the right audience

Profiling

Experienced direct marketers use what is known about their existing customers to attract new customers. One of the benefits of a customer database which tracks individuals by their personal details, transactions and promotional history, is its value in forming acquisition strategies, especially in respect of targeting.

Knowledge of extant customers can be used to decide not only how and where to advertise, but also likely recruitment costs – by media, method, target prospect (eg age), etc.

The technique used for identifying denominators common to established customers is known as "profiling". Key discriminators include:

- ✔ Socio-demographics
- ✔ Geodemographics
- ✔ Lifestyle, psychographics
- ✔ Method of acquisition (recruitment source)
- ✔ Customer behaviour, eg recency, frequency, value of purchases
- ✔ Responsiveness to specific promotions

The "Identikit" profiles of known customers, built up from the above, are compared with the profiles of media readerships, lists, geographic areas (postcodes), etc, in search of a close match. The closer the match the more likely it is that prospects will behave like your established customers. In this way you can pick your target audience with some precision.

A simple example is where **neighbours** of customers are recruited through direct mail and door-to-door promotions, because their profiles (primarily the type of area in which they live) suggest similar purchasing propensity for certain types of product or service.

Business-to-business

In business-to-business, profiling looks for similarities and differences in such areas as:

- ✔ Type of business (SIC, Standard Industry Code)
- ✔ Size/turnover
- ✔ Type and number of sites
- ✔ Number of employees per site
- ✔ Level of decision maker(s)
- ✔ Anticipated demand level
- ✔ Customer transaction data, eg purchases: recency, frequency, value, etc

Member-Get-a-Member

Customer recommendations are an interesting extension of the profiling principle. Prospects identified and/or recommended by customers (eg friends, neighbours, relatives, colleagues) by means of a "Member-Get-a-Member" scheme (MGM) usually show a high degree of correlation with the people who put forward their names. Hence "recommend" schemes are a vital part of any successful direct marketer's repertoire.

More of the same

One of the most important pieces of advice that can be given to new direct marketers is to remember the principle of profiling: what you are generally looking for is not new and different types of customer, but more of the same.

Exceptions to the "more-of-the-same" rule

An important exception to the above rule is when you introduce a product or service which **may** attract a different type of user. For example, if a manufacturer of soil-based fertilisers introduces a liquid version, will customers for the new product be the advocates of his soil-based products – or will they be a different category of gardener altogether?

Another exception is when there are no more ideal prospects to uncover, perhaps because you have contacted them all. **In this case it will be necessary to identify and target secondary characteristics.** For example, previous purchasing behaviour is an ideal characteristic but geographic location might be a useful secondary characteristic.

What if you have no customers to profile?

If, presumably because yours is a new enterprise, you have no customers to profile – what then?

You can still use the techniques of profiling to match the **anticipated** profile of your **likely** customers (drawn up from research, observation, etc) with the known profiles of media readerships, geographic areas, etc.

Profiling and its associated subjects, segmentation and modelling, are dealt with more fully by other authors in this Guide. See Chapters 3.5 to 3.7.

Targeting – let's be realistic

Targeting is vital to modern direct marketing, and so much a factor in its success that the term is often over-used. In practice, there is targeting and targeting – ranging from very specific (eg direct mail to known individuals), to very loose (eg newspaper advertising directed at a broad readership which shows only a slight bias towards your prospect group), to almost non-existent (eg TV bought cheaply to reach as wide as possible an audience).

It is a common error to assume that all targeting is highly precise – unfortunately direct marketing has not yet reached that Utopian goal. In fact, close targeting can be a disadvantage in some situations as we shall see on the facing page.

Don't be so personal!

A supplier was forced to sue its client for non-payment covering the costs of a direct mail campaign. The client counter-claimed on the grounds that the list it had been supplied was not wholly made up of retired people as it had hoped, being based solely on geodemographic codes. The court, having read submissions by advertising experts, decreed that it was unreasonable to expect any form of targeting to be 100% accurate.

Never assume, therefore, that because a list comprises a higher than average percentage of people of one or other characteristic, that all its members will fit that description. Don't make the mistake, as another marketer did, of opening your letter "Dear Retired Person" simply because it was being targeted to a geodemographic area with a high retired population. Sixty percent of recipients were not retired.

In fact, the "loose" targeting of newspapers, television and radio serves acquisition programmes very well, for two reasons:

1. You may not always know exactly who is attracted to your product, or why. In the early stages of a product's life, you may be relying on new users to tell you things you will employ later, in more closely targeted media.

2. Your best prospects may not yet appear on a close targeted list, for example if they have just taken up a pastime, or started a business, or entered a new lifestage.

– all of which brings us back to the pyramid we saw earlier, where the less targeted, higher volume media formed the base and the close targeted, low volume opportunities the apex.

Timing

The ideal timing for a customer acquisition campaign, like most decisions in marketing, depends on many factors. Chief among these are the product (is it a lawnmower or a snowplough?) and the state of the market, especially competitive activity, eg is it necessary to pre-empt your rivals?

There are several aspects to timing that are less obvious.

For example:

1. Response is often seasonally biased despite no apparent seasonality in the product or market. A review of competitive direct marketing activity will usually throw light on data of this kind. (See Chapter 4.1.)

2. Certain times of the year are generally reckoned to be more productive in response terms. These do not always correspond with periods of highest media cost.

HIGH RESPONSE January – March Mid August – October	**BEST VALUE** Early January August
June – July Late November – December **LOWER RESPONSE**	April – May November – December **WORST VALUE**

Sum(mer) total

It is often assumed that "everybody goes away in the summer holidays". The mistaken belief is that the entire population is out of the country throughout July and August.

In fact, only a minority goes abroad while an even smaller minority is away from home during any given week. Holidays are times of low-cost offers from many of the media (who also believe everyone is away!).

This situation can lead to some extremely attractive customer recruitment opportunities for wide-awake direct marketers.

3. For some products customers' buying cycles may be long and difficult to predict (we must remember direct marketing isn't used only for mail order).

   In fact, customers' personal buying cycles explain why responses often come in over a long period, and why follow-up mailings are sometimes as successful as initial campaigns.

   The following example points to several different opportunities for manufacturers and dealers to win over the customer.

Wannabe a BMW owner?

A driver's decision to buy a BMW may come at the end of a long process of making mental lists of cars which project his/her desired self-image. There will then be a period of fact-gathering as the need to purchase looms. (Opportunity).

The decision, whatever else is involved, will be primarily about image – derived from PR, showroom displays, cars and their drivers on the road, and, of course, advertising. (Opportunity)

A BMW is expensive. The customer needs to be sure he or she is making the best decision and needs plenty of support. (Opportunity)

Cars are complex. Some help in understanding the features/benefits of a BMW would be appreciated, if only as justification for a decision already taken based on image. (Opportunity)

A new car is an infrequent purchase, meaning not only that the customer needs time to make the decision, but also that time is available – perhaps as much as two or three years. (Several opportunities)

Finally, the customer will contact a BMW dealer – who will themselves have been promoting their wares. (Opportunity)

The growth of data-driven marketing has led to many advertisers collecting relevant information on the seasonality of individuals' purchase behaviour, ensuring that their promotions to these prospects are well timed. This is particularly true of financial services and motoring.

Creating the recruiting message

Copy, design, formats

The "creative" component is said by most experts to be low in the order of what is most important in the direct marketing communication. But it is the creative execution that will attract the consumer's attention and communicate the benefits of the product and the excitement of the incentives and offers. What Drayton Bird calls, "The Moment of Truth".

The creative approach should identify the key elements of the offer and express them in a way that will attract, excite and convince the sort of person whom you expect to buy your products. In a "one-stage" advertisement, copy will usually be long. The promotion has to take the customer from knowing little and being wary about the product, through the benefits, overcoming objections, all the way to completing the coupon or making the 'phone call.

Newcomers to direct marketing often puzzle over why long copy is used when seemingly it isn't always essential. One answer must surely be:

For prospects who know nothing about a product, long copy is necessary to ease them through the stages of the selling process. **For prospects who know a great deal about a product**, long copy is simply enjoyable.

Using data to create the message

Increasingly the skilled direct marketing creative uses existing customer data to shape recruitment communications. It's never too late to learn something new about what makes customers respond:

You mean it's really free?

Which? Magazine had run a no-risk three months' free trial for many years. It then conducted focus groups amongst subscribers who had responded to the free trial offer. One of the strongest findings was that new subscribers were surprised when the free trial turned out to be ***really*** *free – they had expected a catch. This led to a new headline "COMPLETELY FREE OFFER" with more emphasis on the fact that it really was free with no strings attached. This approach led to a significant increase in response.*

The subjects of copy, design and format are all covered in detail later in this Guide by specialist authors. See Chapters 6.1 to 6.6.

Response mechanism

As we said right at the beginning of this section, to be effective an offer must be easy to respond to.

If you are using print media, include a well-designed coupon with lots of room for information. With direct mail, pre-enter the prospects' name and address and other information, giving them an opportunity to correct it. Be careful about asking for ancillary information – it would be "nice" to have your customer's telephone number, but unless there is a good reason for requesting it you may find it lowers response. Give a telephone number for ordering but always include a coupon as well where possible.

The coupon is a critically important element of any printed communication. However persuasive your copy and offer, if the customer gets to the coupon and can't understand it, or read it – or can't find it! – your careful work will come to nothing. **The positioning, size and copy of the coupon is so important it should form a central consideration of the design process – not be tacked on as an afterthought.**

An apparent exception to the "easy to respond" rule is the success of prize draw promotions which incorporate complex and involving formats. Direct mail-packs and inserts that use involvement devices, eg scratch-offs, stamps, coins, tokens, have a fun factor that leads the customer to get involved in the pack and then in the offer. Involvement devices can be equally effective in non-prize draw promotions.

Fulfilment and conversion

As part of planning your acquisition programme, you will also set up your fulfilment and customer service routines. Your fulfilment resource should be fully informed to ensure that responses are handled swiftly and efficiently; the product despatched correctly with any appropriate additional material; and customer services personnel able to answer any queries.

Give careful thought to what material will go out with the product and what you will use to fulfil enquiries.

Your initial communication hopefully created a good impression of your company. Those same values should be reflected in the material that accompanies the product, which should arrive as quickly as possible. If the promotion is two-stage, the quality and persuasiveness of the conversion programme will determine the cost effectiveness of the promotion as a whole.

The subject of fulfilment is covered in detail in a later section of this Guide. See Chapter 7.9.

Capturing the data – ready to begin the retention process

The key to direct marketing is that it should be on-going. Every direct marketing activity you undertake will give you information, on media costs, response by source, payment and bad debt, levels of complaint or problems, test results of new media, new lists, new creative, new offers, etc.

As much can be learned from the promotion failures as the successes. Ensure that systems are set up with your suppliers or in-house facilities to capture, record and above all **use** this data, to better inform your planning for your next campaign.

The subjects of data capture, processing and usage are dealt with in Chapters 3.1 – 3.7, also 7.1.

The spiral of prosperity

The continuity of successful direct marketing can be represented by an upward spiral. Other authors may prefer analogies like building blocks and stepping stones, with tomorrow's sales being raised on today's customer foundations. But the so-called spiral of prosperity perfectly describes direct marketing's continuum: increased investment follows improved profits, which in turn spring from enhanced customer knowledge, and so on, in what is hopefully an ever-upward direction:

The spiral of prosperity

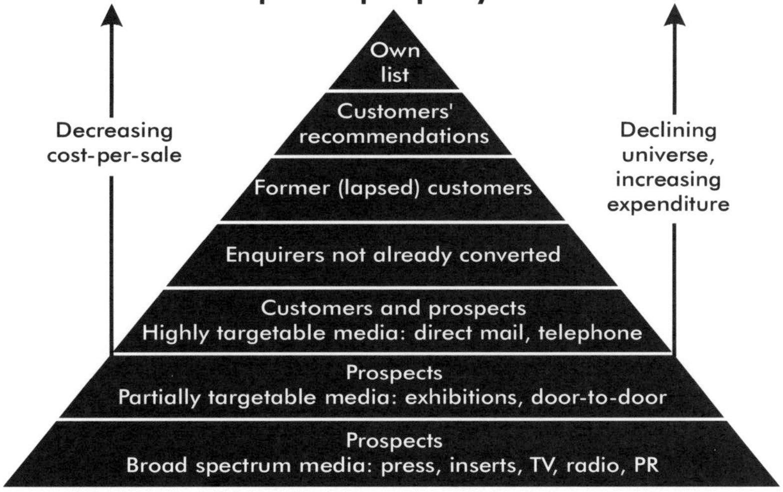

We end this introductory chapter on acquisition with a reminder that acquiring the right customers and settling them in is the first stage of the retention process, the subject of the next chapter.

Chapter 1.4

Retaining customers through genuine loyalty

This chapter includes:

- **Degrees and types of loyalty**
- **Short-term promotions versus long-term loyalty**
- **The weakness of reward-only schemes**
- **The true motivators: 3 types of bonding**
- **The business benefits of loyal customers**
- **The "Laws of Loyalty"**
- **The "Moments of Truth"**
- **The language of loyalty**
- **Loyalty case studies**

In the previous chapter we looked at how we acquire customers and prospects, the first stage in building a customer database. Acquiring the right customers, we noted, is the first crucial step towards retaining them: the better the match the longer and more rewarding the relationship. In this chapter, Angus Jenkinson looks at how customer relationships can be fostered and developed.

Not long ago even eminent marketers could be heard extolling the view that a good product backed by satisfactory service would automatically lead to repeat sales. Today we know that to be simply untrue; research proves without doubt that so-called "satisfied" customers are often among the most promiscuous.

Loyalty begins, says Jenkinson, with understanding each and every one of your customers. It is no longer a matter of what you can do to compel or persuade them, but how to behave so that they will positively **want** to keep doing business with you.

New in this edition. Such is the rapid growth in the importance of long-term loyalty that our first edition did not carry a chapter specifically devoted to the topic. In this edition it could easily be deemed one of the most important chapters in the Guide.

Angus Jenkinson, founding director, Stepping Stones

Angus began his career with IBM, in sales and marketing, before joining IBM's midrange systems partner, JBA International. In 1986 he was appointed Managing Director of The Computing Group, then the fastest-growing company in direct marketing information systems and services. In 1991 he founded Stepping Stones, a thriving consultancy with a reputation for originality, excellence and results.

His long list of achievements includes Chair of the Institute of Direct Marketing Management Forum; Chair of AIMS (Association of Information Systems for Marketing and Sales); and Chair of Database Advisory Panel for the International Montreux Direct Marketing Symposium. He has written numerous papers, contributes to seminars, conferences, corporate events and academic programmes, and is the author of "Valuing Your Customers" (McGraw-Hill, 1995). He has also run personnel development programmes on Leadership, Innovation and Change.

Stepping Stones' achievements include facilitating the launch of a loyalty programme for a billion-pound leisure business; project management of the pan-European mail order division of a major charity; and negotiating a cross-subsidiary marketing database for a leading financial services provider.

Angus lists among his wide-ranging interests: nature, science and art (a fair blend with which to tackle direct marketing); also exploring the mind and spirit, becoming human, enjoying people and having a good time.

Angus Jenkinson M IDM
Stepping Stones Consultancy Limited
16 High Street
Chesham
Buckinghamshire HP5 1EP
E-mail: angus@stepping-stones.ndirect.co.uk
Tel: 01494-792477

Chapter 1.4

Retaining customers through genuine loyalty

What do we mean by loyalty?

We all know what the word "loyalty" means, but what does customer loyalty amount to in practice – and how is it achieved? First of all we need to understand that there are different degrees of loyalty. Loyalty may be:

either ersatz **or** genuine

either passive **or** active

either profitable **or** unprofitable.

What do we mean by ersatz loyalty?

Loyalty based upon cut-price offers, too low prices, or blatant reward schemes (especially money-back schemes) is ersatz. Not surprisingly customers who exhibit this type of loyalty buy because they like price deals, will always look for price deals, and don't respond to anything other than price deals.

This truth was recognised over eighty years ago as evidenced by this quotation from a latter-day retail expert:

> The old-established houses are those that have a reputation for trading in reliable goods. Concerns which cater for cheap trade are always more or less ephemeral, for the simple reason that the buyers of cheap commodities are seldom well-established and their existence is precarious. There is always, it is true, a large demand by short-sighted people for inferior goods, but this is a custom that must be constantly sought for it is fickle and uncertain.
>
> – D N Dunlop, 1916

So what, you may ask, is the purpose of price promotions? Later in this chapter we look at a comparison between old-fashioned price and reward promotions and modern loyalty programmes.

What do we mean by genuine loyalty?

A good example of genuine loyalty is Clarks Shoes.

Clarks Shoes are a British institution. For generations children have been shod by Clarks, their parents valuing the care that goes into good fittings for growing feet. When the children grow up and make their own decisions, they move away from a brand associated with parental choice, at least for a few years. But it is this very same group who, as parents, come back to buy shoes for their own children and so keep the Clarks brand strong. A deep and residual loyalty and trust are carried forward.

Genuine loyalty may or may not be arrived at as part of a conscious loyalty building programme, but most organisations which enjoy this kind of loyalty are also active in encouraging it. It is more likely to derive from service and product quality than from low prices and special deals.

What do we mean by passive loyalty?

Perhaps 90–95% of so-called "loyal" behaviour is passive: it may be founded, for example, in habit, laziness, a lack of knowledge or a dearth of convenient alternatives. In other words: if the conditions remain right the customer will go on buying.

However, **passive loyalty is vulnerable**. Who knows how long before a competitor offers more and better information, improved service, or a more convenient location?

Research shows that customers who are retained merely because they are "satisfied" do not make good long-term prospects, whereas "very" satisfied customers are likely to stay and be profitable. Rank Xerox found that their "very satisfieds" were **six times** more likely to repeat-buy than their "satisfieds".

What do we mean by active loyalty?

Active loyalty is **not** the same thing as active promotion.

In loyalty terms, "active" signifies **emotional involvement**: it implies the customer enjoying affinity, involvement, even affection, with you, just as exists between friends. It means they choose you **consciously**.

Active loyalty leads to commitment, even through difficult times, as well as some forgiveness should something go wrong. It almost certainly involves feedback about disappointments in the expectation that the outcome will be mutually beneficial – just as a loving spouse can still enjoy a relationship despite having something critical to say about his/her partner's performance!

Studies show we need to probe customers' emotions about our brand, product or service – not just their evaluated satisfaction score. All decision-making is emotionally based, so smart marketers focus on **retention behaviour and emotional attitudes** to their brands. Emotional attitudes are just as much a factor in business-to-business relationships as with consumers, as the following example suggests:

Taking the long view

In the late 1980s, The Computing Group, a UK computer bureau providing services to the direct marketing industry, realised it could look at clients as providing monthly fees of £2,000, £5,000 or £10,000; or it could think of them as worth £120,000 or £300,000, or £600,000 over five years. This has a wonderful effect on customer service attitudes and problem solving, and resulted in a long period of zero defections. The Group became market leader with steadily improving financial results.

What do we mean by profitable and unprofitable loyalty?

It is not always realised that it can be extremely unprofitable to devote energy and resources to boosting loyalty among the wrong types of customers, a theme to which we shall be returning several times in this chapter and throughout the Guide.

Sales promotion schemes versus loyalty programmes – a comparison

At this point it is not unusual for students of direct marketing to question the difference between conventional sales promotions and long-term loyalty programmes.

Old-fashioned promotions tend to assume that customers can be bribed, if not compelled; its exponents use the terminology of war (campaign, hit, blitz, etc) rather than of relationships.

In the table below we summarise briefly some of the chief differences between sales promotions and loyalty marketing programmes:

	Promotion scheme	Loyalty programme
Time	Periodic, short-lived	Continuous and evolving
Rewards	Extrinsic, hard	Intrinsic, firm, soft
Branding	Loose	Woven through
Communication	Infrequent, transactional	Appropriate, relational
Aim	Short-term sales	Profitable relationships
Posture	Defensive, militaristic	Optimistic, sharing
Customer attitude	What's in it for me?	It's for me
Employee role	Give the rewards, know the rules	Total involvement, enjoyment; trained and empowered
Process status	Outsourced? Customer collects and receives	Multiple processes to achieve objectives
System status	Point-of-sale driven	Holistic, organisation driven

We can see that true loyalty marketing goes well beyond collectable incentives and should not be reduced to loyalty "schemes". In summary, the difference is the way in which customers are regarded and treated **in the long term**.

Reward-only schemes

The weakness of reward-only schemes

Reward systems, such as points for miles or stamps for gifts, do change behaviour. Green Shield stamps were a powerful pioneer programme and millions of households avidly collected them. So popular are points programmes today that many firms have turned to one or other variant. Their greatest advantage is that they let you recognise the customer – **the points are a price for the information which finds its way onto your database**.

The problem with reward systems is that they affect temporary behaviour, not attitude. Sales last as long as rewards are sustained – Shell lost perhaps 15% of sales when it temporarily removed its Smart Card programme.

In 1972, two believers set out to prove that rewards such as privileges or treats could generate permanent change. Their conclusion showed that **removal of the rewards leads to a decline in desirable responses and a return to base line levels of performance** (Cazdin 1982).

> *In a study of children rewarded for drinking Kefir, a fruit-flavoured yoghurt, the children were divided into three groups:*
>
> *1. Those who were simply given the drink.*
>
> *2. Those who were praised for drinking it.*
>
> *3. Those who were given a free movie ticket if they finished the glass.*
>
> *Which produced the best results? Not surprisingly, those who were rewarded with the free movie ticket were most likely to drink and finish the yoghurt. The movie tickets are a good reward for drinking a glass of yoghurt.* ***But, a week later, they were the least likely to drink it.***

We can damage a great product by giving an unnecessary reward. We may induce purchase but not loyalty. We may even devalue the brand in the long-term – or induce loyalty to the scheme rather than to the product, which is an inherently unstable state of affairs. And, of course, giving costly rewards may damage profits.

To sum up:

✗ Rewarded retention is a junky habit: it costs ever more to sustain.

✗ Blatant rewards are easy to copy (and improve upon).

✗ Rewards divert attention of both company and customer from the real product.

✗ Rewards can be perceived as manipulative; people increasingly try to resist manipulation.

Finally, rewards can prevent you asking the fundamental question: Why? If customers are not buying from you, why is it? Only by identifying the root causes of the problem will you have the opportunity to make the fundamental changes which will affect attitudes and ideas. The reward mechanism can operate like the painkiller that disguises the athlete's growing injury until it is too late.

Positive aspects of reward schemes

Despite all the foregoing, reward schemes have an important place in marketing, especially in providing a means of collecting customer data. Furthermore rewards can and do contribute to loyalty, especially when:

✔ The base product offer is already good and differentiated
and

✔ The reward is intrinsic, ie perceived as an extension of the product
or

- ✔ The reward is genuinely valued and perceived as taking some effort or cost by the company to deliver
  and
- ✔ There is a strong personal element inherent in the reward.

Using rewards within loyalty programmes

If rewards are to be employed in the context of a loyalty programme, the following "rules" have been found to be worth adhering to:

1. Reduce the prominence of the extrinsic motivator. Make rewards as intrinsic to the base product as possible.
2. Create personalised surprises. These rewards should not be published.
3. Don't make rewards a contest. Published rewards should be available to everyone who meets a certain standard.
4. Give people as much choice as possible about how rewards are used. (Where do you want to fly? What do you want to choose?) This reduces the manipulative effect of the reward.
5. Make sure you do not raise the profile of the rewards so high that the product itself disappears. Keep reminding people that the reasons they like the product are to do with the product.
6. Make rewards true to the brand.

True loyalty

What customers really want: The true motivators

So much for rewards. Let us return to the subject of more deep-seated loyalty. True loyalty starts by thinking from the customer's viewpoint. (One interesting way to do this is to act it, sometimes with the help of drama and role-play techniques.) Get physically and imaginatively into the role of customer and see what it is like. Being a mystery shopper is another way to **feel** how customers feel.

What you will discover is, just as research shows, that **intangibles are more important than tangibles** in determining customer satisfaction. Key service experiences, in order of importance, are:

- ✔ Reliability
- ✔ Responsiveness
- ✔ Assurance
- ✔ Empathy
- ✔ Tangibles

Others are: competence, access, courtesy, credibility, security, and understanding or knowing the customer. Customers typically rate **reliability** as the most important service experience. What they are really looking for is something they can trust.

The three fundamental types of bonding

Behind all successful loyalty programmes, and all cases of genuine active loyalty, lies at least one of the following bases for a bond between customer and marketer. Excellent schemes embrace all three:

✔ Financial bond

✔ Social bond

✔ Structural bond

Financial bonds include price, points, discounts, rebates, profit/share dividends, gifts, rewards and vouchers. Financial bonds are the easiest to create, the most popular with the average marketer and salesperson, and the least effective over time. You need a value proposition which satisfies the customer at the financial level – both core price and added value benefit – but financial bonds are too easily copied and often too superficial to secure enduring benefits. In fact, **the danger is that we simply educate our customers into loyalty to the promotion and not to the brand, making them ever more fickle**.

A successful financial bond contributes to brand values and is integrated into the product concept. A company that is organised to guarantee low prices obeys this rule. So does an airline company that lets you earn free airline seats. A petrol company that gives away free mugs does not.

Classic examples of the financial bond in database marketing therefore include frequent-user programmes, like KLM's Flying Dutchman and Tesco's reward card.

Social or relationship bonding develops affinity and relationship values through brand building, personal service, knowledge, communication, club membership, welcome packs and other "Moment of truth" interactions. **Loyalty marketing sees personalised marketing messages and personalised service messages as the left and right hand that work together to craft loyalty.** The customer then feels an **emotional** connection with the brand (or its representatives) and what it stands for. Social bonds are harder to create: they require a passion for the brand, for service, for quality, for clients. But, for this very reason perhaps, they are more durable. Social bonds build trust, which is the most important prerequisite for true loyalty.

When the client feels **"this is my brand"**, he or she demonstrates some sense of community with the brand's values and those of other users. The brand lives in the soul of customers. If all the people who value a brand die, the brand dies.

Because direct marketing is a one-to-one medium, it is the ideal social bonding discipline. Database marketing becomes the means of building the brand one-by-one, person by person. The secret is recognising, appreciating and acknowledging the individual in the customer.

Example of social bonding: Huggies

Huggies recognised that only a finite number of people is in the market for nappies (ie young mothers and fathers) and, while each sales transaction is worth only a few dollars, the nappies used during a baby's early years generate a value in excess of $1,000. So they developed a programme that communicates with new parents throughout their baby's nappy usage.

The main contact vehicle is a magazine "The Beginning Years" which is produced in a number of editions each focused on a period in the child's early life. Each is a beautifully researched and produced little compendium of fun, hints and help designed to demonstrate how Kimberley-Clark Huggies care. "Selling" is minimal, yet powerful, eg when the child might be about to outgrow its current size of nappy (and the mother becomes vulnerable to a product change), they send a free sample of the larger size and some advice to change up.

This is a classic use of database marketing based upon a social bond. The programme has been running successfully for over ten years.

Structural or connection bonds are mechanisms which reinforce the relationship. When you can negotiate a contract or installation, retention is much stronger. A finance company provides a loan for a term and charges a cancellation fee for early termination. A vending machine company installs a unit for a contract period. A mail order book club offers low-cost introductory books in return for a minimum number of purchases per annum. A charity gets a covenant.

A credit card is a mechanism to interact with the company, a frequent-flyer card a mechanism to inform the airline that one is travelling with them. The points received are really a reward for the information given, **not the basis of loyalty**. The points are the reason that a traveller uses the card and using the card lets the airline company know who he/she is. British Airways use that information to tier the value of their customers and reward those who are most important to them with preferential benefits.

A structural bond is therefore a physical or practical mechanic which extends or facilitates personalised interaction with the brand. These connections can range from very powerful and formal mechanisms, such as a joint venture between business partners, to nice little "touches", such as the home insurance company that provides a refrigerator magnet with its 0800 careline number for use in a home crisis.

Every good database can form the basis of a structural bond. At the point when they become known, customers cease to be anonymous transactions and can be welcomed into the family of the brand. The more communication becomes a structural service, the more likely it is that it will be valued by customers.

Most people open their bank statements. A bank statement is a classic piece of structural bonding. It reinforces the social and legal contract between the client and bank each time it is sent. Some marketers think a bank statement is not direct mail. They think that true direct mail is something which the customer doesn't really want! In reality, **the best direct mail is either anticipated and expected, or a joyful surprise**.

A smart connection bond is perceived by the customer not as an imprisonment but as a reliability factor. (The trouble with imprisoning customers is that they escape as soon as the contract period is over.)

Structural bonding: Nationwide ADV

A billion-dollar US office supplies company, Nationwide ADV, operates through dealers who are provided with a dealer-personalised catalogue. Despite listing 25,000 items, they offer next-day delivery in packages bearing the dealer's ***own*** *logo for onward despatch to end-customers. Dealers are provided with a computerised system to give them availability and product information which enables them to place orders direct.*

But Nationwide go one step further – they put terminals on the dealer's ***customers'*** *desks. The dealer's customers perceive they are connecting to the dealer to place orders which are actually fulfilled by Nationwide.* ***This is sophisticated relational, interactive, database marketing*** *– and a powerful example of structural bonding.*

The business benefits of loyal customers

Established customers tend to buy more, are predictable, and usually cost less to service than new customers. They tend to be less price sensitive and may provide free word-of-mouth referrals and advertising. **Acquiring a new customer costs more than retaining an existing one.** The longer the relationship the lower the cost of acquisition. Retaining customers makes it difficult for competitors to increase market share.

A pinta profit

One of the most powerful examples in Britain of the ability of service to deliver long-term value is the milkman delivering the daily pinta. Each delivery is worth very little, but the net present value from a household over 40 years can be around £8,000.

Companies earning greater loyalty can typically:

- ✔ **Charge more money.** Happy customers may pay more, and don't need discounts.
- ✔ **Expect greater share of wallet.** Loyal UK shoppers allocate between two and four times as much more of their monthly budget to their "first choice" store than promiscuous shoppers.
- ✔ **Reduce administration costs.** Falls of 18% were noted in one study of the insurance industry. In the US retail chain store environments, a 2% retention improvement leads typically to 10% reduction in costs. Imagine if every customer needed to have every product line explained in full!
- ✔ **Reduce marketing expense.** Existing customers are more willing to buy from you, often by a factor of 5–8 times.

✔ **Reduce fixed costs as a percentage of sales.**

✔ **Expect more referrals.** The experience of customers filters into the marketplace through Member-Get-Member programmes and spontaneous referral. The leading UK direct insurance writer, Direct Line Insurance, has the highest referral rates in the industry.

✔ **Grow faster.** Since it is common for a business to lose 15–20% or more of its customers each year, simply cutting defections in half will more than double the average company's growth rate. In one exercise, improving retention from 80% to 90% had the same effect in building the customer base as increasing customer acquisition rates by 50%. In another, **it took a 92% increase in customer acquisition rates to produce the same discounted profits as a 5% improvement in retention rate**.

✔ **Enjoy increased employee retention.** This feeds back into greater customer longevity.

✔ **Improve merger and acquisition decision-making.** The retention rate is a simple and powerful indicator of the future.

Sell them more or keep them longer?

How do retention and loyalty manifest themselves in higher profit? We need to compare the relative opportunities that come from selling more to existing customers with that of keeping them longer, ie mere retention versus long-term pro-active development. Usually marketers will seek to sell more **and** retain customers longer, since both represent opportunities to increase customer **value**, as the graphic below demonstrates:

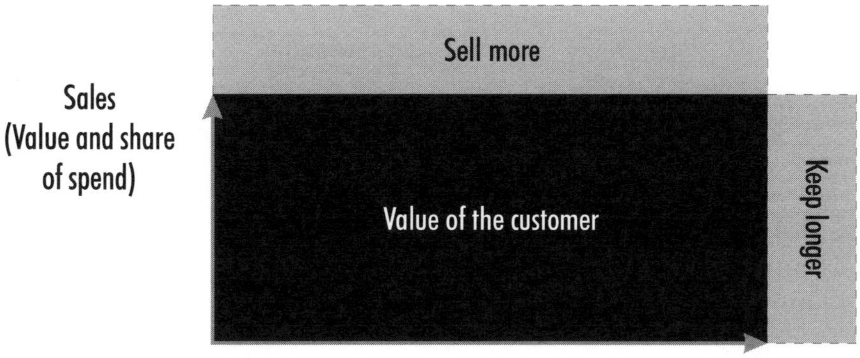

Sometimes, however, only one option is available. Perhaps product change can help. Huggies developed Pull-Ups to extend the sales cycle (keeping customers longer) when children grew out of nappies. Amex created its Gold Card to upgrade its best customers (selling them more).

In many retail and brand markets, retention means simply keeping or improving your percentage of the customer's buying portfolio: the share of spend. Improving retention might mean increasing share of purchase from 30% to 70%.

Ideally a retention plan should not only retain or renew a customer, but maximise individual value during the entire lifetime of a customer. To do this it needs to focus on three areas:

✔ The spending power of customers.

✔ Your share of the customer's spend.

✔ The strength of the emotional tie beyond you and your customer.

All customers are not equal

In practice, not all customers will perform equally. You will have on your buyer file: super-active high-spending customers, occasional high spenders, frequent low spenders, infrequent low spenders, inactives and lapsed customers. Some customers are probably costing you money. So it's doubly important to focus on the best customers. Hence our opening contention that retention and loyalty can be unprofitable, eg if concentrated on the wrong customers.

A surprisingly small proportion of customers provides the profits for most companies. A number of studies show that one-third or fewer customers provide two-thirds or more of profits in virtually every category (the Pareto principle). **Database marketing addresses this by developing communication and relationship strategies where they count most**. One of the most important tests of every interaction with a customer is: Is it contributing to the long-term lifetime value of the customer?

The differences in individual customer performance will stem from many factors: age, income, geographical location, lifestyle, and the source from which they were recruited. Some customers will be responsive to certain forms of promotion, others less so.

Possible customer contact points

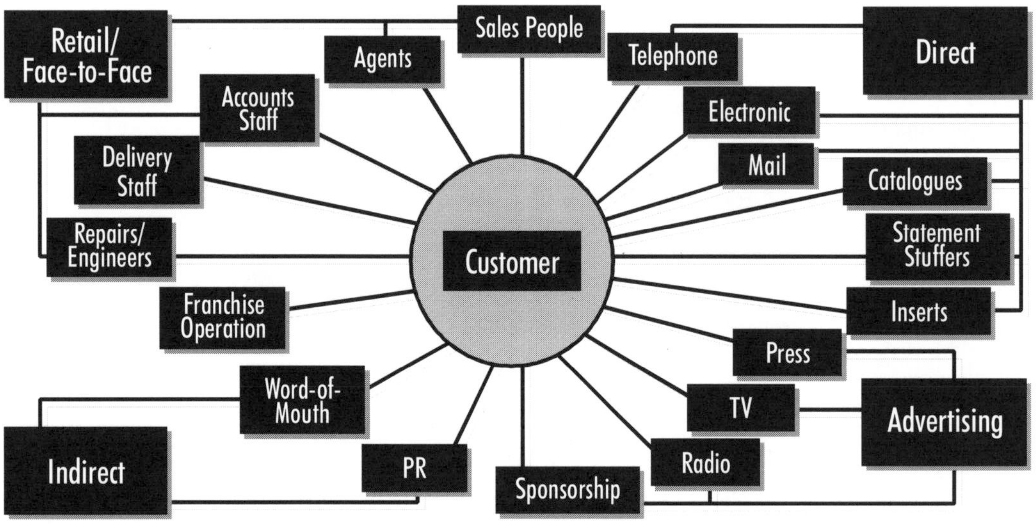

This diagram shows the huge array of points at which you and your customer may make contact. The direct marketer will generally have access to all of these while the customer will often be exposed to most of them. Each point of contact represents a "Moment of Truth". Such an array of opportunities demonstrates the need for a holistic approach to staff training and proves that loyalty is not simply a responsibility of the marketing department. Neither is it a short-term scheme: instead it is a long-term attitude.

The "Laws of Loyalty"

- ✔ Rewards do not buy loyalty, they buy only data.
- ✔ Loyalty **to** customers creates loyalty **from** customers.
- ✔ Relationship efforts must respect the preferred boundaries of customers.
- ✔ Loyalty is not behaviour, satisfaction or attitude. **It is best summed up as "active affection"**, but arises from the integration of thinking, feeling and action **based on trust**.
- ✔ Loyalty is personal and individual and arises out of the holistic experience of a succession of "Moments of Truth".
- ✔ Loyalty is generated through the deployment of financial, social and structural bonding programmes (or processes).
- ✔ Not all customers are equal. Not all companies can recognise that.
- ✔ The attitudes of all stakeholders are mutually reinforcing.
- ✔ Loyalty is a journey, not an arrival.
- ✔ Loyalty is a moral issue. Its deployment will emphasise "marriage" over "military" metaphors.
- ✔ Loyalty stems from loyalty values. Company and customer share a set of values based on fair-sharing, the everybody wins principle.
- ✔ Over-hyping loyalty programmes can itself lead to dissatisfaction.
- ✔ The best customers are those with a propensity to loyalty and to spending. They are already somebody's best customers. Before you court them, make sure you've looked after the customer you already have.

The language of loyalty

Each of these phrases (examples only) can be linked to the "Moments of Truth" in a relationship between customer and company. Before you read on, spare a few minutes to absorb the mindset of a good loyalty marketer. What objectives or circumstances would you expect to trigger a communication based on each of the above?

The language of loyalty

1. Making friends:

"Welcome and Thank you"

Some hard-headed direct marketers, perhaps still committed to yesterday's single sale mentality, believe firmly that you should never contact a customer without attempting to sell something. This is nonsense. You should try to establish a personal touch from the outset and this may or may not involve selling.

Many modern direct marketers take the opportunity to welcome new customers whilst deliberately **refraining** from any overt selling. Instead they offer reassurance, explain their procedures, tell customers how much they are appreciated, and invite new customers to volunteer more information about their needs and wants. Sometimes such messages are linked to a check-up call. In one market, Amex got a 14% increase in retention when they called new cardholders to welcome them and check up.

Whether such a welcome policy is appropriate will depend on many factors, primarily the anticipated lifetime and potential value of the customer. One airline has enjoyed demonstrable success as the result of writing to thank passengers for flying with them.

Whether or not a separate welcome is planned, it will pay you handsomely to recognise a customer's important new status in any early communications. One airline uses the speaker system in its aircraft to welcome on board its frequent flyers.

2. Up-selling:

"Will there be anything else, Mrs Jones?"

The logical development of a mutually beneficial relationship is likely to be an up-selling programme. Up-selling may mean directing customers to more expensive options, or interesting them in longer-term commitments. It may also mean, depending upon your business, persuading customers to accept more of your merchandise. Increasing customers' Average Order Values (AOV) is a proven means of dramatically increasing profitability at low cost. Sometimes, however, it's easier to get the customer to buy more often than to spend more per transaction.

Numerous techniques can be employed for up-selling customers, ranging from discounts and incentives for volume purchases to demonstrating an attractive range of related goods by means of newsletters and catalogues.

Holding on to gold

American Express launched a brilliant concept: the Gold Card for Frequent Travellers. Existing Gold Card holders with the right profile were quietly offered a handsome package of Membership Rewards, insurance and service benefits and four additional cards for family and colleagues for an upgraded price. Customer profitability increased significantly.

The optimum time for introducing up-selling measures can be determined by an examination of established customers' buying patterns where these are available. Timing should also be the subject of constant testing.

3. *Cross-selling:*

"This will also interest you, Sir"

Cross-selling is closely related to up-selling, the only difference being that cross-selling generally refers to introducing products or services to customers that perhaps they had not expected to be offered by your company. The credit card company introducing a gold card is up-selling; the same company offering membership of its wine club would be cross-selling.

4. *Repeat-selling:*

"Will you be ordering the usual, Miss Smith?"

Repeat selling means the continuation of the relationship through the next cycle of consumption.

As we have said, active emotional loyalty involves the customer being **willing to seek out** a particular service location (eg a shop) and/or brand. For example, a customer may choose a shop because it sells a particular product, or may give up product in order to shop in a particular store. In contrast, passive loyalty tends to be more motivated by impulse, convenience and habit. If **the conditions are right, then the customer will buy the product**. Therefore, making it easy makes sense.

Removing the hassle

Bell wanted to keep more customers advertising in their directory. One problem they found was the hassle for small businesses to get an ad together that they liked. So Bell sent customers samples to inspect. A computer programme produced a fully personalised directory page accurate in size, type and style with a personalised cover letter from the salesperson. Ninety-eight variables could change with each letter or directory page. Bell printed five different variations of the customer's potential advertisement using different style, size and copy features to show alternatives and make it easy to choose and order. Production was done automatically by laser printing, so the system provided a complete and convenient personalisation process. The salespeople followed up as needed.

5. *Inviting membership:*

"Madam, would you like to join our club?"

Clubs and affinity groups can build loyalty. The secret of all "clubs" is to get customers to feel they belong. How you do it is just a mechanic. Customers will tell you how if you listen. For example:

Most major hotel chains now offer some sort of frequent-stay programme. In general, members appear to be willing to pay more per night for a hotel room than non-members. Frequent user programmes are often presented as clubs offering exclusivity to their "members".

Elvis lives on

The United States Postal Service wanted to broaden its base of stamp collectors by appealing to a new, younger and more casual saver segment, so they turned to the Elvis Community of Supporters. First, they designed and produced Elvis-related products, especially stamps. Then they mailed 700,000 people who had already either purchased an Elvis stamp or registered an interest in so doing: developing; ***not*** *initiating the relationship. The programme was designed to promote additional Elvis-related commemoratives and stamps and to enhance the value of saving Elvis stamps. It received a 22.65% response rate at a cost of $1.84 each. More than 3.6 million take-ones were placed in lobbies, pulling a 3% response, and 3.13% response was obtained from the 25,000 information requests. In total the revenue generated was 25 times promotion costs. This is a good example of designing add-on products to meet a core customer group need through a club-style affinity programme.*

6. Customer care communications:

"Good morning, Mrs Roberts, how is little Johnny?"

Customer care is, of course, a huge subject in its own right touching every sinew of an organisation's being. Customer retention is the logical outcome of caring about customers and their needs.

Just as the old-fashioned grocer recognised his best customers, served them personally, threw in some extra carrots and gave advice on cooking beetroot, so the modern marketer must do likewise. This means you must:

- ✔ Acknowledge the customer, both as an individual and as a valued customer.
- ✔ Create dialogue that enables warmth and knowledge to be developed.
- ✔ Form a personal relationship, with any problems promptly and courteously dealt with.
- ✔ Give regular added value as a natural extension of the basic transaction.
- ✔ Show special attention during relationship development.
- ✔ Give graceful surprises.

7. Warding off competition:

"Stay with us, please"

When a powerful new entrant to a market comes along – either a major brand or a new technology – you can quickly lose a large part of your market. Yet this is exactly the time when, if you exploit your relationship equity to the full, you can get the most value out of it. The secret is to hold on to customers, either reaffirming what you've done or will do, or both.

An injection of loyalty

Glaxovet's 25-year near-monopoly with its product Dictol, a preventative treatment for lungworm in cattle, was threatened by a new brand, so they developed a powerful retention programme. Farmers bought Dictol via injections by vets. A direct mail campaign was targeted to new and existing users. New users received an offer of a videotape showing the effect of lungworm on the lungs. The new user mailing was also more emotionally charged. Existing users were reminded of their past participation and the benefits, appealing to rational good sense. Both groups were incentivised to fill in a form and a computer then generated a complete specification of requirements in the form of an order for them to take to their local vet. At the same time, the information was added to the existing bank of knowledge provided to the salesforce so that they could visit and brief the vets, in detail, thus adding to their air of professionalism. Only 8% of the market was lost, a fraction of the possible damage.

8. Lapsed customer reactivation:

"Please come back to us, Mr Williams"

Lapsed/inactives strategies may include making especially attractive offers, introducing new products, apologising for any possible misdemeanours on your part and, most important of all, finding out precisely WHY your previously active customer is no longer buying from you.

In many product categories it is simply a matter of recognising the "natural" lifetimes of customers. Gardeners, for example, frequently stock their gardens in the early years of their relationship with a supplier, until they reach the point where they can barely fit in another sapling even if it is offered free.

Whatever the reasons for a customer's inactivity **beware investing large sums, as many companies still do, in communicating with people who are no longer there or who are no longer in the market**. Customer status can often be established with special list-cleaning mailings or telemarketing activity.

But what if the customer is still there but simply not active? By soliciting feedback from defecting customers, companies can ferret out the weaknesses that really matter and strengthen them before profits start to dwindle.

Businesses commonly do not hear from 96% of their dissatisfied customers. For every complaint received typically another 26 customers have problems, six of them serious. Customers with bad experiences are often said to be twice as likely to tell others as those with a positive story. British Airways believes that every 1% increase in **customer comments** equals up to £400,000 revenue won back from potential defectors. They point out that Pan Am had one of the lowest rates of complaint amongst trans-Atlantic carriers just before going bust. IBM found that a 1% improvement in customer satisfaction translates into $500 million in increased sales over five years. But, to improve satisfaction, the causes of dissatisfaction must be understood.

Only 84% of British consumers are satisfied with the goods and services they purchase by direct mail. Although only 8% are actively dissatisfied, and satisfaction rose 2% between 1991 and 1993, given a £12 billion industry, that 8% could be worth £5 to £10 billion over five years.

If you lose one customer for every five who have a problem, a common statistic, then each problem costs 20% of the lifetime value of a customer.

Toyota salespeople in the Corolla division meet together for a day a month, and instead of puffing up their egos by celebrating supposed success, they spend the day doing root cause analysis to overcome problems.

9. Complaints handling:

"Leave it to me, I'll get it put right"

When complaints and problems arise, research shows that customers expect to:

- ✔ Receive a prompt, personal apology, with someone taking responsibility.
- ✔ Be offered a fair solution: the customer must see an effort being made towards reinstatement.
- ✔ See that the company cares with demonstrable empathy, compassion, and understanding.
- ✔ Be offered some value-added, symbolic atonement: this is a token of sorrow, not a pound of flesh.
- ✔ Receive a follow-up check, especially if the customer felt victimised.

One company found that in two out of every three cases in which the customer had a complaint about a product, the problem had nothing to do with the product itself. The problem was caused by the user not understanding how to use the product for the purpose it was designed to serve. Here is precisely an example of how database marketing can serve the customers, overcome problems, and possibly build opportunities for further sales. Why not call to check, or at least make it easy for customers to call you?

Faultless service

Hewlett Packard found that 40% of its returned printers had no fault, so they built a European Call Centre to talk customers through any problems, solving four times as many problems, saving themselves millions, and getting higher retention.

A customer panel or association is one way to work on issues of service and performance and can provide the means for valued feedback. Group 1 Software, a Washington company which is the world's leader in deduplication software, meets with its customers twice each year as well as having regular dialogue. **Remember, direct marketing doesn't just mean the mail and 'phone. Any targeted dialogue is direct marketing.**

But why wait for complaints to materialise when systems can automate communication, whether by post or 'phone? For example, when a flight is delayed, the airline knows who its frequent flyers are through their card registration. Instead of ignoring the problem and hoping it will go away, they could spring into action not only at the terminal but afterwards. The tannoy could be used to call the most important customers to the desk in order to make special arrangements and apologies. The company can then write to all customers immediately after the event apologising and, if appropriate, providing some compensatory offer (which might be a fun experience rather than a financial payment).

10. The ultimate reassurance:

"It's guaranteed for life, Sir"

A **guarantee** is a powerful direct marketing tool to build trust and keep the supplier in the customer's mind. It helps companies stand out from the crowd and delivers a message not only to customers but to the workforce and management. Its promise gives assurance and its feedback mechanism provides a means for customers to talk to the company and not to the rest of the world when something goes wrong.

Depending on the brand, **research shows that disappointed customers will speak to between five and twenty people, delivering anti-brand messages which pollute its image in the marketplace**. Yet research also shows that if customers can be induced to talk directly to the brand representatives, then their disappointment can frequently be transformed or appeased. Loyalty may even be increased. Customers who do **not** complain are often the least loyal to the company. Furthermore, customers who have had a problem and experienced a professional and responsive resolution are often up to **a third** more loyal than customers who have not experienced a problem.

If the guarantee delivers a simple, effective and hassle-free route to communicate, then it is also a structural bond for customers. The complaints can be fed into a database and used to guide future communications and interactions with the customer. They can also be used to understand corporate weaknesses and to identify the root causes of defection. Barclays Bank has a database of problems and empowers all frontline staff to send flowers or chocolates if there is a problem.

A guarantee must:

- ✔ Promise what customers want and expect, ie be relevant.
- ✔ Be simple and clear and free from conditions which fog its impact.
- ✔ Not be risk-free or a joke; it must deliver something real.
- ✔ Be measured on its long-term lifetime value effects.

The Vermont Teddy Bear Company provides teddy bears of high quality, backed by this 100% guarantee:

"As teddy bear makers, we like teddy bears and we love the bears we make. If you are not happy with the bear for any reason we will refund your money or exchange the bear with no question asked. If your bear gets hurt in any way, we will fix the bear free of charge. That means, if your bear gets run over by a truck or the neighbours' kids have a tug of war or if, while sharing a bottle of Beaujolais with your bear, he happens to spill some on his chest ... we will fix him up free of charge for the lifetime of the bear. Since we expect our bears to live a very long time (like for as long as you will live) this is a pretty good guarantee."

11. Customer attitude research:

"Please spare a moment to tell us ..."

There is often a fine line between pure research and the type of concerned enquiry into customers' individual attitudes which the database makes possible.

Many problems arise because marketers have little knowledge of their specific customers and their value and interactions with the brand. This leads to generalised value offers which are less relevant to key customer clusters.

Take a supermarket that withdraws a specialist product off its shelf. It may have no idea whom it is affecting by the change. It could be a product which is bought only by infrequent, low value customers **OR** by the most frequent and highest value customer group. If the latter, its value to the organisation may be out of proportion to its own sales value. Only by knowing who is going to be affected can marketers take decisions effectively.

The smartest marketers focus on learning about and relating to **specific** customer groups and **individual** customers. The role of the database in managing these interactions is self-evident. It can tell you who is really buying the product. It can also provide the perfect sampling frame for conventional market research, especially for postal questionnaires and structured telephone research.

Research is an important ingredient in the best customer care programmes. **What is really different in loyalty marketing is that research focuses almost exclusively on the needs and attitudes of BEST customers.** What you really want to know about your core customers is:

- ? What is important to them?
- ? How good is your service in those areas?
- ? What is NOT very satisfying?

12. Communication triggered by events:

"I'm telephoning you, Mrs Potter, because ..."

The most effective loyalty programmes are built around the moment of truth cycle for individual customers and **triggered by individual behaviours, attitudes and events**. The most advanced marketing database systems enable marketing management to respond to certain events, such as:

✔ The customer's first purchase.

✔ A complaint.

✔ An anniversary or a birthday.

✔ The purchase or non-purchase of a specific product.

✔ A specific period since a purchase.

✔ A change in the customer circumstance, eg marriage or birth of a child.

✔ Management reorganisation, eg corporate merger, etc.

"Good luck in your new job"

Dutch Postbank designed a series of communications to target specific moments in the relationship of an individual from birth to death. For example, school leavers are offered tailored products/services based on whether they are going to a job or to a university. In the UK, First Direct bank use this technique.

Smart marketers don't just measure the effectiveness of a mailing by its immediate response. The important question is, does the communication enhance the lifetime value of customers?

Each moment of truth is a point when the customer has the potential to evaluate the quality of the brand, its service, and its relationship. If a man forgets his wedding anniversary, this says something about the quality of his relationship with his wife. If he is too busy telling her about his day to listen to her day, this also says something about the quality of the relationship; it is a moment of truth. So it is between customers and marketers.

3 loyalty programmes: Advantages and disadvantages

To conclude this chapter we include three celebrated loyalty programmes and discuss some advantages and disadvantages of each.

Students:

The three programmes discussed below and overleaf, in many respects, represent state of the art developments. Yet each has drawbacks. You might like to gather information and collect samples of the creative material in each case so as to make your own assessment of their strengths and weaknesses.

The three programmes are those for

- ✔ **East Coast Rail**, first-class travellers' reward scheme.
- ✔ **Tesco** club card scheme. Compare also with Sainsbury's.
- ✔ **Air Miles**, as used by Shell, Nat West, etc.

East Coast Rail

East Coast *is the largest of the ex-British Rail franchises. To differentiate itself it set up a loyalty programme aimed primarily at frequent first-class travellers.*

Customers appreciated the benefits, which included on-train perks like free tea or coffee, "two for the price of one" drinks, and a free half bottle of wine with meals. Customers noticed they were getting a better service than expected and loved a hotel break taking in "The Phantom of the Opera". Staff felt positive too.

Advantages

Demonstrated that customers' attitudes could be changed through the ***right*** *choice of benefits and rewards.*

Disadvantages

They were not able to recognise individual customers: they had no idea who was travelling when, and so could not make full use of personal data. Their scheme also included dubious "benefits" such as a free mobile 'phone (the customers mostly already had one!) and discounted rooms in hotels not favoured by their customers – suggesting a need for more and better research into customer tastes and aspirations.

Tesco

*The **Tesco** loyalty programme has been a huge success. It has generated eight million cardholders (6.5 million active) and taken market share from competitors. Profitability has increased.*

*Some commentators argue that since Tesco also upgraded their service the impact of different elements can't be judged. Certainly, measuring the relevant weight of different elements is important – and can be achieved through analysis – but the real point is that Tesco **did** add service and social values, not just price promotions. That's why it has been successful. In one focus research programme a customer said:*

> I used to shop at Sainsbury. I tried Tesco because of the points and card. Then I went back to Sainsbury. But now I noticed how slow their queues were, so I went back to Tesco again.

Tesco has also introduced a comprehensive satisfaction guarantee. So far though, Tesco is still learning how to use its data really effectively. Its targeting and added value is still fairly primitive – but better than anyone else's in their market.

Air Miles

***Air Miles**, launched in 1988, provides a currency for other companies' loyalty programmes although it is not itself a loyalty programme. Key UK users are Shell, Nat West, British Airways, British Telecom and Sainsbury. Multiple-user collection schemes have several pros and cons.*

Advantages

- ✔ *Participating companies can immediately plug into customers' collection habits.*
- ✔ *It is easier for customers to earn valuable rewards – because they have many ways to collect – and so may feel more prone to join the programme.*
- ✔ *There is an infrastructure in place.*
- ✔ *Participants can share knowledge about individual customers and their lifestyles.*
- ✔ *There can be a halo effect: sharing the strong values of great brands.*

Disadvantages

✗ *Each user is one of a number of companies and is not therefore offering customers something exclusive.*

✗ *The currency becomes a focus of loyalty, potentially diverting attention from the brands. See earlier advice on reward schemes in this chapter.*

NB: **Shared schemes do not have to feature only large well-known companies. There are several successful programmes uniting small enterprises in, for example, town centre schemes.**

The last word on loyalty

The most important words in the marketer's lexicon are not "New", "First" or "Best" but "**Thank you**".

Chapter 1.5

Direct marketing in practice – making it happen

This chapter includes:

- ❑ **Identifying key tasks**
- ❑ **Anticipating likely problems**
- ❑ **Who does what in the campaign process**
- ❑ **Why you need a formal process**
- ❑ **Designing and running the management process**
- ❑ **Key information: what it is, who provides it**
- ❑ **Some do's and don'ts of campaign administration**
- ❑ **Tasks, campaign statuses, responsibilities, key information areas**

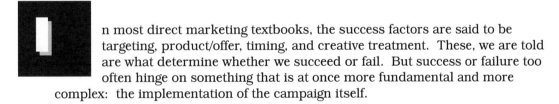

In most direct marketing textbooks, the success factors are said to be targeting, product/offer, timing, and creative treatment. These, we are told are what determine whether we succeed or fail. But success or failure too often hinge on something that is at once more fundamental and more complex: the implementation of the campaign itself.

In practice, many failures or performance shortfalls result not from poor strategy but from flawed execution – a lack of planning and insufficient attention to the thousands of details that make up the typical direct marketing campaign.

More specifically, failure can and does result from such weaknesses as the absence of a clear-cut management process, a dearth of systems, inadequate training and, above all, poor communication between all those involved in delivering even the simplest direct programme.

In this chapter, Professor Merlin Stone restores the balance between theory and practice, between strategy and its implementation. Advocating the use of proven project management techniques (direct marketing is a highly technical process), he provides a number of useful checklists that will help you to mount a successful campaign, not just once but every time.

New in this edition. The guidance in this chapter has not altered significantly since the previous edition.

Professor Merlin Stone

Merlin is a leading expert on direct and relationship marketing, customer care, customer loyalty and customer information systems. He is a Director of QCi Ltd, specialists in relationship marketing, and of Swallow Information Systems Ltd, a software house specialising in customer management software – especially complaints.

His clients include companies from all over the world and in all sectors. He is well known for his propensity to minimise the length of business trips – including the famous "day return to Hong Kong". This is part of QCi's promise to deliver in hours what other consultants deliver in days, and in days what others deliver in weeks.

He is the author of thirteen books on marketing and customer service, including "How to Market Computers and Information Technology", "Database Marketing", "Competitive Customer Care", "Relationship Marketing" and "Direct Hit". He is also the editor and author of the IBM-sponsored SEMS briefing papers series – "Close to the Customer". He is a frequent speaker at national and international conferences – often giving the keynote speech. He has become an expert in giving a marketing spin to time-honoured Jewish jokes.

He is a Founder Member of the Institute of Direct Marketing and an editor of the Journal of Financial Services Marketing. He has a First Class Honours Degree and a Doctorate in Economics. He contributes frequently to academic journals.

Merlin's hobbies are notable by their absence – just coping with work and family absorbs all his time and energy. But his principal aspiration is to become a couch potato, watching southern hemisphere rugby on Sky Sports, interspersed with foreign travel when the younger of his two daughters goes to university (known in the family corporate plan as liberation!).

Prof Merlin Stone M IDM
Surrey European Management School
University of Surrey
Guildford
Surrey GU2 5XH
Tel: 01483 259347
E-mail: m.stone@surrey.ac.uk

(Professor Stone's biography is continued in Chapter 3.2, which he has also written.)

Chapter 1.5

Direct marketing in practice – making it happen

Before the campaign

Start by identifying key tasks

Once a campaign is given the go ahead, the process of implementation begins. The first step is to identify the key tasks you need to do to implement your campaign. On pages 1.5-10/11 will be found a master checklist which includes key tasks. These can be simplified and arranged as a project plan, showing where different tasks can be carried out in parallel instead of sequentially.

The project plan shows the kind of timings you should allow from the time that your campaign is given the go-ahead.

Tasks can be defined at different levels of details. The simplest level is of course just:

- ✔ Plan
- ✔ Implement
- ✔ Monitor

We believe you should plan at the most detailed level. If you find this difficult, choose some level which ensures that all the tasks you **should** carry out **are** carried out and that their completion is communicated to the team. One approach is to focus on major milestones, which also provide good points at which to review progress.

Enter the campaign details onto your system

The next step you will normally take is to translate your campaign into systems language. This translation ensures that:

- ✔ The right selections are made.
- ✔ Details of customers selected are prepared in the right format.
- ✔ These details are conveyed to those responsible for outbound contact.
- ✔ Files are prepared to handle response data; and so on.

Entering the campaign details onto your system is, therefore, an important bridge between planning and implementation. How this is done in your company depends on whether your marketers (specialist direct marketers, brand managers, sales managers) have direct access to the system. The kind of direct marketing campaigns likely to be run by most large companies are very complex in terms of selections and contact strategies. It is enough for marketers to get the marketing side of it right without expecting them to programme the main customer database system. The best that you can expect is for marketers to enter their **requirements** on a management system. This disciplines them to cover all eventualities. Although great advances have been made in database software and design in the last few years, in larger companies it may be more sensible to have a specialist database administration team responsible for the integrity of the data and of campaign programming.

If you have a good central team, they will have in-depth knowledge of the database, the selections that have been made from it, and the results of campaigns run on these selections. Their knowledge and skills enable them to advise marketers on targeting and contact strategy. In some companies this central pool of expertise is one of the main marketing assets – so vital that the team is given the authority to control access to the database. They are – so to speak – the custodians of the customer base.

In some cases, particularly in companies with a very varied product range and constantly changing priorities, it may not be possible to adopt this centralised approach. In this case, marketers may be given direct access to the system. The only restriction is a few basic controls to reduce the chances of misprogramming or campaign clashes. In this case, it is critical that users are properly trained. They must be given the chance to enter “dummy” campaigns, be encouraged to trial small real campaigns, and be given support where they feel they need it.

Communicate the plan to the implementers

It is one thing to plan a project, another to make it happen. Much of the work involved is not in your hands, but in the hands of external suppliers or staff outside your control. Imposing a plan on them without consultation is unlikely to produce results. **Other parties have to agree that what you are asking is feasible.** You should therefore draw up a draft plan and discuss it with them.

The two major causes of promotional projects departing from their agreed timetable are:

- ✗ lack of communication
- ✗ lack of attention to detail

Communication covers everything from clarity and comprehensiveness of the brief, communication of the project plan, and provision of speedy and clear feedback at every review stage. **You must, therefore, allow enough time for communication.**

Attention to detail means not letting anything slip. The annals of direct marketing are filled with examples of reply devices going out without media coding or return addresses, the fulfilment packs being sent to the wrong customers, the wrong telephone numbers being publicised, campaigns going out before telephone response handlers have been trained, and so on.

Today, there are many campaign management software packages which not only facilitate planning, but if used correctly ensure that all the important campaign details are entered.

Anticipate the likely problems

Problems in promotional project management are of several kinds. Chief of these are:

- ✗ You find it difficult to meet your deadlines.
- ✗ Your suppliers find it difficult to meet their deadlines.
- ✗ Staff's and/or suppliers' work is not up to standard.

Most of these problems stem from the same origins, typically:

- ✗ Not identifying all the tasks required to take the project through to completion.
- ✗ Not knowing how much time each will take, or not allowing the time.
- ✗ Not allocating the tasks clearly among the different parties (staff and suppliers).
- ✗ Not briefing people clearly, or asking them to respond to an unclear brief, particularly when there is no time to clarify it.
- ✗ Slack budgeting.

None of these problems is peculiar to direct marketing; other areas of marketing and selling have their own horror stories. Most of them are likely to occur if not enough time is allocated for developing and delivering the campaign. The more hurried the campaign, the less time there will be to **manage it properly** and the more likely you are to have problems.

How to avoid the most common problems

If you follow these steps, you are less likely to experience the kind of problems outlined above:

✔ Do your pre-brief planning thoroughly, so that you are totally clear on campaign objectives, strategies, accountability and timetable.

✔ When planning, ensure that you communicate and consult. Ensure that all relevant parties agree that your objectives, plans and timetable are feasible.

✔ Make sure you do not confuse your customers. Your communication may be one of a series of communications received by them – whether direct or through other media. **Position your offer, therefore, not only relative to competition but also to other offers contained in your other communications.** Customers need to understand where your offer "fits" relative to the others. Also, make sure that your customers know exactly what you want them to do. Otherwise, they will call all sorts of people in your company and you will be unable to handle or trace many of the responses you are so keen to get.

✔ Follow your campaign briefing procedures correctly. Where appropriate submit top-level campaign details (targeting, timing etc) to your database administration early enough for them to comment, suggest modifications, and prepare to meet your needs.

✔ Complete the rest of your campaign planning as soon as possible, and communicate your plans to all parties (internal and external) working on the campaign.

✔ Work out the timings for each step of the project plan, and get them agreed with your collaborators.

✔ Identify important milestones, use them to manage, and get your collaborators to do the same. Make sure suppliers (especially agencies) have the right management process and discipline to meet agreed deadlines.

✔ Measure your progress towards campaign launch, and learn from the experience if things don't go according to plan.

✔ If your suppliers don't understand the process by which you work, brief them on it and if necessary train them to use it.

✔ As elements of the campaign start to emerge (eg the target list, the mailshot), use the appropriate section of the checklist to check them off.

During the campaign

Keep a close eye on your performance

Direct marketing works through measurement. Measurement during campaigns helps you check if your strategy is working. Measurement after a campaign enables you to find out what worked and what did not work. In setting up your campaign, you need to make sure that the right **right information** is reported at the **right time** to the **right people** (ie those who are in a position to do something about it). This means you should:

- ✔ Decide what key performance indicators you wish to use. They must, of course, be measurable as well as useful.
- ✔ Make sure that these indicators are actually measured. Ideally they should not require special measuring techniques but be picked up as a normal part of the campaign.
- ✔ Make sure that the results are communicated to the right people.
- ✔ Ensure that actions indicated by the results are taken.

What should you measure?

The information needed to monitor a campaign is fairly straightforward and derives from the logical flow of a campaign. Below are some examples. Note that many of the measurements are simple checks on the volume of flows (of communication) or stocks (of material to be communicated). The measures are as follows:

- ✔ The number of customers actually selected by your selection criteria (or the number of valid names on a list).
- ✔ Availability of stock of mailing material; check that numbers match selection/ list numbers.
- ✔ Volumes actually despatched; record timings of despatches.
- ✔ Where the first communication is through broadcast or published media, record whether the advertisement/insert appeared according to schedule, and whether the forecast number of people actually received it.
- ✔ Media timings achieved.
- ✔ Numbers responding to the first communication, by category of response.
- ✔ Availability of response packs.
- ✔ Response pack mailings – timing and volumes (applying to every subsequent action step).
- ✔ Results of response pack mailings (category and timing), eg sales.

The flows of outbound and inbound communications are very important. They are the key to checking inventory of mailing material. The inbound rates are also critical in forecasting the final result, but obviously can only be understood if we know when the relevant outbound step took place.

Where does this essential information come from?

The above information comes from many sources. Where it comes from suppliers (eg media buying, mailing, response handling), the contract should include the supply of high-quality, up-to-date statistics. Many companies new to high volume direct marketing have had significant problems in this area. These can easily be avoided by attention to detail at an earlier stage.

Failure to get these statistics from suppliers means that at any one time, no one knows the exact status of the campaign. Supply of these statistics should, therefore, be part of the conditions of the contract and also specifically detailed in the brief for each campaign. Most of the problems in this area are caused by campaign managers failing to specify their requirements in enough detail.

Each supplier should be told:

- ✔ The data required.
- ✔ The frequency of reporting expected.
- ✔ Procedures for signalling problems.

What else can go wrong?

One of the most important skills the direct marketer must have is knowing what to do when initial results do not correspond with expectations. You should, therefore, consider contingencies for such a scenario. Examples include:

- ✘ Responses too high or low.
- ✘ Problems with stocks of mailing or fulfilment material.
- ✘ Media schedules altered for reasons beyond your control.

For example, **if response is too high fulfilment pack stocks may run out**. Can additional stocks be ordered quickly (this needs to be established during initial negotiations with suppliers), or can a later wave of outbound communication be deferred? Before taking a snap decision, the **reason** for the high volume needs to be established. Was the outbound mailing larger than expected? Was there a special reason why more people than usual might have seen the press advertisement? Has there been a high volume of responses from "friends and family" as well as from the target respondents?

If response is too low, the achieved media and mailing schedules should be checked. So should the selection criteria or list used. Perhaps there were delays in the outbound communication. Were all the components of the pack included? Did the right response packs go to the right respondents?

The statistics you receive are an important line of defence in ensuring quality. Let us assume you have chosen the right selection criteria (lists and/or media), have designed the offer well, and it has been well presented creatively. Your control statistics tell you how well you organised and briefed your internal and external suppliers, and how well they observed your brief. **Analysing control statistics over several campaigns will give you a good idea of whether there is a fundamental problem in a particular area.** For example, does a particular mailing house always mail out late, or does a fulfilment house always notify stock figures too late? Has staff absence on business or holiday caused problems in the management of a campaign, suggesting that a sharing arrangement with colleagues would help?

The problem with learning after the event is that you may already be on to the next campaign. Control statistics may be forgotten. **They should, therefore, be kept, ideally in simple graphic format, as a permanent record of the campaign's progress.** This will help you review, for example, the performance of particular agencies over several campaigns, as well as evaluate your own judgement.

After the campaign

Learning from your final results

Monitoring and control during a campaign are closely related to final evaluation, except whereas during a campaign we usually evaluate basic flows and stocks (responses in and packs out), after a campaign we typically evaluate rates and ratios (eg profit per contact).

There are many ways to measure a campaign's effectiveness. Some are non-monetary (eg response rates). Some are cost ratios (eg cost per response, relative media cost/ productivity). **In the end, the most important results are customer satisfaction and brand support, and how these are translated into financial measures such as revenue and profit.** We can use intermediate criteria to judge effectiveness. These are based on the **chain of productivity**, the ratios which determine the relationship between input and output. A simple example of such a chain is:

- ✔ Profit = Unit profit x Number of units sold
- ✔ Number of units sold = Sales per response x Number of responses
- ✔ Number of responses = Responses per customer reached x Number of customers reached

Using intermediate measures, the campaign could be evaluated by:

- ✔ The number of customers reached.
- ✔ The number of responses generated (of each type).
- ✔ Number of bookings/orders generated.
- ✔ Incremental profit from the campaign.
- ✔ Effect on customer lifetime value, etc.

Each campaign must be evaluated against, as well as in conjunction with, other campaigns. Thus, you might evaluate mail **parallel** to telemarketing, or **with** telemarketing as a combined contact strategy.

The "cost/productivity" statistics we use to judge the effectiveness of different inputs into the marketing process include:

- ✔ Cost per 1000 mailed, or per 'phone call
- ✔ Cost per decision maker contact
- ✔ Cost per lead achieved
- ✔ Cost per sale

These should be compared for different media. The cost of different elements of the sales process (outbound contact, enquiry handling and fulfilment, concluding sale) should also be evaluated. These should be set against revenue and margins achieved (including any selling of products which were not the subject of the promotion).

Quality statistics should also be accumulated. These include database quality statistics (eg gone aways) and measures of the quality of the response handling process (eg average elapsed time before fulfilment pack sent out).

The subject of direct marketing measurements is dealt with more fully in subsequent chapters of this Guide (see Chapters 2.4, 2.5 and 2.6).

Managing the direct marketing process

Why you need a process

Much of the content of this chapter may seem a tall order to the average beleaguered direct marketing manager. But the fact is without a proper management process you have little hope of making it all happen. Even if you do once, you'll have to work just as hard next time to make it happen again. This is where the management process comes in.

Yet many direct marketers still have to design and deliver campaigns without any management process. Some are simply given a list of "stages of campaign development". This was fine in the days when direct marketing consisted of the odd tactical campaign. Today, when direct marketing has become central to the strategic marketing of many companies, it is not good enough. You **need** a process.

What kind of process you need depends very much on the kind of company you're in, and how it organises its marketing. What follows are detailed suggestions as to the kind of approach you might adopt, and the information requirements of that approach.

But first let us look at the benefits of having a process:

Process benefits: (1) resource allocation

A good management process allows resources to be based upon a clear understanding of the future workload of every member of the team. This improves resource utilisation and the quality of work carried out. Direct marketing departments tend to commit to a large number of campaigns before working out whether they have got the time and resource to do the job properly. A good process avoids this fundamental error.

Process benefits: (2) management support

A good process provides management support to members of the team including suppliers and internal customers (eg brand managers, sales managers). Direct marketing is a very detailed and information-intense activity. At every stage of a campaign many decisions have to be made, and much information is needed. **A good process ensures that the right information is available at the right time to the right people.** In particular, information on the status of campaigns is readily available.

Tasks and stages in a direct marketing campaign

Different campaign types may differ in terms of which tasks are required and in what order. Many tasks may run in parallel, so this checklist is arranged by topic. If a campaign has already been tested, many stages may be omitted (eg creative/media development, market targeting, etc). A test campaign should involve the same tasks as a roll-out campaign.

Strategy tasks

- ❒ Develop marketing plan
- ❒ Within marketing plan, determine market focus for campaign
- ❒ Identify customer needs in target market
- ❒ Select product or service for promotion
- ❒ Check customer database system for previous similar campaigns: type, product, customer coverage, level of success, etc.
- ❒ Confirm consistency with timing of other campaigns
- ❒ Run trial selections to confirm numbers in target market
- ❒ Determine budgets
- ❒ Set up outline campaign on database and management system
- ❒ Prepare draft timings (main milestones, not detailed project plan)
- ❒ Circulate draft timings to all suppliers and internal customers
- ❒ Receive supplier and internal customer comments and modify draft timings

Campaign management tasks

- ❒ Determine project management accountability – overall and in each supplier/ department
- ❒ Prepare contact list and circulate to all suppliers
- ❒ Confirm product and service details
- ❒ Agree campaign timing
- ❒ Prepare draft agency brief using forms
- ❒ Issue draft brief to agency (or agencies if competitive tender being used)
- ❒ Invite agency comments on draft brief
- ❒ Finalise brief and confirm
- ❒ Agency to develop strategy concepts, proposals and detailed timings
- ❒ Prepare detailed project plan in consultation with suppliers
- ❒ Prepare reporting forms
- ❒ Review forms with management
- ❒ Agree forms
- ❒ Agency to submit initial recommendation (creative, media, etc)
- ❒ Select agency (if competitive pitch)
- ❒ Evaluate costs of recommendations against expected response
- ❒ Comment on recommendations, using checklists in this Guide
- ❒ Agency to revise recommendations?
- ❒ Agency to present revised creative and media proposals
- ❒ Agree agency creative proposals finally
- ❒ Agree agency media proposals
- ❒ Prepare campaign flowcharts
- ❒ Circulate campaign flowcharts to all suppliers/departments

Mailing and fulfilment

- ❒ Prepare copy and layouts (letters, brochures, envelopes, etc)
- ❒ Prepare illustrations and photographs
- ❒ Review copy and layouts using checklists
- ❒ Revise copy and layouts if required
- ❒ Approve final copy (text)
- ❒ Prepare artwork
- ❒ Check artwork
- ❒ Revise artwork
- ❒ Approve artwork
- ❒ Prepare complete pack dummy
- ❒ Check pack dummy
- ❒ Approve pack dummy
- ❒ Print sample run for distribution to all involved in campaign
- ❒ Distribute samples
- ❒ Order all print for production runs

Internal communication

- ❒ Brief all sales and marketing staff
- ❒ Brief all customer-facing staff
- ❒ Receive confirmation from customer-facing staff that briefs received, understood and agreed and that mechanism exists for handling results of campaign (lead-handling, follow-up)
- ❒ Schedule training and motivation meetings if required
- ❒ Prepare training and motivational material
- ❒ Hold training and motivation meetings

General and system logistics

- ❒ Make go/no go
- ❒ Check campaign logistics with mailing, telemarketing, response handling and fulfilment agencies
- ❒ Check data links between all parties
- ❒ Agree selection/list
- ❒ Determine testing strategy (including test & control cells)
- ❒ Determine list size
- ❒ Select contact strategies

- ❒ Confirm selection rules and timing for initial target customer groups for each action/ treatment, allocate codes and enter into system
- ❒ Confirm rules for allocation to follow-up groups, allocate codes and enter into system
- ❒ Write custom selection routines if required
- ❒ Run trial extract/selection on test basis
- ❒ Check trial extract/selection
- ❒ Modify extract/selection programme if required
- ❒ Run extract/selection on production basis
- ❒ Check output file
- ❒ Transfer to desired medium
- ❒ Despatch output
- ❒ Check with recipient(s) that output correct/ readable
- ❒ Go live!
- ❒ Update promotion histories
- ❒ Receive updates from fulfilment/ telemarketing agencies
- ❒ Update contact records
- ❒ Report production
- ❒ Report campaign closed
- ❒ File outstanding enquiries for future
- ❒ Prepare final campaign report and issue

Print and mail logistics

- ❒ Brief mailing and fulfilment houses using briefing format
- ❒ Develop print production schedule
- ❒ Issue print production schedule
- ❒ Prepare artwork for print
- ❒ Prepare laser letters with variations to match source and targeting and (for fulfilment letters) outcome of customer response
- ❒ Check sample letters
- ❒ Confirm outbound mailing envelope description
- ❒ Confirm fulfilment pack envelope description
- ❒ Define mailing and fulfilment packs on system
- ❒ Confirm media slots and timing
- ❒ Issue final media schedule
- ❒ Print outbound mailing
- ❒ Check samples of outbound mailing
- ❒ Deliver outbound packs to mailing house
- ❒ Outbound stock arrives and correct stock level confirmed
- ❒ Print fulfilment packs
- ❒ Check samples of fulfilment packs using checklists
- ❒ Deliver fulfilment packs to fulfilment house
- ❒ Check fulfilment stocks arrived and confirm correct stock levels
- ❒ Plan and buy media
- ❒ Check advertisements appeared correctly
- ❒ Send mailing tapes/data to mailing house
- ❒ Despatch mailing
- ❒ Receive response to media advertising/ mailing/telemarketing
- ❒ Process response information to determine fulfilment pack required
- ❒ Initiate fulfilment
- ❒ Print personalised laser letters
- ❒ Make up fulfilment packs to customer requirements and dispatch
- ❒ Monitor fulfilment stocks and replenish if required
- ❒ Receive progress reports and monitor
- ❒ Dispose of unwanted print stocks after campaign close

Telemarketing

- ❒ Prepare draft telemarketing agency brief
- ❒ Issue draft brief to telemarketing agency (or agencies if competitive tender being used)
- ❒ Receive agency comments on draft brief
- ❒ Finalise brief and confirm
- ❒ Receive agency recommendation on campaign approach
- ❒ Select agency
- ❒ Evaluate costs of recommendations against expected response
- ❒ Comment on recommendations
- ❒ Agency to revise recommendations
- ❒ Agency to develop decision trees
- ❒ Circulate decision trees internally and to client for comment
- ❒ Agency to presents revised decision trees
- ❒ Agree decision trees for testing
- ❒ Agency presents draft scripts
- ❒ Scripts circulated internally and to client for comment
- ❒ Agency to present revised scripts
- ❒ Agree scripts for testing
- ❒ Design script screen displays
- ❒ Check screens
- ❒ Brief training and 'phoneroom management, and receive comments on screens
- ❒ Amend screen displays and implement
- ❒ Determine data entry procedures, including return of questionnaire data to customer database
- ❒ Implement data entry procedures
- ❒ Select test team
- ❒ Train test team
- ❒ Make test calls
- ❒ Check hard copy output
- ❒ Revise trees and scripts after testing
- ❒ Revise screens and data entry procedures after testing
- ❒ Agree final trees and scripts
- ❒ Confirm target customers
- ❒ Set live date!
- ❒ Determine customers to be called and provide telephone numbers
- ❒ Select main calling team
- ❒ Train calling team (products, offer, etc)
- ❒ Confirm timing of calling
- ❒ Begin calling
- ❒ Despatch call results to system for processing
- ❒ Check tapes and follow up
- ❒ Receive progress reports and monitor

A good process reduces the time wasted looking for information. It reduces time spent in meetings exchanging information. Meetings are expensive and should make the most of the "brain-time" of those involved for discussing options and making decisions. A good process has the added benefit of identifying problems early. It also reduces the time staff spend on sorting out administrative complexities, and improves overall morale.

Process benefits: (3) managing suppliers

A good process improves the management of suppliers. It starts with supplier selection and continues through briefing and quotation to tracking suppliers' work. This enables suppliers to work more effectively with your team and your team can in turn manage your suppliers more tightly, leading to budget savings. Why? Because a good process identifies when supplier inputs are required and ensures that time is set aside to deal with them. These inputs range from quotations and negotiations to actual delivered work.

Process benefits: (4) improved lead times

A good process improves lead times, allowing time for better, more cost-effective implementation and for more pro-active management of opportunities. This is a "chicken and egg" situation. Initially, implementing a process may increase lead times as your team gets used to working with it. But eventually, because campaigns are managed more efficiently, they can be completed more quickly.

However, this does **not** imply that briefs can be left until later. The benefit of an improved process should be increased quality of campaigns, not quicker turnround. Indeed, we are arguing for campaign development cycles which are on average **longer** than in most companies. Ideally the campaign development cycle should begin, at the latest, as soon as the marketing plan is drawn up. With campaigns well managed and properly paced you can then deal with urgent campaigns more speedily, while maintaining quality.

Process benefits: (5) campaign quality

A good process helps to ensure quality in all the key elements of a campaign: targeting; contact strategy and media; timing; offer design; and creative. **The right information is provided to the right person at the right time.** Accountabilities are clearly allocated and milestoned. The whole campaign will be managed better and produce better results. This is likely to be visible first in mistake avoidance, and later in better results.

Before we go on to look at the management process in practice, let us recap its purpose and its benefits:

Good campaign management means getting the right information, to the right people, at the right time.

Designing the management process

What exactly is a management process?

A management process is simply an organised way of going about things. More simply, it is a statement that when we do something, we do it this way. The elements and visible signs of a process include the following:

The broad components of a management process	
Planning and decisions	Analyses Task planning Problem resolution Progress chasing Progress management Meetings
Information handling and reporting	Regular reports Exception reports Communicating progress Review cycle Output evaluation Result publication Enquiry handling Notifying requirements Computerisation Form filling Data entry Documentation Filing
Resource processes	Budgeting Resource allocation Negotiation/influencing
People processes	Role definition Accountabilities Motivation Management action Staff appraisal

Work cycles: Days, months or years?

There are many ways of viewing how a process works. One way of describing a process is according to the length of work cycle that it manages. The following distinctions have been found useful by many leading practitioners:

Day in the life – the everyday job of managing work. This includes filling forms, data entry, filing, diary management, back-up provision and meeting management. The focus here is on balancing individual tasks on a daily basis. At the human level, the focus is on such things as checking that events are proceeding according to plan, managing problems, helping people complete tasks, and supporting and giving lift through motivation.

Month in the life – slightly longer-term activities or projects. These include putting together plans, implementing campaigns, briefing suppliers, recruiting, developing, communicating with and motivating staff and measuring performance.

Year in the life – major activities and very important projects. These include launching a major new product, development and implementation of a strategic campaign and production of a business-wide plan. Also included here are longer-term people activities, eg appraisal, long-term development and promotion.

Running the process

Some rules for successful campaign management

Some processes can be self-administered, particularly if tasks are simple and routine and all involved know what the tasks are, why they're necessary, and the consequences of not doing them. Self-administered processes also work well if managers concentrate on managing the exceptions. This should be by strong positive reward for successes **and** for working to the process, as well as negative reinforcement for staff not observing agreed processes. Self-administration usually consists of following a checklist.

But if tasks are not simple or are required only occasionally – or if understanding about the need for them is not widespread – then a more hands-on approach to management may be required. In some cases, a document-intensive process may be used to ensure that people know what they are doing and communicate it to each other.

"Process" and "procedures" are related. **"Process" describes the general way you want people to deal with tasks. "Procedures" are the detailed steps involved in running the process.** If a process and/or set of procedures is to work, these conditions must hold:

✔ Staff must understand and be committed to the process.

✔ Roles must be allocated clearly and staff must understand them, eg what they are accountable for, what they can decide or influence.

✔ Staff must have the skills to carry out the roles and the time and resource required to do so.

✔ The process should produce clear benefits for staff, eg help them work better, reduce tension or conflict, give them clear standards by which to judge their own performance.

✔ Staff commitment to the process must be reinforced by management action (managers must be seen to be involved in implementing the process, setting clear priorities, administering rewards and sanctions). Appraisals must take into account contribution to the process.

✔ Management must know when someone is or is not carrying out their role, otherwise individual reinforcement cannot take place. In other words, managers must keep their ears to the ground!

✔ The objective of the process must be "right for the business".

✔ The process must be designed to support that objective (ie right for the business), or allow staff to work more effectively to achieve it.

Ideally, most elements of the management process should be computerised. This applies particularly to planning, information preparation and distribution.

Process management in an imperfect world!

Running campaigns without an overall marketing plan

We have seen that campaign planning **should** start when marketing planning starts. In practice, many companies' marketing plans lack the basis for this approach. A plan may be too general, lacking the detailed objectives required. It may be produced too early and be irrelevant by the time it is applied, or it may be produced too late. If this Guide were to recommend a process which depended totally on the existence of a properly documented marketing plan, its advice would be dismissed as irrelevant by half its readers!

So, in what follows, we describe how campaigns can be handled irrespective of the state of your marketing plan. A good marketing plan will help you handle campaigns better. But you can still develop and run good campaigns without a proper marketing plan, provided you do your bit professionally. However, if your company doesn't give you the right support for campaign planning, you must develop an approach of your own. If you don't get clear guidance on objectives and priorities you must develop them yourself.

Campaign planning and co-ordination are not theoretically complex. It is just a question of making sure that your campaigns deliver messages whose content and timing are co-ordinated and which contribute to the development of your brand(s). This means co-ordinating every aspect of campaign development.

Important: Remember to co-ordinate your direct and non-direct marketing activities!

Co-ordinating targeting and contact strategies

In companies whose main marketing channel is direct, such as mail, and which have good customer databases, co-ordinating its selections is the key activity. **This is so important that some companies treat access to the database as the most important marketing decision.** Brand managers and sales managers are required to submit their briefs to the database manager. His job is then to determine who are the best prospects for each campaign, and when they should be contacted. In deciding, he takes into account the targeting, timing and offers of other campaigns.

In some companies, the database manager himself suggests which campaigns should be run and what contact strategies should be used. He moves from being a gatekeeper of the database to the initiator of campaign ideas. By analysing the database he can determine what campaigns are required. He plays the customer-advocate, with customers speaking through him on the basis of which campaigns they have responded to, and which they have not received.

Co-ordinating multiple products and offers

In companies where heavy investment goes into producing a variety of products, and where direct marketing is a central sales channel, co-ordinating products can be difficult. The company's need to run a campaign can clash with its need to run campaigns for other products. As direct marketers, we have to accept this. The earlier the warning about the need to promote a particular product, the more time everyone gets to develop ways of differentiating products through offers.

Where products differ greatly in their nature and target market, co-ordination is not a problem. **But where products are similar, with overlapping target markets, you must develop ways of positioning products relative to each other.** You need time to test how far the target markets actually do overlap, so that you can identify the non-overlapping segments and promote differently to overlapping and non-overlapping segments.

Offer and product co-ordination depend on having a deep understanding of target markets and product benefits. The secret of offer/product co-ordination lies in early briefing on product benefits, clear and early-stated views on target markets, and decent warning of the required timing of campaigns.

Co-ordinating and organising the team

At the risk of being repetitive, it is worth stressing once more that co-ordinating and forewarning personnel are the most important single function of a campaign process.

Many companies organise their co-ordination by committee. Incoming briefs are collated and submitted to a campaign co-ordination committee. This meets regularly (typically monthly) to review all briefs and slot them in. In other companies a planning department receives all briefs and allocates them a budget and timing slot.

Whichever approach you use, the most important achievement is getting briefs submitted in good time and ensuring that the output of the planning process is properly communicated, so that the whole team knows what it must do and when.

Defining the status of a campaign

Where are we at today?

Because it genuinely takes time to decide whether and when a campaign should be run, a campaign can have different statuses, from being a gleam in the idea of a product manager to being finished. It is essential to recognise this in your process.

Opposite, we set out the kind of status that a process may be at, which can be easily determined by anyone who needs to know. We have divided the possible statuses into "operational" and "management".

The eight operational statuses	
Provisional	The campaign has been identified as needing consideration, but has not yet been submitted for formal consideration by your campaign co-ordination process. Normally, a deadline for such consideration should be set. The campaign proposal should contain an outline brief, timing and suggested budget.
Submitted	The campaign has been formally submitted for consideration through your campaign co-ordination process, with the brief and timing firmed up. Again, a deadline for approval or otherwise should be set.
Approved	The campaign has been approved by the campaign co-ordination process, with timings for development, launch and close agreed.
Budgeted	Although an outline budget should be considered when a campaign is at earlier stages, we believe that you should not budget until you have received quotes from suppliers. There is no point in getting detailed quotes before the campaign is approved, because this wastes suppliers' time, and may slow down other projects. The outline budget should be based on your experience with earlier campaigns. An outline budget also stops you wasting time if your suppliers think your requirement is totally unfeasible within the outline.
Under development	Serious work has started on the campaign, suppliers have been briefed, and money is being spent!
Live	The campaign has hit the market.
Completed	The campaign has been completed, as no further actions in the market will be undertaken.
Closed	The results of the campaign have been analysed and properly documented.

The eight Operational Statuses describe where a project has reached in its normal process of development. However, things do not always run so smoothly. Campaigns may be cancelled, deferred or even absorbed into other campaigns. So we need four further statuses, known as Management Statuses, as follows:

The four management statuses	
Current	The campaign is at one of the above statuses and progressing normally.
Cancelled	The campaign will not go ahead. This may be determined at any stage before the campaign is live. You should keep a record of work done for the campaign as it may be needed later.
Deferred	The campaign is deferred. No new timing has been specified and it will require resubmission through the co-ordination process.
Absorbed	The campaign has been absorbed into another campaign.

The four Management Statuses have important resource implications and possible legal or contractual implications with suppliers. For example, cancelling a campaign may risk a breach of contract with suppliers.

If you observe the above statuses, then it becomes much easier to manage your campaign co-ordination and resource allocation processes. Your whole team, including suppliers, will know at any one time which campaigns you are considering, planning, working on, and finishing.

Who makes the decisions?

Who is responsible for making the decision at each stage and managing the campaign through depends on how you are organised. Here is a suggestion as to how you might allocate what we call "authorities" at each of the main campaign statuses:

Who does what in the campaign process?

Status	Person responsible and action required.
Provisional	The person initiating the request (the brand or product manager, sales manager, service manager, database manager, etc) is responsible for providing an outline of the brief, requested timing and likely budget.
Submitted	The person initiating the request is responsible for submitting the campaign unless you have some more formal process of allocating the progression of projects.
Approved	The manager of the campaign co-ordination process is responsible for making it happen. Any revisions to the brief agreed during the process – especially targeting and timing – should be circulated by him.
Budgeted	This depends on how you are organised. If your promotional budgets are centralised, this may be the responsibility of your financial controller. If budgets are allocated to internal customers (eg brand managers), they may be the appropriate authority (solely or jointly with you).
Under development	The campaign manager is finally responsible for all work during this and the next two stages, live and completed, and for documenting the results at campaign close.
Cancelled, deferred and absorbed	The manager responsible for the last stage of a campaign is responsible for maintaining the data available. However, ideally the data should be centralised with the manager responsible for campaign co-ordination.

... and who carries out the various tasks?

One of the most neglected aspects of direct marketing management is recognition of the different functions needed to ensure that campaigns are delivered properly. We have already discussed some implicitly, eg the campaign manager, the person responsible for co-ordination. But there are other roles that management must fulfil as listed at the top of the facing page.

What else must be done?

Initiation/ origination	Coming up with the ideas for campaigns.
Workload/ resource control	Ensuring that the resources of the team – including suppliers – are adequate to meet the demands upon them, and that work is scheduled so as to optimise these resources.
Campaign administration	Ensuring campaigns are correctly documented and communicated, and that everyone in the team meets their deadlines.
Delivery/ production	Actually bringing the campaign to market.
Sponsoring	Providing the funds.
The internal customer	The person benefiting from the campaign, typically a product, service or sales manager.

In some companies, all the above functions and roles are combined in the job specification of the direct marketing manager. But in very big companies heavily committed to direct marketing the roles are often split. The most under-rated of all these functions is campaign administration. Although quite a junior person often occupies this role, a good campaign administrator is worth his/her weight in gold.

The complete campaign process in detail

What should be done and by whom

On the next page is a checklist showing what should happen at each stage of a campaign and who should do it. The information required will typically be organised into a number of computer screens or parts of screens, which should be completed as the campaign progresses and which together constitute the campaign file. In some companies, this process is still largely manual with the only computerised information being that required to trigger actions (eg selections). However, without properly documented campaign files you are likely to commit more errors of commission and omission than otherwise. With the information properly organised, you'll at least have the basis for quality.

Make a copy of this checklist (overleaf) and refer to it regularly – it will save you many an embarrassment and earn you many a plaudit!

Note: Each of the stages referred to in this checklist is dealt with more fully in other specialised chapters in this Guide. Use the index to locate further advice.

The campaign process – key information areas and responsibilities

1.	**Campaign definition and accountabilities**	Describing the requirement in brief and saying who is involved in delivering it: staff, suppliers and internal clients.
2.	**Campaign coverage**	Testing and market coverage issues.
3.	**Objectives and strategy**	Where the campaign fits in overall marketing and promotional strategy and what the campaign needs to achieve.
4.	**Product or programme detail**	What exactly is being promoted, and what its features and benefits are.
5.	**Market detail**	Who the campaign is targeted at, what their perceptions are, who the competition is and what they're offering.
6.	**Campaign elements**	What are the detailed requirements of the campaign.
7.	**Initial estimates**	What you think the campaign's going to cost and what revenue you expect.
8.	**Management and media timing plans**	The main milestones in campaign planning including above-the-line media (press, TV, etc).
9.	**Mail and telemarketing timing plans**	The main milestones for direct marketing media implementation.
10.	**Formal agency quote**	What the agency believes it should get!
11.	**Outbound list selection brief**	Which specific customers you want to target.
12.	**Internal list selection brief**	As 11, but for when your database is organised into lists.
13.	**External list selection brief**	As 11, but for when you need to rent lists.
14.	**Contact and fulfilment strategy**	What you're going to do with each group of customers you target.
15.	**Contact and fulfilment details**	How you're going to do this in detail.
16.	**Contact strategy diagrams**	A diagrammatic representation of 14 and 15.
17.	**Data format and delivery**	How you want the data to be provided by your customer database system.
18.	**Reports**	What reports you want from the database system.
19.	**Systems feedback report**	How many customers have been selected by your selection criteria.
20.	**Outbound telemarketing**	Detailed brief to telemarketing agency for outbound calling.
21.	**Enquiry management/inbound telemarketing**	As above, but for inbound.
22.	**Questionnaire summary**	To record details of questions asked in telemarketing or mailing programmes.
23.	**Media – broadcast**	Brief to media buying for TV and radio.
24.	**Media – press**	Brief to media buying for press.
25.	**Fulfilment pack summary**	Details of contents and suppliers.
26.	**Fulfilment letter summary**	Details of letter/literature to accompany pack.
27.	**Print production & distribution**	Handling of printed items.
28.	**Print delivery advice**	To ensure print gets to the right place.
29.	**Campaign close report**	The results!

Some tips for administering a campaign

The checklist on the facing page may seem a rather complex set of actions, but it represents what goes on in most companies – albeit often verbally or on the back of an envelope. All that we have done is to rationalise it.

All you need do now to implement such a process is to work to a clear set of administrative procedures, as follows:

- ✔ Do maintain a master file for the complete campaign (campaign administrator).
- ✔ Do physically document the entire process including management decisions and actions taken.
- ✔ Do package the file properly, into clearly marked sections, so absence or incompleteness of any information can be detected readily.
- ✔ Do ensure that forms are kept up-to-date. Certain items should be mandatory at particular stages.
- ✔ Do ensure all information is copied to the entire team even where it is addressed to "principal recipients".
- ✔ Do issue amendments whenever a change is made.
- ✔ Do ensure the team keeps its information files up to date by recording each change.
- ✔ Do **date** amendment sheets.
- ✔ Do insist that suppliers produce simple summaries which should also be kept on file.
- ✔ Do circulate outputs from each process, eg draft copies and targets, scripts, etc.
- ✔ Do develop standard forms to convey essential information, eg changes of campaign status.
- ✔ On very large projects, do automate communications with direct links to suppliers and customers. There are obvious benefits in computerising a campaign process. Without computerisation, running the process will be very cumbersome. In particular, reporting will be very slow and paper-intense. The kind of reports that will need to be issued include the following:
  - Projects at different statuses
  - Date each form was last updated
  - Milestones due and missed
  - Budgets allocated
  - Quotes accepted
  - Data missing
  - Results summary
  - Work loading on staff

Using software to manage the process

Today it is commonplace to maintain and communicate campaign schedules using proprietary software available on Windows, DOS or Mac. The output is usually in the form of a chart, either Gantt or PERT; examples of both are shown below. The advantage of software is that updating is vastly simplified and virtually instant.

Gantt chart

Below is a Gantt chart detailing the stages of a direct mail campaign. It shows the order in which tasks must be started and the effects of delays on the project as a whole. Critical tasks are those that must be completed before other tasks can commence, indicated by capital letters.

```
5    Days Per Symbol   06      09      13    20    21    29    03    07    11    16
ID   Task Name         Dec 94  Jan 95  Feb   Mar   Apr   May   Jul   Aug   Sep   Oct

001  Define market     X ------------------------------------------------------------
002  Campaign plan     XXXX ---------------------------------------------------------
003  Produce brief     ----X---------------------------------------------------------
004  Agency response   ----XXX ------------------------------------------------------
005  Agree strategy    -----XX ------------------------------------------------------
006  Confirm budget    -------X------------------------------------------------------
007  Go/no go          ------M ------------------------------------------------------
008  Contact strategy  -------X------------------------------------------------------
010  Media plan        ------xx>>>> -------------------------------------------------
014  Determine lists   ------xx>>>> -------------------------------------------------
012  Creative work     -------XXXX --------------------------------------------------
021  Plan fulfilment   ------xx------------------------------------------------------
009  Do selections     -------xx-----------------------------------------------------
015  Order lists       --------xx----------------------------------------------------
011  Order media       ---------xxxxxxxxx > -----------------------------------------
013  Creative submit   --------X-----------------------------------------------------
016  Creative agreed   ---------M----------------------------------------------------
017  Copy/artwork      --------XXXX -------------------------------------------------
018  Copy/art agreed   ----------M---------------------------------------------------
019  Pack finalised    ----------XX -------------------------------------------------
020  Production begin  -----------M--------------------------------------------------
022  Printing          -----------XXXX-----------------------------------------------
023  Lasering          ---------------XX --------------------------------------------
024  Packs made up     ----------------XXX ------------------------------------------
025  Ads appear        -----------------m -------------------------------------------
025  Mailing begins    -------------------XX ----------------------------------------
026  Fulfilment        ------------------XXXXXXXXXXXXXXXXXXXXXXXXXXX ----------------
027  Campaign close    ----------------------------------------------------X --------

xxx  non critical      m    milestone               >>>   float/delay
XXX  critical          M    critical milestone      XXX   final delay
```

PERT chart

Opposite is an example of part of a PERT chart for a multi-media campaign (mailings and press advertising).

Example of a PERT chart

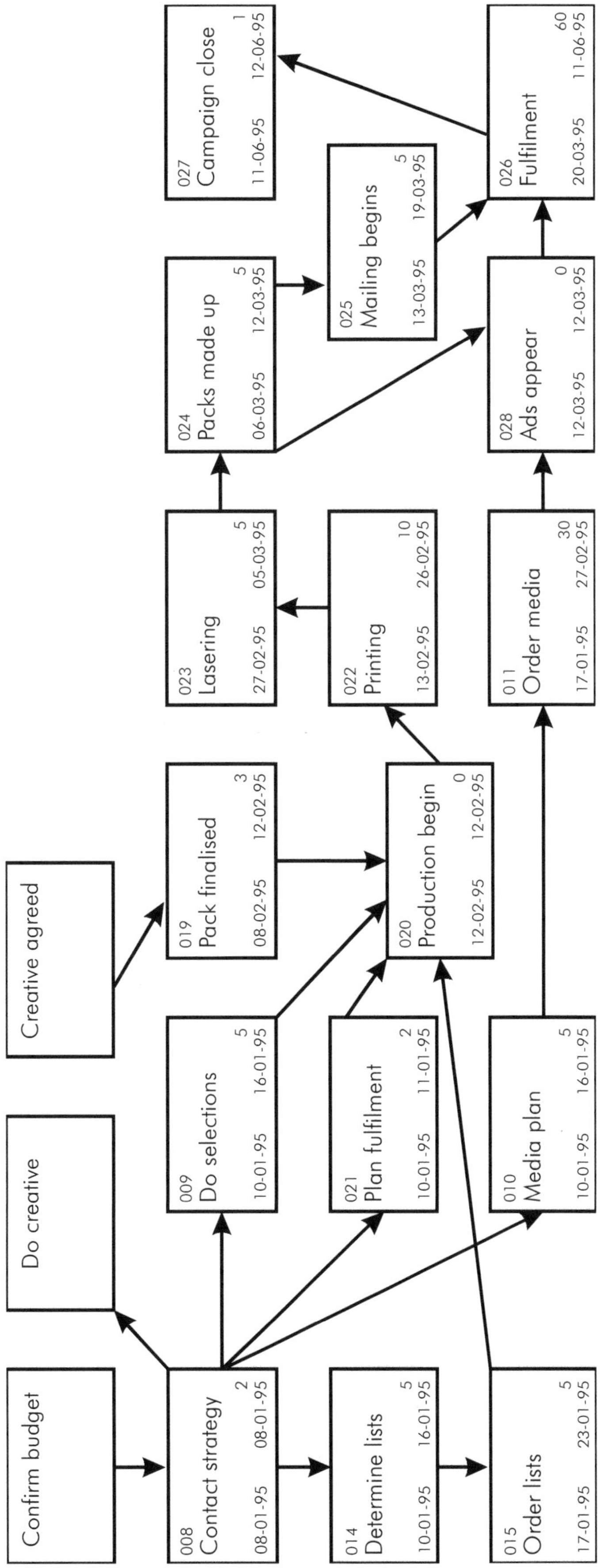

A PERT chart provides a graphic representation of:

- ✔ The tasks
- ✔ How the tasks are interconnected and interdependent
- ✔ How long each task takes
- ✔ When each task should be completed

A PERT chart may indicate that a particular chain of events forms **the critical path**, ie the longest timescale of any mutually dependent series of actions.

Either Gantt or PERT can be used; it makes no difference as long as the timescales are realistic and displayed clearly.

Summing up: The campaign process

A good campaign process is designed to ensure that the **right information** reaches the **right people** at the **right time**.

The purpose of this chapter has largely been to remind you of processes and procedures that you will encounter, to ensure that none is overlooked, and to put them in some sort of logical sequence. Use the foregoing checklists to build management documents which suit your particular needs.

Chapter 2.1

Direct marketers turn to market research

This chapter includes:

- Why direct marketers need market research
- Basic types of research: secondary and primary
- Conducting a research survey
- 3 types of interview, advantages and disadvantages
- Using the database for market research
- Postal research, how and why
- Panel, omnibus and syndicated surveys
- Media surveys and data fusion – a new technique
- 8 case studies: pre-testing products and communications

Traditionally direct marketers believed that practical testing provided answers to almost all their questions about products, markets, communications, even likely sales. It was, they argued, inexpensive, fast and incapable of bias; furthermore it described the behaviour of customers and prospects in real-life situations rather than simply reflecting their intentions or attitudes. The development of predictive databases added weight to those claims.

In the first edition of this Guide Peter Mouncey pointed to the weaknesses of this “testing only” approach and showed how direct marketers could use their databases to answer hitherto unanswerable questions. Only market research, he demonstrated, could tell us WHY people behave as they do – leading to increased success, reduced risk, lowered costs and the exploration of ideas that might otherwise not see the light of day.

Today, says Mouncey, market research is as relevant to direct marketing as it is to any other promotion and distribution method. One major advantage available to the direct marketer is that a list of customers – and information about them – is usually available from a computerised database and this can be used for conducting research.

New in this edition. Eight studies showing how market research has been used to pre-test communications and products prior to more orthodox live testing.

Peter Mouncey, General Manager, Group Marketing Services, AA

After gaining an HND in Business Studies and the Institute of Marketing Diploma, Peter worked for a spell in the market research department at the Gas Council, joining the Automobile Association in the early 1970s. His first two years at the AA were spent in market planning before taking over the Market Research Unit, becoming Market Research Manager in 1978. These responsibilities were widened in the mid-1980s to include developing the AA's first marketing databases.

He is currently General Manager, Group Marketing Services, providing market research, customer satisfaction research and managing database systems and services to support the AA's marketing activities. He is also responsible for stewardship of the AA brand and for co-ordinating the AA's marketing plans.

After being elected to the MRS Council in 1986, he went on to serve as Honorary Secretary/Treasurer and then Chairman from 1990 to 1992. Between 1988 and 1990 he was Chairman of the Association of Users of Research Agencies (AURA), the main research buyers' trade body. He is an ex-Council Member of the Institute of Direct Marketing and worked on the sub-committee which developed the transformation to institute status.

He is currently Chairman of the Research Development Foundation, the "think tank" of the market research industry, which has recently completed a major study of respondent co-operation in the UK. He has also published many articles and papers, presented at conferences, seminars, etc, is a past lecturer on the IDM Diploma Course and has recently been appointed a Visiting Fellow at Cranfield University.

Interests outside work and family include walking and reading.

Peter Mouncey M IDM
General Manager
Group Marketing Services
The Automobile Association
Norfolk House
Priestley Road
Basingstoke
Hants
RG24 9NY
Tel: 0990 448866

Chapter 2.1

Direct marketers turn to market research

What is market research?

The Chartered Institute of Marketing defines market research as "The means used by those who provide goods and services to keep themselves in touch with the needs and wants of those who buy and use those goods and services ... It is basically a fact-finding activity and services management by decreasing the field of uncertainty within which often vital business decisions are taken."

A rather stricter definition in terms of the collection and use of survey data (not necessarily for business use) is contained in the Market Research Society Code of Conduct to be used in registration under the Data Protection Act:

What do we mean by Confidential Survey Research?

Academic, Market or other Survey Research including the collection and analysis of personal data, with no disclosure of identifiable personal details about survey respondents to any third party (including any client for the research) and no use of the personal data for anything other than statistical and research purposes.

Market research and direct marketing

The application of market research to direct marketing has tended to lag behind usage in other marketing processes. One of the main reasons for this might well be that the industry was founded on a basis of small companies run by independent entrepreneurs. This resulted in:

- ✗ An emphasis on current campaigns with little or no long-term planning.
- ✗ No desire to try and discover insights into consumer behaviour.
- ✗ Market research viewed as yet another expense rather than as an investment for future development.
- ✗ Low marketing and promotion budgets coupled with tight margins in often highly competitive markets.
- ✗ Testing either viewed as synonymous with research or preferred to research.

Even in the 1990s research versus testing remains a live debating issue within the industry. Some direct marketers still advocate that the sophisticated nature of today's customer databases and associated analytical tools and systems render traditional market research techniques unnecessary.

However, market research remains a very cost-effective step prior to undertaking test campaigns – especially in developing products, promotion material and targeting. It is also the only way to discover WHY customers behave the way they do. For example, why they do or don't respond to a specific campaign, which, of course, helps enormously in creating alternative approaches.

The fact is market research techniques are now becoming increasingly applied in direct marketing. Three reasons might be cited for this change:

- ✔ Current and future growth in direct marketing is now primarily by large established companies where marketing management expects to have at its disposal the full range of professional expert services, including market research.
- ✔ The value of market research in providing an understanding of consumer behaviour and a competitive edge in the marketplace has been increasingly recognised.

✔ The trend towards relationship marketing, which demands a very detailed understanding of customers' needs, attitudes, etc, and a high degree of market segmentation in which customers demand increasingly individual treatment.

Where direct marketers use research

Areas in which market research is of particular value to direct marketers and where it is being employed by more and more organisations include:

✔ Product/concept testing.

✔ Recognising customers' usage of and preference for different distribution channels.

✔ Guidance in developing creative messages and materials.

✔ Quantifying, profiling and segmenting target prospects and existing customers.

✔ Targeting direct response off-the-page/DRTV campaigns.

✔ Defining consumers' needs and understanding behaviour patterns.

✔ Developing and maintaining loyalty programmes.

✔ Understanding the overall marketplace, including overall trends and competitors' activity.

✔ Checking the accuracy of database information.

✔ Identifying customers' usage of competitors.

Later in this chapter we show a few case examples of how market research has been used in a variety of direct marketing situations.

The two basic types of market research

Market research activities can be broken down under two main headings:

Confusingly, secondary research normally takes place **before** primary research. It is called secondary because it is not usually the main research activity. For example, it does not include surveys directed at specific customers or customer groups, but instead **makes use of existing data** including published data already in the public domain.

Secondary market research

Secondary market research uses existing data which may be drawn from any or all of the following:

- ✔ Previous research surveys
- ✔ Government statistics
- ✔ Trade association data
- ✔ Company statistics
- ✔ Industry reports
- ✔ Published research surveys
- ✔ Databooks
- ✔ Computer-linked services

Secondary research may be used to help design primary research, to provide researchers with background to the subject being researched and to help calibrate the results of more specific surveys. For obvious reasons it is also sometimes known as "desk research".

Since secondary research is generally understood by most direct marketers – and involves little more than looking up and understanding already pre-digested data – in this chapter we concentrate mainly on our other category of research: primary research.

Primary market research

Primary research is **original** research which is undertaken **to ascertain information not already known or recorded elsewhere**. It may also be used to update findings of an earlier survey – in which case if the researcher expects to uncover new data then it is, in fact, still original research.

Most of the time when we talk about carrying out research we mean primary research. Primary research involves the design and implementation of field surveys, focus groups, depth interviews, etc. It may be carried out in person, by telephone, postally or by other forms of interactive media.

Primary research may be further sub-divided into:

We shall discuss the differences in methods and objectives between these two categories in a moment.

How to commission and manage a research survey

The diagram overleaf shows the many stages involved in conducting a typical **quantitative** market research survey, starting with the definition of the marketing problem and ending with the debriefing stage where findings are presented and recommendations made for future action.

The steps include **qualitative** research to help define the issues and a **pilot** to test the questionnaire. Then comes the **interview** which may be conducted in person, by 'phone, by post, or possibly by some form of electronic reply.

Stages involved in conducting a Market Research Survey

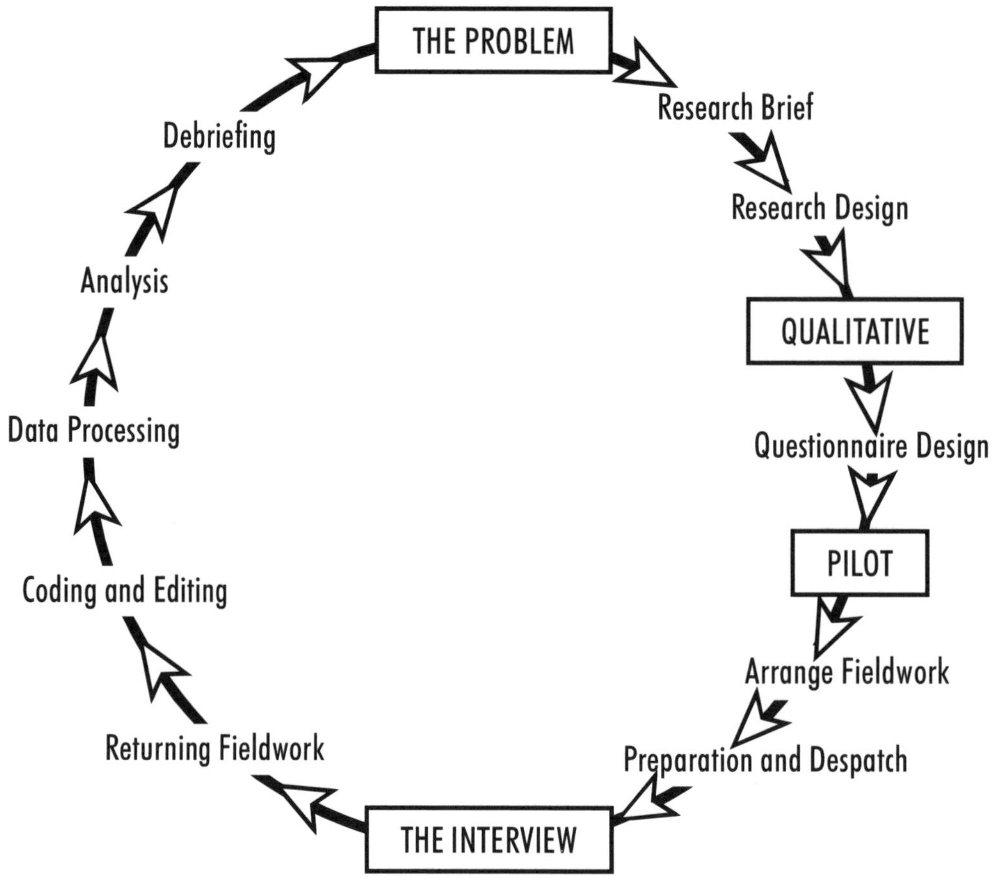

We now look at some of the key stages shown above in more detail, up to and including methods of interviewing. Following the collection of data comes a number of highly technical and specialised stages, such as coding and analysis, which we do not deal with in this Guide.

Briefing your research agency

The first step in commissioning a survey is usually to find and select a research agency. Later in this chapter will be found details of industry organisations whose help can be sought at the outset.

Having selected your research agency the next step is to brief them thoroughly. Use the following checklist to ensure that you have included all the main items in your brief.

Briefing the research agency

- ❑ Background to the brief (ie the market problem)
- ❑ Objectives of the research
- ❑ Anticipated type of study (qualitative, quantitative, etc)
- ❑ Expected uses of results (eg will they be published; used in assembling a forecast?)
- ❑ Statistical/sampling theory issues (eg key sub-groups in the analysis)
- ❑ Description of the target population from which the sample will be drawn
- ❑ Potential source(s) of the sample (eg customer database)
- ❑ Previous relevant research findings
- ❑ Customer profiles
- ❑ Other relevant materials and references
- ❑ Constraints on the survey design (eg geographic areas where interviewing should not take place; availability of the sample; seasonality factors in purchasing behaviour, etc)
- ❑ Requirements (eg fieldwork only, full survey, report or no report, etc)
- ❑ Budget
- ❑ Timescale for the project
- ❑ Stimulus material which will be provided (eg promotion roughs, product concepts, etc)
- ❑ Competitive or not (ie is more than one agency being asked to tender?)
- ❑ Organisation and staff credentials (ie background on the company and relevant staff) including internal contacts for the project

The Association of Users of Research Agencies (AURA) has produced a Quality Check List that relates in full all the factors which those commissioning research surveys should bear in mind when managing a survey research project.

Designing an effective survey

There are three key points which should be kept in mind when assessing the likely effectiveness of any particular survey:

? Are the people who are going to be interviewed a reasonable cross-section of those relevant to the survey?

? Are the questions to be asked easy to understand?

? Are the individual questions designed from an objective viewpoint or do they try to "lead" the respondent into giving a particular point of view?

Sampling theory, which is the basis of survey research as well as of the direct marketer's traditional testing, is fully described elsewhere in this Guide. The three key issues which need to be considered when commissioning a research survey are:

? What is the population/universe (from where the sample can be drawn)?

? How many people should be interviewed?

? How should those to be interviewed be selected from the population/universe?

Apart from the need to determine that the sample is statistically representative and adequate in size to give reliable statistical data, a key determinant for the size of the total sample is the extent to which it is likely to be broken down into sub-groups at the analysis stage (eg age bands, occupation classification groups, geographic areas, geodemographic codes, etc). **If reliable comparisons highlighting real behavioural differences are to be made from the data, then sub-group size is an important consideration.**

How market research data is collected

The two main methods of data collection for primary research are **qualitative** and **quantitative**. Each uses a variety of techniques and methods and has its own objectives.

Which method? Which purpose?

Qualitative	Quantitative
✔ Group discussions	✔ Postal
✔ Depth interviews	✔ Field ("face-to-face")
✔ Extended creativity panel	✔ Telephone
✔ Other techniques derived from clinical psychology	✔ Hall tests
	✔ Observation
✔ Investigates attitudes, beliefs, motivation, etc	✔ Panels
	✔ Technological: Eye Movement Recorder; Tachistoscope
ANSWERS THE "WHY" AND "HOW" QUESTIONS	ANSWERS THE "HOW MANY" QUESTIONS

Collecting qualitative data

Qualitative research answers the "why?" and "how?" questions and is often used in the early stages of a major quantitative survey for in-depth exploration of consumer motivations, attitudes, beliefs and behaviour. It also provides detailed feedback to help:

✔ Understand the language used by consumers when discussing the product field in order to aid questionnaire design.

✔ Identify the main topics to be covered.

✔ Look for any basic differences between population sub-groups.

Qualitative research may be the only research conducted in certain situations, for example in the development of advertising creative material.

The two most commonly used techniques for qualitative data collection are:

✔ Group discussions

✔ Depth interviews

Group discussions are the most commonly used qualitative technique. Small numbers of people (normally 6–9) are recruited to discuss a particular issue or topic in detail, normally at a private home, hotel or a special centre close to where those recruited live (equipped with viewing and listening facilities to allow observation by other researchers or clients to take place). They will cost between £1,250–£2,500 or more (1996 prices) per group, depending on the complexity of the sample and the length of the interview.

The discussion, led by a trained and experienced moderator, whilst following a prescribed path, will not be a question-and-answer session but an attempt to explore in-depth attitudes, motivations and beliefs concerning the topic under discussion. Projective and other psychologically based techniques may be used to help those present express their views.

Groups are frequently used to help develop advertising, with part-finished material being used to stimulate the discussion.

Depth interviews follow a similar pattern to group discussions but on a one-to-one basis and may be particularly useful to explore feelings or attitudes on sensitive topics. This technique is often used in business-to-business research as group discussions are often impractical. Depth interviews are unlikely to cost less than £100 each and may be several times this amount where, for example, senior executives are being interviewed.

Variations are **paired depths** or **mini groups**. Some agencies provide mini in-depth interview services at central locations or telephone-based qualitative interviews. Qualitative research, by its very nature, does not provide statistically reliable information unless very large numbers of depth interviews are carried out.

Collecting quantitative data

Quantitative research answers the "how many?" questions. The main methods of obtaining this type of data are as follows:

- ✔ **Field interviews.** Still the most commonly used method. These are usually conducted in the street or in the respondents' homes.

- ✔ **Telephone interviews.** Increasingly important in consumer research. Especially used for business-to-business research.

- ✔ **Postal questionnaires.** Often thought of as the "Cinderella" method, but a reliable and low-cost alternative and especially interesting to direct marketers with access to a customer database. (The use of postal research is further discussed later in this chapter.)

- ✔ **Hall tests.** Respondents are recruited in shopping areas to be interviewed at a central location nearby. This method is often used for testing out new products, especially foods and drinks.

- ✔ **Combination methods.** For example, non-respondents to a postal survey are contacted by 'phone, or material is sent through the post to form the basis of a telephone survey; hall tests may include a proportion of qualitative mini depth interviews.

- ✔ **Panels and omnibus surveys.** These are covered in a separate section of this chapter and are especially used for gauging trends in attitudes and behaviour in the longer term.

How they compare

The main advantages and disadvantages of the three most frequently used quantitative collection methods are summarised in the checklist opposite.

The importance of good questionnaire design

Expert guidance on questionnaire design will be found in the next chapter of this Guide, but no section on market research would be complete without stressing the main attributes of good question design.

The objective of a good questionnaire should be to achieve a conversation between the interviewer and the respondent. Here are some of the key points to consider when designing a questionnaire:

- ? Has the respondent got the information (ie will he or she have adequate knowledge or experience of the topic to answer the questions)?

- ? Will the respondent understand the question (see below)?

- ? Is the respondent likely to give a true answer (for example, are the questions or the topic either too hypothetical or too sensitive)?

In the cause of accuracy and a good response, the following advice related to question design is particularly important:

- ✘ Don't use unfamiliar words/phrases.

- ✘ Don't use difficult and abstract concepts.

	ADVANTAGES	DISADVANTAGES
Field interview	✔ High-quality data ✔ Special trained interviewer ✔ Fewer constraints on content, format, order of questions and length of questionnaire ✔ Visual material can be used ✔ Prompted recall can be used ✔ Feedback from interviewers	✘ Most expensive method (although not necessarily least cost effective) at £20 or more per interview ✘ Samples now usually clustered to reduce costs ✘ Particularly expensive if names and addresses are pre-selected ✘ Possibilities of interviewer bias ✘ May necessitate call backs to verify data ✘ Quota sampling where interviewers select individual respondents
Telephone interview	✔ Medium cost at £15 or more per contact ✔ Samples need not be geographically clustered ✔ Can be completed to very tight time schedule ✔ Central control – often conducted from single location ✔ Training easily standardised, leading to uniformly high quality	✘ Difficult to contact specific individuals especially if names and addresses must be matched to telephone numbers from separate lists ✘ Easy to refuse ✘ 'Phone ownership is still not universal, growth in ex-directory 'phone owners, answer machines and caller-identity methods ✘ Content and length of interview may be limited
Postal questionnaire	✔ Low cost (around £7 per "interview") ✔ Response as good as, or better than, other methods (when used appropriately) ✔ Central control ✔ Samples need not be geographically clustered ✔ No interviewer bias ✔ Does not require immediate availability of respondent ✔ Allows reference to other members of business or household ✔ Questionnaires can be pre-tested at low cost ✔ Better prospect of contacting specific individuals, eg from a customer list ✔ Matches promotion/distribution channels of direct marketing leading to more accurate demand forecasting	✘ Used inappropriately, response rates will produce statistically unreliable results ✘ No guidance available to help respondents to interpret questions, probe for additional comment, or explain why certain questions are necessary ✘ Question type and content may be limited, eg it is difficult to probe attitudes ✘ Assumes respondents read all questions before beginning to complete the questionnaire ✘ Reference to other people and/or sources of information before responding may be undesirable ✘ May not be fully or correctly completed ✘ Needs longer time span. Lacks "top of the mind" spontaneity, may bias awareness ✘ Time scale can be drawn out if a series of reminder letters is employed ✘ Risk of responder bias, eg only those with positive/negative attitudes bother to respond

- ✘ Don't use questions which tend to lead respondents to provide a particular response or which are biased.
- ✘ Don't pose hypothetical situations.
- ✘ Don't ask over-long questions.
- ✘ Don't ask two questions in one.

Qualitative research and piloting the proposed questionnaire will help ensure that potential question problems are sorted out before the main survey is conducted. Whilst most types of questions can be administered in fieldwork surveys, telephone and postal surveys have limitations, especially for certain types of attitude questions.

Obviously, the order of questioning is important with initial questions providing a "lead in" to the main areas. Careful thought should be given to routing within the questionnaire as it is highly likely that not all respondents will be required to answer all questions. The positioning of awareness and attitude questions needs to be thoroughly considered to ensure that earlier topics do not provide a source of information that you do not wish the interviewee to have at that stage. This problem cannot easily be resolved in a postal questionnaire – a limitation of the method.

Questions are usually either PRE-CODED, where respondents are presented with a fixed list of possible answers from which to make a choice, or OPEN-ENDED where respondents answer in their own words.

Questionnaires should also usually contain a detailed section for classifying respondents (eg age, occupation, TV region, etc). These questions are normally for analysis purposes when they are used to help segment respondents. They may include specific items held on a database to enable results to be compared with customer profiles.

Data analysis and reporting

All market research agencies will provide detailed analysis data from the survey – including cluster, factor, CHAID and conjoint techniques. In addition, sophisticated but user-friendly PC-based software specifically designed for analysing survey data is available for use in-house by agency clients.

The Market Research Society Code of Conduct advises that all market research reports should always contain the following key information to ensure that the structure of the survey can be clearly understood:

- ✔ How many people were interviewed.
- ✔ How they were selected.
- ✔ What questions were asked.

Using your database for market research

A major advantage, often available to the direct marketer planning a market research programme, is that a list of customers and information about them is often already available from a computerised database.

Databases provide an excellent sampling frame due to the amount of information usually available about individual customers, for example:

- ✔ Name, address, status (eg married, single, pensioner)
- ✔ Postcode
- ✔ Geodemographic code
- ✔ Telephone number
- ✔ Demographic/profile data
- ✔ Promotion/response history
- ✔ Customer value
- ✔ Purchase history and status (eg lapsed, active)

Databased personal information enables the classification section of the questionnaire to be reduced and provides a range of additional analysis variables.

Customer databases provide a very important resource for market researchers in selecting samples of customers for:

- ✔ Qualitative research
- ✔ Field interviews
- ✔ Telephone research
- ✔ Self-completion/postal questionnaires

Additional analysis variables and lifestyle/psychographic data can be added as well as data modelled from other surveys such as:

- ✔ Target Group Index (British Market Research Bureau)
- ✔ Financial Research Survey (NOP)
- ✔ Family Expenditure Survey (Government)
- ✔ National Readership Survey (JICNARS)
- ✔ Customised surveys, etc

Some of these data sources have been used by leading market analysis companies/ bureaux to enhance commercially available database information.

Care should be taken not to break data protection legislation or the Market Research Society Code of Conduct when using personal data drawn from surveys in the ways described in this section (see Choosing a Market Research Agency at the end of this chapter).

A plan for integrating market research and the database

The full integration of market research and the database can lead to the successful development and launch of a new product or service by direct mail. The six-step model below is a proven formula for successful integration.

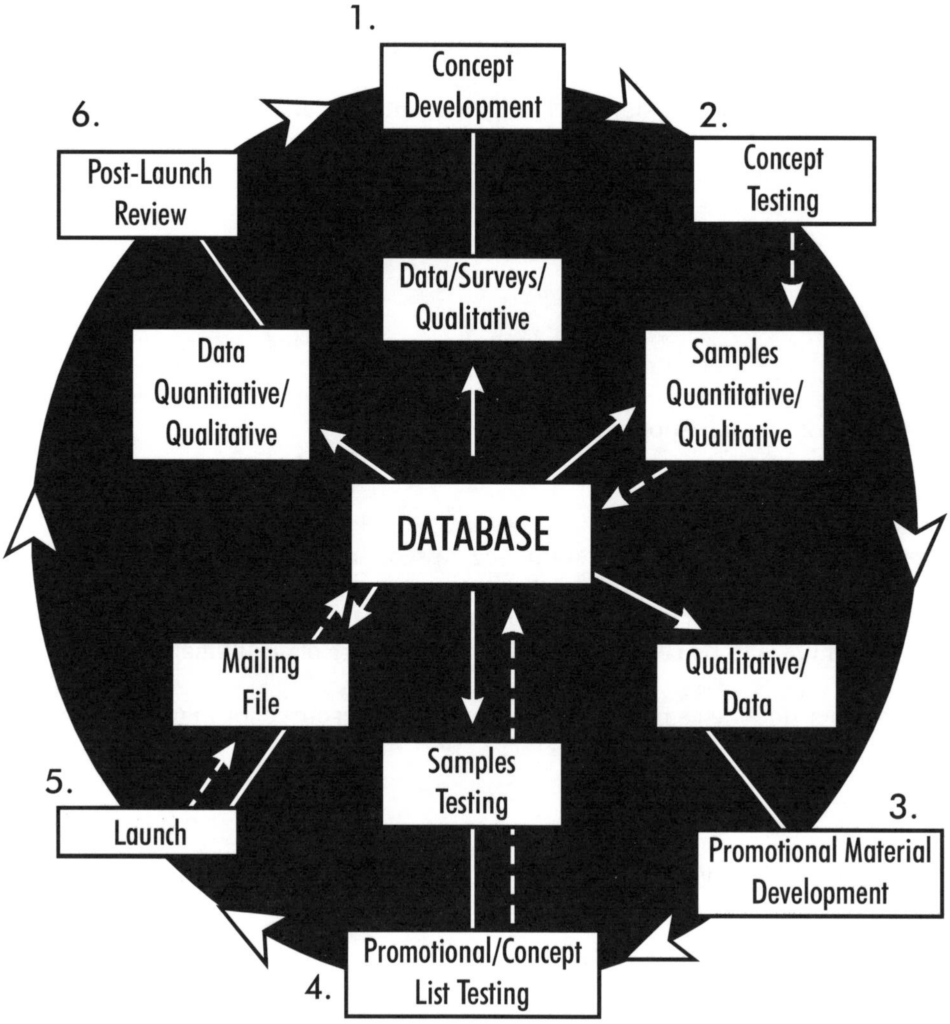

Step 1: Concept development

Develop product and service concepts using previous market research and customer data. Select samples from the database for qualitative developmental research on the concepts.

Step 2: Concept testing

Use postal quantitative research to assess attitudes to the product/service concepts. Materials should replicate the actual promotion and product distribution method as far as possible. The results will aid demand forecasting, indicate target segments, and enable price and concept variants to be tested at low cost.

Step 3: Promotional material development

Use qualitative research, customer data and the results of the concept test stage to develop promotional material which will be tested quantitatively at the next step.

Step 4: Promotional/concept and list testing

Test list selections using the results of the stages to date. All the information from this step will be fully analysed and fed back into the database.

Step 5: Launch the campaign

Step 6: Post-launch review

Fully analyse the results of the launch. This should include post-facto market research amongst responders **and** non-responders, in order to gain a full understanding of consumer reactions both positive and negative.

Postal research – the direct marketer's best friend

Earlier we looked at methods of collecting quantitative data. Postal research, we noted, is particularly relevant to direct marketing. One reason for its suitability is that many of the design factors required to achieve a good market research response are similar to those required to produce response to a direct marketing campaign and are well understood by direct marketers, among them:

- ✔ Sampling frame and selection process
- ✔ Value of prior contact (postcard or letter)
- ✔ The mechanics of mailing
- ✔ Use and design of covering letter
- ✔ Use of low-cost relevant incentives or prize draw
- ✔ Questionnaire design
- ✔ Importance and design of reply devices, envelopes, etc
- ✔ Follow-up approaches (letters, second questionnaire, 'phone calls)

Just as response to direct marketing can be improved by the use of specific "response boosters", so can the response to market research postal questionnaires. For example, the use of a postcard or letter to pre-announce a forthcoming sample has proved especially productive.

The response increases tabled overleaf show the benefits of various other components of a well-run postal survey:

Component or technique	% Response increase
A clean up-to-date customer file for sample selection	+150
First reminder (letter)	+26
Second reminder ('phone)	+25
Introductory questions of high interest to respondents	+19
Relevant incentive	+18
Second reminder (letter + questionnaire + reply envelope)	+12
Second class post	+8
First class post	+5

Source: Market Research Development Fund: Increasing Response, November 1985

Postal research can provide a very cost-effective data collecting method. The key issue in achieving reliable results is to ensure that it is the most appropriate method for the intended survey. Agencies will advise on this but qualitative and pilot research will also help provide feedback to judge whether postal research will be an effective method.

Sharing the costs of data collection

Beside the more familiar techniques discussed, there are a number of market research techniques whereby data is compiled on a **collective** basis for a group of clients, using the same sample. Some of the data may be available to all subscribers whereas other data may be confidential to individual clients. **The three best-known techniques for sharing data are research panels, omnibus surveys and syndicated research.** Others are media surveys and a new technique, data fusion.

Research panels – a continuous process for gauging trends

A research panel is a representative sample of individuals/households selected from the universe to be studied. Measurement is ideally a continuous process based on data collected at regular and frequent intervals. Data collection methods are usually via a home audit or the customer's diary of purchases, although agencies are starting to use bar-code scanning pens for panel members to record product purchases. The data can be fed via a modem direct from the household to the research company to provide very up-to-date information.

Marketing information which can be gleaned from research panels includes:

- ✔ How many people buy the product
- ✔ How much they buy
- ✔ How frequently they buy
- ✔ Where they buy
- ✔ Competitors' situation
- ✔ Brand share trends
- ✔ Profile of users/non-users
- ✔ Regional factors
- ✔ Impact of advertising, point of sale incentives, coupons, price discounts, etc

The advantages of research panels include the amount and accuracy of data and the depth of analysis that can be achieved. The chief disadvantages are what researchers call "product purchase conditioning" and sample stability over time. The former simply means that belonging to a panel **may** affect members' behaviour.

Some examples of research panels include:

- ✔ TNAGB: Home Audit
- ✔ TNAGB Television Consumer Audit (TCA)
- ✔ BARB (television viewership)
- ✔ Produce Studies: Farmstat
- ✔ TNAGB/Royal Mail Communications Panel (Letterbox Research)

The TNAGB/Post Office Communications Panel, marketed by the TNAGB subsidiary company RSGB as Letterbox Research, is of particular relevance to direct marketers. Letterbox Research monitors the flow of mail (including non-postal door drops) through the letterbox and use of the postal service by panel households. It provides, for example, the total size and growth of direct mail including seasonal fluctuations. This can be analysed by the demographics of recipients and users of direct mail and by product service category.

Omnibus surveys – large scale research at low cost

Omnibus surveys enable a few questions, or even a short survey, to be administered at low cost to a relatively large sample. An omnibus questionnaire is composed of several sub-questionnaires covering topics/projects exclusive to individual clients. For example, you may use an omnibus survey to ask a few salient questions about, say, lawnmowers and the results will be exclusive to you. **But the administration and classification data are shared with other organisations asking questions about other products/markets.** Cost-effective field or telephone interviewing is used for large-scale samples and entry is by a fixed-rate card of charges.

Omnibus surveys are typically used for experimental designs, pre- and post-advertising research, product launches, split runs, minority samples, and tracking/trend data. They can also be effective for smaller scale surveys. Opinion polling is sometimes undertaken on omnibus surveys.

Examples of omnibus surveys operated by research companies for specific markets include:

Household/Adults	NOP, BMRB, MORI, Gallup, ASL, TNAGB
Motorists	Sample Surveys
Children/Teenagers	Carrick James

Syndicated surveys – sharing an interest in a market

The idea behind syndicated surveys is to allow organisations with an interest in a particular market to share the data from a relevant survey. The survey may be continuous or conducted at less frequent intervals. Examples include:

- ✔ British Travel Survey (BTA)
- ✔ Financial Research Survey (NOP)
- ✔ Books and the Consumer (Book Marketing Limited)
- ✔ Maps and Guide Books (Strategy Research and Action)
- ✔ Direct Mail Information Service (DMIS)

The Direct Mail Information Service undertakes a major "establishment" survey every two years on attitudes towards and usage of direct mail. Although not strictly a syndicated survey, copies of the report can be bought from their London headquarters.

Media surveys – media information and much more

There is one more group of shared research services which the direct marketer is advised to consider: audience research surveys. These are generally conducted by the television, press and radio joint industry committees.

The main purpose of audience research is, of course, to assess advertising opportunities. However, some of the surveys contain a great deal of additional useful information.

Examples of major media and related surveys include:

- ✔ BARB Panel (TV viewership)
- ✔ JICNARS (newspaper/magazine readership)
- ✔ JICREG (readership of regional newspapers)
- ✔ JICRAR (radio listening)
- ✔ OSCAR (poster and outdoor advertising)
- ✔ Business Readership Survey (Research Services Ltd)

✔ Target Group Index (BMRB). Provides very detailed information on product/service purchasing, including brands, as well as media exposure

A number of research agencies provide specialist services for pre-testing and tracking advertising (see Choosing a Market Research Agency).

Data fusion – a new technique

Data fusion is a new technique whereby data collected on one survey can be input to responses from a second survey using a set of matching rules through a specially developed algorithm. For example, it is possible by fusing data from BARB and TGI to plot product usage by television viewership time-bands. This could show, for example, the proportion of 25–34 year old Guardian readers, new car owners or wine drinkers, etc, likely to be watching a particular TV programme.

International and business-to-business market research

All of the principles mentioned in all the sections of this chapter apply equally well to consumer, international and business-to-business surveys. The Market Research Society's Organisations Book will enable you to identify agencies which specialise in any of these areas.

Market research in action

Over the next four pages we show examples of many of the techniques discussed above, as used by a wide variety of marketing organisations including direct marketers. They demonstrate:

1. Testing video as a direct mail support medium
2. Researching direct mail for an fmcg company
3. Publishing research using field interviews
4. Hall testing of direct mail for a charity
5. International research using telephone interviews
6. Postal research for a mail order book publisher
7. Researching fit between mailing and market
8. Researching audience reactions to mailing

Market research in action

1. Testing video as a direct mail support medium

Prize Draws are commonly used in direct marketing to boost response. A company was considering sending a video as a precursor to the usual direct mail to raise awareness of the forthcoming draw. They required guidance on its likely success and creative development.

*The Qualitative Consultancy used its branded technique "**TACTIX**" to provide focused qualitative interviews with a precise target audience. They conducted the equivalent of two hall days of interviews (around forty 45-minute interviews) with a sample of non-customers. Three video executions and seven packaging options were shown. The project delivered three clear benefits:*

- ✔ *Demonstrated that a video mail shot is likely to be registered, noticed and watched, enabling the client to draw conclusions about its effectiveness relative to conventional direct mail.*
- ✔ *Gave clear guidance on the optimum details to put on the video packaging (about the company as well as the Prize Draw), and on the choice of presenter.*
- ✔ *Gave actionable recommendations on the content of the video itself, in particular key features which would motivate recipients to play it.*

Source: The Qualitative Consultancy

2. Researching direct mail for fmcg

A leading fast-moving consumer goods company, traditionally reliant on TV advertising to gain sales and market share, began to look at direct marketing to reinforce its advertising as a means of building "share of repertoire" among users. Three direct mail routes were developed by its agency.

The Qualitative Consultancy was asked to explore consumer reactions to each of the mailing routes to assess their effectiveness, relevance and motivational power. Four group discussions were conducted, recruited from the client's lists of users, and the three routes explored in depth. The research showed that:

- ✔ *Route One, which used a product demonstration message, was essentially seen as a generic, not a branded message.*
- ✔ *Route Two, whilst being the most popular even among direct mail "cynics", did not communicate the brand or its proposition clearly.*
- ✔ *Route Three had a clear, emotional point of entry with which consumers were able to identify, which was closely linked with the brand proposition.*

The depth of understanding provided by the qualitative approach allowed the company to avoid a potential disaster by choosing the most popular option on a first-past-the-post basis.

Source: The Qualitative Consultancy

3. Publishing research used field interviews

A publisher wished to conduct research into a new product. Research was commissioned to ensure that the most suitable topics were included in the publication, and that the direct mail promotion was interesting to a large number of potential customers.

In-home face-to-face interviews were conducted amongst the target sample defined as:

- ✔ *Book purchasers by mail order in the past twelve months and/or subscribers to a continuity programme or magazines.*
- ✔ *Respondents who had stated their willingness to purchase by mail order.*
- ✔ ***Excluding** people employed in advertising, marketing, market research, journalism, public relations, publishing, print and retailing of magazines and/or books.*
- ✔ *Those selected were women, aged 18–69, with an interest in the topic of the publication and who, after reading a concept statement, showed an interest in the product.*

The most important part of the survey was the ranking of potential contents. Using a 7-point scale from "Extremely Appealing" to "Extremely Unappealing", respondents were asked to rank each topic, taking as much time as they needed to make a considered judgement. Topics were rotated to ensure no order bias existed.

The results showed which topics should be developed for the publication and the order in which they should be arranged. In the past, prolonged trial-and-error testing would have been required to achieve the same result.

Source: Sample Surveys Ltd

4. Charity uses central hall to test direct mail

A leading charity commissioned a study to establish its positioning relative to other charitable organisations. A wide range of prompt material was used and the research conducted in a central hall.

Direct mail appeals are an important means of generating funds for the charity and part of the research was designed to test reactions to outer envelopes and images within their packs. Respondents were asked which envelopes they would be likely to open – and why.

Respondents were also presented with a range of photographs depicting people in various states (eg happy, impoverished, etc) and asked which images were "appropriate" for the charity and which would encourage them to "give".

These results identified which images created the greatest empathy, by establishing the most suitable and most impactful pictures. They also provided the charity with clear guidelines as to the most effective image/ message mix.

Source: Sample Surveys Ltd

5. International research using telephone interviews

A company that designs and sells high-quality products with broad consumer appeal, by mail order, believes that a better understanding of its existing customers enables it to develop new products and increase profitability. Their research aimed to produce demographic, attitudinal and lifestyle profiles of loyal customers and to segment them accordingly.

Research was conducted in 16 countries, covering four major subject areas. Since no prompt material was required, telephone interviewing was considered the most cost-effective and accurate form of data collection.

A minimum of 350 interviews was conducted per country/per product giving a total of 12,250. Each interview was approximately 15 minutes long and was well received by the majority of current customers.

The findings are being used for new product development, marketing and editorial direction.

Source: Sample Surveys Ltd

6. Postal research used for mail order book publishing

To help develop the future publishing programme for hard-back books to be sold by mail order, four-page A4 questionnaires were compiled, each comprising:

- *Front page covering letter.*
- *Double-page inner spread containing brief descriptions of up to five concepts – including price, size and number of pages – plus a 5-point "likelihood to order" scale for each concept.*
- *Final outer page containing classification questions (demographics, area of residence, previous purchases by mail order, hobbies, interests, etc).*

The questionnaires were mailed to samples of previous book buyers drawn from the customer database. Several questionnaire variants were compiled to test different versions of the concepts and price elasticity.

The results were used to build a short-list of future titles based on likelihood-to-order data, and to provide an initial estimate of demand prior to testing actual direct mail promotional packs. Qualitative research was used to help develop the most effective concept descriptions and the promotional material for the test programme.

Source: AA

7. Greater fit between communication and product

A new publication launched by a major UK publisher was failing to reach predicted sales. The publishers had previously had great success with this product in other world markets and were perplexed by the product's under-performance. Research was commissioned to assess response to the product, in conjunction with the mail-pack, and to explore the fit between communication and product.

Research identified that the numerous in-pack devices, which had worked well across other publications, were inconsistent with the self-view of the target market. The market considered themselves sophisticated and discerning whereas the promotion appeared to them to be fussy and downmarket.

By simplifying and refocusing the pack, an overall impression consistent with the product's strengths and its target market personality was achieved. Take-up figures responded accordingly.

Source: The Research Business

8. New targeting and feedback mail-packs for a major charity

A major UK charity has been operating a specific recruitment scheme, alongside its main donor recruitment programme, designed to offer people the chance to sponsor specific projects rather than the charity per se. As such, it was designed to reach a different audience, but the charity was concerned that it was not reaching its intended new audience.

Research revealed that the audience's interpretation was one of generally being "kept in touch" rather than being offered a new scheme. Therefore the mail-packs were appealing to people who were already likely to be involved, rather than reaching a new audience. A revised communications programme, involving different donor recruitment advertisements and a new mail-pack, was developed.

Source: The Research Business

Choosing a market research agency

Background to the market research industry

In 1994 around £650 million was spent in the UK on market research services by an industry that can be divided into suppliers or agencies and users or buyers. The former are the organisations and individuals who either undertake complete research surveys or provide particular key services such as interviewing or data processing. Users are organisations who use market research services and buyers are their employees.

There are over 7,000 members of the Market Research Society, ie individuals deriving their livelihood primarily from market research. The Society publishes an annual Organisations Book which contains details of over 450 agencies or consultants who supply research services. It is available from the London-based Market Research Society, and contains the following details:

✔ Supplier companies or consultants with one or more Full Members of the Market Research Society

✔ Addresses and telephone numbers

✔ Annual turnover per supplier

✔ Services provided (including specialities such as qualitative, panels, advertising pre-testing/tracking, omnibus surveys, etc)

✔ Key executives/MRS Full Members

✔ Brief descriptions of member companies

✔ Date formed

✔ Ownership

The Market Research Society's Code of Conduct

The Market Research Society has a Code of Conduct binding on all members. It has four main sections covering:

✔ Responsibilities to Respondents

✔ Responsibilities to the General Public and the Business Community

✔ Mutual Responsibilities of Clients and Agencies

✔ Conditions of Membership and Professional Responsibilities

The Code is designed to protect the confidentiality of individual respondents and the information which they provide and states that **no activity shall be mispresented as research**, thus data and personal information collected through market research must never be used to compile lists or databases for non-research purposes. Similarly, no attempt should be made to sell under the guise of market research, ie "sugging".

Standards are also maintained through schemes, linked to the Society and endorsed by (but not binding on) companies providing research services. These are:

- ✔ Interviewer Identity Card Scheme
- ✔ Freephone Market Research (to enable respondents to validate the authenticity of telephone and self-completion surveys)
- ✔ The Research Mark (to authenticate self-completion surveys)
- ✔ The Interviewer Quality Control Scheme (prescribes standards for interviewing/ interviewer training)

A new quality award scheme for research agencies run by the MRQSA has recently been launched under BS/ISO standards.

There is also now a separate registration under the Data Protection Act for those involved in market or survey research activities where the data is de-personalised and used only at an aggregated level as required by the MRS Code.

To help market researchers cope with the increasing complexity of dealing with personal data and keeping within the Code of Conduct and data protection legislation, a new set of guidelines has also recently been published by the Market Research Society.

Useful trade associations

- ✔ Association of Market Survey Organisations or AMSO (36 research agencies).
- ✔ Association of British Market Research Companies or ABMRC (196 research agencies).
- ✔ Association of Users of Research Agencies or AURA (senior buyers in companies spending over £25,000 per year on market research services); currently around 150 members.
- ✔ Market Research Quality Standards Association (MRQSA).
- ✔ Association of Qualitative Research Practitioners (AQRP); currently 840 members.

Further information

For a list of useful names and addresses connected with market research, also for further reading, refer to the third volume of this Guide.

All marketers requiring specific information about research panels, omnibus surveys, syndicated surveys, and media surveys are advised to contact one of the above trade associations in the first instance. Alternatively, refer to a recognised market research agency.

Chapter 2.2

How to write effective questionnaires

This chapter includes:

- **The basics of a good question**
- **Problem questions and how to avoid them**
- **Laying out a questionnaire**
- **Self-completion questionnaires**
- **Some useful guidance on postal research**
- **Asking questions by telephone**
- **How to design and use rating scales**
- **Extracts from a questionnaire demonstrating good practice**

In the previous chapter we looked at the range of research techniques available to marketers. At the heart of market research is the interview – whether conducted face-to-face, by telephone, or by post. At the heart of the interview is a series of carefully worded questions. Question design, together with sampling, coding and analysis, is a highly skilled task best left to experienced and qualified market research professionals.

But the simple act of showing interest in customers, as we saw under "Loyalty and Retention", can often help to cement lucrative long-term relationships with customers. Marketers and creatives, therefore, increasingly find themselves penning questions for inclusion in customer service questionnaires which may, in truth, fall far short of pure research.

In this chapter Graham Read sets out the proper way to formulate unambiguous questions. In so doing he dispenses useful advice on posing questions by post and by telephone.

New in this edition. In the first edition of this Guide, telephone research was referred to as less widely used than postal research. Today, due to increased telephone ownership, telephone is now more widely used than postal research in many markets. For examples of telephone research in action refer to Chapter 2.1. Also included are extracts of a questionnaire from the Automobile Association, demonstrating the theoretical points made.

Graham Read, Managing Director, RSVP Research

Graham Read graduated in Geography at Birmingham University in 1965, where he also obtained an MSc in Meteorology and Climatology. After a period of post-graduate work in Meteorology at the University of Reading, he began his market research career at BMRB in 1970.

At BMRB he worked in fast-moving consumer goods research, and media and special research, becoming Ad Hoc Research Director in 1977. He was also extensively involved in the company graduate training programme and in graduate recruitment.

In 1982 he moved to the Mars Company as Market Research Manager for the confectionery business, where he worked on a range of projects including the Mars Retail Audit. Returning to the research agency side in 1984, he set up the Product Research Division in RSGB and took over as Managing Director of the company early in 1986.

Following the Maxwell takeover of the AGB Group in 1991, Graham moved to Martin Hamblin before returning to BMRB as MD of its international division in 1993. He then moved to Harris Research in 1994 before setting up his own research and training consultancy, RSVP Research, at the start of 1995.

Graham has written papers on Trends in UK Teenage Markets (ESOMAR), Qualitative Research Methods in Business (Henley Management Centre), and Quantitative Market Measurement (Institute of Marketing).

Graham J Read
RSVP Research
18 Cairn Avenue
Ealing
London
W5 5HX

Chapter 2.2

How to write effective questionnaires

The importance of skilled questionnaire design

Questionnaire design is an extremely skilled craft which is much underrated. The chief reason for this is that we are all "experts" – we ask questions and answer them all day long in the course of our general lives. Furthermore, unlike errors of sample design, errors of question design are not measurable and often go unnoticed. They can also be blamed on people other than the perpetrator, ie the interviewers, data processors and respondents, with little risk of discovery.

However, the effects of poor questionnaire design can be enormous. Biases due to question-wording and question-order are potentially much greater than those from any other source. For example, small changes in wording or in the order of questions can give very different results – so different, that different conclusions would be drawn and different action taken.

Basics of a good question

There is no magic about the characteristics of a good question. A question should be:

✔ Clear and unambiguous

✔ Easy and quick to understand

✔ Simple to respond to

✔ Relevant to the respondent

The important test of a good question can be summed up in three questions of our own:

1. Will the respondent have a reasonable chance of **understanding** the question?
2. Will the respondent, having understood the question, be **willing** to answer it?
3. Will the respondent, having understood the question and being willing to answer it, have a reasonable chance of **being able** to answer it?

Below are the causes of some common question errors. The checklist on pages 2.2-5/6 shows examples of each of the errors below and suggests ways in which you can avoid making the same mistakes.

Will the respondent understand?

? Unfamiliar words and concepts

? Ambiguous or imprecise words/concepts

? Complicated wording

? Too many qualifying clauses

? Multiple questions (eg two questions in one)

? Abstract or vague concepts

? Arithmetic concepts/terminology

Will the respondent agree to answer (honestly)?

? Taboo, embarrassing, personal subjects

? Biased or leading questions (answers "put in respondent's mouth")

? Questions where the respondent's answer is likely to be blunt or rude and so cause them embarrassment

Is the respondent able to answer?

? Too trivial to bother

? Too detailed to remember

? Too intricate to phrase

? Hypothetical

? Requires feat of memory

How to ask questions about attitudes

Market research often entails attitude measurement. The ideal attitude measurement technique, besides being reliable and valid, enables us to distinguish groups of people whose attitudes towards an object or an act are:

✔ Similar to each other

✔ Different from other groups
- in a known direction
- with a known degree of difference

Below are the main methods of asking questions about attitudes so that the result can be measured, followed by a résumé of chief attributes of each method:

✔ Open-ended questions

✔ Choices between statements

✔ Adjective ascription

✔ Rating scales
- verbal
- numerical
- diagrammatic

✔ Semantic differential scales

✔ Questionnaires that form scales

Open-ended questions – easy to ask

Open-ended questions range from the simple "Why do you say that?", to more elaborate questions such as "What do you think are the main problems facing the country today?" They have the advantage of being easy to ask but the disadvantage of being difficult to analyse. The two main consequences of the difficulty of analysis are a large amount of inaccuracy in coding the data and a high cost for processing and reporting on it.

On the facing page and overleaf will be found examples of common question problems – and how to avoid them.

Some common question problems – and how to avoid them

Problem	Avoidance
Will respondents understand the question? *Use of unfamiliar words:* "Biscuit countlines" "Denture fixatives"	✓ Use familiar words ✓ Explain meanings
Ambiguous or imprecise words and concepts: "On a typical day how many envelopes does your establishment send out?" *Complicated wording/too many qualifying clauses:* "On a typical day, about how many envelopes does your establishment send out, excluding any parcels, rebate-posted items or pre-paid envelopes?"	✓ Check understanding by piloting ✓ Split into basic elements ✓ Ask a series of questions about each type of envelope, etc ✓ Show a clear idea of what you want on a card ✓ Repeat the essence of the question at the end
Multi-questions, eg two questions in one: This is common with attitude questions but also occurs with factual questions, eg: "Are your two major suppliers British?" This does not allow for one being British and one not. The respondent in this situation may reply: "One is, one isn't" but also possibly "No" (ie they aren't both British).	✓ Separate the questions, eg: "Is your major supplier British?" "If more than one major supplier, what is the nationality of each one?" Follow with a grid to accommodate the answer in respect of several major suppliers.
Abstract/vague concepts: Remember most people are not good at generalising, eg: "I would like you to give me as much detail as you can about a typical purchase."	✓ Be specific "I would like you to list the last six purchases you have made and give me as much detail as you can about each." Follow with a list of detailed questions, and a grid to accommodate the answers, for each purchase in turn.
Arithmetic concepts: Business people can also be bad at understanding arithmetic concepts, eg: Percentages Proportions Ratios, etc	✓ Simplify to a verbal scale, eg: "all" "more than half" "less than half"
Will respondents be willing to answer? *Taboo, embarrassing, personal subjects, eg:* *Sex* "Have you had sexual intercourse in the past week?" *Money* "How much do you earn?" "What is your turnover?"	Almost anything can be a subject of a question provided it is sensitively treated. ✓ Ensure the respondent understands the relevance of the question to the rest of the interview ✓ Use prompt cards with letters (eg for income bands)

Continued overleaf →

Problem	Avoidance
Bodily functions "Have you ever wet the bed?" In all these areas there will be a large number of refusals to the question and even to the continuation of the interview, unless great care is taken.	✓ Do not ask for greater detail than you require for analysis purposes ✓ Use good interviewers ✓ Ask delicate questions towards/at the end of the interview
Biased/leading questions: "Were you prompted to contact the supplier because you had seen advertising for this supplier?" Here we are dealing with the respondent's willingness to answer the question accurately/ honestly.	✓ Ask an open-ended question or supply an exhaustive list of alternative reason/factors ✓ Split into two questions: "Did you consider any other brands?" If YES: "Which other brands did you consider?"
Respondent does not wish to appear rude: "Were you prompted to contact us because our salesman visited you?"	✓ Don't divulge the sponsor until the end of the interview or until all the necessary prompted responses have been gathered ✓ Alternatively suggest that a "rude" answer is perfectly acceptable
Will the respondent be able to answer? *Too trivial* "What is the wattage of the electric light bulbs in each of your rooms?" *Too detailed* "How many copies were made in this machine in each of the last three months?" *Too intricate* "Can you tell me the route you followed and the stands you looked at as you went around the exhibition?"	✓ Observe the behaviour you are interested in Interviewees can be asked to inspect (a sample of) light bulbs and an observer can follow people around exhibitions. Some questions are almost certainly unnecessarily precise: insert "approximately" to improve them.
Feats of memory "How many times have you put petrol in your car in the past year?"	✓ Avoid asking respondents to perform amazing feats of memory either for very infrequent or very frequent occurrences ✓ Look carefully at frequency/importance/distance in time of event(s) ✓ Ask for an approximate answer, or break down question into series of questions ✓ Use prompt cards which allow a category to be chosen that best fits the response without over-taxing the memory
Hypothetical questions "Would you be prepared to pay 10% more for the model you prefer?"	✓ These are often unavoidable ✓ If hypothetical questions are the only way to obtain the information, be wary of treating the results as literally true

Choices between statements – possibly misleading

These are questions where respondents are asked to select from a number of alternatives the statement which most closely corresponds to their view, eg "Do you think that on the whole the activities of large companies are a good or bad thing for this country's economy?" This sort of question can be misleading because it tends to over-simplify issues and many respondents find it hard to choose.

Adjective ascription – less tiring for respondents

The technique of ascribing adjectives to propositions can often be very useful especially in brand image measurement, eg:

> "Here is a list of brands of washing powder. I'm going to read out a series of statements and I'd like you to tell me to which of the brands, if any, the statement applies. You can mention as many or as few as you like for each statement. Now which do you think ...
>
> (a) "Are kind to hands?"
> "Are not so kind to hands?"
>
> (b) "Get clothes really clean?"
> "Don't get clothes quite so clean?"

The respondent is given a card listing brands to choose from.

This technique is useful because it enables the researcher to examine both the **strength** of the image (ie the proportion of respondents who mention a brand at all on an image dimension) and the **character** of the image (ie the proportion of all those who mention a brand who mention it in a favourable light).

Adjective ascription is less tiring for respondents than many other methods of image measurement because it does not require them to rate every brand on every dimension.

Verbal rating scales – easy and familiar

Verbal rating scales are probably the most common form of attitude measurement used in market research. Questions run something like:

> "I'm going to read out a number of things people have said about Fairy Liquid and I'd like you to tell me from this card how much you agree or disagree with each of them."

The respondent is given a card listing a number of response categories from which to choose, eg:

"Agree a lot"

↓

"Agree a little"

↓

"Neither agree nor disagree"

↓

"Disagree a little"

↓

"Disagree a lot"

Watch out for these points when asking verbal rating questions:

✔ Include a "no opinion" or "don't know" category in your coding frame (this need not be shown to respondents).

✔ Take care to avoid double concepts or double negatives.

✔ Try not to point all the statements in the same direction (either favourable or unfavourable).

✔ Scales do not *have* to be balanced, but if they are not balanced you should have a good reason.

✔ Four- to seven-point scales are usually better than a larger number of categories.

✔ People tend to choose from the top of the list, so rotate the list between respondents.

Semantic differential scales – verbal and visual

Semantic differential scales are a combination of verbal and diagrammatic scales. The concept or product is rated on a diagrammatic scale, the end-points of which are defined by opposite pairs of adjectives or phrases, eg:

"My boss is ..."

1.	"Extremely understanding"	[ ]	[✓]	[ ]	[ ]	"Not at all understanding"
2.	"Witty and amusing"	[ ]	[ ]	[✓]	[ ]	"Boring"
3.	"Delegates the right amount"	[✓]	[ ]	[ ]	[ ]	"Doesn't delegate enough"

Note: Some of the above scales are monopolar (1 and 3) and some bi-polar (2) – thus the mid-point means different things. It is important also to have a "no opinion" category to distinguish "no answer" from where the respondent deliberately selects the middle position.

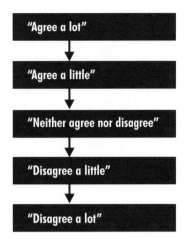

Numerical rating scales – keep it simple

With numerical scales the positions on the scale are given numbers, but the numbers should appear only at the **end** of the scale and not at the beginning.

Very suitable	☐	4
Fairly suitable	☐	3
Barely suitable	☐	2
Not very suitable	☐	1
Not suitable at all	☐	0

Numerical rating can also be achieved by asking people to "give marks" out of 10 for dimensions. But it is important not to have too long a scale as many of the points may not be used.

Diagrammatic rating scales – a visual assessment

In diagrammatic rating the positions on the scale are expressed not in words or numbers, but in diagrammatic form. Diagrammatic scales can be represented by any of the shapes below, or by anything else you can think of.

Marks on **a continuum**

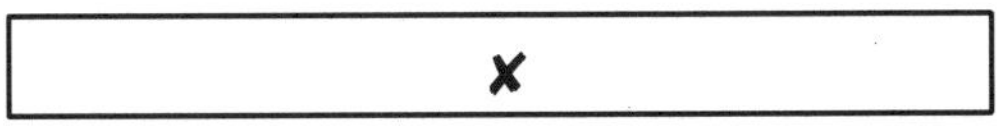

boxes

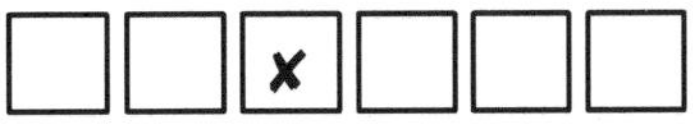

a ladder

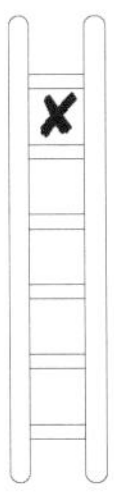

a thermometer gauge

different-sized squares

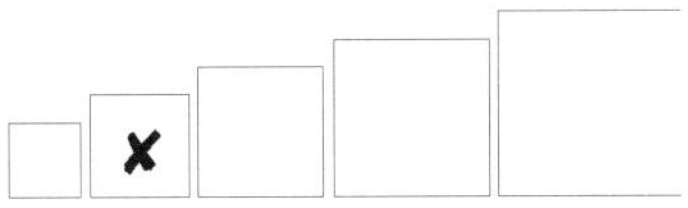

The importance of rating scales

In Chapter 1.4, during our discussion on loyalty, we noted that there is a marked difference between the on-going performance of customers who describe themselves as merely "satisfied" from that of customers who say they are "very satisfied". We saw that customers who are "satisfied" are among the most promiscuous and easily poached, whereas "very satisfied" customers are denoting their likelihood of remaining loyal purchasers.

Such a marked difference demonstrates one area in which regularly and properly conducted customer satisfaction questionnaires can be of immense value to marketers; it also shows why it is important to ask the right questions and provide for respondents to record their true feelings.

Making the most of your questionnaire layout

The way in which a questionnaire is laid out – whether for personal interviewing, postal or telephone use – can make a great deal of difference to its success. In addition to being well laid out for the respondent, it must be designed with the **interviewer**, the **coder**, the **puncher**, and the **tabulator** in mind.

The importance of coding

In general a questionnaire that is well laid out for the interviewer will also be easy for the coder to follow. If you use a good filtering system and allow sufficient room for open-ended answers, this will facilitate efficient coding.

Remember: pre-coded questions create a lot less "aggro" than open-ended ones. Pre-code where possible, do not be lazy.

However, the practice of partial pre-coding must be looked on warily as it tends to produce more answers in the pre-coded categories than would occur with either full pre-coding or a completely open-ended question.

On the facing page are some useful tips for better, more efficient coding:

Tips for better coding

- ✔ Pre-code if possible throughout the questionnaire.
- ✔ Leave plenty of space between questions.
- ✔ Ensure answer and code space are aligned or clearly related.
- ✔ Ensure that "Office Use Only" boxes or headings are included in the appropriate places.
- ✔ Leave enough space for interviewers to answer. If they abbreviate or truncate, coding will be more inaccurate.
- ✔ Ensure space is available for "others" to be written in; in grid questions, if "others" are allowed for more than one question, ensure space is provided for *each* question.
- ✔ Ensure enough space is available for coding where there can be multi-coding.
- ✔ Ensure sufficient columns are available to allow coding of the complexity you require.

Tips for successful punching/data entry

- ✔ Keep all coding to the right of the page.
- ✔ All coding to be preferably vertical – particularly for grids.
- ✔ Do not split columns over pages.
- ✔ Where columns are to be skipped, be sure to include instructions to this effect.
- ✔ Where information is to be transferred, instruct carefully.

Tips for successful tabulating

- ✔ Card numbering is essential for a multi-card survey.
- ✔ Start a new question with a new column.
- ✔ If repeated information is being collected, ensure columns follow a regular pattern.

For an example of effective questionnaire layout, clear coding, and unambiguous questions, refer to the Automobile Association questionnaire on pages 2.2-18/19.

The importance of piloting

The importance of piloting questionnaires cannot be overstated. Even one or two completed can tell you a lot about how to improve your questionnaire. Pilot in the office, pilot on respondents where possible – but *not* the most important ones! However you do it ... pilot! Use piloting to learn more about and improve:

✔ Question wording

✔ Question phrasing

✔ Question order

✔ Questionnaire layout

✔ Pre-coded categories – appropriateness
– comprehensiveness

Self-completion questionnaires

There are many instances in market research where self-completion questionnaires are a valuable tool, among them:

✔ Within a personal interview, for example where a response is required to a long list of attitude statements

✔ Separate from a personal interview but involving personal placement and personal collecting, eg:
- where the informant is required to do some "homework"
- where data is required from more than one individual (in a company or household)
- where data is required about behaviour **as it takes place** (eg purchases)

The postal questionnaire is the most obvious example of a self-completion questionnaire. Whilst **most** of the principles of personal interview questionnaires apply to self-completion questionnaires, there are some major differences which we look at next – with special reference to postal research for direct marketing.

Getting the most from postal research

Postal research is particularly appropriate to direct marketers for the reasons given in the chapter on market research by Peter Mouncey (Chapter 2.1).

The main disadvantage of postal research is that response rates are usually lower than for personal interviewing.

Generally speaking, response rates are higher where the population is **interested** in the subject of the survey (eg a survey by a society amongst its members) and where the contact is **hot** (eg amongst a personally recruited group of the relevant population).

There are a number of generally recognised tips for maximising response to a postal research questionnaire, many of them learned from the techniques of direct response marketing, among them:

Tips for maximising response to postal questionnaires

✔ Enclose a covering letter which should:
- attempt to interest the informant
- explain the purpose of the study
- if possible give the informant an "angle"
- stress confidentiality

✔ Make the questionnaire as attractive, interesting and relevant as possible, and not longer than necessary.

✔ Despatch one or two reminder letters (ideally with a further copy of the questionnaire) to those who have not replied 7–10 days after the initial mailing.

✔ Consider offering an incentive (eg a summary of selected survey findings in the case of a business-to-business survey or a free prize draw for a consumer survey).

✔ Enclose a reply-paid envelope.

✔ **For business research**, despatch on a Monday (using first class mail) to arrive early in the working week and not on a Friday night when it will be consigned to the waste bin!

✔ **For consumer research**, Thursday is the favourite despatch day so that the questionnaire arrives in time for the weekend.

✔ Use typed envelopes as opposed to computer labels.

✔ Address the letter "Dear Mr Smith" as opposed to "Dear Sir".

✔ Mail a preliminary letter in *advance* of the questionnaire.

✔ Use a personal signature to the covering letter as opposed to a printed facsimile.

✔ Use a stamped as opposed to a franked outer envelope; stamped reply envelope as opposed to a pre-printed Business Reply Paid envelope.

Whatever the advice, remember to judge each tip on its merits. If the effect on response rate is likely to be marginal, the additional costs may not be justified.

For further advice on maximising replies to questionnaires using direct marketing response techniques, refer to the creative sections of this Guide, Chapters 6.2, 6.3 and 6.4.

Laying out a self-completion questionnaire

Some tips for good postal questionnaire layout

Remember the whole questionnaire can be read before completion, so the order of questions should be logical and in line with what people expect. There is no point in "hiding" certain questions until later in the interview as one often wants to do in a personal interview.

Here are a few tips for questionnaire layout which apply particularly to postal and other forms of self-completion questionnaire:

- ✔ Good appearance is important. Give the impression that you care about standards.
- ✔ But – do not make it too glossy. It should look like professional research rather than a promotion.
- ✔ Spell out filter instructions in detail. Informants are not aware of the conventions we take for granted with interviewers.
- ✔ Include prominent section headings to break up the whole into "manageable chunks".
- ✔ Give worked examples for the more complex questions, eg attitude batteries, questions involving grids.
- ✔ Explain why certain questions are required if they are not obviously related to the main subject of the study, eg business classification questions.
- ✔ If you pre-print computer codes point them out to informants and ask them to ignore them.
- ✔ Do not cramp the questions: it is better to be generous with space than to save a sheet of paper.
- ✔ Allow space for the informants to amplify their answers should they so wish; otherwise they might feel frustrated/insulted.
- ✔ Reassure the respondent that we still need to hear from him even if he can't answer some of the questions.

Open-ended questions are often valuable to give informants an opportunity to express views not catered for elsewhere, but, a self-completion questionnaire cannot probe like an interview. The volume of comment to open-ended questions is less in the self-completion situation, therefore:

- ✔ Pre-code as much as you can. Pre-code **all** the options or otherwise the pre-coded answers will get too many endorsements relative to those that have to be written in.
- ✔ Regarding awareness questions, remember that informants can mug up on things before completion.

How critical is questionnaire length for a postal questionnaire?

It is often said that postal response rates are sensitive to questionnaire length. This is true only up to a point. If properly designed, a postal questionnaire equivalent to a personal interview of 30–40 minutes can work perfectly well.

There are sometimes good reasons for deliberately extending the length of a questionnaire beyond that dictated by data needs, eg:

✔ To make the questionnaire more interesting for the respondent.

✔ To camouflage the sponsorship. (Remember the informant can read the whole questionnaire before completing it.)

✔ To include questions which people *expect* to be asked.

✔ To include "something for everyone". A questionnaire which immediately filters out a particular group is likely to achieve a lower response from that group, some of whom will regard themselves as not relevant to the researcher.

Telephone research – special considerations

The telephone interview has more in common with the field interview than with a postal questionnaire. It is quick and capable of great accuracy (especially where interviewers work under direct supervision in central locations).

Here we look at some of the unique features of telephone research that have led to its phenomenal growth in recent years.

1. Telephone ownership – now well over 90%

Until recently, telephone interviewing was less widely used than postal methods for consumer research. Its main drawback was that telephone ownership was restricted. Now it is more widely used than the post.

The reason is that use of the telephone has become almost universal with penetration now well above 90% of UK households. (Although, as might be expected, ownership is highest among AB households and in the Greater London area.)

Today, for many markets, the telephone provides satisfactory access to representative samples of the population.

2. The perfect tool for interviewing businesses

In business-to-business research telephone interviewing really comes into its own, since:

✔ Virtually all business premises have a telephone.

✔ Reasonably good sampling frames exist – with 'phone numbers.

- ✔ A potential informant is more likely to give up a few minutes on the 'phone than make an appointment for a personal call.
- ✔ Secretarial defences are probably stronger against unsolicited mail (eg a postal questionnaire) than against a persuasive interviewer's telephone call.
- ✔ Samples are usually too widely dispersed to make face-to-face interviewing economic for short interviews.
- ✔ It is better to rely on a telephone call to establish who is the right person to interview than trust a postal questionnaire to reach the right person.
- ✔ Business people are **used** to the telephone: it is less likely to inhibit their response than that of consumers.
- ✔ The telephone can set up "hot contacts" for a postal survey by means of a screening 'phone call. Frequently your sampling frame is establishments (eg from Yellow Pages) and you don't know whether the establishment qualifies or whom to speak to. Telephone screening ideally resolves such questions:
  - it defines eligibility
  - it puts you in contact with the correct respondent
  - it enables you to "sell" the survey and thereby improve the response rate.

The follow-up postal questionnaire will then collect more information than by the telephone alone.

3. The risk of being too intrusive

In the case of consumer research, a telephone call penetrates the respondent's home directly and can rapidly cause antagonism and refusal unless appropriate preliminary action is taken to reassure the respondent (eg regarding confidentiality).

The introduction is therefore all-important and should cover the interviewer's name, company, location and the method of sample selection.

4. How long for a telephone interview?

The evidence on questionnaire length is inconclusive at present, but major users of the medium suggest that a warning is needed if the interview is likely to exceed 15 minutes.

5. Overcoming the absence of visual stimuli

With telephone research visual stimuli cannot be shown. Questions must *sound* well rather than *read* well. In order to make the respondent's task easier, in the absence of prompt cards, responses may need to be built into the question and scales may need to be "unfolded" in stages rather than reeled off all at once.

For example, an agree–disagree scale may need to be handled as follows:

"Do you agree or disagree?"
IF "AGREE"
"Do you agree a little or do you agree strongly?"
IF "DISAGREE"
"Do you disagree a little or do you disagree strongly?"

6. Telephone needs even greater clarity

During a face-to-face interview the interviewer can build up a rapport with the respondent and easily spot misinterpretation. In a postal questionnaire the informant can work through the questionnaire at his own pace and go back over his answers to check what he has said.

Neither of these advantages applies to the telephone. Hence a telephone questionnaire must be particularly clear and unambiguous.

7. Avoiding the tendency to rush responses

There is evidence that respondents feel greater time pressure when being interviewed on the telephone than in a personal interview.

There is thus a tendency for respondents to rush their responses, particularly to open-ended questions, and provision should be made for this in terms of prompts and probes.

8. Holding respondent's attention on the 'phone

With all telephone research there is a greater likelihood of serious distraction than for other types of survey.

Hence when designing a telephone questionnaire be particularly aware of the need to maintain the respondent's attention and concentration by keeping his/her interest.

The above considerations add up to particular care still being needed for telephone surveys. The telephone is still not quite such a "natural" part of life in the UK as it is, for example, in the USA and Scandinavia.

CATI and CAPI – the computer to your aid

CATI (**Computer-Assisted Telephone Interviewing**) can be of significant help in telephone questionnaire design, eg through the randomisation of question order and the order of responses to questions, and with complex routing.

CAPI (**Computer-Assisted Personal Interviewing**) is the face-to-face interviewing equivalent of CATI. It is an extremely important development from the point of view of quality enhancement and can save significant amounts of time at the questionnaire transmission, data-return and data processing stages. However, even **greater** care is required with CAPI than with CATI in view of the difficulties involved in checking the questionnaire set-up before the fieldwork takes place.

How the Automobile Association researches its services by post

Here are some extracts from an AA questionnaire into how well it responds to the needs of its members. The questionnaire was sent to members to investigate attitudes about the breakdown service. We have chosen 7 questions from a total of 28 to demonstrate good practice. The questionnaire is accompanied by a clearly worded covering letter which tells the respondent how to answer the questions, ie ☑

SECTION 1: BREAKDOWN

Q1. Which one of the following best describes where you broke down?

At or near to own home	☐ 1	Motorway (hard shoulder)	☐ 7
At the home of friends/relatives	☐ 2	Car park	☐ 8
On a country road or road in a village	☐ 3	At a garage	☐ 9
In a town/city centre	☐ 4	At work	☐ 10
In a town/city suburb	☐ 5	Other location	☐ 11
Motorway service area	☐ 6		

Question 1. The motorist should have no problem in recognising and identifying the site of the breakdown from these clear and unambiguous options.

Q2. What were the driving conditions like at the time you broke down? (PLEASE TICK ANY THAT APPLY IN EACH COLUMN)

TEMPERATURE (3)		WEATHER (4)		ROAD SURFACE (5)		LIGHT (6)	
Very hot	☐ 1	Raining	☐ 1	Wet	☐ 1	Daylight	☐ 1
Warm	☐ 2	Snowing/sleet/hail	☐ 2	Dry	☐ 2	Dark	☐ 2
Cool/cold	☐ 3	Foggy/misty	☐ 3	Icy	☐ 3	Dusk	☐ 3
Very cold/frosty	☐ 4	Sunny	☐ 4				
		Cloudy/overcast	☐ 5				

Question 2. Visual aids help postal questionnaires but only when used sparingly, as here. Occasional symbols add variety/interest without interfering with coding and tabulating work.

SECTION 4: OPINION OF STAFF – TELEPHONE

Q15a. Please could you rate your opinion of the telephone staff on the following features, using a scale of 1 to 10, where 10 is the most positive answer and 1 is the most negative answer

	10	9	8	7	6	5	4	3	2	1	
Efficient	☐	☐	☐	☐	☐	☐	☐	☐	☐	☐	Inefficient (48)
Courteous/Polite	☐	☐	☐	☐	☐	☐	☐	☐	☐	☐	Rude/Abusive (49)
Helpful	☐	☐	☐	☐	☐	☐	☐	☐	☐	☐	Unhelpful (50)
Professional	☐	☐	☐	☐	☐	☐	☐	☐	☐	☐	Unprofessional (51)
Warm/Friendly	☐	☐	☐	☐	☐	☐	☐	☐	☐	☐	Cold/Unfriendly (52)

Question 15a. Example of a simple but effective rating scale.

Q20. Other than fixing/diagnosing the problem with the car, what else, if anything, did the AA patrol/garage mechanic do, or offer to do? (TICK ALL THAT APPLY)

(95)

Rang me to say they were on their way/had arrived	☐	1
Offered to contact a relative/friend to let them know I had broken down	☐	2
Let me sit in his cab while he fixed/diagnosed the problem with the car	☐	3
Carried out general checks on the car/sorted out another minor fault/advised me on other areas of the car which might need attention	☐	4
Obtained extra parts needed for the car, which he did not have with him	☐	5
Followed me: home/to my destination/for a while	☐	6
Organised Relay for my car	☐	7
Towed me home/to garage/off road	☐	8
Took me home/to garage in AA van	☐	9
Advised me on how to avoid the same problem occurring again	☐	10
Advised me on what work would need to be done on the car for a more permanent repair	☐	11
Advised me on how to continue driving my car, until a more permanent repair was possible	☐	12
Other advice/action (Please write in) ______		
No advice given	☐	99

Question 20. This could have caused problems for respondents had the designer not provided the guide lines between statement and tick box. Note space for respondent to write in additional responses.

Q21. How do you think the service you received from the AA patrol/garage mechanic compared with your expectations?

(96)

Much better than I expected	☐	1	A little worse than I expected	☐	4
A little better than I expected	☐	2	A lot worse than I expected	☐	5
As I expected	☐	3			

Question 21. Another simple rating scale.

Q25e. In what way(s) was the service better or worse than you expected? (Please write in below) (122)

______

______

______

______

Q25f. What else, if anything, could the AA have done to improve any part of the overall service you received on this occasion? (Please write in below) (123)

______

______

Question 25. These open-ended questions appear at the end of the survey. The respondent has had time to reflect and should now be able to compose a constructive and useful answer.

Source: Corinne Green, Automobile Association, 22.8.97
Thanks to: Mr Nigel Caulkin – University of Hertfordshire

Chapter 2.3

Testing – the theory and the practice

This chapter includes:

- What is testing?
- The benefits of testing
- The first rule of testing
- Designing a test programme
- Testing multiple variants in direct mail
- Practical testing in press media
- The statistical principles of testing
- Using statistical tables
- Sample sizes and confidence levels
- How testing can go wrong

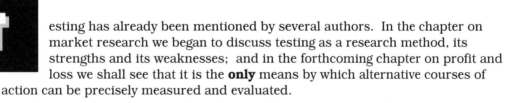

Testing has already been mentioned by several authors. In the chapter on market research we began to discuss testing as a research method, its strengths and its weaknesses; and in the forthcoming chapter on profit and loss we shall see that it is the **only** means by which alternative courses of action can be precisely measured and evaluated.

Today the old conflict between "pure" research and "real-life" testing has all but evaporated. Modern direct marketers appreciate that not only are the two disciplines complementary but also indispensable: whereas market research seeks to tell us why people behave in certain ways, testing tells us how they actually behave and, more to the point, how they are likely to behave in the future.

In this chapter, Terry Forshaw looks at testing in depth, its uses, benefits and methodology – and the science which underpins it. Should you riffle through these pages and be disturbed by the complex scientific equations on offer, have no fear. Subsequent pages will show how you can design statistically valid testing by simply reading data from a table.

New in this edition. A 12-step process for mounting a test campaign, cases, additional examples, a new matrix for testing multiple variants.

Author/Consultant: Terry Forshaw

Terry Forshaw, Director, Institute of Direct Marketing

Terry has an honours degree in Business Studies from Kingston Polytechnic and a Diploma in Direct Marketing which he passed with distinction. After working for Save & Prosper where he was developing an integrated customer loyalty programme, he joined The Bradford Exchange as Head of Client Promotions. There, he was responsible for an on-going mailing programme to an existing database of half a million customers.

In 1989 he joined The Institute of Direct Marketing as Marketing Manager and in 1991 was appointed Board Director with special responsibility for marketing its courses and services. Terry has a wide knowledge of print production and project management, and also advises several clients in financial services and IT on both tactical and strategic aspects of their direct marketing activity.

Terry Forshaw M IDM
Marketing Director
The Institute of Direct Marketing
1 Park Road
Teddington
Middlesex TW11 0AR
Tel: 0181-977 5705

Chapter 2.3

Testing – the theory and the practice

PART I: What is testing and what can it do?

Despite its unsophisticated label, testing is a sophisticated form of research. At its simplest, testing means a direct one-to-one comparison between two marketing options, eg between a high price and a low price.

For example, by presenting two different offers to identical samples of a target audience, an exact measure of the selling power of each offer can be obtained. Similarly, by presenting an identical offer to two different market segments, the responsiveness of each audience can be measured.

The simplest test of all would be to compare a single isolated variant with a known control. The example below shows how a simple test programme can be developed to evaluate marketing options:

Control	List A	Proven offer
Test 1	List A	New offer
Test 2	List B	Proven offer (as control)

A simple set of tests such as that above sheds light on a potential new market (List B) and a new offer (eg a lower price or a new incentive). So long as the samples are representative and the sample sizes are sufficient, tests can predict the outcome of future marketing activity with a fair degree of accuracy.

A more esoteric definition of testing, properly designed and implemented, is as follows:

What is testing?
The planned and scientific inclusion and measurement of alternative marketing elements (or combinations) in a campaign in order to improve systematically future campaign performance and profitability.

How testing differs from research

In the earlier chapter on research, the author pointed to the drawbacks of testing. In this chapter it is as well to remind ourselves of the benefits of testing over conventional market research, among them:

✔ **Low cost.** For large strategic applications, the costs of conventional market research may be insignificant, but for smaller operators market research may well be prohibitively expensive. Testing can offer a low-cost means of establishing important market data.

✔ **Simplicity.** Virtually any direct marketer can design and implement effective tests. The test of a headline, for example, whilst possibly generating a great deal of extra revenue, need involve few changes and almost no additional effort.

✔ **Real.** The chief advantage of testing, whether for large or small applications, is that it measures recipients' behaviour in a realistic environment, ie in their own homes or offices, confronted by an actual proposition which they must either respond to or ignore.

Whereas market research is almost entirely based on what people **say** they do, or would do, testing measures what they **actually** do in everyday situations.

More benefits of testing

Testing has numerous benefits in common with other forms of research. It also has benefits unique to itself, among them:

✔ **Minimises financial risk**
Testing minimises financial outlay, and therefore risk, by restricting test activity to test samples of customers or prospects. Later we shall see how relatively small samples can be used to assess the likely behaviour of whole populations. For example, a few thousand names, if carefully chosen, can be truly representative of entire markets.

Beyond a certain minimum level required for statistical validity, it is not the size of a sample which determines its usefulness, but the extent to which it is representative of the market as a whole. In Part III of this chapter we deal at length with sample sizes and whether or not a sample is statistically valid.

✔ **Protects your greatest asset, customers**
Another major benefit of testing, using smallish samples, is that only a minor segment of your customers or prospects needs be exposed to each test you devise.

Thus, if a test is unsuccessful, it will have consumed only a small proportion of your overall customer base. The bulk of your customers can still be treated to a proven offer, or to further tests, unaware of and unaffected by any unsuccessful tests you carry out.

✔ **Helps to maximise response**
Testing allows you to optimise your marketing activity at every opportunity. In essence, direct marketing testing is about expanding your most responsive or profitable activities and cutting back, or eliminating, the least successful activities.

Direct marketers talk of "rolling-out" successful tests, a term referred to throughout this Guide.

✔ **Helps to trim costs**
Testing can not only improve results, but also uncover ways in which you can obtain the same results with reduced costs.

Once a successful marketing offer has been established (the control), it may be fruitful to test cheaper formats (eg smaller brochures or fewer components), less expensive incentives, fewer stages (eg direct sales versus enquiry and conversion), and so on.

✔ **Validates research**
As explained in the research chapter, conventional market research gives broad directions to be followed. For example, it can help to show **why** people have product preferences. Testing, on the other hand, provides an objective and measurable assessment of people's behaviour in a true-life marketing environment. It can validate (or repudiate) research findings as well as suggest areas for further market research and product development activity.

✔ **Predicts the future**
Testing, in combination with the other direct marketing skills, is a means of removing a great deal of uncertainty about the future of your business.

As your test programme and your database activity become more sophisticated, so you will be able to predict your future with greater confidence.

Of course, testing cannot completely **remove** uncertainty. What it can do is **lessen** uncertainty about specific issues.

✔ **Stimulates creativity**
Testing provides a continuous spur to creative development. With each new campaign, the experienced direct marketer will call for further tests to "beat the control".

By setting yourself the task of designing tests that will hopefully be successful, you drive the entire business onward in its search for continuous improvement.

Testing can be summed up as a search for continuous improvement, with each successful test being further refined and tested again, represented by the schematic opposite.

Testing – a source of continuous improvement

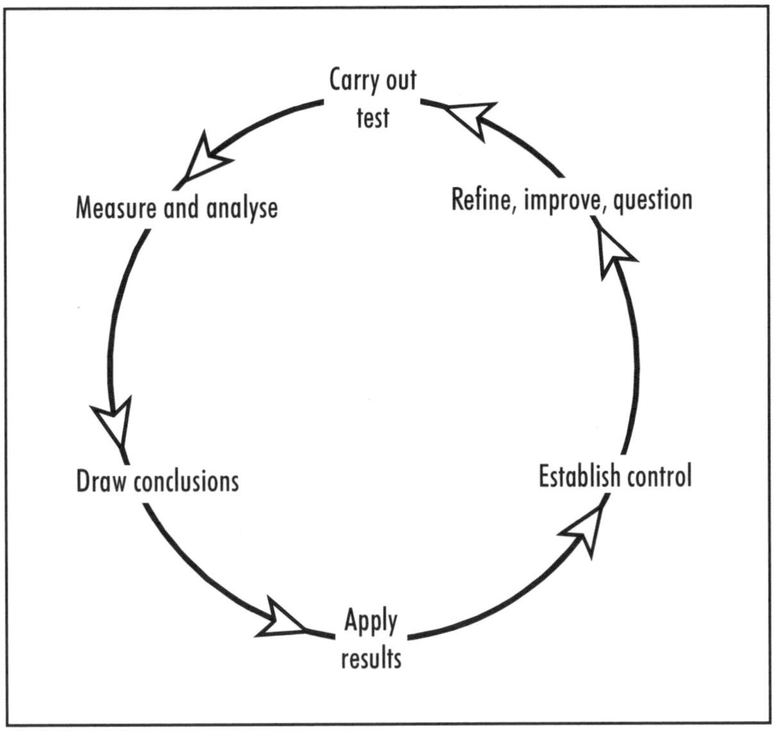

If it ain't broke ...

A memorable way of looking at the benefits of testing is to turn on its head that popular adage "If it ain't broke, don't fix it." As Graeme McCorkell points out in another IDM publication, the huge advances made in Formula 1 racing car technology would never have occurred if things that hadn't broken were never replaced. Science advances precisely because innovators constantly pose the question: How can we improve what is already working very nicely?

So in direct marketing the rule is:

If it ain't broke, fix it – so that it'll work even better and be even less likely to break in the future.

A suitable case for testing?

One of the great virtues of direct marketing is that almost **anything** can be tested and its effect measured. To show how testing is used and how it differs from market research – and how professional direct marketers differ in outlook from some marketers engaged in image advertising – let us take a hypothetical (only slightly tongue-in-cheek) example.

The sweet smell of failure?

Take the case of a new national environmental charity we shall call The Fresh Air Campaign Team (FACT). After a good start fuelled by massive press coverage, FACT decides it is time for a major donor appeal. It knows that all the major charities use direct mail for this purpose and it asks a direct marketing consultant to draw up a list of proposals and present some persuasive copy. It also knows that charities rarely bypass the opportunity in their donor mailings to draw attention to their goals and achievements. "Facts about FACT" is their theme.

But FACT wishes to remain loyal to its advertising/PR agency and asks them to design the printed literature. Someone has the bright idea of emphasising what FACT stands for by impregnating the mailing envelope and letter with the aromatic essence of wild meadow flowers. "Smell the fresh air" exhorts the copy. So far so good, except that this process is inordinately expensive, adding 50% to the cost of the mailing. It's worth it, argues the blue-sky lobby faced with doubts from the down-to-earth department.

They agree to research it. Market researchers set up tests in halls all over the country. The research is too expensive to test just the meadow flowers idea, so this is tacked onto the end of a policy/image debate. So as not to bias the result, some attendees are exposed to the meadow-scented literature without being told about it. They mostly don't notice the aromas, or not consciously anyhow. Others are told about it and enthuse wildly, admiring the technology.

They all vote on whether or not it would make them want to donate to FACT: a lot more, a little more, no difference, less, or not at all? Results confirm that the idea smells good. They go ahead with the impregnated mailing and lose their hair-shirts – money they can't afford to waste at this stage of their development.

What would the professional direct marketer have done faced with this enticing but expensive idea?

Hands up anyone who said **"Test It!"** Test it on a matching sample of the target market, against an unimpregnated control? Test it, with and without drawing attention to the aroma to see if it worked at a subliminal level? Test it in varying strengths of fragrance? Test? Test? Test?

Well, no! The chances are that such an idea wouldn't get past first base with a skilled direct marketing agency.

Why?

Because it breaks the first rule of testing.

The first rule of testing

Many tyro direct marketers – and non-direct marketers with a smattering of direct mail knowledge – often become preoccupied with their new toy: measurable response. All too often they channel all their creative energies into formulating (and testing) relatively unimportant variables, almost always those involving creative elements, eg copy style, layout and design, paper folds, envelope colours, etc, etc. Such tinkering rarely, if ever, pays off.

The golden rule of testing is that tests must be meaningful. **Only significant marketing variables should be tested.** As one of the modern industry's founding fathers puts it: "Test the BIG things."

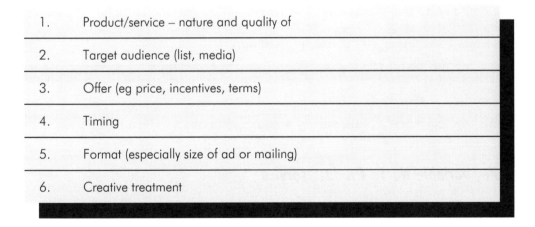

> Test the BIG things.
>
> – Bob Stone, "Successful Direct Marketing"

Testing **marketing** variables will normally have a much more dramatic impact on response and/or profitability than any esoteric creative test, and your test programme should reflect this.

The 6 key marketing variables

The following six factors are the key elements responsible for the success or failure of **all** direct marketing ventures. Experts go as far as to rank them in the following order of importance:

1.	Product/service – nature and quality of
2.	Target audience (list, media)
3.	Offer (eg price, incentives, terms)
4.	Timing
5.	Format (especially size of ad or mailing)
6.	Creative treatment

Fortunately, this hierarchical order of importance corresponds with the normal chronology of planning and implementation, ie in a normal sequence product and audience are planned first and creative treatment last. So there is no excuse for overlooking the most important variables.

Testing is not only about response

Bear in mind, as we discuss the impact of each of the six chief marketing variables, that their impact will vary greatly from one situation to another. Remember also that we are not simply concerned with which will deliver the highest response.

As well as response, our test plans should take into account:

- ✔ Potential cost savings, effect on profits
- ✔ Outlay costs, absolute expenditure – affordable or not
- ✔ Competitive pressures (change may be unavoidable)
- ✔ Risks incurred or avoided (not necessarily financial)
- ✔ Long-term implications (you can't always go back)
- ✔ Overall marketing objectives (not always response and/or immediate profit)

Matching test objectives to marketing objectives

Company A's marketing objective was to recruit 10,000 new clients at a cost per new client of £10 each. Its list/media test programme was structured to identify new lists or media to generate new clients within this threshold using a proven offer/creative approach.

Company B's marketing objective was to reduce mailing costs by 10% while maintaining volume. The variables it selected for testing included cheaper formats and fewer enclosures per mailing.

We now look at each of the six key marketing variables in turn:

Key variable No 1: Product/service

In many situations the product or service on offer will be pre-determined. Test programmes will be built around the other five key variables.

However, the benefits of testing can be profound in the area of product design and development. If the product or service has insufficient appeal then all else will fail, and small scale product tests will have limited the cost and risk at the launch stage. More significantly, testing can take place prior to expensive product development. This may involve "**dry testing**".

Using dry testing a number of product concepts and promotions can be tested simultaneously. Only successful products need go forward to more expensive product development stages.

What is dry testing?

Dry testing means developing a product concept and promotional package without producing the final product. Promotions must make clear to prospects that the product will not be available immediately and should not request payment until the order has been fulfilled. To overcome negative reactions, dry-test products are often offered on special terms, eg a pre-launch discount. Subsequent production can be based upon responses to dry tests. Beware! Dry testing can cause serious hostility among prospects if it is not fairly and openly conducted.

Not surprisingly, the opposite of dry testing, ie when the product is established, is wet testing. Some exponents also use the term damp testing to cover situations where a product is in an advanced stage of development but not quite available.

Key variable No 2: Target audience

The selection of lists, choice of media (and programme content in the case of TV and radio) are absolutely critical to the success of direct marketing. It is often stated, but is worth repeating, that the wrong creative approach to the right audience may succeed but the right creative approach to the wrong audience is doomed to failure.

The questions of list, media selection and targeting generally are fully dealt with elsewhere in this Guide, and much advice is given on testing and measurement of their performance.

Sufficient to remind ourselves here of some of the many different types of lists and media available, all of which can be tested before committing to a full-scale roll-out.

Mailing test options include:

- ✔ Customer lists
- ✔ Enquirers
- ✔ Lapsed or dormant customers
- ✔ Affinity groups
- ✔ Lifestyle databases
- ✔ Cold lists (ie bought or rented lists)

Media test options include:

- ✔ Newspapers
- ✔ Magazines
- ✔ Inserts
- ✔ Home delivery (door-to-door)
- ✔ Direct Response TV

- ✔ Radio
- ✔ Directories (eg Yellow Pages)
- ✔ Telephone
- ✔ Electronic media (eg Web Sites)

Key variable No 3: Offer and price

A strong offer can greatly enhance a product's appeal and increase its sales. As Jim Kobs says "The right offer can sell almost anything". The key word is "right". The offer needs to be relevant to the target market.

Offers may be as simple as the product at an attractive price. Or they may be multi-faceted including optional extras, special packaging, incentives, terms, payment options, guarantees, etc.

Elsewhere in this Guide (Chapter 6.6) a large section is devoted to offers, and the author contends that from a basic selection of over 50 offers, several thousand combinations can be created.

The important point, as far as testing is concerned, is that offers not only affect response, they also lead to further variables, ie different offers produce different levels of on-going customer performance. For this reason, sophisticated marketers track the results of offer tests for several years.

Price is often as critical as the product itself in terms of whether or not a sale is made. Its effect is something which most experienced exponents find impossible to predict without testing. For example, a high price can occasionally pull the best response while a low price may not guarantee you a sufficient number of orders. For this reason, and because of the impact of price on profitability, price testing should be considered wherever possible. Chapter 2.5 sets out a realistic price test and demonstrates the effect of different prices on ultimate profit and loss.

To non-marketers the concept of price testing is often suspect, but if the exercise is carried out sensitively there should be no problem. After all, the aim of price testing is not to find the highest price at which goods can be sold. It is to find the **optimum** price and this may well be a lower price than customers might otherwise expect to pay.

In a direct high/low price test, it is important that customers buying the product at the higher price are refunded the difference and the reason for the lower price should be explained, eg lower production costs resulting from higher volume responses. Conversely, where a higher price is subsequently settled upon, test customers paying the lower price should be informed that the low price they paid will be honoured.

In today's highly competitive and consumer-needs-focused marketplace, where competitive products are frequently similar in function and price, the emphasis is shifting to added-value extras and service benefits. Direct marketing is especially adept at evaluating added-value offers through controlled testing.

Key variable No 4: Timing

Although timing tests are often neglected in test programmes, timing can play a very significant role in direct marketing success and failure. There are obvious situations where the product has a link with seasonality, eg a gardening product, a Christmas hamper, a holiday, an educational product coinciding with the commencement of the academic year, etc.

However, seasonality is often far more subtle. For example, when would you expect private motor insurance applications to peak, if at all – at the beginning of the registration year, in January, at the beginning of summer, none of these? Certainly until recently the peak was in March, one explanation being that motorists used to lay up their cars for the duration of the winter! Who would have guessed that?

The missing 95%

*There is a continuing debate between non-direct and direct marketers about the so-called missing 95%, ie why do so many target prospects **not** respond to offers tailor-made for them? One major exponent in the IT industry concluded, after prolonged research, the reason is **timing**. At any given time only a proportion of prospects are actually ready or able to transact. Their reasons may include financial contingencies, a desire to see how a new product performs in the market, domestic upheavals (eg moving house), etc. This question of timing helps to explain why repeat mailings and follow-ups are often successful. It may also help to explain why roll-out results are often different from test results when, in theory, they ought to be identical.*

Timing can vary from season to season, so that tests evaluated one year may have to be revisited the next. One example is the packaged tour industry which appears to go in cycles. First new business enquiries peak early as holidaymakers vie for their first choices; then bookings fall back as they wait for late-booking bargains. Tour operators are often torn between advertising early and conserving their budgets for the later booking period. Replies to enquiry ads are an excellent measure of such fluctuations.

Since timing tests based on identical advertisements or mailings repeated at regular fixed intervals inevitably decline and fail in the end, they are sometimes known as "destruction" tests. They shed light on stamina as well as timing.

Clearly it is difficult to generalise about timing. Some mail order companies' tests have shown July to be a strong selling period – maybe as a result of less "clutter" in the press and mail from competitors. Others typically favour January–February and September–November. Timing should therefore always be included in any serious test programme if results are to be maximised. Not surprisingly media owners have become aware of these peaks and troughs and now adjust their rates accordingly, so that planning should take into account savings from using less popular, cheaper time slots.

One of the surest guides to seasonality and timing is directories such as Yellow Pages where an ad may sit unchanged year in, year out. A simple tracking of enquiries/ sales will accurately pinpoint peaks and troughs of interest.

Some like it hot

When would you expect swimming pool enquiries to peak? Remember a pool may take several months to plan and build and so, to be ready for the first hot day of summer, you might expect prospects to make their plans just after Christmas, or perhaps March at the latest. When do they peak? Many suppliers report enquiries peaking on the first hot day of summer! No doubt the same goes for other summer-related capital goods: sun awnings, conservatories, garden furniture, etc.

Key variable No 5: Format

The physical format of a mailing piece or advertisement is another important area for testing. For example, it has been known for a large C4 pack to more than double response when tested against a smaller DL pack. Conversely, small packs have triumphed over large packs in different situations, especially when their lower costs are taken into account.

Possible format tests include size, number of components, paper weights/qualities, types of envelope (eg paper or polythene), addressing method, etc.

However, an important word of caution here: to reiterate Bob Stone: *test the big things.* It is often tempting for new direct marketers to get carried away with trivial differences and lose sight of more significant variables. Remember a variable need not show an increase in response; if it shows a significant cost reduction (as many format tests can do) it is significant.

Experience shows that the following tests are **not** usually significant: colour of paper, label versus direct addressing, blue versus black signature, name and style of signature, franking versus pre-printed postal impression, etc – yet all of these are regularly tested by marketers at the expense of more meaningful marketing variables such as, for example, payment methods.

Key variable No 6: Creative treatment

Although low on the hierarchy list, creative elements (copy, layout, typography, colour, etc) can significantly affect results. However, care must be taken when drawing conclusions. A well-written letter clearly stating benefits, proposition, product details and action required may increase response, but it is easier to conclude **that** it works rather than **why** it works.

In press advertising, variables can include basic appeal, headline, dominance given to coupon and/or telephone number, type of illustration, etc. Where space is limited, it is vital that the major variants are those likely to have the greatest impact on results. The emphasis given to testimonials and guarantees can be an important creative variable as we shall see in the chapters on creativity.

Whose garden is it anyway?

A manufacturer of garden tools decided to find out whether results were affected by the use of male or female gardeners in illustrations. To his surprise, although his garden implements were heavy and difficult to handle even for professional gardeners, both enquiries and sales were enhanced by some 20% when female models were employed. This does not mean more gardeners are female, although it ***might*** *mean that. It is a typical example of how testing shows* ***what*** *happens, while research is needed to know* ***why*** *it happens.*

Creative testing, whilst rarely the most productive in terms of profit and loss, is an endless source of fascination for marketers at all levels. As with conventional research, results of creative tests can point to profitable new directions and spark off stimulating avenues to explore. This is why, despite its lowly place in the key variables hierarchy, at least one creative test usually finds its way into most comprehensive test programmes.

Later in this chapter we include a couple of actual tests. See how you fare in picking the winners. Creative options will be discussed at length in later chapters of this Guide, Chapters 6.1 to 6.6.

So what to test?

The list below demonstrates only a fraction of the number and variety of tests regularly carried out by direct marketers.

- ✔ Product, product name, with and without accessories, deluxe or standard versions
- ✔ High price vs low price; payment terms, paid or free trial, size of discount
- ✔ Free gift vs no free gift; nature and number of gifts; reason for gift
- ✔ Prize draw: nature and value of prize(s)
- ✔ Media tests, eg newspapers vs magazines, positions, sizes, timing
- ✔ Lists
- ✔ Formats, eg envelope size, number of components, use of colour
- ✔ Copy, tone, positioning, length

If you're still looking for your big break in direct marketing, take your ideas for tests along to the interview. They'll get you a lot further than waltzing in with a head full of creative ideas!

PART II: Practical testing

How to design a test programme

Before we begin to design a test programme we need to fully understand the campaign of which it is to form a part.

On the facing page is a 12-step checklist for planning and executing a test programme, from initial campaign objectives to final analysis and reporting on test results.

As you will see, the final step is a return to the beginning: testing should be a continuously upward spiralling process leading inexorably to greater profitability.

Warning: if tests are not correctly set up they will be difficult to implement, cause havoc to the main body of your campaign, and be impossible to evaluate.

Setting up a practical test programme

We now explore the three practical steps in setting up a test programme, Steps 4, 5, and 6 from the master checklist on the facing page:

First, establish the CONTROL

A control is simply your best-performing package, insert, advertisement, or script. It is the base against which all test results should be measured. The control is the approach you would use if you were unable to test alternatives, what some exponents term “the banker”. Test programmes should monitor the continued effectiveness of the control while at the same time trying to beat it.

If yours is a new venture you will have to research industry norms to establish a control; if using direct mail you will probably start with a fairly standard pack (eg letter, brochure, order form, outer and reply envelopes). This need not inhibit you from being more adventurous – it simply means that you will have a baseline against which to judge more ambitious departures. Hopefully you will conserve your creative energies for testing the key marketing variables!

An important reason for testing – perhaps **the** most important reason – is that at some point your control will tire and cease to perform adequately. At this point you will need a replacement control, developed and honed from your test programme.

Next, decide the test STRATEGY

There are many possible test opportunities in direct marketing, as we have seen. Previous results and analysis will help to determine which new tests are likely to be the most fruitful.

At this point it is advisable to produce a simple test strategy statement like the one on page 2.3-16 for a direct mail campaign.

A testing strategy statement like this will have many uses including briefing, estimating costs, and evaluation of results. Remember to file copies for future reference. It is surprising how often hard-earned test history is lost or misplaced in a busy department. Include the results when these become available.

The 12 steps in building a test programme

Step 1	Define the overall campaign objectives	What is important to the campaign's success? What are the real objectives?
Step 2	Understand the parameters of the campaign as a whole	How many mailings? Available list size? Opportunities for testing? Budget? How are responses to be handled? Time span? Is response device logical and clear? Data to be captured? Etc?
Step 3	Decide list selection criteria	Remember test lists must be representative of the market universe. See Part III of this chapter.
Step 4	Establish the control/s	See facing page and next few pages.
Step 5	Decide the test strategy	
Step 6	Construct test matrix	
Step 7	Carry out tests	
Step 8	Observe responses	Is any cell responding far better than others? Can this be explained? Are all cells contacted at the same time? Is bad weather affecting overall response? Note your conclusions for future reference.
Step 9	Check back	Was the programme executed as planned? If changed, will this affect results?
Step 10	Analyse results	Plot key variables and record what worked and what failed to meet objectives.
Step 11	Study analysis	Can you spot any correlations between winners and losers? Any key variables among responders to tests, eg age, gender?
Step 12	If possible, undertake other forms of analysis, eg regression analysis	Try to gain a subjective view of who is responding to tests, and why.
Step 1	Define overall objectives for the next campaign	Begin the process again.

Test strategy statement

Project name: SPRING 1998 WIDGET MAILING
Issued: 11/9/97
Control: C4 control pack with 2-page letter, control brochure and reply card

	Test	Objectives	Method
1.	Format test: C5 v C4 outer	To reduce mailing pack costs whilst maintaining control response	All internal elements as control pack, folded to fit C5 outer envelope
2.	Free gift added – low-key presentation	To improve response and profitability by offering a free gift, without affecting the basic tone and structure of the control pack	Mention free gift in the letter copy and PS
3.	Free gift added – heavy emphasis	To improve response and profitability by offering a free gift and featuring the gift heavily throughout the pack	Include separate four-colour "free gift" flyer. Refer to gift in letter copy and PS and include on order card with illustration
4.	New creative	To achieve a "break-through" against the existing control by using a very different approach	All new elements

Why archive your tests and results?

One successful direct marketing agency explained part of its success over many years, as follows:

"Whenever we took over a new client, instead of immediately pushing our own ideas, we began a detailed investigation of its past results going back several years. Inevitably we would track back to the company's halcyon days and find an offer, a pack, a product, or ***something****, that had worked incredibly well for many years – but which had been abandoned. Further probing would discover that a long-serving control had begun to falter (for reasons we were often able to deduce) and had been replaced in desperation. Further disappointment led to more ideas, more tests – until eventually the stalwart controls were lost in the sands of time. Frequently new marketing personnel arrived in the interim, keen to press on, never daring to look back. We called it "creative wandering" – often the new tests were creatively oriented.*

We would dig out the old controls, update them, and return to basics in terms of media planning (usually the cause of the original decline). Having set them back on the right road, we then proceeded to look for new directions – and new controls. This procedure served the clients – and ourselves – very nicely for several years."

The agency believes, incidentally, that this demonstrates that not all good advice needs to be served up as a bundle of new work. But it's a brave client who's prepared to admit they lost their way. Usually only shareholder-managers were prepared to sanction the investigations!

An important rule when constructing a test strategy is: **do not allow more than one variable to affect the results of any one test.**

There are, however, two major exceptions to the rule of single-variable testing:

✔ In some situations it may be wise to break right away from earlier thinking and test a completely new approach, in which case the more different the new approach, the better. This should **never** be done in the absence of a strict control or the effect in future years may be literally to lose one's bearings and not know which way to turn next ("wandering").

✔ Multiple factor tests can be carried out if a strictly scientific basis is used to determine sample size and test structure, as we explore below.

Finally, construct your TEST MATRIX – direct mail

At the most advanced level of direct marketing, where large amounts of money are at stake, multi-factor test matrices are constructed and monitored by statistics specialists.

For the lay reader, some guidance is given below on compiling direct mail test matrices to compare several variables at once.

Let us suppose you want to compare three lists (A, B, C) and three offers (1, 2, 3). Strictly speaking you would need to cover all possible combinations of list and offer, each to a statistically significant sample. If your minimum sample size was 6,000, your test matrix would look like Test Matrix I below. It would consume 54,000 valuable names (always assuming that you had 54,000 names available!).

Test matrix I

	Offer 1	Offer 2	Offer 3	Total
List A	6,000	6,000	6,000	18,000
List B	6,000	6,000	6,000	18,000
List C	6,000	6,000	6,000	18,000
Total	18,000	18,000	18,000	54,000

Consuming too many names in a test, even if available, can be a serious error, and so an alternative matrix may be needed. It is possible to reduce the number of test names used by making some careful assumptions.

If we assume that the three lists (A, B, C) are sufficiently similar and the best offer is likely to work across all three lists (ie the lists and the offers are independent variables), then the test matrix can be revised as follows. Test Matrix II uses only five test samples and reduces the name requirement to 30,000 overall. The likely outcome of the blank cells can be extrapolated from those mailed.

Test matrix II

	Offer 1	Offer 2	Offer 3	Total
List A	6,000	6,000	6,000	18,000
List B	6,000	–	–	6,000
List C	6,000	–	–	6,000
Total	18,000	6,000	6,000	30,000

However, an even more efficient method is a **block design** which can be used to combine all the test factors in one matrix and further reduce the number of test names used. In Test Matrix III below, only 18,000 names have been consumed. The minimum mailing quantities of 6,000 per test are arrived at by adding up the columns. The required results are the totals for each column, both horizontally and vertically.

Test matrix III

	Offer 1	Offer 2	Offer 3	Total
List A	2,000	2,000	2,000	6,000
List B	2,000	2,000	2,000	6,000
List C	2,000	2,000	2,000	6,000
Total	6,000	6,000	6,000	18,000

The benefits of multi-factor or block designs like the one above (Test Matrix III) are twofold:

1. The total sample size is kept to a minimum.

2. Some light may be thrown on the effects of different combinations of factors. Remember, for these interactive effects to be regarded with certainty, each individual cell total would need to be 6,000 names, which brings us back to Test Matrix I and a total of 54,000 names.

By keeping the numbers within each test cell to a minimum you run the risk of an occasional freak result. If, in a multi-factor test matrix comprising small volumes, the result of one of the cells is abnormally different from the other cells, it may be wise to ignore the result for that cell. The discrepancy may be caused by some operational problem and not the test variable itself. Alternatively, you would need to investigate the "freak" result very carefully and ascertain the likely cause.

Test matrix IV			
	List 1	**List 2**	**List 3**
Offer 1	Copy A	Copy B	Copy C
Offer 2	Copy B	Copy C	Copy A
Offer 3	Copy C	Copy A	Copy B

In Test Matrix IV – a "latin square" – we see that **nine** variables have been included: three lists, three offers, three copy variants. To test these nine variables in straight head-to-head tests would consume approximately 100,000 names for the results to be meaningful.

But by using a latin square, these tests can be carried out with only 45,000 names, or 5,000 per cell, saving hundreds of pounds on the programme.

Note each offer, list and copy variant appears in three cells. To design and evaluate the results of a complex matrix like this requires either a software package or a statistician.

How to test in print advertising

For direct marketers developing customer acquisition programmes across a range of media, testing print advertising can be as important as direct mail testing.

But, whereas direct mail permits testing a wide range of variables very quickly, space advertising opportunities for testing are fewer. Advertising tests must accommodate the physical limitations of print media.

Several techniques are used for testing advertising in space and inserts, as follows:

Perfect splits using inserts

A number of versions of an insert can be interleaved or ganged up at the print stage before being supplied to the publication. In this way a number of options (usually no more than six) can be tested in any one issue of the host medium. This method is ideal for accurate testing of such variables as product, price, incentive, headline, copy, illustrations, etc, ie anything printed on the surface of the insert.

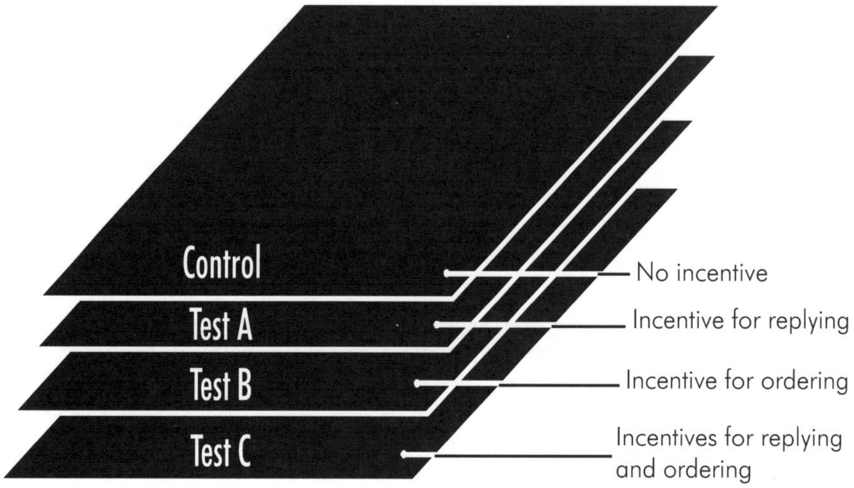

It is more difficult to test different **formats** of inserts (eg unequal sizes, shapes, or thicknesses) by this method, since printers and publishers cannot so easily arrange random distribution of unalike items. However, many publishers do offer test facilities for unalike inserts by ensuring that batches of test inserts are delivered to matching areas in equal quantities:

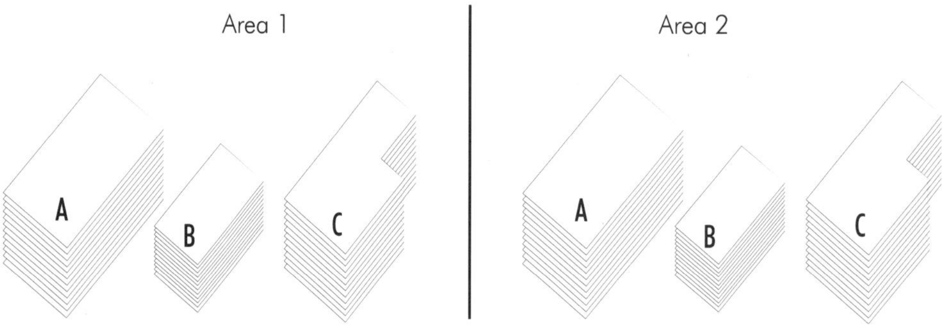

You will occasionally discover different inserts for the same advertiser when examining consecutive copies of a publication. If you are keeping tabs on a competitor – or a market – you may need to buy several dozen copies from several regions of the country in order to acquire knowledge of who's testing what.

A further advantage of insert testing is that any number of media can be included on the test schedule with no increase in cost or complexity. Results can be measured not only by test, but also by medium. Interaction between medium and test can also be observed in this way.

It is always advisable to discuss your requirements for inserts with the media at the time of booking to ensure that your inserts are acceptable in terms of size, weight and format, especially if tests are planned. See section on inserts in Chapter 4.1.

Space advertising: A/B splits

Many publications are printed two-up, meaning the printer produces two copies simultaneously from each machine. By changing a plate affecting half of the press sheet, a perfect 50/50 or A/B split can be achieved. In this way you can arrange for each alternate copy of a publication to contain either advertisement A or advertisement B.

Some publications offer split-run facilities using several machines printing simultaneously. You can arrange for half the machines to print your A copy and half the machines to print your B copy.

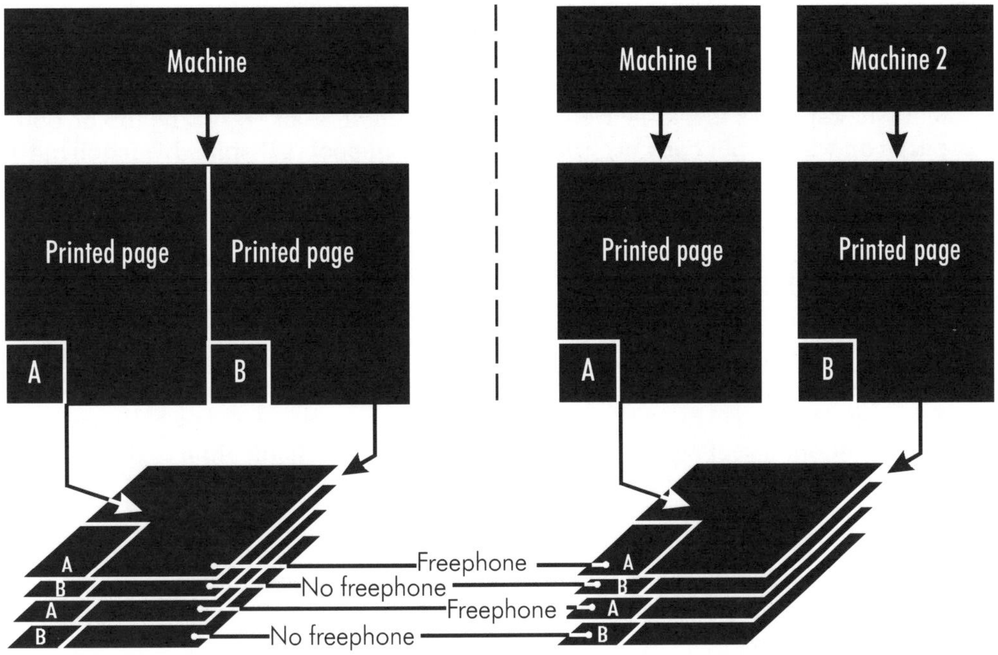

A/B splits can be used to compare a wide variety of variables but always two at a time. To test colour versus mono (black and white) advertisements, you will need to pay for colour in the whole run and sacrifice the colour in half the number of copies – a technique very much frowned on by media owners and only rarely available nowadays.

Some advertisers have on rare occasions used A/B splits to test the effect of size, but this requires you to re-sell, give away, or otherwise utilise any surplus space, eg for another offer or brand. (The media owners will not be keen to co-operate!)

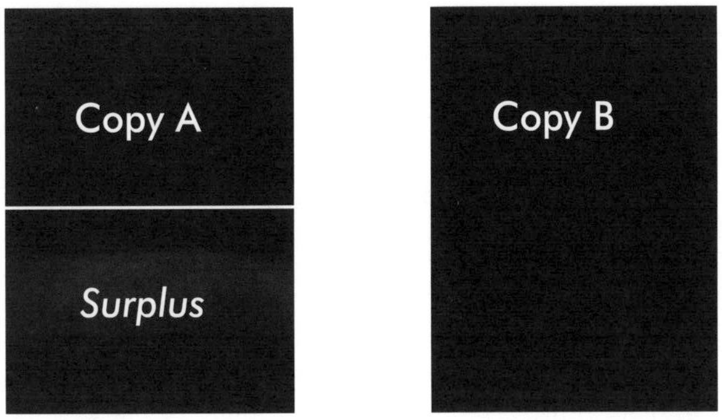

In theory, A/B splits are perfect samples, since each alternate copy of the publication contains Copy A and Copy B respectively. Excellent samples of several million copies can be achieved with national newspapers, or combinations of magazines.

However, the results of A/B splits, whilst extremely useful, are not **individually** reliable. For example, due to breakdowns or other operational reasons, a printer may not always print equal numbers of your A and B advertisements, although this fact will be unknown to you. A/B splits are a facility offered to advertisers at a nominal cost and are generally outside the publisher's legal obligations, therefore no redress will be available.

The golden rule of A/B splits, especially when using newspapers, is not to attach too much credence to a single result. Always repeat important tests several times before drawing far-reaching conclusions.

Many newspapers mark their editions with a small "A" or "B" at the top or bottom of pages on which split copy occurs so that you can spot A/B splits by acquiring several consecutive copies.

Cross-over testing

Cross-over testing is a technique sometimes used where individual publications do not have A/B split capabilities but where tests are important for the product. Cross-over testing can also be used for testing pairs of advertisements which are different in size, position, use of colour, etc. It is, however, less reliable than A/B split testing and far less reliable than testing with inserts.

Using two similar publications, advertisement A is first run in one magazine with advertisement B running in the other. Then, in a subsequent issue, the advertisements are switched. The results are aggregated over the two issues and comparisons drawn, as in the example below:

Example of cross-over test

	Magazine 1		Magazine 2	
	Copy	Response	Copy	Response
1st issue	A	240	B	120
2nd issue	B	180	A	160
		420		280

In the example above, advertisement A might be regarded as the winner – after aggregating the results of the two publications. If, however, only the second issues are considered it is possible to conclude that advertisement B outpulls advertisement A.

Clearly, extrapolating results from this cross-over test is not an entirely satisfactory basis for important decisions. As with A/B splits, it is unwise to base decision-making on isolated tests but to repeat important tests several times.

Telescopic testing using regional splits

Where only simple A/B splits are available, but a number of advertisements need to be tested, this can be solved if regional editions are also available. With a large circulation publication which offers A/B splits within regions, it is possible to structure a test combining A/B and regional splits, called telescopic testing, eg:

Examples of telescopic testing

		Circulation	Test
Region 1	Two-way split	250,000	A vs B
Region 2	Two-way split	250,000	A vs C
Region 3	Two-way split	250,000	A vs D
Region 4	Two-way split	250,000	A vs E
Region 5	Two-way split	250,000	A vs F
Region 6	Two-way split	250,000	A vs G

Using this method, each new advertisement (B, C, D, etc) is compared with the control (Copy A). By indexing the results, comparisons can also be drawn **between** advertisements B, C, D, etc.

Using inserts to test press (space) advertisements

One method of testing, not so far mentioned, is the use of inserts for testing space advertisements.

For example, where your campaign relies on press advertising, but testing by the split copy method is not available or too slow, inserts can be used to replicate your space ads and placed in similar media (or media targeted at a similar audience to that intended for your product). This method produces extremely reliable data.

Timing and frequency testing

It is possible, through the use of regular advertisements featuring identical copy, to ascertain seasonal bias for a product by measuring the changing levels of response over time. However, this is only viable with small spaces, since larger, higher impact spaces are quickly affected by diminishing returns. As already mentioned, directories such as Yellow Pages and Thomsons, besides being effective response generators in their own right, are also very useful for assessing and predicting levels of interest throughout the year for almost any product category.

A common question posed by would-be press advertisers is which day of the week to advertise. The answer will depend on many factors, among them your product category and the rates charged by the media for different days. Ultimately only experiment, rather than testing, will yield the correct answer.

The ideal frequency for a product or offer, ie a frequency which can withstand the effect of diminishing returns, can also be ascertained only by trial and error. By running an advertisement in similar media, at different frequencies, the effect of diminishing returns can be measured. This topic is dealt with more fully under media planning, Chapter 4.1.

Testing in practice – 2 case studies

To put some meat on our discourse on testing we conclude this practical section with a couple of cases – a chance for you to try your hand at guessing the outcomes of creative executions. (We use creative tests here because the differences between the tests are more apparent.)

Direct mail envelope test – colour or mono?

On the facing page is a mailing envelope test for the Craigandarrach holiday complex near Balmoral. The 1990 campaign was to promote subsidised inspection visits to middle-aged professionals earning over £35,000 pa – so the test cells would have comprised representative samples of this target market.

Despite our earlier advice to test only significant marketing variables, this is a test of a full-colour envelope versus a monochrome alternative. Is it a mere creative test? Not really; it is a test of a major cost element, since colour costs significantly more than black-on-white, but of course there are also creative and motivational implications.

To whet your appetite for the creative chapters to follow, let us pose you the problem facing the marketers at Craigandarrach:

A quality white envelope with an elegant typeface printed in black is known to convey opulence, quality and style – but may also be deemed austere by some recipients. Full colour helps to depict the beauty and atmosphere of the Highlands and is the norm for holiday offers – but full-colour envelopes often fail to pay for themselves ... a suitable case for testing.

We cannot, of course, give you the company's profit and loss statistics but we are permitted to tell you the result of the test. Perhaps you might like to hazard a guess as to which was the winner. Remember testing not only tells you which test won, but also by how much.

The winner was the full-colour envelope resulting in 15% more response, 15% more visits arranged, and 150% more sales revenue (due to the high value of incremental sales).

Source: John Watson, WWAV Rapp Collins, 15.10.97

Testing broad product appeal – conservation or entertainment?

Our second test (opposite) again looks like a test of creative interpretations, but was designed to be a test of broad product appeal to a given target market.

The campaign for London Zoo included this head-to head comparison between what the advertiser described as a conservation approach (Save The Lions) and an appeal to parents of animal-loving children to take them on a zoo outing (the fun approach).

Given that you wished to test such a differential, which medium would you use? Bear in mind your market is virtually all parents and children living within just over an hour's drive time from London, and your selling season is brief. The advertiser used interleaved inserts carried in local and regional newspapers.

And which approach would you have put your money on to produce the most visits?

The "conservation" approach was three times as productive in terms of identified visits.

There is an inherent danger in attaching too much significance to the broad conclusion that "conservation" is the winning appeal in this example. How many other variables can you spot between these two versions, any or all of which could have affected the outcome? And you know what we said about not testing more than one variable at a time? What were the possible exceptions to that rule? Which other alternative way of assessing the relative appeal of the "conservation" versus "fun" approach might you have investigated?

Exercise for students

The foregoing case, its conclusions and any reservations surrounding it would make a very useful exercise to debate. Be prepared to discuss such a case as this when applying for your first post in direct marketing, especially if you are aiming to join an agency.

Source: *Nick Moore, Barraclough Hall Woolston Gray, 28.10.97*

Press testing: Some rules of thumb

✔ When testing a publication for the first time, use your control advertisement where possible.

✔ If your control advertisement is particularly expensive, experiment with smaller or cheaper spaces.

✔ Different media and copy often produce widely varying on-going customer performance (the so-called "back-end"). It is therefore wise to calculate back-end results carefully before settling on control advertisements and media.

✔ Never rely on single press test results. The more critical the decision, the more tests should be carried out (say 4–6). Fewer tests than this may yield inexplicably contradictory results.

✔ Where two advertisements regularly produce similar, satisfactory results, regard this as a good outcome. It could mean you have a second winner!

In summary, testing in press (inserts or space) offers less flexibility than direct mail. It is also less scientific. But there is no other way to compare the response-inducing power of advertising in newspapers and magazines. The important point is to be aware of the deficiencies and to re-test frequently.

For more advice on media planning, refer to the appropriate section of this Guide, Chapters 4.1 to 5.3 as follows:

4.1 Press advertising and inserts
4.2 Door-to-door
4.3 Direct response TV
4.4 Radio
4.5 Electronic media/the Internet
4.6 Catalogues
4.7 Outdoor advertising/posters
5.1 Direct mail lists
5.2 Direct mail/exporting
5.3 Telephone

Exercise for students

Each of the above media offers its own advantages and disadvantages for testing the content and nature of communications. You might like to draw up a table of comparisons showing the main differences in test facilities provided by each medium.

PART III: The statistical principles of testing

All prediction based on the outcome of tests relies on the theory of probability. The theory is used to assess the chances of a given test result being repeated.

By using statistical probability direct marketers can interpret response data and make decisions on the basis of objective criteria. Statistical principles provide a better decision-making foundation than "gut-feel" or partial experience. **By balancing statistical probability with sound judgement, direct marketers can make the best possible decisions.**

While a thorough understanding of probability theory is unnecessary for testing, an understanding of its statistical basis is nevertheless valuable. The numbers, of course, are mostly crunched by computer.

The role of statistics

Statistics are used to **generalise**, eg to summarise the characteristics of customers in a particular target market. In direct marketing, the aim is normally to use the characteristics of past and present customers to **predict** the character of future customers, although the direct marketer should never forget that predictions based on test results are conditional on other factors remaining equal.

The three statistical concepts discussed in this chapter are:

- ✔ INFERENCE
- ✔ SIGNIFICANCE
- ✔ CONFIDENCE

The laws of statistical probability are encapsulated in the following equation or formula which we shall be making full use of later:

$$E = Z \times \sqrt{\frac{R \times (100 - R)}{N}}$$

In this equation Z represents the level of confidence (the likelihood); R is the expected or estimated percentage response from a representative sample of the target market; N is the sample size; and E is the amount of error which can be expected from the calculation.

The good news is that most of this information has been distilled into a simple set of tables as we shall see. But first some explanation:

Inference: Accuracy depends on sample size

Direct marketers not only generalise from past and present customers to future customers, they also analyse part of their target market to describe their entire target market. This process of generalisation is called "statistical inference". The term "inference" is used for good reason: it is never possible to prove that a future response rate will be X%. **This can only be inferred.** The smaller the group that is studied, the less certain one can be that the inference is a good one.

Even if it were possible to analyse the whole of a target market, any forecast of future response rates would still be an inference, since other factors might change. Because analysing the whole of a target market is usually expensive, time-consuming and often impractical, tests are performed on **samples**.

A sample should be of sufficient quantity, and of a suitable character, to render it unbiased and wholly representative of a total "universe".

We shall look at sample sizes and how samples are selected in a moment. Remember: sample size is represented by N (number) in our master equation.

Significance: Is that test difference meaningful?

Significance is what you are hoping for when you plan and execute a test: you want to know if one course of action is more productive than another, by how much, and – this part is often overlooked – whether the result is **statistically** significant. Not whether it is significant to you but whether it is significant scientifically, ie not simply the effect of chance.

To assess the significance of a result, therefore, you need to analyse the difference between the actual (or "observed") result and the result you were expecting. If it is within the realms of normal statistical error, then it is **not** significant.

Significance is closely related to confidence. Once you know the significance of a test result you can decide whether or not to take a calculated risk on the outcome of a "roll-out".

Significance is all about the probability and limits of statistical error (E in our equation), which again is inextricably linked to the size of the sample.

Confidence: How reliable is the test overall?

Because all tests are probabilistic, we need one more assessment of the accuracy of a test before we can be sure of its value. This is the confidence level, more accurately defined as the "confidence interval". The confidence interval represents the degree of assurance that the test sample and its result are representative of the total market.

The probability that a test response lies within a given range is its **confidence level**. Typically this would be set at 80%, 90%, 95% or 99% depending on the required accuracy and importance of the test.

As the marketer you must set the level of confidence required. What you are stating is how different a test result must be from its control before you can be confident of its significance.

A confidence level of 95% means that if a given test were repeated 100 times, on 95 occasions the result would be as the test, all else being equal. Confidence is represented by a constant (K) in our master equation, K being decided by the level of confidence that **you** require.

Samples and sampling methods

A sample is a **representative** selection from the proposed market or universe. For a sample to be truly representative care must be taken to ensure that no bias exists when samples are selected.

The following sampling methods are designed to achieve representative samples:

✔ **Simple random samples**
Each individual selected for a sample is picked on a completely random basis, ie each has an equal chance of being selected.

✔ **"1 in N" samples**
The familiar method for direct marketers is a "1 in N" selection. Individual records are systematically taken at intervals (every Nth name), so that when the end of the file is reached the required quantity of sample names has been selected.

For instance, to select 10,000 names from a list of 250,000 starting from an arbitrarily chosen name in the first 25, every 25th name would be picked.

Nth sampling provides an acceptably randomised selection, with only a slight possibility of bias (other than that inherent in random sampling anyway), which can just possibly occur due to the order in which the list has been compiled or sorted in the first place. Vary the way you select, eg select 1 in 10, 1 in 12, 1 in 25 alternately, so that there is less risk of the same names being picked each time.

Remember, names selected as test samples should be flagged and excluded from other test activity, thus ensuring purer roll-out results in due course.

✔ **Stratified samples**
Where a particular characteristic of the universe (eg buying pattern) is a key response discriminator, it is important to stratify or order the file by that characteristic **prior** to selecting a sample. The test sample will then accurately reflect the total universe to be tested. For example:

Example of stratified test sample

Universe		Sample		
Recent Actives	20,000	1 in 10 sample	=	2,000
Older Actives	60,000	1 in 10 sample	=	6,000
Inactives	30,000	1 in 10 sample	=	3,000
	110,000			11,000

Setting the sample size

There is no "right" sample size. In practice, sample sizes are a trade-off with the **accuracy** required of a test, ie the required **confidence** in its results. The more confident you want to be, or the greater the required accuracy, the larger the sample needed.

An important point to note about sample sizes is that they do not depend on the total size of the list, market, or population but on the degree to which the sample is representative of the whole.

The size of sample required for a test can be determined by adjusting the equation, or formula, we have already introduced, as follows:

$$\text{Sample size} = \frac{Z^2 \times R \times (100 - R)}{E^2}$$

Where: Z is a constant related to the level of confidence required. The constants most commonly used by direct marketers are:

1.281 for an 80% confidence level
1.645 for a 90% confidence level
1.960 for a 95% confidence level
2.575 for a 99% confidence level

R is the estimated percentage response from a sample.

E is the required limit of error – a measure of the accuracy required (it is expressed as a percentage variation on either side of R).

NB: "percentage" difference in these calculations refers to percentage points, ie the difference between 1% and 2% is not 100% here, but 1% (one percentage point).

What sample size?

What sample size would be appropriate if you expect a 2% response to a test mailing and want to be 95% confident that the roll-out response will be within +/- 0.3% of your projected response, ie between 1.7% and 2.3%?

In this case *Z = 1.96 (for 95% confidence)*
R = 2.00 (%)
E = 0.30 (%)

Using the formula:

$$\textit{Sample size} = \frac{1.96 \times 1.96 \times 2 \times 98}{0.3 \times 0.3}$$

= 8,366 (say 8,400)

In other words, if you take a sample of 8,400 and the estimated response is 2%, then you can be 95% confident that the roll-out response from the total audience will be between 1.7% and 2.3% ***subject to consistent conditions****.*

Rolling-out a test

In practice, roll-out conditions are rarely consistent with test conditions, and many factors need to be considered when assessing the viability of rolling-out a test. For example, the timing of the roll-out, the level of competitive activity, and general economic circumstances, could all significantly affect response.

After a test has been run and the actual percentage response is known, the formula can be converted to adjust the confidence interval thus:

$$\text{Limit of error} = Z \times \sqrt{\frac{R \times (100 - R)}{N}}$$

How reliable is it?

If the test mailing of 8,400 names gave a response of 1.8% at the 95% confidence level, what is the confidence interval?

Z = 1.96 (constant for 95% confidence)
R = 1.80% (actual response)
N = 8,400 (number in sample)

$$\textit{Limit of error} = 1.96 \times \sqrt{\frac{1.8 \times 98.2}{8400}}$$

$$= 0.28432 \text{ or approx } \underline{0.28}\%$$

The 95% confidence interval thus becomes:
1.8% +/- 0.28 = 1.52 to 2.08

Statistically this means that if the exercise was repeated 100 times, 95 would give a response rate within the range calculated.

Testing alternative approaches

The foregoing formula is designed for setting sample sizes and projecting roll-out responses from test samples, but it does not determine statistically valid **differences** between alternative approaches. In cases where a number of variations are being tested against each other and against an established control, a formula is needed to compare each possible pair of variations.

The following formula will establish whether the differences in response between each of the pairs is significant at an agreed confidence level. If it is not, then the observed difference could have been due to the sampling error inherent in any testing.

The formula used for comparing alternative approaches is:

$$\text{Limit of error (of the difference)} = Z \times \sqrt{\left(\frac{R1 \times (100 - R1)}{N1}\right) + \left(\frac{R2 \times (100 - R2)}{N2}\right)}$$

R1/N1 and R2/N2 relate to the two respective sample results and sizes.

Is the difference significant?

A test sample of 10,000 was mailed with an established control pack and a further 10,000 received a variation. The question is: are the different results statistically valid?

The response percentages were:	*Control*	*2.14%*
	Test	*2.68%*

To be 95% confident of the test results the formula looks like this:

Limit of error (of the difference)

$$= 1.96 \times \sqrt{\left(\frac{2.14 \times 97.86}{10{,}000}\right) + \left(\frac{2.68 \times 97.32}{10{,}000}\right)}$$

$$= 0.425$$

The difference observed was 0.54 (2.68 – 2.14) so the confidence interval for the true difference is:

$$0.54 - 0.425 = 0.115$$

$$0.54 + 0.425 = 0.965$$

You can thus be 95% confident that the difference in response between the test variation and the control lies in the interval 0.115 to 0.965 and that the observed difference ***is*** *statistically significant at the 95% confidence level.*

If, in the above example, you wanted to be **99%** confident that the results were statistically significant, or if you reduced the respective mail quantities to 5,000 and got the same observed difference, you would find after applying the formula that the true difference in each case was zero and therefore **not** statistically significant.

Statistics are an essential part of good direct marketing. They enable test programmes to be developed at a strategic level. They allow large amounts of data to be meaningfully analysed and structured decision-making to take place.

However, statistics must always be applied with good business sense and care must be taken to ensure that results are painstakingly analysed and methodically evaluated.

Using statistical tables

We have made much of the statistical formulae in this chapter to demonstrate the principles involved. In day-to-day direct marketing it is far more likely that you will refer to published tables of sample size and probability.

Opposite will be found a useful table of sample sizes covering responses from 0.5% to 10%, the range most frequently used in consumer direct marketing.

The table shows the minimum sample size required for different response rates and accuracy levels.

Table of minimum sample size for a test or control mailing

95% confidence level

Acceptable plus or minus error on anticipated % response

Anticipated response rate to the mailing	0.1%	0.2%	0.25%	0.3%	0.4%	0.5%	0.6%	0.7%	0.75%	0.8%	0.9%	1.0%
0.5%	19,100	4,800	3,100	2,100	..	..	..	..	..	..	..	..
1.0%	38,000	9,500	6,100	4,200	2,400	..	..	..	..	..	..	..
1.5%	56,800	14,200	9,100	6,300	3,500	2,300	..	..	..	..	..	..
2.0%	75,300	18,800	12,000	8,400	4,700	3,000	2,100	..	..	..	..	..
2.5%	93,600	23,400	15,000	10,400	5,900	3,700	2,600	..	..	..	..	..
3.0%	111,800	27,900	17,900	12,400	7,000	4,500	3,100	2,300	2,000	..	..	..
3.5%	129,800	32,400	20,800	14,400	8,100	5,200	3,600	2,600	2,300	2,000	..	..
4.0%	147,500	36,900	23,600	16,400	9,200	5,900	4,100	3,000	2,600	2,300	..	..
4.5%	165,100	41,300	26,400	18,300	10,300	6,600	4,600	3,400	2,900	2,600	2,000	..
5.0%	182,500	45,600	29,200	20,300	11,400	7,300	5,100	3,700	3,200	2,900	2,300	..
5.5%	199,700	49,900	31,900	22,200	12,500	8,000	5,500	4,100	3,500	3,100	2,500	2,000
6.0%	216,700	54,200	34,700	24,100	13,500	8,700	6,000	4,400	3,900	3,400	2,700	2,200
6.5%	233,500	58,400	37,400	25,900	14,600	9,300	6,500	4,800	4,200	3,600	2,900	2,300
7.0%	250,100	62,500	40,000	27,800	15,600	10,000	6,900	5,100	4,400	3,900	3,100	2,500
7.5%	266,500	66,600	42,600	29,600	16,700	10,700	7,400	5,400	4,700	4,200	3,300	2,700
8.0%	282,700	70,700	45,200	31,400	17,700	11,300	7,900	5,800	5,000	4,400	3,500	2,800
8.5%	298,800	74,700	47,800	33,200	18,700	12,000	8,300	6,100	5,300	4,700	3,700	3,000
9.0%	314,600	78,700	50,300	35,000	19,700	12,600	8,700	6,400	5,600	4,900	3,900	3,100
9.5%	330,300	82,600	52,800	36,700	20,600	13,200	9,200	6,700	5,900	5,200	4,100	3,300
10.0%	345,700	86,400	55,300	38,400	21,600	13,800	9,600	7,100	6,100	5,400	4,300	3,500

To use the statistical table on the previous page, given the most commonly used 95% confidence level, you need to have a broad idea of the response rates that you anticipate. These will probably be based on previous controls. As the minimum size of sample increases with higher response rates, you should slightly overestimate your anticipated response levels when deciding on minimum sample size.

Then, you must decide on an acceptable level of accuracy. The accuracy will affect any calculations of break-even or profitability. For example, are you going to be satisfied by results which are within $\pm$ 0.5% of your expected response, or do you need to be sure to within 0.2%? The decision often depends on the lower limit as this may represent break-even or budget cut-off points.

Testing for smaller users

Many smaller users will, of course, never achieve the minimum sample sizes required to be 90% or 95% confident about their test results.

This does not mean that small operators should not test. On the contrary, testing is as important for small users of direct marketing as it is for the giants of the industry. It simply means that you should not accord too much credence to isolated tests. You should also not attempt to test minor departures from your control, but only major marketing differentials.

The golden rules for smaller operators include:

✔ Repeat important tests several times.

✔ Validate test results by other research methods, eg follow-up interviews, customer feedback, staff reports, etc.

✔ Keep tests to absolutely significant differentials.

✔ Test only one or two **major** departures per campaign/season.

✔ Keep tests to criteria which cannot be verified by other means.

✔ Don't overlook alternative forms of testing, eg the interleaving of different inserts discussed earlier.

The cost of testing

One argument often advanced for testing, compared with market research, is that it costs nothing – tests being carried out as part of a revenue-generating programme.

This is not quite true. Testing has a cost – and therefore requires a budget. The cost of testing stems from such items as:

✘ **Higher print and production costs.** Shorter runs and more variants inevitably result in higher unit costs.

✘ **Loss of discounts.** Variations of materials and timing can lead to forfeiture of volume discounts on print, postage and media buying.

✘ **Executive time.** The cost of devising, implementing, controlling and reporting upon a complex test programme is extremely significant and should not be overlooked.

✗ **Higher proportion of fixed costs.** Developing a number of new test approaches can involve additional fixed costs such as creative origination charges or agency fees.

Your test budget should be seen as an investment in the future, and needs to be carefully weighed against projected changes in profitability. Enhanced profitability will flow only from worthwhile tests of important differentials – in other words: test only the things that can significantly improve your bottom line, or do not do it at all.

Test only the things that can significantly improve your bottom line, or do not do it at all.

Depending upon their commitment to direct marketing, many operators devote between 10% and 40% of their marketing budgets to testing. Interestingly, this figure is **not** lower for more established operators. Dyed-in-the-wool direct marketers know that only by devoting significant resources to testing will they continue to prosper.

It should also be remembered that testing is not necessarily expenditure that cannot be recouped. As part of an on-going programme, tests may well earn a higher return on investment than the remainder of the programme even in the short term, if the tests have been well chosen and implemented.

For an example of testing in practice and its effect on profit and loss, refer to Chapter 2.5.

Test ideas

Use this space to make a note of good ideas for testing as they occur to you:

eg Free gift for orders over £40

Direct debit vs standing orders

PART IV: Monitoring and evaluating test results

A carefully structured test programme will count for nothing if the results are not **properly** monitored, analysed and evaluated.

Systems and procedures should be established to ensure that campaign results are carefully monitored, sources of responses and sales trackable, and final results carefully and thoroughly analysed and reported upon.

Monitoring and evaluating systems can be divided into five stages as follows:

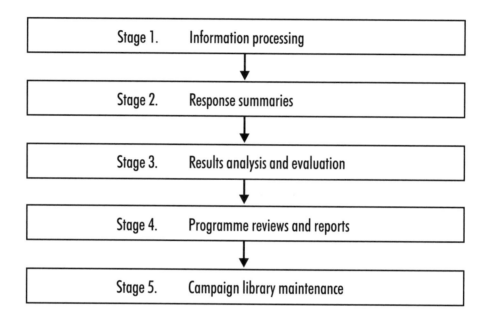

Stage 1. Information processing
↓
Stage 2. Response summaries
↓
Stage 3. Results analysis and evaluation
↓
Stage 4. Programme reviews and reports
↓
Stage 5. Campaign library maintenance

Stage 1. Information processing
Personnel who physically handle responses must be briefed with relevant campaign details (products, timing, source codes) and should also appreciate the need for accuracy.

The response handler's brief should include:

? **When** response should be counted (daily, weekly).

? Exactly **what** should be recorded (single/multiple orders, order values, source codes).

? **Checks** to be made to ensure source codes are not wrongly captured. The system should recognise current promotion codes and input data should be verified.

Stage 2. Response summaries
When the first orders or enquiries are received, systems should be in place to provide on-going response summaries. Although it is dangerous to draw too many conclusions from early results, where response is exceptionally high or low early warning allows immediate adjustment of fulfilment resources. The following should be considered:

? How should response be summarised and reported, how frequently and to whom?

? Will response actuals be shown against response projections?

? Who will perform what analyses and how often?

? Has an analysis schedule been set up?

The temptation to make early judgements from interim response summaries is ever-present. However, it is vital that campaign results are fully and carefully analysed, and formally reviewed, to ensure that subsequent marketing decisions are sound and early observations either qualified or rejected.

Stage 3. Results analysis and evaluation
Once campaign results are final (or if final results can be **accurately** projected), they should be carefully analysed. Results analysis is two-stage:

Initial response analysis establishes that results are statistically sound, ie the absolute number of orders received is adequate and differences statistically significant.

Back-end (subsequent customer performance) analysis. Once all campaign costs are known and performance rates established (eg conversion from enquiries to sales), the profitability of the test programme can be calculated. Depending on test objectives it is often not until this stage that meaningful conclusions can be drawn.

For example, "two incentives" may outpull "one incentive" at the enquiry stage, but a poor conversion rate may mean that "one incentive" is the most profitable approach.

Remember, when test results are analysed, additional costs attributable to testing must be taken out of the calculation. Roll-out cost **projections** should be compared with control costs to establish which is the more cost effective, test variation or control, in the long-haul. **Higher origination costs, higher costs associated with smaller print-runs, discounts, etc need to be deducted to reflect the roll-out conditions.**

Stage 4. Programme reviews and reports
To avoid some of the problems inherent in testing it is important to set up formal review meetings or, at the very least, structured test programme reports in order to:

✔ Confirm the validity of test results.

✔ Objectively assess results and evaluate against test objectives.

✔ Balance the results with judgement and past experience. Do any external variables or circumstances need to be considered?

✔ Agree key decisions affecting future marketing activity and adjust future programmes accordingly, ie should the control be changed, should you adopt the low price, do you re-test or drop the new incentive?

Stage 5. Campaign library maintenance
A well-maintained campaign library is essential and should provide a permanent record of all key marketing information for future reference. Details of test programme results and objectives, analyses, recommendations and decisions taken should all be accessible together with appropriate sample packs or ads.

All too often such an information base is not properly maintained or is made the responsibility of a junior member of staff. Having invested time and money in acquiring direct marketing knowledge you should carefully record, maintain, and refer to it regularly.

How to ensure the reliability of testing

At several points during this chapter we have stressed that test results should be valid when compared to the control, **all else being equal** or, as the scientists say, "subject to consistent conditions".

The phrase "all else being equal" rolls nicely off the tongue but it can mask situations that are decidedly unequal – between tests and control, or between actual test results and expected outcomes.

We have dealt with statistical error, but what about operational error and other factors outside our control? The graphic below draws attention to some of the many factors which can lead to forecasting being rendered inaccurate and thus to disappointing outcomes.

To ensure the reliability of testing and of the resultant predictions, careful attention should be paid to all the areas highlighted, many of which are dealt with more fully by other authors in this Guide.

How testing and forecasting can go wrong

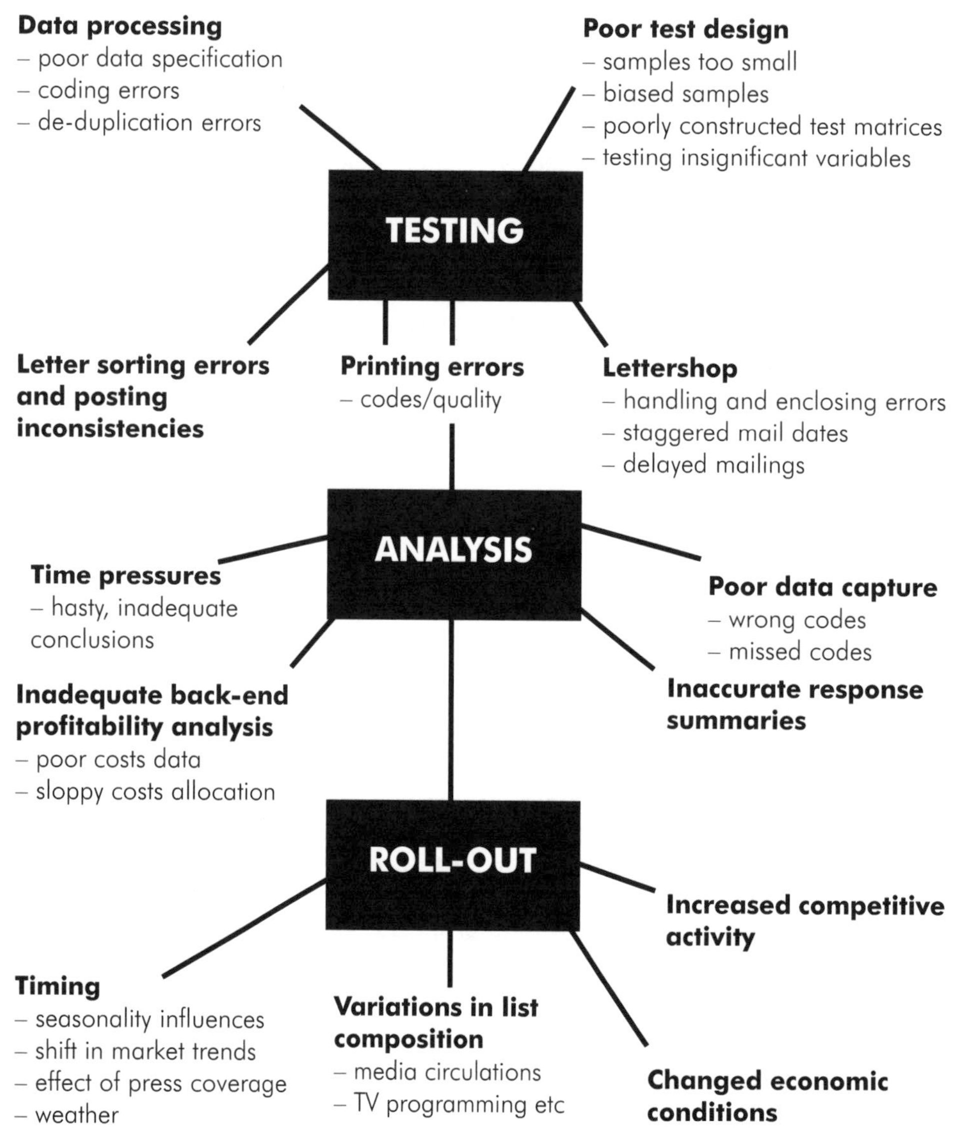

The role of judgement

The theory and principles behind direct response testing are sound. The statistical concepts used are reassuring. However, it must be stressed that testing is an **aid** to judgement and **not** a replacement for it. Test-based experience must be modified with judgement in order to reach decisions.

Testing can provide invaluable guidance and can dramatically improve long-term profitability but it is an imperfect science. Many variables outside your control can and do affect test results. It is as well to be as aware of the pitfalls of testing as of the opportunities it affords.

An important testing rule to remember is: never believe a single result however convincing it appears. The following continuous programme of testing holds good for direct marketers large and small.

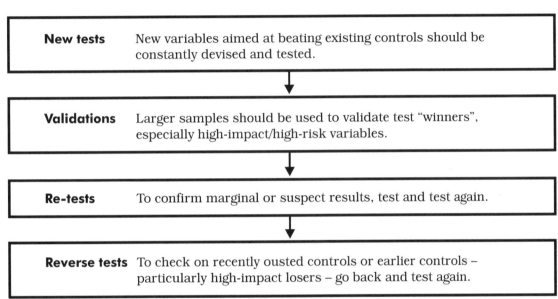

New tests New variables aimed at beating existing controls should be constantly devised and tested.

↓

Validations Larger samples should be used to validate test "winners", especially high-impact/high-risk variables.

↓

Re-tests To confirm marginal or suspect results, test and test again.

↓

Reverse tests To check on recently ousted controls or earlier controls – particularly high-impact losers – go back and test again.

Chapter 2.4

Compiling a direct marketing budget

This chapter includes:

- **The standard direct marketing measures**
- **Calculating allowable cost-per-order**
- **How direct marketing costs behave**
- **Fixed, semi-fixed and variable costs**
- **Cost components of a direct campaign**
- **Sample campaign budget**
- **Introduction to customer lifetime value**

The chief attractions of direct marketing are, for many users, its targetability, its unique ability to forge and maintain one-to-one relationships with customers and prospects, and its power to reach and satisfy niche markets which can often not be accessed by any other means.

But for many direct marketers, old hands and new converts alike, the legendary measurability of direct marketing remains its overriding appeal. We are talking about a near-instant assessment of profit and loss whether for a specific event from a single advertisement or mailing, to a complete campaign, or the value of a customer's lifetime activity.

Central to the management of direct marketing finance is, of course, the budget. In this chapter, Russell Weetch sets out some simple rules for the management of direct marketing in monetary terms, and shows us how to prepare the all-important budget. His advice: never attempt to compose a budget in one hit. Instead build it up piece-by-piece using manageable chunks.

By way of introduction, Weetch explains some of the more common direct marketing measurements.

New in this edition. Following feedback from readers, an additional explanation of the campaign budgeting process has been included on page 2.4-17.

Russell Weetch, Systematic Marketing Limited

Russell is a founding director of Systematic Marketing, a company specialising in the development of direct marketing systems and database related Internet and Intranet sites.

After graduating in Economics from University College, Cardiff and later gaining an MBA from Middlesex University, Russell worked in direct marketing within the Barclays Bank Group. He was responsible for the introduction of profitability models for marketing evaluation as the means of driving both the database and marketing development. He was also extensively involved with developing large marketing databases and other marketing related delivery/ processing systems.

Systematic Marketing develops systems such as customer databases, campaign tracking and customer support systems. Systematic have been working with the Internet for the last four years and sees this as a natural evolutionary step for direct marketing. Having developed UK Index (www.ukindex.co.uk), the major UK Web search engine, the company has developed other sites such as the Official National Trust Web site (www.ukindex.co.uk/nationaltrust).

Russell Weetch
Systematic Marketing Limited
11–12 Tottenham Mews
London W1P 9PJ
E-mail: russell@sysmarketing.co.uk
Web site: http://www.sysmarketing.co.uk
Tel: 0171-636 0400

Chapter 2.4

Compiling a direct marketing budget

The basic direct marketing measures

In this chapter we look at the basic direct marketing measurements and show how they are used to compile a campaign budget. In subsequent chapters, other authors will look at profit and loss, and the lifetime value of customers, more deeply. We start with a few simple but very important reminders:

Easy ways to manage numbers

In direct marketing we often find ourselves looking at numbers at two extremes: on the one hand we talk of mailing quantities, or customer databases, or media circulations, which sometimes reach into the **millions**, eg:

"The XYZ Publishing Co has 4,000,000 active subscribers"

On the other hand, when looking at the response to certain offers, we are often looking at values of **fractions of one per cent**, eg:

> "Response to XYZ's continuity series offer was 0.012%"

We need, therefore, a way of presenting and comparing extremes of data that is immediately informative, so that, for example, we can contrast two quotes or two results with only a quick glance at the figures. What direct marketing has evolved is a series of STANDARD MEASURES.

The standard "per thousand" measure

Direct marketing's answer to its numerical extremes is the standard "per thousand" measure. Thus print costs are measured "per thousand" units, media in "per thousand" readers, and so on.

Beware how you express "per thousand". Old-style direct marketers, mathematicians and students of Latin have a penchant for the expression "per mille" or "per m". This, of course, can easily be confused with "per million". Better to stick to "per thousand" (or "per thou"), per '000, or even per k (for kilo), to avoid any risk of confusion.

If you do insist on using "per mille" or "per m", make sure that everyone connected with your organisation is according it the same meaning.

Standard production measure

In the area of production most suppliers now quote on a "per thousand" basis. But if you are comparing two quotes make sure you are comparing like with like:

Comparing supplier quotes

You have received two quotes for different campaigns, one of 15,000 mailings and one of 22,000. The cost of the first mailing is £7,550 and the second £11,200. How do you compare the quotes?

Converting into cost-per-thousand, we find:

Quote no 1

$$\frac{£7,550}{15,000} \times 1,000 = £503.33 \text{ per '000}$$

Quote no 2

$$\frac{£11,200}{22,000} \times 1,000 = £509.99 \text{ per '000}$$

You can now compare the quotes on a similar basis.

Standard analysis measures

The commonly used measures for analysis are either **per thousand** based or **per order/sale** based. By using these measures we can quickly compare campaigns in terms of the response or sales we receive per thousand households mailed or per thousand door-drops, for example.

Below are three simple calculations which occur throughout direct marketing:

Cost per thousand

$$\text{Cost per thousand} = \frac{\text{Total cost}}{\text{Total quantity}} \times 1{,}000$$

$$\text{Total cost} \div \frac{\text{Total quantity}}{1{,}000}$$

Response per thousand

$$\text{Response per thousand} = \frac{\text{Total response}}{\text{Total mailed}} \times 1{,}000$$

Cost-per-order

$$\text{Cost-per-order} = \frac{\text{Total cost}}{\text{Total orders}} \quad \text{or} \quad \frac{\text{Cost per thousand}}{\text{Orders per thousand}}$$

Postal costs – a rule of thumb

Be especially aware of confusion when comparing postage costs on a per thousand basis. It all too often happens that, when carrying out rough calculations, a postage cost of 20p per item is put down as £20 per thousand. Not so! 20p per unit is £200 per thousand. Remember to add the "0" and change the pence to pounds.

Allowable cost-per-order – where it all began

One of the simplest measures used to control direct marketing activity is the ALLOWABLE COST-PER-ORDER, an approach which is as old as direct marketing itself. Other authors will term it allowable cost-per-sale (CPS). In fact, orders and sales are not always synonymous since unpaid orders do not equate to sales.

Allowable-cost-per-order is reached by building a mini profit and loss account for an average sale **including** the desired profit but **excluding** promotional costs.

The result is the amount we can **afford to spend to secure the sale**: the allowable selling or promotional cost or the allowable cost-per-order (CPO).

Calculating the allowable cost-per-order (£)

Selling price			50.00
Less returns			5.00
Net order value			45.00
Costs:	Cost of goods	15.00	
	Fulfilment	5.00	
	Bad debt	2.25	22.25
Contribution to breakeven			22.75
Desired profit			5.00
Allowable promotional cost			17.75

Calculating required response

Once we have calculated the allowable cost-per-order, by building in the cost of promotion and quantity to be mailed we can calculate **the response required** to produce a desired profit.

Calculating the required response from allowable cost-per-order

Say that the cost of a promotion is £12,000. How many sales are needed to cover this sum? If we allow £17.75 to be spent for each sale, the allowable cost-per-order, then our requirement is 676 orders.

$$\frac{12{,}000}{17.75} = 676 \text{ orders}$$

We need 676 orders to achieve the desired level of profit per sale.
So, if we are mailing 50,000 people, we need a net response rate of 1.35%.

$$\frac{676}{50{,}000} \times 100 = 1.35\%$$

Advantages and disadvantages of the allowable-cost approach

The advantages of the traditional allowable-cost approach to direct marketing are twofold:

Advantages

✔ Requires the discipline of setting targets; also the targets have to be realistic.

✔ Imposes the discipline of evaluating campaigns before they are agreed to.

Clearly the allowable-cost approach has served many organisations well. But in this basic form it has at least five limitations which have to be recognised if not addressed, as follows:

Disadvantages

- ✗ There is an assumption that the product price is fixed and predetermined, and cannot easily be altered.
- ✗ Sales have to be predicted to establish the unit cost.
- ✗ It treats promotion as a function of price and sales.
- ✗ Decisions are not based on profit maximisation, but rather on profit satisfaction at the individual sale level, overlooking the larger campaign issues. It can become a self-fulfilling prophecy.
- ✗ It does not take into account subsequent purchases a customer might make.

What is needed is to build on the allowable-cost approach, to obtain more flexibility and to address these problems, as in the approach which follows.

Allowable costs – 5 steps towards a more flexible approach

Step 1. Overcoming fixed prices

The first limitation we identified in the basic allowable cost-per-order approach is the fixed or predetermined price. That is easily addressed. All we need do is re-run the numbers based on different prices. See table below.

All other things being equal, a lower price will require a higher response rate to achieve our objectives, and a higher price will require a lower response rate. We must then judge whether these are reasonable or not, based on our experience.

Calculating allowable costs and required response using different prices

Mailing	50,000		
Cost	£20,000		
		Price A (£)	Price B (£)
Price		50.00	39.99
	Less returns	5.00	4.00
		45.00	35.99
Direct costs		22.25	22.25
		22.75	13.74
Required profit		5.00	5.00
Allowable cost		17.75	8.74
Response needed		1,127	2,288
Response percentage		2.25%	4.58%

Step 2. Overcoming the need to calculate unit costs

The second problem of the basic allowable-cost approach is calculating unit costs. To do this we need to predict the sales, which may be difficult. However, this can be an important part of our decision-making process and can be used as the base with which to compare expected sales with **needed** sales, so it is not all bad!

Step 3. Overcoming the promotion presumption

The third constraint of the basic allowable-cost approach is the presumption that promotion is a function of price and sales (ie the more we sell and the higher the margin, the more we can spend on promotion – the allowable cost). On the one hand, this suggests that the level of sales is independent of the promotional effort. On the other hand, it suggests the more we sell, the more we should spend on the promotion – rather than maximising profit.

Obviously neither of these suggestions is a true reflection of the business environment in which we operate. First, sales **are** a function of promotion, price (usually inversely related) and other factors. Second, while we can set profit-per-sale targets, the costs of a promotion are not determined by our sales but by market forces, ie competition for the services of our suppliers.

It is not the cost of a promotion (eg mailing) that changes with our level of sales but the profit we make from it.

If we accept that response is at least partially a function of price, then our comparative example opposite using different prices is misleading and we must calculate a different set of allocated costs.

Step 4. Overcoming the narrow view

The answer to the fourth limitation of simple allowable-cost calculations, ie that they overlook the large campaign issues, is to move up a level in our evaluations.

Rather than use a single sale as our base level, why not use the campaign? And rather than judge a required response rate against our experience, why not use our best estimate of a response rate and judge whether we proceed with a campaign or not on the profit likely to be generated?

We can always work out individual sales profitability from the overall campaign calculation as the example on the following page shows:

Campaign based budgeting

	Price A	Price B
Price	£50.00	£39.99
Number mailed	50,000	50,000
Response	2.25%	4.00%
Number	1,125	2,000
Returns	10%	10%
Sales	£56,250	£79,980
Less returns	£5,625	£7,998
Net sales	£50,625	£71,982
Cost of sales	£25,031	£44,500
Gross profit	£25,594	£27,482
Promotion cost	£20,000	£20,000
Campaign contribution	£5,594	£7,482
Contribution per gross sale	£4.97	£3,74

Comparing the two preceding calculations, the first (price comparison, page 2.4-6) illustrates, on the basis of simple allowable cost, that if we felt that the response would be 4% we would not choose to accept a selling price of £39.99 because this would require a response of 4.58% to achieve our target of £5.00 profit per sale.

The second calculation (campaign based budget above) shows that choosing the higher price would mean sacrificing £1,800 worth of contribution, despite the higher profit per sale. An example of the classic marketing conundrum of whether or not to go for higher volumes at lower cost, or vice versa.

Step 5. Overcoming the short-term objection

The fifth and final limitation of the simple allowable-cost approach is its failure to consider the on-going value of a customer. This is easily addressed in theory, but can prove very tricky in practice, as discussed later. (A full explanation of the long-term value of a customer will be found in Chapter 2.6 of this Guide.)

How direct marketing costs behave

Before we go on to look at budgeting and decision-making models more closely, it is important to understand costs: what they are and how they behave.

Costs in direct marketing, as in every area of business, fall into two basic groupings: fixed costs and variable costs. In building the cost component of a budget we are concerned with what costs we shall incur, whether these costs are fixed or variable and, if variable, on which element(s) they are dependent.

Variable costs, fixed costs and overheads

The definition of costs changes depending on the level being addressed. Some costs may be fixed when looking at an individual campaign, but variable in the context of a year's worth of campaigns.

Variable costs
are defined as costs which vary with the amount of a given activity. For example, the cost of a list will vary according to the quantity you choose to rent; postage will be directly proportional to the number you mail; data capture of responses will be linked to the number of people who respond.

Fixed costs
are costs which are not influenced by changes in activity. For example, the cost of artwork is fixed at the campaign level (although it could be seen as variable at the strategic level).

Overheads (indirect fixed costs)
are costs which are incurred whether or not an activity takes place. For example, rent is likely to be a cost which is not only independent on the quantity mailed in any one campaign but also independent of the number of campaigns in a given period (within reason).

On the next page are some examples of how variances in these costs can be dependent on each other, and in the next chapter will also be found some examples using actual product costs.

Exercise for students

In a two-stage mail order advertising campaign would you expect the following cost components to be fixed or variable, and if variable on what might they depend?

Agency costs for designing advertisement/s?
Cost of freepost service for replies?
Cost of capturing and processing response data?
Enclosing and handling brochures requested?
Setting up fulfilment agency routine?
Cost of product?

For answers, see table on next page.

An example of cost relationships

A.	Press advertisement	
1	Agency costs	Fixed
2	Media	Fixed
B.	Initial response	
3	Response	Assumption
4	Freepost	Variable to 3
5	0800 etc	Variable to 3
6	Handling	Variable to 3
7	Data capture	Variable to 3
8	Processing	Variable to 3
C.	Mailing	
9	Number to be mailed	Variable to 3 less duplicates
10	Agency costs	Fixed
11	Production	Variable to 9
12	Text set up	Fixed
13	Processing	Variable to 9
14	Lasering	Variable to 9
15	Enclosing and handling	Variable to 9
16	Postage	Variable to 9
D.	Purchase response	
17	Response	Assumption and variable to 9
18	Freepost	Variable to 17
19	0800 etc	Variable to 17
20	Handling	Variable to 17
21	Data capture	Variable to 17
22	Processing	Variable to 17
E.	Fulfilment	
23	Agency costs	Fixed
24	Cost of product	Variable to 17
25	Handling	Variable to 17
26	Packaging	Variable to 17
27	Postage	Variable to 17

The two-way effect of quantity

Some direct marketing costs increase with quantity. For example, overtime processing costs can result from an unexpectedly high response to a mailing or advertisement. On the other hand, some costs, eg the unit cost of printing, can be dramatically reduced with increases in quantity – as the following example for a fairly standard C5 mailing pack demonstrates.

Effect of quantity on print costs (C5 mailing)

Quantity	Total cost	Cost per pack
5,000	£1,450	£0.29
50,000	£10,050	£0.20
1,000,000	£161,000	£0.16

From the example above it can be seen that straight-line extrapolation from test mailing costs would seriously distort the financial implications of a roll-out: the cost of 1,000,000 mailings projected from the cost of the 5,000 mailout would be £290,000 rather than the £161,000 it actually cost.

However, if you were to run on a further 1,000,000 copies there might be hardly any further reduction for quantity, as you would have already amortised the set-up costs and used up the "economy of scale". Eventually, when ordering very large volumes, the unit cost may become virtually constant.

Understanding the effects of quantity is critical if the correct inferences are to be drawn from a test campaign about the financial implications of a roll-out.

How to handle overheads

The handling of costs is probably one of the most contentious areas of budgeting. Variable costs, by definition, can easily be allocated and do not present a problem. Fixed costs, directly related to an activity, eg artwork for a mailing, also do not create a problem. It is the allocation of overheads (indirect fixed costs) which causes most of the heartache.

We can attempt to allocate overheads to products or campaigns, but there are problems. For example, say a product manager has planned twelve campaigns for the year, we could allocate 1⁄12 of his salary to each campaign.

But what if two of the campaigns take twice as much of his time as the others?

What if one of the campaigns is cancelled (maybe after he has done a lot of the work) or another campaign added during the period?

One answer is to instigate a method of decision-making that does not require us to allocate overheads to specific activities. We are talking of the **contribution** or **relevant costing** approach.

The contribution approach

When looking at a campaign, the most useful level for decision-making is the contribution level. This takes into account **all** the revenue and costs directly associated with an activity.

Example of contribution approach

Assume you are evaluating whether to undertake a mailing to 100,000 people. You expect to receive a response of 10% and the cost of your product is £10.50. The costs you expect are:

Goods in at £2.50 each

List £90 per 1,000

Artwork and agency fees £8,000

Production and postage £500 per 1,000

Product manager to handle 12 such campaigns in the year, salary £15,000 pa

Office costs (rent, heat, lighting, etc) allocated to the campaign: £5,000

Responses handled in-house: £1.00 per response

Putting this together you calculate

Mailing		100,000
Response @ 10%		10,000
Revenue		£105,000
Cost of goods		£25,000
Gross profit		£80,000
Cost of list	£9,000	
Production	£50,000	
Agency/Artwork	£8,000	
Staff	£1,250	
Office costs	£5,000	
Handling	£10,000	£83,250
Profit/(Loss)		(£3,250)

According to your calculation the activity makes a loss. But there are three indirect costs you have included which you are going to have to pay whether or not the campaign goes ahead. These are: the staff cost; the office cost; and the handling cost. Together, these costs add up to £16,250.

A **relevant costing** approach would say that the campaign generates an income of £105,000 and as a result of undertaking the campaign costs of £92,000 will be incurred. This leaves you with an income of £13,000 to contribute towards your overheads, ie if you don't undertake the campaign you are likely to be £13,000 worse off at the end of the period.

This contribution (or relevant costing) approach, based on identifying the **relevant** costs associated with a campaign, looks to see if undertaking the campaign **contributes** towards the overheads (which will be incurred whether or not the campaign proceeds).

It is important to remember that, although the contribution approach does not attempt to allocate overheads to specific activity, which can be very problematic, **overheads cannot be ignored**. The contributions from all the activities which the overhead supports must add up to more than the overheads if the business is to survive.

The benefit of the contribution approach is that it looks at what additional costs will be incurred, over and above those which will have to be paid anyway, and so helps lead to decisions which maximise profit – as the example on the previous page demonstrates.

When "fixed" costs move: Semi-fixed costs

In practice, to some extent all costs are variable. Some costs, which are technically referred to as "fixed", respond to quantity, although not in a gradual fashion. Rather, they move in steps, or are fixed up to a particular level then increase as a variable cost. We call these semi-fixed costs.

An example of an apparently fixed cost which can move is processing. If a company has a response handling department which employs full-time processors, then the cost of these staff is, for all intents and purposes, fixed. Whether they are fully employed or underemployed within any period, their costs (wages, etc) have to be paid.

If, however, the volume of processing work rises to a level where temporary staff have to be brought in, or overtime has to be worked, the costs start to fluctuate with the level of activity. So, where a campaign forces us to incur extra costs, these need to be considered.

An example where semi-fixed processing costs might come into play is when you move a promotion from test to roll-out. A test of 5,000 might not put any burden on the processing department, but a roll-out to say 500,000 prospects over a short period might require the staff to work overtime.

Opportunity costs: The cost of lost opportunities

The contribution or relevant costing approach we have been discussing readily lends itself to the comparison of alternatives. At the basic level, as we have seen we can compare the benefit of undertaking a campaign as against not doing it.

But the contribution approach becomes even more powerful when comparing alternative uses of resources. Since the approach looks for contribution to overhead, we can look for projects which maximise contribution. This takes us into the realms of opportunity costs.

Opportunity costs are not costs in the normal sense of the word. Opportunity costs are the costs of opportunities forgone – ie how much we could have made by using our resources to do something else. For example, if we have a choice of undertaking either campaign A (which we expect will bring in a contribution of £20,000) or B (which is likely to generate £25,000), and we decide to pursue campaign A, then the opportunity cost of choosing option A is £5,000.

Economics dictate that projects likely to generate the greatest contribution be selected. But, in reality, decisions are not solely based on economic judgement. What contribution analysis does is allow you to make better informed decisions.

Creating a direct marketing budget

What is budgeting?

Budgeting is building a "picture" of the business in numbers. It provides a framework in which to make decisions and examine the impact of those decisions on the business. In building a picture, or model, we are concerned with two interactions:

✔ **External influences**
The effect of external influences on our likely performance, eg "How will the economic climate affect our sales?"

✔ **Internal influences**
The effect of our internal procedures on each other, eg "If we make 500 plates a day instead of 200, what does this mean for the life of our machinery?"

The building block approach

Building a picture of the business does not have to be an all-or-nothing process. It can be put together in blocks, eg campaign by campaign.

In simple terms the annual marketing budget is the sum of all the campaign budgets during the year, plus the overheads needed to run the operation.

The marketing budget is the sum of all the campaign budgets during the year.

Why budget?

Budgeting has many uses and benefits to a company. It should not be seen as simply a form of monetary control. Among the many non-financial benefits of proper budgeting are:

✔ The organisation's objectives are clearly defined.

✔ Key actions are highlighted.

✔ People are forced to think ahead.

✔ Responsibilities are defined.

✔ Measurements of performance are defined.

✔ An overview of the activities is constructed.

✔ Decisions about trade-offs and priorities can be made in an informed way.

✔ Inter-departmental conflict is reduced.

✔ Early warning of problems is given so that corrective action can be taken.

✔ Provides useful checklist to ensure all aspects of the work are covered.

Budgeting – a continuous process

Budgeting should not be a once-off process. It should form part of a cycle which helps manage a business and improve its performance. To achieve this, results must be fed back into the budgeting process so that more accurate assumptions (such as the likely response to an offer) can be made. Thus confidence in the model's accuracy as a decision support tool is increased.

A budget is a pre-event evaluation and should be the basis for comparison of actual performance during the budget period. Providing the budget has been properly constructed, measuring the variance of actual from budget is a powerful tool for the early identification of problems.

What makes for successful budgeting?

Successful budgeting depends upon a number of factors. Failure to observe any one will jeopardise its usefulness and reliability. These factors are:

- ✔ Co-operation and communication between all the people concerned
- ✔ Realistic targets
- ✔ Consistent objectives
- ✔ An easily understood format
- ✔ Accuracy
- ✔ Timeliness
- ✔ Frequent reviews of progress and of the system itself

The first steps

The first step in creating a budget is to define the structure of your campaign. Is it a mailshot, a one-stage press campaign or a two-stage campaign (where the initial response is for more information and the second is the sale)? Having defined the campaign we need to identify the sources of our costs, and the inter-relationship between them.

The schematic on the next page shows a typical campaign structure. It is very helpful to draw up a chart in this way:

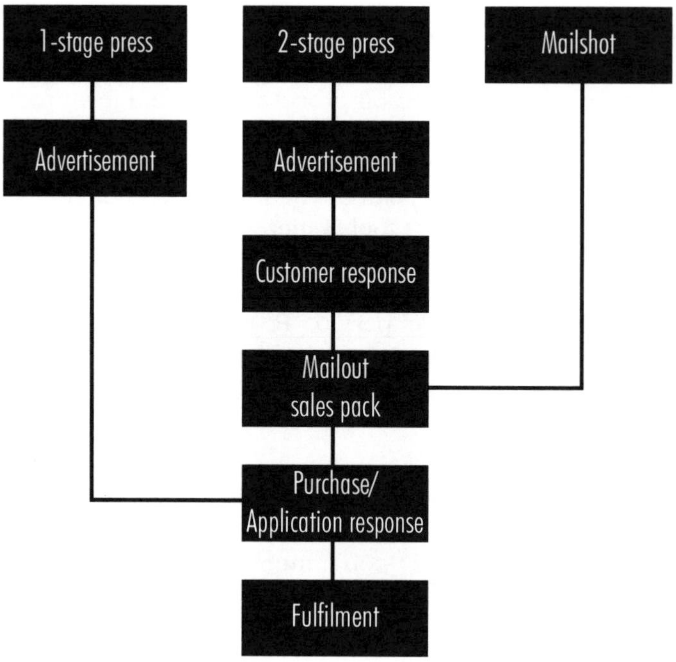

Finding the component costs

We can now take each section of the campaign and start building a detailed picture of what costs we are likely to incur. We can then look at the various elements which influence the costs and build our budget model(s) using the following checklist.

Typical cost components for a direct marketing campaign

- ❒ Press advertisement costs
  - Copy
  - Artwork
  - Media space
- ❒ Agency costs
- ❒ Production and print costs
  - Brochures
  - Letterheading
  - Envelopes
  - Reply envelopes
  - Order forms
- ❒ Bureau costs
  - Text set-up
  - Data processing
  - Lasering
- ❒ Mailing costs
  - List
  - Enclosing
  - Handling
  - Postage
- ❒ Response costs
  - Freepost/Business Reply Service
  - 0800/Freefone
  - Handling
  - Datacapture
  - Deduplication
- ❒ Fulfilment costs
  - Copy
  - Artwork
  - The product
  - Handling
  - Packaging
  - Postage
- ❒ Other costs
  - Consultancy fees
  - Bad debt
  - Returns
  - Insurances

For a more detailed examination of direct marketing costs please see the following chapter in this Guide.

Putting it all together

The final step in drawing up a campaign budget is pulling together all the costs we have already identified. The annual marketing budget can then be compiled, as already discussed, by drawing together the individual campaign budgets.

Of course your budget will have its own requirements and the detail will vary according to the work involved. However, the example campaign budget overleaf should provide a useful guide to starting your own budgeting process.

The budget layout

Our budget layout may look very different from those you have seen before. It is designed like this so that it can be more useful than simply as a financial document. It can be used as a production plan and a checklist; it also enables you to spot any costs that you may have omitted.

As you can see, unlike conventional budgets, it does not begin with revenue but instead has a campaign description at the top, in numerical terms – and it is laid out in blocks.

The top block contains the "global" parameters for the promotion, ie the number of prospects to be mailed, the expected response, and a forecast of returns.

The second block records one-off charges, such as artwork and consultancy fees.

The third block represents activities required to complete the promotion activity..

The final block is a summary. You could add other measures here, such as profit per 1,000 mailed.

The blocks, you will notice, are in chronological order. Within each block the individual items are also entered in roughly chronological order. All this will help to keep your planning on the straight and narrow.

Within the two larger blocks are four vertical columns:

The first column describes the item/action.

The second column sets out the cost basis, eg £150 (per 1,000).

The third column: the unit/s to which the cost refers, eg 1,000.

The fourth column: the revenue; or cost (in brackets).

The fourth column is calculated by dividing the relevant measure in the first block, by the unit of costs (column 3); multiplied by the cost basis (column 2), thus:

List rental: 5,000 (mailed) divided by 1,000 x £90 = (£450)

Freepost: 500 (responses) divided by 1 x £0.185 = (£93)

This approach is particularly useful for computer spreadsheets because it gives a lot of flexibility in asking the "What if?" questions.

Sample campaign budget

Expected quantities & estimates		
Mailing quantity		5,000
Response rate	10.0%	500
Returns/rejects	10.0%	50

Item	Price	Per	Revenue/Cost
Set up			
Creative, Artwork, Fees	£10,000	1	(£10,000)
Total			(£10,000)
Mailing			
List rental	£90	1,000	(£450)
Computer processing	£50	1,000	(£250)
Printing	£50	1,000	(£250)
Lasering	£60	1,000	(£300)
Enclosing	£40	1,000	(£200)
Postage	£0.180	1	(£900)
Total			(£2,350)
Response handling			
Freepost	£0.185	1	(£93)
Data capture & processing	£100	1,000	(£50)
Despatch	£30	1,000	(£15)
Gross sales	£500	1	£250,000
Returns	£75	1	(£3,750)
Cost of goods sold	£350	1	(£157,500)
Total			£88,592
Summary			
Sales			£250,000
Set up			(£10,000)
Mailing			(£2,350)
Response handling			(£161,408)
Campaign contribution			£76,242

This budget layout has the advantage of doubling up as both a production plan and a checklist ensuring that no important costs are omitted.

The future value of a customer

No discussion on budgeting for direct marketing can be satisfactory without reference to customer lifetime value (LTV), even though this topic is covered more fully elsewhere in this Guide (see Chapter 2.6).

Establishing the future value of a customer is a major step in recognising the true value of a campaign. To do this we must forecast the likely average level of future sales from each new customer and what expenditure will be needed to bring this about.

Lifetime value is a very important concept in direct marketing evaluation. It moves us from a transaction-centred focus to one of relationship development. It is an approach which recognises that existing customers are likely to be more profitable than new ones and allows us to reflect this in our evaluation of prospective campaigns.

The lifetime value of a customer is the total revenue received from a customer during his/her "lifetime" with our company, less the costs of servicing and marketing that customer. It is the total profit we get from having that customer over time.

How do we calculate lifetime value?

Calculating the lifetime value of a specific customer is obviously something that can be done only retrospectively. But providing we have enough data we can develop a model of how our average customer performs. This allows us to evaluate campaigns on the basis of our likely average customer lifetime value.

With more data we could segment our customers, for example according to which source they came from (eg which medium they initially responded to). This would allow us to make decisions on the varying profitability of recruitment options, based not only on initial responses but on their on-going value.

The two examples below and overleaf demonstrate how the cumulative value of a few customers who are regularly promoted (campaign A) might compare with the results of a one-off promotion (campaign B) to a large number of customers.

Note: Year or Period "0" means "now". This is not arbitrary numbering as we shall see in the next section.

Value of a regularly promoted customer

Campaign A/ List 1	Year 0	Year 1	Year 2	Year 3	Year 4	Year 5	Year 6
Customers	1,000	500	350	300	250	225	200
Net profit	£30.0	£22.5	£19.3	£18.0	£15.5	£14.4	£13.0
Cumulative	£30.0	£52.5	£71.8	£89.8	£105.3	£119.7	£132.7

Value of a one-off customer

Campaign B/ List 2	Year 0	Year 1	Year 2	Year 3	Year 4	Year 5	Year 6
Customers	3,500	0	0	0	0	0	0
Net profit	£105.0	£0.0	£0.0	£0.0	£0.0	£0.0	£0.0
Cumulative	£105.0	£105.0	£105.0	£105.0	£105.0	£105.0	£105.0

If we had to make a choice between the two campaigns above, we would give up £27,700 worth of profit over the seven years if we undertook an evaluation based at the one-off campaign level rather than over a "lifetime".

A major point, however, to come out of this example, is contained in the words "over seven years". **When** we receive our profit is important, since £1 received today is worth a lot more than £1 received in seven years' time because of its investment value, as the final worked example will show.

Today's cost of tomorrow's earnings: Discounted cash flow

When looking at the value of future earnings from a customer, it is essential to take into account the real value of money over the period in question.

You know how accountants have historically matched costs and sales. If we buy a personal computer today the cost will amortise (depreciate) over, say, three years, even though we have to pay the full cost now. The classical accountancy approach ignores the timing of revenues and payments. That approach says that if you sell something in 1990, then you account for it in 1990, even if you do not receive the money until 1992. This is questionable because there is a time value of money – £1 today is worth more than £1 tomorrow, and so on. Therefore, if we are concerned with lifetime values, or we sell a product which is paid for over a period of time (like life assurance or a loan), we must take into account this time value.

So how do we build this investment value of money into our evaluation? The method we use is called **Discounted Cash Flow (DCF)**.

Discounted Cash Flow looks at actual cash flows rather than accounting profit, and brings all revenues and expenses back to a present value (PV) – it **discounts** them. We take our cash flows and discount them by a rate of interest (the discount rate) which reflects both the true value of money and the risk of our investment.

This interest or discount rate is compounded to reflect the period in which a cash flow happens. The general formula for the discount rate is shown opposite together with a worked example on the following page.

Discounted cash flow example

Formula for discount rate: $\dfrac{1}{(1+r)^n}$

where r = the rate of interest expressed as a proportion (ie 1.0% = 0.01), and n = the period to be discounted.

Assume that the interest rate is 15%. If you receive £1,000 now, in period 0, it would be worth £1,000. If you receive it at the end of year 1 it would be worth:

$$£1{,}000 \times \frac{1}{(1+0.15)^1} = £869.57$$

In other words, if you had £869.57 given to you now, you could invest it and it would be £1,000 in a year's time.

If you receive it in Year 3 it is worth, in today's terms (present value):

$$£1{,}000 \times \frac{1}{(1+0.15)^3} = £657.52$$

You can prove the value of this formula by applying it to the year "0", ie **now**. Currently £1 is obviously worth £1. Thus the formula becomes:

$$£1{,}000 \times \frac{1}{(1+0.15)^0} = £1{,}000$$

Now let us look at the lifetime value calculations we have been using taking into account the discount factor, starting with Campaign A ie regularly promoted customers:

Campaign A	Year 0	Year 1	Year 2	Year 3	Year 4	Year 5	Year 6
Discount factor	1.0000	0.8696	0.7561	0.6575	0.5718	0.4672	0.4323
	£30.0	£22.5	£19.3	£18.0	£15.5	£14.4	£13.0
							£132.7
Present value	£30.0	£19.6	£14.6	£11.8	£8.9	£7.2	£5.6
Total present value							£97.7

Now let us look at Campaign B, the one-time customers:

Campaign B	Year 0	Year 1	Year 2	Year 3	Year 4	Year 5	Year 6
Discount factor	1.0000	0.8696	0.7561	0.6575	0.5718	0.4672	0.4323
	£105.0	£0.0	£0.0	£0.0	£0.0	£0.0	£0.0
							£105.0
Present value	£105.0	£0.0	£0.0	£0.0	£0.0	£0.0	£0.0
Total present value							£105.0

When we look at our alternative options (A and B) with Discounted Cash Flow, we can compare them on a like-for-like basis – ie we have used DCF to calculate a single value for each project, irrespective of the time over which the income/costs are spread. This value is the Net or Total Present Value – the value of the project to us in today's money **after taking into account the time value of money and the riskiness of the project**.

We can see that Campaign A (regularly promoted customers) has a Net Present Value of £97.70 ie value of the profit stream we expect to receive (£30.00 this year, £22.50 next year, and so on) in today's money is £97.70.

Campaign B, however, has only one year in which it delivers a profit. This is the current year and so its Total Present value is the same as its Net Value.

As our aim is to maximise our company's profitability and value, we should always choose the alternative that generates the highest expected Net Present Value, so in this case we would run with Campaign B.

Direct marketing, accountable advertising

The inter-relationship between costs, revenue and activity – combined with the statistical analysis of performance – is the cornerstone of direct marketing. Bringing the information generated by these analyses to the decision-making process has earned direct marketing the title of **most accountable form of advertising**.

But be warned: it is easy for direct marketing's accounting techniques to be abused, although not necessarily intentionally. They do require a lot of effort. The effort, however, is well rewarded. Better decisions are made, not only because better information is available more readily, but also because in building the models, marketers develop a much greater understanding of their business – which is why it is equally vital to non-financial managers.

In the next chapter the author will look at the components that make up revenue and costs in more detail, and show how these are used to arrive at the profit and loss account for a single event.

Chapter 2.5

Revenue, costs and profit – a closer look

This chapter includes:

- ❑ **Accounting definitions made easy**
- ❑ **Why direct marketing P&Ls are special**
- ❑ **Costs: The Famous 5**
- ❑ **Types of cost: attributable, non-attributable**
- ❑ **Using "Relativities"**
- ❑ **Forecasting and Breakeven**
- ❑ **A warning about marginal costing**

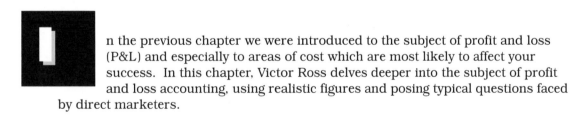

In the previous chapter we were introduced to the subject of profit and loss (P&L) and especially to areas of cost which are most likely to affect your success. In this chapter, Victor Ross delves deeper into the subject of profit and loss accounting, using realistic figures and posing typical questions faced by direct marketers.

There is a lot of confusion about profit, says Ross, some of it to do with moral considerations, but more often, he says, it stems from imprecise definitions and our failure to understand the different accounting conventions.

In most respects, profit from direct marketing is no different from profit derived from any other marketing venture. But – and it is a big "but" – in direct marketing P&Ls are not something to be summarised annually, quarterly or even monthly. They are tools to be used constantly for evaluating alternative courses of action and for allocating resources on an event-by-event basis.

Once more we start with some simple definitions.

New in this edition. This more advanced look at direct marketing P&L accounting did not appear in our first edition.

Victor Ross, Marketing Management Consultant

After a spell as free-lance writer and journalist Victor Ross joined Lintas, then a Unilever house agency, as a copywriter.

From there he made his move to UK Reader's Digest where he spent the next 30 years, doing every kind of job, including that of Chairman during the last four years of his employment.

He was involved in the creation and build-up of many of the Digest's continental editions – most intimately the Swiss, Dutch, Italian and Portuguese companies.

While his main interest has always been the management of creativity, Ross did not neglect the institutional side of the business, believing that he owed a duty where he had reaped so many benefits.

He was founder-president of the Association of Mail Order Publishers, the first representative of direct marketing in the Councils of the Publishers' Association and the Advertising Association; he negotiated the first rebate contract awarded to a mail order house by the Post Office; he was the industry's spokesman on data protection during the protracted negotiations with the Data Protection Registrar which led to the first Code of Practice in that field, and became the first direct marketing representative to sit on the Home Office Data Protection Tribunal.

Both the advertising and the direct marketing fraternities have chosen to honour him, and among many distinctions received, he greatly prizes the award of an Hon. Fellowship of the IDM. Today Ross is active as an author on marketing management, as a speaker and teacher, and as a consultant working with continental direct marketing companies eager to acquire British know-how.

Victor Ross FIDM
Worten Mill
Great Chart
Nr Ashford
Kent TN23 3BS

Chapter 2.5

Revenue, costs and profit – a closer look

What is profit?

Profit is the most widely-used measure of business success for three good reasons:

- ✔ It is the ideal basis for calculating the rewards of owners and managers.
- ✔ It is the basis on which business is taxed.

✔ It reduces disparate commercial activities to a common denominator, thus allowing comparisons and choices to be made, most importantly the allocation of resources.

But what **is** profit? Where does it stem from? Here is a statement of the obvious – or so it would seem:

> Profit
>
> Profit accrues when the revenue obtained from a commercial transaction is greater than its cost, or: <u>Revenue less Cost = Profit</u>

It sounds simple, but ask any three accountants what the profit on a commercial transaction is and they will come up with three different answers. Why? Because they will each have a different definition of what constitutes revenue – and what to include in each area of cost.

What is revenue?

Let us look at revenue first. Take the case of a coupon ad in a magazine offering a pair of earrings on approval, to be paid for in cash or in three instalments. (We shall use this example throughout the first part of this chapter.)

What is the revenue for such a promotion? Is it:

? The number of orders received (including credit orders) multiplied by the price?

? The amount above less the value of orders screened out by credit checks?

? The value of cash plus first instalments actually received, plus payments still outstanding?

? The amount of money banked at the end of the collection process, with all returns credited, money-back claims satisfied, and bad debts written off?

It is easy to see that each of the four totals above can represent a different sum of money (although in an ideal world they'd all come out the same in the end). We could have gone on inventing variations on the definition of revenue.

But for purposes of calculating profit, net revenue has to be:

> Net Revenue
>
> The amount of money banked at the end of the collection process, with all returns credited, money-back claims satisfied, and bad debts written off.

So talk about revenue is loose talk. There are actually **two** basic categories of revenue (as well as several stations in between). They are:

- ✔ Gross Revenue
- ✔ Net Revenue

What is Net Revenue in direct marketing?

We've looked at gross revenue. Its definition is simple: the value of orders received at the selling price.

But net revenue in direct marketing is less obvious, even to experienced accountants. There are four important facts of direct marketing life that lead us to our own definition:

These 4 direct marketing special conditions are:

! Credit checks will eliminate some orders at the outset.

! Distance selling will result in some goods being returned.

! Requests for refunds will occur and have to be honoured.

! Credit offers will inevitably attract some bad debts.

Any or all of these may erode GROSS revenue as follows:

GROSS REVENUE	= Value of orders received (excluding VAT)
Less	Orders not accepted
	= ADJUSTED GROSS REVENUE (AGR)
Less	Value of goods returned under approval
Less	Refunds under "money-back" guarantee
Less	Bad debts, whole or part
	= NET REVENUE

So now we have a new, improved definition of profit, one which is likely to prove a far better starting point for us in direct marketing:

Profit = Net Revenue less Costs

Is that it, then? Well, no. We still have to ask ourselves exactly how "net" is our net revenue? Have we forgotten anything? What about credit card charges? What about the costs of administering all those stages – the credits, the money-back claims, the bad debts written off? We are beginning to see why P&L in direct marketing has its own rules.

Costs: The Famous 5

The scope for argument about revenue is nothing compared with the scope for argument about costs.

Identifying the costs of every activity, tracking down every last one of them, is vital to ensure that we do not kid ourselves about whether a client, a department, a product, or a campaign is profitable or not. More advertising businesses go bust from losing track of costs than from losing track of clients!

It is convenient to group direct marketing costs under five main headings which we shall use throughout this chapter. We call them:

The Famous 5	
1.	Cost of product
2.	Cost of fulfilment
3.	Cost of promotion
4.	Cost of finance
5.	Cost of overheads

Every cost in a direct marketing operation can and must be allocated to one of these five broad categories. The ability to allocate costs correctly, and to be aware of relationships between the categories, is one of the marks of a seasoned direct marketer.

We now look at each of the Famous five in turn:

1. Cost of product

This is the cost of making or buying-in whatever is being sold. It may be a single item, for example earrings, without any value added by the vendor. Or it can be a long list reflecting, say, the complicated editorial-cum-manufacturing process of producing a book with an extended period of gestation requiring research, outside contributors, editors, proofreaders, artists; paper, printing, binding, and so on.

2. Cost of fulfilment

Fulfilment covers the costs of receiving orders, despatching goods, handling returns, collecting the money, and so on. Fulfilment costs bridge the distance between seller and buyer.

Customer service (telephone answering, correspondence) is usually included under this heading, and sometimes service departments like computer operations and the warehouse. But these are arbitrary allocations since an in-house computer (or a computer bureau) may serve a number of departments – from payroll to research – and ought to charge out its services accordingly.

3. Cost of promotion

Promotion includes every cost associated with selling and advertising. In our chosen earrings example, the costs are clear-cut and simple.

But suppose we were selling the earrings by direct mail: we would then have the costs of name selection; designing, printing, addressing and perhaps personalising the mailing piece; sorting and postage; and possibly an incentive. These costs are not difficult to recognise, but they need careful tracking and recording.

4. Cost of finance

The capital employed in financing the operation has a cost, all too often ignored even by sophisticated marketers.

For example, if you borrow money to finance a campaign (eg to pay for the earrings before you have sold them), the interest on the loan is part of the cost of the campaign and should be charged to it.

But if the money is already in the business, does its use still have a cost? The answer is an emphatic YES. The cost of that money is the alternative use you might put it to, which includes depositing it in the bank and collecting the interest.

So, the minimum cost of depriving yourself of the use of money while it finances a campaign, or while you "advance" the purchase price to your customers (waiting for them to repay you on the never-never), is **the current rate of interest which you would otherwise earn on the money**.

These are not just games for accountants to play, but vital decision-making factors when you compare, say, the relative merits of offering one or two years' credit. The latter may increase response, but not enough to pay for the use of money tied up.

5. All the other costs: The Overheads

Finally we come to No 5 in our Famous Five: the Overheads – all those remaining costs which it is impossible, illogical, or too costly to attribute to identifiable chunks of revenue.

An archetypal overhead is the cost of management on the basis that management's efforts are evenly spread over all activities. Another is the office rent. Likewise the cost of clean towels, plants in the reception area, the maintenance man, and so on.

But purists can quite rightly find flaws in this, too. They will argue that there is no reason why senior management should not keep timesheets and charge out their "services" accordingly, as do solicitors and auditors. And why should building costs not be allocated on the basis of space occupied?

There is, of course, opportunity for abuse in blood-hounding every last penny back to what it was spent on, but there is more abuse by idle managers who cannot be bothered to attribute costs at all, shoving everything into Overheads, allowing them to become a monstrous, swollen ragbag. Fortunately, later in this chapter you will be offered a rule of thumb to alert you to such abuses. (Watch out for "Relativities".)

In practice, in the best-regulated businesses, some of the cost of, say, computer operations will appear under Fulfilment, some under Promotion, some in other categories, and only the irreducible, unattributable balance under Overheads.

The 4 fundamental characteristics of costs

Before we start looking at actual examples of direct marketing costs, we must distinguish four fundamental characteristics of every cost. Is the cost we are looking at:

? Attributable (as we have been discussing)?

? Non-attributable (ditto)?

? Variable?

? Fixed?

Is it attributable? If so, to what?

Attributable costs (also called direct costs) are costs that would not have arisen had the revenue-producing activity not taken place, eg there would have been no bill for space if there had been no advertisement for the earrings; the cost is wholly and directly attributable to the revenue produced by the ad.

Is it an overhead, ie non-attributable?

Non-attributable costs include such costs as the marketing manager's salary which would have been paid whether or not the earring ad had run. Senior salaries and office expenses like rent, heat, etc, are not usually attributed but treated as Overheads.

Is it a variable cost? Does it depend upon activity levels?

Does the cost go up or down according to the level of sales? The archetypal variable cost is product cost. The more earrings sold, the more that must be bought in. Closely linked to the number of products sold may be handling costs since these will also vary with the number of orders received and products despatched.

Variable costs may not show a straight-line increase, ie they may not be **directly** proportional to the level of activity because of economies of scale, eg quantity discounts. This point will be taken up under **marginal** costs (page 2.5-21), but the principle remains unaffected.

Is it a fixed cost?

Fixed costs are those that do not vary according to the amount of activity. For example, creative costs may be constant whether our ad runs once only or every week for a year. Sell one pair of earrings or sell a thousand pairs, fixed costs remain the same.

What category of costs?

Now we come to our first worked example in this chapter.

We are ready to list all the costs of a hypothetical campaign, allocate them under the Famous Five headings, and mark each one according to whether it is attributable or not, variable or not. This is the fun bit. We are going to think of every cost that could possibly arise in connection with a campaign (eg to sell earrings through a press ad).

Remember: Some costs under the headings of Fulfilment and Promotion have easily attributable elements, such as the despatch of goods, as well as non-attributable elements such as the maintenance of the database.

Students: you may like to conceal the right-hand columns before attempting this exercise. Some explanations follow.

Costs of a typical direct marketing campaign

	a = attributable cost o = overhead	v = variable cost f = fixed cost
1. Cost of product		
1.1 Manufacture	a	v
1.2 Design	a	f
1.3 Royalty	a	v
1.4 Packaging	a	v
2. Fulfilment		
2.1 Order intake	a or o	v
2.2 Product despatch	a	v
2.3 Product returns	a or o	v
2.4 Warehouse and storage	o	f
2.5 Billing & collection, correspondence	a or o	v
3. Promotion		
3.1 Agency fee	o	f
3.2 Artwork	a	f
3.3 Space (media cost)	a	f
3.4 Reply postage	a	v
3.5 Incentive	a	v
4. Finance	a or o	v
5. Overheads		
5.1 Promotion dept, including research	o	
5.2 Production dept	o	
5.3 Fulfilment & warehouse	o	
5.4 Computer operations	o	
5.5 Building & maintenance	o	
5.6 Accounts	o	
5.7 Management	o	

A closer look at some individual costs

For the previous example we chose a simple campaign. Our allocations are logical and conventional (although this does not mean that another manager might not treat some items differently). **The important point is that every cost item is allocated somewhere and none is forgotten.**

Below we have picked out a few items which call for more comment, as follows:

Royalty

In addition to a fixed design fee for our product, we may have contracted to pay a royalty per item sold. This is common practice in book and music publishing but can occur in other fields.

Packaging

Remember the need for extra cartons for repacking re-usable returned goods.

Order intake costs

These are costs that arise in handling orders as they are received: order entry into customer records, screening, output of despatch documents, etc. They may be dealt with, in practice, in one of the following three ways:

? Time and cost the effort involved and attribute it strictly. This is suitable when the effort is large or unusual, or special accuracy is required.

? Make an estimate of the costs of recurring work and attribute on that basis. This is a compromise method.

? Regard all costs (of computer ops) as an overhead to be allocated by department or revenue source. This ensures "recovery" of the cost but does nothing to further the study of P&L. However, it might be the right approach, for example where a single operator handles hundreds of different transactions in a day.

Product returns

The cost of handling returns tends to get submerged in fulfilment overheads because returns pass through so many hands – unpacking, account crediting, inspection, refurbishing, repacking, etc. It is generally easier to calculate an average cost per unit returned – or treat the entire cost as a fulfilment overhead.

Occasionally a product will be returned in large numbers because it is faulty and extra staff must be hired to handle it. Clearly this has to be a charge against that product.

Warehousing and storage costs

The cost of a warehouse is fixed, certainly in the medium term, although in the long run parts of it can be let (or extra space acquired) and staff levels can vary. Most companies with a warehouse of their own treat it as an overhead.

Promotion

Had we chosen to sell our earrings by direct mail, additional questions would arise, eg how to attribute the cost of name selection and maintenance of the database?

Should we try to allocate these often considerable costs campaign by campaign, selection by selection? The answer almost certainly has to be no: they are an overhead.

The same goes for staff. While it is possible, by means of timesheets, to attribute staff costs to discrete marketing efforts, the system tends to break down. It is therefore generally accepted practice to put inside staff into overheads. Freelances brought in on an ad hoc basis are almost by definition attributable.

Overheads

By now it is obvious that overheads are not an immutable concept. According to circumstance, convention, effort involved, and the transaction, the same costs may appear as an overhead in one company's P&L and as an attributable cost in another's.

More important is the realisation that no cost is fixed for ever. Even chairmen and skyscrapers can be got rid of!

What have we discovered so far?

It is time to recap on what we have learned, and to draw up a few basic rules.

Rule 1. Unless every element of a P&L has been captured, true profit cannot be established. Self-deception will damage your wealth.

Rule 2. P&L brings together net revenue and the costs of obtaining it. The more accurate and painstaking the attribution of costs to the appropriate revenues, the truer the profit picture that will emerge.

Rule 3. It is useful to categorise direct marketing costs under one or more of five headings, and to recognise that every cost falls into one of the following quadrants:

	Variable	Fixed
Attributable	eg Product	eg Original artwork
Non-attributable	eg Corporation tax	eg Buildings, Management

Rule 4. The Famous Five cost headings are really four – Product, Fulfilment, Promotion and Finance, all directly affected by trading – plus one: Overheads, ie the costs that tend to go on regardless and don't belong or don't fit into the four.

Rule 5. Whenever we face the problem of allocating salaries, wages and equipment costs, the temptation to avoid attribution and regard them as an overhead is great. Which of the three options to adopt – ie tracking precisely, estimating, or lumping them together under overheads – is a matter for careful judgement.

Rule 6. In a static situation, the simplest solution is the best. But as soon as something out of the ordinary happens, the red alert should go out. Changing the offer, the copy, the incentive, or any of a hundred other components, may affect costs in the most unexpected quarters; for example, extending the credit period affects Gross Revenue and Finance Costs.

Rule 7. One of the tests of a well-run direct marketing company is low Overheads – not only because they show that the managers are cost-conscious, but also that they have made great efforts to attribute costs to specific headings.

The art of attribution

Good direct marketing management, then, involves careful attribution of as many costs as possible. So let us now look at the purpose and art of attribution more closely.

In the good old jargon-free days, attribution was referred to as good book-keeping, but the purpose has always been the same: to avoid misleading oneself about the state of the business.

Direct marketing is different: with direct marketing, P&L can be studied at the micro level for almost every action, and rough P&L calculations are a daily routine, almost instinctive to the good direct marketer.

This is due to what is often referred to as the accountability of direct marketing. What is actually meant is its countability. Nearly every direct marketing revenue is traceable to its source and therefore to the costs that gave rise to it.

However, the level of refinement at which you practise attribution depends on what you are trying to make a judgement about.

> **If you are comparing one test with another**, only the most meticulous hunt for the respective costs will give you the answer.
>
> **If you are trying to judge an entire department**, it doesn't matter nearly as much if you have not disentangled its attributable costs from its Overheads.
>
> **If you are judging the performance of the entire business**, allocation among the Famous Five is almost irrelevant, so long as all the beans have been counted somewhere.

A digression about accountants – don't read this if you are one!

Before we go any further, perhaps it is time for a kind word about "Suits". Accountants don't always enjoy a good press. Yet they often end up running things like film corporations, advertising agencies, record companies and publishing houses. The sad truth is that creative folk rarely understand the basics of P&L. Accountants know that costs have to be recovered before a profit can be posted. They understand, often better and quicker than anyone else, the connectedness of the Famous Five: that if you make a radical change in one, there may be repercussions in the others. They appreciate the danger of lowering the unit cost of a product by increasing the quantity ordered beyond what can be sold. Yet how many traders (especially publishers) have made this elementary mistake again and again, to the point of bankruptcy.

Respectable accountants would certainly jib at our stripped-down version of the earrings account. But then their business is to consolidate operations rather than look at one in particular. This means bringing in elements we have ignored, such as taxes – both VAT and corporate – which add nothing to the evaluation of marketing effectiveness. Accountants would bring into the equation the value of re-usable returns, write-offs, timing factors such as "expensing" and cash flow, risk management and investment policy. They would have something to say about research and the cost of testing.

But in the context of judging alternative marketing options, these become relevant only when a change of strategy has significant secondary effects, eg when the introduction of a powerful incentive, leading to a higher response, provokes such high returns as to create inventory problems. Meanwhile, as direct marketers, we could do worse than continue to study our micro P&Ls – and stay close to our accountant.

4 more useful P&L tools

Let us assume that we know now which costs produced which revenues. We need a few more useful tools to make full use of this precious information. Four of the most useful tools, which we now explore in turn, are:

✔ P&Ls compiled **after** the event (per ad, per product, etc)

✔ The "Relativities"

✔ The P&L forecast

✔ The Breakeven calculation

The P&L, compiled after the event, tells you how much money has been made from a particular marketing effort (eg a single mailing or advertisement, a TV campaign, or the lifetime of the product). In the following pages we shall discuss two typical P&Ls, a simple one relating to our earrings example (Table I), and a more complex one relating to books (Table II).

The "Relativities" are a useful concept enabling the crafty manager to practise the mental arithmetic of profitability. Again we shall demonstrate in terms of the simple offer (Table I) and the more complex offer (Table II).

The P&L forecast. Forecasting is what direct marketing is all about! It takes a number-cruncher to tell you what has happened, but only a marketer knows what is going to happen – or thinks he knows. How? By practising the wiles described under forecasting.

The Breakeven calculation is what comes to your rescue when you have no precedent or test results to go on. Breakeven calculation has been described as nothing more than "Relativities stood on their head so that the answers drop out at the bottom". How to perform this trick is the subject of Table III and is also discussed as part of forecasting.

... and a useful concept: The Contribution

The Contribution represents the amount of money by which the business will be better off as a result of having engaged in a particular activity. When evaluating tests, one tends to look at the Contribution rather than at Net Profit, since overheads are not likely to vary much between tests.

Post-event P&Ls – useful tool No 1

We now look at a P&L using figures such as might have emerged from running our earrings ad (Table I on the next page).

Let us ask ourselves a few questions (which you may like to answer after studying the table and before reading on):

? Was the effort worthwhile?

? Was the effort profitable?

? Were all the costs correctly attributed?

? Were all the costs recovered?

Table I: Profit and Loss Account of a single advertisement and what it can tell us

Statistics

A. Selling Price	£25 + £2.50 p&p	
B. Orders	1,000	
C. Failed Credit Screen	27	
D. Despatches	973	= (Despatches x Price = Adjusted Gross Revenue (AGR)
E. Returns & Refunds	111	

	Units	£	% AGR	% Net Rev
Despatches (AGR)	973 (1)	26,757.50	100	
Returns/Refunds	111	3,052.50	11.4	
Bad Debts (whole or part)		1,787.50	6.7	
Net Revenue		21,917.50	81.9	100
Product Cost*				
Earnings (per order)	£4.73 x D	4,602.29		
Cartons	£0.11 x D	107.03		
Total		4,709.32	17.6	21.5
Fulfilment Cost*				
Product Despatch (2)	£2.84 x D (3)	2,763.32		
Returns & Refurb	£1.50 x E	166.50		
Billing & Collection (4)	£0.99 x D	963.27		
Total		3,893.09	14.5	17.8
Promotion Costs*				
Artwork and Typesetting		2,000.00		
Space Cost & Freepost Replies		6,300.00		
Total		8,300.00	31.0	37.9
Finance Cost* (5)		210.00	0.8	0.9
Total Attributable Costs		17,112.41	63.9	78.1
Contribution		4,805.09	18.0	21.9
Overheads*		2,192.00	8.2	10.0
Net Profit (before tax)		2,613.09	9.8	11.9

(1) Orders less credit screen failures (B-C)
(2) Includes order intake, cartoning, delivery, postage
(3) Note cost not fully recovered (see A)
(4) Reminders to late payers only
(5) Assume 80% instalments, average outstanding 2 months @ 8%
* The Famous Five

Was the effort worthwhile? If the ad had not run, the business would have been £4,805 worse off – £4,805 is the "Contribution" to Overheads and profit and therefore the amount that has to be exceeded by any alternative activity proposed in place of the ad.

Was it profitable? Yes. A return (net profit before tax) of around 9.8% of the Adjusted Gross Revenue (AGR) is not unreasonable.

Were all the costs correctly attributed and recovered? Yes. In this case Order Intake, often treated as an overhead as we have seen, was allocated to Fulfilment and attributed to Product Despatch.

"Relativities" – useful tool No 2

"Relativities", as the name suggests, show how the Famous Five costs relate to each other in an easily assimilable form. To do this we simply convert them to percentages of the Adjusted Gross Revenue.

In the case of our earrings ad (Table I) these are as follows:

Adjusted Gross Revenue	100
Net Sales Revenue	81.9
Product Cost	17.6
Fulfilment Cost	14.5
Promotion Cost	31.0
Finance Cost	0.8
Contribution	18.0

Once you have established a norm for what your relativities **should** be, such a summary quickly draws your attention to any serious deviations.

In our example, credit checks, returns, and bad debts reduced the gross by about 20% because the ad was initially open to all-comers.

Product Costs were unusually low at under 20%. This raises the question whether we charged too much, or could have added value in some way and thus, by reducing returns, obtained higher net sales leaving us with higher profits.

Finance Costs are negligible because 20% of payment were in cash and 80% of the balance was outstanding for an average of only two months at 8% interest.

You can see that Relativities make you think!

A different P&L example (Table II)

To reinforce the explanations covered so far, and to introduce a few concepts not yet dealt with, we turn to a different P&L example (Table II, overleaf). This time we are looking at a quality book being sold direct by the publishers to a selected segment of their customer list.

Table II: Profit and Loss Account, book sale to publisher's own list

Statistics

A. Selling Price	£25.00 + £2.95 p&p
B. Quantity Mailed	3,000,000
C. Orders	213,804 (= 7.126% response)
D. Failed Credit Screen	840
E. Despatches	212,964 (orders minus failed credit screen (C-D)
F. Returns & Refunds	20,864

	Units	£	% AGR.	% Net Revenue
Despatches	212,964	5,952,344	100	
Returns/Refunds	20,864	583,148	9.8	
Bad Debts (whole or part)		142,856	2.4	
Net Revenue		5,226,340	87.8	100
Product Cost				
Editorial		184,512	3.1	3.5
Art		202,368	3.4	3.9
Inputting		28,808	0.5	0.6
Paper		404,736	6.8	7.7
Printing		220,224	3.7	4.2
Binding		291,698	4.9	5.6
Sub Total Manufacturing		1,332,346	22.4	25.5
Cartons & Cartoning		130,944	2.2	2.5
Total Product Cost		1,463,290	24.6	28.0
Fulfilment Cost				
Order Entry, etc	£0.17 x C	36,346	0.6	0.7
Product Despatch	£1.93 x E	411,020	6.9	7.9
Returns/Refurb/Replace	£1.04 x F	21,699	0.4	0.4
Billing & Collection	£0.61 x E	129,908	2.2	2.5
Total Fulfilment Cost		598,973	10.1	11.5
Promotion Cost				
Name Selection & Addressing	£0.03 x B	90,000	1.5	1.7
Mailing Materials	£0.35 x B	1,050,000	17.6	20.1
Sorting & Postage (inc reply postage)	£0.15 x B	450,000	7.6	8.6
Incentive (contrib to prize draw)	£0.02 x B	60,000	1.0	1.2
Test Costs		112,000	1.9	2.1
Total Promotion Cost		1,762,000	29.6	33.7
Finance Cost				
Editorial – pre-sale		14,000	0.2	0.3
Instalments – post-sale		66,000	1.1	1.3
Total Finance Cost		80,000	1.3	1.5
Total Attributable Costs		3,904,263	65.6	74.7
Contribution		1,322,077	22.2	25.3
Overheads				
Editorial & Art		136,000	2.3	2.6
Production inc salaries		26,120	0.4	0.5
Fulfilment		199,000	3.3	3.8
Promotion		266,000	4.5	5.1
General & Admin		177,000	3.0	3.4
Total Overheads		804,120	13.5	15.4
Net Profit (before tax)		517,957	8.7	9.9

Remember the priorities: correct and complete attribution, total recovery of costs and a realistic approach to overheads.

Let us now compare the difference between our book offer to a house list of likely buyers with our earrings offer to the general public (Tables I and II).

Net revenue is higher at 87.8% of Adjusted Gross Revenue.

Returns and bad debts are lower owing to methodical selection of target audience for this offer.

Product cost is higher at 24.6%, which includes editorial costs.

Fulfilment cost is lower, reflecting economies of scale.

Promotion cost, although lower, at 29.6% is fairly typical of a high-response direct mail offer. We have included 1% for a prize draw (2p per name) and 1.8% (£112,000) towards the cost of product and promotion testing, ie sample selection, creating and mailing of test material.

Finance cost includes cost of stage payments to contributors over the book's three-year gestation, ie editorial costs pre-sale.

Contribution at 22.2% is higher. Note overheads are allocated to ensure full recovery of non-attributable costs. There may be a bit of over-recovery here, which will be adjusted at the end of the accounting period if not needed.

Overheads Production covers salaried staff seeing the book through all stages of its development.

Net profit at 8.7% AGR is not brilliant, **but the mailing has absorbed the full cost of originating the product** (£570,808), ie editorial, artwork, typesetting, etc. Future sales will be free of this burden. (It would have been possible to spread origination costs over more than one print order by anticipating future sales, but to recover these costs with the first edition is the prudent course.)

Reading the Relativities again

The Relativities (cost percentages compared to Adjusted Gross Revenue) for our books example are shown below and compared with those for the earrings ad:

Books (Table II)		**Earrings (Table I)**	
AGR	100	AGR	100
Net Sales Revenue	87.8	Net Sales Revenue	81.9
Product	24.6	Product	17.6
Fulfilment	10.1	Fulfilment	14.5
Promotion	29.6	Promotion	31.0
Finance	1.3	Finance	0.8
Contribution	22.2	Contribution	18.0

For the books offer we have some 22% of AGR to cover Overheads and Profit. Since it is unlikely that we can do anything about Overheads in the short run, any improvement in profit (if this is what we ask of ourselves) is likely to come from aspects of either the Product or its Promotion.

At this point we could ask ourselves:

? Could we make the promotion more effective, eg by introducing another incentive that puts up net sales by more than its cost?

? Could we save on the product without losing elsewhere?

? Could we affect net sales in any other ways, eg 1% fewer returns (other things remaining equal) could add nearly £60,000 to profits.

Although the Relativities are no more than a template, you can see how useful they are to a marketing manager. For example, if your promotion percentage went up to 40%, your contribution would drop to under 12%, which would barely cover your overhead. Then what would you do? We'll leave you to think about that!

Forecasting – useful tool No 3

Most of the marketer's time is spent looking ahead rather than back. Forecasting what will happen, what **should** happen based on testing, is the direct marketer's main preoccupation. This is why we test and calculate and test again. And this is where the Relativities become invaluable. But what to test?

As the marketing manager, your instinct may be to test every possible deviation from a successful norm. But there is a limit to how many tests you can afford, set by time and money (and by the names at your disposal – never forget that testing consumes names as well as other resources).

Question: My creative department has put forward thirteen good ideas, how do I pick, say, three I can afford to try?

Answer: You use the Relativities as a simple mathematical model and interrogate it about the prospects for the tests.

For example, suppose your objective is to increase Contribution, and the test suggestions include (a) a 20% price increase; (b) manufacturing the item to a more expensive specification to add value; (c) using an advance letter to soften up prospects. In other words: (a) increasing revenue, (b) enhancing the product, or (c) beefing up the promotion – how do you assess the chances of success before the event?

Breakeven calculations – useful tool No 4

You answer the question by using the Relativities to perform breakeven calculations. This is both clever and simple. Instead of trying to guess what a 20% price increase will do, you turn the question on its head: how much lower a response, how many more returns can you accept and be no worse off? This lays a floor to the risk you would be prepared to accept. Once the figures have been calculated it is not too hard to judge whether there is a chance to come out with additional profit.

Let's do some Relativities and Breakeven forecasts

The Relativities model, as we have said, helps us to forecast what is likely to happen if we change any of the cost elements significantly. Let us now see this procedure in action by arming the model with some actual figures. We shall continue with our books example using the base data from Table II and the Relativities model drawn up from it. Please note that we ignore Overheads on the assumption that they will be the same whatever changes we make.

We are now looking at Table III below using the pro-rata values for 1,000 book despatches from Table II (percentages have been rounded).

Students and established marketers alike are invited to work through these calculations as they tell a lot about the differences between direct marketing P&Ls and those for more straightforward retailing ventures.

Table III: Relativities as a forecasting tool (books example continued)

		Original		Higher selling price £30					
		Column 1		Column 2		Column 3		Column 4	
		@ £25 + £2.95		@ £30 + £2.95		@ £30 + £2.95		@ £30 + £2.95	
		%		* Same contribution ***amount*** as control		* Same contribution ***percentage*** as control		* **Contribution increased by 4%** over control	
1	AGR	100	27,950	100	32,950	100	32,950	100	32,950
2	Returns	10	2,795	12	3,954	12	3,954	12	3,954
3	Bad Debts	2	559	3	989	3	989	3	989
4	Net Revenue	88	24,596	85	28,007	85	28,007	85	28,007
5	Product Cost	25	6,978	21.2	6,978	21.2	6,978	21.2	6,978
6	Fulfilment Cost	10	2,795	8.5	2,795	8.5	2,795	8.5	2,795
7	Finance Cost	2	559	1.8	600	1.8	600	1.8	600
8	Direct Cost – before promotion	37	10,332	31.5	10,373	31.5	10,373	31.5	10,373
9	Contribution – before promotion	51	14,264	53.5	17,634	53.5	17,634	53.5	17,634
10	Allowable Promotion	30	8,385	35.6	11,755	32.5	10,715	28.5	9,397
11	Direct Cost – after promotion	67	18,717	67.1	22,128	64	21,088	60	19,770
12	Contribution*	21	5,879	17.9	5,879	21	6,919	25	8,237
	% Response	6.6%		4.7%		?		?	

What we are going to do is introduce a higher selling price (£30 instead of £25) and see what promotion costs we can afford and hence the level of response we are likely to need, whilst still achieving specified levels of Contribution as explained below:

Column 1 is the Control, our established pattern of trading or our currently favoured option, showing a bottom-line Contribution of £5,879, or 21% of AGR.

Column 2 asks what level of response will be required at the higher price in order to maintain the same **amount** of Contribution, ie £5,879.

Column 3 asks what level of response will be required at the higher price to maintain the same **percentage** of Contribution, ie 21% of AGR.

Column 4 asks what level of response will be required at the higher price in order to deliver **a 4% increase in percentage contribution**, ie from 21% to 25%.

We now look at Column 2 taking each line in turn:

Adjusted Gross Revenue. Obviously this has increased over control as a result of the higher selling price.

Returns. We have increased these by 2% since responders are more likely to reject at the higher price. Actually they may not, but this is a useful precaution.

Bad Debts. We have increased these by 1% since higher prices tend to attract more bad debtors; again it may not happen, especially as we shall not mail known offenders.

Net Revenue. This has fallen from 88% in the control to 85%, the result of deducting the 2% and 1% for returns and bad debts respectively.

Product Cost. The unit cost does not change as the result of the higher price, although it is a lower percentage of AGR.

Fulfilment Cost. No change.

Finance Cost. There is a small upwards adjustment in this amount, since more money will be outstanding at any point during the collection cycle (although again it represents a slightly reduced percentage of AGR).

Direct costs BEFORE promotion. Asking a higher price will mean fewer orders per 100 pieces mailed. We must discover how much we can spend to get 1,000 orders, ie what our new allowable promotion cost will be. To do this we first total direct costs (product, fulfilment and finance) **excluding** promotion. In Column 2 this becomes £10,373.

Contribution BEFORE promotion. This is net revenue minus direct costs excluding promotion (lines 4–8).

Allowable promotion cost. Now we come to the line we have been waiting for. Remember we know what final contribution we are looking for (£5,879, as control). So what we have to spend on promotion now, at the higher price, is:

Contribution **before** promotion	£17,634	
Required contribution **after** promotion	£5,879	
Allowable promotion	£11,755	(lines 9–12)

Direct cost AFTER promotion. To complete our Relativities model we can now add the new allowable promotion cost we have calculated to our direct costs (line 11).

So what is the answer?

We know (from Table II) that the promotion cost of 1,000 mailings is £550 (or 55p each).

The control promotion budget (£8,385) therefore allows us to despatch 15,245 mailings to attract 1,000 orders, a required response of **6.6%**.

The Column 2 test promotion budget (£11,755) allows us to despatch 21,372 mailings to attract the same 1,000 orders, a required response of **4.7%**.

Is it likely? Is it acceptable? What do you think?

Our Relativities breakeven forecasting exercise has shed light on several questions. Is it **likely** that putting up the price of our book to £30 will cause a drop in response to 4.7%, the lowest response level we now know we can afford and still maintain the required contribution? If the response drops only to 5.5% we shall have increased the contribution; if it drops below 4.7%, we shall be worse off at the higher price.

Try these further breakeven calculations

Using Table III Columns 3 and 4, what percentage response will be needed at the higher price to maintain the levels of contribution stipulated for each, ie £6,919 (Column 3) and £8,237 (Column 4)?

Whilst no one can be sure of the outcomes of such experiments, at least using these so-called "R-Models" you will be better placed to answer confidently. What would you have said if someone had posed the question: "What will be the response if we increase the price to £30?", and you hadn't done your homework?

The cost-per-order conundrum

To close this chapter we examine a common marketing fallacy, ie that minimising cost-per-order (CPO) always equates with maximising profit. (Relativities tend to reinforce this impression.)

The fact is, the number of despatches is not infinitely expandable at a given cost. Suppose you have exhausted your best buyers lists, but there is another list which you can rent which produces orders more expensively, perhaps at just enough to cover Overheads and leave a small net profit. In such a case you would probably ignore the Relativities and do it. But ...

A word of warning about marginal costs

There is another way of looking at maximising profit. We can argue that the true costs of extending promotion into new territory are lower than our costs for the main campaign – because the **run-on** costs of manufacturing the product and producing the promotional materials are lower once fixed costs have been recovered.

In other words we can argue that we ought to be looking only at the **marginal costs** of any extra marketing effort. The same could be said for overheads. The whole contribution from additional activity would then go straight into net profit.

These are seductive arguments – and dangerous! There are times when "borderline" activity is justified; there are times when it leads directly to bankruptcy!

What advice can we give you, the marketing manager, to conclude our chapter on profit and loss? If in doubt, talk to your accountant!

Summary: Direct marketing IS different

One message of this chapter is that Direct Marketing has several unique features, chiefly because distance selling means goods returned, refunds, and (if credit is offered) orders eliminated by screening, bad debts, and the cost of instalments and their collection.

But there is another difference: in direct marketing we can often change our plans rapidly following, say, an unexpectedly high or low response. And this is where some quick P&L calculations will stand you in good stead.

The most important message is that because of the measurability of the effect of every action in Direct Marketing, you can construct a model of how revenues and costs will interact, and use it to get answers to the question: "What if ... ?"

Chapter 2.6

Calculating the lifetime value of a customer

This chapter includes:

- Why lifetime values?
- How long is a "lifetime"?
- Factors affecting lifetime span
- Two ways to calculate lifetime values
- Historical and projective approaches
- Discounting for the cost of capital
- Example calculation

One of the traditional benefits of direct marketing is its ability to generate immediate and measurable results. So far we have looked at profit and loss primarily in respect of single sales and short-term promotions.

But there is a measurement far more important than that for any single activity: the value of a customer during the entire period of their involvement with you, called the customer "lifetime". As customers have become more difficult and costly to recruit, the lifetime value of a customer (or LTV) has become **the** critical statistic. Once you know it, you are better placed to set allowable costs for recruitment and to allocate funds between different methods of acquisition.

In this chapter, Rick Courtheoux repeats his advice from the first edition of this Guide on precisely how to calculate lifetime values.

It is tempting to believe that, even if you do not actually calculate the LTV for each of your customers, recognising its importance is a good first step. Not enough, says Courtheoux, without accurate predictions you are just as likely to under-invest as to over-invest in customer acquisition.

New in this edition. Three new case studies plus an explanation of the discounting procedure.

Richard Courtheoux, Senior VP, Direct Marketing Technology

Rick has a BS degree from Yale, an MBA from the University of Chicago and an MS in Computer Science from the Weizmann Institute of Science. He has been a direct marketing consultant since 1978. Senior appointments have included Head of Quantitative Methods at agency Kestnbaum and Founder-President of Precision Marketing of Illinois. He is now Senior Vice-President and Head of Consulting Division at Direct Marketing Technology.

He has consulted for many of the world's best known direct marketing organisations, including L L Bean, Nieman-Marcus, Sears, Time-Life Books, Microsoft and Dell Computer. Services have included strategic development, statistical analysis, and database development.

Rick has presented the DMA's database seminar and is a member of several advisory boards representing direct marketing, including The National Centre for Database Marketing (USA). He is a frequent speaker at database and direct marketing conferences in America and Europe.

His areas of special interest include segmentation, statistical modelling, lifetime value estimation and product affinity analysis.

Richard Courtheoux
Senior Vice-President
Direct Marketing Technology
955 American Lane
Schaumburg IL 60173
E-mail = RickC@dmti.com

Chapter 2.6

Calculating the lifetime value of a customer

Why customer lifetime value is critical

New businesses must acquire customers before they can begin to cherish and nurture them. Even established businesses with high levels of loyalty need to recruit customers in order to replace those lost through attrition. Without new customers every business must eventually atrophy.

Yet, in every sphere of marketing the cost of recruiting new customers is escalating as businesses mature and competition intensifies. In order to grow, companies need to invest in customer acquisition, but the investments must be carefully justified to avoid quick ruin.

Customer lifetime value is the concept used by progressive database marketers to manage the customer acquisition and reactivation process. It is used to:

✔ Control customer acquisition investments.

- ✔ Identify critical target segments.
- ✔ Guide reactivation and retention efforts.
- ✔ Monitor and project business prospects.
- ✔ Make decisions about products and offers.

With customer lifetime value estimates a marketing manager can address each of the above issues in a financially justified, long-term oriented way. Customer lifetime value puts customer management at the core of the marketer's activities and decision-making.

Here are two real-life examples in which customer lifetime value has proved to be of enormous importance:

Car buyers stay loyal for decades

A major motor manufacturer wants to attract young adult customers to its brand, but is uncertain how much it can afford to invest to induce a first purchase. Studies of long-term car buying behaviour reveal that consumers are very likely to repeat purchase within a brand. This year's marketing spending, therefore, may influence very large purchase decisions for decades. This longer-term perspective justifies larger investments in new customer acquisition. And if this manufacturer does not take a long-term perspective, it is very likely that one or more of its competitors will. In other words, the manufacturer needs to estimate the long-term, or lifetime, value of each expensively acquired new buyer in order to know how much to invest in recruiting him or her.

Charity spends money to acquire future donors

A leading UK charity found that the cost of recruiting new donors significantly exceeded their first-year contributions. Analysis of its donor file showed, however, that over a ten-year period the value of a new supporter – in terms of donations, purchases, introductions to friends, etc – amounted to many times the initial cost of recruitment. Thus it could afford to invest in new donors. The question was: by how much? Calculating the lifetime value of each donor provided the answer.

In each of the above examples marketers who looked only at a one-year budget would make decisions which ignored long-term opportunities. Today's marketing databases allow managers to examine multi-year time spans to see how customer value develops over years.

What is "customer lifetime value"?

Lifetime value is a summary of the future profit expected from each name on your customer database. More precisely we can say:

> **The lifetime value of a new customer is the net present value of all future contributions to profit and overhead expected from that customer.**

This definition is particularly useful because it supports the decision areas listed above in a financially rigorous way. In fact, one of the benefits of using the lifetime value concept to manage marketing is that it facilitates understanding and communication between marketers and financial management.

How long is a "lifetime"?

The number of years you choose to describe a customer's lifetime will depend upon many factors concerned with your business, your market, and your objectives.

For example, each of the following will be highly relevant:

✔ **Product category.** Replenishment products tend to have longer lifetime value horizons. Durable products also tend to be associated with longer lifetime value periods.

✔ **Type of customer.** For example, businesses marketing to particular age ranges will have lifetime value periods which cover only the relevant age range.

✔ **Market stability.** High tech businesses or industries undergoing rapid regulatory reform may have shorter lifetime value horizons since long-term customer buying behaviour is especially difficult to project.

✔ **Company objectives.** Financially strong, strategically oriented companies will take a longer view of their customers' worth.

There is no industry standard number of years to use in estimating lifetime value, but it is usually reasonable to project over 5–10 years. One or two years more or less do not usually make a huge difference to the overall estimate. **The big mistake is not looking several years into the future, ie not taking any account whatever of lifetime values.**

The mistakes you are likely to make if you do not take account of customer lifetime value, in the simplest terms, are:

Overestimating a customer's value, believing that customers will return again and again, spending more as they become more "loyal" – and so you invest too much in their initial recruitment and early promotions.

Underestimating the customer, preferring to extract too large a contribution from the initial sale, overlooking the value of future sales – and so you invest too little in their initial recruitment and early promotions.

Factors affecting customers' lifetime performance

The lifetime value of a customer – or group of customers – will be affected by a large number of additional factors, among them:

Method of recruitment. For example, heavily incentivised recruits may well perform less well than customers who were not offered extraneous incentives.

Medium. Respondents from certain newspapers, eg the quality press, might be more expensive to acquire than those from other media, eg the so-called down-market tabloids, but perform better in the medium and long term.

Lists. Names on some lists will undoubtedly perform better over time than those on other lists, depending on how they were originally recruited and how they have subsequently performed (this information may not be fully known to you when you acquire the list).

Geodemographic factors. For example, owners of larger gardens may be better long-term prospects for garden products than small-to-medium house owners, although the differences might not be obvious at the time of recruitment.

In fact the list is virtually endless. Three popular differentials with catalogue marketers are:

- Source
- Type of merchandise first purchased
- Size/value of first order

Some hypothetical examples (based on real-life case studies) are shown in the charts that follow. They show how different factors typically influence the lifetime value calculation of different groups of customers.

Lifetime value by source of customer acquisitions

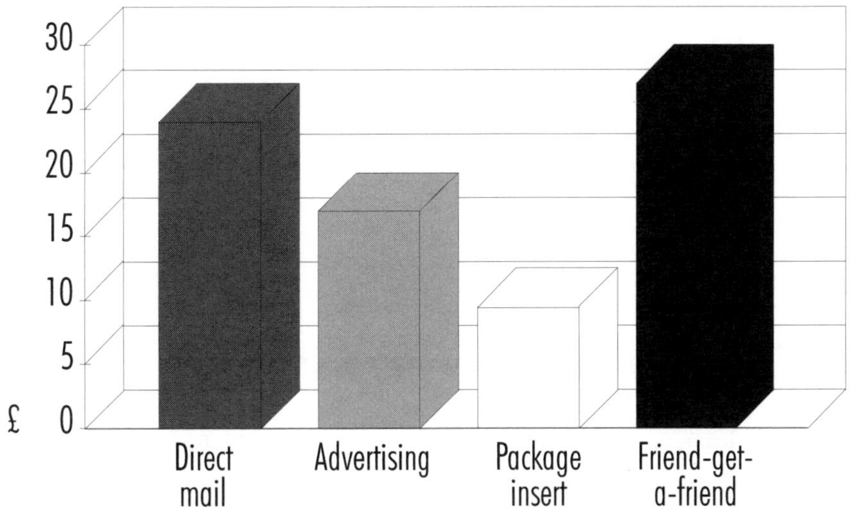

Lifetime value by merchandise first purchased

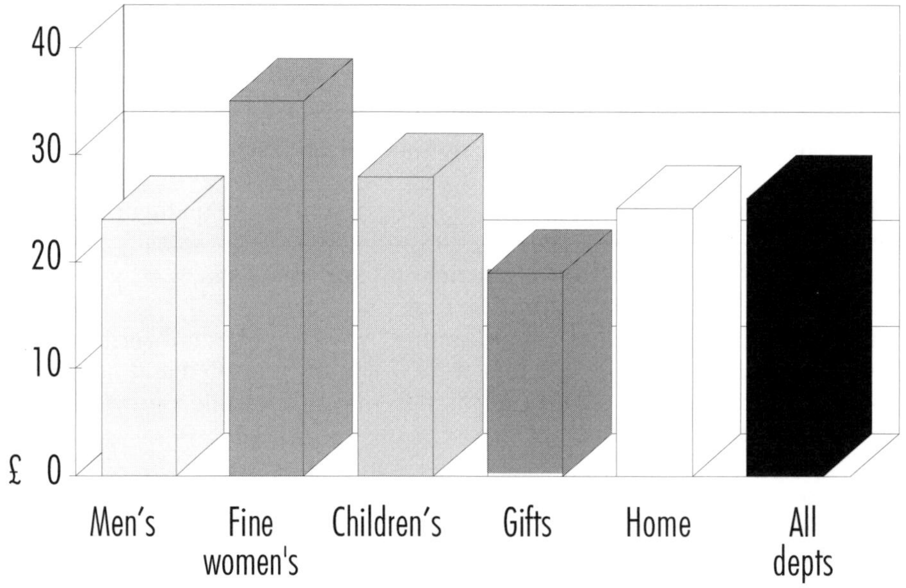

Lifetime value by size of first order

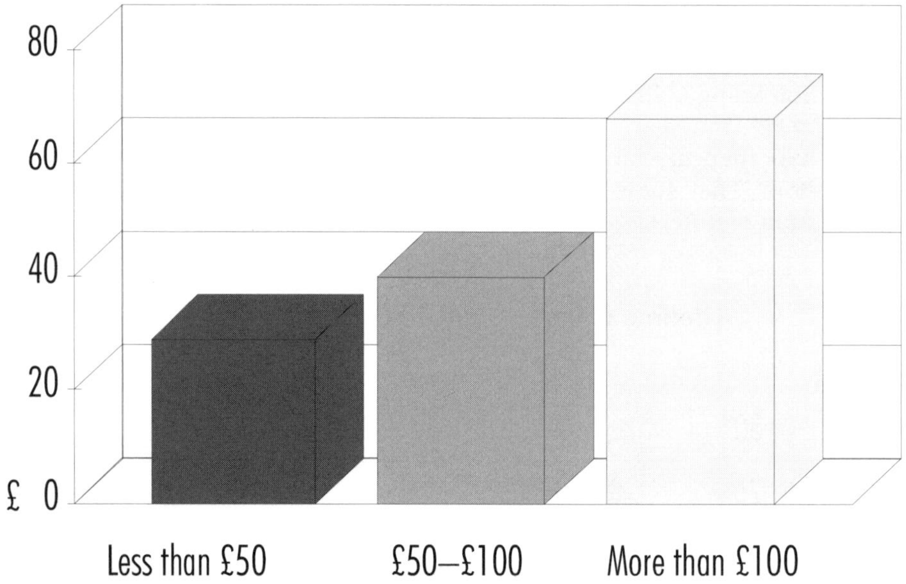

Making use of customer lifetime value

Lifetime value is a **number** that should be used to support marketing **actions**. The most important of those actions are now described.

1. Setting target customer acquisition investment limits

The most effective way to set target customer acquisition investment limits is to create a **ratio** of lifetime value to acquisition investment that has to be exceeded. **One reasonable limit is that lifetime value always be at least double the acquisition investment.** This provides a cushion against being too aggressive, since the lifetime value can deteriorate considerably without harm. On the other hand, all very beneficial investments will be pursued.

To grow or not to grow?

Marketing management at a catalogue company are planning its multi-year business development strategy. They are considering the possibility of not investing in new customer acquisition, investing only enough to replace existing customers who are lost. If no investment in customer acquisition is made, then the file size will shrink substantially. A modest investment in customer acquisition will maintain the current business size. However, a more significant investment in customer acquisition – ***but still less per name than the customer lifetime value*** *– will yield a file which grows in size over time.*

5-year file size by customer acquisition investment strategy

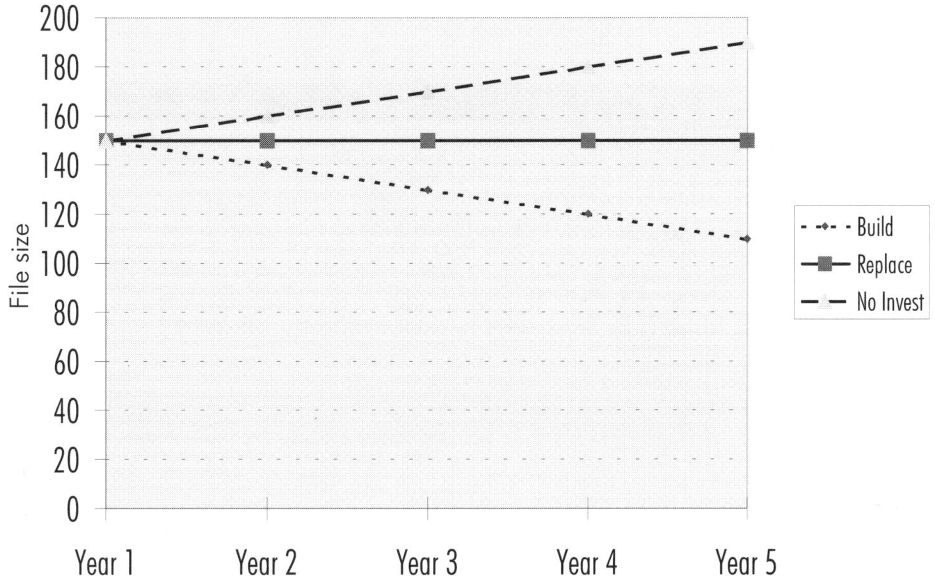

2. Allocating acquisition funds using lifetime value

Different sources of acquisition produce customers with different lifetime values. As already stated, different newspapers and magazines, different rented lists, and different segments of your own list will all affect the long-term value of customers recruited from each source.

Naturally, you should invest more in acquiring a highly valuable new customer than in acquiring a below average value customer.

When looking at possible sources of new customers it may be helpful to calculate the lifetime value-to-acquisition ratio for each of them. Then rank the sources based on that ratio. The resulting ranking can be used to prioritise the sources so that the best get used first and lower ranked sources are used only if the budget permits.

Which source produces the best customers?

A magazine publishing company analysed the lifetime value and acquisition cost per name of its subscribers. It then compared those two measures in the table below to develop a key perspective on its customer acquisition strategy. Which source do you think is most valuable to this publisher?

Lifetime value and acquisition cost by source

Source	Lifetime value	Cost per name	Ratio
A	12.59	4.32	2.91
B	3.87	1.68	2.30
C	20.41	5.67	3.60
D	7.37	2.27	3.25

Although Source B yields new customers at the lowest cost per name (1.68), the value of those names (3.87) is quite low relative to other sources. This company is better off acquiring the higher quality names from Source C at a higher cost per name. By examining the lifetime value-to-cost per name ratio in this example, it is clear that Source C should be used first, then Source D and so on.

3. Choosing customer acquisition products and offers

The lifetime value of a customer can depend on the type and value of their initial purchase. This can lead to decisions about which products and offers to use in the acquisition media. For example, **advertisements in acquisition media should feature products which produce customers of the highest lifetime value.**

Creative approaches and incentives might be used to build the number of people responding to an offer, but this sometimes produces customers of lower overall value. Different products and offers can be evaluated in terms of their lifetime value-to-cost ratio.

Which activity produces most long-term income?

An Association markets memberships, subscriptions, products and training seminars. It has to make important decisions about how to allocate its marketing funds among these various areas. To make those decisions correctly, it needed to see how much its members/customers were worth to it over several years. It found that there were some very different values in each line of business as illustrated below.

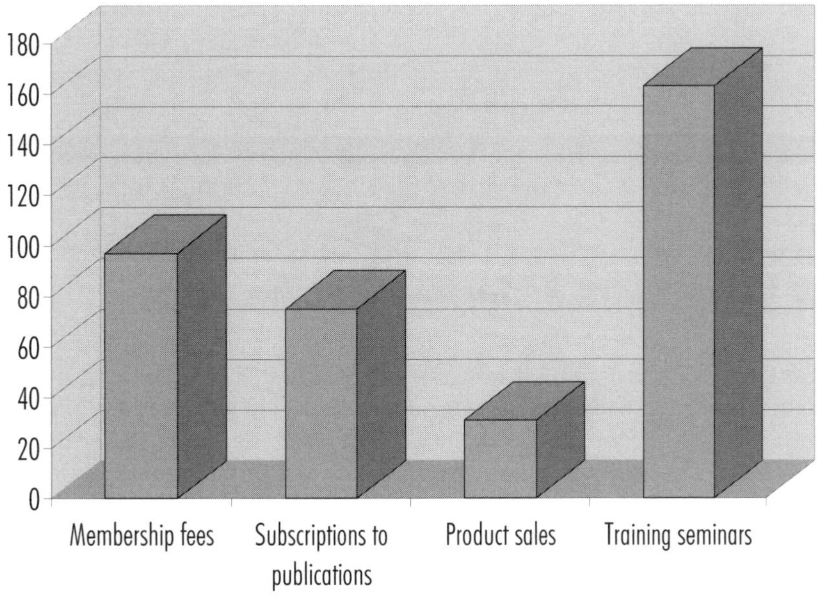

These results showed that the training seminar participants were by far the most valuable segment of customers while product buyers were the least valuable. Up to this point the largest effort was devoted to acquiring product buyers because they were the least expensive customers to acquire. It further emphasised that getting customers to buy training seminars was of strategic importance in developing the value of the customer base.

Two ways to calculate lifetime value

Businesses of any size can (and should) estimate their customers' lifetime values. Good estimates can be made using PCs and spreadsheet tools such as Excel or Lotus. The two approaches which have been found to be effective in estimating lifetime value are:

- ✔ **Historical.** This approach takes a group of customers acquired in the past and tracks all revenues and costs associated with them.

- ✔ **Projective.** This approach takes the most recently observed trends in customer behaviour and projects them into the future.

In stable businesses the two approaches will produce very similar results. However, the historical approach embeds in its calculations all the business decisions and market conditions for many prior years. Where a business – or its marketplace – is changing rapidly, these prior conditions may not be representative of the future, so the projective approach will give much more useful results. The relative advantages of the two approaches are summarised below.

Advantages of historical and projective lifetime values

Historical	Projective
Relatively simple to calculate and implement	Reflects most recent business conditions
Result is factual, not speculative	Can be done without many years of historical data
Easier to tie to financial statements	Easier to do "what if" analyses

How to calculate historical lifetime value

In practice, the historical lifetime value of a customer is calculated from that of a group of customers with similar characteristics. They might be a certain type of customer recruited from a specific source at a specific time. It is critical that the calculation be done by tracking a group which started at the same time.

Here are the four basic steps you will need to calculate an **historical** lifetime value:

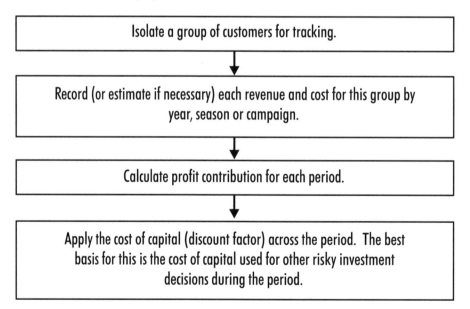

1. Isolate a group of customers for tracking.
2. Record (or estimate if necessary) each revenue and cost for this group by year, season or campaign.
3. Calculate profit contribution for each period.
4. Apply the cost of capital (discount factor) across the period. The best basis for this is the cost of capital used for other risky investment decisions during the period.

An example of an historical lifetime value calculation is shown on the facing page:

Historical lifetime value calculation

In this example we calculate the lifetime value of 1,000 customers who first bought in Autumn 1992, having just concluded the Spring 1996 campaign.

- *Autumn 1992 revenues, costs and contributions are subsequent to the first purchase. This is because it is much more informative to see the customer value separate from the investment costs.*

- *For simplicity all costs are grouped into one column. A more realistic calculation would enumerate the major distinct costs.*

- *The cost of capital (discount factor) used is 6% **per season**. This value was chosen to express the need for a very healthy financial return on investment in customer acquisition.*

Season	Total Revenues	Total Costs	Total Contribution	Discounted Contribution *	Cumulative Discounted Contribution
Autumn 92	4,000	2,400	1,600	1,600	1,600
Spring 93	18,000	10,000	8,000	7,547	9,147
Autumn 93	15,000	8,600	6,400	5,696	14,843
Spring 94	12,600	7,400	5,200	4,366	19,209
Autumn 94	10,600	6,300	4,300	3,406	22,615
Spring 95	8,900	5,500	3,400	2,541	25,156
Autumn 95	7,500	4,400	3,100	2,185	27,341
Spring 96	6,200	3,700	2,500	1,663	29,004
Total	82,800	48,300	34,500	29,004	

Cumulative discounted contribution

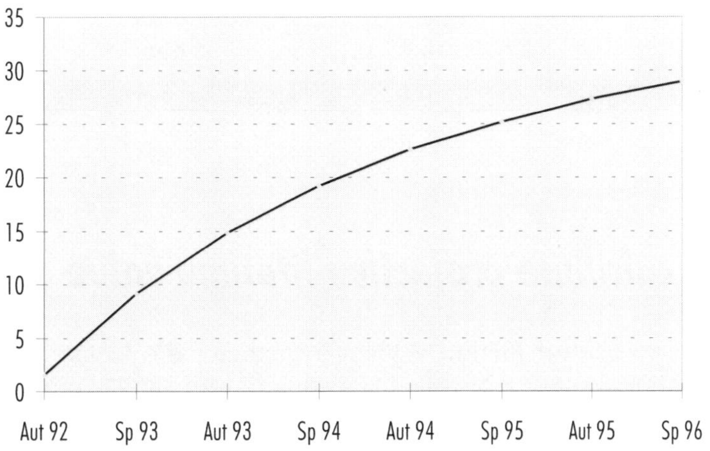

Conclusion

These 1,000 customers acquired in Autumn 1992 have an average lifetime value to date of 29.00 each. It is reasonable to assume that their value will increase in future seasons.

* For explanation of discounted contribution, see the following table and also the previous chapter.

How to calculate the discounted contribution

The reason for discounting the contribution is that revenue earned **now** is clearly worth more to the organisation than money earned later. Any future profit expected from a customer should be discounted according to how long we must wait for that profit. Remember, money was invested originally to acquire the customer, and there is always a cost of having money tied up.

To allow for this, lifetime value calculations must "discount" future earnings by an agreed percentage. In the example on the previous page, 6% **per season** was chosen. Using twice-annual adjustments is more accurate than once a year discounting.

In very simple terms, to calculate the discounted value of a season's contribution in our example, you divide the contribution by 1.06 (1 + 6%), and "power" it to the season number.

Thus:

Autumn 92	1,600 (no discounting for first season)	
Spring 93	8,000 divided by 1.06	= 7,547 (one season's discount)
Autumn 93	6,400 divided by 1.06^2	= 5,696 (two seasons' discount)
Spring 94	5,200 divided by 1.06^3	= 4,366 (three seasons' discount)

If you do not wish to use the "squared"/"cubed" mathematical notation, you can equally divide by 1.06 once, twice, three times according to the number of seasons/ years elapsed. Thus:

Autumn 93	6,400 divided by 1.06	= 6,038
	divided by 1.06	= 5,696

How to calculate projective lifetime value

The projective or future lifetime value of a customer is calculated on the basis of recent actual performance by cells of customers with similar purchasing characteristics. Cells may be defined in terms of score ranges, Recency/Frequency/ Value breaks, or other criteria.

Here are the basic steps for calculating projective lifetime value.

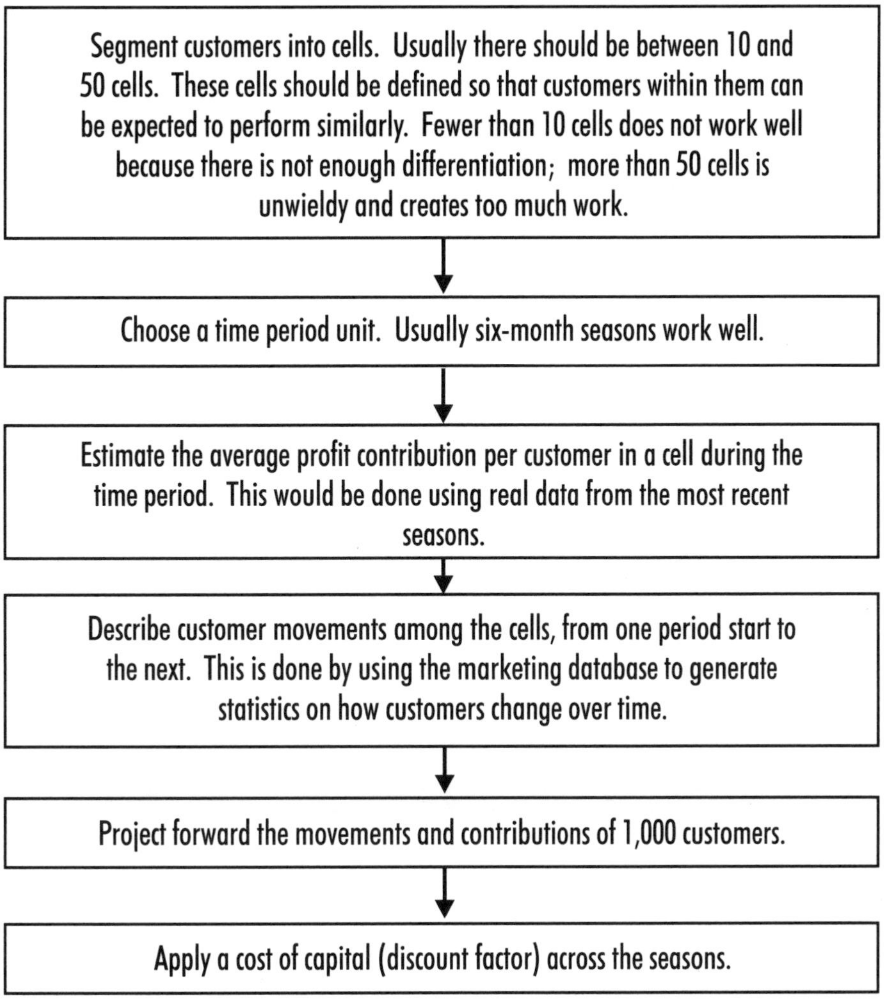
Segment customers into cells. Usually there should be between 10 and 50 cells. These cells should be defined so that customers within them can be expected to perform similarly. Fewer than 10 cells does not work well because there is not enough differentiation; more than 50 cells is unwieldy and creates too much work.
Choose a time period unit. Usually six-month seasons work well.
Estimate the average profit contribution per customer in a cell during the time period. This would be done using real data from the most recent seasons.
Describe customer movements among the cells, from one period start to the next. This is done by using the marketing database to generate statistics on how customers change over time.
Project forward the movements and contributions of 1,000 customers.
Apply a cost of capital (discount factor) across the seasons.

An example of a projective lifetime value calculation is illustrated overleaf.

The need for calculations, not guesswork

In today's highly competitive environment a company's major asset is its customer base. To grow this customer base, most companies need to invest in acquiring new customers and retaining or reactivating existing ones. This process is financially quite sensitive.

Customer lifetime value is the concept which brings together the marketer's need to grow the customer base with the financial division's need to optimise the impact of company investments. Marketers can find in it the justification for long-term oriented spending on customers. Financial analysts can use real database summaries of customer behaviour to estimate financial returns from marketing programmes.

It is not sufficient, however, to simply make general statements about customer value and long-term financial orientation. **For these concepts to have actionable meaning they must be attached to real calculations leading to estimates of customer lifetime value.** This chapter deals with two respected and time-tested methods for performing those calculations.

Projective lifetime value calculation

In this example we calculate the lifetime value of 1,000 customers who first bought in Autumn 1992.

- *Customers are segmented by recency of last purchase and grouped into six-month categories.*
- *Six-month seasons are used as the basis for all calculations.*
- *The discount factor is 6% per season.*

Season contribution per cell

Recency Group In Months	Average Revenues	Average Costs	Contribution per Customer
0 – 6	34.54	25.76	8.78
7 – 12	23.28	18.88	4.40
13 – 18	15.86	13.82	2.04
19 – 24	10.58	9.44	1.14
25 – 30	6.64	6.50	0.14
31 – 36	3.56	3.74	(0.18)
37+	0.00	0.00	0.00

This shows, for example, that an average customer who bought in the most recent six months will spend 34.54 in the next period. There will be 25.76 in costs associated with these sales leaving a contribution to profit and overheads of 8.78, and so on.

Season customer movements among cells

Start cell	End cell	Probability
0 – 6	0 – 6	0.25
	7 – 12	0.75
7 – 12	0 – 6	0.17
	13 – 18	0.83
13 – 18	0 – 6	0.12
	19 – 24	0.88
19 – 24	0 – 6	0.09
	25 – 30	0.91
25 – 30	0 – 6	0.06
	31 – 36	0.94
31 – 36	0 – 6	0.03
	37+	0.97
37+	37+	1.00

Here movements are expressed as a probability of moving from one cell to another. For example, among customers who last bought 0–6 months ago, 25% are expected to purchase again in the upcoming season based on recent history. 75% will not buy and will become 7–12 month recency buyers at the start of the next period.

These foregoing calculations, derived from the marketing database, are then used to make a projection for 1,000 typical new customers. The projection is driven by the projections of customer counts which are then combined with profit contribution calculations.

Customer lifetime value projections

Recency group	Seasons									
	1	2	3	4	5	6	7	8	9	10
0 – 6	1,000	250	190	154	130	108	86	62	48	37
7 – 12	0	750	187	142	115	98	81	64	46	36
13 – 18	0	0	622	155	118	95	81	67	53	38
19 – 24	0	0	0	547	136	104	84	71	59	47
25 – 30	0	0	0	0	498	124	94	76	65	54
31 – 36	0	0	0	0	0	468	117	89	72	64
37+	0	0	0	0	0	0	454	568	654	724
Contribution	8,780	5,486	3,758	2,916	2,120	1,636	1,370	1,042	802	620
Discounted Contribution	8,283	4,883	3,155	2,310	1,584	1,153	911	654	475	346
	Total 23.750									

Cumulative Discounted Contribution: 23.75 per customer

An average new customer results in 23.75 in discounted contribution over 10 seasons. To help you follow the calculations illustrated above, here are some example components:

- *Example migration. At the start of season 2 there will be 250 customers with 0–6 month recency. Of these, 25% (62.5) buy and are 0–6 month recency customers at the start of season 3 while 75% (187.5) do not buy and are 7–12 month recency customers as of the start of season 3.*

- *Another example migration. At the start of season 2 there will be 750 customers with 7–12 month recency. Of these, 17% (127.5) buy and are 0–6 month recency customers at the start of season 3 while 83% (622.5) do not buy and are 13–18 month recency customers as of the start of season 3.*

- *The 0–6 month count as of the start of season 3 is 190 which is composed of 62.5 customers from the 0–6 month season 2 group plus 127.5 customers from the 7–12 month season 2 group.*

- *Profit contribution for season 3 is 3,758 which is composed of (190 x 8.78) plus (187 x 4.40) plus (622 x 2.04). This is calculated by reference to the two tables on the previous page, eg contribution per customer per recency group (eg 8.78) multiplied by residual customers after seasonal movement among cells (eg 190), thus 190 x 8.78, and so on.*

- *To put the season 3 contribution in terms of acquisition season (ie, season 0) funds, 3,758 is divided by 1.19 (= 1.06^3) to get 3,155, its discounted value. See earlier explanation on page 2.6-12.*

To summarise

Long-term or lifetime value is the measure of a customer's worth. It can vary according to the method by which customers are acquired. It can be used to inform decisions in many key marketing areas. It is at its most valuable when compared with the cost of acquiring a customer, ie when viewed as a ratio of value-to-cost as in the following equation:

$$\frac{\text{Lifetime value}}{\text{Cost of acquisition}} = \text{Lifetime value/cost ratio}$$

The higher the ratio, the more valuable the customer.

It could, of course, be mistaken to invest only in customers with the highest lifetime values if these are in such low numbers as to cause a shortfall in the company's volume objectives. Lifetime value is therefore not the only measure to be taken into account, but it remains one of the most important.

Chapter 3.1

Getting to know your database

This chapter includes:

- ❑ **How names are captured**
- ❑ **The 5 stages of building a relationship**
- ❑ **The 4 types of data**
- ❑ **Business-to-business data**
- ❑ **Using indicators as shorthand**
- ❑ **Lifestyle and employment indicators**
- ❑ **The database in action (simplified example)**
- ❑ **The test of a good database**

Our first chapter gave us the following definition of direct marketing: "produces or uses data from interactions with customers ... to target marketing activity, generate continuing business and maintain control over marketing expenditure". What makes such a process possible? The database.

With a properly constructed and well maintained database you can select and target customers and prospects individually, delivering a relevant personalised message to each one. Once you know what really motivates them to buy your products or services, you can offer them more. You can also recognise and cultivate prospects who are like your customers – and so acquire new ones. And you can do all this in ways that you can predict will succeed.

In this introductory chapter, Russell Logan sets out the basic principles for building, using and maintaining a marketing database. He makes it sound deceptively simple. But before you hasten to read subsequent chapters you might find a second reading well worthwhile.

One Institute of Direct Marketing lecturer describes this chapter as the most useful and interesting dozen pages ever written on direct marketing. If we were to highlight the important parts of Logan's text every word would be underlined, italicised, boxed, or smothered in yellow marker!

New in this edition. This chapter, one of the most popular in the first edition, has needed only slight updating.

Russell Logan, Senior Partner, Business Aid

Russell is a highly experienced direct marketing professional with special skills and knowledge in the areas of database installation and management. Senior appointments have included board directorships of Book Club Associates (BCA) and Kaleidoscope during their rapid development in the 1970s.

In 1979 he formed the management consultancy Business Aid which specialises in computer systems and the management of databases for direct marketing, particularly the technical aspects of database systems and techniques.

He has worked with many top direct marketing companies and their agencies as well as with major manufacturers, retailers and charities wishing to use direct marketing more efficiently. His client list reads like a Who's Who of direct marketing and includes The Daily Telegraph, Mars Pedigree, RNLI, Help The Aged, The Folio Society, Eurostar, Boots Opticians Ltd, and the Chartered Institute of Marketing.

Russell has always been active in trade associations, having sat on the board of, and helped to develop, the British Direct Marketing Association, forerunner of today's Direct Marketing Association UK. He set up and chaired the DMA's Database Marketing Group, and devised and organised its annual Database Marketing Seminar for the first ten successful years. He is a founder member of the Institute of Direct Marketing and a much-requested speaker at trade conferences. He is also a member of the ICFM.

Russell has "another life" as a crime writer, being the author of several paperbacks under his pen-name Russell James. His books, low-life thrillers set mainly in London, are published in Britain and the United States. He denies that his inspiration for low-life thrills derives from his formative years in direct marketing!

Russell Logan M IDM
Business Aid
30 Sydenham Road
Cheltenham
Gloucestershire GL52 6EB
E-mail: business.aid@dial.pipex.com
Web site: http://dspace.dial.pipex.com/found/
Tel: 01242-514992

Chapter 3.1

Getting to know your database

Database – the marketing alternative

Database marketing does not necessarily replace existing sales channels. It works with them. Often, in consumer and business-to-business marketing, a face-to-face relationship with the prospect is uneconomical or impractical. Direct marketing – or preferably database marketing – may be the **only** practical contact strategy.

Database marketing meets a variety of objectives with numerous advantages over traditional marketing methods. Examples of database applications, referred to throughout this Guide but worth restating, include:

- ✔ focus on prime prospects

✔ avoid poor prospects

✔ evaluate new prospect lists

✔ cross-sell related products

✔ generate incremental and follow-up sales

✔ launch new products to receptive prospects

✔ site new outlets in high usership areas

✔ identify new channels of distribution

✔ build customer loyalty

✔ convert occasional purchasers to lifetime customers

✔ target minority markets and niches

Both direct and database marketing are expensive, so there is no commercial sense in using these costly techniques in order to acquire new customers without at the same time laying the foundation for an on-going trading relationship. Database marketing provides the methodology for building relationships on an **individual** basis, allowing **you** (the supplier) to know **me** (an individual among your customers). No matter how many customers (or prospects) you have, you should know who I am, what I want, when I want it, and how I can be persuaded to buy.

The database dialogue

Building a database begins with the capture of a name. We do this in order **to begin a relationship** – a crucial point to bear in mind throughout this Guide.

As direct marketers, our goal should be to build a bank of customers who stay with us, buying our product, hopefully introducing more customers to us – ultimately becoming advocates for our service.

Even if customers do not knowingly recommend us, we can use them to locate new customers. We get to know them, discover who they are, find out what **sort** of people they are, in order to help us recognise more people like them.

Step-by-step – the direct marketer's goal

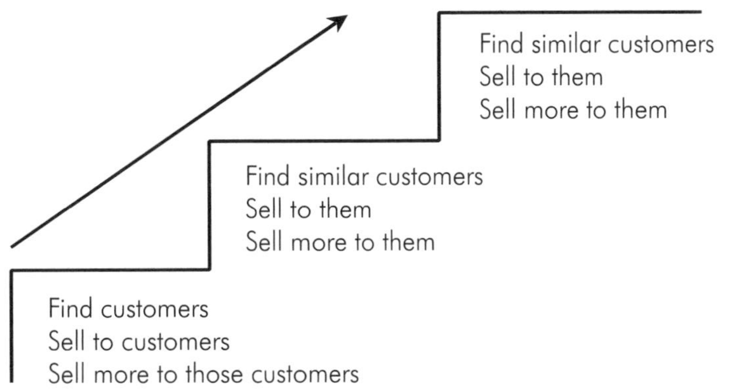

But how do we capture customers' names in the first place?

Elsewhere in this Guide will be found many references to customer acquisition and "name-gathering" techniques. Here are just a few to set you thinking:

- ✔ Direct sales
- ✔ Special offers
- ✔ Gifts or discounts
- ✔ Games and competitions
- ✔ Questionnaires
- ✔ Enquiries for product information
- ✔ Guarantee cards
- ✔ Credit or payment schemes
- ✔ Service calls
- ✔ "Friend-Get-a-Friend" schemes (Member-Get-A-Member)
- ✔ In-store registration
- ✔ Exhibition visitors

Dialogue begins not only with the capture of a name, but with the capture of vital extra data about customers and prospects.

You do not need to "wheedle" data from your customers. Most will volunteer information freely if they believe it will be used to service their needs more efficiently.

New car, Reg?

A motor manufacturer asked motorists for their vehicle model and age, annual mileage, brand preference, frequency of purchase, other automotive products bought, etc. The manufacturer then had an indication of potential value per customer in the most valuable form: knowing what type of product each customer bought, and when they were likely to do so next. Some customers even disclosed ***exactly*** *when they intended to make their next purchase.*

Where charity begins

A charity asked for details of other charities supported, topics of concern, hobbies and sports participated in, and even educational status (pupils and teachers were treated differently from each other, and differently again from other members of the public). In this way they were able to identify and contact potential participants and organisers for such events as sponsored walks, sponsored swims, etc.

Gradually, additional data can be applied to each name to form a unique and individual picture of each prospect on file. These customer "profiles" can then be used to drive relevant marketing to them. It is this approach that underlies the science of database marketing.

The 5 stages of building a relationship

There are five stages in building a one-to-one customer relationship. Each has its own objectives, strategy and mechanisms. The five stages are:

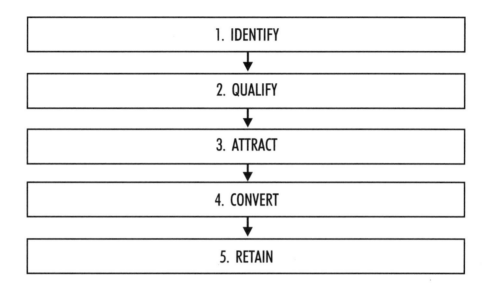

1. IDENTIFY
↓
2. QUALIFY
↓
3. ATTRACT
↓
4. CONVERT
↓
5. RETAIN

For example, in order to **identify** a prospect it may be necessary to develop a campaign that allows prospective customers to identify themselves (this is your **objective**). At its simplest, the **strategy** might be mass-communication style advertising, and the **mechanism** a coupon offering further information.

The table overleaf comprises a checklist of the five stages together with some typical examples of strategy and execution. The database is used throughout to facilitate each stage, becoming more useful as the data grows in relevance.

What information should be collected

What distinguishes a true database from a mere "list" (the two are still frequently confused) is the amount and quality of **marketing** data on file. Data might be collected for customers (previous purchasers), prospects (eg enquirers) and contacts (eg non-respondents).

The information on a typical marketing database can be sub-divided into **four** main classifications:

1. People data

2. Address data

3. Accounts data

4. Activity data

The 5 stages of building a relationship

Stage	Objective/strategy	Typical mechanisms
		"Mass" communication with an individualised approach.
1. Identify	To develop campaigns where people identify themselves as potential (or existing) customers.	❒ Send-for offers (direct sales) ❒ Redemption-at-outlet offers ❒ Information offers (two-stage)
2. Qualify	To develop mechanisms whereby prospects can indicate the volume of product they buy or might buy.	❒ Account records ❒ Proofs of purchase ❒ Incentivised questionnaires
3. Attract	To increase prospects' knowledge of products, services, outlets etc.	❒ Newsletters ❒ Bulletins about new products/benefits/offers ❒ Lists of stockists ❒ Maps of outlets
4. Convert	To attract prospects to try (new?) products by means of personalised trial offers.	❒ Direct mail ❒ Door-to-door ❒ Trial vouchers ❒ Free-trial samples ❒ Purchaser competitions
5. Retain	To develop loyalty building schemes aimed at keeping and developing customers.	❒ Members' magazines ❒ Catalogues ❒ Events/invitations ❒ Membership cards ❒ Reward schemes ❒ Recognition schemes ❒ Bonus entries for competitions, games, etc ❒ Advance previews of new products/services ❒ Delayed payment schemes

1. People data – more than just names

The difference between a true database and a simple list becomes immediately clear when we look at the type of personal data contained in a typical marketing database:

Consumer records:

- ✔ People record key
- ✔ Name
- ✔ Age
- ✔ Marital status

- ✔ Number of children
- ✔ Income bracket
- ✔ Lifestyle indicators
- ✔ Job codes
- ✔ Credit indicators

For business-to-business marketing, as opposed to consumer marketing, records must be constructed differently. Some of the detail, of course, will vary according to the nature of business being transacted, but as a minimum records should include:

Business person records:

- ✔ Individual record key
- ✔ Name
- ✔ Job code
- ✔ Job description (as it should be printed)
- ✔ 'Phone number
- ✔ Fax number
- ✔ Department or division (as it should be printed)
- ✔ Authoriser/influencer/buyer
- ✔ Area of business (Standards Industry Code (SIC) or similar coding)
- ✔ Company code (address record key)
- ✔ Personal address record key (if relevant)

2. *Address data – not as simple as it sounds*

Correct address data is as pivotal to database marketing as a name. Much direct marketing activity hinges on the availability of a correct address. By address we might mean:

Consumer address records:

- ✔ Address record key
- ✔ Full address
- ✔ Address type
- ✔ ACORN, MOSAIC or other geodemographic codes
- ✔ Region code
- ✔ Sales area
- ✔ Media area code (eg TV region)

For business-to-business marketing, records will be constructed differently. Business address records might include all of the following:

Business address records:

- ✔ Address record key
- ✔ Group indicator (parent company, subsidiary, sole)
- ✔ Parent company record key
- ✔ Full company name
- ✔ Short company name
- ✔ Full address
- ✔ 'Phone number
- ✔ Fax number
- ✔ Telex number
- ✔ E-mail address
- ✔ Region code (sales area)
- ✔ SIC (or similar coding)
- ✔ Principal product types
- ✔ Importer/exporter indicator
- ✔ Number of employees indicator
- ✔ Turnover range indicator

In both consumer and business-to-business, more difficulty in database marketing is associated with incorrect address data than with almost anything else. Other authors in this Guide deal thoroughly with the problems of recording and reproducing addresses, and help you avoid the more obvious pitfalls. (See Merge-Purge, Chapter 3.3).

3. *Accounts data – the prospect's financial status*

Direct marketing relies on targeting prospects with relevant messages. One indication of whether a message is relevant or not is a prospect's ability to pay. Few prospects wish to be continually exposed to literature about products they cannot afford.

Likewise, no self-respecting marketer wastes his budget on despatching offers to customers whose financial status clearly rules out any such purchases – ie even if they wanted it, would their credit status allow them to have it?

Information to be included as Accounts Data should include:

- ✔ Account record key

- ✔ Reference number
- ✔ Account type
- ✔ Start date
- ✔ Last used date
- ✔ Average balance
- ✔ Account worth indicator
- ✔ Accounting codes as required

Accounts data is frequently deployed to arrive at a score for credit worthiness, a major component in name selection for further offers.

4. *Activity data – how the customer behaves*

Another distinguishing characteristic of database marketing is that it provides an on-going record of customer responses and purchase behaviour – not what customers **say** they will do, but what they actually do in practice.

Elsewhere in this Guide much is made of the "RFV" formula (Recency, Frequency, Value of purchases), a key element in a true predictive database.

Activity does not mean simply purchases – it may also describe a customer's responses, eg whether or not they entered a competition or accepted a trial offer.

A basic activity record would include:

- ✔ Activity record key
- ✔ Activity code (eg media or source code)
- ✔ Activity date(s)
- ✔ Response type
- ✔ Recency of last response
- ✔ Frequency of responses
- ✔ Value of response(s)

Any activity is an indication that the customer is still communicating with you. **No** activity is an alarm call.

That last statement comes under the heading of one of those golden rules of direct marketing that ought to be reiterated and emphasised, so here it is again:

Any activity is an indication that the customer is still communicating with you. No activity is an alarm call.

Avoiding clutter in your database

Using "indicators" as shorthand

Over a period of time, given a happy customer and a dynamic marketing department, you will begin to collect more data than you can ever make use – or sense – of!

Rather than clutter up your database with gigabytes of transactional data, use **indicators** to summarise subjective data.

For example, "Lifestyle" is a major force in modern marketing. But lifestyle can be described in many ways. Your indicators should therefore be both descriptive and succinct. Here is a sample spread of indicators covering lifestyle:

Typical lifestyle indicators

01	Youths and children
02	Students
03	Young adult single
04	Young adult married
05	Family with children
06	Dual-income family without children
07	Older family, older children
08	Older family, children left home
09	Near retirement
10	Retired

The above list of lifestyle indicators is clearly not exhaustive. Yet even that short list might usefully be replaced by four simpler **attitudinal** lifestyle indicators, eg:

Examples of attitudinal indicators

"Live now"	(2, 3 and 6 above)
"Family"	(4, 5 and 7 above)
"Spare income"	(7, 8 and 9 above)
"Scraping by"	(1, 2 and 10 above)

Of course, it isn't always that simple. For certain individuals (eg students with spare income), more relevant indicators, or combinations of indicators, may be needed.

The point is: there is nothing sacrosanct about these examples – they are for illustration only. Decide the most relevant categories, descriptions and indicators for your own marketing needs.

Employment indicators – a valuable extra

In consumer marketing, experience shows that it is often useful to add **simple** employment indicators, eg:

Employment indicators
"White collar"
"Blue collar"
"Self-employed"
"Casually employed"
"Unemployed"

Simple employment codes can often be easily applied to consumers even if the consumers themselves will not give them – for example, as shoppers pass through a retail outlet.

In business-to-business marketing, employment codes can be specific. As well as job title/function and department of the person named, add such company discriminators as:

Company discriminators
Size of company
Turnover
Number of sites
Number of employees
Equipment (eg number of computers, etc)
Nature of business
SIC (Standard Industry Classification)*

* SIC is not always obtainable or necessary. You probably have more relevant descriptors in use in your company. Talk to the sales force: ask them how they currently describe their main business sectors – then adopt their classifications.

However, if you wish to use SICs, here are the ten UK Standard Industry Classifications for reference:

Standard Industry Classifications (SICs)

1.	Agriculture, forestry & fishing
2.	Energy & water supply industry
3.	Extraction of minerals & ores & other fuels, manufacture of metals
4.	Metal goods, engineering and vehicle industries
5.	Other manufacturing industries
6.	Construction
7.	Distribution, hotels and catering, repairs
8.	Transport & communications
9.	Banking, finance, insurance, business services & leasing
10.	Other services

Learn from your database

Stripped of its complexities and jargon, the database is a relatively simple marketing tool. It serves two functions which differentiate database marketing from conventional marketing.

These two vital functions are analysis and selection (or segmentation).

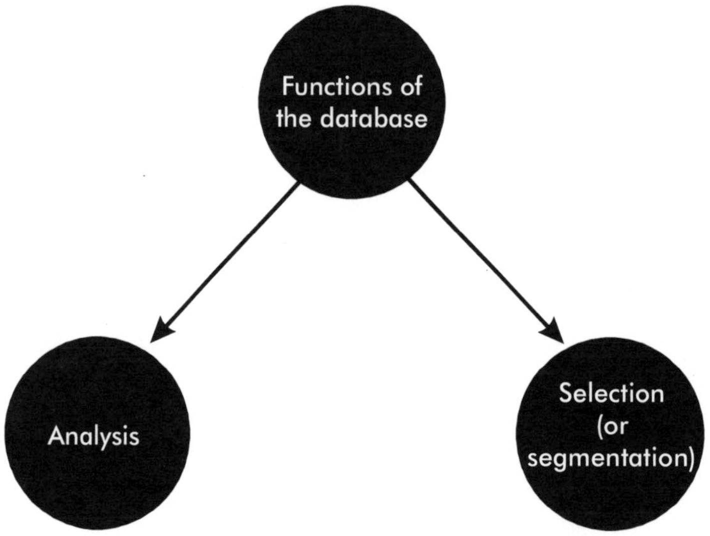

Using the database for ANALYSIS

A database must be capable of easy and frequent analysis.

Certain analyses will be required regularly and can be incorporated in normal processing routines. Others will be ad hoc, required only on occasion for specific purposes. Typical reports will be in grid or matrix format, comparing the numbers and values of customers in given categories who have performed in given ways.

Marketing executives should be able to undertake analyses themselves using simple report-generating software or file extracts on a PC. It is never a good idea if, every time a report is required, marketing personnel have to specify their requirements to another department (eg Management Services) where the necessary programming will have to be slotted into already crowded schedules. With today's PC technology this should rarely be necessary.

Using the database for SELECTION and SEGMENTATION

The database is the prime means of selecting prospects for further activity. The selection process frequently uses a combination of criteria, taking data from different parts of the overall database.

As part of the selection criteria, you will occasionally need to perform calculations. **Some selection programmes cannot do this: make sure that yours can.** Simple selection tools will not be enough: invest in powerful selection software.

When you make a selection from the database, there should be an optional facility to record which names have been selected into which marketing segment. You will then know who has been offered what, how many times, and how they responded – it is just as valuable to know who never responds to your offers as to know who does.

The example overleaf shows how a database can be used for analysis and selection using a token group of just four people being considered as prospects for a range of financial products.

It demonstrates, most importantly, the simplicity of coding. Of course, it is over-simple, with just four records. But the principle of analysis remains simple whatever the file size, **provided that an uncomplicated system of coding lifestyles, campaigns and products is used**.

What appealed to whom?

The example shows the transactional records of **four** customers (of course, a sample of four would be meaningless statistically but we can imagine them as being representative of four much larger groups with similar or identical purchase behaviour).

The four customers have been offered **six** products (1–6) via **two** different mailing packs (X and Y). Each customer belongs to **one of two** lifetime categories (A or B). The results for each cell are given. But what do they tell us?

Using a database for analysis and selection

Customer 1

Lifestyle: A
Products purchased: 1, 3
Mailed: Packs X and Y
Responded to: Neither pack

Customer 2

Lifestyle: B
Products purchased: 1, 2, 4, 6
Mailed: Packs X and Y
Responded to: Pack X only

Customer 3

Lifestyle: B
Products purchased: 2, 4, 5
Mailed: Packs X and Y
Responded to: Both X and Y

Customer 4

Lifestyle: A
Products purchased: 3, 4
Mailed: Packs X and Y
Responded to: Pack Y only

Which product(s) appealed to which customer?

Product	Customer	Lifestyle
1	1, 2	A, B
2	2, 3	B, B
3	1, 4	A, A
4	2, 3, 4	B, B, A
5	3	B
6	2	B

What have we learned? What can we predict?

Products 1 and 4 appeal to Lifestyles A and B
Products 2, 5 and 6 do not appeal to Lifestyle A
Product 3 appeals only to Lifestyle A
Half the product range appeals to Lifestyle A
Virtually everything appeals to Lifestyle B
Pack X worked to Lifestyle B but not to A
Pack Y worked equally to both Lifestyles
Lifestyle B was more responsive than Lifestyle A

This example is indicative only. Wherever possible statistical cells should contain at least 200 members per cell.

How does your database match up?

The ideal database provides – **without disturbing the administrative procedures** – a file structure that is people-based and not transaction-based.

To achieve its objectives a marketing database must be:

✔ Comprehensive

✔ Accurate

✔ Simple to use

Your database will be comprehensive if it contains relevant data accessible by individual customer or prospect. It should give a complete picture of activity, overlaid with demographic and simple psychographic data.

Your database will be accurate if it is the database used by your core administration systems – otherwise it will have the synchronisation problems inevitable with any "parallel" database. A parallel marketing database may be unavoidable, in which case it must be frequently refreshed with the latest changes to administration files.

Your database will be simple to use if the information is collated in a form that is easy to access, easy to use, and easy to maintain.

Remember: successful database marketing does not depend on complex, incomprehensible technological techniques. The whole point is to increase comprehension. To know what is happening ... to know your customer. The computer is there to serve you. It does not call the tune.

Chapter 3.2

Putting your database to work

This chapter includes:

- ❑ The 5 types of marketing database
- ❑ The 3 main types of database applications
- ❑ Data reduction, data warehousing, and data mining
- ❑ Choosing the right applications
- ❑ Deciding who owns the database
- ❑ Phasing in applications
- ❑ Step-by-step through a typical application

The previous chapter introduced us to the database: what it is, what it does and how it works. Over the next few chapters we shall be delving deeper into some of its more technical and specialised aspects.

In this chapter Professor Merlin Stone expands on the different types of marketing database and the applications to which they can be put. Essentially the latter can be termed either marketing (customer) applications or management (planning) applications, or combinations of the two. Whatever you do, says Stone, avoid choosing applications simply because they are possible. The right way is to decide your applications before building or developing the database on which they are to run.

As in his earlier chapter on project management, the author lays great stress on the importance of making sure everyone involved fully understands your objectives. And he warns against over-sophistication in the early stages – first, he says, you need to build a history of properly mounted and successful campaigns.

New in this edition. Explanations of techniques for obtaining and processing data which were not widely used in direct marketing as recently as five years ago.

Professor Merlin Stone, relationship marketing consultant

Merlin is a leading expert on direct and relationship marketing, customer care, customer loyalty and customer information systems. Until 1993 he was a Faculty Dean at Kingston University, where he is now a Visiting Professor and teaches part-time. He also teaches part-time at Surrey University. He is a leading researcher on relationship marketing strategies, media and technologies. His clients include companies from a wide range of sectors, including financial services, utilities, airlines, retailers, automotive, energy and IT.

In 1997 Merlin was appointed IBM Professor of Marketing at Surrey European Management School, University of Surrey. His task there is to build their research, teaching and general reputation in the area of customer management.

Merlin has been conducting research on relationship marketing and information technology for several years, involving in-depth interviews with leading clients and suppliers. The results are published by Policy Publications as a series of briefings of which he is the editor and principal author, entitled "Close to the Customer", sponsored by IBM and Surrey European Management School.

Many companies from the financial services sector have also participated in his research, and these results were published in 1997 by Financial Times-Pitman in the report, "Winning New Customers in Financial Services". His research is sponsored by IBM, the Royal Mail and Equifax. He also works on business development with these three organisations.

Professor Merlin Stone M IDM
Surrey European Management School
University of Surrey
Guildford
Surrey GU2 5XH
Tel: 01483-259347
E-mail: m.stone@surrey.ac.uk

Chapter 3.2

Putting your database to work

The 5 types of database

Before we can understand how a database can assist, let alone **solve,** marketing problems, we need to be clear about the database itself: what type of database it is, what it contains, what it was primarily designed for, and what it is capable of. All too often we hear marketers talk of "the database" as if all databases were alike. They aren't.

It is useful to distinguish five types of database which hold marketing data as follows:

The master customer file – holds basic customer details such as name, address, etc.

The operational (or transactional) database – used for everyday management of sales and service transactions with customers, eg accounting records.

The customer database – a current view of the customer, eg policies (of businesses), relationships, nature of business, etc.

The marketing database – details of current and past customers, promotions, results, etc.

The data warehouse – may contain data from several of the above as well as from others.

The table on the following page describes each of the above in more detail. Each is used for different applications as we shall see.

Could all these types, and the applications associated with each, be combined in a single customer database? Many very large companies have been optimistic about the extent to which a single customer database can cope with all the operational, marketing and strategic needs of a business, and have come badly unstuck as a result.

Direct insurer warehouses its data

A major direct insurer had all of its customer data within its operational databases – one for each product. Any cross-selling was preceded by a complex process of analysis, extraction and further analysis, eg to identify "good" customers from one product database and see if they fitted the "good" profile for the product to be cross-sold. The company then constructed a data warehouse, which put together data from all of its product databases. This allowed analysis and profiling to be carried out much more quickly, and also permitted within-campaign response analysis to be accelerated.

What types of application are there?

Customer database applications can be split into two categories: customer applications and management applications. A third category – which broadly covers dialogue and relationship applications – is effectively a combination of the two.

✔ Customer applications

✔ Management applications

✔ Dialogue and relationship applications

We now look at each of the above in turn:

Customer applications

Customer applications are those uses of the database which involve the creation and maintenance of contacts and relationships with customers.

The 5 types of marketing database

Database type	Basic characteristics	How it is used and other characteristics
Master customer file	Holds the basic details identifying and allowing access to the customer, ie name, address, telephone numbers.	Often held within another database. In companies which transact directly with their customers (eg banks, mail order), it is held within the transactions database. For businesses which do not transact directly with their final customers, but through agents (eg airlines, fmcg), or where transactions are anonymous (eg retailers – although this does not apply to those with customer loyalty and credit cards) it is more likely to be held on the customer database.
Operational or transactions database	Used to manage sales and service transactions with customers.	There are usually several of these in most companies, perhaps used to manage transactions for different products or services.
Customer database	Provides a single, current, view of the customer – policies, relationships (household, family, commercial, etc).	This is built from operational data, which has been merged, cleaned, deduplicated, sometimes using semi-automated or even manual processes, and often dependent for its quality on a highly skilled database administrator. It may be supported by customer notes. It may have different interfaces and will almost certainly be used by many different people, eg tied or franchised agents, telemarketing personnel, mailing houses. It should have smooth access to its source operational systems and becomes the accepted source of quality information about the state of the company's customer inventory.
Marketing database	Supports business and marketing planning. It provides a view of the business over time, because it holds details of current and past customers, and campaign prospects.	It is used to drive campaigns and assists tracking of prospects and proposals. It tracks and supports development of customer relationships over time. This database may include data from external sources – lifestyle, psychographic and demographic, any segmentation codes, responses to test campaigns, questionnaire responses, etc. It is here that campaign selections are likely to be held. Note that some operational data may not be here, as it has been found not to be useful for marketing purposes. Note that segmentation codes and scoring algorithms may be written back into the customer database, as they will be used at point of sale to a) determine which segments new customers belong to and how the customers are to be handled b) calculate appropriate, customised prices.
Data warehouse	This contains data from many of the above databases and possibly from still further databases, eg customer service (complaints and compliments).	This is constructed either for analysis or to provide a master standardised data set which other applications can use. A sub-set of a data warehouse is usually called a data mart. A warehouse may be a batch warehouse, compiled specifically for analysis or marking a customer database, or an on-line warehouse built to ensure that a uniform dataset is available for a specified set of on-line applications, eg inbound telemarketing.

The main customer applications of a marketing database are:

- ✔ **Direct mail** – using the system to select customers to receive relevant mailings.
- ✔ **Response handling and fulfilment** – using the system to record your customers' responses and manage the next step in the contact strategy – fulfilment.
- ✔ **Telemarketing** – using the telephone to manage your customers, by contacting them or allowing them to contact your company, recording the results of the dialogue and initiating the required next contact.
- ✔ **Dealer, distributor or agent management systems** – providing data to intermediaries to help them meet their customers' needs better, whilst monitoring their performance.
- ✔ **Club or user group marketing** – creating an "inner circle" of your customers who receive special additional benefits in return for their loyalty.
- ✔ **Consumer promotions** – eg coupon distribution and redemption.
- ✔ **Business promotions** – eg salesforce incentive schemes, competitions.
- ✔ **Credit card management** – using the system to recruit credit card customers, record their transactions, invoice them and promote to them.
- ✔ **Targeted branding** – using the system to deliver branding messages to individuals identified as being either specially receptive to your brands or at risk from competitive actions.
- ✔ **Data marketing** – selling or renting the customer data on the system.
- ✔ **Any other dialogue or relationship application** – ie one which involves a sustained series of communications with customers in a target market.

Listed in this way, these applications look very familiar. However, as we shall see, making them work is quite a task.

Management applications

Management applications are those applications which change the way marketing managers plan, implement and assess their marketing activities.

Management applications include:

- ✔ **Analysis and planning** – using the data on the system to identify customers to target or avoid; to select customers for particular campaigns or offers; or to measure the effectiveness of entire campaigns or their individual elements (media, offer, creative, etc).
- ✔ **Campaign co-ordination** – using the system to ensure that campaigns fit into a logical sequence resulting in a sensible dialogue with customers, rather than confronting them with clashing and inconsistent messages.
- ✔ **Project management** – using the system to manage the delivery of communications projects.

✔ **Campaign performance and marketing mix productivity analysis** – using the system to identify which elements of the mix are best for managing different kinds of customers and which campaigns are most successful.

✔ **Campaign monitoring** – using the system to provide interim data on campaign performance, so remedial actions can be taken where necessary.

Which applications should you implement? These should be determined by marketing strategy. They should not be chosen simply because they are possible. In fact, it is best to plan the database and applications as an integral proposition. The fact that this is so rarely done gives you a competitive opportunity. **If you plan your applications from the outset, you'll get much better results from your database.** But if you rush ahead with customer applications and don't pay attention to management applications, your use of your database is likely to be very inefficient.

Some common misuses of the database

A major retailer *with one of the best known and productive customer loyalty schemes in the business spent very large amounts on bringing its data in-house from a bureau. Just before the completion of this project, it discovered that it had no management process for developing strategic use of the database. Rather, the database was used whenever the company decided a tactical campaign was necessary. The result was that large groups of very loyal users were effectively unmanaged by the company.*

Another retailer *with a similarly strong database discovered that it had no process or software for analysing its database, other than through guesswork (eg "let's see how many customers behave like X").*

A national utility *spent very large sums on developing its customer database and direct mail applications, enabling it for the first time to address its target markets with coherent messages. However, it had no system for co-ordinating the work of the many different marketing managers who used the system. The result was very high campaign expenditure, and clashing communications, with customers sometimes receiving several conflicting communications in the same week.*

In the above examples, the companies focused on customer applications, leaving management applications trailing behind. Much potential profit was lost because they were not able to use the right consumer applications. This in turn was due to failure to develop the right management applications.

Dialogue and relationship applications

A dialogue is defined as a structured series of contacts – involving an approach to the customer and the customer responding – giving information, making purchases, etc. The concept of dialogue is central to maximising profit from customer data. A dialogue is more effective than a monologue – a one-way series of contacts with no response – or than a single conversation (a one-off promotional contact).

In a dialogue, you ask your customer questions such as "When do you intend to buy?", "When will you next need help?" and "What other products might interest you?" You effectively programme your database system to analyse these responses, and the outcome of the analysis is the triggering of future contacts – of a type and timing the customer wants. This is how you develop a dialogue with your customers. The aim of this dialogue is to:

- ✔ Move your customers towards purchase.
- ✔ Keep them satisfied after the purchase.
- ✔ Ensure they buy additional or replacement products later on.

Without such a dialogue, there is just a one-way flow of contacts and literature, most of which is wasted.

Your database system is essential in ensuring that the right communication reaches the right customer at the right time. It selects the initial contacts. It analyses the customer response pattern. It plans the follow up. Your aim should be to develop contact strategies and dialogue applications that suit all your target customers and prospects, and to have management applications that ensure that you are able to do this properly.

Card company segregates best customers

A leading credit card company has identified that customers can be segmented according to their propensity to take credit and their propensity to respond – the two key determinants of customer profitability. It has developed different communications streams – with customers segmented according to their profitability – and uses this to develop a dialogue with more profitable customers.

Strategic issues before you develop your database

Earlier in this chapter, we listed five different types of database where customer data is to be found. Your first step – one that many companies forget to take – is to turn your customer information into a customer database.

If you sell to customers directly (eg via a field salesforce), you are likely to have a reasonably high-quality **customer file** already, possibly several files, containing details about your customers. You will almost certainly have a **transactions file**, showing which customers have bought what and when. You need to turn these into a **marketing database**.

Remember, a marketing database contains more than just customer records. It also holds details of:

- ✔ The marketing and sales campaigns you run.
- ✔ The resulting contacts with your customers.
- ✔ The outcomes of these contacts.

However, your customer and transactions files may be hard to convert to a marketing database. You will have to decide whether to merge all your information, or keep the source files separate and use them to update a new marketing database on a regular basis. Costs are likely to be high, and issues such as frequency of update from the main database, data quality and data ownership will be prominent.

Your transactions file may contain useful source data on recency, frequency, value and category. But it may not be stored in the right way for you to target customers and find out what purchasing histories are associated with high potential for future purchases. Other information which indicates likely customer needs (organisational, psychographic, etc) may not have been collected methodically or at all. You may need to enhance the database through imported or questionnaire data.

If you have no direct contact with customers, you have three main options in database and application development, which you can pursue simultaneously:

1. Compile, through list purchasing, testing and research, a database of those **likely** to be buyers of your products.

2. Create marketing applications which by themselves generate the data through direct contacts, often through "plastic" (credit cards, club membership, promotional entitlement records/cards, etc).

3. Switch (partially or wholly) to channels of distribution which do involve direct contact, eg direct sales.

Airlines forge links with customer

Most airlines sell their tickets via agencies and their most profitable customers buy nearly all their tickets through agencies or corporate travel agents such as American Express and Carlson-Wagons-Lits. Airlines' own card-based loyalty schemes not only help them manage their final customers directly (through service differentiation and reward programmes), but have also been used to develop different marketing applications (eg credit card and mobile 'phone programmes) which have added significantly to their profit – and in one case provided ALL an airline's profit.

With indirect sales, key transaction data (frequency, recency, value and category) will not be available except through customer questionnaires or if your bargaining position is strong enough to enable you to extract data from third parties, eg automotive suppliers.

If you cannot get transactions data, you must find other data indicating propensity to buy your products. In consumer markets, you may be able to source this data from a lifestyle data supplier. Otherwise, a questionnaire may be needed.

The problem of getting the right data is often compounded by the fact that companies often go into database marketing at times of strategic uncertainty. They may not be sure which products they will be marketing to whom over the next few years. This means that it is not easy to determine which data will be needed. If this is your situation, your best strategy may be to start a programme of testing the importance of different variables in explaining buying behaviour for different kinds of products, combined with data reduction (see page 3.2-10) and profiling wherever possible, to simplify the data set, which could otherwise get out of hand.

Acquiring and developing data

Having understood that there are different types of database, and that each is suitable for different applications – and having decided which applications you wish to pursue – you are now ready to begin to develop your own database.

A data acquisition and development strategy is your next need. This strategy determines:

- ✔ Which data you need to support your marketing strategies.
- ✔ How sources of data are to be identified, qualified and tested (including different questionnaire programmes).
- ✔ How the data is to be maintained.

You need this strategy whether or not you have started with a customer file, and whether or not your aim is to sell more to existing customers or to recruit more customers.

Retailer eyes ageing customers

A leading retailer has developed a database combining out-sourced lifestyle data with its own transaction data, and is using this data to identify how customers purchasing patterns develop as they age. It is using the resulting database to support new strategies for helping it to challenge its major competitor, which has always been successful with older customers.

Motor company sorts enquiries

A leading motor company is using lifestyle and demographic data – on-line in its out-sourced call centre – to qualify enquirers and decide what their likely value will be. According to its estimates of customer value, it allocates enquirers to different communications streams with different costs and contact strategies.

There are so many new data sources these days that it is important to keep informed about what lists and databases are available. Although the golden rule is still that your own data is best of all, there is always room to enhance it – particularly if you are moving into new areas (eg recruitment of a different kind of customer, launch of a radically new product).

Although a questionnaire may contain relevant data, the costs of entering it onto the system – and of analysing it for the segmentation you need – means that your plan for obtaining, entering and testing the data must be carefully laid out to prevent acquisition of high volumes of information when low volumes would do. An alternative is to build a partnership with non-competing companies to share the information and cost.

One concept that you will need to embrace at this point is known as **data reduction**. Data reduction is important because, unless you use it, you could find yourself collecting masses of data which prove unwieldy to use.

Data reduction – science within a science

Data reduction is the science of finding a few variables to explain a complex set of data. This is done by statistical techniques. For example, you may use a long questionnaire to find out whether your customers are satisfied with their relationship with you, and use statistical techniques to find out which questions account for most of the difference between customers. Or, if you wish to segment your customers for targeting purposes, you might use a questionnaire on buying attitudes and behaviour, and find which questions enable you to divide your customers most neatly into different groups.

Another concept that you will probably invest in at this stage is **profiling**.

Most database marketing users invest in profiling to give convenient measures of customer characteristics/susceptibilities. The idea is to develop (usually from an analysis of your existing data) one or more profiles (eg of a type of customer the company would like more of). Credit scoring is the "home" of this kind of work – where it is used to develop profiles of customers that are definitely not wanted.

The benefit of this approach is that it provides scorecards or directories which can then be applied to any file, provided that the latter contains the variables which the scoring technique uses. For example, in credit scoring the variables include income levels, home ownership and credit card history. This reduces the volume of testing required and increases the response rates of campaigns. However, campaigns may be required just to bring in the right data.

Data reduction identifies customers likely to switch

A telecommunications company used data reduction and found the likelihood of business customers to switch could be determined by their answers to three questions – satisfaction with the brand, satisfaction with the service, and satisfaction with the category (ie did they feel their overall telecommunications set-up met their needs). This allowed it to design a customer questionnaire which could be used to predict likely switchers.

A timely word about database maintenance

Before we go on to discuss applications in greater depth, now is a good moment to remind ourselves that:

✔ If you have a database you need to maintain it.

✘ If the database isn't maintained, your applications will collapse.

Best practice is that the database should be largely self-maintaining through the applications run on it. But the paradox is that databases which are easiest to update may be the least valuable. If all competitors are in monthly direct dialogue with their customers (eg in the credit card market), data on monthly purchasing patterns and repayments is plentiful. **Competitive advantage will come not from having data but from turning it into a form that can be used for marketing purposes.** Dialogue applications (ones in which you are informing and selling to customers, and they are responding with information and orders) provide the best data, but are the most expensive to create and manage.

If dialogue is intermittent and conducted through third parties (eg dealers and wholesalers), building a database is hard work, involving questionnaires, promotional programmes and so forth. Heavy investment in hand-raising promotion (persuading customers and prospects to identify themselves) may be required. Once built, it can be used to understand replacement cycles and to target promotions more effectively.

Do you really need that database?

Once the database is in order, it is worth re-examining your objectives to see whether the database still supports them or justifies more aggressive objectives.

A worthwhile application or not?

A branded durable goods company develops a database to target promotions more accurately and discovers that some of its customers want to buy mail order (they may already be buying from a mail order company). A small catalogue may be in order, with carefully timed promotion. It may discover that its list is valuable and start to market it. Service contract marketing may prove viable. Related products may be marketed. ***But all this should be judged against the strategic objectives of the company and the costs of running the database for these purposes.***

Which applications for you?

In most large companies, database users are not simply direct marketers. The database is used by marketing analysts, sales managers, retail planners, brand managers, and so on. The marketing applications they need could be any combination of those already mentioned.

Because of the variety of possible applications, **database marketing can be a destabilising influence when introduced into a complex marketing and sales organisation**, if the changes which result from its introduction are not understood beforehand and managed proactively. It helps if database marketing policy (campaigns, support resources, systems capabilities) is developed together with marketing planning and organisation policy.

Developing the applications plan means aligning database plans with strategic marketing plans. If you have a large number of customers who buy moderate amounts but not enough to justify a field sales call, the first applications you need are direct mail and telemarketing. On the other hand, if you want to use the system to gather information about customers buying your products through retailers, then the first applications needed may be high-volume, low-cost coupon processing and questionnaire management.

Here is a four-step process for choosing the applications you need:

How to determine which applications you need	
1.	Identify the kinds of contact you have with your customers (pre- and post-sales). This is called the contact audit.
2.	Identify whether there is a requirement for more frequent or different contact, and what the benefits of these contacts might be.
3.	Produce a list of possible marketing applications (as detailed earlier, plus any others that are relevant to you).
4.	Identify the combination of applications which is most likely to be cost-effective, using standard techniques of cost-benefit analysis.

And a process for managing your applications ...

Once the database and its marketing applications are set up, a process is required to make the database work as a management tool. Here is such a process:

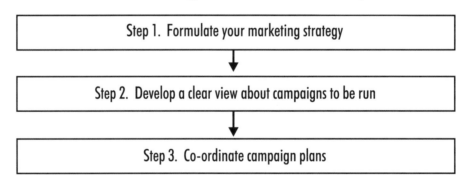

Step 1. Formulate your marketing strategy

↓

Step 2. Develop a clear view about campaigns to be run

↓

Step 3. Co-ordinate campaign plans

Step 1. Formulate your marketing strategy, including considering the different ways (channels, products, etc) of relating to (now known) customers. This is critical to making the database deliver value to general users. The management application should include ways of extracting data about different groups of customers and how your company has performed with each of them. It should also enable you to model the effects of different strategies.

Step 2. Develop a clear view on the kinds of campaign to be run, and whether they will follow particular themes. Develop a structured approach to maximise learning and effectiveness, minimise costs and reduce conflict. Different kinds of campaigns have different pay-offs, use different kinds of data, and have different priorities. The further you progress with database marketing, the more your campaigns will increase in sophistication, placing a greater load on marketing, and statistical and systems services. Without a proper medium-term campaign plan, you may run into bottlenecks or, worse, conflicts. Your management applications should enable you to run simulations of individual campaigns and of several campaigns together. This will help you evaluate different options.

Step 3. Co-ordinate campaign plans to ensure maximum effectiveness and minimum overlap. Make sure campaigns make sense in terms of the dialogue with individual customers. A campaign planning and co-ordination application, showing what campaigns are planned when, and to whom, will help ensure this. In some parts of the "classic" direct marketing industry, rolling campaign plans – from one to five years' duration – are used. In some companies, the database system has a full management process application attached to it. This shows not only what campaigns are planned to be run when, but what are the different stages in getting these campaigns to market, ie a project management application.

Deciding who "owns" the database

As soon as you start to use your marketing database to sell to customers, you may run into a series of ownership and accountability problems. In due course the applications themselves will show you where the data is being used most effectively, and by whom.

For example, companies with a territory salesforce, regional marketing teams and product or brand managers, may find that all these groups want to contact the same (usually the most loyal) customers and claim the benefits of resulting sales.

The solution to problems like this is partly political – your senior management must make it clear that the company as a whole owns the data, and accountability is therefore **shared. But the effectiveness of the campaigns run by different centres of marketing power should be measured and compared!** Your database should make performance achievement much clearer. Eventually, it should become the foundation for a "marketing mix evaluation" application. This shows which elements of the marketing mix are being used cost-effectively, by comparing spend with results.

One area where financial evaluation is particularly important is the media mix. Database marketing provides more accurate data on media effectiveness. It provides a firmer basis for the development of a media usage strategy, overall and for particular markets and segments. There could, for example, be different departments recommending direct mail, press advertising and press relations. But, your financial evaluation may show that **no** media are cost-effective for accessing a particular market. You may need to develop new media to access it (eg your own newsletter, a customer Helpline). The development of a media analysis application (which simply means that the data on media effectiveness must be gathered, through coding of all response vehicles, and analysed properly) can lead to dramatic savings in advertising budgets.

Are all users using your database effectively?
Is your marketing strategy developed in consultation with all potential users of the database?
Does your direct marketing campaign plan lock in with other advertising campaigns and field sales initiatives?
Will all your campaigns sustain your brand image?
Have all your campaign plans been "sold in" to your staff? Will they benefit the whole company?
Do the timings of your campaigns clash with any other communications going out from your company – like renewal notices, safety warnings?
Have you taken all the steps you can to reassure other departments about the database's use and its benefits, including external suppliers such as advertising agencies?

The system holding your database must have an executive system/decision support element, which makes manipulation of data for analytical (research, analysis of effectiveness) and policy purposes much easier.

Without a management application, managing the database can become a nightmare. It may take you a long time to find out exactly what is on the database, or what the results of a particular campaign were. Without fast access to this summary data, bad marketing decisions are likely to be taken: the wrong campaigns will be run, leading to low responses, customer alienation and deterioration of data quality.

Make sure everyone understands your aims

Your database must be **internalised**. That is to say, a clear view must be developed of how it will be used in practice, by the many kinds of staff who will want to use it.

This requires understanding the perspective of the different users. They must be trained to use it and to feed back information. A reporting process must be developed which incorporates database marketing reports.

When your users feel happy about the value of the database, they will be happier about using it more proactively to manage customer relationships.

You must identify how users can incorporate the database into their traditional disciplines, their planning processes and their day-to-day working, with clear benefit to them. This may mean building a number of simple reporting applications into the system, so that it produces the outputs required by different kinds of staff to fulfil their jobs. You may need to combine data from the system with output from your other systems. It may cost more in terms of programming, maintaining data compatibility and sustaining data links, but if it achieves the objective of making the database approach a way of life, it may be worthwhile.

When to introduce more sophisticated applications?

The initial benefits of having a customer database are straightforward, ie you know what your customers want and what effect your marketing is having on them. However, as experience accumulates, sophistication increases and your staff become familiar with management processes. A good "history" of properly mounted campaigns is accumulated. Carefully and regularly presented reports on these campaigns can then really help sell the benefits of using database marketing internally. A good statistical capability becomes essential for understanding the true determinants of effectiveness (eg through new ways of segmenting, targeting, and managing contact strategies via scoring).

But, be warned, too much experimentation too early can lead to waste of resources on statistical analysis before the fundamental characteristics and quality of the database are understood. You'll best understand how your customers react to your marketing efforts by exposing them to a consistent series of communications, not a few, one-off, poorly co-ordinated promotions.

Testing strategies are another form of sophistication, although important for prospecting programmes, in which it is easy to invest a lot of resource for little return. Testing is, however, vital to establish which contact strategies are right for different customers.

Digging deeper for data: Data mining

Many companies are now using data mining to develop an understanding of their customers, using information from one or other of the database types already discussed.

> **Data mining**
>
> Data mining is "extraction of previously unknown, yet comprehensible and actionable information from large repositories of data", used to make crucial business decisions and support their implementation, including formulating tactical and strategic marketing initiatives and measuring their success.

Data mining is not a miracle science. In companies with large customer bases, with a reasonable degree of stability in the marketing staff and in the service agencies supplying them, there will normally be a wealth of knowledge about customers. Data mining will often confirm their beliefs, but add a more quantitative or practical edge.

Most users of data mining are already quite advanced users of other data analysis methods. This simply reflects that the culture of the company is one of investigation and curiosity, based on a belief that business decisions require complex data sets to support them and the tools to analyse them.

The key to getting results out of data mining is wherever possible to start with an available computerised data set, whatever the variety of sources from which it is compiled, and consolidate this into a data warehouse for analysis, to ensure consistency across different business uses.

Although some earlier projects were feasibility studies, data mining is now accepted as highly likely to deliver useful results. The outcomes demonstrate its ability to cope with very large volumes of data and to come up with very detailed segment profiles.

Senior management commitment is very important as without it a small data mining project can be dismissed as an interesting piece of technical analysis. In most cases, outside consulting expertise has been needed to assist the company to use the mined information and to get value from it.

How essential is a Data Warehouse?

Data warehousing and data mining are not synonymous. The data warehouse, although ideally required for data mining, is not an integral part of it. There is some evidence that, if the total dataset required for mining is likely to lead to a long period of constructing a data warehouse, it is better to take a subset of the data and start to mine it while still building the data warehouse.

Airline discovers frequent flyers in data warehouse

An airline which warehoused its frequent-flyer data discovered for the first time exactly how many frequent flyers it had inside its largest customer. The problem: this customer had made a number of name changes, and this had not been updated on the database.

Building a data warehouse for data mining is necessary only if the source data is not in a state which can be analysed, ie if it is distributed over several different, often incompatible, databases.

Once a data warehouse has been constructed, however, many other methods of analysing it can be used. For example, it is not unusual to find that the data warehouse allows the company to count certain frequencies for the first time.

New flyers given helping hand

A leading airline used data mining to identify the characteristics of future frequent flyers. It used the results to revise its frequent-flyer scheme, ensuring that "early stage" flyers were treated better during the critical period when they were increasing the frequency and variety of their flying, and forming their portfolio of preferred brands.

Insurance company finds "customers in a million"

An insurance company identified that many customers were letting their policies lapse. In an analysis of tens of millions of customers over a ten-year period, classification and prediction analyses were used to determine the characteristics of customers who lapse in terms of their age, sex, policy type, and so on. Identifying the main classes of lapsing customers enabled a risk and profitability analysis to be carried out which determined the value of retaining some or all of these customers. The most valuable customers could then be approached (by agent, mailshot, etc) to encourage them to stay loyal by offering special services or other inducements.

Phasing in your applications

Steps on the path towards full integration

How you phase in use of your database depends very much on your company's structure and strategy. Take the example of an integrated company with a structure of local branches/offices in which some marketing and most selling is done, and with a central marketing unit. This company might start with central outbound calling and mailing combined with central response handling and fulfilment.

This is not really relationship marketing or long-term investment. There is low involvement of local sales and marketing staff. Contact strategies may be very simple, scoring may not be used and offers may be just one type per campaign. Later, local outbound telemarketing may be introduced, to generate local leads. Then more advanced, central campaigns may be introduced, involving local fulfilment – integrated with central or local response handling, but still not as part of a long-term relationship. Campaigns will still be product-based, but better co-ordinated. However, this is still not relationship marketing.

Eventually, the company may move to fully integrated local and national **"virtual account management'**. More complex contact strategies will be used, their design driven by a scoring capability. Offers will be much more varied to suit different customer types. **For some companies, the ideal will be when the database is used by real account managers**, contacting customers on a regular calling cycle, using database marketing disciplines. Campaigns for particular products and services are then treated as a highlight to the relationship, helping focus customer attention on additional benefits.

The fully integrated system and its applications

At the centre of a fully integrated marketing system is the customer database. If your organisation is multi-branch or multinational, then this database may have central and local elements. Where these are and how they are used depends on the degree of variation between local and central campaigns, the costs of communicating data and of distributing computing equipment to handle local databases.

Specialist support staff will need to work with company management to plan and help implement campaigns. Leads generated by the system will need to be passed out to the appropriate channels. Lists of various kinds may be needed to build the database. Further lists are generated from it as the basis for tests and full campaigns. Leads and enquiries from various sources (eg mail, telephone, branch customer service) are handled using pre-tested contact strategies, and the results placed on the database, which leads to firm orders being placed with the distribution function. Marketing analysis is carried out to show the profitability of different approaches and to allow tactical changes to be made to campaigns currently being undertaken.

"Stepping through" a typical database system

One of the main justifications for database marketing is that it serves the needs of marketing managers who have responsibility for particular groups of customers (or the entire market) or for particular products. These are the "internal customers" of database marketing. One way to understand how a fully fledged database marketing system works to serve the needs of "internal marketing customers", is to go through the steps by which the application runs, eg through which a campaign is designed and implemented.

For the example overleaf we trace a typical application through a typical system, from marketing plan to fulfilment via development of the campaign. The channel of distribution being used is a direct salesforce.

Step-by-step through a typical database application

1. A **marketing plan for a brand, product or sector** is formulated. It identifies the need for one or more marketing campaigns. Initial work identifies which campaign types are likely to be most successful for the product or sector, and which customers should be targeted in them.

2. A **campaign brief** is drawn up. This includes campaign objectives, targeting, timing, the precise nature of the product or service to be promoted, the offer to be made to the customers, the benefits, how the campaign will help build company brand values, the resources required to implement the campaign, the way in which the campaign's success will be measured and the expected returns. This brief is the basis on which all work is carried out and ultimately executed.

3. The brief is used to derive a **campaign specification**, which is entered into a computerised campaign co-ordination system. This co-ordinates the planning, execution and implementation of all marketing campaigns. It ensures that the approach to customers is co-ordinated and prioritised, taking into account the importance of different target markets, budget availability and the need to avoid clashes. One of its principal outputs is an agreed schedule of campaigns to be run. Without this, database account management is impossible.

4. A **campaign is designed** to achieve the marketing objectives within the permitted budgets. Data about customers and past campaigns are used to define the target market more closely and to identify which broad kinds of campaign are likely to be most successful for the product or sector.

5. Campaigns are devised to **test the different elements** of the design on statistically significant sample lists extracted from the database. Testing normally covers the main elements of the campaign, ie which customers are targeted, which offers they receive, the timing of contacts with them, how they are to be reached and how their responses are to be handled.

6. The **test campaigns are implemented and the results are analysed** to determine which campaign elements (eg media, contact strategies) produced the best results.

7. The detailed design of the **campaign is developed**. As the contact strategy determines a high proportion of the costs of a campaign, contact strategies should be tested very thoroughly and prioritised. The tests provide the basis for prioritising. This occurs in various ways, eg by including some customers in the campaign and excluding others, by handling customers in different ways.

8. The **details of the campaign** are agreed and an outbound list is selected. This determines which customers will be contacted in the first step of the contact strategy. The list is selected using a formula derived from analysis of tests.

9. The **main campaign runs**. The customer receives a communication, which is part of the campaign. This prompts him to respond, eg by coupon or telephone. If the response is to an inbound telemarketing set up, the operator at the latter finds out which campaign or "offer" the customer is interested in. The operator, cued by a sequence of on-screen displays, asks the customer a series of questions. These include confirmation of the customer's identity (possibly including telephone number, address and job title), specific needs concerning the product or service in question, and the customer's needs for further contact. The operator enters the answers into the system. If the enquiry is by mail, the respondent is contacted by an outbound telemarketing call and a similar process takes place.

10. The **enquiry information** gathered from the customer is matched to the existing customer file (if any) and merged with other information on the database.

11. The computer uses rules derived from tests and agreed with the campaign originator and project manager, to prioritise the enquiry according to the likelihood of a customer ordering. These rules may be based on predetermined campaign profiles (ie the kind of customer the company is trying to attract) and may use **data gathered** during the customer's response.

12. A particular **contact strategy is recommended**, based on the type of product and on the priority.

13. **The fulfilment organisation receives information** indicating, among other things, what kind of letter and additional material should be sent to the customer or, if the product is mail order, what product should be sent.

14. **Local sales offices, sales staff or dealer outlets receive information** about the enquiry on their computers, follow up enquiries, and feed the results of the follow up back to the database.

15. The results of all enquiries and responses are analysed to provide regular reports on the **effectiveness of activities** and to help improve the effectiveness of future campaigns. Detailed performance data plus expenditure data from financial systems are used to evaluate financial performance and plan new campaigns.

How far have we come?

In just two chapters we have gone from an introduction to the basic principles of database usage and management through to a fully integrated system. On the way we learned that the road to database marketing begins by defining the applications your database is to support, rather than by building a database. We've seen that there are two types of application – customer applications, or what you want to do with customers, and management applications, which help you structure these customer-facing activities and ensure they take place efficiently. A key issue for both types of application is how you acquire, use and maintain your data. We also saw what happens when you leave consideration of applications until after you've built your database.

Database building is a process which doesn't take place overnight. It is a phased activity, which never ends. As your data grows and improves the more you will use it as your foundation for contacting customers.

We are now ready to look at how the database can be used for profiling, segmentation and selection. But first we must make sure that our data is as reliable as possible through the process we call merge-purge.

Chapter 3.3

The how and why of merge-purge

This chapter includes:

- ❑ **What is merge-purge?**
- ❑ **The 7 steps of a merge-purge project**
- ❑ **How names and addresses can cause problems**
- ❑ **PAF, MPS, multi-buyers and seeds**
- ❑ **The 4 levels of deduplication**
- ❑ **Special lists, including user lists**
- ❑ **Analysing the outcome of a merge-purge**

Without a proper understanding and application of merge-purge, no direct marketer can hope to succeed in anything but the shortest of short terms. In this chapter Ian Goodman explains the mechanics of merge-purge and sets out a 7-step process for carrying it out.

The problem is essentially one of names occurring, or appearing to occur, more than once – possibly several times in a given list, as happens frequently when a master list is compiled from several other lists or sources. Removing duplicates automatically would be a doddle ... if it were not for those names occurring in a multiplicity of forms: sometimes variations, sometimes incomplete, sometimes inaccurate.

In combination all these probabilities (duplicates, errors, etc) can and do create havoc for anyone who tries to carry out a sensible mailing or build a marketing database. The risks (and costs) of using incorrect personal data are nothing short of horrendous.

Merge-purge, then, is a highly technical scientific procedure at the very heart of modern direct marketing. So how does it work, what does it achieve, and what are the benefits? Let Goodman, one of the world's foremost merge-purge innovators, guide you through it.

New in this edition. A fuller explanation of the merge-purge process has been included in response to popular demand.

Ian Goodman, Head of System Development, Printronic International Plc

Ian is Head of System Development at Printronic International plc, one of Europe's largest independent computer bureaux specialising in direct marketing.

After obtaining his degrees in mathematics and physics, and training in computer system design with ICT Ltd and sales management with Fabri-Tek Inc, he entered direct marketing with Acxiom – becoming a director of Acxiom UK and of R & D with Acxiom Inc, USA.

He is credited with the design and marketing of the first UK charity database system (MAPS) which managed the direct mail promotions for over thirty charities. It included the first UK postal address correction system (ATLAS) subsequently installed by such companies as American Express, Standard Life, Renault UK, and Rank Organisation. He designed merge-purge and database management systems before taking a 4-year secondment to work in R & D in the USA.

"I proposed an unorthodox design for an international postal address management system," says Ian. "It was so unusual that everyone liked it, but no-one was willing to fund the development. So I returned to the UK and found backing for the project with Printronic."

At Printronic, Ian has seen his ideas mature into a new generation of postal address correction and merge-purge systems which harness the unusual concept of converting PAF data from each country into a series of formulae to control postal address management functions internationally.

Ian teaches at the DMA Advanced level workshop and writes occasionally for the trade press. He played rugby at county and regional level and represented the South of England in a final England trial. He views his early experience of contact sports as an invaluable preparation for a career in direct marketing!

Ian Goodman
System Development Manager
Printronic International Plc
1 Endeavour Way
London SW19 8UH
E-mail: iangoodman@printronic.co.uk
Tel: 0181-946 7537

Chapter 3.3

The how and why of merge-purge

The consequences of unrecognisable names and addresses

An obvious consequence of trying to manage a mail campaign, or build a database, with incorrect or poorly presented name and address data, is that many names will occur several times in remarkably different guises, and not be recognised. Think about your own name and address, at home or at work, and recall the number of variants in which it occurs – perhaps perpetrated by yourself!

You may, for example, occasionally use a house name as well as, or possibly instead of, a number. You may sometimes include in your address a tiny district or locality which is not part of your postal address, in order that visitors can pinpoint you more easily on the map. You may or may not include your job title; you may abbreviate the name of your company in the knowledge that your contacts (and your local post office) know all the permutations. You may be a member of a trade association which entitles you to use a suffix, eg M IDM (Member of the Institute of Direct Marketing); and so on.

But whilst you, your friends and colleagues, and your local postie may recognise all these variants as being you, practically nobody else will. To a computer, certainly, each variant will look like and be recorded as a separate entity unless, that is, it is a computer programmed to merge all the versions and then purge all the unwanted variants.

How duplicates arise

Duplicates arise in almost any list of customers or prospects for a variety of reasons. These include: the same customer making multiple purchases from a company and being treated as a new account each time; several members of a household or employees of an organisation all responding to offers or initiating orders; customers moving house and their old name and address records not being deleted, and so on.

Of course, it would be relatively simple to recognise and remove, or consolidate such records if they all appeared in an identical format that any computer could easily pick out. But, as explained, they do not – and that is where the real problem starts.

The cost in mistakes, money, and annoyance

The effect of names and addresses occurring several times in a list of customers is chiefly in two areas. **In terms of statistics** it is, of course, a disaster – each variant being counted as a new name, hopelessly distorting and exaggerating the number of true prospects, customers, inhabitants, etc. **In terms of communication**, eg by mail, the risk is that many intended recipients will receive several identical messages quite probably in a very short space of time (the same day!).

If your message is meant to be individual and discreet, you've blown the gaffe when the customer receives six copies of your carefully personalised billet-doux. You will also have spent six times as much on envelopes, paper, and postage as you should have done. But the real catastrophe is that your personal contact realises that, despite what you may be **saying**, you've taken precious few steps to really get to know him or her. **In short, you haven't recognised them, and what bigger insult is there than that?**

Hopefully we've said enough to demonstrate why merge-purge, which can correct inaccuracies and remove duplicates from virtually any number of lists, is so vital to modern communication techniques. It can be used to unify and "condition" any computerised list or assembly of lists, whether they be rented, bought, specially compiled, or already existing within an organisation, eg held by different departments, in different forms.

In the process of merge-purge many other improvements can be made to a list and to the names and addresses it incorporates, as we shall see, with many additional benefits.

Examples of name and address abuse and misuse

Above (left) shows how a computer can be abused by typing narrative into the space reserved for a postal address. The system has tried to form the message into an address – surprisingly it didn't try to convert "Hurrey" into Surrey.

(Right) Computer has added a Northern Ireland postcode to a Channel Islands address. Why? In seeking to add a missing postcode, the system referred to a Royal Mail file (PAF) and found a locality called "Islands" in County Fermanagh – hence the Belfast code.

What is a merge-purge?

In its simplest form, a merge-purge is a computer process in which a number of different lists of names and addresses are "merged" together and then "purged" of any duplicated and otherwise superfluous names and addresses.

The merged list is called a "Gross List", which is usually sorted into postal address sequence which highlights any duplicates which can then be removed. After deduplication, it is called a "Net List" which can be used for direct mail purposes or become the basis of a master database.

The more powerful merge-purge systems can also cross-reference the names of people to households, families and companies within a postal address, and can consolidate marketing information (eg purchase history supplied with each name and address) to all of these levels.

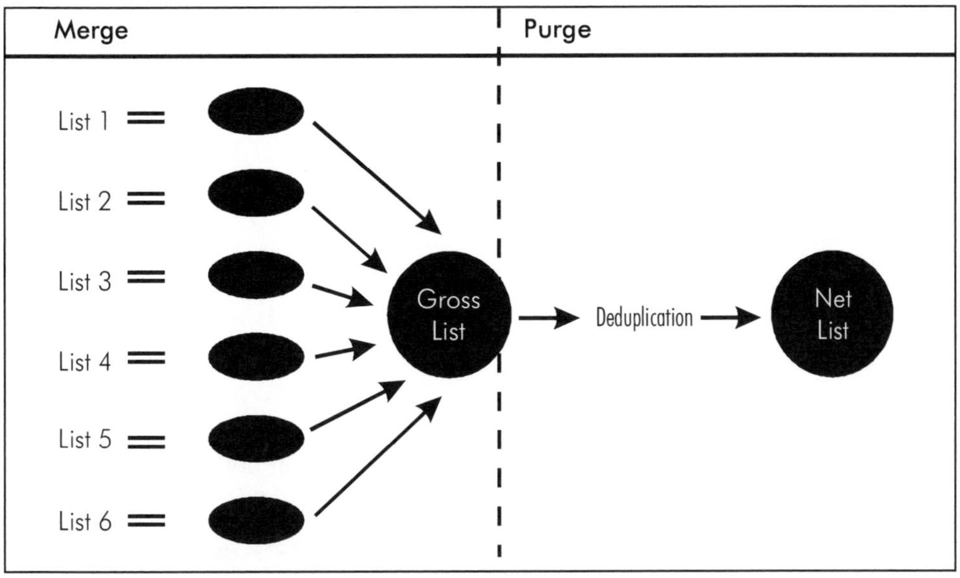

Creating lists and building databases

A modern merge-purge system is one of the most powerful weapons in the direct marketing arsenal. It can be used to deliver a finely targeted mailing campaign using hundreds of rented mailing lists, or it can be used by an organisation to create a marketing database by combining lists and the information held on separate in-house computer systems.

A good merge-purge system can accept information recorded by different computers in a variety of formats and on different kinds of electronic media. It copes and deals with the problems of poor presentation of name and address information. It merges, sorts and cross-compares the information in alternative sequences until it establishes the best postal address-based sequence for all the names and addresses.

The very best merge-purge systems can correct errors in postal addresses and produce an address-sequenced Gross List of names and addresses ready for deduplication. The deduplication process can then work with the names within each address to establish relationships between people at the household, family, company and individual level. Selection of the best quality name at each level and the aggregation of any supplied marketing data to each level are the final steps towards the creation of the Net List.

We can see that the skills and techniques invested in merge-purge systems put them among the most powerful computer systems in everyday commercial use.

The two types of merge-purge project

There are two main applications of the merge-purge process:

✔ To merge and purge a number of rented lists for a direct mail acquisition programme.

✔ To merge and purge data from different systems/departments to create a single marketing database.

More examples of problem names and addresses

Ambiguous addresses. The following address could refer to Bolton in Lancashire, or to Boston in Lincolnshire (there is a Church Road in both towns).

1 Church Road
Bolton
Lincs

Old-style addresses. The following address is shown in both old and new styles (Royal Mail alters hundreds of thousands of postal addresses every year).

Old-style (pre-1993)	New style
149 Central Avenue Gretna Carlisle Cumbria CA6 5AA	149 Central Avenue Gretna Dumfriesshire DG16 5AA

Offensive mis-spellings. The following address refers to the town of Whitstable.

2 Church Street
Shit-stable
Kent
CT5 1PJ

Multiple errors. The following address is presented with a small area name (Tankerton) which is known locally, but is not required for correct addressing purposes. The postcode is also incorrectly positioned.

2 Church Street
Tankerton
ShitstableCT5
1PJKENT

Hoax entries. The following will need to be erased once they have been proved to be hoaxes:

Margaret Thatcher
Ghengis Khan
Donald Duck *
Deceased (when not true)

(* When a genuine donor called Mr Donald Duck tried to give a donation to the Salvation Army it caused a technical problem!)

Multiple variations. In the extreme case below the executive has used her professional nom-de-plume; one company is a subsidiary of the other; the addresses are two different entrances of the same building. Otherwise they are the same person although merge-purge will not detect it.

Liz Smith WWAV 31 St Petersburgh Place London WC 7LA	Beth Vaughan Compton & Woodhouse 35 Cheapside London W2 6LB

Mistakes? Are they or aren't they the same person? Could Bobby Smythe be a misspelling of Mrs Smith's husband or son? Could her first name be Bobby? And if they are one family (or even one person) do they live at No. 34? Are there **two** families, with two different postcodes?

Mrs John Smith Peters Court Upper East Hayes Bath BA1 6PL	Bobby Smythe 34 Upper East Hayes Bath BA1 7LB

Straightforward variations. Below is an everyday type of duplication which merge-purge can quickly highlight and remedy but which can cause serious problems if not remedied.

Mr W Smith Managing Director Direct Editorial Services Quay House Christchurch Dorset BH23 1DR	Bill Smith Account Manager DES 11 Quay Road Christchurch Dorset BH23 1DR

Simple duplicate. Two name and address records which most of us would guarantee are duplicates, but which a computer might not recognise without benefit of merge-purge.

John Smith Coburg Villas Bath BA1 6LD	Mr J Smith 3 Coburg Villas Bath BA1 6LD

A merge-purge project involving rented lists for a direct mail campaign is usually planned with the assistance of a list broker and advertising agent, and executed by a specialist computer bureau and mailing house.

To create a marketing database from data held on a variety of in-house systems will normally involve in-house management working with information specialists. Again, the services of a specialist computer bureau are usually required to execute the process.

In either case, the functional capabilities of the merge-purge process, which are described on the following pages, need to be understood at the planning stage. A detailed specification must be created to select and control the project.

The 7 steps of a merge-purge project

Most merge-purge projects involve a series of seven sequential steps comprising human and computer activity. These are summarised below and explored more fully in the remainder of this chapter:

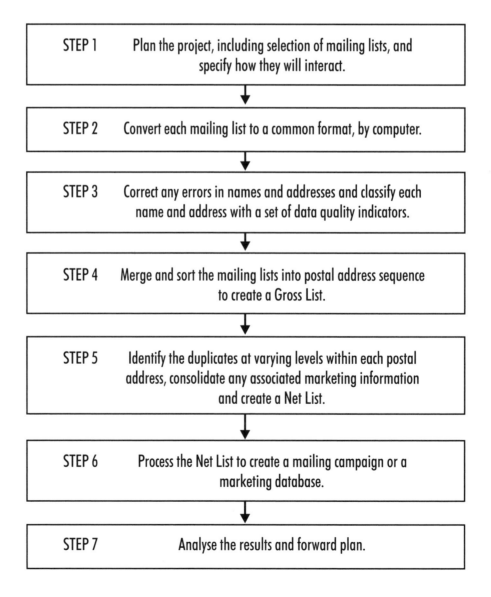

STEP 1 — Plan the project, including selection of mailing lists, and specify how they will interact.

↓

STEP 2 — Convert each mailing list to a common format, by computer.

↓

STEP 3 — Correct any errors in names and addresses and classify each name and address with a set of data quality indicators.

↓

STEP 4 — Merge and sort the mailing lists into postal address sequence to create a Gross List.

↓

STEP 5 — Identify the duplicates at varying levels within each postal address, consolidate any associated marketing information and create a Net List.

↓

STEP 6 — Process the Net List to create a mailing campaign or a marketing database.

↓

STEP 7 — Analyse the results and forward plan.

Step 1: Planning the merge-purge project

At the all-important planning stage each of the following sub-steps should be carefully considered:

✔ **Business objective**
Define your business objective. Write this down, then make sure that all the parties involved in the project have a copy. Include a statement under the title "Criteria for Success". This will tell everyone what you intend to achieve and which measurements you will take to judge the outcome of the project.

✔ **Partners**
Identify, select and meet with those who will be directly involved in the project. Include external suppliers, eg list brokers, computer bureaux, advertising agencies, printers, mailing houses. Contact your peers who will be affected, including those representing finance, customer relationships and fulfilment. Talk to those involved in concurrent initiatives that may impact your plans.

✔ **Data sources**
Review, define and quantify the sources of data. A list broker or advertising agent will help to produce a "list of lists" for a typical merge-purge. This will specify the name of each mailing list, the number of name and address records, the geographic coverage, the type of names, any special selection criteria for these names, rental costs and associated terms. Remember to include any special suppression lists (like MPS) and "seed" lists. Decide if List Priorities are required or if name and address selection from a set of duplicates is to be random or driven by data quality criteria.

> MPS = Mail Preference Service, an industry-funded scheme which offers consumers the facility to have their names and addresses deleted from mailing lists.

> "Seeds" are names inserted into mailing lists deliberately in order to recognise rogue users and/or to discreetly monitor the performance of those who handle lists, eg mailing houses.

If the project involves the manipulation of information recorded against each name and address, then you may need the services of an information technology specialist to create a specification of the data sources and the Net File.

✔ **Name and address management**
Assess the expected quality of names and addresses from each source and what special processing may be needed. Will any/all of the following apply?

? Postal address text correction

? Postcoding

? Mailsort or Walksort postal discount

? Mail barcoding

? Name salutation

? Default salutation

? Special exclusions (names and addresses to be excluded by geography, by company type, by type of name, etc)

✔ **Deduplication level(s)**
Define what level of deduplication is required within and across the mailing lists. For example, in a company do you wish to remove all but one contact, or retain several contacts whose names may occur on the lists? Different levels may be required when comparing some lists against others (eg suppression lists against rented lists). Decide if you wish to select multibuyers for special promotional treatment.

Multibuyers are names that appear on several different buyer lists (possibly from different companies). They are often reckoned to be especially valuable since their propensity to respond to direct offers has already been established.

✔ **Test segments**
Plan the tests you wish to include in the project, eg pilot projects or test mail-packs containing special offers. Decide on selection criteria and volumes. Agree on how these tests will be controlled and measured.

✔ **Timings**
Draw up a schedule of events and identify suitable checkpoints for the review of progress.

✔ **Costs and contingencies**
Finalise your budget and payment schedules and identify potential contingencies.

✔ **Response and other reports**
Plan how direct mail response will be measured. Plan how the results of an information development project will be measured. Consider what by-product information might be useful and when this should be available to you.

For example:

- Name and address exception reports
- Reviews of other data being processed
- Deduplication reports
- Print proofs

✔ **Forward planning**
Consider having your response properly "profiled" and how you will use this information to exclude unprofitable names and addresses from future mailings.

Step 2: List conversion

Mailing lists supplied for merge-purge processing are normally sent to the receiving computer bureau on magnetic media or via electronic transmission. Some of the more commonly used media include:

- 3.5 inch floppy disk
- 5.25 inch floppy disk
- DAT cartridge
- 3480 cartridge
- 0.5 inch magnetic tape
- telephone modem
- Internet

Disk data is usually preferred as a plain text file with a "carriage return/line feed" delimiting the records, or with a fixed number of bytes per record. Individual fields in the records should be delimited or fixed length. Files recorded by MS Excel, MS Word, dBase, Lotus 1-2-3, MS Access are usually acceptable.

DAT data is usually recorded using a back-up or archive product of which PKZIP, Seagate Backup, or TAR are commonly used.

3480 cartridges and 0.5 inch magnetic tape for mainframe computers should contain logical records, either variable or fixed length, recorded in ASCII or EBCDIC.

Transmission of data via telephone modem or via the Internet should be arranged beforehand with the communication specialists employed by the computer bureau.

Step 3: Correct errors and classify names

The next step is known as Postal Address Management and involves correcting errors, removing discrepancies and classifying names and addresses.

In many situations lists to be merge-purged will have been poorly managed over a number of years. The quality of the supplied postal addresses can therefore vary, from the sublime to the downright ridiculous, as we have already seen. Reasons for such errors include mishearing, ignorance, illegible writing, forgetfulness, mischief, incompetence – the lot! Sometimes errors are quite innocent. How many versions of your own name and address have you used because of space constraints, for example.

Merge-purge systems can identify ambiguous postal addresses and other alternative potential corrections. They can also automatically correct a wide range of other postal addressing errors of the kind we have depicted, by reference to the Postal Address File (PAF).

PAF

The Postcode Address File (PAF) is a computer file containing the correct postal address details for every UK address. PAF is issued by Royal Mail at monthly intervals to reflect new, deleted, and amended postal addresses.

Beware ambiguous postal addresses

Some mailing lists which you acquire and intend to merge-purge may have been previously processed by an address management system, in which case the lists may be advertised as "100% postcoded" or "verified against PAF". **This does not necessarily mean that every postal address is perfectly accurate.**

Some address management systems can make mistakes when they add postcodes to addresses, and these mistakes can create addresses which are postally ambiguous. The problem is: Royal Mail may accept an envelope carrying an ambiguous postal address – and may deliver it. But to what address?

In the examples shown below, you can see some ambiguous addresses which were detected in an actual 1997 merge-purge project. Each ambiguous address is shown together with the real address alternatives. In fact, it is the addition of the postcode that rendered the original address ambiguous.

Ambiguous	Is it this address?	Or this address?
66 College Road Harrow HA3 6EB	66 College Road Harrow Weald Harrow HA3 6EB	66 College Road Harrow HA1 1BE
23 Carmunnock Road Busbyby Glasgow G76 8SZ	23 Carmunnock Road Clarkston Glasgow G76 8SZ	23 Carmunnock Road Glasgow G44 4TZ
3 The Green School Lane West Kingssown Sevenoaks TN14 6JW	3 The Green Idle Hill Sevenoaks TN14 6JW	3 The Green School Lane West Kingsdown Sevenoaks TN15 6JW
School House Dorrington Shrewsbury SY4 4QL	School House Rodington Shrewsbury SY4 4QL	School House Church Road Dorrington Shrewsbury SY5 7JL

A merge-purge can trap these ambiguous postal addresses and can report them in the style shown above. You will have to apply some other form of verification or interrogation to determine which is the address that should be adopted. Otherwise, Royal Mail is given only a 50% chance of delivery to the correct address.

"Conditioned" names and addresses

Names and addresses which have been processed by the methods described so far are known as conditioned names and addresses. A name and address record which has been conditioned can be described as shown in the following schematic:

Source/list identity	Given name and address	Conditioned name and improved address	Quality indicators (see below)	Other source data

The components of a conditioned name and address record are:

Source list identity – the list on which the original or "given" name and address was supplied.

Given name and address – the name and address in the original form in which it appeared on the list supplied (the source list).

Conditioned name and address – revised version of name and address that meets specific (laid down) quality criteria.

Quality indicators – the criteria by which the quality of a name and address can be judged (see below).

Other source data – any other information for the name and address which was available in the source list is preserved in this final field of the record.

What are postal address quality indicators?

Most of the postal addresses in a merge-purge are verified as accurate or can be corrected to become postally accurate. A minority may only be partially correctable. Some may be so bad as to be totally unrecognisable.

The precise condition of each postal address can be assessed and described by a few address quality indicators which the merge-purge can add to each name and address record. Some specimen indicators are:

Indicator	Description
A.	This is a PAF-perfect address.
B.	This is a PAF-perfect address with an embellishment (eg a postally not required locality).
C.	The address premises could not be verified.
D.	The address premises and thoroughfare could not be verified.
E.	The address locality details could not be verified.

The merge-purge bureau will normally advise what indicators are available and will expect to receive instructions on how to deal with any addresses that are less than perfect. For example, if the merge-purge project is required to exclude any potentially undeliverable postal addresses, the instructions to the bureau would require the exclusion of records with quality indicators C, D and E. If the requirement was for PAF-perfect addresses only, the instructions to the bureau would also require the removal of embellishments from records with a quality indicator of B.

How can you be sure of postal address quality?

The quality of the postal address recognition and correction system operated by the computer bureau has a major impact on the success of a merge-purge project. It will affect every subsequent step in the project, including merging, sorting, deduplication, mailing, response analysis – and the recipients' attitudes towards your organisation.

You can assess the quality of a postal address correction system by asking the computer bureau to demonstrate it on a mailing list of your choice. It may also be possible to obtain a written statement from them defining the scope of the service.

On the following page is a specimen Quality Statement published by a computer bureau. As you can see it lists ten points on which you will need to be reassured.

Managing names, including prefixes and suffixes

So far we have talked mainly about managing addresses. There is also the name to consider: it, too, may appear in a variety of forms – sometimes with and sometimes without a variety of prefixes and suffixes.

A merge-purge system will try to identify every part of a person's name as given in a name and address record. This includes the personal prefix, forename, initials, surname and any suffix. An example for the name Lt Col James B Wellington-Smith MC is shown below.

Prefix	Lt Col
Forename	James B
Surname	Wellington-Smith
Suffix	MC

This identification process is vital, since each item of information can be compared only with another item of similar classification during the deduplication process to follow.

The merge-purge may also create an appropriate letter salutation for the name (Dear Colonel) and may add some useful indicators (army, male, double-barrelled surname, military decoration) to the name and address record for subsequent analysis and selection.

All these functions are controlled by computer reference tables which are a part of the merge-purge system. A computer reference table is simply a list of words and phrases which are cross-compared to the words and phrases in a given name and address. Some examples from a computer reference table are noted on page 3.3-16.

Example of a postal address quality statement

The following is a typical statement issued by a computer bureau to reassure clients about the postal quality of lists produced by the merge-purge process.

1. *The text recognition and correction rules for each and every locality in the UK will be available for inspection by our clients at our offices.*

2. *Postal addresses will be corrected to the text defined in one of the two most recently documented releases of the Royal Mail Postal Address File (PAF).*

3. *The system will recognise and correct the name of a dependent locality, post town and county which was previously associated with an address but which has subsequently been changed by Royal Mail.*

4. *Postcodes will be allocated or corrected for all addresses that contain a recognisable premises. Thoroughfare names will be corrected for all such addresses.*

5. *Ambiguous postal addresses will be identified as uncorrectable because they can refer to two or more differing premises on PAF. The software will report on the alternative PAF addresses.*

6. *The status of postal address text (thoroughfare, locality, town, county) will be identifiable and selectable by the following criteria:*

    * *correct*
    * *correct, but with a removable embellishment after the thoroughfare*
    * *correct locality, town, county*
    * *address not recognised*

7. *The status of a postcode will be identifiable and selectable by the following criteria:*

    * *accurate (confirmed to premises level)*
    * *confirmed to thoroughfare level*
    * *confirmed to dependent locality level*
    * *confirmed to Post Town level*
    * *missing or unverifiable*

8. *All counts reported by the software will be verifiable by printing the corresponding addresses. Sample cases of postal address correction will be selected at random and will cover <u>all</u> combinations of:*

    * *the change in the number of address lines*
    * *the change in the number of address words*
    * *the nature of the first spelling correction in the address (character omission, transposition, etc)*

9. *The system target is that software errors will affect fewer than 0.001% of corrected addresses (fewer than 1 in 100,000 addresses).*

10. *The system will be re-tested with new releases of PAF using every PAF locality to ensure there is no data mis-recognition or mis-correction.*

What's in a name?
Prefixes
Male forenames
Female forenames
Joint forenames
Suffixes
Job titles
Departmental words
Company prefixes
Company suffixes
Prefixes and salutations
Rude words and phrases
Equivalents in foreign languages

Below is an extract from a name reference table. There are many thousands of titles, which shows the scope for confusion (and annoyance if wrongly transcribed onto an envelope).

From Air Commodore (A/Cdr) to Zonjusha and Zoti

Abbreviation/common form	Full title/accepted title
Squadron L	Squadron Leader
Squadron Ldr	Squadron Leader
Sr	Senor
Sr D	Sr D
Sr Ing	Sr Ing
Sra	Sra
Sra Dona	Sra Dona
Srta	Srta
Staff Sergeant	Staff Sergeant
Sub Lieutenant	Sub Lieutenant
Sub Lt	Sub Lieutenant
Sub Ltnt	Sub Lieutenant
Sur	Surgeon
Surg Capt	Surgeon Captain

Step 4: Sorting names and addresses into postal sequence

The next stage involves the merging of all the mailing lists to create a unified Gross List. This Gross List will be repetitively sorted into different sequences and the names and addresses cross-compared with each other **in each sequence**. Each sort is designed to bring more duplicates together for identification, as the following comparisons show:

For example, a sort to **surname** and **initial** sequence brings the names BILL E.GOLD and B.E.GOLD together, as follows:

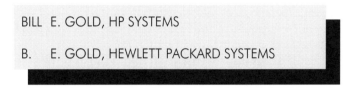

BILL	E. GOLD, HP SYSTEMS
B.	E. GOLD, HEWLETT PACKARD SYSTEMS

A further sort to **company name** sequence will identify another potential duplicate, as follows:

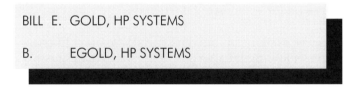

BILL	E.	GOLD, HP SYSTEMS
B.		EGOLD, HP SYSTEMS

The process of looking for potential duplicates in alternative sort sequences is a means of overcoming spelling variations in the uncontrolled and uncorrected data elements in a name and address.

When these successive sorts and comparisons are complete, the computer will "force" the potential duplicates to appear next to each other in a final postal address sequence, as follows:

BILL	E.	GOLD HP SYSTEMS,	UPPER FLOOR, ETC
B.	E.	GOLD HEWLETT PACKARD SYSTEMS,	TOP FLOOR, ETC
BILL		EGOLD, HP SYSTEMS,	PENTHOUSE, ETC
WILLIAM	E.	GOLD, HEWPACK SYSTEMS	UPPER FLOOR, ETC

A group of potential duplicates like the above, which are deemed to be at the same postal address (despite small variations in the actual address details), is called "a match group". The list is now in the form of a Gross List.

At this point in the merge-purge, the computer bureau has established the total number of postal addresses involved in the project and is ready to begin the process of final deduplication and selection of records for inclusion on the Net File.

You may wish to see a specimen set of "match groups" before the final deduplication process begins, so that you can influence the final outcome according to your requirement. Most people find it easier to define their deduplication requirement by using real examples of match groups.

Step 5: The process of deduplication

Deduplication is now ready to go ahead to your requirements. For example, you may stipulate that you want to include several names within one company, or at one address – just so long as you can be fairly certain that they are not variants of the same person. Or, alternatively, you may wish to include as many names as possible and risk some of them possibly being duplicates.

How accurate is your name management?

There have been tremendous technical advances in automated postal address management over the past few years, to the extent that it is now a dependable science, not an art. Today, a computer bureau which corrects a postal address should guarantee the result as an improvement. It should also be able to give the logical reason why a particular address could not be corrected. This is due in no small part to the existence of PAF in the case of consumer names.

By contrast there is no such up-to-date, official, definitive and centralised reference file covering personal names, job titles, departmental names and company names. It follows that merge-purge systems have not yet evolved which can offer comprehensive error correction services on these items of information.

Instead, most merge-purge systems offer a data recognition and interpretation capability. But even this is less than foolproof. For example, do the following items of information refer to People? Companies? Ships? Pubs? Jobs?

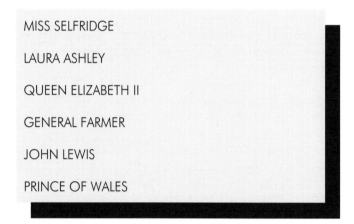

MISS SELFRIDGE

LAURA ASHLEY

QUEEN ELIZABETH II

GENERAL FARMER

JOHN LEWIS

PRINCE OF WALES

It all depends on the context which may, or may not, be supplied by the postal address. Some bureaux can cross-check a mailing list against the Electoral Roll to confirm a given personal name for a home address. But an unconfirmed name is not necessarily inaccurate. One reason: all the residents of an address may not be included on the Electoral Roll.

Are we ready to produce the Gross List?

The conditioned and improved name and address records are about to be merged into a Gross List ready for sorting into postal address sequence prior to deduplication. Clearly, from all the foregoing, you can see that accurate deduplications would be impossible without the processing so far outlined.

It is the computer bureau's responsibility to let you know about data problems in a mailing list. **The acceptability of all the mailing lists must be confirmed before the next step of the merge-purge can begin.**

If you go too far in either direction (eg too many **ex**clusions or too many **in**clusions), you risk what are known as “Overkill” and “Underkill”, each with its own advantages and disadvantages.

Overkill

A term used to describe a deduplication biased towards the elimination of all possible duplicates by making more tenuous comparisons. The Net List is smaller, with fewer residual duplicates.

Underkill

A term used to describe a deduplication biased towards the elimination of probable duplicates only. Stricter comparisons are made. The Net List is bigger, with more residual duplicates.

Deduplication levels – you decide on your needs

Even where there is no risk of incorrect names or addresses, there may still be duplicates, ie people, addresses or companies occurring on several lists, which call for a decision from you.

Merge-purge systems can compare names and addresses at all these different levels. A “match” can be made at the address level, company level, family level, or at the individual level, as follows:

ADDRESS LEVEL: (The same address)	Mr James Smith 1 Endeavour Way London SW19 8UH	Mr Bill Jones 1 Endeavour Way London SW19 8UH
COMPANY LEVEL: (The same company name and address)	Mrs Gwen Lloyd Aybe Ltd 2 Church Street Whitstable CT5 1PJ	Mr Fred Parr Aybe Ltd 2 Church Street Whitstable CT5 1PJ
FAMILY LEVEL: (The same family name and address)	Miss P Starr 12 Hidcote House Devonshire Avenue Sutton SM2 5JL	Michael Starr 12 Hidcote House Devonshire Avenue Sutton SM2 5JL
INDIVIDUAL LEVEL: (The same person)	Peter Woods 2 Bridgefield Court Whitstable CT5 2PL	Peter Woods 2 Bridgefield Court Whitstable CT5 2PL

The computer bureau needs to be told at which level to operate the deduplication process. An "address level" deduplication will result in only one name and address per postal address.

A deduplication at any other level may result in several names (different companies or individuals) per postal address.

Some merge-purge projects may require deduplication at two or more levels, depending on which lists are involved. For example, a merge-purge where all lists are to be compared at the individual level, but where the Mortalities list is to be compared at the address level (because no mailing is to be sent to an address where someone has died recently).

The deduplication level chosen will obviously affect any counts of duplicates detected by the merge-purge. It is essential that the deduplication level is taken into consideration when you review a printed report of the number of duplicates detected.

Multiple-level deduplication – different levels for different objectives

Some merge-purge systems can review potential duplicates at all levels before making a decision on which names and addresses are to be kept and which are to be deleted.

Below is a set of names detected at the same postal address "match group". The merge-purge has "flagged" these names to indicate that they will be selected for inclusion on the Net List depending on the required level of deduplication.

Flags			Name	Company
A	C	E	Michael Smith	ABC Ltd
-	-	-	Mike Smith	ABC Ltd
-	-	E	Peter Brown	ABC Ltd
-	C	E	Ann Jones	XYZ Ltd
-	-	-	Ann Jones	XYZ Ltd

Flag A: Address level
Only one record has been given a flag A and it can be selected if deduplication is required at the ADDRESS level (eg a one-per-address mailing).

Flag C: Company level
Two records have been given a flag C and they can be selected if deduplication is required at the COMPANY level (eg a one-per-company mailing).

Flag E: Employee level
Three records have been given a flag E and they can be selected if deduplication is required at the EMPLOYEE level (eg a one-per-employee mailing).

How to handle the multiple-customer household

This example presents another problem for you and your bureau: what to do with the multiple-buyer household. It shows why every merge-purge programme should be tailored to the marketer's specific needs.

Take the case of a department store whose customers include a husband, wife and daughter all at the same address. The husband may have a budget card and a charge card; the wife, a budget card and a lifestyle card; the daughter, a budget card only. Three members of a household holding five cards in three different combinations at one address with one surname.

To promote a special offer to lifestyle customers presents no problem: there is only one lifestyle card holder in the family so only one mailing would go. But suppose there was a promotion for the budget card? Three identical mailings to one household would be wasteful and unwanted. So the conversion program allocates a code to each name's title – say 1 for Mr; 2 for Mrs; 3 for Ms; and 4 for Miss. The merge-purge program takes the "lowest" code as the one to be mailed (in this case 1 – Mr, the husband) and then purges the rest.

But when notifications of changes in interest rates are sent out, a different merge-purge program is necessary because it is a legal requirement that ALL card holders receive a personal notification. So here all three would receive the communication, but the husband and wife would be purged from one of their lists so that despite having two different cards they need only receive one mailing each.

Mailing purpose	**Husband budget card charge card**	**Wife budget card lifestyle card**	**Daughter budget card**
Promotion to lifestyle customers		✔	
Promotion to budget customers	✔ (serves all three family members)	Purged	Purged
Interest rate notification (budget card)	✔ (also covers charge card)	✔ (also covers lifestyle card)	✔
Interest rate notification (lifestyle card)		Purged	
Interest rate notification (charge card)	Purged		

Intra-list and inter-list duplicates – useful measures of list quality

A merge-purge will detect duplicates within a mailing list and across mailing lists, as we have seen. These are usually counted and analysed separately, under the following heads:

Intra-list duplicates	The number of duplicates detected within a particular mailing list.
Inter-list duplicates	The number of duplicates detected across two particular mailing lists.

The count of INTRA-list duplicates is an important measure of the quality of the list. A high count indicates poor list management, ie the count relates to duplicates detected at the individual level. The same would be true for a list of company names and addresses, ie the count referred to duplicates detected at the company name level.

The count of INTER-list duplicates is an important measure of the synergy between two lists. A high count indicates that the lists are similar and are likely to respond at similar rates to a particular offer. (List owners in non-competitive markets, who find that their lists have a high rate of inter-list duplication, will sometimes consider a list swop.)

Multibuyers – proven responders?

A "multibuyer" is a person who appears on more than one mailing list; in other words an inter-list duplicate at the individual level. Multibuyers may, in fact, not be buyers but responders in other ways, eg enquirers, attendees, etc.

Multibuyers are often considered to be the most responsive segment of a net mailing list. This is most likely to be true if they appear across mailing lists which have been built from direct mail response. Most merge-purge systems can identify and select multibuyers from the net mailing list so that they can be treated as a special segment for a campaign.

Choosing the right duplicate – three forms of priority

Where a name and address are identified as a duplicate featuring on several lists (whether all versions are identical or nearly so), it is necessary to make a decision about which list they are to be selected from, since you want to retain them only once.

If the name and address appear in more than one form, it will be necessary to select only one version.

How do you ensure that your deduplication process selects the best version of each name and address and the best list to select them from. The answer is to allocate them a ranking or **priority** as follows:

- ✔ **List priority**, giving priority to the name as it appears on one list rather than another.
- ✔ **Postal address priority**, giving priority to a version of the name and address which is thought to be the most accurate or complete.

✔ **Name priority**, giving priority to the version of the name which is the most likely to be accurate, probably because it is more complete.

List priority – choosing the name from the least cost list

The owners of rented mailing lists may agree to a so-called "net names deal", where they will be paid rental fees only for names and addresses mailed. Fees may be waived, in whole or in part, for names and addresses which are deselected because they duplicate with names and addresses on other mailing lists.

There can be a considerable difference in the unit rental costs of different mailing lists, so it makes sense to bias your selection of net names and addresses towards the cheaper rented lists. In the example below, we can see a multibuyer who appears on three different rented lists A, B and C.

Mailing list	Priority	Rental cost per '000	Name and address
A	1	£100	John Doe, 15 High Road, Oxford
B	2	£120	John Doe, 15 High Road, Oxford
C	3	£150	John Doe, 15 High Road, Oxford

Mailing list A has the lowest unit rental cost and we would like the name and address to be selected from that list. To facilitate this, each mailing list has been pre-allocated a "relative list priority code" of 1,2 or 3 where 1 is the highest and 3 the lowest priority code.

The merge-purge will select the name and address with the highest list priority code. In our example, the name and address selected for inclusion on the net mailing list will be those from List A.

The merge-purge will print a summary report detailing how many names and addresses were selected in this way from each mailing list. In a "net names deal" this report provides the basis for calculating the fees due to each list owner.

List priorities should therefore be an important part of the instructions given to the merge-purge bureau. They are normally specified in a "list of lists" delivered to the bureau. This list of lists is drawn up in descending list priority and given to the bureau before the deduplication. The list of lists is sometimes called a "List Hierarchy".

Postal address priorities – cheapest not necessarily best

Despite what we have just said about list priorities and choosing the cheapest, as in many other walks of life the cheapest is not necessarily the best or most cost-effective course of action. Merge-purge systems which use List Priorities to select names and addresses from the cheapest lists can fall into the same trap.

We said earlier that most merge-purge systems offering automatic postal address correction will add a Postal Address Quality Indicator to each name and address record. These indicators can be used to identify the best quality postal address in each match group. Sometimes a better quality address is worth paying for – occasionally it is imperative.

In the example below we see names and addresses, each occurring on three different lists A, B and C. These lists have been allocated list priorities of 1,2,3 in descending priority order according to cost. In this example, the record on List A would normally be selected for inclusion on the Net file; it is the cheapest list with the highest priority. But look at the postal address quality indicator for each list ... what does that tell us?

List	Priority	Name	Address quality indicators	
			Address text	Postcode
A	1	Michael S. Smith	Poor	None
B	2	Michael S. Smith	Perfect	Correct
C	3	Michael S. Smith	Fair	Incomplete

The record on List A cannot qualify for a Mailsort or Walksort postage discount because it has no postcode. It is better to select the record from List B which has a correct postcode and can qualify for a postage discount. The savings offered by a postage discount nearly always exceed the savings in unit rental costs offered by the cheapest list. (For more on Mailsort refer to Chapters 7.8 and 7.10 in this Guide.)

Quality of name priorities – preferring the more complete name

We have seen how a merge-purge can examine the records in a duplicate match group and can select a name and address on the basis of a highest list priority code, or on the basis of the best quality postal address. It is also possible for selection to occur on the basis of the quality of the name, the third type of priority.

In the example below, we can see three different presentations of a name (all at the same postal address). Which would you prefer to use for a mailing or to transfer to your master database?

List	Name
A	Ms Smith
B	M.S. Smith
C	Michael S Smith

At first sight, the name from List A appears as a female name. But List B suggests that the prefix MS is a set of initials. This is confirmed by List C, from which it is apparent that it is a male name. **Usually the more complete the name, the more accurate it is.**

A merge-purge system which can assess the relative quality of names can also, as in this case, perform a useful service in determining the gender of a name and can go on to generate a correct letter salutation, eg Dear Mr Smith (rather than dear Ms Smith).

What to do when the above priorities conflict?

Sometimes names and address priorities may be in conflict.

For example, in the specimen match groups shown below, we can see three duplicated name and address records which were sourced from Lists A, B and C. List A has the highest priority, but the record from List B has the best postal address. The record from List C has the best personal name. What would you do in this situation?

List	Priority	Name	Address text	Postcode
A	1	Ms Smith	Poor	None
B	2	M.S. Smith	Perfect	Correct
C	3	Michael S. Smith	Fair	Incomplete

In an ideal world, you would create a final name and address using the name from List C and the postal address from List B (and pay the price for List A!). Indeed your in-house database development people may demand such an amalgamation.

In this case, the merge-purge programme may be required to report on such cases so that any final amalgamations are controlled by clerical support staff.

Clearly, in a direct mail project using rented lists, the computer would attribute a gender and salutation to the record with the best postal address.

Step 6: The Net List is ready

After removal of all unwanted duplicates from the Gross List, you arrive at the Net List. Your merge-purge is complete. Your Net List is now ready for whatever application you have in mind, a direct mail campaign for instance.

At this point you will know the quality of your combined list, the number of duplicates rejected, the number of multibuyers earmarked for special treatment, and how much you will be paying for the names you have used. You may wish to make selections from this list based upon "other information" preserved from the original source lists. Whatever you do, you can be sure you are working with the best possible name and address data.

Using rented and merge-purged lists

As we have seen, one of the most common uses of a merge-purge is to consolidate a number of rented mailing lists into a Net List for use in a direct mail campaign. The owners of the rented lists must approve the purposes of the campaign and may require a preview of the advertising literature that will be mailed.

The administrative work involved in dealing with list owners, including negotiation on list availability, selections, pricing, delivery, etc, is often done by a list broker or advertising agency. A list broker acts as an agent between the list user and the list owners. The list broker will also ensure that the rented mailing lists are delivered on time and in a form which is suitable for merge-purge processing at a selected computer bureau.

Negotiation	Merge-purge	Direct mail
List user → List broker → List owners →	Computer bureau →	Mailing house → Mail

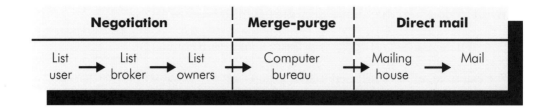

Computer bureaux which provide merge-purge services have strict security and control procedures that respect the commercial interests of all the parties involved in the project. The security of the rented mailing lists in the bureau premises is a paramount concern.

Incorporating "special" lists into your merge-purge

Net lists can be further refined by including additional or "special" lists in your merge-purge procedure. These may be used to suppress names, to augment the information available for names, and for several other purposes, eg security and monitoring.

The table below shows examples of some special lists together with their uses and destinations.

Special list	Uses	Examples/description
Suppression List	Names and addresses which must not be allowed onto Net List, subject to certain exceptions (eg seed names which must be "forced" onto the Net List – see below).	**Mail Preference Service (MPS)** – List of people who do not wish to receive unsolicited direct mail. **Mortalities** – List of people who have died recently. Users may wish to suppress all names at the deceased's address. **Gone-aways** – List of people known to be no longer resident at the address listed.
Seed Lists	Names and addresses which cannot be de-duplicated or removed by a Suppression List, ie all seed names must be "forced" onto the Net List. Usually included for security and monitoring purposes.	**Monitor seeds** – People whose role it is to report back to the user on a mailing, eg when it was delivered, whether it was correctly presented, etc. **Security seeds** – Fictitious names (to preserve anonymity) whose role is to report any unauthorised use of the list, usually to the owner.
User Lists	Names and addresses which may be deduplicated but cannot be removed eg by suppression list (possibly because they have positively requested inclusion). User lists take priority over rented lists where duplication occurs.	**Users** – Customers/prospects (who would expect to be included). NB: Merge-purge provides an ideal opportunity to de-duplicate and otherwise improve names on the user list.
Overlay Lists	Items of information for transfer to matching names and addresses on the Net List.	Telephone number lists. Lifestyle data. **Change of address lists** (Royal Mail National Change of Address List, NCOA) – used to substitute new addresses for old.

Step 7: Analysing the results: What can we learn?

The merge-purge has been done. You have built or added to your marketing database, or have perhaps carried out a direct mail campaign. The response is now available. The next step is to analyse that response and to use the lessons learned wisely in your next merge-purge. Direct marketing, as we have seen in other chapters, is a continuous process.

The analysis procedure is quite straightforward and is an integral part of most computer bureaux services. The steps are noted below:

✔ **Exploratory analysis**
Perform a response analysis which identifies the response rates for different segments of the mailing. A segment is a set of names and addresses which have been similarly classified according to UK or EU demographics, geodemographics, compiled business data, name and address characteristics, and from established customer data. (See segmentation, Chapter 3.5 of this Guide.)

✔ **Data selection**
Use the response analysis to identify data elements with a significant effect upon response rates. For example, is your response greatest in a geographical area, in a certain industry, or among a particular age group?

✔ **Response modelling**
Build a statistical model to predict an individual's response rate and validate the model using a set of names and addresses withheld from the model building process – then build a gains chart. See modelling Chapters 3.5 and 3.7 of this Guide.

Specimen gains chart

% of the mailing file	Response rate – %	Cumulative response rate – %	Response index
Top 10%	3.20	3.20	160
2nd 10%	2.80	3.00	150
3rd 10%	2.60	2.87	144
4th 10%	2.20	2.70	135
5th 10%	2.00	2.56	128
6th 10%	1.90	2.45	123
7th 10%	1.70	2.34	117
8th 10%	1.50	2.24	112
9th 10%	1.20	2.12	106
Worst 10%	0.90	2.00	100

✔ **"Matrix Day"**
This is a workshop where list buyers and bureau analysts can work together to build a mailing matrix. Selections are made by the model list scores, and by list, to ensure maximum gains from the next campaign. Different selections are made from different lists, according to performance, as illustrated in the following diagram:

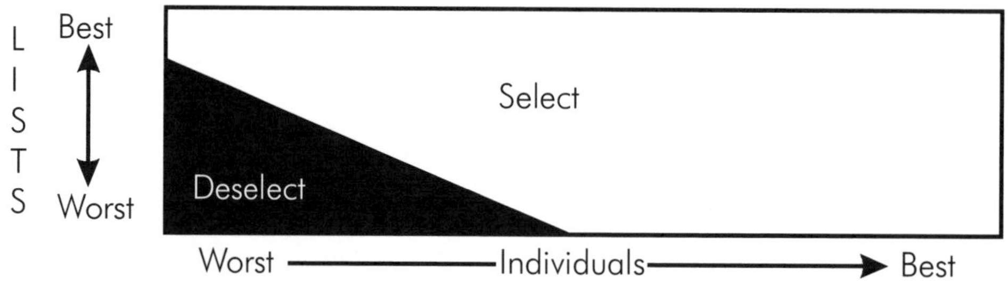

✔ **Validation**
The model can be validated in a test mailing in which segments are selected by reference to the model and compared with other segments created without the benefit of the model. A comparison of response from these segments will confirm how good the model is at selecting highly responsive individuals. (A model should also be revalidated at periodic intervals in live mailing campaigns to ensure it remains effective.)

International merge-purge

In the UK, market demand for merge-purge services on international mailing lists is very small in comparison to the demand for services on UK mailing lists. Consequently, very few computer bureaux have invested in research and development of software to handle foreign mailing lists. Certainly, there is no bureau which would claim that its expertise in foreign name and address manipulation is anywhere near as good as that for its own country.

Nevertheless, there has been a steady increase in the number of foreign national and multinational mailing lists available for rental in the UK and there are a few computer bureaux who can offer a fair degree of expertise in processing these lists. In most cases, multinational merge-purge will more than pay its way by the elimination of duplicates and by the savings offered by a response analysis leading to the deselection of unresponsive list segments.

It is therefore important to use a bureau which can demonstrate expertise in these two areas, processing and analysis, and which can demonstrate competence in dealing with foreign name and address formats and foreign character sets. For more information on international direct mail lists see Chapter 5.2 of this Guide.

How much does merge-purge cost?

Finally, how much does all this highly complex computer servicing cost? Actually, these services cost **nothing**. They are **free**. In fact, they are **less** than free, because they actually save you money. The savings made by deleting duplicates almost invariably outweigh the cost of removing them. Likewise, the discounts on postage obtained by supplying pre-sorted mail are significantly more than your bureau will charge for rebate-sorting – as the following example demonstrates:

Financial benefit of merge-purge	
Cost of mailing	£450 per thousand (say)
List rental volume	100,000 records
Average processing charge	£16 per thousand
Total computer charge	£1,600
Level of duplicates	5%* (say)
Number of duplicates therefore	5,000
Saving (at £450 per 1,000)	£2,250

* In practice it is not uncommon for 15% duplicates to be removed.

Remember to add to your saving: Mailsort discounts and increased responses due to list selection improvement. Merge-purge is at the very heart and is the lifeblood of successful personal communication. It is as important as that. And it pays!

Chapter 3.4

Choosing your database software and system

This chapter includes:

- **The 4 basic software options**
- **Step-by-step, choosing a software package**
- **Using bureaux and their software**
- **Ready-made versus custom built**
- **How computers store information**
- **Sequential files and relational databases**
- **Choosing a computer bureau**

Not long ago database technology and software development were the exclusive domain of data processing specialists. Today it is universally accepted that, where direct marketing is concerned, it is marketing management who must lead the project – because the systems required by direct marketers are significantly different from those required for finance, manufacturing, stock control, etc.

You no longer have to be a systems designer to influence major database design decisions, but you will need an understanding of the options available. You must also be able to comprehend the advantages and disadvantages of the different types of database and weigh the pros and cons of the many external services available.

In this chapter Neil Woodcock concentrates on the three major questions: the software options open to you, the main types of database, and external services – bringing a much-needed simplicity to a subject all too often overburdened with jargon.

New in this edition. The list of software packages has been completely updated. It will, of course, begin to date even before this edition goes to press, but it should provide you with an excellent starting point for your own researches. Also new is the 17-step process for shortlisting and selecting packaged software.

Neil Woodcock, Director, QCi Ltd

Neil holds a BSc (Hons) and, before becoming a computer consultant, held sales and marketing management roles with Unilever and Mobil Oil. He then spent almost a decade as a business consultant with Andersen Computing before co-founding QCi Ltd.

He has worked with blue chip companies in the UK, Europe, the Far East, South Africa and USA. This experience, coupled with the knowledge gained from the extensive research carried out with Professor Merlin Stone and QCi, has contributed to a detailed insight into many different markets and industries. He is a regular speaker at international marketing events and is widely published on the subject.

His books include "Relationship Marketing" with Professor Merlin Stone (Hogan Page) and "Winning New Customers in Financial Services", in association with IBM (F T Pitman).

Neil is a specialist in helping organisations understand how they can develop, apply and measure customer management strategies using IT. He defines this as (1) planning effectively across sales, marketing, service and IT functions, (2) optimising the use of direct channels such as mail, telemarketing, field sales or indirect channels, eg dealers, resellers, retailers, field marketing, franchises, developing and managing dialogues with customers, and (3) analysing customer behaviour and attitude. He is an industry expert in call centre strategy, set-up and management.

With QCi, he has led the development of the QCi Customer Management Diagnostic Tool, the first software tool of its type, which enables a company to quickly diagnose its customer management capability and identify ways to improve it.

Recent projects included call centre design for a major oil company, resource planning for a large telecommunications organisation, developing a customer management strategy for a credit card issue, and direct marketing development for a personal finance house.

Neil Woodcock M IDM
Director
QCi Ltd
1 Gaston Bridge Road
Shepperton
Middlesex TW17 8HH
Tel: 01932-252993

Chapter 3.4

Choosing your database software and system

So you're ready for a database?

The key to successful long-term direct marketing is, as we have seen, the database. Not just any database, but a database developed for marketing – it must be **flexible** and it must be **usable**.

A database means, of course, **software**. Once you have decided you need a database, your next requirement will be to select the most appropriate software to meet your objectives.

There are four basic options open to you:

Option 1	Buy or lease a software package designed to support your requirements.
Option 2	Use proprietary software provided by a computer bureau, ie employ a bureau.
Option 3	Custom build your own database from scratch.
Option 4	Adapt your existing database, possibly merging several databases to form a master.

The right choice for you will depend on your particular needs and also on the stage you have reached in database marketing. A marketing **system** may involve two or even three of the basic options above.

Let us now take a look at the steps needed to choose the right option as well as the advantages and disadvantages of each.

Option 1: Buying or leasing a software package

A wide range of packages to choose from

The number of marketing and sales software packages continues to escalate. There are plenty of good packages on the market to support a huge variety of applications: market research, telemarketing, direct mail, geographic mapping of customers, etc – all usable with a personal computer. They can be bought or leased. You'll find some suggestions on page 3.4-11.

Remember, software manufacturers invariably claim multiple functions for their packages. But how well they support your task is what matters. In short, do not rely on manufacturers' claims. Check them out!

In the next few pages we show you how to whittle down the vast list of available software to the one or two packages that will be suitable for you.

Overleaf is a master step-by-step checklist that it will repay you to refer to regularly as you work through your software selection procedure:

Steps in selecting a database software package

Step	Action
1	Select your project team
2	Decide your overall time span
3	Define your business objectives for the system
4	Define your functional requirements for the system
5	Analyse your capacity and performance needs
6	Consider individual versus company use
7	Check your security and back-up needs
8	Identify your current system weaknesses
9	Define your technical requirements
10	Carry out a cost-benefit analysis
11	Identify potential packages
12	Draw up an Invitation-to-tender
13	Define your software selection criteria
14	Evaluate shortlisted software packages
15	Meet the two top-scoring suppliers
16	Ask for a prototype
17	Make your decision!

We now look at each of the above steps in turn, stressing the main issues. This will take us up to page 3.4-16.

Step 1: Select your project team

Selecting the right team to set up your database is the most critical step of all. Selection should **not** be led by computer staff (they won't be using the system), but by business managers, preferably from sales or marketing.

Develop a core selection team comprising the following members:

The ideal software selection team	
Project Manager	Senior business manager (usually marketing or sales)
Technical analyst	Systems manager
Functional analyst	Business person who can develop and understand the overall process which the system must support
User(s)	User(s) of the current system (ideally they will have been instrumental in the drive for change)
External adviser	Someone who has been through the process before and understands all the complexities and issues involved

Give them enough time. Ensure the team selected has sufficient time for the project. Too often staff cannot devote enough quality time to master the details – they remain at the "veneer" level.

For the selection of a 10-station telemarketing system, for example, time allocations may be as indicated in the table below.

How much of their time?	
Project Manager	50%
Technical Analyst	60%
Functional Analyst	60%
User(s)	30%

Step 2: Decide your overall time span

The time span required to select a software package depends on the project and the team time available.

To progress through the steps discussed here (ie for selecting a package to support only a **mildly** changed business process) typically takes about three months.

However, if **major** changes are being considered, simply defining your objectives (our next step) may take several months. Similarly, finalising your decision may take several months, especially if protracted negotiations are involved (eg as with a 100-operator licensed system).

With the help of someone who has carried out these functions before, plan and publish your intended time schedule which may look something like this:

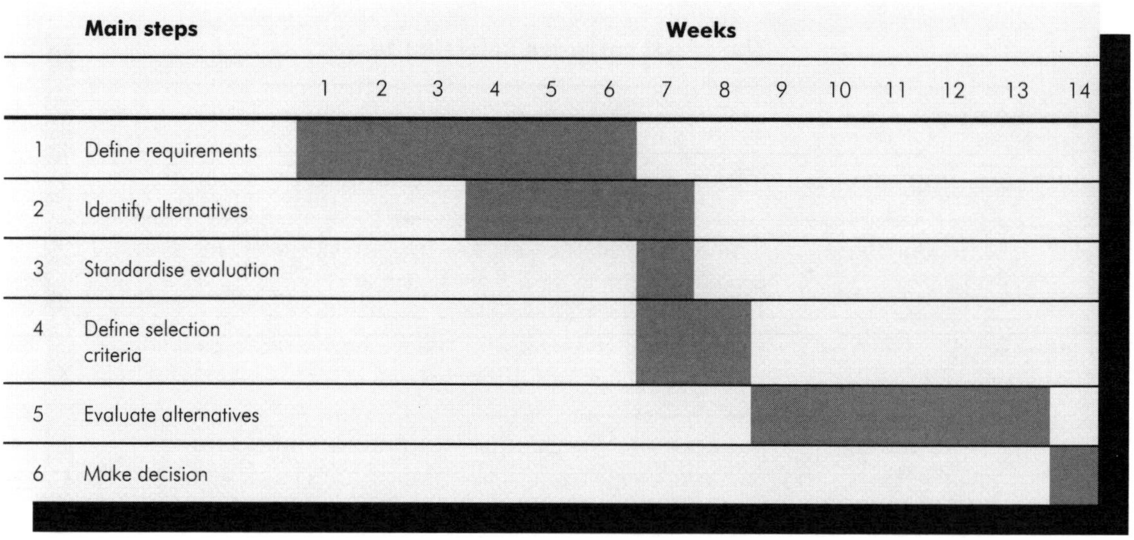
Main steps
Weeks
1 2 3 4 5 6 7 8 9 10 11 12 13 14
1 Define requirements
2 Identify alternatives
3 Standardise evaluation
4 Define selection criteria
5 Evaluate alternatives
6 Make decision

Step 3: Define your business objectives for the system

We now come to another very important step in the software selection process: defining your business objectives for the system.

If you do not identify your requirements for the database software and system in detail, at this stage, your new software will NEVER sit comfortably with those who must use it.

Just look at the risks of getting it wrong:

✘ Wasted project team time.

✘ Wasted cost of software package, licences, customisation, etc.

✘ Cost of user training on unsuitable system.

✘ Wasted internal time developing interfaces.

✘ Lost "face" of all concerned.

✘ Lost business through poor support.

✘ Customer frustration at being handled badly.

✘ User frustration and annoyance.

✘ User apathy in future.

The important point here is to define objectives for the business **and** for the system – clearly these must be totally compatible.

Ask yourself these questions:

? What do I want the system to do?

? Can I state my objectives clearly?

? Can they be measured?

? Can they be achieved in the timescale?

Below are two examples of agreed business objectives linked with the system benefits:

Is yours a retention objective?

If you have a problem retaining, say, medium-sized customers who, research has shown, are effectively unmanaged by the company – and you are developing a database to better manage the inbound and outbound contacts with them – the link would be with customer retention, maybe improving it from 60% to 75%, or perhaps from 75% to 79%.

Is yours a cost-cutting objective?

If you are looking to reduce the cost of sales by introducing a telephone account management unit to support field sales and manage some of the smaller field sales accounts, you might stipulate a percentage reduction, say 30%, at which you are aiming.

Step 4: Define your functional requirements for the system

The software package you choose must also fit with your technical strategy (the "how" as well as the "why"). The processes which the software is to support must be developed in detail.

Ask yourself (and the users):

? Who will be affected?

? What information will they need?

? How and where can the system support them?

? What functions and features should the system have?

Prioritise your answers provisionally; the final priorities will be decided by management.

System benefits you can look forward to

Here are some examples of system benefits you might look for from your new software and systems:

✔ **Increased efficiency**, eg a reduction in unit costs of sales and marketing through alternative channels (telemarketing to support field sales?); also improved controls and measurement.

✔ **Extra revenue from existing customers**, eg through cross-selling, up-trading, reactivating dormant customers, enhancement of lifetime values, etc.

✔ **Extra revenue, new customers**, through better targeting, prospecting, and enquiry management.

✔ **Increased loyalty and retention**, through better customer management; more and better information (to and from customers); more timely and relevant contacts; better handling of complaints; additional contacts through alternative sales channels; fewer invoicing errors, etc.

✔ Employee motivation, less absenteeism and reduced staff attrition.

One way to ensure that you achieve the goals you want is to adopt the kind of systematic software selection process we are advocating here.

Step 5: Analyse your capacity and performance needs

Capacity and Performance Analysis (CPA) will help you determine:

✔ How many users will be involved.

✔ Where they are located.

✔ The likely complexity of the processing.

✔ The amount of data to be accessed.

✔ Task and response times (especially for telemarketing systems).

This form of analysis should rule out some of the single-use packages on offer, further helping you to narrow down the field.

Step 6: Consider individual versus company use

Surprisingly, most telemarketing and salesforce automation packages were conceived, designed and built for individual use – **not** for companies. Typically these packages attach little or no importance to company requirements, which may rule them out.

Do your **business** requirements include any or all of the following:

? Multi-level security (see following Step 7)?

? Frequency distribution reports?

? Summary business reports?

? Data centralisation?

? End-user configurability?

? Data compatibility and integrity control?

? Data transfer and synchronisation?

? International applications (language compatibility)?

It reads like a thesaurus of business jargon, but stop and consider each point for a moment and imagine the impact on your business if any one, say data centralisation, was not possible.

Step 7: Check your security and back-up needs

Security and back-up may well be a major requirement of your database software. Most software packages are very weak in this area – a few more options bite the dust.

Ask yourself:

- ? What type of data will be on your system?
- ? How sensitive is the data?
- ? Will it contain personal data on customers' health, finances, relationships, etc?
- ? Will customers accept the data uses being proposed?
- ? Will your data contain business "secrets", eg about the overall profitability of products?
- ? Who will be able to access the system?
- ? What authorisations will be issued?
- ? Will external data sources be incorporated, possibly exposing the system to "hacking", viruses, etc?

If security is important to your company, it should be highlighted and transferred to your key criteria checklist.

Step 8: Identify your current system weaknesses

This is an area which is often overlooked; surprisingly, since dissatisfaction with current processes is often the driving force behind change.

Analysis of your current system, especially what users do and do not like about it, can lead to refinements. It can also identify discrepancies between what users **say** they want and what they actually **need**.

Beware specifying a system to fix one problem (eg to supply supervisors with call data), which then causes another problem (eg damages the telemarketer's customer relationship, demotivation, time wasted, etc).

Trace through all the possible outcomes of introducing a new system. Serious change issues can emerge from a fairly simple system requirement.

Step 9: Define your technical requirements

Now is the time to develop your technical and strategic requirements for the new system.

For example, each of the following can be used to rule in or out software packages from your original list:

- ? Hardware requirements?
- ? Operating systems?
- ? Type of database?
- ? Programming language?

It is often tempting for business users to try and override this stage, especially if the project manager is a business project manager. This should be avoided because the support of IT personnel for the system will be critical.

Step 10: Carry out a cost-benefit analysis

An outline cost-benefit analysis will demonstrate the level of finance required for the software and systems development: whether more can and should be afforded, or whether some applications will have to be trimmed. Such an analysis may rule out some advanced packages.

Never allow the company to be swayed by price alone, certainly not until you are certain that you have defined all your requirements **very** meticulously.

Step 11: Identify potential packages

By now you will be in a position to make initial enquiries about software packages which may suit your needs.

The table on the facing page will give you a start. If, by the time you reach this stage, some of the contacts we have listed are out of date, at least you will be able to begin your own process of tracking down suitable suppliers.

By contacting the suppliers we've provided, also trawling through software directories, external consultants and internal specialists – and by using all the information deduced – you should be ready to make an intuitive shortlist. **Four or five possible packages is all you need.** This process should not take long, except in the case of the most complex requirements.

In practice you will have neither the time nor the patience to visit every supplier. Even if you were to try you would rapidly become punch-drunk with functions, features, and sales talk! So keep some distance between you and your potential suppliers at this stage.

At this stage, or certainly the next, you need answers to such questions about your potential supplier as:

- ? Number, qualifications and experience of personnel?
- ? Relevant background of personnel and supplier company?
- ? Strengths and abilities in your own weakest areas?
- ? Attitude towards your business?
- ? Successes with other clients, etc?
- ? Any weaknesses admitted by them or perceived by you?

Examples of marketing software packages

Package	Contact	
ACT	Symantec	0800-526459
Brock	Co-Cam (UK) Ltd	0181-490 7100
Goldmine	AVG	0171-454 1790
Mailbrain Telemarketing	UCL Computer Factors	01203-555466
Market Force	Market Solutions Ltd	01628-32517
Market Pulse	CCA	01628-781255 (fax)
Maximiser	Modatech	01732-742626
NPRI	'Phone Power	01734-880216
Oxygen	Integrated Sales Systems	0181-740 7440
Sales Action Manager	Tranzline	01276-686968
SPS	Saratoga Systems	01344-875170
Symmetry	Workstations Ltd	01628-603284
Tel-Athena	Alpha Numeric	01628-475661
Telebusiness Edge	Datapoint (UK) Ltd	0181-459 1222
T.O.P.C.A.T.	Independent Software, Marketplace Ltd	0181-543 2211
Tracker	Tracker	01628-488866
Unitrac	Unitract Software	0181-781 1994
Viper	Brann	0117-927 7790

Step 12: Draw up an Invitation-to-tender

Now that you have your shortlist and answers to some basic questions, it is time for either an ITT (Invitation-to-tender) or an RFP (Request for proposal).

(If you **haven't** already asked those questions at the bottom of the previous page, now must be the time.)

Overleaf we give an example of a typical Invitation-to-tender showing the type and arrangement of questions to be completed by the supplier.

Invitation-To-Tender Document
In Confidence

Date:

From:

To: ***This ITT is the responsibility of:***

Potential suppliers must agree, and sign off to, the following. The recipient must:

1. Keep the number of copies of this document to a minimum.
2. Keep all copies in-house (not to any subcontractor, unless previously agreed by us).
3. Destroy all copies at the end of the tender process, if not successful.
4. Have signed the Confidentiality Agreement before reading the document.
5. All personnel involved in the project must also have signed the Confidentiality Agreement before reading the document.

Proposal instructions

Date required:

To whom:

How many copies:

Format:

Presentation format (if required):

Project timescales:

Contact person: Tel No: Fax No:

Overview of requirement:

Overall processes to be supported (chart)

(Use separate sheet of paper if necessary)

	Requirement	Comment
Part 1		
	1. Functional requirement	
Overview		
	2. Technical requirement	
Overview		
	3. Data relationship and integrity	
Overview		
	4. Capacity and performance reqs	
	5. Back-up and security	
Part 2		
	6. Supplier/supplier's clients	
	Biggest client and % of income represented by this client during year ended 31.12.97	
	Installed base	
	Client list	
	Reference sites available	
	Experience with similar companies	
	Experience with similar functions	
	No. of versions/release dates of version/next release date	
	7. Supplier details	
	Owning company	
	Years in operation	
	Accounts, last three years	
	Software ownership	
	No. of staff (and by year)	
	Years of employment of key staff	
	8. Supplier's cost areas	
	Cost breakdown for this project	
	Site/User Licence cost	
	Customisation cost	
	Training (x users by type)	
	Day rates for consultancy/ programming/account management	
	Upgrade/new version costs	
	Help desk support (opening times/ support time included/ongoing costs)	
	Experience of our industry	
	Proven software	
	Supplier stability and confidence	
	User acceptance of solution	
	Timescale for development	
	Ability to migrate to other technical platform	

As you will have seen on the sample ITT document on the previous spread, the Invitation-to-tender lists eight requirement areas to be covered:

✔ Functional

✔ Technical

✔ Data relationship and integrity

✔ Capacity and performance

✔ Security and back-up

✔ Supplier assessment

✔ Supplier details

✔ Supplier costs

Remember, when you come to meet the shortlisted suppliers, or have preliminary talks with them over the telephone:

✘ Don't keep secrets from them; tell them everything that will help them to give you sound, reliable advice.

✘ Don't be blinded by functions and features that are not your main requirement.

✔ Do channel all contacts through a single interface.

✔ Do hold project meetings internally to review any important new requirements/obstacles, etc, that come to light as the result of your discussions with suppliers.

Step 13: Define your software selection criteria

We are nearing the final stage of the selection process now and we must identify the **key criteria** you will use to evaluate and differentiate supplier proposals.

This will be a diluted version of the ITT, focusing on the "must haves" rather than the "nice to haves". This process can be painful. If it is not painful, it probably means that one person's personality or wishes are being progressed at the expense of debate. It is surprising how far one person's (internal or consultant or supplier) view can distort reality. **The "sexy" functions and features will often not provide the main benefits and should not be on the key criteria list.**

The key selection criteria can include anything to do with the requirements, hardware, software, experience in the industry, supplier stability, approachability of the people, in-depth technical support, etc, included in the ITT. Often, supplier stability and seeing the package in action at a known competitor provide enough confidence.

Step 14: Evaluate the shortlisted software packages

Here, an evaluation spreadsheet will help record suppliers' responses to your key criteria.

		Suppliers				
	Weighting	**A**	**B**	**C**	**D**	**E**
Requirement 1	10	8	6	4	7	3
Requirement 2	5	3	1	3	1	2
Requirement 3	7	4	3	2	2	-
Score		15	10	9	10	5

An overall score can be developed objectively from this process. Objective scoring is a guide only, but if the key criteria have been carefully agreed, it is an important guide.

You can now overlay on your top-scorers the "nice to have" criteria and bring in your team's subjective views. You should by now be down to a couple of possibles.

Step 15: Meet the 2 top-scoring software suppliers

The final stage of the selection process is to meet the two best suppliers face-to-face ("eyeball" them, in US slang). Ask if you may review a client site, preferably without their being present all the time.

There may be no such thing as a free lunch, but a lunch that you sponsor can work wonders in extracting real information about suppliers and their products which might not otherwise emerge.

Step 16: Ask for a prototype

Ask your favoured suppliers to develop a detailed working prototype, not for the whole process but for a complex part of it. Prototyping is often the best way to gain confidence that a supplier's software meets your functional requirements. This may be offered free, but if done properly will demand supplier time, so some payment to show good faith may be advisable.

Unfortunately, this is an industry where "all packages can do anything" (maybe they can if they are totally redeveloped!). The way to be sure is to believe nothing until you see it demonstrated, either at a client site or in a WORKING prototype. So select supplier's client visits where the most unproven part of the package can be demonstrated.

Step 17: Make your decision: Choose your package

It's nearly all over. There's not a lot more to be said about making your final selection ... so we'll say it anyway!

- ✔ Rework your cost-benefit analysis now that you know all the costs.
- ✔ Agree any reworking of the package that may be needed.
- ✔ Agree cost parameters if it is difficult to arrive at an inclusive fee.

Remember, software suppliers' bread and butter, and their biggest source of incremental income, comes from their established customers. That will be you once you buy their package. Make sure you know their daily rates before you sign!

So far we have looked at choosing software to buy or lease but there are other options which we now deal with, eg using a bureau or developing your own database from scratch. Whichever option you choose you will find a step-by-step process similar to the one we have been working through will serve you well.

Option 2: Using a bureau's proprietary software

Instead of buying or leasing software – and going through the process of selecting the right package, as we have just done – **one** alternative is to employ a bureau to run your database on their own proprietary software.

Marketing computer bureaux who offer this service are listed in the software directories regularly published by the marketing trade press (see "Precision Marketing" and "Direct Response" in the third volume of this Guide).

The chief differences between software packages offered for sale and bureau packages are these:

Unlike software packages, bureau software is not designed for use by companies unless they have experience of running something similar – although it is occasionally offered for sale or lease to experienced users. Bureau software is not as user-friendly as packages. But, unlike software packages, bureau (proprietary) software can be customised to meet your needs.

Proprietary software can thus be defined as a cross – or halfway house – between buying or leasing a software package and developing your own custom-built database software.

Whether you buy or lease a package, or opt for the bureau's proprietary alternative, you will need to work through many of the steps we have already discussed.

Advantages and disadvantages of ready-built software

Before you decide on a ready-built software solution – either a bought-in package or a bureau service – let us look at the advantages and disadvantages of using ready-made solutions.

Advantages of packaged and proprietary (ready-built) software

Low development cost	Almost certainly cheaper than a custom development – at least in the short term. Software support and maintenance, provided by the supplier rather than by in-house data processing specialists, may alter the picture over time.
Proven in use	If the software has been available for some years, it should be relatively bug-free.
Users	Usually you can contact other users of the software to find out whether it really does work in the way the supplier says.
Support available	The software company should be able to offer professional system support, maintenance and training.
Timescale	The development time needed to get your system up and running will be reduced.

Possible disadvantages of packaged and proprietary software

Unproven?	Many packages on the market are fairly new and relatively unproven.
Documentation?	Check the quality and thoroughness of the documentation. A badly written and documented package will cause severe headaches when you attempt to adapt it to fit your needs. You may find that, even for small changes, you have to call in the supplier to help. This can be expensive.
Expandable?	Make sure the software is not stretched to its limits in supporting your requirements. Can or will the supplier tailor the package to your requirements? Your requirements are bound to become more advanced in future, and selecting, purchasing and re-training people on new software will be time consuming and expensive.
Hidden costs?	Costs could escalate if the software needs to be customised to fit your requirements. Most packages can be customised to some degree, but a great deal of customisation, maybe to support as yet undefined requirements, may cause problems despite what the supplier may say. It is important to budget for additional costs. Costs do not simply end when the database is initially installed. Maintenance and development costs can add up to 40% per annum of the installation costs.
Can it be moved in-house?	Operating proprietary software at the direct marketing bureau is almost certainly the most efficient option. But ensure bureau-operated package software can be moved in-house later if desired.
Supplier stability?	Check that the supplier is stable and financially secure, and that he will continue to support the package for the foreseeable future.

Option 3: Building your database from scratch

There are several reasons why you may wish to build your own database software – or why building your own database software is the only option.

This is likely to be the case if you cannot find a package/supplier/bureau combination which will:

? Handle your size of customer base

? Provide the specialist functions or data structures you require

? Integrate with your other systems

? Fit with your hardware/software strategy

Before you even begin to contemplate building a database, you will need to think a great deal about the alternatives open to you, and their advantages and disadvantages.

But, even before we reach the point of looking at this option (or the next), you will need to understand how computers store information, which we are about to explore commencing on the following page.

Option 4: Adapting your existing databases

In an ideal world, every marketing database would be built from scratch for the express purpose of marketing.

In practice, the marketing database is often adapted by customising existing databases – **either** databases originally set up for other purposes (eg order processing, accounting or administration) **or** acquired from other sources, eg via company takeovers.

Adapting a database is often more complex, and more difficult, than starting from scratch, and carries more risk to the business. Your first step will therefore be to hire the necessary skill and experience, either in-house or via a consultant.

You will also need to understand the ways in which different types of database store their information.

How computers store information

The advice contained in the remainder of this chapter will form a useful background for either building or adapting a database.

At the time of our first edition we listed four types of database: four ways in which computers store information. They were:

✔ Sequential files

✔ Network

✔ Hierarchical

✔ Relational databases

Of these, we can ignore network and hierarchical databases as both are now outdated. Most direct marketing applications are now either sequential files or relational databases.

We now look at each of these two main types – the sequential file and the relational database – how they work, together with their advantages and disadvantages.

Sequential files – made up of customer records

Traditionally computer data has been stored in "files". A customer file, for instance, would contain data on customers: company name, address, contact name, job title, and so on. In order to select and report on customers, the data must be stored in a set format. The set format (or "record") contains a defined set of data fields of a certain maximum length and type (alphabetic character or number). For instance, the first part of a typical customer record may look like this:

Field	Field name	Length/ Characters	Type
1	Customer Number	8	N
2	Address Line 1	30	A
3	Address Line 2	30	A
4	Address Line 3	30	A
5	Address Line 4	30	A
6	Postcode	8	A
7	Contact Name	30	A
8	Title	4	A
9	Job Title (code)	4	A

N = numeric A = alpha-numeric

A file would be made up of a number of these records. The customer records in a file may be stored sequentially (eg alphabetically or by customer number). The easiest way to search the file is to search it sequentially, to look at each record in turn for the ones you want. For example, in the above record, if you wanted to search for all managing directors you would instruct the computer program to look at field number 9 in each customer record.

However, sequential file searchers are slow and quicker methods of searching have to be employed.

One method is to identify and index those fields which will be used as search fields (eg job title), and hold the indexes in a separate file for speedier and more efficient searching. This method of searching is found in indexed sequential files (eg VSAM, a common IBM mainframe file structure). VSAM file structures are often called databases, but in the technical definition of the words they are simply files.

There is, of course, a little more to it than that. But computers have worked in this basic way for many years, and technology has only fairly recently moved on significantly from this field/record stage. In fact most of the proprietary direct marketing software mentioned earlier is based on this type of technology. It has its advantages but it is also slow, often difficult to use and comparatively inflexible.

Relational databases – a flexible approach

A relational database is a collection of groups of data referred to as "tables" rather than records. Data from multiple tables can be joined together easily in different programs, depending on the selection, on-line, or reporting requirement. These table-joins, or relations (hence "relational"), do not have to be predefined in the database structure as they do in the record structures of other types of database. They can be defined in the programs. **This means that you do not have to try and anticipate all of your requirements at the database design stage.** Applications can therefore be much more flexible than in the past and can evolve over time.

Relational databases have been commercially available since about 1980. Relational databases such as Oracle, Ingres and Powerhouse were greeted enthusiastically by a marketplace which was fast demanding more flexible and user-friendly systems.

In theory at least, with a relational database the power of the computer – its ability to carry out selections and to manipulate the data – is controlled more by the user than by specialist programmers. **This is good news for PC users who need no longer be frustrated by having constantly to ask specialists to extract customer data from mainframe databases.**

The language most used to develop applications on relational databases is IBM's Standard Query Language (SQL). SQL is a fourth generation language (4GLs are much easier to learn and use for developing applications) which is fast becoming the standard for all relational databases.

So what is the bad news? Poor performance (search times and computer processing unit usage) was a characteristic of many relational systems in the early years. Although performance has improved considerably, and will continue to improve, performance remains an issue with all relational databases especially larger customer databases. The cost of operating a relational database may well, therefore, be higher than that of using other database methods such as the older network and hierarchical types.

In practice the performance problem will only affect you if you have very complex data structures and/or a lot of data to store. If your requirement is to hold data on fewer than one million customers, this problem should not affect you.

Sequential v relational: A comparison

Now that we have outlined the basic differences in operation between sequential files and relational database storage methods, it is time to draw some direct comparisons.

To help you make your comparison, and to ensure that nothing is overlooked, there now follow some checklists: the first is a question and answer aid to decision-making featuring some commonly requested marketing requirements; the remainder comprise a summary of the advantages and disadvantages of both main types of database.

How marketing requirements affect database choice

Marketing requirements	Database favoured	
	Sequential	Relational
Your data requirements are clearly defined and unlikely to change	✔	
Your reporting requirements will change		✔
Your market structure is complex and likely to change		✔
You need to integrate with other systems	✔	✔
The system is likely to be enhanced to include other applications in the future		✔
You need quick development	✔	
Initial cost is important to you	✔	
You require to add/modify/browse data on-line		✔
You want a user-friendly, flexible environment		✔
You know what sort of queries you will be making and what sort of reports you require	✔	
You are happy for selections and queries to be carried out by specialists	✔	
You will be making long batch-processing runs (often)	✔	
You will need to make ad hoc queries		✔

The advantages of indexed sequential files

✔ **Well-proven technology**
Sequential file technology is the type used by the majority of the traditional direct marketing bureaux. It has therefore been well proven for direct marketing work.

✔ **Batch-processing cost**
Arguably, the cost of complex trawls of the database will be lower than with the relational option. DP specialists should be able to provide performance guarantees. (Because relational technology is fairly new, performance guarantees are rare.)

✔ **Quicker/cheaper initial development**
Proprietary software exists which can be customised to meet most requirements comparatively quickly. This keeps the application simple, and has the advantage of reducing cost, risk and time. Later you may wish to develop a more customised, complex database using a different technical approach.

✔ **Available at many computer bureaux**
This may be an advantage if you want to locate your system externally.

The disadvantages of indexed sequential files

✘ **Inflexible**
Sequential technology is generally inflexible if changes to the data structure are needed. But if requirements are very clear and are unlikely to change, this may not be a problem.

✘ **Limited integration possibilities**
Integration with other systems would be limited to flat file extracts. This is cumbersome and slow.

✘ **On-line processing more difficult**
Customer updates probably have to be carried out in batch. Difficult to see and update customer information on-line.

✘ **Higher maintenance costs**
Modifications to application programs due to changing user requirements will need specialist skills. This will also increase the turn-around time of special requests – a traditional problem.

✘ **Harder selections**
Database selections less flexible than any of the other options, although this will depend to an extent on the proprietary software used.

The advantages of relational databases

✔ **Ease of use**
This advantage should not be underestimated. For programmers it means faster development and maintenance. For users it offers the ability to change screen and report layouts fairly easily.

✔ **Flexibility**
Data can be added and relations changed without changing the application programs. Important in a marketing database because, as markets evolve, the systems supporting the markets should be able to evolve.

✔ **Security**
Security controls can be more easily implemented because database access authorisations relate to fields and relationships on the database, eg the field "Credit Rating" could be restricted to the accounts department.

✔ **Programming language**
SQL is a powerful non-procedural language offering quick development and standardisation between databases.

✔ **Strategic systems architecture**
A relational/SQL combination may offer an attractive long-term strategic architecture for a company's systems. The relational systems developed to support marketing and sales could fit well into a company's hardware/software strategy.

✔ **Software availability**
The availability of an increasing number of software packages designed to run on SQL databases – to support different functions such as word processing, spreadsheet, graphics – is an advantage. If your main customer database is relational/SQL, a variety of software packages could be built on later to enhance the number of applications.

✔ **Easier on-line access**
This is important if you constantly want to call up customers, modify their details, or browse through list selections on-line.

Exercise for students

If you are intending to enter the direct marketing business in either marketing management or account handling, your time spent mugging up on the two types of databases, their advantages and disadvantages, will be well rewarded. Try testing yourself using these checklists.

The disadvantages of relational databases

✗ **Batch-processing costs**
These are generally thought to be high in a relational environment. However, they are only part of the cost equation for developing, operating, and maintaining a system. They will be significant if complex selections from the database are made often.

✗ **Licence costs**
A cost would be incurred in either licensing (one of the major relational databases costs about £3,000 per month) or purchasing the software and related environment (the relational database management system or RDMS as it is called).

✗ **Development time**
There are few marketing software packages available in a relational environment. For instance, software to incorporate signatures on letters may not exist in some relational environments. This means that all software may have to be developed from scratch.

✗ **Delay in implementation?**
There is another reason why the relational approach can cause delays in the implementation of the system. The relational approach may suit the strategic systems architecture of the company. But a project designed to analyse the strategic use of information in the company may delay the development of a critical direct mail system. In this case, stop-gap developments using packaged or proprietary software may be necessary.

In-house or external marketing database?

Many companies use external services to operate their direct marketing databases. Why? The reason is an increasing recognition in the industry that data processing is a service, just as the creative element of marketing is a service, which need not be carried out in-house.

However, if you have the resources (both people and computer) available in-house, you may wish, or be persuaded to, develop the database in-house. Be careful! There are clear advantages but some high risk disadvantages with this approach.

Disadvantages of an in-house approach

Cost of hardware, software and consultancy. Your company will have to bear these costs in full. A bureau can take advantage of economies of scale not available to single users and can amortise the cost of the hardware and software across many clients. This may make your initial capital outlay a great deal more attractive to you. Also, your in-house team is likely to need basic consulting help on marketing database structures and processing routines, something that comes automatically from a computer bureau.

Speed of development. Bureaux have experience in direct marketing database development as well as specialist expertise. They know where to cut the corners and where not to, and may have a proprietary software shell which they can customise to fit your requirements. They are likely to develop a working application for you quicker than an in-house development team can.

In-house system analysts often become too complex in their definition of what is required and lose sight of the core functions of a marketing database. Not only will this approach delay development, but the resulting system may be too complex to use effectively.

Service standards. In-house systems departments often have less urgency than a service supplier to deliver the goods, eg to carry out selections, produce tapes, print reports or carry out necessary enhancements to the system. Direct marketing is all about deadlines! Often in-house systems departments simply do not understand and are not structured to support the basic requirements of a direct marketing system. With a bureau you can draw up a set of service standards (which some companies are beginning to do with their internal systems departments) which documents performance guarantees.

Specialist processing. Name and address processing, merging and purging data and identifying duplicate records (discussed in detail in Chapter 3.3), are processes which, especially for large databases, demand specialist software skills. All bureaux have access to this type of software and will be experienced in using it. **Some software will be better than others – and if this is important to your company, the decision on which bureau to choose will be made mainly on which has the best deduplication process.**

It is unlikely that you will want to develop the specialist software in-house, and owners of large customer databases will probably still send files to a bureau for name and address processing even if the database is developed in-house.

Advantages of an in-house development

Strategic orientation. Customer data is increasingly viewed as strategically important to companies of all types. As such, a marketing database containing detailed data on the customers and (sometimes) the prospects of a company may be considered too important and integral to a company's business strategy to be held outside the company.

Integration and on-line access to data. It is often a good deal easier and cheaper to hold marketing databases which are integrated with order processing, accounting, telemarketing and/or service systems in-house, utilising hardware and communication networks that already exist in the company.

Greater control and ownership. Better understanding of the database may result for a database held internally. Most marketing databases take information regularly from other internal systems (eg order processing). If the marketing database resides externally, systems people may not view the database with the importance it deserves. This could cause problems if any changes are made to internal feeder systems without considering the impact on the marketing database. This may seem an obscure point, but in practice a lack of ownership can represent a real risk to the quality of data on your database.

Cost may be more attractive. Operating the database internally may actually be cheaper than using an external supplier. The cost equation is something which is very individual to a company. In costing approaches for companies, consultants have experienced both situations, ie in one case the costs were more attractive for in-house development and in another case, in a not unrelated industry, external development and operation cost about 70% less than the internal cost!

Choosing and using external services

If you decide to use external suppliers you will need to know how to go about selecting the one that is right for you.

There are essentially two types of external service:

- ✔ Facilities management
- ✔ Bureau operation

A facilities management company will manage your entire data processing operation, either externally using their own hardware/software environment, or within your company managing your staff and environment. This type of service is not discussed in this Guide.

A traditional bureau operation will operate your system for you, whether it be a payroll system or, more relevant here, a direct marketing system.

What can a bureau offer?

Many direct mail databases are being successfully handled for clients by direct marketing bureaux. A bureau will obviously charge according to the services required, which usually involve:

- ✔ Loading data from client's and external files
- ✔ Deduplicating the data
- ✔ Storing data
- ✔ Making selections
- ✔ Providing files for mailing and analysis
- ✔ Maybe carrying out the mailing

This is all work which bureaux are used to, using systems they are familiar with, and they are often good at it. As already mentioned, they can take advantage of economies of scale which are not available to many single users, and offer many other advantages.

There are many advantages of using a bureau besides cost-savings, among them:

	The advantages of using a bureau
✔	Systems and skills need not be developed in-house
✔	A high level of expertise and systems at your disposal
✔	Avoidance of fixed costs of computer facility
✔	Speed of start-up
✔	Performance guarantees
✔	Can be used as required

Choosing a bureau – 4 points to watch

If your choice is an external bureau you need to consider carefully the following points when making your choice. Having asked these questions you may want to reconsider the prospect of an in-house operation:

The four key issues to look out for are:

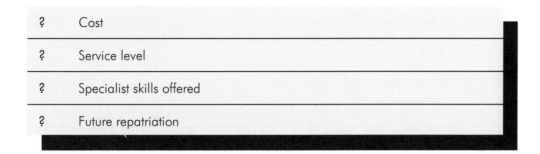

?	Cost
?	Service level
?	Specialist skills offered
?	Future repatriation

Before we close this chapter let us look at each of these points in turn. Their importance cannot be overstressed:

Any unforeseen costs?

It may be cheaper to run the system at a bureau if the data processing resources (both personnel and machinery) necessary to develop and support the system are not available in-house. Obviously the cost picture will change if and when you have the necessary computer capacity and skills in-house (which, of course, incur their own costs).

Look for unforeseen costs when negotiating with a bureau. They all mount up! When considering costs, remember that even if you operate your own system, you may have to use a bureau for name and address cleaning, deduplication, and incorporating additional profiling information.

Examine the costing structure put forward by the bureau very carefully. Unit cost areas could include any or all of the following:

?	Cost per addition of each new name
?	Cost per addition of each transaction (eg order, enquiry) associated with the customer
?	Cost per record read or selected
?	Cost of computer processing time used
?	Printing/output costs

Most bureaux will also charge a fixed cost in areas of:

- ? Data storage
- ? Minimum charge
- ? Cost per customer per year
- ? Account management fee

Service level: Get it right first time

Service is vital. An external supplier of services will supposedly work harder to meet deadlines than your internal people – and there is no activity with more deadlines than direct marketing! It is important that the service offered by the supplier is monitored and reviewed regularly.

As with all service companies, some bureaux are better than others. Although you can in theory switch to another bureau, it will be expensive repatriating your data and applications to a bureau where different proprietary software will be involved. So make your initial choice of bureau carefully.

A service level agreement should be negotiated between the supplier and client against which service levels can be monitored. Key performance indicators covering at least the following aspects should be part of the service level agreement:

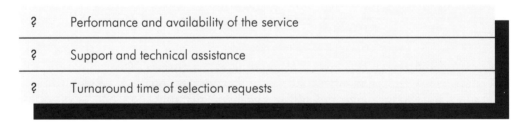

- ? Performance and availability of the service
- ? Support and technical assistance
- ? Turnaround time of selection requests

Specialist skills: Who is teaching whom?

Make sure that the bureau you choose has the depth and range of skills that you require. For instance, how experienced are their account handlers? Are you paying for their personal development or are they able to offer added value to your database marketing approach? Also, if you want the bureau to carry out your data analysis, make sure you know who will do the analysis. How good are they? Who is their back-up? All obvious points but often overlooked by clients who assume that all bureau staff are experts. Some are better than others!

Future repatriation

It is hard to accept that the database, if it is to become the core of the marketing operation, will be operated and maintained externally to the company for ever. Yet repatriation of bureau-operated systems (moving the system to another data centre) is not always possible. If this is a requirement which may be important to you check this point carefully prior to choosing a bureau.

Chapter 3.5

Profiling and segmentation – what your data is telling you

This chapter includes:

- How profiling works
- The 5 stages of profiling and segmentation
- Types of variable
- Defining your key measures
- The 3 types of "average"
- Calculating standard deviations
- The real role of segmentation

With direct marketing, as we have seen, you can measure the performance of each individual customer. Ideally, your database will have a personal record detailing their purchases by value, date, product type, etc. In theory, therefore, you are perfectly placed to engage in the direct marketer's holy grail of one-to-one communication.

In practice, unless you market only very expensive goods, you are more likely to think of your customers – and relate to them – in terms of **groups of people with similar characteristics and behaviour**. To do otherwise would be impractical; there is a limit to how many campaign variations you can produce to meet the needs of thousands, perhaps hundreds of thousands, of different customers.

How you recognise customers and allocate them into manageable groups is the subject of profiling and segmentation – explained here by one of the world's foremost specialists, Clive Humby. It all amounts to avoiding wrong assumptions and understanding patterns in your computer data.

New in this edition. This topic was not explained in depth in our first edition.

Author/Consultant: Clive Humby

Clive Humby, Chairman, DunnHumby Associates

Clive has over twenty years' professional experience in market analysis. He is founder and Chairman of DunnHumby Associates, one of the UK's leading market analysis companies, serving clients such as Tesco, BMW, and Mercury Communications. Since its formation in 1989, DunnHumby has helped numerous blue chip companies develop segmentation and information-led marketing strategies.

Prior to forming DunnHumby, Clive was Chief Executive of CACI where he had held key posts since 1976. He was one of the early pioneers of the application of statistical methods for use in marketing, including such innovations as the widely acclaimed ACORN system, and a range of mathematical methods such as gravity and location modelling, data fusion and use of new data sources in marketing.

Clive is an industrial fellow of Kingston University and regular presenter and trainer for commercial, industry and professional bodies on subjects ranging through statistics, computing and market segmentation.

Clive Humby
Chairman
DunnHumby Associates Limited
7 Devonhurst Place
Heathfield Terrace
Chiswick
London W4 4JD
Tel: 0181-994 2780

Chapter 3.5

Profiling and segmentation – what your data is telling you

Getting to know your customer

Direct marketing stands apart from other marketing disciplines. It is easy to measure. Analysis of patterns in response data or your customer database can lead to informed decision-making throughout the process.

The customer gives you information as part of a response or purchase cycle. Better, more informed decisions can be made by understanding patterns in this data. This is what **profiling and segmentation** are all about.

The applications that stem from a true understanding of your customers are far ranging. It answers such questions as: Which customers are the most profitable? What are the differences between customers who buy Product A and Product B? What is the next opportunity for a particular group of customers?

Towards a sharper customer focus

Often this type of analysis is used as a rear-view mirror, but it can also be used to predict. Used as a planning tool – as part of your strategic development – profiling and segmentation can give your organisation a true customer focus.

Many businesses claim to focus on the customer and his/her needs, but in fact pay them only lip-service. Customers are still mass-mailed resulting in low response rates. Although organisations still make money in this way, it is very wasteful and customers recognise what is happening ... bombarding the many in the hope of finding the few, whilst employing ersatz personalisation to suggest the personal touch. Ultimately, such practices dilute the impact of direct marketing.

Customers are becoming more and more aware that data is used in marketing and increasingly they expect you to use it well, sending them messages that are relevant. Organisations who truly believe in the customer ensure that their communications are timely, relevant and targeted to best advantage.

What do you need to know about your customers?

Profiling and segmentation, then, are not just a rear-view mirror – they are the key to customer understanding which will impact on **all** your marketing processes.

Below is a checklist of some of the questions which your data can answer if you know how to analyse it:

	What your data is trying to tell you
?	What are the characteristics (profile) of your customers? What makes them different from the population as a whole and similar to your market?
?	Is this profile changing over time? Do different media attract different types of customer? Do some customers appear to prefer different sales channels?
?	How can this knowledge improve your advertising and direct mail? How can copy be tailored to optimise what you know about your customers?
?	Do you have different types of customers for different products? Does this help or hinder your ability to cross-sell or up-sell to them?
?	Can you define different customer segments? Might these segments alter what you promote? When you promote it? Which sales channels you use? Possible partnerships with other organisations?
?	Which customers have reached each stage on the loyalty ladder? Which have the highest risk of lapsing or defecting? What are the characteristics which lead to lapsing? Can you avoid recruiting potential defectors, or can you change their behaviour before they lapse?
?	Which customers are ready for their next purchase? And what to offer them?
?	Can you break down next year's business objectives across each segment of your customers? What are the individual goals for each segment and what do you need to spend to achieve this goal?

How profiling works

The first step in profiling is to understand the data you already have on your customers. This will require what we call a "data audit".

Armed with sufficient, reliable data, profiling then takes two forms:

1. **Comparing characteristics between customers.** For example, how does the profile of purchasers of Product A compare with those for Product B? This stage does not demand any new data from outside your business and can be undertaken directly from your own customer data.

2. **Comparing the characteristics of your customers with people who are not your customers.** For example, what is the profile of your customers compared with that of your target market or industry norms, or the population as a whole? This profiling requires external data to enable you to understand the bigger picture.

Sources of external data

There are four major sources of external data for comparison with your own data:

4 sources of external data	
Syndicated (pooled) industry data, eg – CCN and Equifax credit databases – SMMT CARPARC – Neilsen/IRI Grocery Audit – Mortgage Lenders Association	Normally available only to members on royalty terms. Often supplied subject to release rules, eg your own data versus industry average. Often difficult to obtain in computer-readable form. Syndicators often restrict manipulation of data to themselves.
National statistics, ie data collected under legislation directly or indirectly, eg – Population census – Electoral Roll – Companies House Registrations – Post Office (PAF) file – County Court Judgements	Population data is released via census agencies: CACI, CCN, Data Consultancy, Equifax (see Chapter 3.6). Postcode Address File (see Chapter 7.10).
Market research including syndicated research	Examples include National Readership Survey (NRS) and Target Group Index (TGI) (see Chapter 4.1).
Mailing list data	

Searching your data for flaws

Both forms of profiling use similar techniques: first you have to understand the key characteristics of your customers, then you compare them with either sub-groups of your own data or with the target market or population as a whole.

There is another major benefit of profiling: it helps you to understand your customer data in ways that otherwise you might not appreciate.

Here, it is important to remember that most businesses collect their data as part of processing a transaction. This might be account or order processing or other operational system. In other words, the data often isn't collected primarily for marketing purposes and as such may have serious shortcomings.

For example, there may be a world of difference between the record layouts in your computer systems and the data you have actually captured. You may find data missing from such fields as Date of Birth or Gender because omitting it saved the operator time, especially if it was not essential to the transaction.

Before you can properly understand your data, and use it for profiling, you must be aware of any such constraints or deficiencies in its original collection and processing. We shall look at some examples of missing and misleading data in a moment.

Stages in the process of profiling and segmentation

We now begin our study of the five stages of profiling and segmentation, but first a summary:

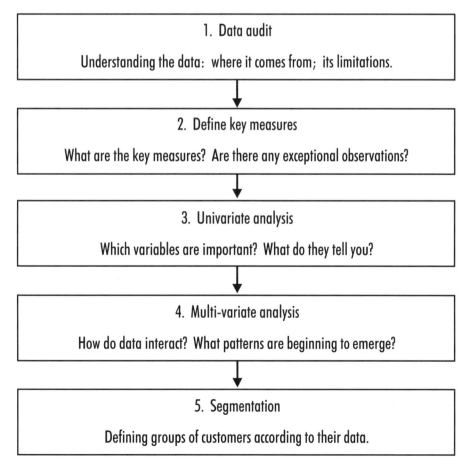

1. Data audit

Understanding the data: where it comes from; its limitations.

↓

2. Define key measures

What are the key measures? Are there any exceptional observations?

↓

3. Univariate analysis

Which variables are important? What do they tell you?

↓

4. Multi-variate analysis

How do data interact? What patterns are beginning to emerge?

↓

5. Segmentation

Defining groups of customers according to their data.

Stage 1: The data audit

It is not the purpose of this chapter to explore the subject of data auditing in detail, only to show why it is important.

The main point to remember is that you must be aware of the limitations of your data before you attempt to use it for profiling and segmentation.

Here is just one example of how and where data is often seriously misleading:

Lazy source coding

Like most direct marketers, the XYZ Company wished to know which types of customer were being recruited from which media. They knew that enquirers do not always quote the media or code number when responding and operators do not always pursue it.

However, operators should always be instructed on how to deal with the missing data. In XYZ's case the operator was instructed to enter the most recently issued code in the absence of the required code.

Thus, despite some media obviously attracting many more responses than others, the media codes did not show this. In fact, the results for each code appeared remarkably similar because the operators were allocating each day's responses, regardless of source, to the code for the day!

Applying the lessons

The first result of your data audit, therefore, is likely to be tightening up your definitions for the variables in your data. You will also establish some rules for defining which data is usable and which is invalid for profiling purposes.

For example, in the case of missing source code data (as with XYZ above), you might decide to analyse only print enquiries where the source code is pre-printed on reply devices and not rely on codes entered by telesales operators. Alternatively, you might devise another method of coding for telephone responses – or decide to retrain your operators.

Ideally, as the result of this stage, you will amend your working practices to ensure that your data can be easily and accurately profiled in future.

The 3 types of variable

During the audit stage you will need to classify each item of your variable data under one of the following categories:

- ✔ Continuous
- ✔ Discrete
- ✔ Categorical

Each type of variable has different applications and tells us different things about the data, so an understanding of their differences at this stage is vital.

Continuous variables. These can theoretically take any numerical value. For example, size of balance, age (measured in years, months or days), height, etc.

Continuous variables can be made into discrete or categorical variables by banding. For example, income between £5–£10,000, £10–£15,000, £15–£20,000, etc.

> Watch out that "zero" is not put into the same category as "missing" or "incomplete" as this will cause significant problems of analysis – another common mistake.

Discrete variables. These are always counts of something. They take a whole number value, 0, 1, 2, 3, etc. For example, the number of accounts held by a customer and how many times the customer has been mailed are discrete variables.

Be careful! Some variables are given codes so that they appear as a whole number (eg £50–£75,000 = 01). They are **not** discrete numbers – they are "ordered categoricals".

Categorical variables. These are often non-numeric data. For example, the make or colour of car a person drives or the title of a recruitment medium. They may also be numerically coded where the number does not imply any order or size. For example, look-up codes to record media source (01 = The Times, 02 = The Telegraph, etc).

Some numerical coding conventions can be misleading. Beware geodemographic systems such as ACORN or MOSAIC and SIC codes. The codes are numeric and may look like discrete variables, but they are actually categoric variables.

Redefining your variables

To use your data for profiling it is a good idea to re-label your continuous measures, eg customer expenditure, so that you can create recognisable bands, eg £15–£20,000. (You will retain the **exact** spend in each customer's individual record.)

One effective way of banding continuous variables such as expenditure is with percentiles, deciles, or quartiles, whereby, for example, your lowest 10% is coded 00, the next highest 10% coded 01, etc. This method permits the use of charts and graphs to compare the performance of all variables.

For example, you may wish to create spend quartiles as a way to band your customers, as in the graphic below:

First 25% is the bottom quartile of spenders

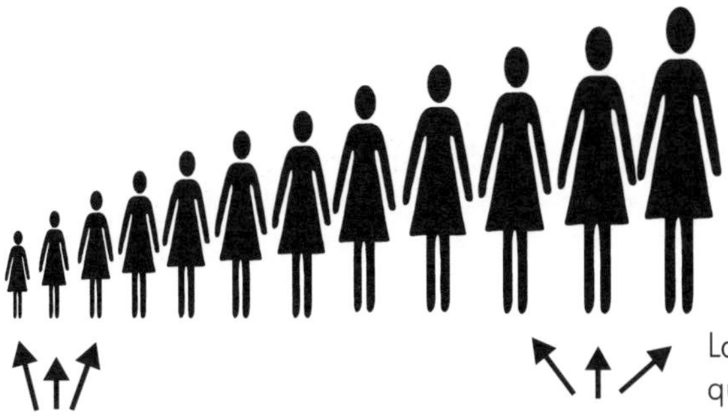

Last 25% is the top quartile of spenders

Remember, the different types of variable are going to be used in different ways. For example, there is no average for categorical variables, and averages of discrete variables have to be treated with great care (eg no families have 2.4 children!). So it is important to properly categorise your variables before you start the next stage.

Stage 2: Defining your key measures

Having completed the data audit, you're ready to start the profiling and segmentation. **The next major decision is to define what you want to profile.** Your choice of measures may influence the methods you take.

You will almost certainly want to profile your customers, beginning with a simple count of the number of records by each major variable, eg 400 customers spending between £100–£120. But for a real understanding, you will probably also want to incorporate monetary and time measures such as average order value, total spend per season, numbers of orders per annum, etc.

In some circumstances you may want to build more complex measures such as profitability. This is especially true if the range of products varies greatly in profit margin or, for example, in business-to-business where customer discount levels often vary by large amounts.

At this stage it is useful to understand the dynamics of the measures themselves, eg how variable or constant they are within themselves. **At this stage you must also identify extreme values which may otherwise distort your key measures.**

Extreme values are known as "outliers". They are so important that we now look at them in some detail.

Beware OUTLIERS!

An outlier is an exceptional observation which can radically distort the true picture and lead to seriously misleading results.

Outliers can occur by chance, eg because of extreme behaviour by one or two customers, or as a function of system limitation where some fields are set to extreme values, such as £9999.99, as part of the system design or to deal with exceptional cases. The data audit phase should have identified the latter.

The exceptional high-spending customer is a more likely outlier. The example on the facing page demonstrates the far-reaching effects that unrecognised outliers can have. One or two exceptional values can distort your analysis very dramatically. You must therefore examine your data very clearly whenever monetary values are introduced.

It is not always realised that time measures can also harbour disruptive outliers. For example, lapsed or dormant accounts may create the "wrong" measure of frequency of purchase. In this case, zero activity should be identified and isolated from the analysis.

Outliers may take many other forms, eg the "rogue" customer for a London department store who lives in Aberdeen, or accounts believed to be dormant because data is incomplete due to operational reasons. Even staff sales have been known to distort sales data in this way, if not properly identified.

Outliers: A cautionary tale

A charity test mailing to existing donors asked for an additional donation for a key cause. It gave donors the option of ticking one of three boxes (£15, £25 or £50) or making a donation of their choice, with this overall result:

	Mailed	Response Rate	Responders	Money	Av. Gift
Overall test result	20,000	2.27%	454	£15,025.00	£33.09

On this basis, a roll-out to 200,000 was undertaken, with the goal of raising over £150,000. But it fell short by over £25,000 despite a similar response rate, as you can see below:

	Mailed	Response Rate	Responders	Money	Av. Gift
Roll-out result	196,380	2.28%	4,477	£124,734.00	£27.86

What happened? Why did the "average" gift value drop so dramatically? Could it have been predicted? YES ... the disappointment was caused by an exceptional donation of £2,500 in the test. The fuller picture can be seen in this more detailed breakdown of the test:

		Mailed	Response Rate	Responders	Money	Av. Gift
Test result showing responses by donation value		20,000	2.27%	454	£15,025.00	£33.09
	Optional gift breakdown:					
		£15	0.66%	132	£1,980.00	£15.00
		£25	0.83%	165	£4,125.00	£25.00
		£50	0.45%	89	£4,450.00	£50.00
		Other	0.34%	67*	£4,470.00	£66.72

Analysis of the test shows that the "average" (mean average) of £33.09 is not very representative of the data. In fact, only 25% of donors gave above the mean, made up of those giving £50 and a small number of other donations. That donation of £2,500 is badly distorting the figures. If it had been removed, the result would have been as follows:

		Mailed	Response Rate	Responders	Money	Av. Gift
Test result after removing exceptional donation		20,000	2.27%	454	£12,525.00	£27.58
	Optional gift breakdown:					
		£15	0.66%	132	£1,980.00	£15.00
		£25	0.83%	165	£4,125.00	£25.00
		£50	0.45%	89	£4,450.00	£50.00
		Other	0.34%	66*	£1,970.00	£29.40

Their predictions for the roll-out would have been very close to the final result and they would have had no nasty surprises. What the charity should have done at the test stage was to look at the median as well as the mean, as explained in this chapter.

Improve your understanding of the measures

Now is the time to further improve your understanding of your chosen measures. This can come from analysis of each measure in terms of its "location" and its "variability". If these measures are poor, then this step will spot the problems and ensure you don't go on to make the sort of mistakes we looked at in the charity example on the previous page.

The danger of "averages"?

As marketers we regularly use the term "average". What do we mean by average? In fact, there are **three types of average**. If we use the wrong type, disaster can result.

For example, what do we mean when we say that an average clothing customer spends £15.21? Customers may spend anything from £5 to £200, so how can we use the figure of £15.21, for example, to predict what any individual customer will spend? We can't!

Is the "average" customer buying only for him/herself? What makes some customers kit out the whole family and thus reach a higher spend? Is it wise to even think in terms of an average customer spending only £15.21 – is this not in danger of becoming a "self-fulfilling prophecy"?

Perhaps we have two different types of customer, some spending only £10 and others who spend £150. Oughtn't we to treat them differently? But we can't treat them differently until we recognise that such differences exist – all perhaps buried within our data "average".

The graphic below is an example of how dangerous so-called averages can be:

Monthly spend for 4 example customers

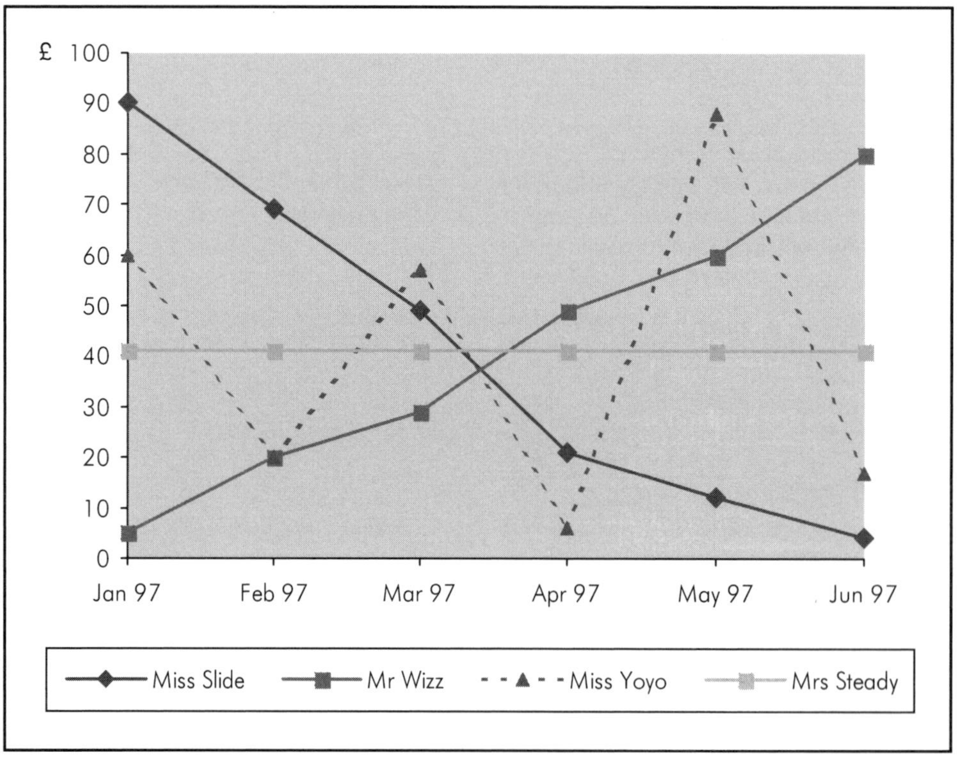

Mr Wizz began slowly and his expenditure is rocketing. Miss Slide began in style but has been slipping away ever since. Miss Yoyo is very erratic. Mrs Steady is unbelievably steady. **Yet each of these four typical customers has an average monthly spend of £41 over the year.**

Such a variety of performances could, for example, be the pattern of response to a regular catalogue mailing. If too many customers have Miss Slide's profile, then the next mailing could deliver a very nasty shock.

The statistician's 3 types of average

There are, as we said, three types of average, each of which may tell us something different about our customer data. These are:

- ✔ The mean
- ✔ The median
- ✔ The mode

The Mean

The mean is the measure most of us have in mind when we describe "the average". You obtain it by adding up all the values and dividing by the number of observations or records. It is simple to do and most database packages can do it automatically.

However, as we have seen, the mean is prone to problems if the data contains outliers. For example, whereas most of your observations may be between, say, £10 and £50, one or two very large values can give a mean of over £50 ... the so-called "average" is considerably in excess of most values being observed.

The Median

The median is obtained by ranking observations in order of size and then counting in to the middle value. (If there is an even number of observations, it is the mean of the two middle values.) The median is more robust than the mean since it is not prone to outliers.

Unfortunately, the median is harder to calculate – the data has to be sorted – and a lot of database packages do not provide it as a standard function. You can use data visualisation methods (graphs, etc) to help you if you do not have the function, but you are strongly recommended to find a way of calculating it. PC stats packages are quite cheap. Taking a random sample of data for analysis is practical for most purposes.

The Mode

The mode is a particularly useful measure for categorical data. It is the most "popular" or frequently occurring value in a data set. For example, for colour of car, the mode might be "RED". The mode is very useful if only a few values occur very often, for example if the measure is one of several standard donations or product types. If all values occur only once, then there is no mode.

Understanding the 3 types of variability

The next type of understanding we need is how variable our measure is. Again, there are three main measures that are commonly used:

- ✔ Range
- ✔ Variance
- ✔ Standard deviation

Range

The range is simply the difference between the largest and the smallest value in the data set. This gives a measure of variability, but is limited to just two observations and so it is not a particularly sensitive measure.

Variance

The variance is the difference between each observation and the mean. If we add the variances in a set of data, the net result will be zero since some will be plus and some will be minus values. So we square each difference which makes all the numbers positive (–2 x –2 = +4). Squaring the differences also gives more weight to values further from the mean (1 x 1 = 1 but 6 x 6 = 36).

We then sum these differences and divide by the number of observations minus 1. **This gives the variance of the data set.**

Unfortunately, the measure is in "squared" units. For example, if the observation was pounds (£s) we now have "squared pounds", whatever they may be!

For this reason we calculate the square root of the variance, which we call ...

The Standard Deviation

The standard deviation is simply the square root of the variance which brings it back to the same units as the original data (eg £s).

The example calculations on the facing page show how we determine the mean, median and mode; and the range, variance and standard deviation.

Understanding and calculating the key measures

The following data contains nineteen expenditure records for Mr A, Mr B, Mr C, etc, varying from £10 to £123 per customer.

Students: *You might like to conceal the answers at the bottom before calculating the mean, median, mode, range, variance and standard deviation.*

A Person	B Value	C Values in B sorted	Difference between B and Mean	Square of Difference
A	£15	£10	(£14.42)	207.97
B	£20	£12	(£9.42)	88.76
C	£12	£12	(£17.42)	303.49
D	£15	£15	(£14.42)	207.97
E	£17	£15	(£12.42)	154.28
F	£12	£15	(£17.42)	303.49
G	£22	£15	(£7.42)	55.07
H	£19	£16	(£10.42)	108.60
I	£32	£17	£2.58	6.65
J	£18	£18	(£11.42)	130.44
K	£45	£19	£15.58	242.70
L	£103	£19	£73.58	5,413.86
M	£16	£20	(£13.42)	180.12
N	£15	£22	(£14.42)	207.97
O	£19	£31	(£10.42)	108.60
P	£10	£32	(£19.42)	377.18
Q	£15	£15	(£14.42)	207.97
R	£31	£103	£1.58	2.49
S	£123	£123	£93.58	8,757.02
Sum	£559	£559	£0.00	£17,065.41

Mean = £559/19	£29.42
Median = middle observation	£18.00
Mode = most popular	£15.00
Range = £123 – £10	£113.00
Variance = 17065.41 ÷ (19–1)	948.04
Standard Deviation = Square Root (Variance)	£30.79

What do the standard measures tell us?

We are beginning to learn a lot about our data that we may not have known before. There are no hard and fast rules, but here are two examples of what your standard measures may be trying to tell you:

Are the mean and median similar? If not, then outliers are likely to cause you problems as you try to progress with your profiling and segmentation, as we have seen.

Try to isolate outliers and then recalculate your measures to get a better picture. (Outliers may, of course, represent exceptional customers whom you wish to pursue – we are not for one moment suggesting that you discard them, only that you recognise them and prevent them from distorting all your other measures.)

How large is the standard deviation compared to the mean? Typically, you should expect about two-thirds of your observations (68%) to be within 1 standard deviation of the mean. If the standard deviation is very large, then check for outliers and also consider splitting the data between lower values and higher values as two separate measures.

Are there any missing values? Decide whether any zero values are actually zero or really missing data. Zero values may also be a form of outlier, in which case they should be removed and treated separately, as discussed.

Create a graph to get the picture

A picture in data terms can be worth a thousand words and can be much easier to interpret than numbers alone.

Look at the graph below. It warns that a **very small** number of customers have spent in excess of £100,000 each, contributing to the total of almost £1¾ million and completely distorting the value of the data as a guide to "average" customer performance. This is a typical business-to-business scenario.

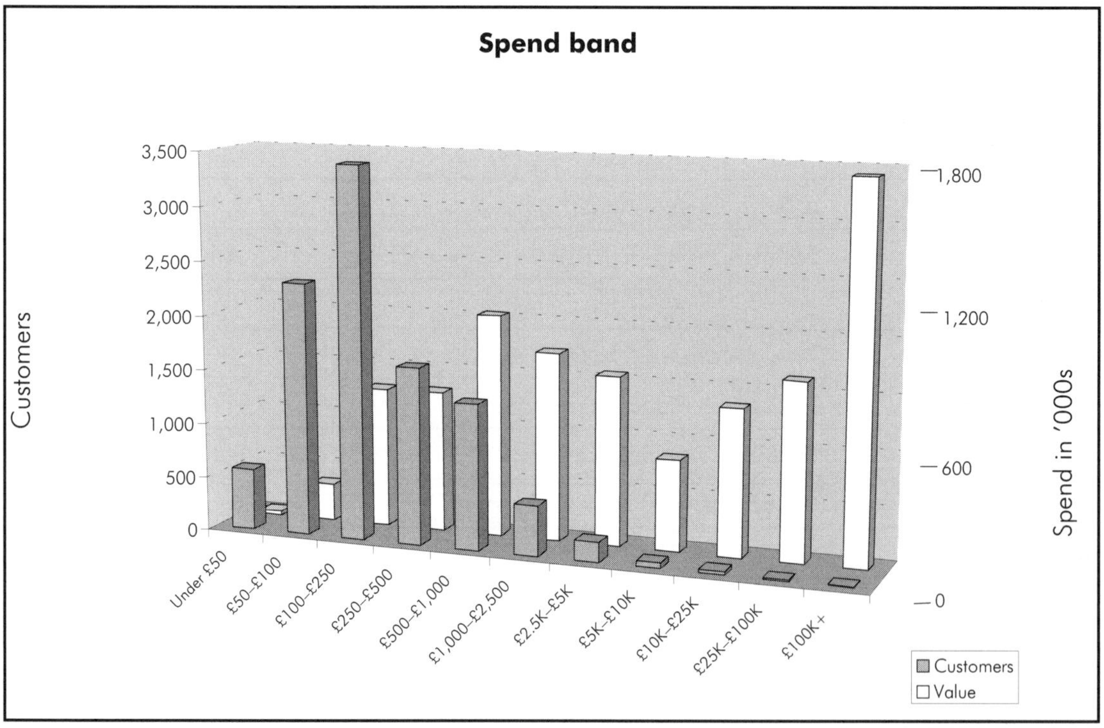

In fact, this graph was plotted from the table on the next page, from which you can see that the mean average spend is £775.35. However, the median for this data, ie for 5,000 observations, occurs between £74 and £188 and is therefore £131. This huge difference between the mean and the median is caused largely by the **seven** customers who spent over £100,000 each.

This example shows how easy it can be to spot distortions using visual representations.

Your attention might also be drawn in this way to the relatively large number of customers (563) who spent under £50. Closer investigation may show that many spent nothing at all, or were **recorded** as having spent nothing, possibly because no other data was available. Perhaps they are no longer customers.

Stage 3: Exploring each of the variables

You are now ready to start true profiling. By now you should have prepared your data for profiling and have a clear idea of which variables you are keen to measure.

We begin with a process called "Univariate" analysis, which simply means looking at one variable at a time. It looks at the "profile" of each variable and compares it to something meaningful.

We have mentioned before that comparisons take two forms. Internal, ie comparisons between or within your own records, and external, comparing patterns to an external measure such as total population or total households.

Profiling against internal data

Examples of internal comparisons are:

✔ Spend versus customers, eg specific customers' spends compared with their percentage of total revenue/profit, etc. (As in the table overleaf.)

✔ A specific type of customer versus all customers, eg the buyer of a given product or recruited from a particular medium compared with all buyers.

✔ Spend versus accounts (especially if customers may have multiple accounts).

✔ Enquiries versus conversions.

Overleaf is a typical profile in which we are comparing the numbers and values of customers within eleven expenditure (spend) bands. **The variable against which customers are counted and valued is their spend band.**

The index in the right-hand column overleaf is the ratio of the two percentage columns (eg 2.2% divided by 23.2% multiplied by 100 = 9.5 for the spend band "£50 – £100").

The author prefers to base the index on 100 as shown, so that the average is 100; low numbers are poor and high numbers good.

Spend band	No. of customers	% of customers	Annual spend	% of spend	Average spend	Index
Under £50	563	5.6	£16,890	0.2	£30.00	3.9
£50 – £100	2,322	23.2	£171,828	2.2	£74.00	9.5
£100 – £250	3,415	34.2	£642,020	8.3	£188.00	24.2
£250 – £500	1,624	16.2	£646,352	8.3	£398.00	51.3
£500 – £1,000	1,332	13.3	£1,018,980	13.1	£765.00	98.7
£1,000 – £2,500	462	4.6	£865,326	11.2	£1,873.00	241.6
£2.5K – £5K	182	1.8	£776,776	10.0	£4,268.00	550.5
£5K – £10K	51	0.5	£420,852	5.4	£8,252.00	1,064.3
£10K – £25K	32	0.3	£672,000	8.7	£21,000.00	2,708.5
£25K – £100K	10	0.1	£812,200	10.5	£81,220.00	10,475.3
£100K+	7	0.07	£1,710,254	22.1	£244,322.00	31,511.3
	10,000		£7,753,478		£775.35	

In this example, an index of higher than 100 means that the group of customers are contributing more to total spend than to the total numbers of customers.

For example, the customers who are in the highest spend band (over £100,000) have an index of 31,511.3, are less than 0.1% of all customers but are contributing over 22% of the total spend. In fact, they have an average spend of £244,322.

Clearly these customers are a key high-spending group who will need to be treated very differently from the majority of customers. The overall mean spend value of £775.35, therefore, is likely to be misleading. It is important to know the patterns within spend before placing any reliance on mean value.

Profiling against an external data source

A similar process can be undertaken by matching your data to an external source, such as a geodemographic or lifestyle database. **In this case it is important to compare like with like.**

For example, if your data is based on accounts and you have multiple accounts per customer, ensure you are fully aware of this when profiling. Ideally, compare accounts and customers internally within your own data, eg do certain types of customer tend to have multiple accounts? This will be reflected in your profile of accounts with the external data.

Also beware of geographic patterns. Always insist that the supplier of third party data allows you to profile against an appropriate base. For example, beware profiling against a national base ... very few businesses are truly national in their profile.

Here is an interesting example of how regional bias can distort data comparisons:

There's a coincidence!

A financial services company had their customer database profiled against a national lifestyle database. They concluded that their products were especially appealing to people with higher incomes and/or who were renting property. Not so! These variables ***appeared*** *to be important because the company's activity is concentrated in the south-east where higher incomes and home rentals are more common. They should have profiled their database with the south-east section of the lifestyle database. When this was done, it suggested quite a different set of discriminators.*

This question of regionality is so important we give below one more example ...

What is "wrong" with the profile for the retailer, below?

Geodem. type	Customers	% of customers	% of UK population	Index
G01	9,835	15.08	8.9	169.5
G02	14,452	22.16	11.2	197.9
G03	4,962	7.61	6.2	122.7
G04	1,159	1.78	7.0	25.4
G05	677	1.04	4.6	22.6
G06	3,581	5.49	6.8	80.8
G07	2,084	3.20	15.9	20.1
G08	14,888	22.83	18.2	125.4
G09	1,370	2.10	6.7	31.4
G10	9,444	14.48	9.2	157.4
G11	2,500	3.83	4.8	79.9
G90	259	0.40	0.5	79.4
	65,211	100.00%	100.0%	

Comparison with the national picture would show that whereas the retailer's share of geodemographic type G01 shows an index of 169.5, it ought to be nearer 200 since this is the pattern for the south-east where their stores feature most prominently.

The analysis below shows that nearly all the retailer's customers are in just two ISBA regions, and so any profiling **must** be done against the populations of these two regions **only**!

Sum of customers

	Total
	4,839
ISBA0	2
ISBA1	5
ISBA10	18,246
ISBA11	203
ISBA12	88
ISBA2	94
ISBA3	318
ISBA4	154
ISBA5	47,841
ISBA6	1,905
ISBA7	28
ISBA8	14
ISBA9	78
Grand total	73,815

ISBA = Incorporated Society of British Advertisers

If you are offered a lifestyle database for profiling and it isn't corrected for regionality, bin it! It really is useless.

Univariate analysis complete?

By now your profiling activity will be raising more questions, which you will answer by reprofiling sub-sets of your records in order to get a clearer picture. For example, you might focus on a particular geographic area or examine a group of dormant customers. As you continue to profile, patterns will begin to repeat and confirm your earlier findings.

Once you have completed your univariate analysis, you should have your first sets of learning. You should be able to say with some certainty:

✔ Which variables show strong discrimination between your key measures.

✔ Which variables could be redefined to make them more useful, eg rebanding.

Of course, making sure that you have understood the impact of any outliers, and dealt with them, is essential before you move on to the next stage.

Stage 4: Finding patterns that interact: Multi-variate analysis

The next stage is the one we call multi-variate analysis. It is about finding significant patterns to show how data interact.

We begin by looking for true patterns within the data which will lead us in two directions simultaneously:

✔ **Better learning.** You will begin to understand how customer characteristics are important in combination. For example, you may get very different spend patterns between young adults living at home with parents and young adults in their own accommodation.

✔ **New measures.** For example, the interaction between frequency of spend and total spend is possibly more powerful than either on its own. This might lead to new measures being created that are functions of more than one variable.

Multi-variate analysis can be undertaken in two ways. You can let the statistics speak for themselves and use various statistical tests, such as the Chi-Squared test, to assess if two variables are associated or not. The choice of technique will be a function of the types of variables you have and your objectives. (See Chapter 3.7.)

Or you can follow a train of thought, seeking to prove or disprove hypotheses about your business. Many experts find this gives them more insight and understanding than wading through reams of statistical output in every conceivable combination.

This latter approach is where profiling becomes more of an art than a science. Some of the variables you find can immediately be exploited in your marketing: the media you choose, the copy, the different messages to key segments of customers ... all of these soon become more important, more "real", more exciting than the raw statistical measures.

Although this is a practitioner's guide, it would be impractical at this stage to give you firm guidance on what to do next. You are learning: learning about your customers, your products and your marketing. Let the data lead you on a voyage of discovery and keep note of the key learning en route.

Again a picture is worth a thousand words. The following retail chart shows the interaction between three measures:

✔ Likelihood of customer lapsing (0–9% probability)

✔ Stability of customer's spend (0–3, very stable to very erratic)

✔ Trend of customer's spending (–6 rapidly declining; +6 rapid growth)

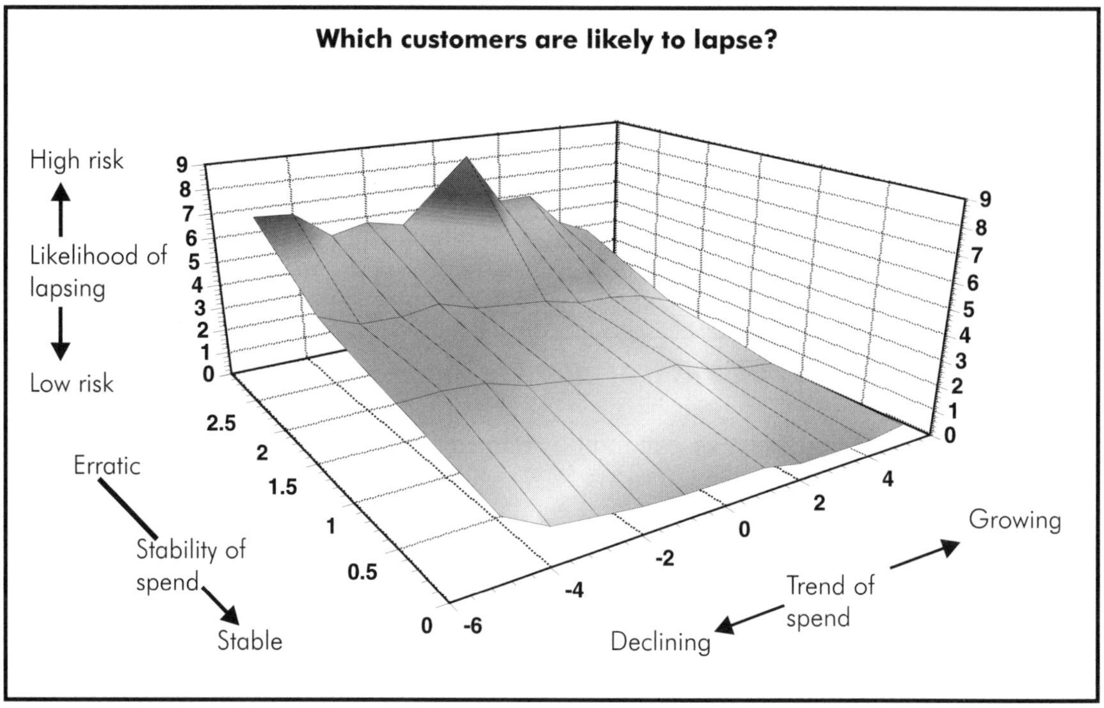

This chart shows that it is customers with high volatility among flat and declining accounts who are most likely to lapse. There is a difference of over 40:1 between the best and worst areas of the chart.

Stage 5: Segmentation begins

We are now ready to move from profiling to the segmentation of customers. Your purpose behind segmentation may be threefold:

✔ **General segments.** To establish some rules for segmenting your customers for general business purposes. For example, classifying customers into "Gold", "Silver" and "Bronze". Objectives for this type of segmentation are general business awareness, perhaps making staff more able to instantly recognise the status of a customer, eg for upgrading them.

✔ **Specific segments.** You may have a key project in mind, eg the launch of a new product. You want to assess and monitor take-up and the segmentation is needed for tracking specific customers by groups, eg by media source.

✔ **Exploratory segments.** Here your objective is to monitor how your general marketing influences customers. The segmentation needs to be rich in variety to get a strong understanding.

We now come to the aspect of segmentation which most people associate with marketing: the use of segmentation for targeting.

Again, there is no right way. Indeed, if you want to be successful, you should probably develop several segmentation strategies to describe your customers.

Once developed, the segments will be used in combination. For example, you may have forty segments in your solution, but you may use various combinations of them in your marketing, eg perhaps only ten segments are reached via certain media, or a particular copy slant is used for only a quarter of your segments, eg a special offer to the least active segment, and so on.

The importance of shared understanding

The key to good segmentation is **understanding**, a word we have used repeatedly throughout this chapter. And this does not simply mean your own understanding. It is vital that your segmentation objectives are understood and appreciated by your colleagues in other departments and by the business as a whole.

> Unless your segmentation can be explained to your colleagues, your advertising agency, your distribution channel, your sales managers and your board of directors, it is little more than an interesting exercise!

Segmentation comes alive when it becomes the way marketing is reported to the entire business. Segments need to be **the** unit of measurement. Apportion your marketing spend to each segment, make the segment the unit of analysis for **all** your marketing.

Then start to set objectives for the segments themselves. For example:

What does an overall growth of 10% imply? What changes do you have to make overall and by segment to achieve these objectives? What movements are we making between segments? What proportion of "New" customers become "Gold" customers within twelve months? What proportion move from "New" straight to "Lapsed"?

When you know **what** is happening, you can begin to ask **why**, and then to do something to curtail or build on whatever is the cause.

What makes a good segmentation strategy?

There are three basic rules for a good segmentation strategy:

1. **Segments must be identifiable.** Unless you can place customers into segments, it is little more than an academic exercise. You want to allocate customers to segments with ease. This often means taking complex statistics and writing sensible business rules that you and your colleagues can understand.

2. **Segments must be viable.** Unless the size and value of a segment deserves your attention, there is little point having it. There's no problem with segments of one customer, if that customer is exceptional and very valuable, eg a large corporate. But all segments **must** be worthy of marketing attention.

3. **Segments must be distinctive.** There must be dimensions or attributes for each segment that set them apart from the other segments, otherwise you may as well merge them back together to keep your life simple!

If you follow these simple rules, you should have something that is easy to communicate and will really work for your business.

How good is your segmentation?

The best way to judge your segmentation strategy is to see how well it explains one or two key measures. A good example of this is the "Gains Chart" or "Lorenz Curve".

You create this by ranking your customers on a key measure and showing what percentage of revenue you can explain as you increase the percentage of your customers.

The chart below shows that we can reach 62% of the revenue from the top 10% of customers, the segments give us 51%.

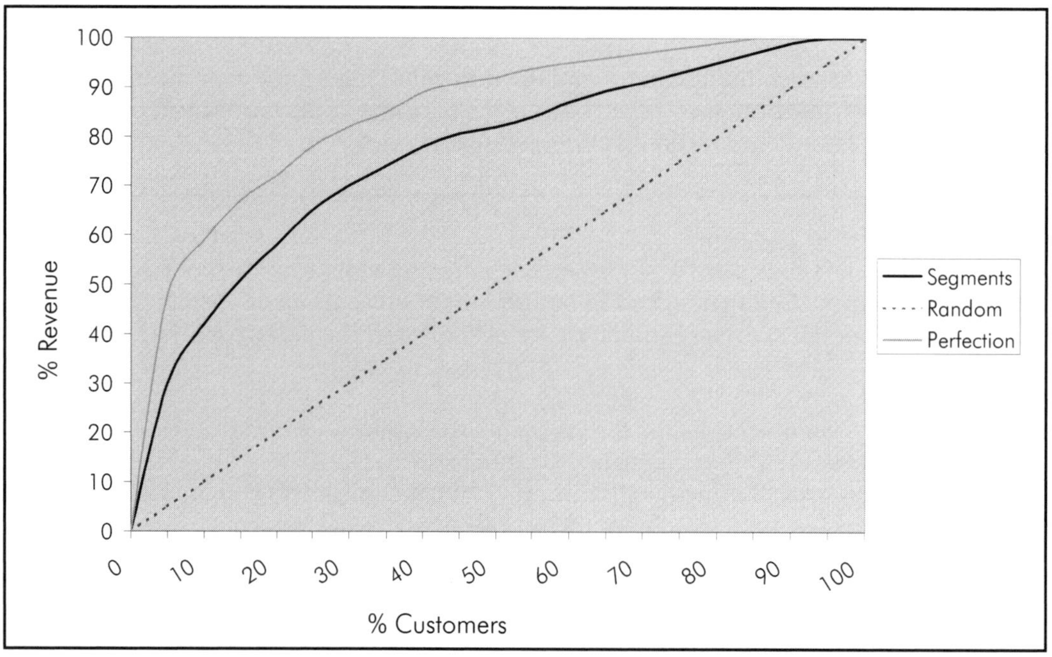

Understanding the gains chart

You obtain a gains chart by ranking customers on a key measure, such as spend.

The chart shows the percentage of the revenue reached, in relation to the percentage of customers. For example, when ranked, 70% of revenue comes from 20% of customers. The segmentation line shows 55% of revenue coming from the top 20% of customers. By chance you would expect 20% of revenue from 20% of customers.

In this case, the segmentation is good, since it explains a high degree of the key measure – revenue.

Methods for building segments

What techniques are available to build segments?

You can use either complex statistical methods, such as CHAID or Cluster Analysis, or start with an intuitive approach. The exact methods will be dictated by what measures and variables you have.

We shall not attempt to guide you in your choice of methodology here. However, we do say **START SIMPLY**!!

Build a segmentation strategy intuitively from your multi-variate findings; one you can understand; one you can communicate to the business and start to apply. Do this rather than abandon all hope at the prospect of complex statistics.

Segmentation is about learning and improving your business. It is not the same as SCORING and a simple strategy can bring huge rewards to the business. Allow it to grow and evolve with you, but don't tinker with it too much. Stick to your guns and revisit and refine it rather than starting again.

CHAID is usually used to "score" customers and needs a dependent variable which you are trying to predict. This might be a customer quality indicator or some similar measure used for general segmentation.

Cluster Analysis creates groups of customers who share common characteristics. It takes into account how diverse each variable is. It does not have a single dependent variable it is trying to predict. See Chapter 3.7.

Segmentation is not scoring

Some readers will be confused at this point on the difference between segmentation and scoring. The first point to make clear is that segmentation and scoring are different techniques used for entirely different purposes.

Segmentation is strategic activity. It sets the scene for all campaigns and marketing and provides a common language to use in your business when discussing customers. You are not looking for an optimal solution, but one which is practical – an efficient and easy way to communicate.

Scoring is a tactical tool. It is especially appropriate when you work with very large volumes and you want to move response from, say, 1.32% to 1.35% between a test and a roll-out. Scoring is usually used in a restrictive way, eg excluding certain prospects for a credit offer using a formula based on electoral roll data, county court judgements, payments records, credit card ownership, etc.

Scoring needs complex methods, such as Scorecards or Neural networks; you may not be able to fully relate to a scorecard, but you know it is about making a bit more money by using it.

There are roles for segmentation and scoring. **But scoring can never be the basis for a segmentation strategy.** It is too heavily influenced by a key task at hand. (See Chapter 3.7.)

Words of wisdom

Profiling and segmentation are basically a commonsense process. They are not necessarily about large databases, fancy statistical methods and sophisticated processing. These latter are simply aids to speed, not quality. In fact, very clever software packages may be so fast that you fail to do the necessary planning, **or thinking**, before arriving at an answer you don't properly understand and can't use!

Start with the small, practical steps. Everything can be done with spreadsheets. Master one step at a time and learn as you go.

If, however, you decide to go the statistician's route, you are advised to begin by reading Chapters 2.3 (on testing and sample sizes) and 3.7 (on modelling) – and then call in a specialist.

Chapter 3.6

Using customers' demographic and psychographic profiles

This chapter includes:

- Demographic data: what it is, where it stems from
- The Census explained
- Strengths and weaknesses of postcode data
- The 4 major uses of demographics
- ACORN, Mosaic, SuperProfiles, DEFINE
- Psychographic data: how it is derived
- Uses, strengths and weaknesses of psychographics
- Demographics and psychographics – a comparison

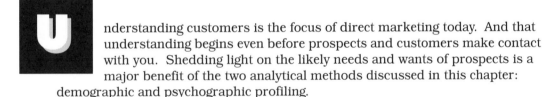

Understanding customers is the focus of direct marketing today. And that understanding begins even before prospects and customers make contact with you. Shedding light on the likely needs and wants of prospects is a major benefit of the two analytical methods discussed in this chapter: demographic and psychographic profiling.

Since the 1970s several companies have introduced demographic profiling services designed to improve the targeting – hence the cost-effectiveness – of a wide variety of marketing methods. Of special interest to direct marketers is their potential to maximise response to a campaign by identifying **groups** of prospects most likely to respond, based largely on Census data linked to the area and type of dwelling in which they live.

Psychographic profiling made its appearance much later, the premise being that large numbers of people can be persuaded to provide comprehensive information about themselves via questionnaires – especially about their interests, purchases, reading habits and, if they are agreeable, their age, family and financial status. This information enables marketers to tailor advertising and direct mail to **individuals** whom they believe to be their best prospects.

In this chapter, Robin Fairlie outlines the systems on offer and the applications to which they can be put, and then evaluates them as marketing tools.

New in this edition. Contact data for the new service providers in this sector.

Author/Consultant: Robin Fairlie

Robin Fairlie, Direct Marketing Consultant

Robin graduated from Cambridge in history before joining the infant computer industry in which he worked as a programmer, systems analyst, and training manager for a leading computer manufacturer. He then joined Reader's Digest as their first computer manager, designing and installing the computer system. He was promoted to Fulfilment Manager and, in 1969, to the Board as Business Services Director – the post he held until 1980.

While with the Digest, Robin co-founded the Mail Users' Association, an extremely aggressive pressure group on postal matters. He served as its Chairman for several years and believes the long, slow (and still incomplete) conversion of the Post Office to a marketing-led, instead of an operations-driven, organisation began at that time.

In 1980, Robin was headhunted to serve as Managing Director of the country's largest library supply company in Nottingham where he worked for two years before returning to London. In 1983, at the request of the Post Office, he set up the Direct Mail Services Standards Board whose purpose was, with the aid of Post Office money, to improve ethical and professional standards in the provision of direct mail services. He served as Chief Executive of the DMSSB for 4½ years.

In 1987 Robin became a freelance consultant and numbers the Royal Mail among his long list of blue-chip direct marketing clients. He has written the chapter on Mailsort, Chapter 7.8, where his biography is continued.

Robin Fairlie M IDM
Business Consultant in Database & Direct Marketing Systems
1 Broadlands Road
London N6 4AE

Chapter 3.6

Using customers' demographic and psychographic profiles

Know your customers – by group or as individuals

This chapter is about two very different methods of describing customers and prospects. The common denominator is that they enable marketers to understand their prospects even before any direct contact is made.

The first method we look at – demographic profiling – sheds light on **groups of people** who may have similar characteristics based upon the type of neighbourhood in which they have chosen to live. Postcodes, as we shall see, give pointers to lifestyle and hence to the possible needs and wants of the people who inhabit them.

The four systems of demographic profiling we shall be looking at are known as:

- ✔ ACORN
- ✔ Mosaic
- ✔ SuperProfiles
- ✔ DEFINE

The second method – psychographic profiling – seeks to assess the lifestyle of individual **prospects** by asking them straightforward questions about themselves using questionnaires. In this way much detailed information can also be obtained about their interests and purchases.

After discussions about both methods we offer a table comparing their relative strengths and weaknesses – and introduce a third approach which is a combination of them both.

PART I: Demographic data and population groups

What is demographic data?

Demographic data is simply statistical information about population **groups**. It is extremely important to bear this in mind. Although some of the systems on offer do use information about individual persons or households, **the basis of them all is the group**. Information about the group can be ascribed to individuals in it only on the basis of probability.

Retirement forecast

If we know that 35% of the people in a given group are retired, we know that the chance of any one individual in that group being retired is slightly better than 1 in 3. We also know that a promotion directed to retired persons will be 250% more effective in reaching its target if addressed to this group (rather than to a similar sized group of which only 10% are retired). What we must ***not*** *do is think of the first group as though it consisted solely, or even mainly, of retired persons since 65% of it does not.*

In an ideal marketing world, we would have a wealth of available information about individuals. In the real world, collection of such information across a population of 43 million adults (or 23 million households) is inordinately expensive. What we do have, readily, cheaply, and plentifully, is information about **groups**. The most plentiful source of such information in the UK is the decennial Census.

The Census – basis of the 4 demographic systems

The Census in Britain takes place every ten years.

The last UK Census was taken in 1991. Every householder is obliged by law to complete a Census form; the data from these forms are collated by the Office of Population Censuses and Surveys (OPCS).

Responsibility for collecting Census forms lies with an army of enumerators, each of whom deals with a small geographic area containing an average of 150 households and known as an Enumeration District (ED).

The ED is the smallest available building block of Census data. Anyone can buy from OPCS a library of magnetic tapes containing full Census data about the 150,000 EDs in England, Scotland and Wales (similar data can now be obtained for Northern Ireland).

Census data are broadly of three kinds, describing:

- ✔ The people who live in the ED: total numbers, numbers by age band and by marital status, for example.
- ✔ Socio-economic conditions, such as numbers in certain types of occupation; levels of car ownership, etc.
- ✔ Types of housing.

The amount of data available is very large indeed: for each of the 150,000 EDs there are some 19,000 variables, or pieces of data, plus a further 1,500 that apply only to parts of the United Kingdom (eg Scotland, Wales).

NOTE: It is important to recognise that no data on individual households are ever available from OPCS. Data are available only on Enumeration Districts, ie blocks of approximately 150 households.

The theory behind demographic systems

The root need of all marketing activity is better targeting. This question underlies the siting of a new shop, the stocking of a range of products, the placing of a newspaper or TV advertisement and the sending of a direct mail promotion. Targeting means ensuring that our message reaches as many as possible of the people we are interested in, while wasting the least possible effort in reaching people we are not interested in (or who are not interested in us).

The object of looking at information that describes groups of people is to differentiate one group from another. Our hope is that differences in the demographic make-up of groups will be reflected in different responses to our marketing initiatives.

Demographic systems must begin by establishing population groups that are demographically different. We can then consider how to test marketing hypotheses about those groups.

Whatever their demographic differences – our chosen population groups must not be so small that observed behavioural differences between them have no statistical significance.

Creating significant groups

Suppose a toilet soap manufacturer were to use the full 150,000 EDs as his population groups, and then applied to those groups data from a random national survey of 30,000 consumers showing which brand of soap they habitually bought. The majority of EDs would not contain any person from the survey; those that did would have one or two persons. It would therefore be impossible, from this survey data, to use the demographic differences between EDs as a way of differentiating people's purchases of toilet soap.

If, however, he divides the population into only 30 larger groups instead of 150,000, then each group will contain on average 1,000 persons from the survey. This should be enough to observe differences in brand preferences between groups with different demographic characteristics. The larger groups are arrived at by banding together several EDs.

The first requirement, therefore, is to band together EDs with similar demographic profiles so as to form groups whose demography is significantly different each from the other, **and whose populations are sufficiently large** that even quite modest research samples will show up at significant levels within each of them.

Reducing the number of variables

Before a demographic system can arrive at a suitable method of grouping, there is another problem: 19,000 variables is far too large a mass of data to handle for each ED – the more so when we recognise that many of the data are either of no interest for marketing purposes, or repetitive.

All demographic systems, therefore, begin by reducing this number to a more manageable total of significant items. These pieces of data are then expressed proportionally, eg:

- ✔ Proportion of ED residents aged 15–24
- ✔ Proportion of ED permanent dwellings rented unfurnished

The systems commercially available use between 70 and 150 principal items of data from among the 19,000 Census variables.

Having determined which Census variables to use, the demographic system will then examine how best, by reference to these variables, the 150,000 EDs can be banded together in groups whose members have broadly similar characteristics. The four systems available derive (by a computerised statistical process known as cluster analysis) 50 to 160 groups of EDs. These groups can then be further aggregated into smaller numbers of super-groups.

So we now have a limited number of groups of EDs, where each group has a substantial population, and all the EDs in each group have broadly similar demographic profiles as determined by the most significant of the Census variables. So far, so good. But when we try to correlate EDs with postcodes, in order to, say, direct mail their populations, we run into problems.

Type 8 Home Owning Areas, Well-Off Older Residents

A
3
8

These are areas of classic seaside retirement bungalows. Although they are found all over Britain, the largest concentrations are in the Isle of Wight, Dorset, Sussex (East and West) and Devon. 44% of the population of Christchurch is ACORN Type 8.

Demographics

These neighbourhoods have very high proportions of elderly people and very few children. Almost 40% of the population is aged 65 and over and over 50% of households are either pensioner couples or single pensioners. With almost 18% of the population suffering a long-term illness (a level 50% above average), healthcare is a major issue.

Socio-Economic Profile

40% of the population are retired. Of the working population, the majority are professional and white collar occupations. Other key features of the socio-economic profile are above average levels of self-employed, home based and part time workers.

Housing

Almost 60% of homes are owned outright in ACORN Type 8. This is a level almost 2.5 times the national average. There are very few rented homes, and few flats or terraced homes - over half the houses are detached with a further quarter being semi-detached.

Food and Drink

The proportion of people who do grocery shopping daily is 52% higher than average. Most grocery shopping trips are made by car. Freezer ownership is slightly above average and consumption of frozen ready meals is well above average. Consumption of frozen foods such as beefburgers and fish fingers, however, is low. Consumption of most packaged and fresh foods is low, except tinned and packet soup and fresh fish. Beer consumption is well below average but consumption of sherry, port and vermouth is high.

Durables

Car ownership rates are modest - the majority of households have only 1 car. The proportion of people who have owned their car for 5 years or more is almost double the average, while there are many fewer new cars than average. Cars tend to be medium sized and priced. 61% more people than average are buying video cameras. Other durables purchased more frequently than average in these areas are washer/dryers, dishwashers, built-in ovens and hobs. Twice as many homes as average are having secondary glazing fitted.

Financial

The income profile peaks in the £5-10,000 and £25-30,000 bands. The proportion of people earning over £40,000 is less than half the average. Ownership of National Savings Certificates is over twice the national average, while share ownership is 40% higher than average. Credit cards are more popular than debit cards. Mortgage and hire purchase ownership are below average.

Media

Daily paper readership is largely concentrated on 3 titles - The Telegraph, The Express and The Mail. All are read much more by people in this ACORN Type than on average. The Sunday Express is the most popular Sunday paper with 62% above average readership. Other Sunday titles with above average readership are The Sunday Telegraph and The Mail on Sunday. ITV viewing is medium and commercial radio listening is light.

Leisure

Winter holidays are much more popular than average, as are European destinations. The proportion of people staying in their own holiday home or timeshare is 78% above average. Gardening is a popular activity and 82% more people than average have a greenhouse. Propensity to visit pubs, clubs and wine bars is low, while the proportion of people eating out regularly is slightly above average. Steakhouses, in particular Berni Inns, are very popular. Participation rates in all sports except bowls are below average but people are more than twice as likely as average to go to theatres and art galleries regularly.

Attitudes

People in this ACORN Type are much more likely than average to believe that a woman's place is in the home. They are generally content with their standard of living and are not terribly concerned with searching for low prices when shopping. They like to holiday off the beaten track. They are more likely than average to respond to direct mail, but are not particularly keen on other forms of advertising.

19

How geodemographic data is used and promoted.

Locating groups by postcode – a problem area

Let us suppose that a marketing manager possesses data – from market research sources or whatever – about the behaviour of a number of people. He wishes to relate this behaviour to the known demographic characteristics of the areas in which these people live, in order to see whether demography is a significant predictor of this particular behaviour. How does he discover in which ED each person in his survey lives?

The key to this whole process is the postcode: if we know an individual's postcode (for which we have a map reference) we can "allocate" him to an ED (for which we also have a map reference).

However, the migration from postcode to ED is not easy. The average postcode comprises 15 households – ie there are 10 average postcodes to the average ED. But the boundaries of each have been allocated independently. Consequently many postcode areas lie in more than one ED.

Each of the four demographic systems uses a different method to relate the two entities; there is as yet no perfect answer. All end up by allocating each and every postcode to an ED, and hence to a group of EDs with a common demographic profile. By this means a demographic profile can be assigned to any individual household in the country.

But, for the benefit of newcomers to direct marketing, it needs to be stressed: **there is no guarantee that a profile will be in any way accurate for a particular household.** If we say that a given address falls in a neighbourhood of "Private Houses, Well-Off Elderly" it may still be the case that every member of that household belongs to the 40% of people in that neighbourhood who are under 45: the neighbourhood description deals only in relativities, and indicates merely that well-off elderly people living in private houses are characteristic of this neighbourhood.

There is no guarantee that a profile will be in any way accurate for a particular household!

Demographic systems and individual data

All four demographic systems use, sometimes in different ways, further data beyond Census data. Some of these data, unlike the Census statistics, are about individual persons. They are broadly of three types:

- ✔ Sample data
- ✔ Universal data
- ✔ Mapping data

Sample data. There is a wide range of market research data available from such sources as the Target Group Index (TGI) and the Financial Research Survey (FRS). These indicate the relationship of a sample of individuals to one or more items in which the survey is interested. Thus, FRS will tell us who, and what proportion, of a national sample are shareholders. By allocating these individuals to their appropriate ED groups, based on their postcodes, we can determine whether one ED group contains significantly more shareholders than another.

Universal data. The Electoral Register tells us the names of the individuals who live in each ED (via their postcodes). The next most frequently encountered example is the Lord Chancellor's list – of County Court judgements, satisfactions, Bills of Sale, and bankruptcies. Since all of these are recorded on the list, it is possible to know the total number occurring in each ED, or group of EDs.

Mapping data. It is also possible to obtain information about road networks and journey times which can be related to the areas in which people live. This can be used to indicate how many people, in which groups of EDs, live within a given area, or within a given journey time of a particular spot. Illustrated below is a drive-time map, and opposite a postcode breakdown showing the deliverable leaflet quantities in each postcode sector for the Southampton area.

Bath 10 minute drivetime
Prepared by The Leaflet Company

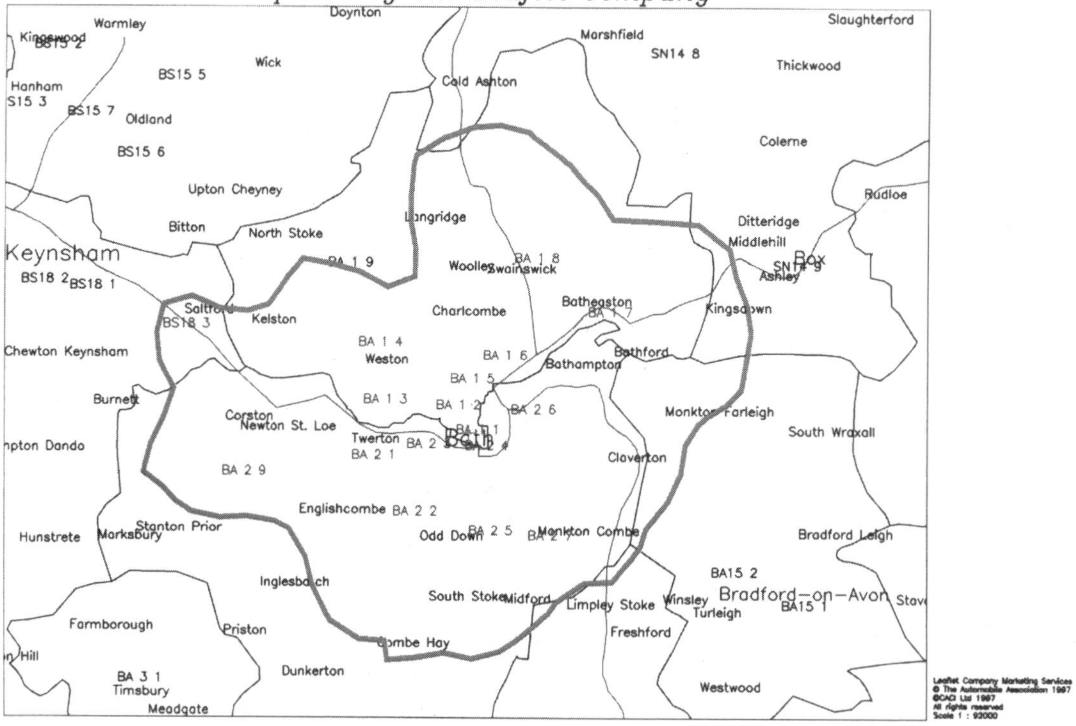

Source: Mark Young, The Leaflet Company, 11.11.97
Allie Oldham, CACI Information Services 11.11.97

Theoretical limitations of demographics

The major value to marketers in linking demographics to postal geography is the ability to take virtually any data that can be mapped and to express it in a way that relates to population – and to population groups differentiated by demographic characteristics.

We now consider the extent to which differentiation, given by clustering enumeration districts on the basis of Census variables, can produce usefully differentiated markets for products and services.

There are a number of reasons for being sceptical about an over-reliance on demographics for this purpose, among them:

- ✗ Historic nature of Census data, ie it is "old" data
- ✗ Imprecise map references

Postcode sector breakdown (sample)

prepared for The Institute of Direct Marketing

Area: Southampton

Postcode sector	Total households	Deliverable quantity	Cumulative del qty.	Publication Title
BH25 5	4,633	4,813	4813	New Forest Post
BH25 6	2,710	3,423	8,236	New Forest Post
BH25 7	2,876	3,262	11,498	New Forest Post
PO 1 5	4,244	4,023	15,521	Portsmouth & Southsea Journal
PO 2 0	4,918	5,006	20,527	Portsmouth & Southsea Journal
PO 2 8	3,731	3,325	23,852	Portsmouth & Southsea Journal
PO 2 9	3,211	3,216	27,068	Portsmouth & Southsea Journal
PO 5 3	2,569	2,492	29,560	Portsmouth & Southsea Journal
PO 6 3	3,522	3,503	33,063	Portsmouth & Southsea Journal
PO 6 4	3,958	3,743	36,806	Portsmouth & Southsea Journal
PO 7 5	4,359	4,292	41,098	Havant & Waterlooville Journal
PO 7 6	3,687	3,727	44,825	Havant & Waterlooville Journal
PO12 1	3,095	3,199	48,024	Fareham & Gosport Journal
PO12 2	4,148	4,416	52,440	Fareham & Gosport Journal
PO12 3	4,923	5,053	57,493	Fareham & Gosport Journal
PO12 4	5,667	5,770	63,263	Fareham & Gosport Journal
PO13 8	1,460	971	64,234	Fareham & Gosport Journal
PO13 9	4,165	3,405	67,639	Fareham & Gosport Journal
PO14 2	3,348	3,313	70,952	Fareham & Gosport Journal
PO16 8	4,191	3,431	74,383	Fareham & Gosport Journal
PO16 9	3,746	3,766	78,149	Fareham & Gosport Journal
PO30 1	2,568	2,800	80,949	MC Promo
PO30 5	3,405	3,000	83,949	MC Promo
PO33 2	3,298	3,300	87,249	MC Promo
PO33 3	3,384	3,000	90,249	MC Promo
PO33 4	2,246	2,000	92,249	MC Promo
SO14 3	891	1,380	93,629	Southampton Advertiser
SO14 5	400	733	94,362	Southampton Advertiser
SO14 6	1,526	1,660	96,022	Southampton Advertiser
SO15 8	451	1,398	97,420	Southampton Advertiser
SO16 0	554	369	97,789	Southampton Advertiser
SO17 2	2,364	2,523	100,312	Southampton Advertiser
SO18 1	3,703	2,974	103,286	Southampton Advertiser
SO19 0	1,750	1,584	104,870	Southampton Advertiser
SO19 2	2,131	2,612	107,482	Southampton Advertiser
SO20 6	1,825	1,123	108,605	Andover Midweek Advertiser
SO41 3	0	1,135	109,740	New Forest Post
SO41 8	2,981	2,375	112,115	New Forest Post
SP 5 2	2,226	1,705	113,820	Avon Adv: Sailsbury/Andover
SP 5 3	2,293	2,424	116,244	Avon Adv: Sailsbury/Andover
TOTAL	117,157	116,244		

Source: Mark Young, The Leaflet Company, 11.11.97

Historic Census data. In the UK a Census happens only once every ten years. At the time of going to press, the 1991 Census data is already over seven years old. By the time the next Census is available, all the currently available systems will be working with 12-year-old data. Since it is generally reckoned that some 10% of the population moves house every year, it is clear that after twelve years we are not looking at anything like the same population in the same place as represented by the Census.

How much this matters will vary from one application to another. Clearly EDs in which significant numbers of new houses (even 15 houses constitute 10% of the average ED) have been built since 1991 will be incorrectly described by Census data – just as the sale of council houses and the development of London's Docklands, overtook the 1981 Census.

City centre EDs can change their demography radically in a few years – through slum clearance, or by gentrification. Areas which had, in 1991, a high proportion of children aged 0–4 (eg new housing estates, or new towns) are likely to show different characteristics seven years later, and so on.

Imprecise map references. As already noted, there is a theoretical problem with relating postcodes to EDs, caused by the non-coincidence of their boundaries. The real problem is worse: the whole process of matching depends upon using the Central Postcode Directory (CPD), which provides a grid reference for every postcode, with grid references for EDs. Difficulties arise in two ways:

1. The CPD map references are imprecise: they define a square on the ground of only 100 x 100 metres (although 10 x 10 metres in Scotland). In the case where one or more ED boundaries run through this square, a postcode can be allocated to an ED in which no part of it actually falls. This can affect up to 50% of the postcodes in city centres. (The effect is less where EDs are geographically larger.)

2. A substantial number of CPD map references are actually wrong, due to mistranscription of data and careless or non-existent verification. This can result in postcodes being allocated to EDs not just yards, but many miles astray.

What differences do these theoretical problems make in practice? It is extremely hard to say. Where a postcode, for instance, is allocated to the ED next door to its "true" ED (certainly much the most common error), the probability is that the two EDs are sufficiently similar to end up in the same cluster anyway – in which case no harm is done.

For the future, work is allegedly in hand (as it has been to little effect for the past five years) to enhance and correct the CPD – which would benefit all the systems discussed here. Unfortunately, the chance to make ED boundaries co-terminus with postcodes was not taken for the 1991 Census (except in Scotland). It is to be hoped that this situation can be looked at again.

These are serious theoretical problems. But marketing is a pragmatic art rather than a theoretical science: the real test of the methodology is how well it works in practice. Beyond doubt it has worked well for some users. It is also capable of very considerable improvement. Ultimately, however, it is liable to be limited by the ageing of its base data.

Beyond doubt demographic profiling has worked well for some users.

How demographic profiling is being used

Despite the theoretical limitations, undoubtedly demographic profiling systems can provide you with useful information about your markets, customers, and prospects.

The main uses of demographic profiling in a marketing environment are:

- ✔ Refining customer lists.
- ✔ Making outside list selections more cost-effective.
- ✔ Understanding markets generally.
- ✔ Optimising store siting and stockholding.

We now look at these different uses, together with some observations on their value.

Using demographics to refine customer lists

The owner of a list of names and addresses can have the codes for demographic clusters (as determined by one or more profiling systems) added to each record on his file, and can use these codes as a discriminating factor (on their own or in conjunction with other data) to determine whether or not to mail individuals with a particular offer.

In practice, it is unlikely that the very generalised and imprecise data underlying demographic codes will make more than a marginal difference to the particular and precise information that a list owner should have about his own customers.

But there can be no harm, and only a small cost, in mounting a test to discover whether the extra discrimination offered by one of these systems results in extra response.

However, it is not generally recommended to include demographic data, or codes, on your own customer files without testing their value first.

> Do not include demographic data on your own customer files without first proving their value.

Making outside list selections more cost-effective

If you are using an outside list on which there is little discriminatory information except codes for demographic clusters, you may use demographic data to choose groups of people to mail. You can determine which clusters to use by one of a variety of methods eg:

- ✔ **By looking subjectively at the demographic profile of each cluster** and comparing it with your knowledge of your own product or service.
- ✔ **By taking a profile of your own customers**, to see which clusters they preponderantly fall into, and choosing from those.

(There is danger of a circularity in this method. If, for example, you find that your customers come predominantly from "Affluent Suburban Housing" this may mean that you have been advertising exclusively in media confined to such households. This own-list profile method will work properly only if the source from which that list was recruited is compatible with the list being researched.)

✔ **By running a test to a sample of the proposed list**, and seeing whether response is conditioned by the clusters in which promotees live.

In terms of list selection, all four commercial systems do succeed in creating homogenous population clusters with widely differing demographic profiles. There is also ample evidence that a wide range of purchasing behaviour is significantly different from one cluster to another.

What these statistically significant differences amount to in terms of profit and loss is something only you can determine – by looking not merely at the relative discriminatory power of the systems, but at the absolute number of real prospects they will deliver, and at the cost of reaching those prospects. (See example below.)

The effect of demographic profiling

Take the case of a marketer who considers Guardian readers as being among his best prospects.

There were, in 1982, 1,524,000 readers of the Guardian. Allocating a representative sample of these readers to the ED clusters produced by one particular demographic system indicated that the cluster categorised as "High status non-family areas" scored 271 for Guardian readers, against a national average of 100, or a penetration of 9% against 3.5%.

Suppose that our marketer has a product proven to be attractive to Guardian readers. He mails the 1,874,000 households known to be in this cluster, knowing he will reach 169,000 Guardian readers. Let us further suppose that the response pattern is:

Guardian readers	*5%*	=	*8,450*		
Others	*1%*	=	*17,050*		
			25,500	=	*1.36%*

If he had mailed a similar number of households from random EDs containing an average number of Guardian readers (ie 65,590 of them) he would have achieved:

Guardian readers	*5%*	=	*3,280*		
Others	*1%*	=	*18,084*		
			21,364	=	*1.14%*

The difference between 1.14 and 1.36 could represent a lot of money, or even the difference between profit and loss – it is, after all, a 19% difference. The improvement may, or may not, be sufficient to pay for the costs incurred. But it isn't anything like as large as the difference between 271 and 100, or between 9% and 3.5%.

The reason for this is that we are looking at only a small part of the whole. If we had an ED cluster in which Guardian readers had a 90% penetration, against a national average of 35%, then, on the same assumptions, the difference in response would be 4.5% versus 2.3% – an improvement this time of 96%.

Data used in this example is derived from application of a 1982 NRS survey to ACORN Group.

As a general rule, for lists devoid of other discriminants, demographic clusters are an advance on nothing: whether the advance is great enough to recoup the cost is an open question.

> Do remember: demographic systems are rather better at distinguishing bad marketing prospects than good ones.

For example: in the 1982 National Readership Survey, households of Social Grade A have, unsurprisingly, a score of 1 in "Poorest Council Estates" compared to a norm of 100. Yet the highest ED cluster achieved a score in this context of only 253. One of the highest scores in the whole survey was 367, for households with oil-fired central heating in "Agricultural Areas"; yet another cluster had a low score of 17 – one-sixth of the norm.

This is probably just a way of stating the fairly obvious – that poor areas are more homogeneous than affluent areas – but it has implications for demographic marketing which are worth thinking about.

Using demographic data to understand markets

Demographic systems were first developed in this country for direct mail use. But in recent years other uses have been developed, some of which may be far more valuable than for direct marketing. Some of these newer uses are highly specific; others are about offering a deeper insight into the nature and composition of one's market – a benefit that may be hard to quantify, but that no marketing person would turn down out of hand.

The general principle is that one can define a geographic area in a number of different ways, eg:

- ✔ As a collection of postcodes, or postcode sectors, or enumeration districts.
- ✔ As everything within a certain radius of a given point, eg a store.
- ✔ As anywhere within a certain journey time, eg a leisure venue.
- ✔ By country, county, local authority, constituency, or ward.
- ✔ By TV region, radio catchment area, etc.

– and any or all of these can be related via grid references and postcodes to the people who live within them. See the following page for an example of a radio catchment area. Through market research surveys, existing or specially commissioned, one can characterise the buying habits of people in these areas against the national norm and subdivide by demographic clusters if required.

As an aid to defining market areas or providing insight into market characteristics, demographic profiling has a great deal to offer.

As an aid to defining market areas or providing insight into market characteristics, demographic profiling has a great deal to offer.

Radio Bristol Catchment Area
Prepared by The Leaflet Company

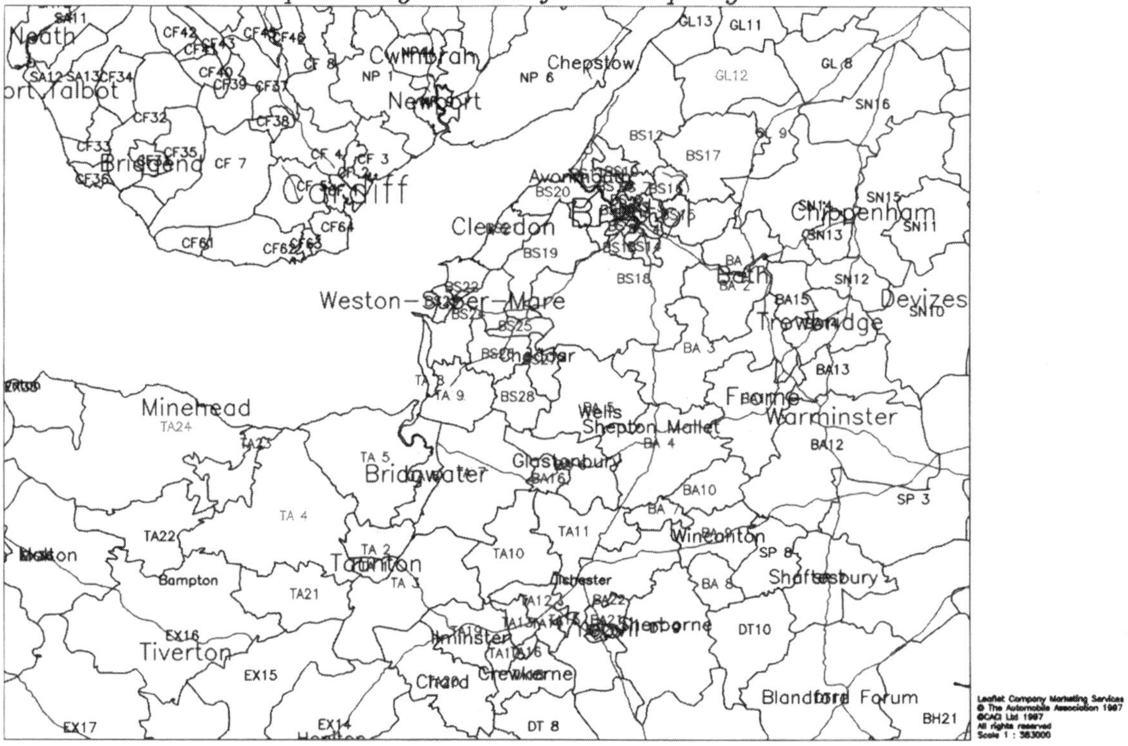

Source: Mark Young, The Leaflet Company, 11.11.97
Allie Oldham, CACI Information Services 11.11.97

Retail applications of demographic profiling

One of the best-known and most successful applications of demographics in non-direct marketing areas is that of siting retail stores.

One can map the propensity of people in urban or rural areas to travel for their shopping: the more expensive the product, the farther people travel for it; wealthier people travel longer distances for more things than poorer people. None of this is surprising, but being able to express it in precise numerical terms, and to plot its incidence on a map, is new.

From this welter of data one can draw all manner of inferences about shopping patterns. These may help determine policy on the siting of a store, or become ammunition in discussing rental levels. They are certainly a basis for a scientific approach to optimising stock-holdings of different lines.

Who provides demographic profiling services?

Ultimately, there are only three questions that practitioners ask about demographics:

? What systems exist?

? Do they work?

? Which one is best?

We have looked at how they work (all are similar in most important respects), but who provides them? There are four commercial systems available, as follows:

System	Operator/owner
ACORN	(A Classification Of Residential Neighbourhoods) owned by CACI
Mosaic	Owned by CCN (a subsidiary of Great Universal Stores)
SuperProfiles	Owned by Credit & Data Marketing Services (CDMS, a subsidiary of Littlewoods)
DEFINE	Owned by Infolink

ACORN is the oldest and most widely-used of these systems and its owner (CACI) is the most experienced of the four companies (although some of their original staff are now working for competitors). ACORN is alone among these systems in using only Census data in the clustering process, although it makes use of purchase data outside of this process.

Mosaic, being the product of a credit reference agency, has added to data derived from the Census area, data about judgement summonses – a highly relevant variable for many users. It describes areas where, for example, you might not want to make credit offers.

SuperProfiles, the system with the most impressive academic backing, has added data from the Target Group Index, renewed each year. The structure of these two latter systems (SuperProfiles and Mosaic) goes some way towards compensating for the loss of power implied by the ageing of the Census data.

DEFINE, like Mosaic, uses credit reference data to supplement Census data. Mosaic uses credit data as part of the clustering process – ie the cluster in which a given postcode falls is determined by a mixture of Census and credit data. DEFINE, by contrast, clusters on Census data and then subdivides each of its 47 clusters into credit-related groups.

All four systems have achieved profitable results for a number of clients. They are all better at locating areas of poverty than of affluence, and better at broad-brush descriptions of geographic areas (invaluable to retailers) than at picking out individuals for direct mail promotion (the purpose for which, ironically, they were designed).

However, even at an individual level, they are all capable of providing a deeper insight into the needs of the marketplace.

Scotland and Northern Ireland?

Both ACORN and Mosaic offer special versions for Scotland as well as general versions for Great Britain (systems based on the 1981 Census dealt with Great Britain only). Census data from 1991 are now available for Northern Ireland.

PART II: Psychographic data – a guide to lifestyle

A behavioural profile of individuals

Whereas the use of demographic data in marketing has been growing in the UK since the mid-70s (earlier in the USA), the use of psychographic, or lifestyle, data is a more recent phenomenon dating back to the early 1980s.

The basis of psychographic profiling is that very substantial numbers of people can be persuaded to provide comprehensive information about themselves, their households, possessions, behaviour, and interests. In marketing, psychographic data can be used for two purposes:

✔ It can provide you with specific information about the kinds of people who buy your products, enabling you to tailor your advertising approach according to their characteristics.

✔ It can provide generalised information about a very large marketplace, making possible extremely precise targeting of prospects based on self-submitted individual characteristics.

How psychographic profiles are compiled

There are four main psychographic databases in the UK, as tabled below:

National Lifestyle	Owned by ICD
Behaviour Bank	Owned by Computer Marketing Technologies (CMT), a subsidiary of Calyx
The Lifestyle Selector	Owned, operated and marketed by National Demographics and Lifestyles (NDL), a subsidiary of Calyx
Lifestyle Focus	Owned by Consumer Surveys Ltd, a subsidiary of Dudley Jenkins Group plc

All four operations are based upon questionnaires distributed to consumer households, resulting in a wide range of information about individual consumers being stored on a database. The method of distributing questionnaires varies between companies – this is likely to be significant for certain users. All operate a system whereby particular questions in the survey can be sponsored by individual companies. The returned questionnaires are handled by the operating company and the information on each is data-captured.

Sponsoring companies receive full reports on the survey results in a pre-agreed format. Certain information (for example, anything that is brand-specific) is regarded as confidential to the sponsoring company, which may also have continuing rights in further use of the data.

Other data, including names and addresses, becomes part of the general database which may be used on a selective basis for direct mail. A number of highly sophisticated tools are available for profiling lists, modelling, scoring, producing gains charts, and so on.

Sponsoring companies each pay a fee to cover the distribution of questions and related services; as a by-product the operating company obtains voluminous information which can be sold – again with added-value services – to other clients.

Psychographics and direct mail

Direct mail has always aimed to target sales efforts to specific individuals likely to be interested in a given offer. How can psychographics help?

If you already cultivate a database of your customers with records of their purchases, payment methods, changes of address, and so on, you are most likely already targeting individuals using relevant data. In this situation it is doubtful whether additional lifestyle information about customers' possessions, habits, and tastes can effect great improvements in a system already acquainted with their purchases.

If you are directing your sales efforts at cold prospects, however, acquired from the Electoral Register or a list broker, being able to select prospects from a database of persons **known to** have responded to a questionnaire through the mail, **known to** be willing to receive advertising material by post, and **known to** be segmentable by reference to their self-submitted characteristics, is a big step forward.

Whereas segmenting a potential mass audience by reference to demographic characteristics – a practice that has become widespread over the last ten years – can help to a rather limited extent, segmenting by known individual characteristics goes a long way to making direct mail a **very** precise instrument – provided that the data is trustworthy – an important proviso as we shall see.

Psychographics and advertising

Advertising can make use of lifestyle databases in three main ways:

- ✔ You can determine whether your existing advertising policy is consistent with what lifestyle profiling tells you about the customers who do/do not respond to your message.
- ✔ You can use lifestyle databases to select groups of individuals to receive a direct advertising message appropriate to their needs or interests.
- ✔ You can vary the terms of your advertising message or offer to suit the particular circumstances of individuals.

Since several other chapters in this Guide are devoted to the subject of addressing individual customers with relevant messages, it is sufficient to note here that psychographic profiling is the springboard to truly personal advertising and direct mail, subject to some of its weaknesses discussed shortly.

Psychographics and market research

The manufacturer of consumer goods who wants to discover more about the end-users of his products – perhaps to determine whether his choice of advertising media is optimal – faces a problem: almost certainly he has no record of who these end-users are, and no established means of communicating even with a small sample of them.

Gradually this situation is changing: motor manufacturers, for instance, now obtain from their dealers the names and addresses of customers, together with basic details of each purchase, which can be built into a database. This enables the manufacturer to communicate with his customers directly rather than through blanket advertising media. Such a database, however, is in itself unlikely to contain significant information about individual lifestyles, or to be of much value from a market research point of view.

The traditional solution to this problem is to commission a market research survey. The value of even the most basic database, in this context, is that it provides a sampling universe for the market researcher. With or without this assistance, he will then, probably in a series of face-to-face interviews, record the lifestyles of a sample of buyers, extrapolate to cover the universe, and note the differences in his findings from what is known about the population at large.

Unlike the psychographic approach, conventional market research has three serious limitations. The strengths of the lifestyle database approach are the reverse of these weaknesses, as the comparison below demonstrates.

But conventional market research and lifestyle database research are not necessarily competitive. One of the hardest problems in market research is knowing before the event what questions one wants to ask. Because the lifestyle questionnaire is a cheap way of obtaining large quantities of data, it may make sense to use it as a sort of saturation coverage. From the results one can construct a small-scale, more precise piece of conventional research. Such an approach will make it easier to frame one's ultimate questions better, and to economise on overall research costs.

Psychographic and conventional market research: A comparison

Conventional research	Psychographic approach
High cost Even at the minimum level required for statistical significance conventional research is expensive; extended to any substantial scale it becomes extremely expensive, with costs closely related to numbers of persons surveyed.	Low cost The methodology is cheap: the design, printing and distribution of questionnaires, the datacapture of responses, and the analysis of results, should give a cost measured in pence per respondent.
Limited use The statistical tabulations produced from this kind of research are its sole output: the rules of the Market Research Society positively forbid the attribution of names to research data.	Valuable list The chief by-product of the whole process is a potentially valuable list of self-submitted names and addresses, with a wide range of information about each.
Inflexible The methodology requires 20/20 vision at the time of designing the questionnaire: it really isn't practicable to look at the response and discover some interesting further question one would like to explore with certain respondents.	Ease of follow-up Because this list of names is available, any kind of follow-up suggested by the results of the original questionnaire is simple.

Weakness of psychographic profiling: Self-selection

There are two major drawbacks to the psychographic questionnaire which particularly apply to its use in a research context.

The essence of conventional market research lies in obtaining response from a representative sample of the universe that one is trying to profile. Thus, one might go to a representative sample of the total population in order to discover what proportion of UK adults regularly drive a motor car. Alternatively one would pick a representative sample of Porsche buyers in order to determine the age breakdown of all Porsche buyers. And so on.

The trouble with lifestyle databases is that they seldom – never in the case of the systems discussed here – constitute a representative sample of anything definable. It is therefore not possible to extrapolate from a lifestyle study to a universal statement. The very fact that the information on a lifestyle database is volunteered by the persons to whom it refers – an enormous strength in a direct marketing context – means that **it contains a self-selected and therefore non-representative sample**.

There is a further difficulty: how credible is this kind of self-submitted data? We may believe a consumer who says he reads the Daily Telegraph (or we may not!); we will probably believe the consumer who says he owns a dog ... but what are we to make of a statement such as "Yes, I would consider supporting National Heritage". What does "consider" mean? What does "supporting" mean?

Of course, these problems may not matter greatly: it is perfectly possible to obtain a worthwhile insight into one's market without having to quantify it to three places of decimals. We are, after all, in business to record profits, not statistics. And the larger the proportion that our sample forms of the total, the less its technically non-representative nature will matter.

So, if we have access to a lifestyle database on which are recorded 30% of this year's customers for a given item, we will give more credence to it than we would if the same records constituted only 3% of the total. **It is important to recognise the theoretical limitations of what this kind of data can tell us; it is not necessarily important to invoke the last degree of precision for our calculations.**

Weakness of psychographics: Size of databases

One of the early difficulties in the use of psychographic profiling lay in the relatively small size of the lifestyle databases. Although the quantity of information available on any one name is large – thus very complex selections are possible – this may not make too much sense on a list of, say, 250,000 households, where a complex selection may give a very small output. This raises the whole question of the size of these lifestyle databases.

If we regard the useful life of a single, non-updated, database entry as being between two and three years, then the size of the database is going to depend on the number of questionnaires that a company can distribute in this period, and on the response rate. This in turn will be affected by the different methods of distribution used by current practitioners, and on the incentives offered to consumers to respond. Different practitioners have different expectations.

Most experts agree that a lifestyle database of fewer than two million households (which is close to 10% of the population) is not likely to be viable long term. The systems considered above are able comfortably to exceed that target. (However, CCN has launched a lifestyle database called Chorus which is as yet rather small.)

PART III: Demographics and psychographics – a comparison

To conclude this chapter we look first at a broad comparison between the two profiling methods, before looking at ways to get the best from both.

The table below compares demographics and psychographics: their history, development, uses and strengths.

After several years of discussion and argument over the relative merits of geodemographics and lifestyle data, systems are now being developed which aim to bring together the best features of each.

Demographics and psychographics: A brief comparison

Demographics	Psychographics
Pioneered by the direct mail industry in the 1970s.	Introduced to the UK in 1983.
Aim: to segment huge but undifferentiated lists such as the Electoral Register.	Developed by consumer goods manufacturers who were finding conventional advertising and market research methods either inadequate or poor value for money.
Data relates not to individuals, or households, but to groups of households of a roughly homogeneous kind.	Data relates to individuals.
Data relates to whole country.	Data relates to a limited number of self-selected individuals.
Based on census data – an aggregated snapshot of the population at an increasingly remote point in time.	Based on data about individual behaviour and preferences, usually volunteered by consumers and collected by questionnaire.
Uses: the geographic analysis of population groups.	Value: allows direct mail to become the highly selective and carefully targeted medium it has always claimed to be.
Direct marketing potential: limited, since data apply to groups not individuals and decay with time.	Direct marketing potential: limited by self-selected nature of data providers.
Best use: the geographic analysis for marketers whose prime interest is groups not individuals, eg retailers.	Uses include advertising, selling and market research.
Suppliers: the Big Four demographic profile services: ACORN: CACI Mosaic: CCN SuperProfiles: CDMS DEFINE: Infolink	Suppliers: Behaviour Bank: CMT The Lifestyle Selector: NDL Lifestyle Focus: Consumer Surveys Ltd National Lifestyle: ICD

Three "combination" systems already in use are:

Lifestyle Plus	Data from CACI and ICD
Lifestyle Census	Data from NDL and CAT, marketed by MIC
Portrait	Data from Infolink and NDL

These new systems offer combinations of data from:

- ✔ Electoral register
- ✔ Census
- ✔ Lifestyle questionnaires
- ✔ Surveys (TGI, FRS, NSS, etc)
- ✔ Credit records

It is with comprehensive systems of this kind that the future must lie. But the older systems have many years of experience and expertise built into them which will require some catching up.

Further information

For contact numbers and addresses of organisations mentioned in this chapter please refer to the information volume of this Guide.

Chapter 3.7

An introduction to data modelling

This chapter includes:

- What modelling can achieve
- The 3 stages of modelling
- Descriptive and predictive analysis
- Cluster analysis
- Regression analysis
- CHAID
- Neural networks
- Advice to non-statisticians
- Software packages

Since the first edition of this Guide interest in statistical analysis and modelling has leapt sky high. Reasons include improvements in computing power, reductions in costs, the growth in large databases, new analytical theories emanating from academia, the improved education of our marketers, and stories of its proven success.

Keeping step with these trends have been the purveyors of software packages on which to run these new techniques.

Before you leap off into the unknown, spend a few minutes reading Huw Davis's succinct introduction to basic and more advanced modelling. What it does. How it works. The pros and cons of the various methods at your disposal. And, most important of all, what you need to do to prepare your data before you even contemplate investing in advanced modelling.

But make no mistake, modelling **is** the future. If your organisation isn't yet participating, this chapter couldn't be a better place to start.

New in this issue. Data modelling techniques did not feature in the first edition of this Guide.

Author/Consultant: Huw Davis

Huw Davis, Director, Data by Design

Huw is a household name in his own household. Since graduating from Heriot Watt University with a Mathematical Statistics degree, Huw has worked in the marketing industry for over fourteen years, specialising in the strategic use of data. His approach to statistical modelling and data analysis is more Uxbridge than Oxbridge – providing solutions which are actionable rather than theoretical. Huw is founder and senior director of Data by Design, a consultancy specialising in data analysis and database design within marketing. Data by Design is now part of the US company Metromail Corporation, one of the world's largest information services providers, with turnover in excess of $300 million pa.

Huw is one of the key lecturers on the IDM Direct Marketing Diploma course and for the last eight years has taught the statistics and modelling units of the course. He is a regular conference speaker both for the Direct Marketing Association and The Institute of Direct Marketing. He is also a renowned after-dinner speaker at business and charity events and barmitvzahs.

He is also Chairman of the DMA's Targeting and Statistics Interest Group.

Huw is married, which surprises many people; and has a daughter, Alice, which was a surprise to him!

Huw Davis
Director of Analysis and Consultancy
Data by Design
Lower Ground Floor
Bain House
16 Connaught Place
London
W2 2ES
Tel: 0171-664 1000
E-mail: HuwDavis@aol.com

Chapter 3.7

An introduction to data modelling

Background

Sophisticated statistical analysis is not exactly new to direct marketing. Reader's Digest, back in the early 1960s, used multiple regression analysis to predict which names on its house list were most likely to respond to its mailings for magazines, books and records. By concentrating its efforts on its best prospects, it saw profits increase dramatically.

Since those days, and particularly in the 1990s, many new techniques for modelling have been developed, tested, and found profitable.

Some of the techniques now in use by direct marketers are frankly **very** sophisticated, and many require the attention of an experienced statistician.

This chapter, therefore, sets out to explain the basic principles of data analysis and modelling. Then it's over to you to pursue your interest in whatever direction you choose.

What does modelling achieve?

Modelling, in direct marketing, is often used to maximise response to a given campaign. (That's by no means its only use as the author of Chapter 3.5 stressed.) The fact is that in any large-scale mailing there will be names that oughtn't to be mailed, or be sent a particular offer, and so on.

Basic modelling techniques in this situation can, for example – by breaking down the customer database into more and less profitable segments – select the names that will produce the best response, or the best order value, etc.

Advanced modelling improves significantly on basic modelling, and should therefore earn even higher profits. The table below shows the results of a publishing house modelling exercise. Half the audience produces almost twice the profit.

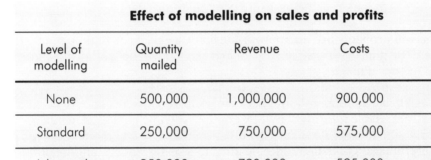

Effect of modelling on sales and profits

Level of modelling	Quantity mailed	Revenue	Costs	Profit
None	500,000	1,000,000	900,000	100,000
Standard	250,000	750,000	575,000	175,000
Advanced	250,000	790,000	595,000	195,000

The 3 essential stages of modelling

This being a practical guide, we start at the beginning – with a summary of the steps which **all** modelling exercises should follow, whether basic or sophisticated.

The three key stages are:

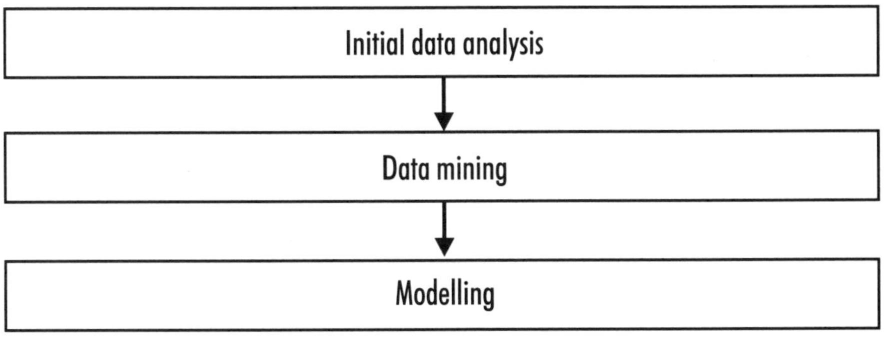

Initial data analysis

The first requirement in any modelling process – as explained by the authors of earlier chapters – is to summarise and understand your data. **A clear understanding of your data is imperative before any kind of modelling can be contemplated**.

The initial data analysis should take the form of identifying shapes and trends within your data (as we did in Chapter 3.5).

At this stage you will be looking at the three averages – Mean, Median and Mode – and at variances and standard deviations.

You will also establish which variables are likely to be your key measures in your models, and you will highlight and remove any extreme values (outliers).

Your data is now "clean" and ready for processing.

Data mining

The next stage is to look much closer into your customer data.

For this you will probably use an appropriate software package (although much of the work can still be done with simple spreadsheets). You will be looking for patterns and trends in your data.

This stage is known as "data mining" because, at its most basic, you "drill" into your data and extract usable information. Most of the available packages highlight patterns for you to investigate further by other methods. All of them allow you to visualise several layers of data at once, leading to a better understanding of the way in which variables can interact.

The more complex – and more expensive – "data mining" tools do not enable you to get any closer to your data. Their purpose is to speed up project times for the professional statistician, so be warned.

Here's another warning:

Many software systems that purport to undertake data mining are, in fact, glorified "cut and slice" information-and-reporting tools. Some packages that are likely to disappoint aren't even on the market yet, so we can't help you here except to say: ask an expert when the time comes.

Modelling – its 2 applications

Once your data has been analysed, described, and understood, you're ready to prepare for the modelling itself.

(But first make sure your objectives are clear **and** agreed. This will help your stats person to know what he/she is expected to deliver, which data is required, and whether the data is ready to deliver it.)

Modelling can be either **descriptive** or **predictive**.

Descriptive models, as the name suggests, describe the status of groups of customers. The most important descriptive modelling technique is **cluster analysis**.

Predictive models are those normally used in direct marketing to improve response, conversion, order values, etc. Many of these methods have been around for years and some for centuries. The most common are **regression** and **CHAID**, with **neural networks** recently becoming popular as a predictive tool.

Whether you choose descriptive or predictive modelling will depend upon your objectives. Basically, if your model is required to produce "yes/no" or "go/no-go" answers, you will use a predictive model.

Examples of yes/no answers include whether to mail active or lapsed customers; whether to include high or low order values, etc.

Cluster analysis DESCRIBES groups

Many variables, when plotted in isolation, can create uniform reliable patterns; for example, the normal curve of distribution. Predictions can be read off such a curve with some precision.

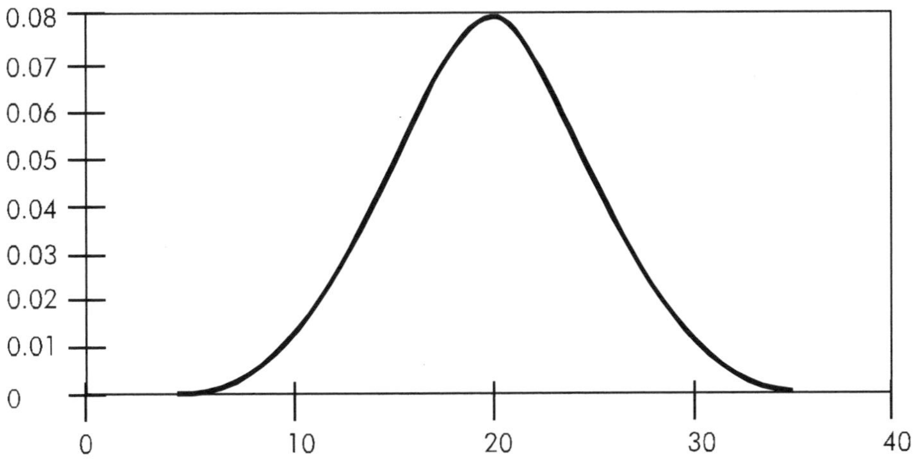

But suppose you plotted your customer base and found two peaks (nodes) on your graph? Now you have two distinct groups to consider.

For example, if we were to plot the heights of all the people within a junior school building, we might discover two nodes – one clustered around the average height of the children, and one around that of their teachers.

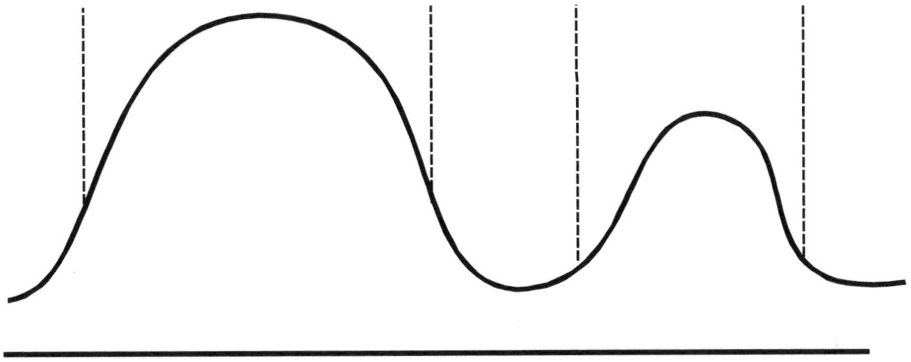

We are beginning to explore the principle of clusters and this is where cluster analysis comes into our reckoning.

In the simplified example below, we begin our analysis by creating clusters using just **two** variables.

In practice, statisticians will create clusters based on several variables. If you're thinking of trying this, remember it can take several years of practice.

Remember also the variables MUST be completely independent of each other, ie not highly correlated, or they cannot be clustered.

And a final reminder: all modelling must begin with clean data, ie with outliers removed.

Creating clusters based on shoe size

Let us assume we run a shoe catalogue and we want to know more about our sales to men. We know only three relevant facts about them: shoe size, age, and purchases over the past two years. So we plot them by age and expenditure:

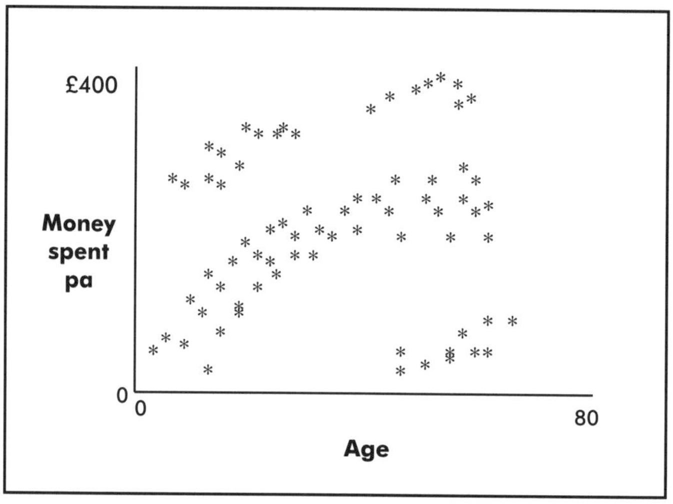

From this plotted data we can identify patterns, in this case three clusters (ringed):

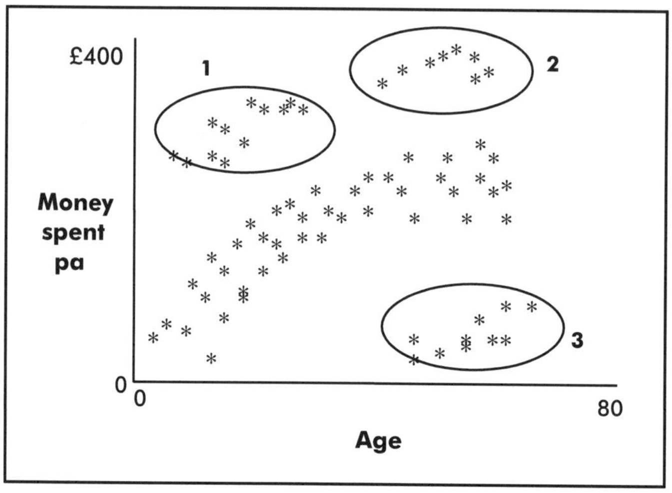

Cluster 1 is young people with high spends. Cluster 2 is older people also with a high spend. Cluster 3 is older people with a low spend (possibly infrequent purchasers – perhaps they don't wear out their shoes, or prefer to have them repaired rather than buy new). We need to know more about Clusters 1 and 2. So we apply our only other piece of data and plot them by shoe size:

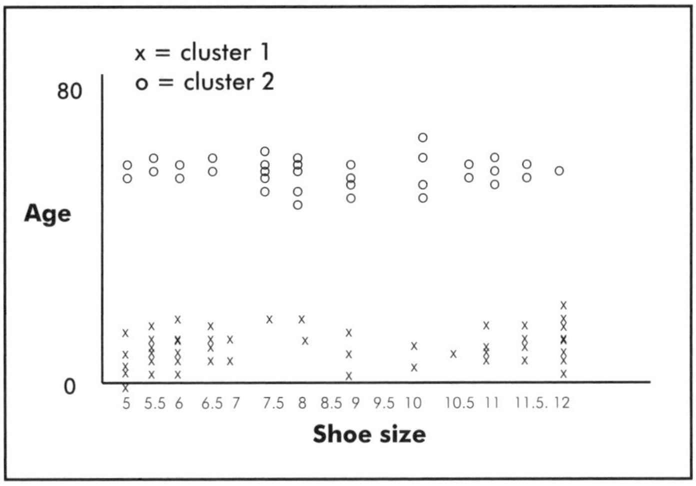

We see older men buying across all sizes – no clue there. But younger men are clustered around "extreme" sizes (5, 6, 11, 12) which are difficult to find in many shops. Perhaps we should do some research? More tests? We may have discovered a niche market. We can now target our messages, perhaps create special editions of our catalogue for older buyers who like the convenience of buying from us, and for younger buyers who can't find their sizes anywhere else.

Cluster analysis describes customer groups according to key variables.

Regression analysis PREDICTS customer behaviour

For several decades regression analysis has been used very profitably by direct marketers.

The basic principle behind regression is that if we have two or more variables to compare, it is possible to find a single line that will closely fit the data.

When the "best" line has been established, it can be used to "read off" the characteristics of customers and thus seek out further customers whose profile falls on or near the line.

Overleaf, we show a simplified example to demonstrate the theory.

Example of simple regression analysis: Shoes

Looking at our earlier shoe business data, we see that our clusters were scattered. If we remove those clusters, we are left with a broad swathe moving upwards from left to right. We can draw a line to represent this central core of the data, as shown:

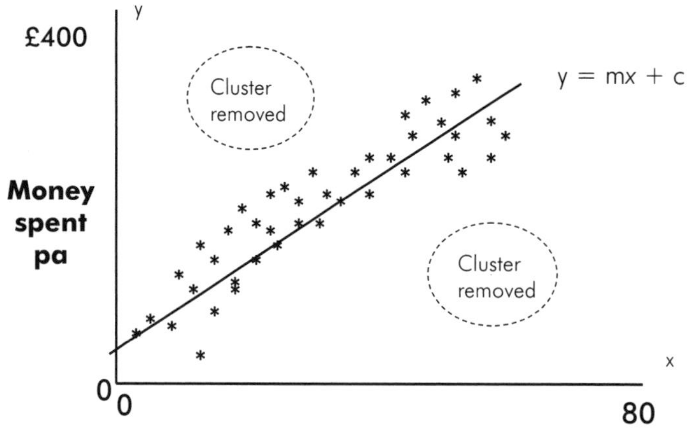

The graph above shows a clear relationship between age and money spent, ie older customers spend more through this channel. As the data tends towards a linear relationship, **an equation can be created which approximately represents the age/ spend relationships** as follows:

$$y = mx + c$$

where:

y is the **dependent variable** (spend)

x is the **independent variable** (age)

m is the **gradient**, calculated from:

$$m = \frac{y}{x}$$

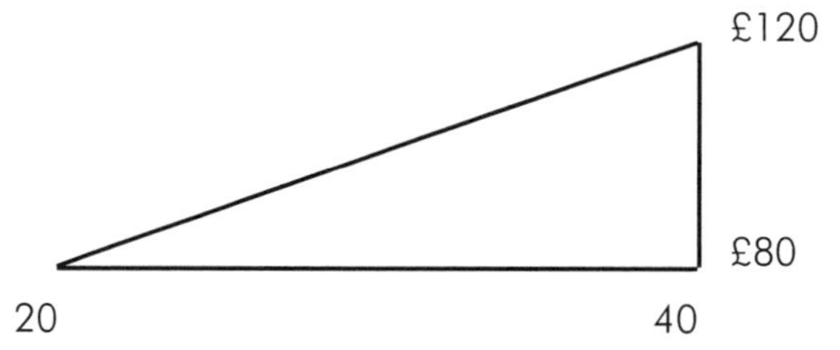

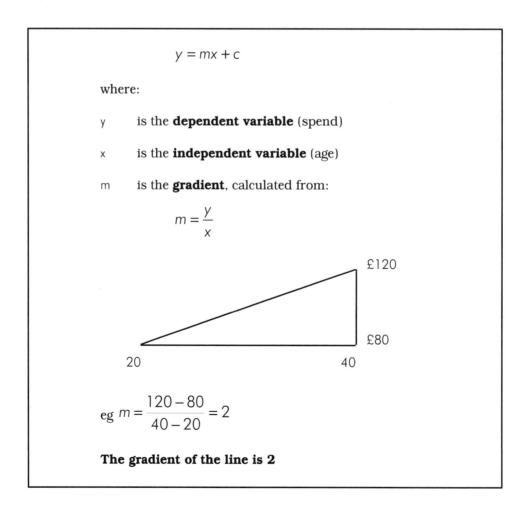

eg $m = \dfrac{120 - 80}{40 - 20} = 2$

The gradient of the line is 2

C is the **intercept**

The intercept is where the line crosses the y-axis when x = 0

Thus, using our data:

$$y = 2x + 10$$

So, what we have done is literally "regress" the individual points to a single line, hence "linear regression analysis".

We can now predict that if a man who responds is aged 30, he will spend £70 on shoes in the next two years:

$$\begin{aligned} y &= (2x30) + 10 \\ &= 70 \end{aligned}$$

The most important factor in this equation is the gradient (m), because it shows how influential the age factor is on expenditure. The gradient is often known as the **weight** or **score** of x. In our example the score for age is 2.

The example above is very simplistic in its outlook and prediction of how a customer will behave. The risk of getting the prediction wrong using this equation is high.

To reduce the risk in regression models we add further variables. The more variables that we add to the equation, the more accurate the final model will be, which brings us to our next level of modelling.

Multi-dimensional direct marketing model

In direct marketing the dependent variable is linked to a campaign, ie **whether a person has, or has not, responded to a mailing**. Response is normally represented by 1 and no response represented by 0. The dependent variable could also be actual order value or **likelihood** to buy.

Using the knowledge we have of our shoe company, we can create a response model based upon age, shoe size and total spend in the last two years, and create a regression model of **likelihood to respond**.

To reach the final stage of the equation we need to go through several stages, as follows:

1. Assuming we have no response history we must first mail a random sample of customers. During selection we must take a snapshot of their transaction data and marketing history. This will allow us to analyse the responses once collated. We need to know exactly what each individual customer looked like **at the time of mailing**.

2. Once the results are available we need to compare those who responded with those who did not, in order to discover any key differences, eg are older customers more likely to respond than younger ones?

3. Experience shows that splitting continuous variables like age and income into smaller, more discrete variables often improves the overall power of the model. Statisticians call these split variables, **dummy** variables – so this we do next. By splitting variables in this way, we ensure a greater differentiation **within** each variable.

Dummy variables

AGE can be split into YOUNG (18–30), MIDDLE (31–50), OLD (51–65), OLDEST (65+)

TOTAL SPEND can be split into LOW (under £60), MODEST (£60 – £119), HIGH (£120+)

SHOE SIZE can be split into SMALL (6 or below), USUAL (6.5 – 11), LARGE (11.5+)

4. Now we are ready to create a regression model based upon **all** the split variables. The model itself will be developed using appropriate software. The most common of the statistical packages are SPSS and SAS (contact data at end of this chapter). The skill of the statistician is to identify the best solution.

5. There are many approaches to regression modelling, but all eventually create a set of **scores** for the variables in the model. Some scores are positive, others negative. Often variables are allocated a zero score, which implies that the variables are neither a positive nor a negative factor and are not strong enough to influence the customers' decision to respond or not.

The final model for our shoe company mailing will look something like the following:

Response to mailing = a x YOUNG
+ b x MIDDLE
+ c x OLD
+ d x OLDEST
+ e x LOW
+ f x MODEST
+ g x HIGH
+ h x SMALL
+ i x USUAL
+ j x LARGE

Where a to j are the scores.

Multi-dimensional regression is not trying to fit a best **line** through the data, but the best n-dimensional **plane** through it. In our example it is a 10-dimensional plane; this is impossible to either draw or imagine!

6. A scorecard table is created to represent the model factors, for example:

	Variable	Score (a to j)
Age		
	Young	–10 (a)
	Middle	+6 (b)
	Old	+12 (c)
	Oldest	+11 (d)
Total spend in last two years		
	Low	–4 (e)
	Modest	+14 (f)
	High	+21 (g)
Shoe size		
	Small	+13 (h)
	Usual	–10 (i)
	Large	+7 (j)

7. The whole mailable universe is now scored in this way. The scores for an individual are totalled: in theory, the higher a customer's overall score the more likely he is to respond to the next mailing.

Example Scores

Man aged 25, who has spent £90 in the past two years, and wears size 6 shoes; likelihood-to-respond score:

Age score	Spend score	Size score		
–10	+14	+13	=	17

Man aged 55, who has spent £133 in the past two years, and whose shoe size is 9; likelihood-to-respond score:

+12	+21	–10	=	23

At this point, we might surmise our best customer is a wealthy old man who buys all his shoes from us because no one else can fit his incredibly small feet! (If we were engaged in profiling we might be looking for more like him.)

Anyone you know?

Many years ago, in the early days of regression analysis in direct marketing, a leading publisher regressed its customer base and discovered that its best prospect was a man aged 38 employed at the Town Hall who travelled to work on a motor cycle!

8. The next step is to test the model on another past mailing to see if what is predicted actually happened, ie are the predicted scores responding as expected.

9. If the model appears to be predicting properly, then the entire customer base, once scored, can be segmented and a mailing programme planned accordingly.

Modelling other dependent variables

Often direct marketers use modelling, not simply to predict response, but to predict the actual value of an order.

Scorecards can also be used to calculate **the likelihood of a customer ceasing to respond** or to buy a product. They are then known as retention models. (For an example see the earlier chapter on profiling.)

Caution!

1. We have been looking at a very basic approach to regression modelling. Although all methods are based on the same concept, there are many other ways of approaching the task.

2. Regression models often have a short lifespan (12–18 months) and should be continually reviewed and reworked. Models can be affected by economic conditions, new product pricing, fashion changes, competitive innovations, etc.

3. Multi-variable modelling should be tackled only by a qualified statistician using a powerful computer.

4. Scorecard regression works only when used in similar circumstances, ie if developed for shoe sales it should be applied to shoe sales: eg if you attempt to use the model to predict the sales of socks it is unlikely to be useful.

CHAID: Predicting response by comparing 2 variables

We now come to our second major predictive modelling technique: Chi-squared Automatic Interaction Detector (CHAID).

It may sound like a star wars technique for spotting UFOs, and in some ways it is – a technique for spotting patterns at speeds the human eye is unable to detect.

AID techniques are used in direct marketing to automatically segment files into unique combinations. CHAID is the most widely used of these techniques.

CHAID works by repeatedly splitting segments into smaller segments. At each step it looks at a segment (or "cell"), considers all the variables within it, decides which split is the most statistically reliable, and divides the cell into two smaller cells. It then repeats the process until it decides there are no more statistically significant splits to make.

In direct marketing we use CHAID to find the most significant factor to cause a response or non-response. It then divides the segment into two, and repeats the process as in the example below. We call the outcome a tree diagram.

The chief advantage of CHAID is that it results in segments which are clearly defined and easy to understand. The information it supplies can be applied immediately; for example, it can be used to make selections for direct mail as the final cells below demonstrate.

Important

To use CHAID, continuous data, eg expenditure and income, must first be banded into categories. (See Chapter 3.5.)

Example of CHAID analysis: Who buys and why?

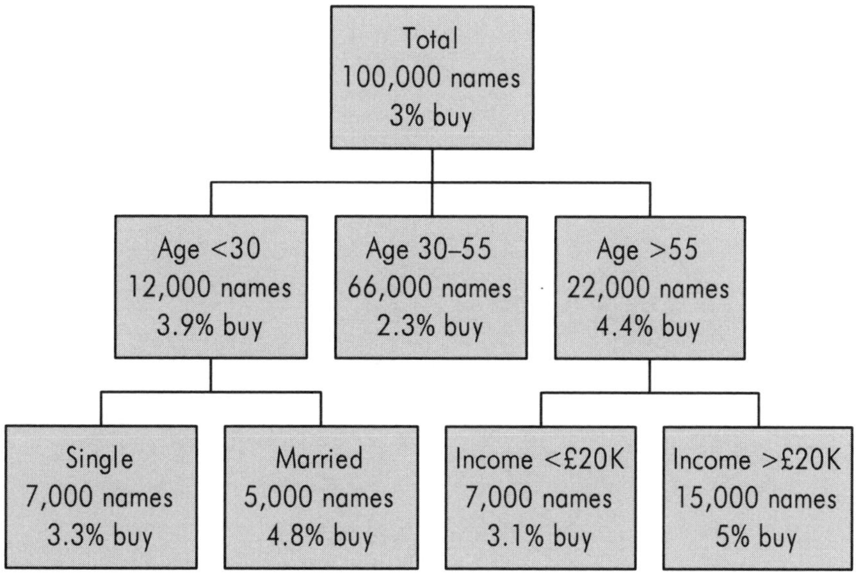

In the foregoing example, CHAID first identifies **age** as the most important differential. The ages will already have been banded, ie under 30; 30–55; over 55 years. So it creates three new cells.

Within the "under 30" cell, it decides that marital status is the key discriminator, and divides into "single" and "married" cells.

Within the "over 55" cell, where marriage is not a major differential, it chooses income bands as the basis for its next division.

Thus CHAID is all the time analysing the interaction of variables, eg if customers are over 55 with incomes of more than £15,000, they are the most likely to buy; whereas people of the same age with lower incomes are the least likely to buy.

If the "married under 30s" were further divided by income groups, we might find that the higher income groups produce a better response than the 5% already recorded, perhaps 6%. (Caution: be sure any further division is statistically significant.)

If we compare all the percentage responses we can see that response from the better segments is well over 200% of that for the least responsive. We are not only seeing how CHAID works, but also witnessing the best possible demonstration of the power of segmentation.

(Students: You might have some fun debating which types of product might lead to an analysis such as the one above.)

Neural networks: Learning from the human brain

A third predictive technique which is rapidly gaining widespread acceptance in direct marketing is modelling with neural networks.

Neural networks try to simulate neuron activity within the human brain and are extremely complex to build. Fortunately, it is possible to use neural network models without an understanding of the physics involved.

Modelling amounts to encouraging the network to train itself: it "learns" how signals (input) relate to output (response). The "neurons" learn to recognise the strength and form of each connection.

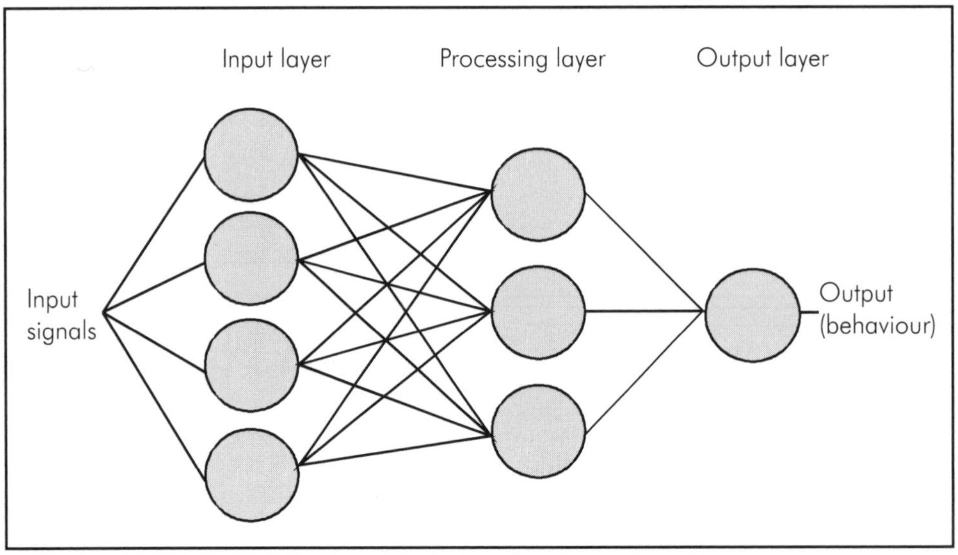

Neural network modelling can be highly automated. However, some experts say that a great deal of experience is required to achieve the best possible results, and that the outputs require specialist skills to implement.

No doubt this will be an area of heightened development in the next few years.

Comparison summary of modelling techniques

Strengths	Weaknesses
Cluster analysis (descriptive)	
Ideal for use where you have no preconceived idea of your target markets	Often results are not specific enough to clearly identify target markets
Reduces large amounts of data into groups that can be clearly described in terms of transactions/demographics, etc	Weaker for targeting than predictive techniques such as CHAID
Helps to suggest and test hypotheses, eg that certain customers like certain offers	
Multiple regression (predictive)	
A very powerful and time-tested technique	Requires considerable expertise to prepare for and run
Can analyse a large number of variables simultaneously	Can be unreliable if insufficient variables are used
Results can be fairly easily explained	Models can have short life-span and may need continually renewing
CHAID (predictive)	
Very simple to understand, use and apply, especially for simple categorical data (eg income bands)	No variable weightings and uses only categorical data
Good at finding interactions between key variables	Needs large samples
Results are easily understood and can be immediately applied to segmentations	Results must be validated by other methods
Neural networks (predictive)	
Very powerful, very sophisticated	Very complex, expensive hardware required
	Requires considerable expertise to set up and use
Fully automatic in use; "trains" itself	Does not readily produce selections (segments). Output hard to explain
Possibly the future of predictive modelling	Very difficult to improve performance if not satisfied

In-house, or call in the specialists?

As a marketer, you may not be a statistician. As an entrepreneur, for example, you may not fully understand (or have time for) the niceties of basic, let alone advanced modelling.

For you, the aim of this chapter is, as its title suggests, primarily one of introduction. Hopefully you are now sufficiently primed to begin talking with your key staff, consultants and suppliers, about techniques which could easily double your profits.

Your first decision, therefore, is whether to pursue the development of modelling techniques yourself, eg in-house, or to call in outside experts.

Here are a few more pointers that you may find helpful:

✔ No one modelling method, however sophisticated, is right for all applications – but **all methods, if suitable, should give similar results**. Nobody's software should produce better results than anyone else's.

✔ Some software solutions are suitable only for basic applications, and some for advanced modelling. **Make sure you don't get saddled with the latter when what you need is the former.**

✔ **Advanced modelling can be very expensive** in terms of software, systems and skilled personnel.

✔ The more advanced the method, the more care and control required to implement its conclusions.

✔ Once you have a model, **always insist on having your model validated**. This is done by using it to predict the performance of a large set of data (ie several thousand files) **not** used in building the model itself. If the two outcomes correlate very closely, you have a good model.

✔ **Some models (especially regression analysis) should be renewed at regular intervals**, eg 12–18 months, if their outputs are to remain reliable.

✔ Remember: we've all heard of cases where high tech has led to high drama. So **keep it as simple as possible**, learn as you go, and if in doubt, call in an experienced statistician.

Software packages for modelling

The two major suppliers of packages used in direct marketing are SPSS and SAS. Each has its strengths and weaknesses.

SPSS is ideal for basic users and those who prefer to work in drop-down menu environments. Their programs run on a variety of platforms, including PC, and they offer a reasonable level of technical support. Contact 01483-719200; http://www.spss.com.

SAS have greater statistical and database depth and a far heavier bias to data warehousing and system application development. They probably have the best support desk and documentation of any software, given the number of users worldwide. These support levels, however, reflect their complexity. SAS is recommended for more technical users and runs on any platform from mainframe to PC. Contact 01628-486933.

There are also specialist companies who develop packages for specific modelling functions, in particular Neural Nets.

Further reading: See bibliography in information section of this Guide. Specially recommended is "Taking the Fear out of Data Analysis" by Diamantopoulos & Schlegelmilch.

Chapter 4.1

Building your customer list: Press advertising and inserts

This chapter includes:

- ❑ **Background to the UK press industry**
- ❑ **Features and advantages of press advertising**
- ❑ **The 5 direct marketing applications**
- ❑ **Media planner's master checklist**
- ❑ **Using media research data**
- ❑ **Frequency versus coverage**
- ❑ **The effects of size, colour, position, etc**
- ❑ **The role and benefits of inserts**
- ❑ **Planning an insert campaign**
- ❑ **Directories, reliable enquiry generators**

Despite the growth in direct mail and newer acquisition methods, space advertising and inserts remain the driving force behind much of today's direct marketing. Many leading exponents of list segmentation and profiling have built up their huge databases by persuading prospects to identify themselves after reading inserts and press advertisements.

In this chapter, Beverly Barker details new data on press and insert opportunities and applies a modern media planner's mind to the tasks of setting objectives and matching prospects to media profiles using media research.

Media planning for direct marketing is no longer merely a question of maximising the response to each and every advertisement. It is about finding and delivering customers with the best long-term potential, whilst also creating the right awareness and positioning climate for those prospects who do not respond immediately.

New in this edition. Latest available industry data on almost every page, plus additional advice on using media research.

Beverly Barker, TMD Direct

Beverly began her career in newspaper and magazine advertising in the classified sales department of Times Newspapers, in 1982. After discovering that there appeared to be more depth and interest, and a greater challenge, on the agency side – and after completing the CAM certificate – she joined Ogilvy and Mather as a radio and television buyer, planning and buying for many of the agency's major accounts.

Her next move was to a senior media buying role with Davidson Pearce working on Fiat Motors, BT Mobile Phones and Matthew Clarke, and then to Media Director of Porton Advertising in 1988. During this period she also read Business Studies at South Bank University.

In 1992 Beverly joined TMD Carat as head of its direct marketing division, TMD Direct, providing media communications solutions to mail order and direct response clients across a wide spectrum of media, clients including American Express, Franklin Mint and Britannia Music. She also advises several traditional brand advertisers as they look to incorporate response techniques into their total communications strategies.

Beverly married Alan after he successfully called on her to sell space for LBC. Their joint campaign to produce a daughter proved successful in 1996, since when they have both been trying to catch up with their sleep! Consequently hobbies, which used to include DIY, skiing and painting, are now on hold.

Beverly Barker M IDM
Head of Direct Marketing
TMD Carat
New London House
172 Drury Lane
London
WC2B 5QR
E-mail: Beverly_Barker@tmdcarat.co.uk
Tel: 0171-611 8000

Chapter 4.1

Building your customer list: Press advertising and inserts

Press advertising – a unique acquisition method

Advertising in newspapers or magazines, whether consumer or business, is a potent source of new customers for many of the UK's committed direct marketers. It offers results in many areas that cannot be matched by any other medium.

Later in this chapter we shall divide our topic into space advertising and inserts, but first we take a broad look at the medium: national and regional newspapers, consumer and business magazines.

PART I: Background to UK press media

The national press

The main national titles comprise 11 "dailies" and 10 "Sundays" in three broad categories: popular, mid-market and quality.

The charts below detail their circulations at the end of August 1997 (*Audit Bureau of Circulations*).

Daily newspaper circulations

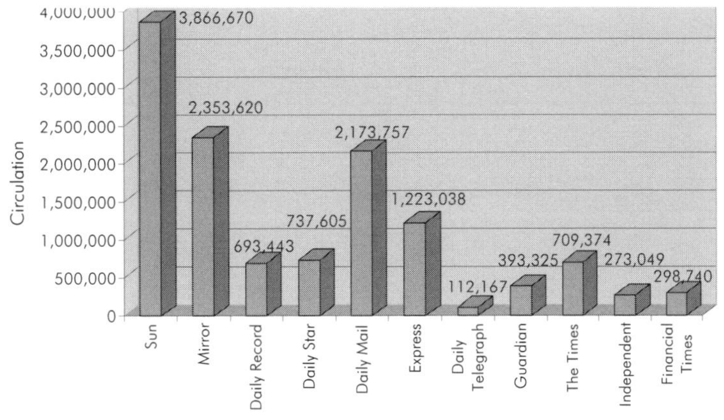

Sunday newspaper circulations

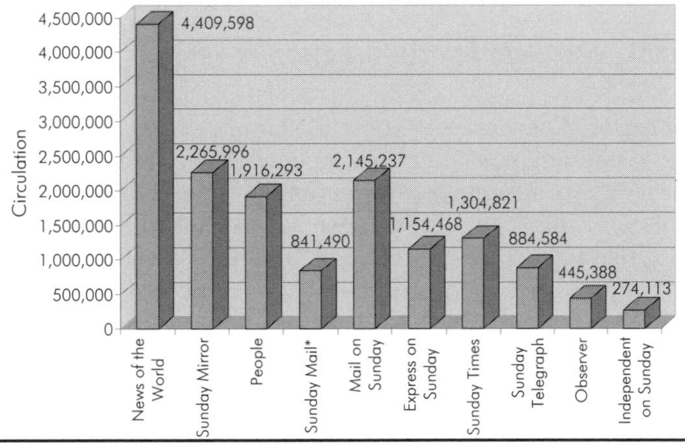

National newspaper circulation trends

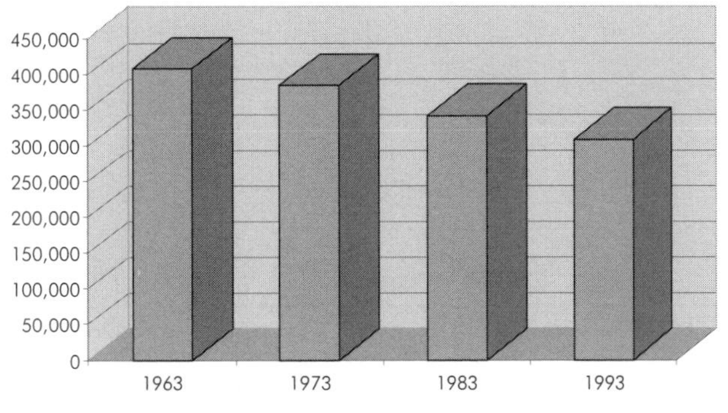

The top chart shows that the popular daily press (Sun, Mirror, Star) accounts for over 10 times the combined circulation of the quality press (Guardian, Independent, Times, FT), while the Mail, Express and Telegraph form a huge middle market. The centre chart shows "Sundays" divide along similar lines.

The bottom chart shows that, despite its huge reach, officially Britain's gross national newspaper readership has declined for several decades. However, this overlooks the fact that each newspaper has added numerous extra sections and supplements – all of which are good news for direct marketers seeking niche opportunities. Doubtless readers have as much to read as they ever did, perhaps more!

In total the national press remains a powerful medium with 35 newspapers and supplements, or almost 4 per household per week, being bought and read.

Publication	Number	Circulation '000
Morning newspapers	11	12,834 (daily)
Sunday newspapers	11	15,661 (weekly)
	22	28,495
Supplements to above	13	21,050 (weekly)
	Total	49,545

The regional press – every conurbation covered

Over 1,200 regional newspapers cover the country's major conurbations and large towns, some assuming near national importance, eg Birmingham Mail, Yorkshire Evening Post, Bristol Evening Post, London Evening Standard, etc. They tend to be dailies (some mornings, some evenings). The sector is dominated by a relatively few publishers which makes for simpler negotiations for nationwide cover.

Regional newspapers do not generally figure in the space schedules of direct marketers but they are extremely valuable as host media for inserts. The problem with regional space is that the cost-per-thousand circulation is much higher than for nationals, as these examples demonstrate:

Newspaper	Circulation '000	Cost of page mono (£)	CPT circ (£)
Cambridge Evening News	42	1,954	47
Bristol Evening Post	83	3,154	38
Mirror	2,355	27,500	12

(CPT = cost-per-thousand copies)

Being around three times as expensive as national press, regional newspapers need to be three/four times more responsive to be cost-effective, which usually they are not.

Local newspapers – town, village and parish

Local newspapers serve medium and small towns and some have editions targeted to individual villages and even parishes. They are usually weeklies, often distributed free, when they are known in the trade as free sheets. They, too, are very effective carriers of loose inserts.

In combination, the national, regional and local newspapers ensure that everyone in Britain has access to at least one regular newspaper.

Women's magazines: Market within a market

Within the broad category of consumer magazines, women's media forms a huge sub-market. Titles fall into six categories determined by the editorial platform, as the graphic below demonstrates:

Because of the close "fit" between editorial and reader lifestyle, women's magazines enjoy strong relationships with their readers which can enhance their pulling power for relevant offers, making them more cost-effective than their rates might suggest.

Consumer interest magazines: Food to football

"Consumer interest" embraces consumer magazines not expressly targeted to women and includes men's magazines. Literally thousands of titles cover every conceivable sport, hobby, pastime, etc. Usually there is more than one title per sector.

Special interest magazines form a natural channel for niche marketing, often delivering responses economically albeit usually in small volumes compared to the national press.

> If an interest is widely subscribed to, eg gardening, its participants can often be reached more economically through national media, eg the Daily Mail reaches more gardeners than all the specialist garden magazines combined.

Consumer magazines are, like non-national newspapers, frequently highly cost-effective vehicles for loose inserts. Subjects indirectly related to the special interest often do particularly well, eg warm clothing offers to readers of outdoor pursuits.

Business and trade magazines – over 2,900 titles

Business magazines cover every trade, industry and profession – and every job function from production to finance. Most are monthly or quarterly, although many trades have weeklies.

There is a further breakdown between paid-for and free subscriptions. The latter, known as controlled circulations, are despatched only to bona fide registered members of an industry or profession.

> The most successful application of business magazines for response advertisers is to direct mail their subscribers. Most publishers offer their lists for this purpose with a high degree of selectivity, eg by job title, region, size of factory, etc.

Features and advantages of SPACE advertising

We now look more closely at paid-space advertising beginning with a review of its general features and advantages (later in the chapter we shall do the same for inserts). This will lead us to its applications for direct marketing.

The benefits of space advertising, most of which are self-explanatory, are as follows (where explanations are needed, please read on):

- ✔ Low relative cost, ie cost-per-thousand circulation
- ✔ High volumes, virtual saturation coverage
- ✔ Wide choice of reader profiles
- ✔ Year-round availability
- ✔ Fast identifiable response
- ✔ Low cost, relatively simple production
- ✔ Short lead-times and last-minute deadlines
- ✔ Fewer personnel needed to plan and buy media
- ✔ Rates published and adhered to
- ✔ Extensive research data on readers
- ✔ Trusted, authoritative environment
- ✔ Test opportunities

Fractions of a penny per reader

The cost of reaching audiences through space advertising, especially in national newspapers, is the lowest of any media. For example, whereas a direct mail package may cost 50p to produce and deliver, newspapers can reach their targets **up to a hundred times less expensively**.

Here are some typical daily newspaper costs-per-thousand circulation (based on 25cm x 4 column space):

Publication	Circulation '000	Rate card £	Cost per thousand
	Jun – Nov '97	25" x 4 columns (mono)	£
Sun	3,799	14,600	3.84
Mirror	2,341	10,600	4.53
Daily Star	631	3,850	6.10
Daily Mail	2,231	10,400	4.66
Daily Express	1,217	8,500	6.98
Guardian	407	3,800	9.34
Daily Telegraph	1,099	8,800	8.01
Independent	264	3,200	12.12
The Times	782	5,000	6.39
Financial Times	326	8,200	25.15

The low-cost argument is less applicable to specialist media with smaller circulations, but often this is compensated by the high responsiveness of special interest markets.

High volumes, blanket coverage

Volume coverage is essential to promote instant awareness of, say, a new brand, but it is also an important factor in direct response planning, as we shall see. Where a market must be blanketed rapidly, eg for a seasonal product, the national press is superbly efficient.

Wide choice of reader profiles

As any direct marketing statistician will confirm, no targeting method is perfect – with the national press it is often quite rudimentary. For example, high-earning professionals read popular tabloids and deprived individuals may be found digesting The Times.

But the "loose" targeting of the national press is also its strength as we shall see. We use its coverage to encourage prospects to identify themselves, a process we call "hand-raising".

Year-round availability

Press media is always available ... if you miss one there's always another one coming along! Published schedules allow you to plan campaigns to break and close on a specific date – a precision not always available with other media.

Fast identifiable response

There is a clear correlation between the "shelf-life" of a publication and the pattern of response it generates. Once you know that pattern you can predict the end-result based on a few days' activity – a very useful facility.

A daily will normally deliver 60% of its total response in the first day or two (depending on whether these are postal or telephone responses). The remaining 40% will be received within ten days. Weekly newspapers and Sundays have a different pattern as shown below.

Typical response pattern for a Sunday supplement

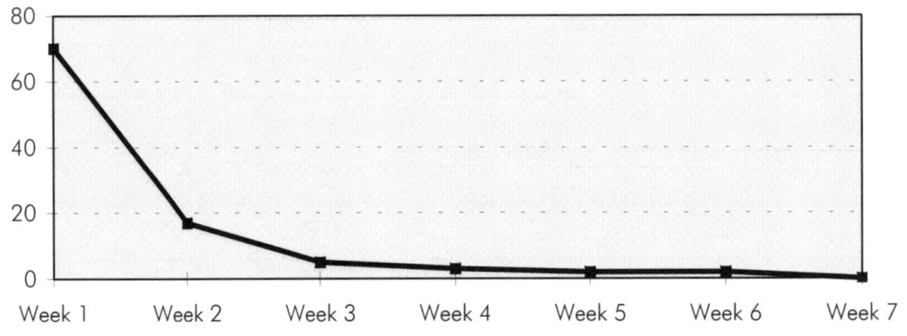

Monthly magazines generate response more slowly, partly because it can take up to four weeks before the full circulation has received its copy. They will then be dipped into on several occasions until superseded by the next issue. Some will be kept for reference, some discarded after a final scan, and some passed to secondary readers. The response tail may therefore be many weeks or months, and in a few cases can be a year or more.

This tail-effect can be a nuisance for some advertisers, but an important source of revenue for others; marketers of high-value goods, where a single incremental sale can make a major profit differential, generally welcome late responses.

Relatively simple to set up

Compared to most media, press advertising costs less and takes less time to set up. Colour reproduction is more complex, of course, although technology is constantly being introduced to simplify the process.

Shorter lead-times for booking and later copy deadlines are further benefits of new press technology.

Don't let shorter lead-times mislead you into leaving space reservation too late. Booking time for some monthlies can be up to four months, and several months longer for specific sites, eg half-page under contents, first right-hand page, facing specific editorial, etc.

Fewer personnel to plan and buy

Extensive press and magazine schedules can be planned, bought, and co-ordinated by a handful of experienced planner-buyers.

Compare the effort, time, personnel and skills involved in reaching a million Sunday Express readers with a full-page monochrome ad (eg to announce a new saving scheme), with that required to source a million suitable names and prepare, print and despatch a relevant mailing – not a wholly fair comparison but a useful indicator nonetheless.

Rates published and adhered to

Press advertising can be costed by reference to publishers' rate cards and industry directories such as BRAD (British Rate and Data). Although published rates leave less room for negotiation, at least you know where you are.

Negotiations do take place, however, for quantity discounts and for filling empty "holes" at short notice, known as distress space, a facility direct marketers exploit to the full.

Overleaf is a typical entry from BRAD showing the wealth of data available for each title, in this case for one of the women's style monthlies:

Elle

Affiliations ABC PPA NRS
Publisher Hachette/Emap Magazines Ltd, Victory House, 14 Leicester Place, London, WC2H 7BP Switchboard: Tel 0171 437 9011. Fax 0171 208 3374. Managing Director Carrie Barker. Publisher Elaine Foran. Editor Marie O'Riordan. Promotions Maurice Mullen. Advertising Manager Rachel Geary. Promotions Manager Sally Scott. Strategic Planner Christina Hartley.
Northern Ad Sales Emap Magazines, Ltd, Unit 3, Claro Court Business Centre, Claro Road, Harrogate, HG1 4BA Switchboard: Tel 01423 565996 Fax 01423 560420. Ad Sales Contact Mandy Sykes, Bev Sanders.
Frequency Monthly – 2nd Thu of month preceding cover date
Price Single copy £2.20
Editorial Profile Elle is an important, high quality directional glossy magazine with a clear emphasis on fashion and beauty. With outstanding photography and witty, intelligent features
Circulation 01 Jul–31 Dec 1996 ABC 205,623
(UK & Eire 182,142 other countries 23,481)
Readership (*precis*)
All Adults Total Readership 1,134,000 (5.4 readers per copy based on Jul 1995–Jun 1996 ABC 172,816 based on All Women)

	A	B	C1	C2	D	E
Profile Index	208	142	138	58	72	37
Coverage %	5	4	3	1	2	1
Coverage '000	70	299	432	148	138	48
	15–24	25–34	35–44	45–54	55–64	65+
Profile Index	261	160	58	74	33	14
Coverage %	6	4	1	2	1	0
Coverage '000	454	357	112	135	46	30

All Women Total Readership 938,000

	A	B	C1	C2	D	E
Profile Index	210	147	133	66	78	33
Coverage %	8	6	5	3	3	1
Coverage '000	52	235	357	127	124	43
	15–24	25–34	35–44	45–54	55–64	65+
Profile Index	287	155	60	53	31	12
Coverage %	11	6	2	3	1	0
Coverage '000	391	272	93	121	35	26

Source: NRS Jan–Dec 1996 National Readership Surveys Limited
Target Readership 18–26 year old women, style-conscious opinion formers, with a high disposable income and a passion for shopping
Rates Effective 1 April 1995
Standard Rates
colour page £7150
mono page £5500
Mono Rates Mono: Dps rop £11000, Page rop £5500, Half rop £3300, Quarter rop £1650
Cover Rates Full colour: Page insert front £12650, Page inside back £11550, Page outside back £15400
Colour Rates Full colour: Dps rop £14300, Page rop £7150, Half rop £4400, Quarter rop £2200
Bleed Pages 10% extra
Special Positions Mono: Page facing matter £6600, Page first half facing matter £8250, Page first half right hand facing matter £9900, Dps first half £13200, Half first half £3960, Full colour: Page facing matter £7920, Page first half facing matter £9900, Page first half right hand facing matter £11000, Dps first half £16500, Half first half £5500, Dps first spread £23650, Dps second spread £21450, Dps third spread £19800
Inserts Accepted by arrangement
Production Specifications Type area dps 269 x 412, page 269 x 190, half horizontal 130 x 109, half vertical 269 x 93, quarter square 130 x 93, quarter vertical 269 x 44. Bleed size dps 310 x 454, page 310 x 232, half horizontal 151 x 232, half vertical 310 x 114. Trim size dps 300 x 444, page 300 x 222, half horizontal 146 x 222, half vertical 300 x 109. All: film, positive, wrong reading emulsion side up, hard dot with Cromalin
Deadlines Copy – 6 weeks preceding publication date Cancellation – 18 weeks preceding publication date

Extensive research data on readers

The publishing industry funds extensive research into the socio-demographic profiles and purchase behaviour of its readers, title by title, essential for refining media selection and targeting. Later in this chapter we look at some of the sources of the data and show how it can be applied.

Trusted environment

The authority, respect and reputation of a printed publication carry over into its advertising columns, whilst the fact that an ad has been accepted by the publisher conveys an element of endorsement.

All the major publishing groups run reader protection schemes to offer readers additional safeguards.

Test opportunities

Press advertising offers plenty of inexpensive test opportunities. See Chapter 2.3 on testing.

So what are the drawbacks of the press?

The first drawback is that it is a public medium. Invariably marketers must also use direct mail, telephone or personal follow-up to transform a press enquirer into a long-term customer.

The second drawback is its high visibility. You can't run a pilot programme in the press without everyone knowing.

And third, there are obvious creative limitations in the case of press, especially space advertising, compared with the reader involvement and reply devices available in direct mail or the moving demonstrations made possible by TV.

Press advertising and the direct marketer

Press advertising is used by direct marketers in five distinct ways corresponding to the strengths of the medium. These are:

- ✔ To produce volume enquiries (two-stage)
- ✔ To make direct sales (one-stage)
- ✔ To reach niche audiences
- ✔ To support other response media
- ✔ To build awareness

These objectives can also be combined, eg to make direct sales and build awareness; or to produce volume enquiries and support other media. Awareness accrues from press advertising whatever its primary objective.

Objective No 1: Volume enquiries

85% or more of all display press advertising carries a response mechanism: coupon, telephone/fax number, or tipped-on reply card. Within "Classifieds" this increases to virtually 100%.

Many organisations thought to be reliant on direct mail have in fact built their databases through response ads in the national press. It is not unknown for a single advertisement (one insertion) to "pull" several hundred enquiries for conversion by mail, telephone or personal follow-up. Increasingly organisations seek responses for reasons of research and customer care as well as sales.

What makes press advertising so successful at inducing cost-effective replies is primarily its low cost and high circulations, as already noted. But there are other reasons: the press is a news medium: readers regard it as a source of news about products and services – including "news" contained in advertising.

The business press also promotes volume enquiries but has an extra dimension, its "directory" effect – readers turn to magazines to locate suppliers of specific goods, much as they would use a directory.

Objective No 2: Direct sales

The use of press advertising to generate direct sales has risen and fallen with the national economy but is now an established method of opening accounts for many marketers – and an enjoyable method of buying for many customers. The boom began in the 1970s with the growth of telephone and credit card ordering.

The majority of mail order or "off-the-page" advertisements appear in supplements to national newspapers (low cost, high volume). Another growth factor has been improved colour reproduction in these media, essential for conveying the attractions of a collector's plate, a floral dress, a stack of CDs, etc.

Off-the-page offers may be cash-with-order (including payment by cheque), free trial, or payment on credit, including plastic cards and direct debit. All direct sale offers, especially cash-with-order, are carefully monitored by the publishers' watchdogs.

(The subject of creating ads for direct response is discussed fully in Chapters 6.2, 6.3 and 6.4).

Objective No 3: Reaching niche audiences

Press advertising can find prospects who cannot easily be identified by any other means, in two ways:

- ✔ Self-selection (hand-raising)
- ✔ Specialist targeting

Where a target audience is highly specialised, but cannot be categorised via a mailing list or niche magazine, the national press can encourage interested prospects to identify themselves by returning a coupon or making a 'phone call. This process is known as "hand-raising" or targeting by self-selection.

Home is where the computer is

Take the case of someone starting up a business from home or a small rented office. Although the SOHO (Small Office, Home Office) market is quite well established, until an individual has subscribed to their first computer magazine or requested a catalogue from a mail-order stationery supplier, etc, no one will know of them or their needs. However, they may be your perfect target market, ready to buy their first business computer, software package, desk or insurance policy. The news and business pages of the national press can be used to reach them.

The business will probably then subscribe to a niche market magazine. Continuing the SOHO example, titles on your schedule will probably include consumer publications devoted to computers, money management and small business opportunities.

Eventually most businesses subscribe to their own trade or industry publications, so that our SOHO prospect will be reachable through their specific interest, whether it be care for the elderly, architecture, dentistry, accountancy, freelance writing, or whatever – all of which have their own publications.

Objective No 4: Support other media

Press advertising, with its high visibility and wide coverage, can provide effective support for other response media such as direct mail or direct response TV.

It is often used to carry detail which cannot be conveyed in image-oriented TV or radio commercials, eg for cars, financial services, travel, etc. It may also be used to promote the "call to action" by providing the necessary coupon or application form. Another example is where the press is employed to convey the broad appeal for a product or service – with direct mail, inserts, door-to-door or telephone used to convert specific sectors of the target market with inducements to respond.

This application is typical of the way business magazines are used to draw attention to a product/service through space advertising with the contact being made through direct mail or personal follow-up.

Objective No 5: General awareness

The first objective of advertising has always been awareness – essential to any subsequent transaction. In direct marketing terms we have already noted that press awareness can be turned to immediate response.

Similarly, by incorporating contact data within image announcements, people who prefer to enquire direct (instead of, say, visiting a store) can be given that option – and their names added to the prospect database. Such a facility is another way of demonstrating customer care.

We are straying into non-direct advertising here. Awareness can be a very real objective – it can also be an excuse for running ads that fail to get replies! You may need to separate the budgets for these two sometimes disparate objectives.

PART II: Media planning using space advertising

The media planner's checklist

We now know the benefits of press advertising and how we can use it. Before we can draw up the media schedule there are many questions we need to address.

The checklist below will help us to work through these:

Media planner's master checklist

Marketing objectives	Number of responses (enquiries/sales) Enquiry-to-sales, expected conversion ratio Allowable cost-per-enquiry/sale Other objectives, eg awareness, support Tests
Target audience	Demographic profile, age, location, etc Interests/lifestyle Purchase behaviour/propensity
Media/audience research	Research data (NRS, TGI, BBS)
Competitor analysis	Register MEAL Observation
Results analysis	Past performance
Production/creative	Lead-times required for production Colour and other special features
Budget	Media Production Follow-up materials
Candidate media	Cost-per-thousand circulation Coverage of target market Test facilities, roll-out potential Editorial environment Deduplication
Specifics	Size Frequency Colour Position, etc

What are the marketing objectives?

The objectives of direct marketing media are normally **numeric** and **response-based**, eg the required number of enquiries and/or sales and allowable costs per enquiry/per sale.

Media planners may also be required to estimate the ratio of 'phone to postal responses (to facilitate handling); enquiries to sales; likely returns and bad debts; spin-off retail sales; and, with business media, the expected number of publishers' "reader service" enquiries.

Other objectives might include awareness and support for non-press media (in which case details of the other media will be needed).

IMPORTANT: Inserts will loom large in the media plan at this stage and are discussed later in the chapter.

Who is the target audience?

Target prospects can be described by socio-economics, geodemographics, age, interests and likely purchase behaviour. Business prospects can be described by industry, job description, title, etc. Accurate "pictures" of likely customers can be gained by profiling existing customers (as we saw in Chapters 3.5 and 3.7).

The essence of media planning is matching the profiles of target prospects with those of media readerships. Here the media planner is helped by industry research:

NRS – The National Readership Survey

NRS tells the media planner about the readers of almost 300 titles, including all the national newspapers, consumer magazines and major regionals.

Information provided by NRS includes:

- ✔ Age and other demographic data of readers.
- ✔ Readership habits by population/demographic groups.
- ✔ Socio-economic status, average household income, marital status, number of children, etc, of core readerships.
- ✔ Numbers of regular readers per title and what else they read.
- ✔ Purchasing habits of readers.
- ✔ Reading habits of purchasers of particular brands or services.

Using NRS for targeting

Below is an example of how the National Readership Survey can be used for targeting readers. This table shows how credit card ownership varies between media as a percentage of all readers.

	% of readers with bank account	% of readers with credit/charge card
Financial Times	90.15	90.91
Daily Telegraph	83.41	81.1
Sunday Times	82.85	79.23
Observer	81.05	76.06
Mail on Sunday	78.75	73.46
Daily Express	76.23	65.67
Daily Star	69.07	52.19
Sunday Mirror	68.03	51.27
Sun	66.65	50.99
News of the World	66.19	49.32

The following NRS extract shows how readers tend to vary by age bands between newspapers.

Daily morning and evening newspapers

	Total		Age group 15–17		Age group 18–24		Age group 15–24		Age group 25–34		Age group 35–44		Age group 45–54		Age group 55–64		Age group 65–99	
Unweighted Sample	38349		1571		3360		4931		6691		6294		6140		5186		9107	
Population (000's)	46150		2105		4917		7023		9039		7943		7446		5618		9081	
	000's	%	000's	%	000's	%	000's	%	000's	%	000's	%	000's	%	000's	%	000's	%
Totals	46150	100	2105	100	4917	100	7023	100	9039	100	7943	100	7446	100	5618	100	9081	100
Sun	10074	21.83	561	26.7	1500	30.5	2061	29.4	2412	26.7	1740	21.9	1452	19.5	1019	18.1	1390	15.3
Mirror/Record	7972	17.27	335	15.9	820	16.7	1155	16.5	1406	15.6	1302	16.4	1307	17.6	1109	19.7	1692	18.6
Mirror	6153	13.33	247	11.7	634	12.9	882	12.6	1012	11.2	988	12.4	1020	13.7	870	15.5	1380	15.2
Daily Record	1887	4.09	90	4.28	190	3.86	280	3.99	408	4.51	332	4.18	299	4.02	253	4.5	315	3.47
Daily Mail	5309	11.5	205	9.74	436	8.87	641	9.13	705	7.8	937	11.8	1030	13.8	850	15.1	1147	12.6
Daily Express	2671	5.79	100	4.75	153	3.11	253	3.6	344	3.81	425	5.35	515	6.92	417	7.42	718	7.91
Daily Star	2079	4.5	110	5.23	360	7.32	470	6.69	578	6.39	428	5.39	292	3.92	171	3.04	140	1.54
Daily Telegraph	2736	5.93	68	3.23	181	3.68	250	3.56	330	3.65	413	5.2	550	7.39	468	8.33	725	7.98
Guardian	1270	2.75	46	2.19	160	3.25	206	2.93	334	3.7	277	3.49	225	3.02	118	2.1	110	1.21
The Times	1954	4.23	78	3.71	197	4.01	276	3.93	352	3.89	392	4.94	368	4.94	263	4.68	302	3.33
Independent	840	1.82	40	1.9	99	2.01	139	1.98	199	2.2	186	2.34	150	2.01	90	1.6	76	0.84
Financial Times	660	1.43	11	0.52	71	1.44	82	1.17	174	1.92	179	2.25	118	1.58	75	1.33	32	0.35

TGI – Target Group Index

TGI is a national survey based on self-completion questionnaires, covering 200 consumer publications. It focuses more on product purchases than NRS, embracing 500 product fields and over 4,000 brands.

TGI data enables close matching of prospect's purchase propensity with that of readers of the media.

The TGI extract below shows how some popular dailies compare in terms of their readers' expenditure on garden plants, bulbs, etc.

		Totals	All adults	ABC1 adults	Students	Adults who spend more than £50 pa on garden stock
Totals	Unwgt	25294	25294	11705	1634	4651
	(000)	46050	46050	22485	3866	8456
	Horz%	100	100	48.83	8.4	18.36
	Vert%	100	100	100	100	100
	Index	100	100	100	100	100
Daily Express	Unwgt	1609	1609	922	95	367
	(000)	2941	2941	1752	211	652
	Horz%	100	100	59.57	7.17	22.17
	Vert%	6.39	6.39	7.79	5.46	7.71
	Index	100	100	122	85	121
Daily Mail	Unwgt	2951	2951	1716	203	746
	(000)	2053	2053	3101	398	1248
	Horz%	100	100	61.37	7.88	24.7
	Vert%	10.97	10.97	13.79	10.29	14.76
	Index	100	100	126	94	135
Mirror	Unwgt	3716	3716	1116	217	538
	(000)	6448	6448	2025	504	948
	Horz%	100	100	31.41	7.82	14.7
	Vert%	14	14	9.01	13.04	11.21
	Index	100	100	64	93	80

More information of TGI can be obtained by contacting BMRB, Hadley House, 79–81 Uxbridge Road, Ealing, London W5 5SU (Tel: 0181-566 5000).

BBS – The British Business Survey

The British Business Survey covers 140 titles, including national press plus selected business magazines.

The candidate media list

When you have surveyed the research you will discover that different titles have different claims to secure your objectives – depending on whether you want volume coverage of your chosen market, the highest penetration of your market within a title, (its profile) or the lowest cost per target prospect.

The table below demonstrates how different candidate media may result from employing these different criteria:

Ranking media according to different criteria

	Coverage %			Profile %			Cost per thousand £s		
1	Cosmopolitan	11.2	1	Marie Claire	43.2	1	Hello!	2000	£3.3
2	Marie Claire	8.7	2	Company	42.3	2	Company	2000	£5.6
3	Woman's Own	7.8	3	Cosmopolitan	40.3	3	She	3000	£6.8
4	Bella	7.8	4	New Woman	38.3	4	Sainsbury's Mag	5000	£8.0
5	Sainsbury's Mag	7.6	5	She	32.1	5	Prima	5000	£8.3
6	Prima	7.3	6	Hello!	27.8	6	OK!	1000	£9.3
7	Hello!	7.1	7	Harpers & Queen	27.2	7	New Woman	3000	£9.6
8	Woman	7.1	8	Essentials	27.1	8	Essentials	4000	£11.4
9	Best	6.8	9	Prima	26.6	9	Cosmopolitan	10920	£11.5
10	Vogue	5.9	10	Sainsbury's Mag	26.2	10	Family Circle	4000	£11.7
11	She	5.5	11	Sky Mag	25.4	11	Marie Claire	9000	£12.1
12	Sky Mag	5.2	12	OK!	24.6	12	Woman's Own	12000	£18.0
13	Company	4.5	13	Vogue	24.3	13	Harpers & Queen	3000	£19.9
14	Essentials	4.2	14	Family Circle	20.5	14	Best	10000	£20.0
15	Family Circle	4.1	15	Woman	19.1	15	Vogue	10500	£22.5
16	New Woman	4.0	16	Best	18.8	16	Bella	15000	£23.3
17	Harpers & Queen	1.8	17	Woman's Own	17.0	17	Woman	14000	£24.3
18	OK!	1.3	18	Bella	16.3	18	Sky Mag	10000	£25.00

NB: Pricing within this chart is totally arbitrary and used for demonstration purposes only.

In practice, you will take note of all three indicators although each will have a different value to you as follows:

✔ **Coverage** is a useful guide if the objective of your campaign is to reach the greatest number of target prospects. This might be the case when launching a new product such as a car, when it is important to get your message to as many prospects as possible ahead of any competitive "spoiler" campaigns.

✔ **Profile %** indicates how many of the total readers are in your target audience. This helps to reduce wastage and may improve responsivity.

✔ **Cost per thousand** is a good guide to reducing the potential cost per response, but only if the title is read by the right people!

Why circulation not readership?

Although much media research is based on readerships (number of readers per copy x number of copies), direct marketers prefer to work with circulations (number of copies only).

This is generally thought to be because only one member per household will enquire or purchase in response to an advertisement regardless of the number of family members reading an issue. Topicality also ensures that the original reader of a medium is more likely to respond than subsequent readers.

Monitoring competitive activity

Monitoring competitive activity can give a clear insight into a market and its use of the media. This is particularly useful to direct marketers since experienced exponents **never** repeat media patterns that are unsuccessful.

There are two chief ways to assess competitive activity:

? Collect all or the main publication on a regular basis and review the advertising – not necessarily a very accurate method.

✔ Buy a competitive analysis report from a specialist supplier such as Register MEAL or Media Monitoring Systems (MMS).

Register MEAL and MMS are long-established services that report regularly on advertising in the consumer press, TV, cinema, radio and outdoor. MMS also reports monthly on the majority of business-to-business sectors including medical and agricultural publications.

Both can provide a detailed view of competitors' advertising including insertions by media, date, position, estimated expenditure, etc. Press expenditure is calculated differently by the two services, but essentially they are both based on rate card costs and include published volume discounts where applicable.

You can also subscribe to a cuttings service to receive copies of new creative executions by your competitors.

Further information on these services can be obtained from:

Register MEAL, 7 Harewood Avenue, London NW1 6JB. Tel: 0171-393 5070.

MMS, Madison House, High Street, Sunninghill, Ascot, Berkshire SL5 9NP. Tel: 01344-627553.

Examining relevant results

Where prior results are available it is important to study these objectively, with no in-built prejudices. Careful results analysis, preferably going back several years, can reveal a great deal about what your customers and prospects are trying to tell you. It may be quite different from what the marketing department believes.

Look especially at media that were once effective and then suffered diminishing returns. Have they been overused? Are they ready for a re-trial? Were they used properly? Have they been supplanted by more powerful media aimed at the same target audience?

It is a fact of direct marketing that certain media tend to produce consistently good responses almost regardless of the product or offer: they are known as "responsive media". These will often be your first choice. Their success usually stems from a low cost-per-thousand advertising rate.

Opposite will be found part of a typical direct marketing results report. Reading from left to right it shows medium, date of insertion, costs, circulation, number of responses, percentage response, number of orders, percentage conversion to orders, cost including response package, initial revenue generated, allowable cost, profit/loss **per insertion**, average revenue. The revenue from future years (lifetime values) would be a major consideration in assessing these results, hence the allowable cost may exceed the revenue at this initial recruitment stage.

Budget and timing requirements

Next on our media planner's master checklist comes the small matter of the budget, which may be for a campaign, a season, a calendar year or a financial year.

In direct marketing there are two types of media budget:

✔ Fixed budget calling for maximum possible number of responses.

✔ Task-related budget, ie amount required to achieve a predetermined number of responses with a known or forecast cost per response.

Combinations of these are also frequently used, whereby a fixed budget is expanded to take advantage of early successes, the "extra" being effectively task-related. Task-related budgets usually come with a caveat to "minimise the cost per response".

How direct media planning differs from awareness

General marketers entering direct marketing will by now begin to see that media planning for direct marketing differs from that for general awareness in numerous respects, as the simplified summary on page 4.1-22 demonstrates.

Title	Date	Size	Media Cost	Cost Inc Vat	Total Cost	Circulation (000's)	Resps	% Resps	Orders	% Conv	Final Cost Inc Fulfilment	Revenue	Allowable Cost	Profit/ Loss	Average Revenue
Daily Mirror	Jan-25	½ page	£13,750	£16,156	£16,156	2353	300	0.013%	77	25.67%	18835.08	14760.13	27306	8470.92	191.69
	Feb-22	½ page	£13,750	£16,156	£16,156	2353	187	0.008%	44	23.53%	17687.01	8700.12	16095	-1592.01	197.73
	Apr-11	½ page	£13,750	£16,156	£16,156	2353	181	0.008%	48	26.52%	17826.17	9060	9234	-8592.17	188.75
Daily Record	Jan-18	½ page	£4,150	£4,876	£4,876	693	70	0.010%	19	27.14%	5537.26	2880.02	5328	-209.26	151.58
	Feb-15	½ page	£4,150	£4,876	£4,876	693	71	0.010%	21	29.58%	5606.84	2646	4662	-944.84	126
	Mar-28	½ page	£4,150	£4,876	£4,876	693	39	0.006%	11	28.21%	5258.94	2273.37	3441	-1817.94	206.67
Daily Star	Jan-20	½ page	£5,236	£6,152	£6,152	737	92	0.012%	28	30.43%	7126.42	4859.96	8991	1864.58	173.57
	Feb-08	½ page	£5,236	£6,152	£6,152	737	64	0.009%	15	23.44%	6674.15	2340	4329	-2345.15	156
	Feb-29	½ page	£5,236	£6,152	£6,152	737	55	0.007%	7	12.73%	6395.83	1330	2109	-4286.83	190
	Mar-28	½ page	£5,236	£6,152	£6,152	737	72	0.010%	12	16.67%	6569.78	1872	2886	-3683.78	156
Sun	Jan-26	½ page	£17,350	£20,386	£20,386	3867	355	0.009%	97	27.32%	23760.88	19582.36	35853	12092.12	201.88
	Feb-15	½ page	£17,350	£20,386	£20,386	3867	389	0.010%	85	21.85%	23343.4	15360.35	28083	4739.6	180.71
Guardian	Jan-21		£7,500	£8,813	£8,813	393	36	0.009%	10	27.78%	9160.4	3060	5661	-3499.4	306
	Apr-09		£7,500	£8,813	£8,813	393	23	0.006%	7	30.43%	9056.03	1019.97	999	-8057.03	145.71
Independent	Jan-21		£7,000	£8,225	£8,225	273	23	0.008%	2	8.70%	8294.58	420	777	-7517.58	210

Direct	Awareness
Coverage measured by circulations	Coverage measured by readerships
Low-frequency repetition to avoid diminishing returns	High-frequency repetition to boost awareness in the short term
Broadest possible range of cost-effective media (to maximise response without attracting diminishing returns)	Relatively narrow band of concentrated media to ensure penetration of message
First insertions normally the most productive, followed by rapid attrition	Awareness builds with repetition of simple message
Planning based primarily on results data	Planning based primarily on research data
Efficacy normally measured by response data, eg cost-per-enquiry/sale	Efficacy measured by research data, eg reading and noting

Below is a graph demonstrating a typical diminishing return from direct response advertising. Whereas awareness of a company/offer grows with the number and frequency of insertions in a given medium, direct responses to individual advertisements fall dramatically with repetition (all other factors, eg seasonality, being equal).

How direct responses diminish with frequency

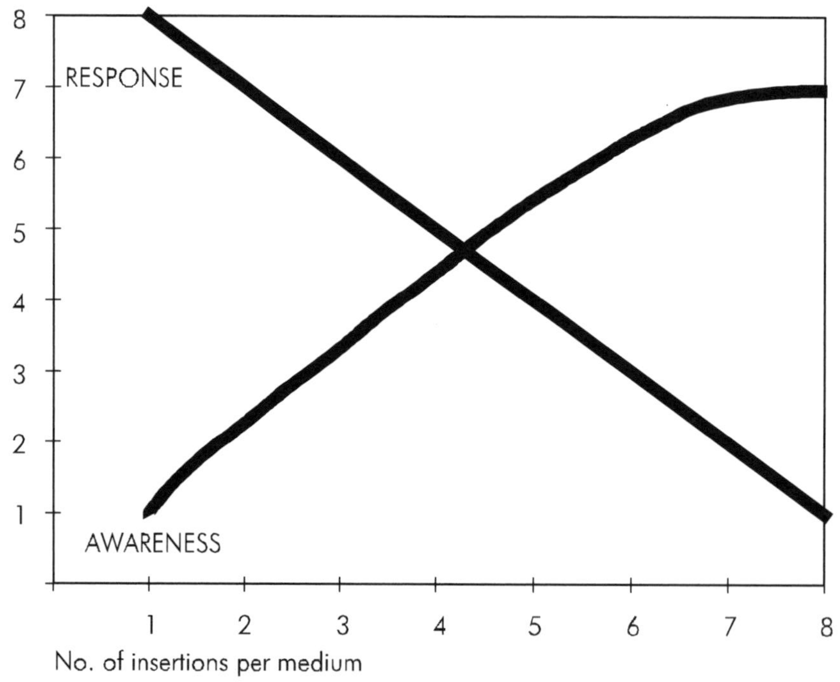

Finalising the media plan

So far we have talked only of selecting media titles – we have not decided space sizes, positions, timing, weight and frequency of insertions, or the use of colour. Of these the most critical are space size and frequency: the "weight" of advertising.

Frequency

Direct marketers normally seek immediate, maximum response. Experience shows that response is highest when an offer is fresh to readers of a given medium. So media planners aim to maximise initial response. Then the ad is withdrawn from a publication long enough for the offer to regain its freshness. How long that is can be determined only by trial and error.

Compare these two scenarios

When the readership of Sunday magazine is presented with the opportunity to buy a cottage plate, it may take 6–12 months to generate sufficient new interest to make advertising again worthwhile ...

... whereas for a product like home insurance, every month the potential audience is refreshed as renewal dates come round.

Direct marketers use a number of techniques to reduce the effects of response attrition due to frequency, among them:

- ✔ Copy variants
- ✔ Change day of the week
- ✔ Change positions, eg from TV page to holiday supplement
- ✔ Vary space size (see below)

The effect of space size

An important way to reduce frequency and maintain response ratios is to begin with a large space and/or to take large spaces less often. Larger spaces normally result in more responses, although not in direct proportion to increased costs.

The term "large" is of course relative, with "small" generally applying to spaces ranging from 5cm by 1 column (a 5 x 1) up to perhaps 20 x 3, or 25 x 4. Full pages and double-page spreads (DPSs) are classified amongst the larger sizes. It really depends on what you term small to begin with.

Experience suggests that the relationship of response to space size is the square root of the increased space, ie doubling the space averagely yields 1.4 times more responses, **not twice as many** – and each response will have cost more.

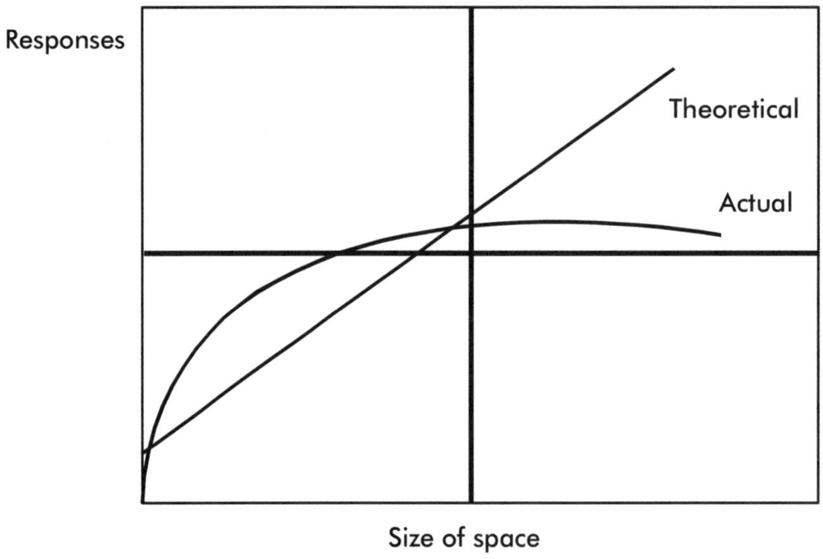

In practice space size will also be arrived at via several other criteria, eg:

✔ One-step ads (direct sale) normally necessitate larger spaces than two-step enquiry generators because of the need for longer copy and mandatory information.

✔ Complex offers require larger spaces to explain.

✔ Small spaces may be deployed to contain the number of responses to levels which can be handled – or large sizes to maximise response.

✔ Large spaces may be used to optimise seasonal potential especially during short seasons.

There are also qualitative reasons for opting for larger sizes, among them:

✔ Greater awareness and impact value.

✔ Improved creative flexibility.

✔ Better potential for negotiation at the buying stage.

Larger spaces (despite their marginally lower cost-efficiency) are therefore generally preferable. However, if in doubt, test. The effect of size can be measured by comparing the results of a cross-over test as described in Chapter 2.3 on testing.

The effect of readership duplication

One final point about frequency: do not forget that frequency applies not only to individual titles **but also to similar titles with a high level of duplication**. For example, 60% of Sun readers also read the News of the World. Thus an advertisement in the Sun may be seen again the next day by 60% of its readers who also take the News of the World, with possibly reduced response as the result.

Duplication among newspaper readerships is surprisingly high – as the table opposite shows – a fact which is rarely appreciated by non-media specialists.

Duplication is often the explanation for a poor response when all other indicators suggest that a good response could be expected. Duplication can often mislead inexperienced media buyers to assume that Publication A is automatically better than Publication B, whereas the truth is that the medium which **first** carries a specific offer frequently attracts the highest response.

Before ruling out a medium from your candidate schedule make sure that it has not consistently appeared during the latter stages of a campaign when it may have been affected by duplication. The first medium to appear may, in fact, carry a later issue date – but it is the time of its appearance on the news-stands, or on executive desks, that determines which medium is "creaming off" the best of the readership.

Examples of readership duplication among newspapers

Readers of	who also read					
	News of the World	Sunday Mirror	Sunday People	Sunday Express	Sunday Times	Mail on Sunday
	%	%	%	%	%	%
Sun	60	32	31	9	4	9
Mirror	41	54	37	11	4	10
Daily Mail	24	20	19	25	12	44
Daily Express	26	21	22	52	8	17
The Times	15	11	9	18	50	16

Readers of	who also read				
	Sun	Mirror	Daily Mail	Daily Express	The Times
	%	%	%	%	%
News of the World	54	29	9	9	1
Sunday Mirror	39	52	10	10	1
Sunday People	43	40	11	12	1
Sunday Express	16	16	19	38	4
Sunday Times	13	11	16	11	18
Mail on Sunday	21	17	42	16	4

The effect of colour

Colour is often thought to be essential to the presentation of certain products, although in practice this is often not so. Readers of newspapers are used to mono reproduction and can envisage colour in a product fairly readily.

Colour, however, does normally boost response and its net effect is much the same as that of larger sizes, ie it costs more, produces more replies, is usually marginally less cost-effective, and above all is a further factor in maintaining volume whilst minimising frequency. It also has a separate image/awareness building quality, of course, and may be regarded as imperative for certain products, eg fashion.

Paying for position?

Another factor to take into account is **position** – both in the journal and on the page. This is perhaps one of the best examples of the need for competitive advertising analysis. This will usually indicate which are the best positions in a given publication.

One argument worth raising here is whether it is worth paying a premium price for what may be an acknowledged superior position, eg outside back cover. Once again, the desirability of greater initial impact, thus allowing reduced frequency, tends to suggest that "special" positions are worth buying. However, on a purely cost-efficiency basis, as with smaller spaces, they are not necessarily superior. The answer, as always, is to test.

The following are usually considered to be superior or special positions:

- ✔ Front cover
- ✔ Back cover
- ✔ Front of publication
- ✔ Outer edges
- ✔ Right-hand pages
- ✔ Facing or next to editorial (next "matter")
- ✔ Next to letters, TV, horoscopes

Testing and roll-out potential

Finally plan media schedules with an eye to testing and future roll-out potential. Especially important are split-run and regional tests, both described fully in this Guide, under testing, Chapter 2.3.

How important is the price of space?

One thing that hopefully you won't let influence your media selection is the promise of bargains. Taking advantage of what appear to be "cheap" media is a common error. In media, as elsewhere, you get what you pay for – the skill is to make sure that you do get what you pay for. Your aim should be to select the best possible position in the right media, at the right time. Only then can you begin to secure the best possible price, knowing that what you are buying **is what you want**. Your results will tell you what you can afford.

It follows that skilled media buying is not digging in your heels and insisting on a better offer. It is knowing your business and the marketplace and applying your knowledge at every opportunity.

Having said that, opportunities to watch out for include:

✔ **Off-season**: eg some advertisers automatically pull out during holiday periods; these can be good response times with lower media costs on offer.

✔ **"Run-of-paper"/"run-of-week"**: better deals are available if the media owner retains some flexibility as to where and when your ad is inserted.

✔ **Forward bookings**: as well as discounts for volume, lower rates may be available for advanced reservations which help the media to forward plan. At least forward booking usually ensures a guaranteed rate when you confirm.

✔ **Stand-by**: very good rates are usually available if you leave an ad with the media for them to run when it suits them – a surer way of securing "distress space" mentioned below.

Short-term buying

A major advantage to the direct response media specialist is that he/she will usually be entrusted to make purchases at short notice without referral to any other authority. Holding a reserve for short-term buying, and thus being able to make quick, sometimes instant decisions, can be a vital factor in securing truly low costs.

Low-cost space offered by media, often late on Friday evenings, sometimes in out-of-office hours, is known as "distress" space, an important aspect of good direct response buying.

Space versus inserts

One of the major decisions to be made at the communications planning stage is the proportion of space to loose inserts in the media mix. We now look at the case for inserts.

PART III: Loose inserts – press advertising with direct mail appeal

Inserts are normally leaflets or folders printed separately from a newspaper or magazine but enclosed with it. They break down further into three types according to the method of enclosure:

Loose – enclosed with the host (or carrier) publication, or delivered alongside it.

Bound-in – stapled or glued into the publication.

Tipped-on – attached to a space advertisement, usually by means of a gummed strip.

Inserts take many forms including single sheets, 4- and 6-page folders, complex multi-fold and one-piece formats, brochures or catalogues (from 8 to 64 pages), cut-out shapes, product mini-samples, postcards, newsletters, unaddressed direct mail-packs, etc.

Other methods of distribution

Inserts are often delivered by **non-press** methods including door-to-door (see Chapter 4.2); in third party communications, eg bills and statements from the gas/ electricity/water authorities; in product despatches, ie contained within the packaging; and in non-competing direct mail on a shared basis.

These additional methods are normally planned by the media planner at the same time as the press schedule, avoiding duplication where possible. Because of the economies of scale at the printing stage, the higher the total volume the lower the unit costs of inserts – providing they are all the same format.

A bounty for new mothers

A good example of inserts being enclosed with products is the Bounty Baby Programme whereby gift samples and information on baby products are presented to new mothers in a bumper pack shortly after the birth.

Why inserts work

Inserts continue to grow in popularity with direct marketers. Why? Because they regularly prove to be extraordinarily cost-effective, often providing affordable sales and enquiries in far greater volumes than are delivered by space advertising.

Inserts are effective for many consumer products, business-to-business, financial services, charities, subscriptions and most other direct marketing applications. Most users of inserts employ them to make offers of literature, ie to elicit names for immediate follow-up or future direct mail activity. For some inexplicable reason inserts are usually less successful for direct (mail order) offers except where a catalogue is involved.

Ill-informed critics will charge that inserts simply drop out on the newsagent's floor and are ignored. "They fall in my lap every time I open a magazine," and "I shake them into the waste bin," are common criticisms.

But the facts are: (1) only a small proportion of inserts fall out prematurely and are ignored; (2) most are noted and looked at before being put aside, which is a major advantage over many other forms of advertising.

Inserts work precisely because they draw immediate attention to themselves before the reader has had a chance to study the news, views and space advertisements inside the publication. Even as it is being picked up, an insert is being looked at.

Partly for this reason, inserts are generally more responsive than space advertising and, although more expensive on a strict per-thousand-circulation basis, are frequently more cost-effective as a result. For some products/services inserts provide 5–6 times the response of a full-page space advertisement, if not more.

The continuing growth of inserts

Since the previous edition of this Guide, the use of inserts has grown in volume in newspapers and general magazines by 72% and in specialist magazines by 92%. The growth in third party and product despatches has been a phenomenal 300%, as the table below shows.

The growth of inserts 1990–1996

Method of delivery/carrier	Volume (billions)			Media spend (£m)			Print costs (£m)		
	1990	1993	1996	1990	1993	1996	1990	1993	1996
Magazines and newspapers	1.8	2.8	3.1	28.8	44.8	49.6	22.4	35	54.2
Specialist titles	1.3	1.9	2.5	20.8	30.4	40	15.4	22.8	43.7
Third party & product despatch	1	1.6	4	30	48	120	14	22.4	70
Door-to-door	5	7	6	60	98	96	60	84	126
Total	9.1	13.3	15.6	140	221	306	112	164	294

The role of inserts

The continued growth of inserts is easy to understand when one considers their uses and advantages. Inserts can be particularly effective in delivering all the following:

- ✔ High volumes of enquiries
- ✔ Cost-efficient responses
- ✔ Creative flexibility
- ✔ High impact
- ✔ Detailed information
- ✔ Measurable test campaigns with good roll-out potential
- ✔ Broad or niche (targeted) coverage

High volumes of enquiries

Insert opportunities exist in the majority of national newspapers, consumer and business-to-business magazines, delivering circulations in excess of tens of millions each month. In addition, "Third y" enclosures are estimated to deliver up to a billion opportunities each quarter.

Coupled to their high responsiveness, inserts account for a huge volume of the enquiries and sales enjoyed by direct marketers.

Cost-efficient responses

In judging the efficiency of inserts the total cost should include the price paid to a publisher/carrier and the price of producing and printing the insert. Both are subject to the laws of supply and demand.

The price paid to the publisher/carrier is negotiable. Inserts can be bought tactically on short term as well as by confirmed volume/date. Ratecard prices for loose inserts vary between £20 and nearly £100 per thousand, specialist magazines (including business-to-business journals with small circulations) being more expensive than large circulation newspapers.

Many advertisers, especially in business-to-business, find the targeting benefits of inserts ideal for high-value goods or services – thus the higher costs of specialist media are not a major concern to them.

The following table lists a selection of host magazines with their comparable cost-per-thousand for loose inserts:

Typical inserting costs

Sector	Title	Instructions/ restrictions	Rate card cost per 1,000 inserts*
Newspapers	Mirror	Fixed day (1–8 pages)	£28
	Observer	Fixed day (1–2 pages)	£35
	Financial Times	Full run (1–8 pages)	£83
Supplements	Telegraph Magazine		£38
	Weekend Guardian		£40
TV listing magazines	Radio Times	1m+inserts (2–8 pages)	£27
	TV Times		£26
Women's weeklies	Woman's Own		£26
	Woman's Weekly		£26
Women's monthlies	Homes & Gardens		£30
	Family Circle		£27
Special interest magazines	Angling Times		£39
	BBC Gardeners World		£30
	Golf World		£40
Business-to-business	Pulse		£50
	Business Life		£68

* *Source: BRAD Insert Guide 1997 Volume 1*

Creative flexibility

Inserts offer immense creative flexibility similar in many ways to that of direct mail. Existing brochures, catalogues and even unaddressed direct mail-packs have all been used, along with the more standard leaflets and folders.

Often inserts can be carried when you are unable to buy space advertising in colour for one reason or another. And, of course, inserts can carry such devices as reply forms/envelopes, scratch-off panels, lucky numbers, mini-samples, etc.

High impact

The combination of interactivity and creative potential ensures that inserts are highly visible, a direct contributor to the higher response patterns that are regularly recorded for inserts of all kinds.

Detailed information

The creative scope allows for the inclusion of as much copy as the advertiser feels will be useful, informative, interesting or convincing to prospects. Entire application forms, full product specifications and details of extensive product ranges can all be included if appropriate.

Inserts are frequently used by industries and governments to publicise information on a wide scale, for example regarding health issues.

Measurable test campaigns with good roll-out potential

Inserts provide the ideal test vehicle. For example, the News of the World can deliver a circulation of nearly 5 million. However, the direct marketer can test the response from this particular publication with an initial run of perhaps 100,000.

Alternatively, you may be unsure which product or creative approach to lead with. Rather than just the two-copy test provided by A/B splits in space advertising, a multi-product test could be constructed using, for example, five products – you simply book 500,000 inserts divided into batches of 100,000 for each product. Successful products and creative can then be "rolled-out" to the full circulation.

Broad or niche coverage/targeting

En masse, inserts can build coverage into any campaign and minimise frequency. However, niche and tightly targeted opportunities also exist:

✔ **Geodemographic targeting**
Many publications will accept inserts into specific TV regions or tightly defined towns and areas within their distribution networks. Others, such as the Radio Times, have invested in Acorn-based systems that allow for the detailed analysis of their wholesale areas and the geo-profiling of inserts.

✔ **Lifestyle targeting**
Special interest titles and third-party carriers can be used to target specific lifestyles such as gardeners, golfers, anglers, new mothers, etc.

✔ **Occupation targeting**
With business-to-business titles there are many opportunities to target prospects by occupation and influence. Some business journals break down their circulations by industry type or job category for insert advertisers.

Planning your insert campaign

As with all marketing activity, the starting point is to define your objective, the role of the advertising and the target audience.

Industry research sources such as TGI (Target Group Index) and NRS (National Readership Survey), described earlier, can be used to identify the readership patterns of your chosen target audience.

The table below illustrates a TGI report analysing the readership of gardening and women's publications by women aged 45+, with household income in excess of £20,000, who are buying or own their own home – an audience that might, for example, be selected by an insurance company to sell a particular policy.

	Readers within target group '000s	Coverage of target group	Target group readers as % of all readers	Efficiency index in delivering target group	Rank
Totals	2,097	100	4.5	100	
Woman's Journal	93	4.43	14.6	321	1
Woman & Home	168	8.01	13.37	293	2
Garden	48	2.29	12.94	284	3
Family Circle	179	8.54	12.79	281	4
Options	75	3.58	12.06	265	5
Harpers & Queen	49	2.34	9.98	219	6
Gardening Which?	54	2.58	9.59	211	7
Your Garden	26	1.24	9.32	205	8
Prima	182	8.68	8.77	193	9
BBC Gardeners World	147	7.01	8.21	180	10
She	98	4.67	8.16	189	11
Essentials	97	4.63	8.11	178	12
Tatler	29	1.38	8.01	176	13
World of Interiors	22	1.05	7.91	174	14
Garden Answers	52	2.48	7.72	169	15
Vogue	133	6.34	7.34	161	16
Garden News	25	1.19	7.06	155	17
Woman's Weekly	173	8.25	7.04	155	18

In the example above, the bias towards particular media (eg the homes and gardening press) can be used to plan inserts in media not included in the research, eg The English Garden, Gardens Illustrated, etc.

On the same basis, you could consider third party mailings by gardening companies, eg for seeds, plants, trellises, wellingtons, etc. These could include Parkers (garden plants and trees), Van Meuwen (seed catalogue), Cannock Gates (trellising, rose arches), etc. Third party programme managers, the equivalent of publication sales representatives, can provide profile information about customers to refine selections beyond the obvious lifestyle interest implied by the company's products. Third party programmes are normally bookable through experienced list brokers (see Chapter 5.1).

Managing the detail

Availability?

Having selected your ideal insert opportunities, planning now becomes a highly detailed function.

First you need to establish whether your chosen publications are able to take your inserts. The majority of publishers/carriers will take up to **three** non-competing inserts in one edition/mailing/product despatch, etc – so clearly the availability of the more responsive carriers is limited by demand.

Size and specification?

Even before booking you may need to confirm with the publisher/carrier that the size, weight, folds, etc, of your insert are acceptable.

There is an infinite number of permutations as to what is acceptable to publishers/ carriers in terms of dimensions, paper stock and total weight. BRAD now produces an insert guide in which the majority of publications' specifications are listed (BRAD Inserts Guide), but inevitably the planner will have to 'phone around to finalise all the information required.

Print economies can be achieved only if an insert design is acceptable to all of your selected titles. This is not always possible as the table below demonstrates:

Publication/carrier	Minimum size (mm) accepted	Maximum size (mm) accepted
Woman's Journal	148 x 105	279 x 205
Woman & Home	150 x 100	279 x 212
Garden	148 x 105	265 x 202
Family Circle	148 x 105	279 x 205
Options	148 x 105	279 x 205
Your Garden	135 x 115	28 x 206
BBC Gardeners World	148 x 105	280 x 205
She	148 x 105	270 x 195
Essentials	148 x 105	265 x 205

Suitability for insertion?

One factor which creates these variations in minimum/maximum sizes is the different inserting techniques and distribution methods employed by publishers and carriers.

National newspapers have to consider the accumulated bulk of inserts when their publications are bundled up. Polywrapped subscriber magazines and third party carriers will be concerned with any additional costs of postage resulting from substantial weight increases.

New technology introduced by many publishers has made the process more automated, which would be a cost saving if it were not for their requirement to amortise the investment costs of the machinery. Some publishers and carriers still rely on hand-inserting – theoretically a more expensive process and one that can place limitations on volumes.

Folds must be planned with the insertion method in mind, the least acceptable being the concertina or fan-type fold.

Finally, delivery deadlines, delivery addresses and preferred methods of packaging and palleting have to be understood and planned for by the media buyer. On the following page will be found a checklist showing how inserts should be prepared for, and despatched to, the printers.

Analysing insert campaigns

As confirmation that an insert has been distributed, printers/media owners should produce a Certificate of Insertion detailing the number of inserts that were actually inserted. It is recommended that no invoice is paid until a Certificate of Insertion has been received.

Where schedules have been planned to target defined regions it is obviously important to break down the total responses according to these regions. This is best accommodated at the planning stage by using regional response codes on coupons and for customers to quote on the 'phone. It is also possible to sort regional response by postcode analysis of enquiries. Systems such as CACI and CCN can be used to do this.

Exercise for students

Collecting loose inserts is an easy and inexpensive way to examine advertisements in newspapers and magazines that you might not otherwise encounter. Ask friends and colleagues to save their unwanted loose inserts for you. See if you can discover any similar but different examples that may constitute a test. Analyse their contents in terms of product, offer, proposition, credibility and action devices before turning to the creative chapters of this Guide (6.1–6.6).

How to supply inserts to the publisher

- ✔ Check the delivery deadline for the specific issue booked.
- ✔ Check the delivery address – it will be the publisher's printer and is **unlikely to be the same as that of the publisher**.
- ✔ Check the packaging instructions – how does the printer want to receive the inserts: pallets, cartons, etc?
- ✔ Pallets must be in good condition to allow them to be stacked.
- ✔ Pallets should be well wrapped to avoid damage during transit and storage.
- ✔ Inserts that are unable to be palletised due to their shape or size should be packed appropriately in cartons.
- ✔ Inserts should be packed with the minimum number of turns, ie all copies stacked in the same direction if possible.
- ✔ Pallets or cartons should be clearly marked with:
  - ❐ Name of advertiser
  - ❐ Name of insert
  - ❐ Number of inserts
  - ❐ Name of publication
  - ❐ Date of planned insertion
  - ❐ Copy of the insert if practicable
  - ❐ Name, address and contact name of advertiser's printer
- ✔ Inserts should **not** be delivered earlier than requested by the publication's printers – with some printers it is necessary to book an appointment for the delivery.
- ✔ Inserts should be accompanied by a **delivery note/instruction sheet** detailing:
  - ❐ Address of the publication's printer/binder.
  - ❐ Description of the insert, including the name of the advertiser and the insert specification (eg 4-page leaflet, 16-page catalogue, etc).
  - ❐ Total quantity delivered and number of inserts per pallet or carton.
  - ❐ Name of publication and date of insertion. **This is very important as many publications use the same printer.**
  - ❐ Editions, regions, quantities and any other inserting instructions.

Directories – the ultimate enquiry generators

No résumé of printed direct response media would be complete without reference to the ubiquitous directories, eg Yellow Pages and Thomsons. These are often misunderstood and underused by nationwide marketers, despite being cost-effective generators of high-quality enquirers for a wide range of industries.

Why misunderstood? Mainly because there is no simple (or at least no **quick**) way to establish how best to use them. Insertion must be booked up to a year in advance of the first appearance of a new directory – and once inserted there is no way of removing an advertisement from public awareness for several years. Thus directories are entirely unsuited to topical information and, indeed, most publishers prohibit the inclusion of prices for this reason.

Other grounds for misunderstanding include the relatively poor quality of reproduction and the cacophony of somewhat brutal announcements from local retailers and services, bold and "bloody" graphics and outrageous puffery being the most dominant treatment.

Hot prospects

As direct marketers we should never overlook the potential of directories to deliver hot prospects. They occupy a unique position in the customer's buying cycle:

1. Prospects turn actively to directories when in need of help or suppliers: they are hotter prospects than enquirers from almost any other source.

2. Directories are used by all ages, groups, professions, etc – absolutely no prior segmentation takes place. A home-owner turning to "kitchens" may occupy a studio flat or a 10-bedroom mansion.

3. Potential buyers often use directories to shortlist suppliers even before making initial enquiries elsewhere.

With so much business on offer, successful advertisers fall back on AIDCA (see creative sections, Chapters 6.2–6.4); stressing **relevant benefits** and especially **credibility** and **positioning**. The prospect is carrying out their own segmentation based on whether, ultimately, they like the look of you or not!

The efficacy of directories – and of specific regions – can be tested by use of the numerous regional editions available, although results will take at least fifteen months to materialise following the decision to take space.

Chapter 4.2

Door-to-door, now with new improved targeting

This chapter includes:

- ❑ **Door-to-door's unique advantages**
- ❑ **Public attitudes to door-to-door**
- ❑ **Door-to-door and sampling**
- ❑ **Targeting by demographics and by database**
- ❑ **The 6 essential features of an effective promotion**
- ❑ **The 5 methods of distribution**
- ❑ **An indication of costs**

Door-to-door is now a viable medium for new customer acquisition programmes after decades of being a short-term promotional tool. What has made the difference is the improved targeting that results from using established marketing databases such as Mosaic and ACORN classifications. Also, the realisation that customers can be persuaded to identify themselves when responding to offers, even though these may be redeemed in stores.

In communication terms, door-to-door has the extended reach of the national press, the impact and immediacy of inserts, and the creative flexibility enjoyed by direct mail – to say that anything can be home-delivered from a pin to an elephant would be only a slight exaggeration. Certainly it is the only advertising medium that can present prospects with a sample of a product whilst at the same time introducing the product's advantages.

In this chapter, Nick Wells explains door-to-door in general terms and invites direct and database marketers to consider how the medium can best serve their needs.

New in this edition. New data on usage and acceptance, new thoughts on targeting, new case study.

Nick Wells, Managing Director, Circular Distributors Limited

Nick is Managing Director of Circular Distributors Limited and its subsidiary Lifecycle Marketing. He was one of four directors involved in a management buyout of CD in 1990 from its parent, the Brunning Group. He joined CD in 1984 as Sales Manager after spending five years in account management for a marketing company. CD is the largest door-to-door distribution company in the UK with a turnover in excess of £26 million.

It has been in the vanguard of the drive to demonstrate the effectiveness of the medium and has commissioned a number of extensive research surveys to prove its suitability for today's consumer-led market.

Nick was instrumental in setting up the door-to-door industry's official trade body several years ago, called the Association of Household Distributors (AHD), and was also the Chairman of The Institute of Sales Promotion (1996–98). He writes and comments regularly in the marketing trade press on all aspects of direct marketing, sales promotion and marketing services.

His background in sales and marketing ensures that he is still very close to many of CD's major clients and their agencies. Many of these clients are from the retail and fmcg sector and include Lever, Van den Bergh, Nestlé, Tetley, Great Mills and IKEA, to name a few.

Nick is married with young children but still manages the odd game of golf and tennis.

Nick Wells
Managing Director
Circular Distributors Ltd
CD House
1–3 Malvern Road
Maidenhead
Berkshire SL6 7QY
Tel: 01628-771232

Chapter 4.2

Door-to-door, now with new improved targeting

What do we mean by door-to-door?

Door-to-door distribution is the business of delivering unaddressed material to houses in defined geographical areas (usually based on postcodes). It differs from mailed communications in that the mail is delivered by the Royal Mail to named persons at specific addresses. Addressed communications are subject to postal charges and restrictions which do not apply to unaddressed deliveries.

Research by RSGB and commissioned by Royal Mail suggests unaddressed items account for approximately one-third of what goes through Britain's letterboxes. While it is impossible to calculate the exact number of items delivered, it is commonly estimated to be in excess of five billion per year, of which the majority is delivered by the three leaders: Circular Distributors (CD), Royal Mail's Door-to-Door, and The Leaflet Company.

The Association of Household Distributors (AHD), through the Advertising Association, estimates expenditure on door-to-door delivery at £129 million excluding print and production. If print and production are assumed to cost twice as much as delivery, the door-to-door market is reckoned to be worth £387 million – more than either radio or poster advertising.

Door-to-door's unique advantages

The fundamental strength of door-to-door is that a leaflet, brochure or sample is delivered through the letterbox, thus offering direct communication to the customer right into the home. It also offers creative freedom, because there are virtually no restrictions as in press advertising – for example, in size, shape, colour or design.

With door-to-door there is no duplication of coverage, because only one leaflet or sample per household is delivered, and it is possible to cover as few or as many households as appropriate to meet the marketing objective. Coverage of virtually every household in the UK is available.

Door-to-door is perhaps most powerful when combined with other media. It is commonly used as a follow-through to a press or TV campaign and is at its most effective when the advertising has been running for a couple of weeks. Then, when a follow-up leaflet reflecting the image created by the advertising arrives through the letterbox, there is instant recognition and the leaflet can play its proper role of triggering purchase.

Door-to-door's national coverage

Door-to-door can cover 96% of women in the UK and 94% of men, proving that it is not merely a "housewife" medium. There is also no bias to any particular age group of householder/ occupier.

Reaching housewives with £200,000

On a relatively small budget of £200,000, comparing

- *A4 leaflet distributed door-to-door*
- *mono page ad, one insertion in every daily and sunday newspaper*
- *page in colour, 3 months in main weeklies/monthlies*
- *30-second TV commercial (delivering 90 TVRs)*
- *30-second radio commercial, 3–4 weeks, all main conurbations*

The door-to-door leaflet reached 85% of housewives
The newspaper campaign reached 75% of housewives
Women's magazines reached 70%
TV reached 50%
Radio reached 40%

Source: *Media Independent*

Geographically, the potential coverage is evenly distributed, as is the coverage of ABC1 and C2DE social groupings – all at between 94% and 96%.

These figures are, of course, before targeting and segmentation have been applied.

How the public regards door-to-door

Door-to-door has been subjected to a great deal of attitude research and some of its findings may surprise you. Of course this research is based on what people **say** they do, a potential weakness; however, some of the comparisons it yields are interesting, for example:

- ✔ 49% claim to recall seeing door-to-door advertising (obviously less than TV but only four percentage points less than newspapers and magazines).
- ✔ Only 12% discard door-to-door leaflets without first looking at them.
- ✔ 33% keep and read door-to-door promotions, becoming 66% for money-off offers on everyday items.
- ✔ 18% have sent for further information.

Perhaps the most important finding in all the research is that offers which promote discounts, gifts, free samples, or other incentives, are better recalled, kept and acted upon – a finding that correlates with direct mail in the popular market.

Who uses door-to-door?

The advent of more accurate targeting in door-to-door helps the marriage with other media. For example, if a new shampoo/conditioner is launched with a heavyweight press campaign targeted to women and a door-to-door coupon drop to encourage trial, then by using NRS, TGI, or demographic targeting (eg 25–45-year-old housewives with children), the distribution can be planned to match the readership profile of the magazines used.

Door-to-door is particularly appropriate for delivering information for public undertakings. It works for the privatised utilities, local authorities, and the Central Office of Information. Leaflets communicating changes of services or timetables, or of policy, have all been distributed.

Door-to-door is now an established medium that plays a crucial role in UK marketing. Most of the major grocery manufacturers and retailers have used it as part of their advertising and promotional strategies. It is also now widely used by mail order companies to recruit agents, and by financial service companies. Many use it consistently as part of their strategic long-term brand building programmes as well as for tactical applications, and it is particularly heavily used for new product launches.

Door-to-door and direct marketing

Door-to-door was until recently associated in many people's minds only with massive distribution of sales promotion leaflets. These often incorporated discount coupons but did not usually call for any other response. Today an increasing number of manufacturers ask customers to write in their names and addresses on coupons before redemption.

Asking consumers to include their names and addresses on redemption coupons not only discourages misredemption at the checkout – the consumer is less likely to mis-redeem if he/she has filled in correct address details – but can also begin to form the basis of a customer database.

Label collection schemes, cash-back offers and many other forms of brand promotion necessarily require a name and address. The more progressive manufacturers already capture such information at the handling house and keep it on file for future direct marketing activity. With the advent of large consumer databases responses to door-to-door promotions can now be matched against existing databases.

Many retailers who use door-to-door already ask for customers' names and addresses. For example, Beefeater and Berni have required those redeeming their vouchers to record their names and addresses.

Mail order companies like GUS and Littlewoods use door-to-door as a direct medium to recruit agents, and financial institutions (life assurance companies, for instance) use door-to-door to generate immediate response. The medium is now as appropriate for this kind of marketing activity as the mail when either a reply coupon or telephone response is required.

More recently car manufacturers, appliance retailers and television rental companies have all begun to use door-to-door to generate leads for their showrooms.

Have a look at door-to-door's many advantages and applications and think how many of them have possibilities for the alert direct marketer:

- ✔ Low-cost distribution of customer recruitment literature, including samples and discount offers.
- ✔ Unrestricted creativity – not bound by the space limitations of press advertising, nor the weight/size restrictions of direct mail.
- ✔ Geodemographic targeting virtually equal to that available for bought-in direct mail lists, at a fraction of the cost.
- ✔ High-speed coverage for most of the country with only a few simple negotiations.
- ✔ Research/feedback facilities – a special benefit in the early stages of building a customer database.
- ✔ The missing link between image advertising and direct sales stimulation – with no need to buy or own a list before you can begin.
- ✔ Testing potential – as for inserts and direct mail, by using alternate or batched leaflets and by comparing regional results.

Clearly door-to-door offers many interesting and unique opportunities for the direct marketer prepared to investigate what has now become an established direct response medium.

Pet project?

A sample drop for Nestlé's cat and dog foods set a UK record when Gourmet cat and Friskies dog foods were delivered to 12 million households. At each house the occupant was asked not only if he or she owned cats or dogs, but also whether the latter were large or small and what food products were bought for them.

Those who owned cats were given a full size retail pack of Gourmet à la Carte; those who owned dogs were given packs of Friskies à la Carte and Friskies Buffet. (Those who did not own pets received sachet samples of Nestlé's Coffee Mate.) Around 500 tons of samples were given away.

The major objective of the exercise was to achieve trial and to encourage repeat purchase. There was no other way of getting to so many cat and dog owners and gathering so much priceless market information so quickly.

The distribution was targeted using AGB data through Pinpoint Analysis to ensure that the right samples got to the right people. And what made the operation unique was that the massive sampling was combined with a mammoth data gathering task.

The information gathered from householders was recorded on questionnaires in such a way that they could be optically character read for analysis to form a database for use in future marketing operations.

Door-to-door and sampling

Door-to-door has been a very popular medium for sampling for many years. As long ago as 1954, four million bars of Sunlight soap were delivered in the north of England. Shortly afterwards, in the first national door-to-door drop, ten million full-size retail packs of the now defunct brand OMO were distributed.

Door-to-door sampling can be divided into two methods:

✔ Letterbox sampling

✔ Personal call sampling

Letterbox sampling

Letterbox sampling is simple and inexpensive. If an item can fit through a letterbox and the product is non-toxic, door-to-door is an option. It is ideal for the delivery of a multitude of products from shampoo to chocolate and toothpaste.

Presentation and packaging add value and attraction to samples. Minipack Sampling Solutions (which specialises in the production of miniature replicas of standard packs) has found that more than 50% of the projects undertaken with its samples have led to repeat business.

Many fmcg manufacturers have used "replica" letterbox sampling, including Lever Brothers, Elida Fabergé, Procter and Gamble, Van den Bergh Foods and KP. A coupon can be included on the reverse of the pack, so that once the consumer has tried the product the coupon is there to encourage repeat purchase. A name-gathering device could equally be applied in the case of a database building scheme.

Personal call sampling

Personal call sampling, although more expensive, enables qualification of the consumer, ie only suitable consumers need be offered the sample. Information can also be collected via a sample doorstep call procedure carried out by interviewers.

Personal call sampling reduces wastage and enables both the collection of valuable market intelligence data and the delivery of bulky samples. The method is particularly favoured if the product costs are high, as when Van den Bergh used it to give away 500 gm tubs of Flora Extra Light to housewives.

Doorstep interviews can also qualify households, eg whether there are children or pets in the home, for the purpose of collecting data.

Attitudes to sampling

The performance of door-to-door is especially remarkable where samples are distributed, one of the chief uses and benefits of the method, as research tends to show.

The figures below are the percentage of interviewees agreeing to the statements on the left.

"Samples tend to give a better idea of the product than advertising"	94%
"If they give samples away it shows they have nothing to hide"	54%
"I usually look for money-off coupons"	53%
"It's not right to give people samples they haven't requested"	8%
"Influenced me to try the product"	71%

Door-to-door and redemption coupons

Coupons delivered door-to-door are a particularly powerful sales promotion tool. According to Nielsen Research, door-to-door redemption levels are around 4.5%, compared with only 1% and 2% respectively for coupons featured in magazines and newspapers. The response rate on door-to-door coupons is bettered by in-pack and on-pack coupons and by direct mail although this does not take into account the high cost of delivery by mail.

Of all coupons delivered just over 5% are delivered by mail, 58% by newspapers and magazines, and 37% by door-to-door.

Geographic targeting using door-to-door distribution

When door-to-door distribution first became popular with mass marketers, its strength was as a low-cost non-discriminate means of reaching everyone, ie the mass market. Later, with the development of socio-economic classifications, a degree of targeting became possible. But in recent years targeting has become highly developed and now rivals direct mail in its geographic selectivity.

The following geographical groupings are widely used in the distribution of door-to-door advertising, each of which can be overlaid on the recognised socio-economic groups ABC1 and C2DE:

- ✔ TV regions
- ✔ Radio regions
- ✔ County boundaries
- ✔ Major urban areas/conurbations
- ✔ Marketing areas, eg Nielsen sales territories
- ✔ Catchment areas, eg around retail stores
- ✔ By postcode sector (averagely 2,500 households)

Targeting with the aid of sophisticated databases

More recently, door-to-door has begun to employ sophisticated computer techniques coupled to established consumer databases (already discussed in other chapters), to target **areas with the highest penetration of likely prospects for a particular product, service or offer**.

First you need to establish a geodemographic profile of your ideal prospect, using either research data (eg TGI, discussed in Chapter 4.1) or by profiling existing lists of customers and prospects.

This profile is then overlaid on one of the following databases or systems, eg:

- ✔ Mosaic
- ✔ Financial Mosaic
- ✔ Electoral roll
- ✔ Retail catchment areas

Finally, the best prospect locations are compared with possible methods of accessing them, eg:

Solus delivery by distributor

Shared delivery by distributor

Delivery with a **newspaper**

Delivery by the **postman**

4 methods of distribution

There are four main methods of delivering unaddressed promotions, namely Solus (by distributor), shared (by distributor), with a newspaper or by the postman. We now look at each option in turn:

Solus – undivided attention for your message

Solus gives total flexibility. You can choose your own timing, precise geographical area and selection criteria. Your message is delivered on its own and does not have to compete for attention. In some cases it is the only practical method. For example, it is not possible with shared methods to make personal calls and place product samples in the hands of prospects, to qualify prospects on the doorstep, or to collect information about householders. Solus is, of course, more expensive than shared alternatives. Nationally this service is offered by Circular Distributors, Royal Mail and The Leaflet Company.

Shared – the low-cost option

Shared delivery is the most economical method, because you share with up to four non-competing brands or products. Flexibility nevertheless exists to choose by geographical area, TV region, socio-economic grouping, Mosaic, etc. Shared delivery was developed in the 1960s to expand the total market and encourage new users of the medium. Small product samples of up to 70 gm can be letterboxed in this way.

News delivery – riding the free newspaper boom

Delivery with newspapers is a technique which was developed twenty years ago. It has grown rapidly with the enormous growth of the free newspaper business in the UK. 86% of the country is now covered by free newspapers, and the medium's advertising revenue is now more than that of the paid-for weeklies. As many as 18 million households can be covered by inserting leaflets into free newspapers.

The reliability of distribution by the reputable operators is backed by VFD (Verified Free Newspaper Distribution) which was founded by ABC (Audit Bureau of Circulation) in 1981 to provide independent verification of circulation figures. Latest research indicates that VFD papers have an average certified distribution rate of 95%.

Unlike solus and shared operations, newspaper deliveries can usually be completed within a 3-day period. Most papers go out on a Wednesday, Thursday or Friday so if speed is vital, News delivery is the answer. Three organisations offer a national planning and distribution service: Circular Distributors, The Leaflet Company and NLM (National Letterbox Marketing).

With the post

Delivery of unaddressed mail is undertaken by the Royal Mail, items normally being delivered by the postman along with the normal post. This service is more fully described in a later chapter of this Guide, see Chapter 7.10.

Door-to-door and creativity

Just as it is possible to deliver a wide variety of different types of weights of samples cost-effectively, so it is also practical to deliver a wide range of different promotional formats. The space limitations imposed by newspapers and magazines do not apply to door-to-door, nor do the weight and bulk limitations of direct mail.

As long as a promotional item can be fitted through a normal letterbox the advertising agency can create any type of novel shape. Promotional items in the shape of the product have become particularly popular with grocery manufacturers. This tactic ensures that when the product is seen on the retailer's shelf there is immediate recognition – a vital function of image advertising.

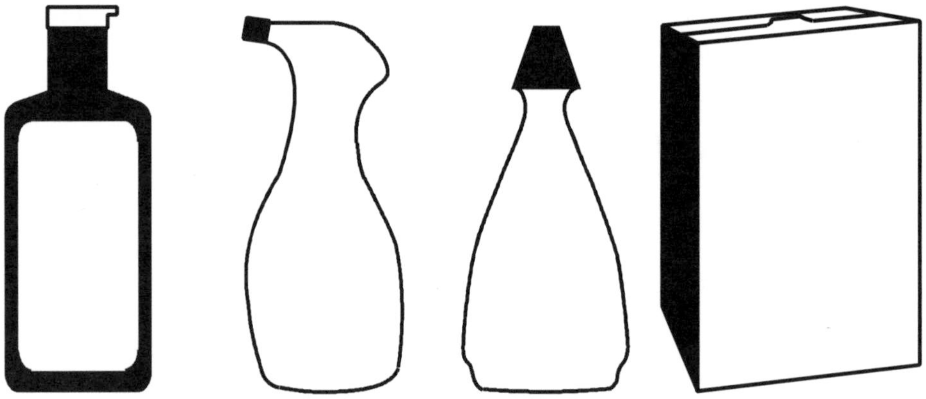

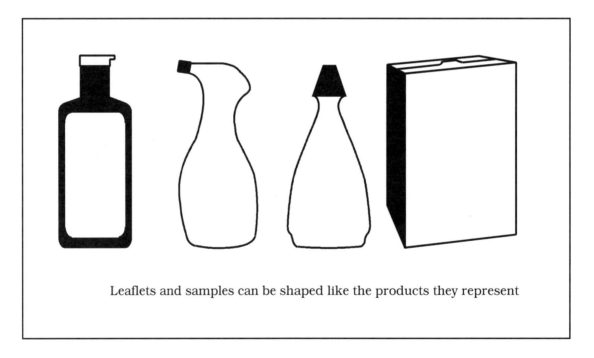

Leaflets and samples can be shaped like the products they represent

There is also evidence to show that large formats, provided that they can be folded to go through the letterbox, are cost-effective. Catalogues and magazines, often quarterly, are a format increasingly used by retailers who want to promote a wide range of merchandise in one vehicle – something that cannot be done in a press ad or a TV commercial. The Co-op's "Your Choice" is a good example of a quarterly magazine delivered around the catchment areas of larger Co-op stores.

Magazines prove highly effective when used by retailers to drive traffic through stores, encouraging loyalty among existing customers and promoting switching among others. There is no reason why manufacturers should not follow this example, as they have done in the US. The house magazine is also a proven vehicle for direct marketers who want to stay in close touch with customers – further evidence of how the separate disciplines are drawing closer together.

What makes for effective door-to-door?

In 1994 Circular Distributors commissioned research to establish the creative factors that determined response, which confirmed the results of an earlier investigation.

According to the research, when consumers receive a leaflet through the letterbox it is either thrown away, retained or, in the case of information leaflets, put to one side for perusal. During the sifting process respondents weed out those items of little or no interest, typical examples being deliveries that are made at high frequency but promote items of low frequency usage, eg double glazing, also confusing or over-complicated material.

Money-off coupons, free samples and multi-faceted offers are considered generally more interesting. The more immediate the reward and the less effort required to get it, the greater is the interest.

As a result of the research, a number of creative guidelines were established for door-to-door. These are set out below in a useful checklist. Keep it handy – much of it applies to other forms of insert and even some direct mail activity.

	Creative guidelines for door-to-door
✔	Brand recognition and message or reward must be almost instantaneous
✔	Strong, simple visual clues (through the use of colour and shape) work best, and can also appear quite creative to consumers. This creativity has to be either brand- or reward-related
✔	Teasers generally serve to confuse and annoy rather than arouse curiosity. Teasers that do work are related to a reward or attractive benefit. In other words, they have to demonstrate relevant creativity
✔	Additional product information has to be communicated with simplicity
✔	Consumers are not generally prepared to read detailed copy, but a product image can still be communicated through mood, tone and style of the leaflet
✔	Information-style leaflets, ie booklets, etc, should have a sense of size and quantity of information, and a quality soft-sell approach

How much will it cost?

The cost of door-to-door distribution is dependent on six straightforward elements:

✔ Size of item

✔ Quantity

✔ Area

✔ Method (eg solus or shared)

✔ Targeting

✔ Supplier

Very broadly shared costs from specialist door-to-door companies can be as low as £12 per thousand; solus £30 per thousand; and leaflets with free newspapers about £12 per thousand. These costs are for simple items weighing less than 10 gm. Less simple items are by negotiation and are subject to sight of intended material.

Costs have gone up comparatively little compared with the leaping costs of other media. In real terms, door-to-door is cheaper than it was in the early 1980s. The reason is a combination of intense competition in the industry and the fact that it has not proved necessary to increase payments to part-time distributors to anything like the same extent as other media costs have gone up.

It is also worth mentioning that for door-to-door it is not necessary to buy a list, insert into envelopes, or engage in expensive personalised printing techniques.

As with every other supplier sphere, buying on price alone almost inevitably leads to poor quality, with reports of widespread dumping and a high incidence of non-delivery. Unless distributors, who are essentially a casual labour force, are properly remunerated and managed there will be trouble. It is therefore important to obtain client references and recommendations, for example from a business colleague or an ad agency.

When buying door-to-door distribution services it is a mistake to accept the cheapest rate on offer. It also pays to ensure the chosen supplier is a member of the Association of Household Distributors (AHD) which sets rigorous membership standards.

Choosing your door-to-door supplier

There are three large nationwide suppliers of door-to-door services: Circular Distributors, The Leaflet Company and the Royal Mail's Door-to-Door. There is, in addition, a large number of smaller regional and local suppliers offering different levels and quality of service.

Having arrived at your shortlist of door-to-door distributors, probing questions should be asked about the operator's field structure. It is important to check the number of area managers within the area network and to ensure that they are wholly employed by the company and bound by proper contracts of employment. Specialists consider that full-time area managers are required for the back-checks to be carried out to ensure deliveries have been properly made in a national campaign.

Details should be requested about back-checking procedures, because this is a vital discipline and a reflection of the company's policy on field control and organisational standards. It is also important to ensure that back-checks are carried out independently of the subcontractor doing the distribution. CD, for example, employs a full-time security officer to ensure adequate policing and professionally executed distribution.

How Wickes uses door-to-door

Wickes, the DIY group, uses Circular Distributors to distribute its booklets (or catalogues) and promotion leaflets (abridged versions concentrating on key revenue generators) to catchment areas around its stores.

▲ The booklet – 96 product-packed pages. Overall size 145 x 145 mm.

The leaflet – 8 A4 pages of key revenue generators – from tools to kitchens and bathrooms. ▶

In 1996, research by Synergism (interviewing shoppers exiting Wickes' stores) was conducted to ascertain the effect of these publications in the following areas:

	{Recognition and awareness
	{Level of reading
Short term	*{Visit and purchase behaviour*
	{Sales/cost of promotion ration
	{Catalogue versus national press advertising
	{Catalogue versus leaflet
	{Brand values
Long term	*{Demographic reach*
	{Longevity of effect

Conclusion 1. *The booklet outperformed press advertising in all areas, its measurable effect being 7 times greater directly after distribution. It was also retained, producing a residual effect leading to subsequent visits. There was some evidence of pass-on readership. The booklet also did more to enhance Wickes' brand values and to raise its profile.*

Conclusion 2. *The leaflet was also more effective than press advertising but at a much lesser degree (+44% purchasers, twice as well read).*

Conclusion 3. *The booklet was more successful than the leaflet in meeting all Wickes' objectives.*

Conclusion 4. *Almost 60% of booklets were kept until superseded by next edition in 2–3 weeks; 53% kept flyers but only for a few days, 35% for one week.*

Conclusion 5. *One group (upmarket younger females) in particular were not reached at all by national press.*

Conclusion 6. *National press was strongest in image/awareness, portraying Wickes as a national chain for serious DIY enthusiasts.*

Door-to-door and overseas markets

Leading companies can mount pan-European distributions through ELMA (the European Letterbox Marketing Association). Different countries in Europe offer differing levels of penetration, price, and sophistication. The UK is more advanced in terms of its targeting abilities than most other countries.

Business-to-business?

Straightforward door-to-door distribution of literature is not usually effective for business purposes, and services in this area are limited. However, personal calls involving literature delivery with research feedback are available from organisations specialising in part-time field sales and demonstrator teams.

Chapter 4.3

Unravelling the mysteries of direct response TV

This chapter includes:

- UK television channels in 1997
- The 6 different objectives of response TV
- The keys to DRTV success
- Branding and direct response – a comparison
- How TV airtime is sold and bought
- Testing and evaluating DRTV
- The importance of response handling and fulfilment

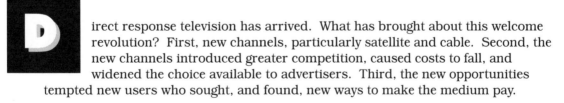

Direct response television has arrived. What has brought about this welcome revolution? First, new channels, particularly satellite and cable. Second, the new channels introduced greater competition, caused costs to fall, and widened the choice available to advertisers. Third, the new opportunities tempted new users who sought, and found, new ways to make the medium pay.

Yes, DRTV is being successfully taken up by more and more advertisers determined to make it work for them, looking to steal a march on their rivals, and searching for new audiences – for not every consumer is an avid reader of newspapers and direct mail.

In this chapter, Simon Foster brings us up to date with this, one of the newest of response media – its uses, costs and rules of thumb – and shows us just what makes it successful for the large number of blue chip advertisers now using it. Where once only music collections and knife sets survived, we now see mortgages being successfully offered on TV – and a lot more besides.

New in this edition. Many of the applications featured here were not known in direct response TV when our first edition was published.

Simon Foster, Head of Integrated Media, MindShare

Following almost a decade in both "above" and "below" the line media, Simon has developed a rare blend of integrated media planning skills.

His direct marketing experience began in 1988 when he joined CACI, the geodemographic pioneer best known for the development of the ACORN family of market segmentation systems. At CACI he worked on a range of direct marketing and database analysis projects.

In 1992 he joined Channel Four Television in a senior business development role responsible for building business across a number of sectors from holidays to financial services. Whilst at Channel Four he worked on the BT/Channel Four DRTV effectiveness studies which became the benchmark for DRTV planning in the UK.

In early 1996 Simon joined Ogilvy & Mather Group as a media planner working on a wide range of response-oriented accounts, including American Express, BUPA, Eagle Star, National Geographic Magazine, Reader's Digest and Save The Children Fund. He was also responsible for all media planning on O&M's BUPA and Eagle Star business whilst remaining the Group's resident DRTV specialist. From May 1998 Simon will be responsible for all direct media planning at MindShare, the new WPP media company formed from the merger of the O&M and JWT media departments.

He is a full member of the Chartered Institute of Marketing and has spoken widely to industry and student groups on issues relating to direct response and integrated marketing. He is a geography graduate whose formal business training includes a postgraduate Diploma in Management Studies and an MA in Marketing which he passed with Distinction.

Simon Foster
Head of Integrated Media
MindShare
40 The Strand
London
WC2N 5HZ
Tel: 0171-345 3000

Chapter 4.3

Unravelling the mysteries of direct response TV

1995–1998: 3 years of unprecedented growth

In recent years there has been a revolution in UK direct response television (DRTV) advertising. DRTV is no longer confined to cucumber slicers and record collections advertised late at night. It has now been adopted by many financial services, motor and travel providers, among others, as a powerful means of initiating a direct relationship with individual consumers.

Of course many attempts had been made before to succeed with response television, notable examples being the Automobile Association's recruitment campaign and before that Time-Life Books' spectacular commercials in the 1970s. But, ultimately, all such attempts were curtailed by the medium's high cost and lack of choice.

The high growth in response generating TV activity since the mid-1990s was fuelled partly by the dramatic increase in the number of TV channels. Ten years earlier advertisers had only two choices: ITV and Channel Four. This limited choice was aggravated by the fact that ITV sales companies sold both ITV and Channel Four airtime, an arrangement that offered media buyers little bargaining power.

In 1990 the UK's two embryonic and competing satellite broadcasters, BSB and Sky, merged to form British Sky Broadcasting (BSkyB). Since then we have witnessed an explosion in the number of TV channels from BSkyB and other new satellite broadcasters.

By 1995 Channel Four and BT estimated that the number of commercials displaying a 'phone number had reached 19%, up from 12% in late 1993. Although no definitive survey has taken place since, it is widely accepted that the growth has continued and the number by 1997 had reached around 25%. In some breaks all commercials now carry 'phone numbers.

UK television channels in the late 1990s

By 1997, in addition to ITV and Channel Four, advertisers and agencies had a third national channel, Channel 5. All three are delivered via a rooftop aerial and are known as the terrestrial channels.

The many satellite transmissions can now be delivered via direct-to-home "dishes" or cable in which case the satellite signal is collected at a central point and distributed via a local cable network to subscribers.

The number of UK homes able to receive satellite channels and cable at the start of 1997 was 6.6 million. By the year 2001 this is expected to grow by 127% to reach a volume of 15 million homes.

Although these audiences are still small compared to terrestrial TV, they already offer DRTV advertisers a number of exciting media opportunities that were simply not available ten years ago, as the table below demonstrates.

1997: UK satellite and cable channels by programme content (or "genre")

Kids	Features	Lifestyle	Mixed	Movies	Music	News	Sport
Cartoon	Discovery	Carlton Food	Bravo	Movie Channel	CMT	CNN	Eurosport
Disney	History	Granada Good Life	Challenge	Sky Movies	MTV	NBC	Sky Sports 1
Nickelodeon	TLC	Live TV	Granada Plus	Sky Movies Gold	VH-1	Sky News	Sky Sports 2
TCC	Travel	UK Living	Paramount	Movie Channel		Channel One London	
			Sci-Fi				
			Sky 1				
			Sky 2				
			UK Gold				

Digital TV is also on the horizon which is expected to offer broadcasters the ability to deliver **hundreds** of channels to subscribing homes. This is, however, medium-term technology and will take time to reach a critical mass – maybe as long as 10 years. In the meantime, cable and satellite are driving the explosion in the UK's number of new channels.

New channels, new opportunities for advertisers

Audience cost and channel choice are two of the most critical success factors in DRTV. The advent of new satellite and cable channels has brought about a gradual move from a sellers' market to more of a buyers' market in TV. This has created a more favourable negotiating environment and an opportunity to buy audiences at a decreasing cost.

The growing number of channels brings with it opportunities to test TV in a myriad of different ways. Channels inevitably perform differently for different products. Increased channel choice opens up the opportunity for DRTV planners to refine campaigns and secure DRTV success through testing and experimentation (see later note in this chapter).

The 6 different objectives of response TV

Because we have moved closer to a buyers' market the opportunities to use DRTV effectively have grown enormously. DRTV has evolved from simple one-stage product selling commercials to a wide range of companies using the medium to generate sales leads. Through this growth the creative community has become more comfortable with developing commercials that carry a 'phone number and invite a rational as well as an emotional response.

Another consequence is that several different types of response-generating TV commercial are emerging, each working towards a different objective, as we are about to see.

Today the traditional discriminators between "DRTV" and "brand" commercials are blurred. If a brand commercial carries a 'phone number does it stop being a brand commercial? Do the philosophies of branding have to be compromised in order to generate leads? If a commercial is written to include a 'phone number does it automatically become a DRTV commercial? Do all commercials with a 'phone number produce similar results?

The need for a clear objective

Sometimes advertisers will say: *"I want a DRTV campaign just like Direct Line ... I know branding and response objectives can be met without being diluted because Direct Line generate response and build a brand."* This is a good example of confusion about response-generating TV. The cause of this misunderstanding is the assumption that all TV commercials carrying a 'phone number generate immediate volume response.

This is simply not true. It requires far more than the presence of a 'phone number for five seconds to make a DRTV commercial generate cost-effective, volume response. It requires the application of a clear response-based philosophy which affects creative and media aspects of the campaign.

It requires far more than the presence of a 'phone number for five seconds to make a DRTV commercial ...

There is a golden rule for DRTV campaigns: **Do not mix your objectives**. If you want to generate immediate volume response cost-effectively, do not produce a branding commercial with a 'phone number as an accessory. You will be very disappointed with the levels and timing of response.

Equally important, if you do want to develop your brand, above all, don't employ the classic sales and lead-generation techniques employed by DRTV copywriters and media planners. Campaigns that do not meet response expectations are usually campaigns which have no clearly written brief.

In order to enjoy a successful DRTV experience, **be very clear about your campaign objectives** and make sure they feed through into creative and media development.

Remember: Not all commercials with telephone numbers are DRTV. There are several types of commercial carrying 'phone numbers, each with a different objective.

Here are the six most frequently used types of DRTV, each labelled with its primary objective. In the next few pages we look at each one in terms of its objective, media and creative considerations, method of evaluation and examples:

1.	One-stage direct sell
2.	Lead generator
3.	Product sampling
4.	Support of primary response activity
5.	Direct brands
6.	Brand differentiation

DRTV type 1 – One-stage direct sell

The main objective of a one-stage commercial is direct sales to viewers at an acceptable cost. This activity is also termed "off-the-screen" in contrast to its press equivalent "off-the-page". Viewers literally order during or immediately after seeing a product or service advertised.

As in the past, one-stage direct sales need low-cost airtime to succeed. As a result, off-the-screen activity is almost always found off-peak. However, with the advent of new channels, low prices are becoming available at other times of the day on certain channels.

Creatively, the style and content of these commercials are usually hard hitting. They use time-lengths of up to two minutes to develop their message and persuade the viewer to act, tending to follow the Attention, Interest, Desire, Action (AIDA) model. They hook viewers with interesting facts or appeals, then develop the selling benefits, establish a clear proposition, and ask for a response.

Direct sale commercials cannot afford to be bashful in displaying a 'phone number or calling for response. They often show the 'phone number at the beginning of the commercial to signal to the viewer that the message will seek a response. Some exponents suggest that the 'phone number should be on screen for 10–25 seconds, while other commercials have been produced with the number displayed for their entire duration.

One-stage direct selling is normally designed to be self-funding, and is therefore evaluated on a highly accountable cost-per-sale or cost-per-lead basis. They are what could be classified traditional DRTV commercials since examples date back to the 1970s.

Recent examples include:

- ✔ Linguaphone
- ✔ Oxfam
- ✔ Reader's Digest
- ✔ Sounds Direct
- ✔ RNLI
- ✔ NSPCC

Interestingly, publishers continue to be among the more successful users of this technique for reasons which students might like to debate. Charities are more recent users (since being permitted to advertise on TV) and for them a direct donation is the equivalent of a direct sale.

DRTV type 2 – Two-stage lead generation

Two-stage lead-generation commercials aim to begin a one-to-one dialogue with the respondent. This will hopefully lead to direct sales followed by cross- and up-selling. Frequently, all that is offered at this first stage is information with a compelling reason for viewers to make contact.

Media planning for two-stage is similar to that for one-stage direct sales. However, for example with mortgages, the allowable cost-per-lead may be considerably more generous than for relatively inexpensive product sales. This means that the media planner can sometimes move into more expensive airtime and so widen the choice of TV channels, times of day, etc. By moving out of regularly used DRTV airtime, such as daytime or late night, the quality of programme and audience can be improved. This can mean a better quality lead and customers with a higher long-term value.

Creatively, lead generators tend to follow the rules for selling off-the-screen. However, as you are asking the consumer for a lead as opposed to a sale, less direct "selling" may be required. As a result, commercials can be shorter – often between 30 and 60 seconds. Tone should be purposeful and businesslike. Humour should be used carefully and should not over-entertain, which can place viewers in a passive mindset not conducive to response.

Two-stage lead generators are evaluated much as one-stage direct sell commercials, with one difference. Some advertisers are prepared to **invest** in acquiring leads, via a higher allowable acquisition cost, giving media planners scope to move into channels and time segments they would not use for low-cost direct sales generation.

Examples of two-stage lead generators include:

✔ Auto Direct

✔ Cornhill

✔ Prospero

✔ Sun Life Over 50 Plan

Currently many successful users of two-stage enquiry generators emanate from the financial services where allowable costs-per-lead can be relatively high.

DRTV type 3 – Product sampling

Response TV techniques are increasingly being used to generate sample requests, much as other types of enquiry are generated. Using TV to encourage consumers to obtain samples is an effective way of building a database very quickly. This can be very important to consumer goods manufacturers who, in many cases, know what **types** of people buy their products, but not exactly who they are and where they live. As retailer strength continues to grow we shall see more moves by manufacturers to get closer to their customers in this way.

Media planning for sampling campaigns follows many of the general rules for one-stage and two-stage DRTV. Planners can make effective use of daytime slots because of their low cost and efficient delivery of "housewife" audiences.

The creative needs to be persuasive and offer-based to get the best results. If an established brand, the style and tone should be in keeping with the brand's character. **It should be made clear that the commercial is offering a free sample.** The 'phone number should be clearly displayed long enough for prospects to capture it. Results may be improved by running tests of different offers, for example in different TV regions.

Evaluation should be on the basis of the number of samples requested, along with the cost per request, but advertisers may also wish to monitor changes in the perception of the brand as a result of offering free samples. The databased relationship is likely to be developed through direct mail.

Examples:

✔ McVities

✔ Kenco

✔ Revlon age defying cream

✔ Fibre One (Cereal Partners)

Much experimental work in this field has been conducted in the US and many exponents are multi-nationals able to learn from their sister operations in other countries. In the US successful campaigns have been conducted using typical branding commercials "topped and tailed" with sample offers.

DRTV type 4 – Support for other response activity

Support TV campaigns are designed to raise awareness of specific direct response offers in other media such as direct mail, inserts or door-to-door. The aim is to increase response rates from the non-TV direct response activity. The activity **being supported** is called the "primary" activity, or alternatively the anchor medium (US).

As support TV is designed to raise awareness of a specific offer in another direct response medium, it is planned for maximum coverage of the response medium's target audience. For example, if it is a product appealing to housewives, then airtime that delivers housewife audiences efficiently is selected. If it is a male-oriented product, such as a DIY item, then male-oriented airtime would be selected.

The ratio of expenditure between primary and support activity is very important. Often the right media mix is specific to a certain product and some pre-testing may be required.

The creative for support TV does not have to be as long and hard-hitting as for one-stage or two-stage response commercials. **The purpose is to raise awareness of a specific offer.** This can be done with comparatively short lengths of between 10 and 30 seconds. The style and tone of the commercials should be informative and draw attention to the offer, for example: "In the next two days watch your letterbox for this offer" etc. (Support advertising is discussed in the creative chapters of this Guide.)

Support TV is evaluated on its ability to uplift response from the primary media. Al Eicoff in his book "Broadcast Direct Response Marketing" cites uplifts in primary media of between 50% and 80% when support activity is correctly planned. However, beware overspending on support media and having insufficient response media to capitalise on would-be responders.

Good example: Reader's Digest *"Win It, Don't Bin It."*

When contemplating support media of any kind, especially TV, remember successful users are invariably advertisers with already proven response campaigns. The basic offer should be successful before support activity is contemplated as TV backing does not in itself render mediocre campaigns successful.

DRTV type 5 – Promoting direct brands

Direct brands are a relatively new phenomenon. They are brands that distribute direct to the consumer and invest in developing a clearly differentiated **direct marketing** position, presenting themselves as modern organisations that deal with customers only by 'phone, fax or post – and thereby cut costs by reducing overheads. They invariably offer services that were previously only available through High Street locations or via intermediaries. Perhaps the best way to describe a direct brand is to cite First Direct Bank.

Direct brands approach media strategically as well as tactically. They aim to secure long-term brand awareness **as well as** short-term call volumes. Their objective is to raise awareness of, and position, the direct brand relative to their more conventional competitors. Their advertising demonstrates and emphasises that the consumer should access them initially by 'phone.

Direct brands employ the more traditional airtime used for brand awareness and development. This means peak time, which is expensive and less responsive than daytime, producing a very high cost-per-lead. However, it is more suited to the objective of raising brand awareness among large audiences. Often direct brands will run a multi-level media plan that includes peak-time brand positioning commercials and harder hitting off-peak DRTV commercials.

Direct brand commercials often exhibit classic brand advertising characteristics. They are short, often less than 30 seconds, with high production values. However, the distinguishing feature of a direct brand commercial is the message, ie that the advertiser should be contacted by 'phone. Not surprisingly a telephone will feature prominently, eg Direct Line's famous red telephone on wheels.

Direct brand commercials are not evaluated on their ability to generate leads alone – if they were, they would not be viable and would not exist. They are evaluated on their ability to raise awareness of, and to position, the direct brand. Higher airtime cost is acceptable because advertisers are investing in the equity of the brand more than in immediate response. The different elements of a multi-level campaign will be evaluated against appropriate criteria, eg awareness and positioning research for the branding element; cost per lead (and/or per sale) for the response element.

Examples include:

✔ Direct Line

✔ Eagle Star Direct

✔ First Direct

✔ Norwich Union Direct

Again we see the dominance of the financial services in this sector, not simply because they can usually invest in a higher acquisition cost, but also because they are better placed to calculate the long-term value of each new lead. Also financial products are more easily developed and can be despatched by post.

DRTV type 6 – Brand differentiation using response offers

As many markets, particularly fast-moving consumer goods (fmcg), mature and become more competitive, it is increasingly difficult to differentiate brands in new and exciting ways. Interactive response devices offer new ways of involving consumers in brand advertising. The objective is to differentiate brands **in an interactive way**, even though gaining response is not the primary objective. Response is simply part of the differentiating process – it can range from an offer, a sample or a competition to an outright gimmick.

Media is planned as for normal fmcg brand advertising. TV airtime for many interactive brands is oriented towards the 16–34 age group, cult status often meaning buying into cult TV programmes. There is no reliance on the traditional types of airtime used by DRTV advertisers despite the response element.

Creatively, with this type of interactivity, **the purpose is always, and only, to differentiate the brand**, ie to develop a personality for the brand that makes it stand apart from its competitors. Depending on the brand's personality, creative work can range from the mundane to the truly bizarre. This advertising has to captivate, fascinate and build brand credibility – the response element being effective only if it reinforces this objective.

Evaluation of interactive branding TV is primarily the traditional brand measures; movements in product sales, changes in market share, and shifts in attitudes towards the brand itself. Whilst high levels of consumer response indicate consumers' willingness to become involved in the advertising, these calls are not the purpose of the campaign.

Examples of interactive brand differentiation include:

- ✔ McCains Pizza
- ✔ Martini
- ✔ Pepperami perfume
- ✔ Tango

Note the youthful common denominator between most of the examples, young people being especially prone to respond to interactive offers and to use the telephone – as well as often being difficult to access by other media.

The keys to DRTV success

Despite our examples of response TV where the level and cost of responses was not a critical factor, for most exponents response is everything.

The **three key measures** which determine the success of a campaign which relies upon response for its success, are:

- ✔ The cost of airtime
- ✔ The cost of responses (airtime ÷ volume)
- ✔ The overall number of responses

In all three measures, the ability of a DRTV commercial to produce volume enquiries or sales is critical. So what drives up the volume of responses?

Driving up the response rate

As with all direct response advertising, whether using direct mail, press, inserts, door-to-door or telephone, response depends on the same six key factors, namely:

- ✔ Product and offer
- ✔ Target audience
- ✔ Media planning
- ✔ Timing
- ✔ Format
- ✔ Creative execution

Choice of product/service. As the earlier examples demonstrate, different types of product tend to be successful with different types of DRTV – some products are clearly suited to one-stage, to two-stage, to sampling, etc.

Partly this is because of their differing allowable costs-per-lead or per-sale. But there also seems to be an affinity between some products and the **method** of selling, especially the timing, eg music collections and low-cost late-night airtime; financial services and peak-time family viewing; "housewife" purchases with the morning coffee break, and so on. Some channels appear to be more successful for certain products.

Unfortunately, only testing, experiment, experience – and watching others – will determine whether **your** product is suited to DRTV.

The offer. As with all good response advertising, the choice and presentation of the offer are paramount. (See offers in the creative section of this Guide.)

Targeting. DRTV is not a highly targeted medium although some of the examples we have already mentioned show that some targeting by channel and time-slot is possible. One problem with TV is that it is sometimes possible to reach a small niche audience cost-effectively, but difficult to expand the activity to a volume audience. In some respects the "loose" targeting of TV is an advantage – see note on "hand-raising", page 4.3-15.

Media planning. We shall be looking at buying TV airtime in a moment.

Timing. Again we deal with this topic in somewhat more detail later in the chapter.

Creative execution. We have already outlined some of the ways in which response advertising differs in creative terms from brand advertising, and how one type of response objective calls for different creativity from another.

Nevertheless there is no harm in reminding ourselves of some of the more important aspects of **all** good direct response advertising which apply equally to DRTV:

✔ Be clear about your objectives.

✔ Make the creative work appeal directly to your target market – to the deliberate exclusion of everyone else.

✔ Arrest viewers' attention immediately.

✔ Have a powerful and motivating offer framed in an irresistible way.

✔ Support selling statements with product facts and features – in the case of TV, **demonstrate** them.

✔ Employ a clear and simple response mechanism.

✔ Capitalise on the brand's established personality.

Branding versus response – a comparison

The question of branding versus response is one that arouses much debate in TV circles. For example, whilst brand development relies on a "big idea" and often uses humour to deliver it, these two powerful communication tools are not the optimum approach for DRTV.

High performing DRTV commercials tend to work best with an opposite treatment. Rather than employing a "big idea", **DRTV attracts the most response by offering a single proposition supported in a number of ways**. For example, "Here is the product and these are the benefits you gain from using it." Humour can be distracting – consumers do not consider spending their money a joke! Efforts to amuse them may result in a sense of over-relaxation which can work against response to your commercial.

Driving down the cost of airtime

The other half of our evaluation measure for response TV is: **costs**.

Airtime costs are critical. Whatever you do, if you don't get the economics right, success will elude you. **The challenge for media buyers working on DRTV is to buy audience at the lowest possible rates.** This usually means working with the **least** demanded elements of the TV contractors' schedule, such as afternoons, night-time, or last-minute sales opportunities which have to be reacted to at very short notice.

The table below illustrates how, if response rates remain stable, reductions in media cost feed directly into lowering the cost-per-lead.

How reducing airtime costs lowers the cost-per-lead

Budget	Airtime cost per '000	Impacts obtained	Responses fixed at 0.03%	Cost per lead
£10,000	£5.00	2,000,000	600	£16.66
£10,000	£4.00	2,500,000	750	£13.33
£10,000	£3.00	3,333,333	1,000	£10.00
£10,000	£2.00	5,000,000	1,500	£ 6.66
£10,000	£1.00	10,000,000	3,000	£ 3.33

Clearly, the challenge for DRTV planners and buyers is to continually push the audience cost as low as possible without reducing the responsiveness. In this way the overall cost-per-lead falls, the campaign becomes more efficient, and runs longer.

The cost of TV production

For very large advertisers the cost of TV production, relative to airtime, may well be a small percentage which can be discounted. However, if the airtime budget is small, the cost of TV production can be considerable, even prohibitive. Some guidance on TV production costs therefore follows:

The first point to make here is that DRTV production does not need to cost the kind of money you hear talked about for image commercials. Very good DRTV commercials can be produced for around £30,000, give or take £10,000.

Some of the ways you can save money include:

✔ Stick to simple creative ideas – they not only cost less, they are also less distracting and therefore work better.

✔ Use location filming rather than a studio, example:

House set in studio:		**House on location:**	
Set cost:	£30,000	Use of house:	£1,000
		Extras (furniture):	£500

✔ Use real people rather than well-known actors. They cost (much) less and there will be no repeat fees to worry about.

Televisual magazine (November 1997) stated that whereas the average branding commercial costs £123,000, the average DRTV 30-second spot costs from £10,000 to £60,000.

How TV airtime is sold and bought

Supply and demand

Generally, the price of TV airtime is governed by the law of supply and demand. If the supply of airtime remains constant, when demand for airtime falls, prices fall. If demand rises, prices rise. But equally, if the supply increases and demand remains flat, prices fall. And if supply increases and demand does not increase at a corresponding pace, prices fall. Nothing new about that, but you might be surprised at the degree to which demand does rise and fall, likewise supply.

The 3 ways to buy TV airtime

Broadly there are three ways to buy TV airtime. They are:

✔ Cost-per-thousand audience

✔ Spot price

✔ Per response

We now look briefly at each of the above in turn.

Method 1: Cost-per-thousand (CPT) audience

In some respects TV audience buying is similar to direct mail list buying. It is generally bought on a cost per thousand (CPT) audience impacts. For example, if a spot delivers 5,000,000 adult impacts at a CPT of £2.00 the cost is:

$$(5{,}000{,}000 \div 1{,}000) \times £2.00 = £10{,}000$$

All TV negotiating is based on the cost of a 30-second commercial. If you wish to use different time-lengths simply multiply the 30-second cost by the relevant time-length factor, as shown below:

Time-length	Factor	Weighted cost
30-second	x 1	£10,000
10-second	x 0.5	£ 5,000
20-second	x 0.85	£ 8,500
40-second	x 1.33	£13,300
60-second	x 2.0	£20,000

Method 2: Spot price

TV spots can be bought and sold on a "spot price" basis. This usually occurs when the audiences are so small that they cannot be accurately measured and the CPT pricing method cannot be used. For example, if a 30-second spot is offered for £200 it may look a bargain. But if it only delivers 5,000 impacts then you are paying the following high cost-per-thousand:

£200 ÷ 5 = £40 per thousand

Even a £20 spot cost for 5,000 impacts would still be a CPT of £4, which is expensive for a DRTV campaign. Using the CPT methods the true value of this spot is in fact only £9.75. Bear in mind if you are offered a spot-priced TV deal, approach it with caution. It usually means the seller has something to hide – namely a lack of audience or very limited demand from other advertisers.

Method 3: Per response ("PI") deals

As the name suggests, these deals are based on the advertiser paying the TV contractor a fixed rate for each enquiry (inquiry in the US, hence "PI") or lead generated. So, for example, if a week's activity generates 2,000 leads at an agreed price of £10 per lead, then the advertiser pays the TV contractor £20,000.

PI deals tend to be offered only at times when demand is light. TV contractors are often unwilling to offer it, partly because they are dependent for their revenue on the sale or lead information the client supplies, and partly because they have no means of judging whether products will perform well and which will produce too few responses for their needs.

So what should you pay?

Most DRTV campaigns need to be bought in a CPT range of £1.00 to £3.00 to have a good chance of success. You can pay more, but only if you have tolerance within your campaign to accommodate an above average cost-per-lead or per-sale.

Airtime costs also vary seasonally because of variations of supply and demand, as explained. The estimated prices for the total 1996 TV airtime market, including ITV, Channel Four and satellite, are listed below for guidance.

Month	1996 adults cost per '000	Month vs annual average index
January	447p	76
February	475p	81
March	532p	91
April	646p	110
May	703p	120
June	729p	124
July	586p	100
August	497p	85
September	645p	110
October	682p	116
November	665p	113
December	496p	85
Average	587p	100

Source: DDS 1996 full year data for ITV/C4/Satellite "all-dayparts" price

If you are buying off-peak airtime, you should plan to reduce the above prices by around 40%–50% on terrestrial TV and by around 60% on satellite.

A 30-second spot in *Coronation Street* costing £75,000 may sound expensive. But if it delivers 15,000,000 viewers, then they are costing you just 500p per thousand, or a staggering half penny per viewer!

The difference between "hand-raising" and targeting

A targeting opportunity on TV is only of value if there is no prohibitive premium attached to accessing it. TV **can** present interesting programme-based targeting opportunities but these usually come with a hefty premium – especially on the terrestrial TV channels. The increase in response generated by the targeting is very rarely sufficient to absorb the premium. This means that programme targeting in DRTV can often be a red-herring.

However, some of the new generic cable and satellite stations, such as Home and Leisure (formerly TLC), Discovery, The Sci-Fi Channel, Carlton Food Network, MTV, etc, can produce audience targeting opportunities at a low enough cost to make them worth exploring.

And, of course, a certain degree of targeting is provided by the choice of channel – as already noted, some products/offers perform better on some channels than others, although you will not easily be able to predict this.

In any discussion on DRTV and targeting it is important to understand the difference between targeting and "hand-raising".

Hand-raising describes the act of prospects identifying themselves from newspaper or TV audiences directed at large numbers of readers/viewers. Within those audiences are "buried" a relatively small number of best prospects who figuratively "hold up their hands" by making contact with the advertiser, saying, in effect, "Yes, I'm a prospect."

DRTV and direct mail – a comparison

It is instructive to compare buying direct mail with buying DRTV at this point:

2 routes to a similar cost-per-response

	DRTV	**Direct Mail**
Media Budget:	£50,000	£50,000
CPT	150p	£100
TV Impacts/Names	16,666,000	500,000
Response rate	0.05%	5%
Responses	8,333	25,000
Media cost-per-response	£6	£2
Production	£35,000	£250,000 *
Total budget	£85,000	£300,000
Responses	8,333	25,000
Overall cost-per-response	£10.20	£12

*Assumes 50p per pack for production and postage for 500,000 items

Direct mail planners pay a premium to reach a highly targeted group of prospects in the expectation of generating high rates of response from them. They may pay as much as £100 per thousand for consumer names and addresses on the basis that their targeted selections will yield well above average response.

On the other hand, DRTV audience is bought so cheaply that "hand-raising" is a realistic objective. TV audience can be bought at as low as 150p per thousand adult impacts in off-peak airtime on some satellite channels. Profitable leads can be generated from a response as low as 0.05% ... **over 99% do not need to respond**.

The example on the facing page shows how, when properly planned and produced, DRTV can be an effective alternative to direct mail. The cost of postage and production for direct mail, although high, is sometimes overlooked when comparing the cost-benefits of DRTV and direct mail. If it is included, the £35,000 cost of producing the TV commercial makes DRTV look very attractive.

More importantly, in many respects, the figures show that DRTV can be used **in addition to** other media such as direct mail – the effective media planner is always looking for ways to broaden the customer acquisition media base and DRTV could be the way to reach prospects who cannot easily be reached by other methods.

Creative and targeting

Whilst DRTV specialists are planning TV on this "hand-raising" basis, **it is vital that the creative work is designed to attract the target audience**. In this sense the creative has another dimension in addition to communicating the offer and appealing for response. If too many of the wrong people respond, call handling resource can be wasted. Alternatively, if too few of the right people respond, the campaign risks being unsuccessful.

Timing: When in the day to advertise?

TV buyers and contractors divide the day into a number of timebands referred to as "dayparts". These are not cast in stone but generally run as follows:

Daypart	Description	Index of price vs average
07.00–09.30	Breakfast	60
09.30–12.00	Coffee time	60
12.00–16.00	Daytime	60
16.00–18.00	Pre-peak	100
18.00–20.00	Early peak	120
20.00–23.00	Late peak	125
23.00–24.30	Post-peak	100
24.30–06.00	Night-time	50–30

You will see that the price of airtime varies dramatically by daypart. As you would expect, peak is more expensive than off-peak. It contains higher quality programmes and, most importantly, delivers higher audiences. Many advertisers need these high audiences to build campaign coverage quickly and are prepared to pay a premium to get them.

Conversely, off-peak is least expensive and reaches smaller audiences, although these may be slightly better segmented, eg a higher proportion of housewives. For the DRTV media planner, off-peak has advantages and disadvantages as the chart below demonstrates.

Off-peak airtime – advantages and disadvantages for DRTV

	Pro		Con
✔	Costs far less than peak on cost-per-thousand basis	✘	Can be a DRTV "ghetto" in which too many advertisers seeking response can tire viewers
✔	Delivers smaller audiences and therefore manageable levels of response	✘	Tends to deliver excessive frequency which can be counter-productive in response terms
✔	A degree of selectivity may be possible, eg home products in daytime slots	✘	Limited coverage, only a fraction of the total TV audience
✔	Unhurried, relaxed viewers who are more likely to respond		

Testing and evaluating DRTV

DRTV offers a myriad of test opportunities and response performance can be compared and analysed across the following three main areas. If the various options available within each of these are permitted, it is possible to identify a staggering 200,000 different test opportunities.

- ✔ Geographical regions/station options
- ✔ Media options
- ✔ Creative options

Testing by geographical region/station option

The fourteen ITV regions and six Channel Four macro regions produce **twenty** basic geographical channel options for testing. In addition, cable, although still a minority medium, is franchised by local authority district which will eventually offer a combination of relatively high-resolution geographical targeting with the advertising power of a moving TV image. Satellite offers only a national option with no opportunity to subdivide the UK – but it does offer some compensation for this through the large number of lifestyle channels its presents.

Testing using media options

The media options in DRTV are enormous. Ten potential testing parameters are listed here. Media planners can look at the comparative performance of:

- ✔ channels;
- ✔ programmes;
- ✔ days of week;
- ✔ times of day;
- ✔ end breaks;
- ✔ centre breaks;
- ✔ positions within breaks;
- ✔ the effects of proximity pairing (putting commercials close to each other, in the same programme or clock hour for example);
- ✔ short- and long-term frequency effects over days, weeks and months.

Testing creative options

From a creative perspective the test opportunities are similarly extensive. Marketers and their agencies can compare the effects of:

- ✔ different creative executions; *
- ✔ commercial time-lengths;
- ✔ phone number types;
- ✔ voice-overs;
- ✔ durations of 'phone number display.

* Owing to production costs, it is usually more expensive to expand the number of creative executions than to increase the number of media or geographical options.

Planning for response handling and fulfilment

Response handling in DRTV has become an industry issue. It is claimed by agencies that handling houses do not have sufficient response handling capacity and should invest more money in its development. Likewise, response handling houses claim that agencies do not appreciate their needs and involve them too late in the planning process. So who is telling the truth? Well, both have a point, but there is a solution.

Advanced planning is the key in all cases

The agency should develop a model that informs it of the level of audience it is able to buy in different geographical regions **without exceeding response handling capacity**. For example, if a handling house can manage 200 calls in a 10-minute period on a campaign that is estimated to produce a response rate of 0.025%, then the maximum audience it can comfortably manage is 800,000. Any audience above this will produce lost calls and irritated prospects.

The response handling house should advise the media planning agency if it is handling other accounts that are likely to produce large volumes of calls and constrain its overall call handling capacity. The drive to maximise revenue may tempt it to avoid this issue, but if the campaign is deemed a failure then it and the agency run the risk of losing repeat business from the client.

Remember: Advanced planning is the key in all cases.

Designing the call answering process

The development of software to run the campaign is of major importance. This applies to live operator and automatically answered campaigns. Live operators require an easy to follow and flexible scripting system which allows them to appear to be part of the company they are representing. Automated systems should be user-friendly for the consumer and make it easy and tempting for them to co-operate.

See also chapters on telemarketing (Chapter 5.3) and fulfilment (Chapter 7.9).

Managing the moment of truth

Advertisers and their agencies must be prepared to invest time and energy in response planning. Although call handling appears to be the least glamorous part of a TV campaign, **it is in fact the most important**. When the consumer interacts with **your** organisation, they are walking into **your** shop and experiencing **your** service. If they are contacting you for the first time, this is where those crucial first impressions are formed. If you fail the consumer here, the campaign fails. The work of everyone involved in other parts of the campaign may be totally wasted.

Call statistics

Through BT's Enhanced Information Statistics (EIS) reports, advertisers can independently monitor the performance of their response handling house. BT can produce statistics that record the total number of calls made to a specific number, the number of calls captured, the date and time they occurred, call waiting time, calls lost and call durations.

So, if you represent a fulfilment house and happen to be studying this Guide, be warned!

For further information on DRTV, refer to BT/Channel Four research into direct response television, 1995.

Chapter 4.4

Radio – getting results at last

This chapter includes:

- How radio "works"
- Who listens to commercial radio?
- Radio as a targeting medium
- Radio response know-how grows
- Advice on scheduling
- How and where to buy airtime
- Research statistics galore

One of the authors of this chapter writes in his biography: "In 1992 commercial radio needed someone with a typical advertising industry attitude to the medium – a mixture of ignorance, prejudice and vague curiosity."

Now, at last, things have begun to change and radio is being taken seriously as a potential source of leads and sales. What has changed? Mainly the structure of the industry, with more stations, more listeners, and more targeting and testing opportunities.

One other thing has changed: the realisation of how radio works. For whilst in many respects it resembles TV without pictures, radio is regarded by its listeners as being more akin to magazines.

In fact, of course, radio is unique. How and why it is unique is what Clive Reffell and Andrew Ingram are about to explain. They also examine the evidence for radio as a serious direct response medium, and give advice on making it pay.

New in this edition. There was no separate chapter for commercial radio in our first edition, which itself speaks volumes.

Clive Reffell, Advertising Consultant, RAB

Clive was one of the founders of the Radio Advertising Bureau which promotes the benefits of commercial radio to advertisers. That was in 1992. In the five years that followed, radio's share of total display advertising expenditure grew from 2% to 5%. Clive's roles are to advise advertisers on campaign ideas and to liaise with radio sales teams on presentations.

His qualification to join the RAB was fifteen years in full-service ad agency media departments. The first was Ogilvy & Mather, which came as a bit of a surprise as he'd answered an advertisement for someone to go on Mediterranean cruises and write brochure notes! He eventually became responsible for media planning and buying for Ogilvy's in-house direct response unit which later became O & M Direct.

Stints of "mainstream" media planning and buying at KMP, Leo Burnett and KHBB led to career highpoints: twice winning the NABS Rugby Sevens in the Carlsberg team and playing for the English Advertising Agency XV against French counterparts in Hong Kong.

Since joining the RAB, Clive has spoken at conferences in Dublin, Barcelona and around the UK, and gained his CAM Diploma in Advertising.

Clive Reffell
Radio Advertising Bureau
77 Shaftesbury Avenue
London W1V 7AD
Tel: 0171-306 2500
E-mail: clive@rab.co.uk

Andrew Ingram, Account Planning Director, RAB

Andrew admits he knew very little about radio when he joined the Radio Advertising Bureau. This was deliberate RAB policy: what they wanted was an account planner with a typical advertising industry attitude to radio – a mixture of ignorance, prejudice and vague curiosity. So no change there!

Account planning at the RAB involves commissioning and analysing research and other projects which help to illuminate radio for potential users. He describes the challenge as finding out what radio is, deciding whether it's any use to anyone, and dramatising the conclusions.

Andrew has a broad-based background in advertising and media, having started in the advertisement department of the Daily Mail, going on through quantitative research (AGB) and qualitative research (he was a director of Winstanley Douglas Partners), eventually moving into account planning in 1989 at Davis Wilkins (which eventually became TBWA). Here his key accounts were the Daily Telegraph and Direct Line Insurance.

He won an IPA Advertising Effectiveness Award in 1992 on the launch of Direct Line Insurance.

Andrew Ingram
Radio Advertising Bureau
77 Shaftesbury Avenue
London W1V 7AD
Tel: 0171-306 2500
E-mail: andrew@rab.co.uk

Chapter 4.4

Radio – getting results at last

How radio came of age

Commercial radio started in the UK in only 1973 (although pirate broadcasting goes back much further), so it is a very young medium compared to press and commercial TV.

Recent developments mean that radio has to be taken much more seriously as an advertising medium. There are some obvious signs of this, for example:

- ✔ Over 200 radio stations now broadcast in the UK.
- ✔ There are now national, regional, local and community stations.
- ✔ The reach of commercial radio now stands at 28.5 million adults per week (1997).
- ✔ 47 of the top spending 50 advertisers in 1996 used radio.
- ✔ Under the Broadcasting Act, the government set up a new body in 1990 – the Radio Authority – to run commercial radio separately from TV.
- ✔ In 1996 copy clearance was separated from that of TV with the setting up of the Radio Advertising Clearance Centre.

As radio has developed, the direct response sector has also begun to take it more seriously (a quarter of national radio ads now have a telephone response mechanism), although knowledge and working norms are not yet as well advanced as for TV and press.

How has radio changed?

The first step in understanding radio is to take a look at the structural changes in the medium. These have occurred in three fundamental areas:

- ✔ Many more people are listening.
- ✔ There are many more stations (and more to come).
- ✔ Radio is eminently more targetable.

In the early years the independent local radio stations tended to broadcast a mixed bag of output designed to appeal to as many people as possible. However, a number of developments changed this situation, as follows:

✔ Policy on awarding new licences (administered since 1990 by the Radio Authority) means that a new station in any given area must offer something which existing stations do not – ie it must extend choice.

✔ As the number of stations increased, individual services became more defined in their output.

✔ New "tiers" of radio station were also established – national, regional and community (also known as incremental). This gave advertisers and listeners a choice which differed not only by type but also by geographic range.

The effects of these changes can be seen in the typical range of options available to Birmingham listeners shown below:

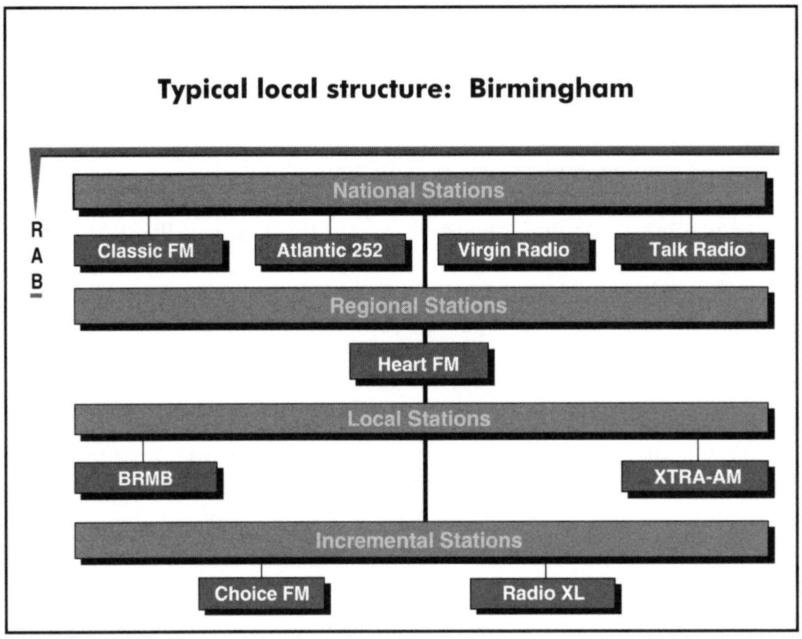

Radio is now defined by content

Although local stations continue to account for the majority of commercial radio listening in the UK (each local station usually offers a different service on its AM and FM frequencies), the newer stations have become increasingly important. The new stations mostly offer a more tightly defined content, eg specific types of music, speech radio, ethnic programming, and so on. The audiences are by definition often niche markets.

This growth in choice for the listener has, not surprisingly, meant a huge growth in audiences, most of whom are people who used to listen to BBC Radio. Allied to greater segmentation, the new audience means new opportunities for all types of advertiser, especially those for whom targeting is vital.

How radio "works" in the marketplace

On the face of it, radio and TV seem similar. They are both broadcast and both **intrude** into consumers' lives. This makes radio ideal for conveying new ideas and for getting listeners to think about issues they might not otherwise consider. But the similarities probably end there.

In many ways, radio is more like magazines, largely because of the way people "consume" it.

According to research, here are some of radio's chief differences:

✔ **Solitary**: radio tends to be listened to alone, allowing the advertiser to speak to the consumer as an individual rather than as part of an audience (that's how presenters are briefed to speak).

✔ **Personal spaces**: most radio listening takes place in people's personal spaces such as the kitchen, bathroom, car, etc. This provides the advertiser with a remarkable opportunity to "sit down next to the listener". Advertising can be timed to coincide with the likely location of the target audience at any time of the day, making the offer more relevant to what they are doing.

✔ **"A friend"**: people invariably describe their radio station as a friend. This allows the advertiser to piggy-back on some of those friend-values (recommendation by a friend always helps credibility), which can be very important for brands seeking to build trust or familiarity.

> When creating radio commercials remember that sergeant-major types shouting and actors putting on silly voices are unlikely to be considered friends – and thereby miss out on one of radio's prime strengths: its friendliness.

✔ **Loyal/habitual**: the majority of listening is habitual – listeners tune to the same stations at the same time each day. Even when there is a wide choice. For advertisers this means a higher exposure of the message (Opportunities To Hear or "OTH") than with TV.

✔ **Secondary/passive**: nine out of ten people listen to radio while doing something else, eg driving, cooking, cleaning. According to the Henley Centre, 79% say they are at least half-paying attention at any given time. 39% say they are paying attention most or all of the time.

But we have to be realistic – listeners can easily be distracted and miss an ad. However, because of the habitual nature of radio listening, if they don't hear your ad in full first time, there will be many subsequent chances. Creative work should take account of this.

✔ **Linear**: because radio uses words in real time, it does not allow the listener to go back over the offer in an ad. It therefore works best when the offer is simple. Again frequency means that the listener will get a chance to hear the ad on subsequent occasions.

✔ **Immediacy/topicality**: radio operates in the present all the time. It's not pre-recorded like TV. Stations exploit this advantage with up-to-the-minute news, weather and travel information. Advertisers can also use this topicality to great benefit.

✔ **Culture of response**: radio presenters thrive on asking listeners to 'phone, fax or write in with their views and requests for freebies, samples, promotions, competition entries, etc. Listeners are thus accustomed to reacting to what they hear on radio, **and** doing so quickly.

✔ **Emotional**: although radio is an information medium (witness the number of news, travel and weather bulletins), it also operates at a very emotional level (one reason why charities find it so effective). For advertisers this can be useful for communicating brand values, especially the caring attitude some advertisers wish to convey. Listeners often judge commercials by "the way the advertiser comes over".

These characteristics of radio have implications for marketers at two levels:

✔ **Creative content** – commercials which will be heard repeatedly should take account of "how they come over". Thoughtful writing and production ensure ads can be enjoyed and remembered by all the listeners, not just those who respond.

✔ **Strategic application** – the linear, invisible nature of radio means it is less good at detail and better at intruding with new ideas or continual reminders. This has led some advertisers to use radio as an "indirect response" medium, generating a desire to respond which is fulfilled via other media.

Who listens to commercial radio?

Many advertisers still do not realise the surprising coverage offered by commercial radio, so let us look at some figures:

The chart below shows that the commercial radio audience comprises 80% of "Under 55" adults over 4 weeks, or around 60% over a single week. The figures for "Over 55s" (who tend to be more loyal to BBC Radio) are nearer 60% and 40% respectively.

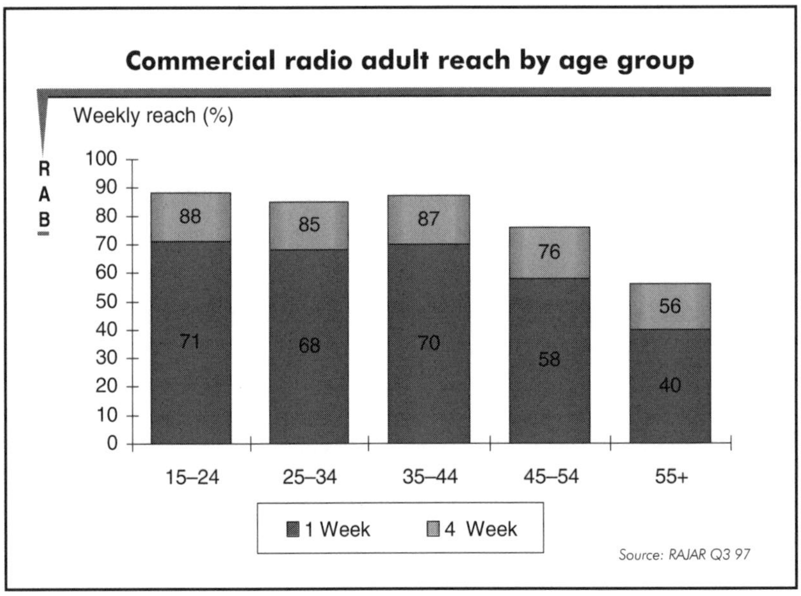

The next graph shows how commercial radio reaches the UK population in terms of socio-economic groupings. The high ABC1 content of the total audience will no doubt surprise some marketers.

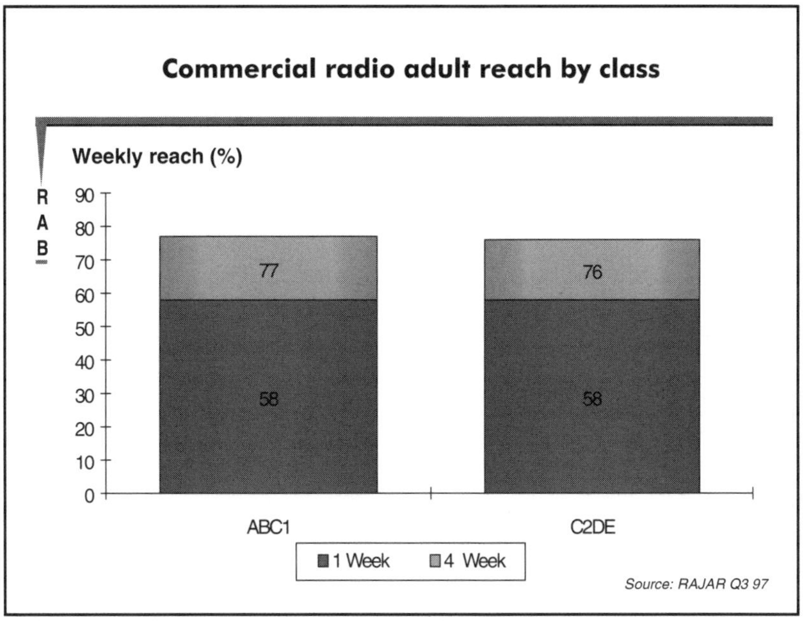

Radio as a targeting medium

Targeting by station content/style

The macro-level analysis above hides the fact that individual commercial radio services offer very effective targeting of certain key groups. While radio delivers to a mass audience, this can also be broken down very finely – as small as a single daypart on a single local station.

Since new radio stations are obliged to offer new choices for the listener in order to secure a licence, the radio marketplace is becoming highly segmented.

London (see graphic overleaf) is the most developed radio market in the UK. But, as we have seen, similar sophisticated choices apply in Birmingham, and to a slightly lesser degree in most other major population areas.

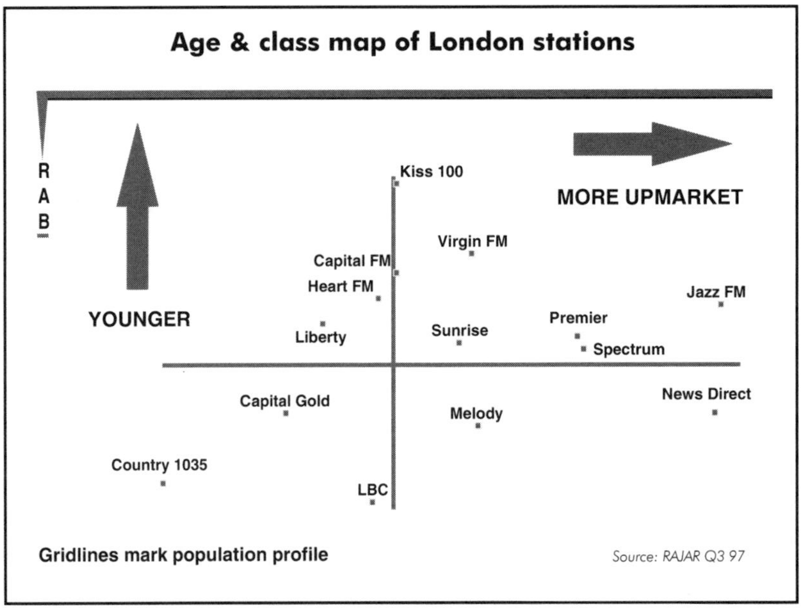

As we have already noted, this choice makes commercial radio much more like the magazine marketplace, offering tightly targeted audiences for the direct response advertiser.

Targeting by time of day

Another useful targeting factor is the time when particular target audiences are at their peak. For most target audiences it is breakfast time, but commercial radio delivers a higher adult audience than commercial TV until 4 pm on weekdays.

Some audience subgroups have very different listening patterns from the all-adult "average". Students, for example, are more likely to listen late at night than first thing in the morning – a fact taken into account by the banks when seeking new recruits by radio.

The chart below traces the adult radio audience for a typical weekday and compares it with that for independent television.

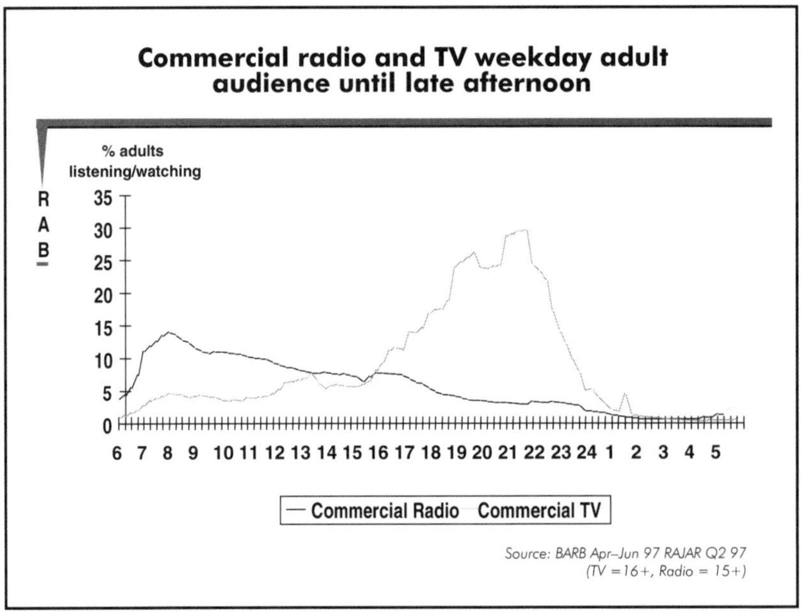

Targeting by listeners' locations

Commonsense says that what listeners are doing, or where they are, may be important to advertisers. For example, research has shown that people are much more "car-minded" when in their car, making it a good time for insurance companies, car dealers, motoring magazines and breakdown services. Similarly, people at work are less inclined to think about products for the home.

Below are two summary graphs of listening location across the day. The first graph is for listeners in full-time work.

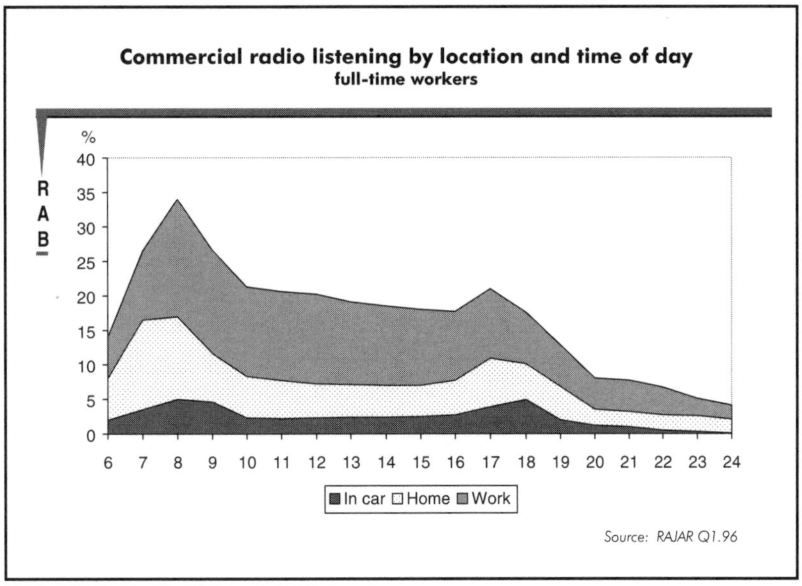

The following graph is for listeners who are not in full-time work. The overall reach is lower – clearly going to work predisposes people to listen to radio.

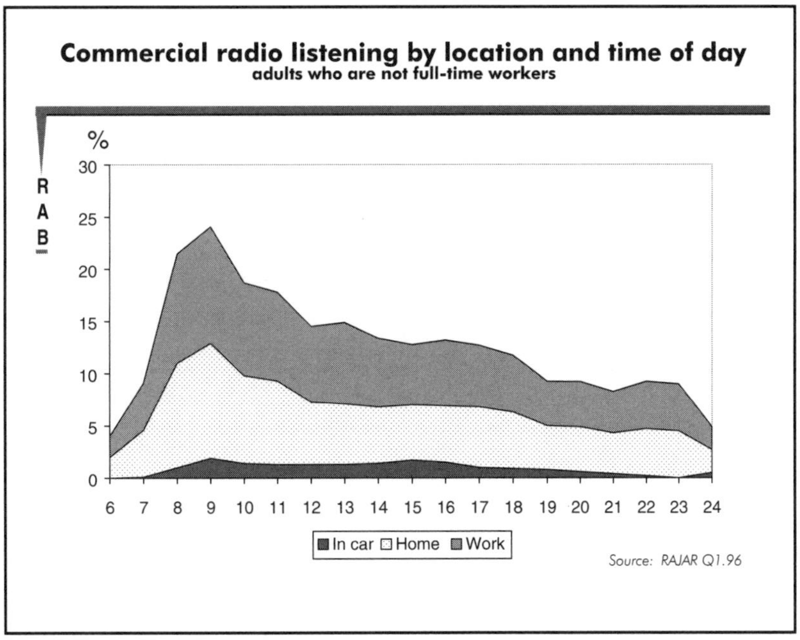

Direct response on radio

It's worth remembering that commercial radio started life as a local medium utterly dependent on response. Local businesses who advertised would simply not continue if they didn't see a tangible upturn in sales, store traffic, visitors, etc. There could be no better demonstration of radio's ability to generate business.

But what about the national level? In common with other media, radio has seen a significant shift towards advertisers running ads with some form of response mechanism. The figures below are based on an analysis by the Radio Advertising Archive which logs radio commercials distributed nationally.

% of nationally distributed ads with telephone response mechanism

	1995	1996
Total	17	26
Financial	50	91
Motors	22	22
Holidays/travel	16	33
Utilities	26	81
Household	9	25
Office equipment	47	44

Source: GWR Radio Group, BT, Classic FM & DMA

Ads with a telephone response mechanism, not surprisingly, tend to be longer – there must be enough time to explain the offer and to read out the 'phone number. Below is a comparison of commercial lengths with and without response data:

% of ads with a 'phone number	Length of ad (seconds)	% of ads with no 'phone number
1	10	3
4	20	13
34	30	47
38	40	23
10	50	3
11	60	9
2	60+	2
100%		100%

Source: GWR Radio Group, BT, Classic FM & DMA

Response plus awareness: Radio's dual role

Are all ads with a telephone number direct response ads?

Clearly not. It is wrong to assume that a response mechanism means an ad is primarily response-based. Ads in most media operate at more than one level. Here again there are parallels with magazines.

Consider, for example, a double-page spread for cars in any consumer magazine. There will usually be some form of response mechanism, perhaps even a coupon, but will the effectiveness of the ad be judged purely on the level of that response?

In other words, the effect of the advertising amongst **non**-responders needs to be planned – and budgeted for.

'Phone company gets right number

A good example is the Carphone Warehouse which has secured huge top-of-mind awareness amongst radio listeners – even amongst those who have no current plans to buy a mobile 'phone. At the same time immediate responses provide the company with a continuous source of leads and sales.

The main point here is to be clear about your objectives. To what extent are response and/or brand promotion your aim? How much are you prepared to invest in brand awareness/positioning, etc. – and how much are you prepared to pay for replies? How many replies do you need/expect from a given expenditure?

Having said that, remember radio **is** used very successfully by advertisers wholly dependent upon immediate and measurable response, eg the music clubs with their offers of CD collections.

Your objectives will also determine the length and creative content of your radio commercial, which will in turn affect your response levels.

Your questions about response answered

As part of its free consultancy service to advertisers and agencies, the Radio Advertising Bureau receives a lot of questions about response on radio. What the industry has done here is to pool its knowledge on the most frequently asked questions. Regrettably, but not surprisingly, the answer to most of them is "it depends"!

We include here findings of research carried out by the GWR radio group (owners of several local stations and Classic FM), BT, and the DMA. Further details can be obtained from GWR Group, Classic FM or the DMA. Contact numbers are at the end of the chapter.

What level of response can I expect?

This is the most difficult question of all. The biggest factor is the offer itself – naturally a weak or generic offer attracts little interest no matter how cunningly phrased and repeated. Conversely, a strong offer can generate immediate results.

Paid £50 for a test drive

A car manufacturer had to cancel a radio campaign after only one day. His offer was to pay motorists £50 if they called dealers for a test drive. Direct marketers will not be surprised to learn that dealers were inundated.

But somewhere between an unconditional offer which is too generous and a less generous or more conventional offer, there lies an offer that could have been just right. What's not in doubt from this experience is radio's ability to convey offers and to generate response.

Below are the findings from the GWR/BT/DMA study. The total average response was 0.15%, but among the Top 10 advertisers the average was ten times higher. This demonstrates the wide range of responses that can be experienced on radio.

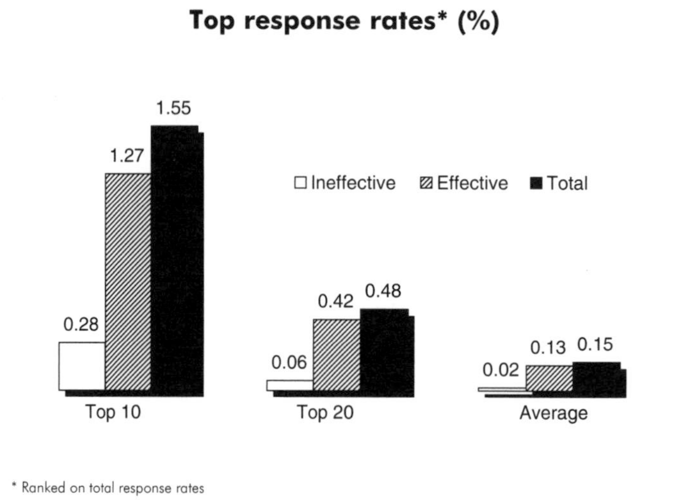

Should I use radio on its own or with another medium?

There are successful examples of both methods. If the offer is complex or beset with terms and conditions, it makes sense to use some form of print in tandem – newspapers, magazines, door-to-door, etc. Using more than one medium can also trigger the well-known "media multiplier" effect, significantly increasing awareness of the offer. (See also support media discussed elsewhere in this Guide.)

Greater inherent awareness of the advertiser helps. The GWR/BT/DMA study showed that advertisers who had previously been on TV enjoyed higher overall response on radio than those who had not. (See next chart, opposite.)

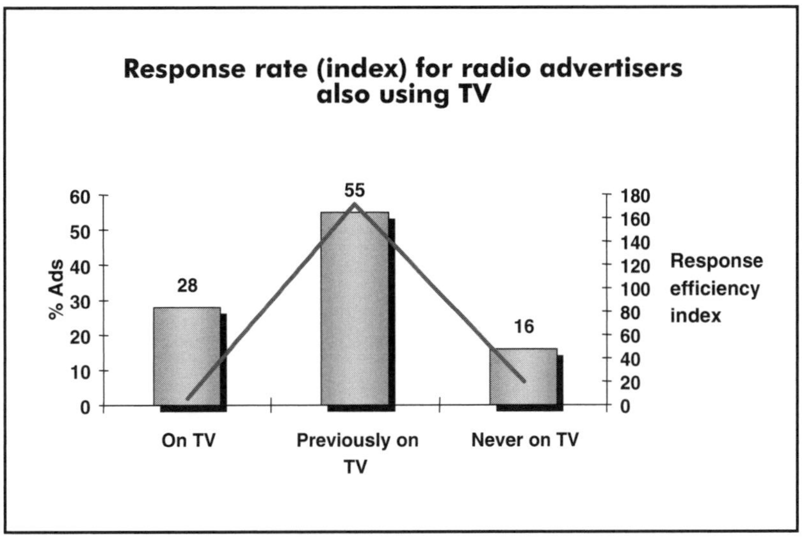

Can I expect response immediately?

This is really two questions:

? How long after my commercial first goes on-air will I start to get calls?

? Once my commercial is recognised, how quickly will the telephone ring – and for how long – after each spot transmission?

Major radio advertisers say that radio response often does not optimise until a campaign has been running for at least a few days. This makes sense when you consider that the first spot may find the potential responder unable to note the number – but still interested, and therefore listening out for the next airing.

The GWR/BT/DMA study says:

The call level in the ten minutes before a radio spot goes on-air gives an indication of the general level of calls. Monitoring the levels of calls after the spot shows how long the increased rate can be expected before it settles back to its general level.

The next chart (overleaf) suggests that most calls generated by a radio ad are received over the next five minutes. This demonstrates the immediate effect – but of course many individuals will remember or note the number and call later, thus adding to the general background level of calls.

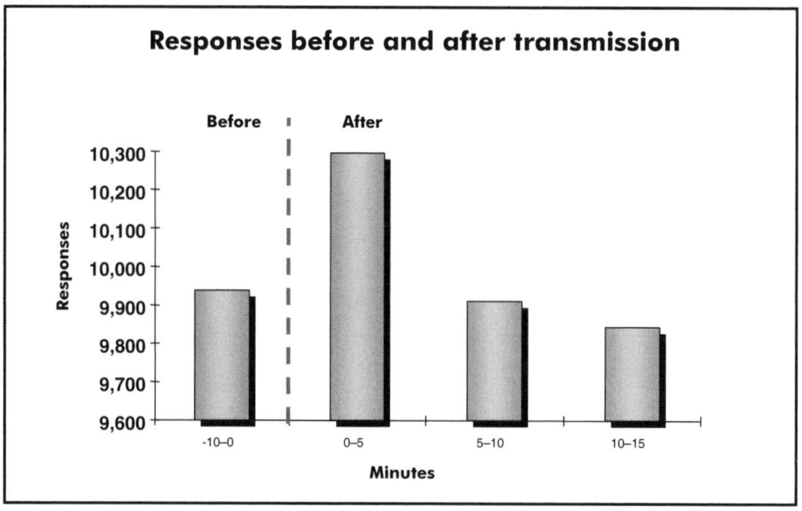

How many times should we repeat the 'phone number?

There are examples of successful campaigns (eg Marie Curie Cancer Care) which use only one mention of the 'phone number – typically at the end, after the persuasive sale has taken place.

However, there is no doubt that repetition makes it easier for consumers to remember. Some direct response specialists, including the marketers of compilation CDs, recommend that the number should be given once during the offer, and repeated once again at the end. This is a convention which listeners recognise, although it can make for tedious listening.

An alternative approach, used by Direct Line Insurance for example, is to refer the listener to a known source, eg "for our number, see the back of the Thomson Local Directory", or "see our ad in the Yellow Pages". For more tactical offers radio commercials can refer listeners to their local evening paper.

How many operators should we have to handle response?

As with response, the answer is very dependent on the offer **and on the type of telephone number you use**. Many listeners are aware of the range of commonly used response numbers varying in cost from free to premium rate.

How awareness varies according to type of number is shown next:

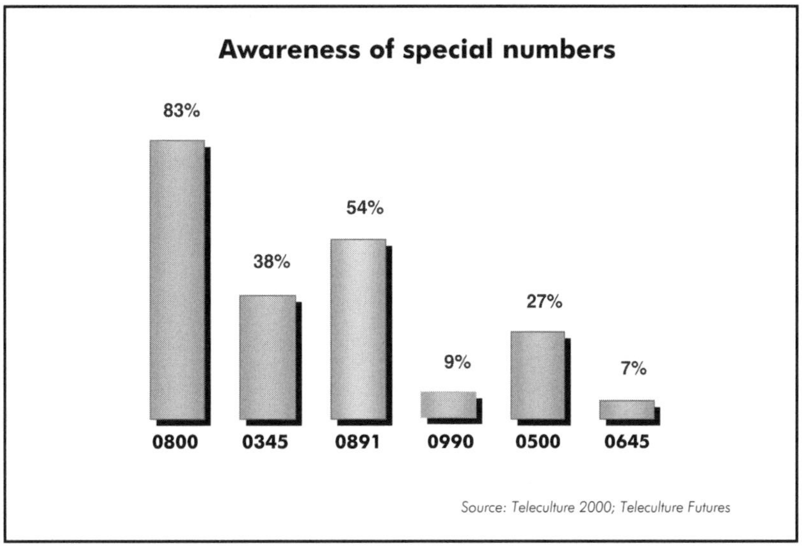

The rule of thumb is that free calls generate the highest level of response, but usually the poorest quality in terms of conversions. If you plan to mail expensively produced material, or offer a personal visit, then a charge-call number may effectively screen out time-wasters who will cost you money.

The following table shows average response rates to free 0800 numbers compared with 0345 local rates and 0990 premium rates. (See also the section in this Guide on inbound telephone marketing, Chapter 5.3 and on fulfilment, Chapter 7.9.)

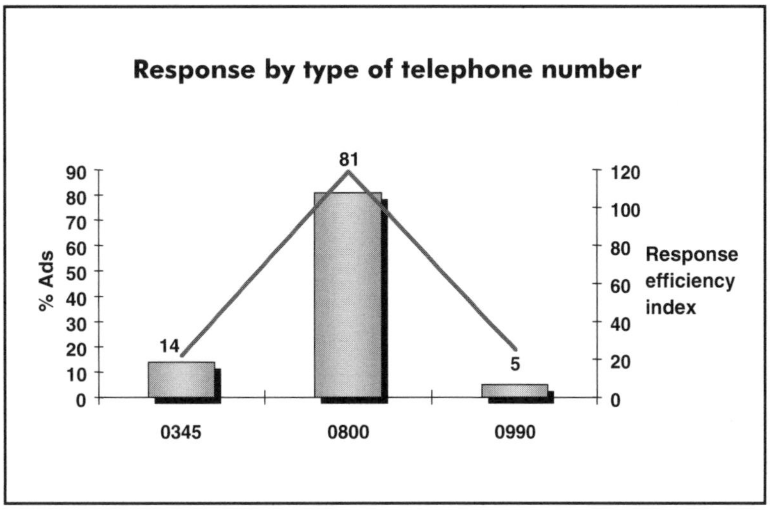

Can radio be used for testing?

Experienced response advertisers on radio continually recommend testing – and radio is the ultimate testable medium. Test campaigns can be local or regional, limited to a single station, varied with different approaches over several stations, with different types of telephone reply number, and so on.

What is the best time of day for response?

The Carphone Warehouse finds that a peak spot reaching 10% of the audience works better than ten off-peak spots reaching 1%. By contrast Abbey Life found that for a critical illness health plan, low-rating, off-peak airtime provided the highest response.

Anyone at home?

An advertiser recruiting arthritis sufferers to test new drugs achieved good results during daytime on weekdays on Melody FM, a London station which caters for slightly older listeners. If they were going to be available for weekday hospital visits, they had to be able to respond to weekday commercials and not be at work.

Below is a chart showing response by time of day, from the GWR/BT/DMA study.

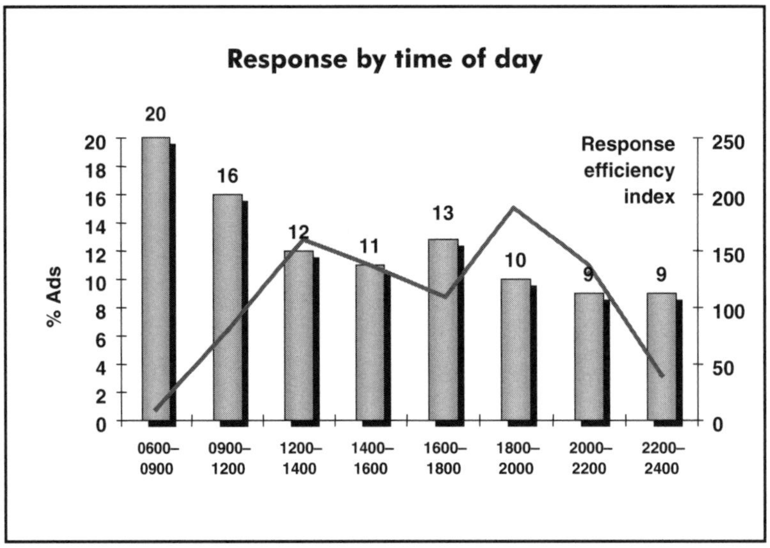

Generally, response efficiency increases after midday. People come home who perhaps could not ring from work or from their car. Access to a telephone is thus a major criterion – **when will your target audience be able to call?** There is also a perception that calling is cheaper after 6pm. However, you may need to build awareness through the day in order to enhance evening responses.

Weekday or weekend can also be a factor. Many business-to-business advertisers, such as business class airlines and mobile telephone companies, use little or no airtime at weekends as they consider their target audience is not in a business-like frame of mind. Overall, though, **response rates tend to be higher at weekends**, despite lower audiences.

Response by time of week

	% of Ads	Efficiency
Weekday	80	89
Weekend	20	146

First come, first served

A clothes shop for young adults was opening in Croydon. They had a special offer on Levi 501s, so decided to open at 5.01 in the morning for novelty expecting few shoppers to turn up.

The shop advertised only late at night on London's Kiss 100 FM in the week of the store opening. After the clubs in Croydon closed in the early hours of the morning of the opening, the police were called to the shop's address. The crowd was so big they had to erect barriers to keep the road clear and prevent people falling through the shop windows.

Targeting – where to start?

The starting point for planning any radio campaign – direct response or otherwise – is RAJAR, the radio audience survey operated jointly for the BBC and commercial radio.

Consumers are asked to fill in a diary detailing a week of their radio listening. The total sample is over 160,000 people a year, so sample sizes are robust (RAJAR is the biggest media research survey outside the USA).

RAJAR results are made available to subscribers on a quarterly basis, on-line and as hard copy. Computer analysis can identify which stations and dayparts offer the best coverage of the target market, and how frequency builds over time.

Apart from listening behaviour, RAJAR also records demographics, home ownership, ethnic group, neighbourhood type (ACORN and Mosaic), and many other variables (more details available from RAB OnLine).

However, the numbers are just the start. While they offer guidance on where the best opportunities are, only testing and experience can reveal the value of different strategies.

Advice on scheduling

The advice always offered to new direct marketers is – **test** (radio is no different from other media in this respect). With this in mind, what follows is some thinking on different ways of scheduling airtime.

Radio is low cost

The costs of media and production are low for radio, so it remains an excellent medium for testing. But make sure that if you test different copy – or stations, or times of day, or weights of advertising – you test only one thing at a time, otherwise the results will be inconclusive. Even a poor response is not a waste of money if you learn what does not work.

Radio is transient

Press ads can be studied at length by consumers and first insertions in carefully selected press titles tend to get the highest response. The reverse is sometimes true with radio: allow time for the message to get home, and for awareness of the offer to build over time. With radio, frequency builds recognition of the offer, which in turn leads to increased likelihood of response.

Habitual listening patterns

Daily listening patterns tend to be the same every weekday – although weekends have their own pattern, as RAJAR reveals. This means that "horizontal slotting" can work very effectively, ie using the same time of day on consecutive weekdays builds frequency very quickly.

Monitor the airtime

In order to understand which airtime has created which effect, it is important to look at the playout times of the ads actually run. Stations sometimes run free additional spots as fillers (although this is rarer nowadays as there is less availability). You need to know whether this has happened.

Geodemographics

RAJAR is fully compatible with geodemographic analysis, making radio an ideal partner for targeting housing types, linking with door-drops, direct mail, etc.

XXXX: four times

*Castlemaine XXXX used geodemographics for the targeting of its "Back of Beyond" door-to-door campaign. With radio support the money-off coupon, redemptions were **four times** the average for alcoholic drinks, according to the Institute of Sales Promotion.*

In-house or bureau?

Long before your radio commercial is due to be run you need to plan your response handling arrangements.

The first consideration is whether to handle calls internally or through a telephone bureau service. For a limited campaign in-house call handling may be sufficient, but bear in mind:

- **?** How many lines has your office switchboard – is it enough?
- **?** Are enough of your staff skilled to handle call taking? This is business, not a conversation with a friend
- **?** If new callers fill your regular telephone lines, what are the consequences for your regular customers who may not be able to get through?
- **?** Have you a system to record and collate respondents' details?
- **?** What would your staff usually be doing if they were not taking these calls? Is it satisfactory for this regular work not to be done on time?
- **?** How will calls outside office hours be handled?

Bureau services offer skilled personnel and sophisticated call receiving and information collation systems, whilst freeing up your own workforce for their regular tasks. But a caller encouraged to respond usually assumes the person taking the call (and in the UK most of us still prefer to get through to a real person) works for the company that placed the advertising. So, it is important to **fully** brief the bureau and involve them in your operation. They become your front-line contact with potential new customers.

The subject of call handling is fully dealt with in this Guide in the chapters on telemarketing (5.3) and fulfilment (7.9).

Keeping the caller waiting?

A variety of types of number is available, as discussed earlier, but particularly relevant to radio is the amount of information you wish to gather.

A caller who is kept on the line answering too many questions may resent having to pay for the call, and hang up. But a Freephone or 0800 number, at no cost to the caller, may encourage time-wasters and hoaxers that will cost the advertiser money. Again, we can only suggest you **test**.

Radio spot times – can they be fixed?

Several direct response advertisers say they have been put off radio because they cannot always be told accurate spot times in advance.

Knowing spot times will help an experienced direct response advertiser to know how many telephone lines and call-takers to have available at particular times during the day, and will help in briefing a bureau.

However, radio is much more flexible than TV. Advertising minutage per hour is not fixed by legislation, the technology is much simpler, and it is possible for advertisers to react to events faster than in other media. Spot times, therefore, are sometimes subject to change at the last minute. But if your total airtime is planned and controlled, the specific timing of each spot (particularly if you use a number of stations) is unlikely to be significant. Individual spot changes across a number of stations will probably even out over your designated time bands.

The alternative is to pay premium rates to guarantee your spots at fixed times, but then you have to consider the additional response needed to offset the higher media cost of perhaps 20%.

Analysing your radio campaign

Within a solus radio campaign

A thorough system would collect details of the number of calls by time of day and by origin. Matched against spot times on each station, it should be possible to determine response levels as a percentage of the target audience listening – by day of week, time band within each day (daypart), and time length. Audience figures at specific spot times can be obtained direct from stations, their national sales house or your advertising agency.

$$\text{Response rate (\%)} = \frac{\text{No. of calls}}{\text{Audience size}} \times 100$$

Try the calculation above using total adult audience and then only those listeners who are in your target audience. This will help show the benefit of specifying times when your audience is likely to be listening.

Such an analysis will not be foolproof, as listeners may write down numbers to call at a later time (perhaps when they reach work, get out of the car, etc). BT claim the peak time of the week for telephone calls is 9.29 on a Monday morning. Perhaps the British reluctance to talk to machines conditions us to call more in office hours.

It should also be possible, through fixed scheduling of test spot times, to gauge the effect of factors such as consecutive breaks or "top and tail" ads in a single break.

Radio in a mixed-media schedule

Few advertisers want to use different telephone numbers in different media for lots of reasons. But when the same number is used across a variety of media, such as radio, press, TV, inserts, door-to-door, posters, and direct mail, it is obviously more difficult to evaluate the relative performance of each medium by call counting.

Whereas callers will frequently have to hand a press ad or leaflet when they dial, callers are unlikely to ring up holding a radio in their hand! Nevertheless, radio may have directed them to the print material, or a press ad may have stood out more as readers made the link with what they had heard on the radio. **A number of case histories demonstrate a higher response to print media among radio listeners.**

Your analysis, therefore, may consider the proportion of population in any area that listens to the radio stations on which you advertised. In Oxford, for example, 35% of adults listen to Fox FM each week. If 75% of adult respondents to your magazine inserts, etc, in Oxford were listeners to Fox FM, it would be reasonable to conclude they had been influenced by the radio advertising. (Actual listening habits could be checked by re-contacting a sample of respondents from within the station's transmission area.)

Beware the misattribution of advertising that frequently disrupts analysis of radio's contribution to a mixed-media campaign. It is often confused with TV advertising – even if TV has not been used.

After a radio-only campaign in London for a regional brewery, one in four of the post-campaign sample who recalled seeing or hearing the advertising claimed it had been on TV.

Where radio and TV are used together confusion is obviously a particularly difficult issue. The simplest questioning techniques may still not uncover the truth about what made callers respond.

Geodemographic analysis

From respondents' postcodes, if response levels are high enough, the resulting database can be profiled by the ACORN or Mosaic systems. RAJAR audience data is compatible with both systems and can be used as target market definitions to aid the scheduling of airtime in future campaigns.

As stated, a geodemographic profile can be taken from existing customers generated by any other means and used for targeting radio. (See chapters on profiling and segmentation, Chapters 3.5–3.7.)

Copy clearance for radio commercials

Since July 1996, commercial radio has been responsible for checking its own copy, through the specialist team at the Radio Advertising Clearance Centre. Their Helpline telephone number is 0171-727 2646.

Their role is:

✔ To ensure commercials conform to the Radio Authority Code of Advertising Standards and Practice;

✔ To provide positive assistance to radio advertisers. They offer genuine help in understanding and implementing the Code's requirements to encourage greater use of the medium.

Commercials including premium rate telephone services must comply with the ICSTIS (Independent Committee for the Supervision of Standards of Telephone Information Services) Code of Practice.

There are several other conditions applicable to direct marketing on radio in Rule 24 of the Radio Authority's Code of Practice. We strongly recommend you obtain a copy. Their telephone number is 0171-430 2724.

Where to buy airtime

National stations

	Telephone	Facsimile
Atlantic 252 } sold by CLT UK Talk Radio } Radio Sales	0171-343 2299	0171-637 3925
Classic FM	0171-713 2626	0171-284 2835
Virgin Radio	0171-434 1215	0171-434 1197

Local & regional station sales companies

Capital Sales	0171-766 6055	0171-766 6150
Choice FM (London & Birmingham)	0171-738 7969	0171-738 6619
Chrysalis National Radio Sales	0171-468 1062	0171-221 6455
Emap On Air	0171-713 0200	
First Choice Radio Sales & Marketing	01372-725662	01372-724289
Golden Rose Sales (Jazz FM, Liberty 963)	0171-706 4100	0171-723 9742
GWR	0171-306 3167	
Independent Radio News (sold by Capital)	0171-383 3000	0171-383 0360
Katz International	0171-388 8787	0171-383 3737
Melody Radio Sales	0171-581 1054	0171-581 7000
Premier Radio Sales	0171-233 6705	0171-233 6706
Scottish & Irish Radio Sales (SIRS)	0171-587 0001	0171-582 1621
News Direct 97.3 FM/LBC 1152	0171-973 1152	0171-312 8470

Where to get more information

Radio Authority, telephone 0171-430 2724, facsimile 0171-405 7062.
Incorporated Society of British Advertisers (ISBA), telephone 0171-499 7502, facsimile 0171-629 5355.

Full details of station group ownership and sales representation are available in the latest Commercial Radio Handbook, and on the RAB's Internet site : RAB OnLine: www.rab.co.uk

The Radio Advertising Archive is a computer-based retrieval system which logs new radio ads as they are broadcast. National advertisers and their agencies can call direct on 0171-306 2599 and ask for a compilation by product sector, style, content, specific advertiser, etc. See RAB OnLine for more details.

RAJAR can be contacted at Collier House, 163–169 Brompton Road, London SW3 1PY.

Sound-bites of most of the stations mentioned in this chapter, and approximately 120 others around the UK, are available on the RAB's CD ROM "Sounds of the Station".

Chapter 4.5

Integration and the Internet – early days

This chapter includes:

- ❑ **Background to the new digital media**
- ❑ **Profile of the typical Internet user**
- ❑ **How people use the World Wide Web**
- ❑ **Ways for marketers to use Web sites**
- ❑ **3 ways to create a Web site**
- ❑ **Constraints and limitations**
- ❑ **Making the best of your site**
- ❑ **Amnesty International: Case study**

The Internet is a global network of hundreds of smaller networks linked together by the international telephone system and easily accessed by a PC and a modem. At the time of this Guide going to print, the Internet is undergoing massive commercialisation and some users believe it is set to revolutionise the way business is done worldwide. Arguably organisations who come on-line early will secure a major competitive advantage.

Most experts, however, warn against talk of a total revolution and stress the many difficulties that the technology still has to overcome. Yes, whole new enterprises have been founded on its advantages, but there are still distinct limits on the performance and capacity that may prohibit universal acceptance and usage.

Better to see the Web, they say, as one more important ingredient in the media mix. In this chapter, Mike Crossman introduces us to some of the basic considerations marketers ought to be addressing and demonstrates an extremely interesting example of a Web site supporting an integrated multi-media campaign.

New in this edition. There was no mention of the Internet or the World Wide Web in the first edition of this Guide.

Author/Consultant: Mike Crossman

Mike Crossman, Managing Director, Bates Interactive

As Managing Director of Bates Interactive, London, Mike leads an experienced team of specialist planners, programmers, designers and account managers who have created award-winning work for a range of blue chip clients. Before joining Bates Interactive he was Managing Director of Marshall Cavendish – one of the world's largest partwork and illustrated book publishers and one of the early entrants into Interactive CD-ROM publishing, with titles including "The Great Artists" produced in association with the National Gallery, London.

His extensive background in interactive multimedia gives him a unique understanding of the creative and communications issues surrounding these new media and their unique applications in a business context.

Among the Bates Interactive clients are BAT, The Halifax, Compaq, Cunard and Pharmacia & Upjohn. The recent work created for Amnesty International (www.refuge.amnesty.org) has won several awards including the Best Use of New Media 1997 at the prestigious New Media Age Effectiveness Awards in 1997. This work is described in the case study included in this chapter.

Mike Crossman
Bates Interactive
121–141 Westbourne Terrace
London
W1 2JA
E-mail: mcrossma@bates-dorlands.co.uk
Tel: 0171-724 7228

Chapter 4.5

Integration and the Internet – early days

What is the Internet?

The Internet is a global network of business, private, government and university computers. Individuals and companies can exchange information via their own PCs and/or corporate computer systems with anybody hooked up to the Net anywhere in the world. From a worldwide base of 40–60 million users now, it is estimated that 200 million people will use the Internet by the end of the decade.

How did it start?

The Internet was first developed as a secure way of linking military computers in case of a nuclear attack. The first four sites were linked to a network called ARPANet in 1969 administered by the US Department of Defense Advanced Research Projects Agency.

In the late 1980s a network was created which linked super computing centres with universities. These, combined with other networks, were the real beginnings of what we know as the Internet. This linking of computers eventually spread into the commercial environment, providing among other things a channel for E-mail which is still one of its most significant uses.

> The World Wide Web is not about connections and cables and PCs. The Web is where people who can't physically sit next to each other can meet to share their hopes and dreams. It's our global village.
>
> – Tim Berners Lee, inventor of the World Wide Web

Digital marketing is naturally gaining attention as the world becomes increasingly "connected". The options available for digital media in the marketing mix range from Internet sites, dedicated CD-ROMs and kiosk applications, through to simple screen savers and, in the near future, interactive television.

The most common of these digital communications tools in use at the moment is the Internet and more specifically the World Wide Web.

> The time is not far off when you will be answering your television, watching your computer and programming your 'phone.
>
> – Raymond Smith, CEO, Bell Atlantic

It was the development of the World Wide Web, a term often wrongly used interchangeably with "the Internet", which created an environment for on-line marketing communications. The Web, which is the most visible part of the Internet, was invented by Tim Berners Lee in late 1990 while he was working at the Cern Research Centre in Geneva.

His innovations made it possible to link seamlessly from one location to another using the digital equivalent of word association. The protocols he developed provided the basis for movement around the World Wide Web. Refinements and improvements to Web construction appear almost daily, providing better interactivity and greater sophistication from Web sites.

Why the rapid growth?

The Internet is available 24 hours a day 365 days a year, is seamless and truly global in reach. It is virtually unregulated and relatively cheap to access. It is an environment where almost anyone can have a voice – many small independent Web sites attract more visitors than some large commercial sites.

A well-developed Web site can respond to individuals and be constantly updated. It can build on sophisticated customer response mechanisms. It can provide an environment for communities who share an interest. The Internet will continue to attract new users with the promise of more on-line shopping, transactions, entertainment, information and communication opportunities.

Who uses it?

Research (NOP) shows that 3.5 million people used the Internet in the UK in the first six months of 1997. Of these it is estimated that around 1.5 million were regular users. These 1.5 million people have been described as "a marketing dream" by the research company BMRB. They are well educated with high disposable income.

Typical UK Internet users have been described by NOP as:

68%	male
77%	ABC1
44%	25–44
58%	earn over £25,000 pa
64%	university educated

Each month 25,000 new connections to the Internet are made, mostly by users in this category. (This was the figure for the early months of 1998.)

The Web in the marketing mix

Advertising on the Internet gets the message to this highly attractive audience in a way never before possible. You can lead the consumer directly from your awareness advertisement to your company Web site. (Imagine taking someone through an outdoor poster site directly into your company's sales office.) You can ask people questions, gain feedback and understand your customer in a new, more instant way.

For the end-user, the Internet is a much more active and engrossing activity than watching television or listening to the radio. The Internet user is in a particularly receptive state of mind, exploring a system full of what's new and different, often seeing themselves at the cutting edge of technology.

An audience of well-educated high earners
+
A truly response-ready advertising medium
=
A significant new communications channel for your message

Web sites will not replace other forms of marketing communications and are best seen in context of the overall communications mix. To be most effective a Web site should be part of an integrated communications package.

For the moment at least, most adult users are driven to Web sites not by surfing, but by a reference in a more conventional medium, eg newspaper ad, magazine write-up, the end frame of a TV commercial, the Web address on the side of a product package, letterhead, etc.

It is the interactive nature which makes the Web so compelling and personal – users are generally very focused on the task in hand and will happily make a series of links to get to information relevant to them. **Remember, the Internet user has made a conscious choice to visit a particular site and will come with expectations which, if met and exceeded, will encourage them to return again and again.**

As with all other communications channels, defining your target and deciding your objectives remain as fundamental as ever. However, it is particularly important to define the role of your digital communication in order to utilise its particular strengths – rather than duplicate a message through what might be an inappropriate channel. This requires an understanding of the users' relationships with the Web and of the "netiquette" (or etiquette of the Net) as it is sometimes called.

Ways for marketers to use a Web site

Web sites can be used in a number of different ways and operate differently for every person who visits them. They can provide a simple source of information which **must** have real value to the site visitor (example: www.costsless.compaq.co.uk). Their main point of interest may be purely the site's entertainment value (example: www.joeboxer.com). Web sites which provide easy, efficient, helpful transactions – such as banking, parcel tracking (example: www.fedex.com) or shopping – constantly reinforce the values of the brand.

Sponsorship is an area where brand owners can find real value on the Web. Extending their activities on-line (example: www.fa-carling.com), they can support like-minded communities and expand the reach of their sponsorship – particularly where the demographics of the Web user match those of the sponsor's target group. The creation of a discussion area can provide on-line research groups and, perhaps and most importantly, an ideal opportunity to gather data about existing and potential customers.

Any Web site can act in some or all these ways. The more interactive a site, the more reason for users to come back. Repeat visits are the key to establishing and building a relationship which is one of the key benefits inherent in the medium.

Examples of some of the above uses will be found in the "screen dumps" on the following double-page spread.

3 ways to create a Web site

Several different types of company work in the new media with varying degrees of expertise and commitment. They range from strategy-based New Media consultants to small production companies whose main concerns are the creative and the programming.

The skills required to initiate and implement a Web site depend on the scope and complexity of the task. The necessary resources could come from in-house or be out-sourced, depending on the skills within your organisation.

There are three different options for developing a Web site and there are pros and cons for each.

The three options are:

- ✔ Web production house
- ✔ New Media consultant
- ✔ Full service agency

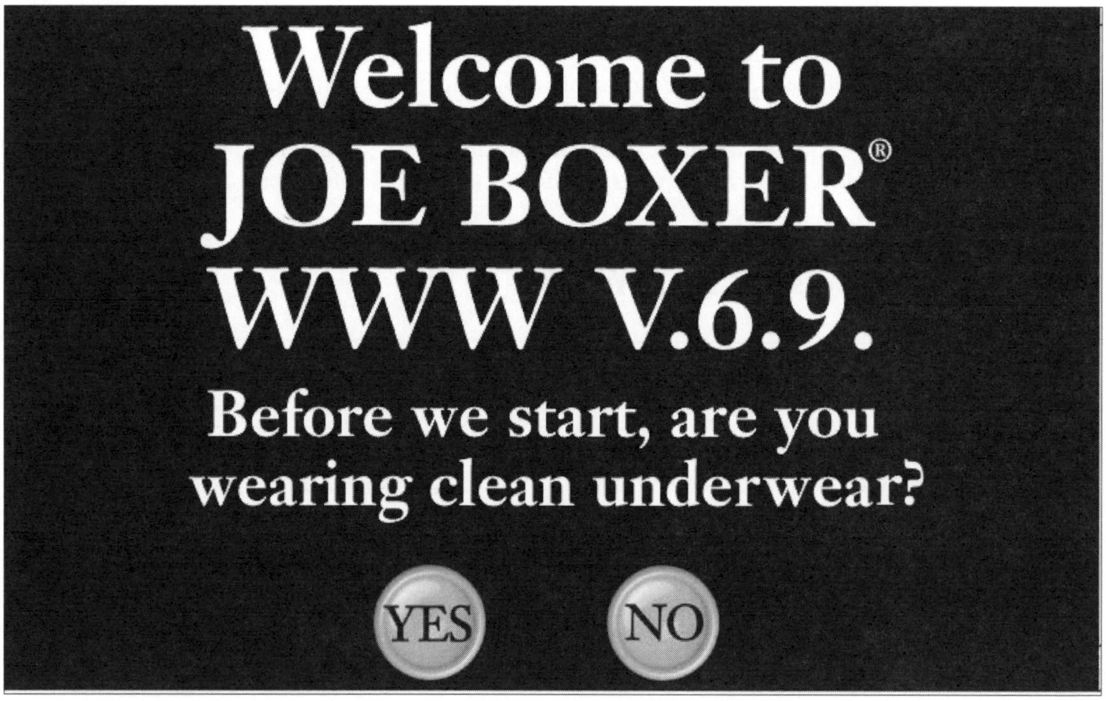

www.joeboxer.com

Entertainment is the key to this site

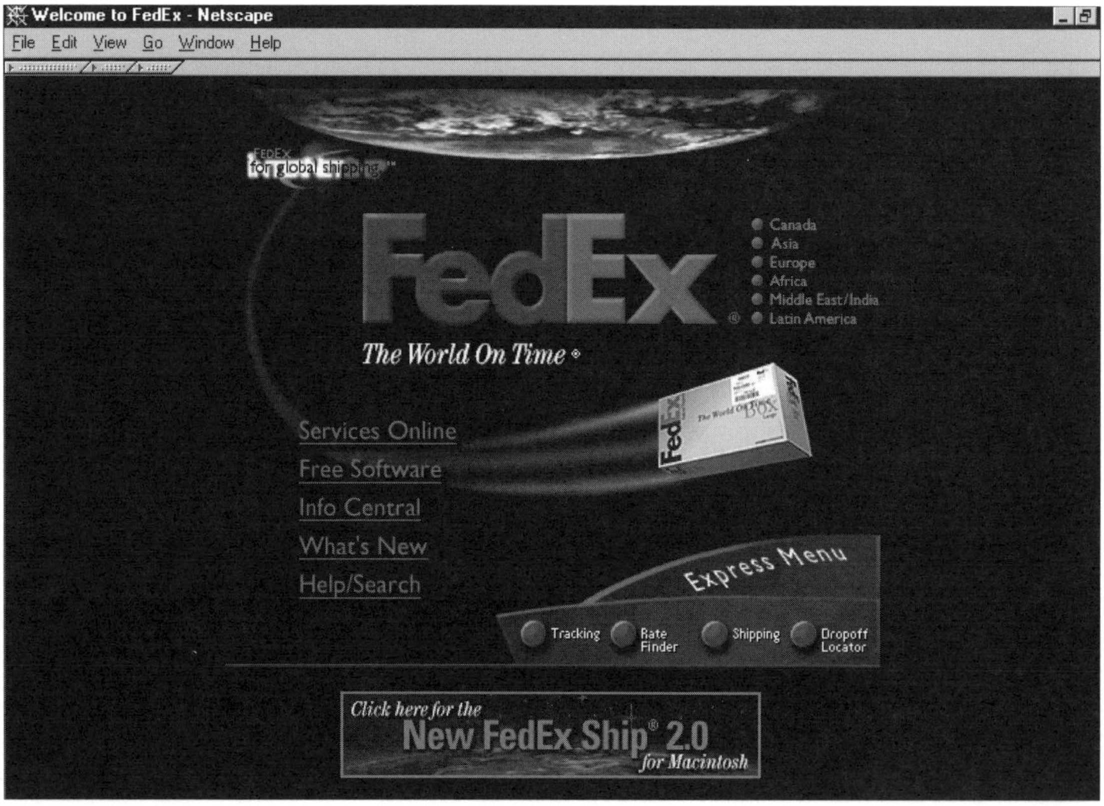

www.fedex.com

Easy, efficient, helpful transactions

www.fa-carling.com
Creating a community among football fans

www.sundaytimes.co.uk
The latest news at your fingertips

Before deciding on your choice of a digital media partner it is worth asking yourself a few questions, for example:

?	What role do I/we want in the process?
?	Who else is involved in advertising the product/service?
?	Do we need help with a digital brand strategy?
?	Do we simply want someone to implement the process?
?	Do we want someone to manage the whole process?
?	Do we want to manage the process ourselves?
?	Are we simply looking for specialist programming and design skills for our Web site?

Web production houses – similar to print or TV production

At one end of the scale lie the many Web production houses. These are akin to any other traditional out-sourced production facility with specialist skills. They tend to be fairly small and concentrate on creating Web sites. They are production-led and often demand a great deal of input from their clients in order to produce something within the overall brand strategy.

Advantages

Their strength is that they often straddle the line between users and creators, keeping up with developments and understanding the netiquette.

With their focus on production, control of the overall process remains firmly with the commissioning agent. This direct link between marketer and production house can eliminate confusion in a situation which may be evolving daily. Production-only suppliers tend to be less expensive, although this is not always the case. In some instances they charge a premium for what is perceived as a specialist skill.

Disadvantages

While production-only suppliers are often at the cutting edge in terms of creativity and technical innovation, this focus sometimes means they have limited understanding of brand values and consumer insight. This can manifest itself in a short-term view and general lack of strategy. At its worst it can mean constant refocusing, reflecting each new design fashion or technical innovation.

Both long-term strategy and clarity of brand communication can, of course, be directed and overseen by the commissioning party but this requires a commitment which many marketers do not have time for. Related to this is the importance of integrating communications. Digital communication is a natural extension of other brand communications so the whole package should be seamless and reinforcing in the eyes of the consumer.

New Media consultants – eyes on the long term

The middle option in terms of a digital media partner is the Digital or New Media consultant. These are frequently part of traditional agencies and are firmly strategy-focused. They operate exclusively within digital media and vary in their understanding of creative and executional issues.

Advantages

The key strength of New Media consultants is their focus on the long-term use and opportunities of digital media. They tend to have an in-depth understanding of the changing nature of the technology as a whole, its marketing applications, and the evolution of the emerging digital landscape.

Disadvantages

At times their focus on the long term can lead to discrepancies between the vision and what is achievable in the short term. Most consultants out-source the production of the actual Web sites and sometimes their suppliers are unable to produce a solution to meet the marketer's expectations.

This reliance on subcontractors also means that consultants can be an expensive option in terms of production. Regarding integration, New Media consultants cannot always extend their expertise to embrace the broader agenda across all media.

Full service New Media agencies – co-guardians of your brand

Your third option in the search for a digital media partner is the full service New Media agency. These specialist suppliers are often part of conventional advertising agencies with an understanding of brands and a focus on communications. Some incorporate production facilities while others buy-in production services in the same way that they buy production services for other more conventional media, such as TV ad production. Full service agencies tend to be relatively large and generally can call on a larger pool of creative and planning resources.

Advantages

As co-guardians of their clients' brands, full service agencies have an in-depth knowledge of consumer behaviour and brand communication. In addition they are ideally placed to position your digital communication firmly within the overall media mix, so that the brand communication is completely integrated.

Disadvantages

Unfortunately, due to the fact that many of these companies come from a traditional ad agency background, there can be a tendency for them to give undue precedence to other more established media. In some cases, their overall understanding of the digital environment is lacking. In other cases, the agency is only paying lip-service to digital media services.

Constraints of the Web – speed problems

Web sites are still restricted by several limitations, not altogether surprising considering the medium is less than a decade old. Much development is focused on getting around these problems, or solving them in creative ways.

Virtually all of the restrictions concern the speed at which information can be transferred. Given the ease with which a user can make an alternative selection, it is crucial that the downloading time is in proportion to the value in the user's mind of the material being downloaded. **If a site does not respond quickly, the average Web user will simply make another selection and look elsewhere.**

Even though someone using the Web makes an active choice in selecting a particular Web site, if that choice is perceived as not being worthwhile then the potential outcome is a negative view that the owner of the site has wasted their valuable time.

Although performance is fundamental to the success of a site, it is even more important that the balance between performance, impact and real value is appropriate for the site **and** the target audience. If there is real value in the assets taking a long time to download, users will wait. But if there is not, then the site will do little more than leave the users frustrated.

Factors in Web performance

Downloading time is based on the following four main factors:

? Speed of the end-user's modem

? Amount of traffic on the Internet at the time

? Volume of text and images, and other assets, needed to create a particular page

? Bandwidth of the hosting server and its connection to the Internet

Modem speed

The user's modem speed controls the rate at which information is transferred to and from the computer via the telephone line. Although there is no official standard at the moment, the most common rate is 14,400 bits per second with 28,800 bps and 33,600 bps becoming more and more common every day. The higher the bps rate the faster the modem. A site which is painfully slow on a 14.4 modem could be very frustrating for an average user. However, if the site is targeting high-end IT professionals where the average modem speed is assumed to be 28,800, for example, it might be perfectly acceptable.

Traffic volume

The amount of traffic on the Internet at the time of usage limits the performance in the way you would expect. You may have the equivalent of an 8-lane motorway but if everyone decides to go home early there will be traffic snarl-ups! The same thing applies to the Internet: if everyone wants to access the same site at the same time, the site itself will not be able to handle the demand. For example, in the UK there is a noticeable drop in performance of many USA-based sites after about one o'clock in the afternoon as the east coast of America wakes up and starts to go on-line.

Text versus image: Effect on download times

Downloading time is also dependent on the quality and quantity of the various "assets" which make up the site. While text is relatively data friendly, high resolution graphics and images are much hungrier in data terms and require much longer download time.

Many techniques have been developed to create more efficient assets and compression is the key. **When planning a Web site it is important to bear in mind the limitations of the medium and to adapt or create assets appropriately.** With images for example, work to screen resolution of 72 dpi (dots per inch) rather than the much higher print resolution unless there is a particular reason to do otherwise.

Legal pitfalls and how to avoid them

Consistency with other elements in the communications mix is essential to the effectiveness of a Web site. Consequently existing assets are often a major source of material for the creation of the site. One of the pitfalls here is the use of intellectual property. Often no agreement has been reached with the copyright owners.

In many cases it is cheaper to create new assets than renegotiate usage rights after the event. Consequently even if there are no immediate plans to use digital media, set up a process for acquiring digital rights when commissioning or buying rights to intellectual property. If this is too expensive, or seems inappropriate, negotiate digital rights usage when you are buying other related rights with payment deferred until digital use is required.

Making the best of your Web site

Although a Web site can only be ultimately judged by the way it meets or exceeds your initial objectives, there are some criteria which contribute to the success of any site.

✔ **Sites should be highly creative and make full use of the interactive nature of the medium.** There is no point in simply putting a brochure on-line when it would be better delivered in its printed form. It is much better to complement the information in the brochure, or reorganise it so that it can be accessed in bite-sized chunks via some simple navigation system.

✔ Include plenty of high-value content and keep it constantly updated.

✔ Give users a reason to return to the site frequently.

✔ Capture data on site visitors and respond to their interests and usage patterns as the site grows and evolves.

✔ Stay at the technical leading edge but bear in mind users with limited specifications on their systems. There are different browsers which people use to access the Web: Netscape and Microsoft's Internet Explorer dominate the market but even these have a variety of versions which handle material differently.

✔ Always balance performance with value to the user.

✔ Constantly create PR opportunities as the site develops; and cross-fertilise with other parts of the communications plan.

Very few Web sites can ever be considered finished. Most need updating and on-going maintenance. Allow sufficient budget to keep yours fresh and responsive to the developing needs of users.

Once the site is built make sure that every opportunity is taken to drive people to the site. Print your Web address on all other communications including brochures, letterheads, business cards, print ads, product packaging, point of sale, direct mail communications, DRTV frames, etc. Interweave the message with lines such as "See our Web site for more information."

Not surprisingly drawing up the creative brief for a Web site is much like preparing for any other element in the marketing mix. In its short form (see briefing, Chapter 6.6) here is a checklist of questions to ask yourself before commencing the task of designing the site.

?	What is the objective of the communication?
?	Who are we talking to?
?	What do they currently think of the brand/product/service?
?	What do we want them to think?
?	What key thought must be taken from this communication?
?	What must be included to justify this perception?
?	What should the tone of voice be?
?	Executional mandatories/guidelines
?	Requirement
?	Production budget

An effective Web communication will obey the principles of AIDCA discussed in the creative chapters. Although the execution might at first appear different from that for any other medium, closer inspection will show that the differences are mainly related to the interactive opportunities and, of course, the limitations. At the end of the chapter will be found a comprehensive case study which demonstrates how to make the most of the opportunities whilst overcoming the limitations.

The costs of creating a Web site

A Web site can operate on many different levels from transaction to research, so it is reasonable for the budget to be shared by several different departments. Set aside budget and sufficient time for planning and strategy **before** you begin constructing the site.

Far too many companies embark on the process without first looking at the role the Web site will have in the longer term – either as part of the overall communications mix or in defining the brand.

Depending on the function of the site, a considerable budget could be needed to populate the site with engaging material.

Construction begins

Once the objectives have been clearly defined and agreed the next stage is Web construction. Typically this is broken down into the creation of assets which are Web appropriate and actual programming.

Existing assets such as images and graphics **may** be reusable but usually have to be adapted for use on the Web. Even company logos designed for high resolution print work need to be adapted for the limitations of the screen.

Next comes the programming which drives the site. This, too, can range from the straightforward to the cutting edge and may require sophisticated links to a database.

What about on-going maintenance?

Once a site has been built, there will be some on-going costs.

Firstly, the site needs to be housed somewhere with a suitable link to the Internet. There are many options depending on the anticipated demand to the site. They range from a dedicated server with a dedicated link to the Internet for a heavily accessed site, to taking just a part of a commercial server and Internet link via an Internet service provider.

The appropriate solution depends on the anticipated site traffic, the frequency and amount of updating, and the resources available. Depending on the construction of the site and the type of maintenance and updating required, these can often be carried out quite simply within a password protected administration area. But each site is different and these costs must be anticipated at the outset.

Web site case study: Amnesty International

Background

Amnesty International is a worldwide human rights voluntary organisation whose remit is to publicise and promote issues relating to human rights.

On March 19th 1997, the organisation launched its first international campaign to promote awareness of the refuge crisis and refugees' rights to protection. The ultimate target was the world's governments who could save refugees from having to flee and ensure a respect for their human rights. The campaign was given the title of "Refuge! Human Rights Have No Borders" and was supported by an integrated programme of communications including press, posters and television, all of which were spearheaded by the launch of a Web site designed and produced by Bates Interactive.

Given the voluntary nature of the organisation, marketing and communications budgets were limited. As a result the site was produced on a shoestring, with the huge amounts of time and effort devoted to its creation being a reflection of the agency's belief in the campaign objectives rather than a commercially profitable exercise.

Objectives

A major component of the campaign was the need to change the public's perception of refugees as its negativity towards them endorses governments' failure to live up to their obligations. Therefore, apart from supporting the Refuge! Campaign, there was a "wish list" that it was hoped the site could address:

- ✔ *Raise awareness of the plight of refugees*
- ✔ *Make people identify with refugees on a personal level*
- ✔ *Encourage people to take action*
- ✔ *Provide links to the campaign manifesto and further documentation*
- ✔ *Ensure the site is functional on low specification computers and modems*

Branding

Amnesty International has a strong brand property in its "candle" which was included on all the main pages as an animated image. The resultant creative synergy across the communication programme helped to maximise the impact of the campaign. The agency took the theme of the first press execution and embraced its proposition and imagery within the site. As further press treatments were launched, these were also incorporated within the site.

Source: *Mike Crossman, Bates Interactive, 13.11.97*

Web site case study: Amnesty International (cont'd)

Strategy

The perception that Amnesty International sought to change was that of faceless masses of refugees, at best seen as dependent and needy, at worst a drain on scarce resources. The desired public perception of refugees is of people who flee from human rights violations, the threat of death, torture or harassment – who flee because they are afraid, not because they want to.

The approach, shared by the advertising agency Bates Dorland, was to personalise the issue and bring it into the sphere of the comprehensible. The strategy was to make the plight of refugees about "us" rather than "them".

Campaign summary

As a result, the Web site incorporates the following functional elements to help reinforce and deliver the strategic direction.

Site visitors are introduced to individual refugees and basic facts are presented which dovetail with existing Amnesty International resources on the World Wide Web.

The on-line community is given the opportunity to take action through an on-line petition. This can be openly or anonymously signed.

The Refuge! Campaign advertises itself through the Web site, offering printable posters (in Amnesty's four core languages: English, French, Spanish and Arabic), plus a downloadable screensaver to ensure continued awareness of the campaign and exposure of the main message beyond the World Wide Web.

Technology considerations

Amnesty International is sensitive to the variable standards of technology throughout the world. The agency therefore produced a site that would not frustrate the efforts of users with older equipment. The end result is very memory efficient whilst achieving high design standards and graphics content. It is equally appealing on small and large screens and easy to navigate with minimal scrolling on individual pages.

Methodology

A news-style approach was adopted, providing a high-impact, visually stimulating and easily navigable Web site aimed at attracting attention and raising awareness of the Refuge! Campaign. It was based on the premise of "How would I feel if it were me?" The site was designed to have minimal content, but to incorporate links to the main Amnesty International Web site which is extremely rich in content. Cohesion between the digital environment of the Web and the traditional print medium was achieved by communicating the strategic messages of the press executions.

(continued)

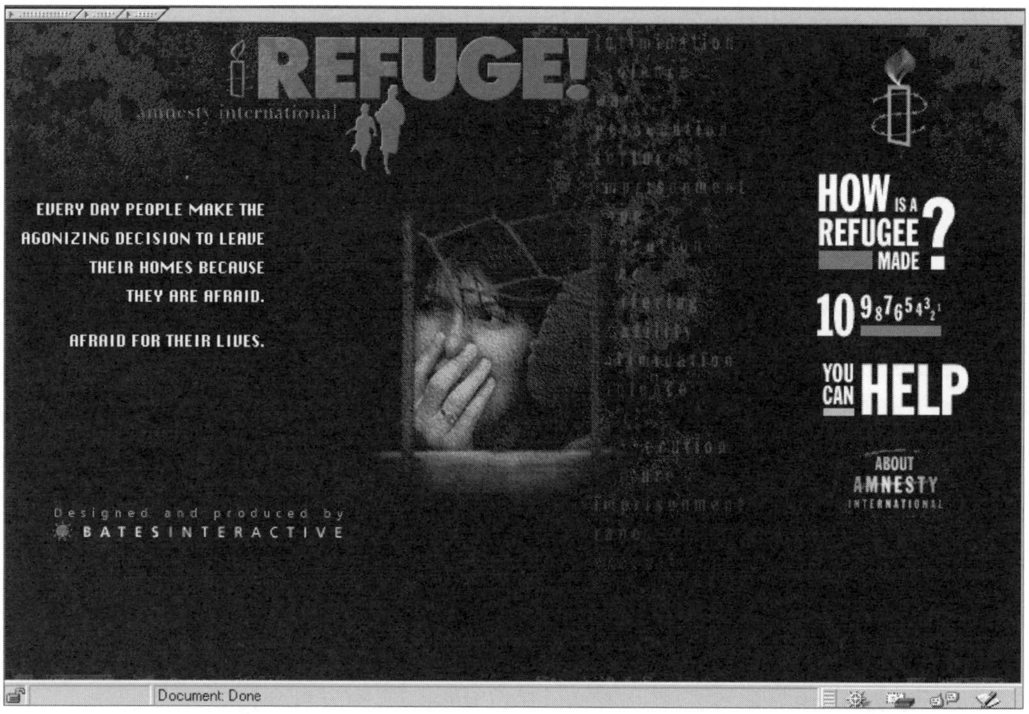

How Is A Refugee Made? *Takes the headline from one of the press executions and gives five refugees' personal stories. Each was carefully selected by the agency to reflect the range of issues affecting refugees and provide an accurate representation of nationality and sex.*

"10" *provides 10 key facts about refugees and reflects another press execution entitled "You've got 10 minutes to get out – what would you take with you?" This section also includes 10 images of refugees, all of which can be clicked on to learn further facts about refugees. These images are highly evocative and designed to help further represent and reinforce the extent of the refugee crisis.*

"What You Can Do?" is the site section which allows people to take action. Through appropriate use of design and programming technology, it is easy to use. The on-line petition which allows people to express their support for Amnesty's Refuge! Campaign can be signed either by entering an E-mail address or registering an anonymous "click".

A printable poster, in Amnesty International's four core languages – English, French, Spanish and Arabic – is also available. Simply designed to allow for all printer specifications, the poster bridges the communications spectrum from digital to traditional print. The poster can be pinned to noticeboards or faxed to friends and colleagues to help further the campaign message. Another element of this section is the provision of a downloadable screensaver, aimed at extending the reach of the campaign beyond the World Wide Web. Finally, "Want to do more?" provides links to the main Amnesty site, local section offices with E-mail addresses where available, together with advice on what else can be done to help.

Web site case study: Amnesty International (cont'd)

Results

Within three weeks of its launch the site was registering an average of 170 user-sessions per day, without the support of any public relations activity to promote the site and with the initial press execution running in only one international market. Within six weeks the on-line petition received 1,113 signatures which increased incrementally as the campaign gathered momentum. Within the same period 1,679 individual user-sessions were registered on the "Want to do more?" *pages and the poster was downloaded 1,598 times.*

Chapter 4.6

Creating a successful catalogue from scratch

This chapter includes:

- The changing catalogue market
- The 4 main success factors
- Pagination, product density, and "pace"
- Image, personality & positioning
- Format and design
- "Hot spots" in every catalogue
- Creative do's and don'ts
- 3 ways to find catalogue customers

Catalogue marketing in the UK has undergone a revolution in the past twenty years – and is still changing fast. For over fifty years the giant 1,000-page catalogues of GUS, Grattan, Freeman, Littlewoods and Empire dominated the scene.

Then, in the 1970s, along came Scotcade and Kaleidoscope, quickly followed by Innovations and Next. At first the catalogue establishment took little notice – but then the implications began to dawn. In America, legends like Montgomery Ward and Sears, pioneers of the big catalogues, closed their doors. J C Penny, the largest of them all, reduced its book by over 50% and introduced **seventy** specialist catalogues to compensate.

Who better to talk about the catalogue revolution than Geoff Cotton? And who better to show you how to go about launching that catalogue you've been talking about for years? Whatever you do, says Cotton, **don't** start by scouring the world for new merchandise. There are some very important decisions to be made before you spend another pound on goods or gimmicks.

New in this edition. Lessons from the post-Racing Green and Lands' End launches; also finding catalogue prospects and transforming them into customers.

Geoff Cotton, Managing Director, Geoff Cotton Partnership Limited

With 30 years' catalogue experience, Geoff is one of the senior figures in UK direct marketing and especially mail order.

Educated at Salford Grammar, he joined GUS, the UK's largest mail order company, in 1968 whilst studying business and marketing at Manchester Polytechnic.

A short period in sales was followed by four years in the computer department where he rose to Senior Systems Analyst, having successfully implemented significant marketing and merchandise information systems.

A move to merchandise followed and he soon became Merchandise Controller responsible for all non-fashion. Here he continued to develop his innovative catalogue skills, increasing sales of non-fashion by over 300% and pioneering sales of co-ordinated soft-furnishing and off-the-page selling. Promoted to Marketing Director of the direct division, he used tried and tested database techniques to considerably boost the company's internal promotions and customer acquisition.

He left GUS to set up his own product-sourcing agency and was retained by several leading companies. He then joined WWAV, the UK's largest direct marketing agency, with a brief to develop their mail order business. He quickly won Racing Green and Scotts of Stow, two high-profile launches.

For his own agency, GCP, Geoff has won the Harrods account, launched The Peruvian Connection in the UK, gained the Disney Selection and Thomas Burberry catalogue launches for GUS, and begun consulting for the Royal Mail's Home Shopping division.

A sought after speaker, he lectures on the IDM Diploma course and has run key business briefings at the IDM Symposium. He has also been invited to join the Home Shopping Council of the DMA and is a regular speaker at the European Mail Order and Catalogue Conference in London.

When not reading or writing about mail order, he is a Manchester United freak, part-time golfer and American football fan. He has an extensive music collection and reads modern literature and anything about Vietnam.

Geoff Cotton M IDM
Geoff Cotton Partnership Ltd
Portland Tower
Portland Street
Manchester M1 3LF
Tel: 0161-238 4936

Chapter 4.6

Creating a successful catalogue from scratch

The new generation of UK catalogues

The late 1970s and early 1980s saw the first stirrings of modern catalogue development in the UK, led by industry visionaries Bob Scott (Scotcade) and Nigel Swabey (Kaleidoscope and Innovations). But the most important and far-reaching breakthrough came in 1987 with the launch of The Next Directory, the Next store group's first catalogue venture.

Next changed not only catalogue design but also cataloguing's whole approach to customers, with 48-hour deliveries, elegant packaging and, of course, an established brand built up through the successful chain of High Street stores.

Next's "upmarket" High Street image brought instant credibility – **a vital mail order ingredient** – and earned it a loyal following of young, middle-class customers who had little or no previous propensity to buy by mail. It brought panache to a scene which had been synonymous with poor quality merchandise, out of date style, and a working-class dependence on extended credit.

The major cataloguers were intrigued but not scared and did little about the impending change. After all GUS, the market leader, had a share of over 45% at this point and the "Big Five" of GUS, Littlewoods, Freeman, Grattan and Empire had over 90% of the market between them.

Enter Racing Green and Lands' End

But the change had begun. In 1991, two clothing catalogues were launched on to the market that were as radically different from Next as Next was from GUS. Racing Green and Lands' End pushed the boundaries of the mail order market even wider.

UK-based Racing Green, emulating successful USA lifestyle catalogues such as J Crew, appealed to an affluent, young, busy market and traded only on cash-with-order (cheques, credit cards, etc) and from a catalogue of fewer than 100 pages. Lands' End, on the other hand, brought a highly successful formula to the UK by simply anglicising its US marketing.

Both catalogues overcame the fact that their products were more expensive than those in other catalogues through the use of superior photography and excellent copy. This skill was born out of the owners' genuine love of their products, their total involvement with every aspect of the catalogue process, and their merchandising and marketing skills.

The scene was now set and newcomers to the market arrived in numbers, from Bob Scott's new catalogue Scotts of Stow, to Divertimenti aimed at cooks, and Kingshill and Elegance aimed at the highest of fashion markets.

All these new catalogues had one thing in common. They were aimed at specific segments of the market. They were targeted at socio-economic groups qualified by interests, special needs or other identifying characteristics.

The rules for successful catalogue marketing in this environment differ totally from the skills required in the old days, as we now explore.

Let's plan a catalogue

We now begin to look at the process of producing a new catalogue and making it successful. Where shall we begin?

As with all forms of marketing, planning is the key to success. Without a detailed strategic plan any catalogue operation will struggle. Every activity should be carried out with the plan as the road map, and the outputs of each step matched against it.

A catalogue plan is not just theory – not just words on paper. It must very soon be made real. It is a good idea to have a dummy catalogue in your hands at the earliest possible stage. No doubt, if you are diligent, you will have other people's catalogues in front of you, too.

It also helps to appoint a custodian of the plan who can remain objective about every decision. This guarantees that product, pricing, creative and marketing decisions are not overly influenced by personal feelings and experience.

Short-term profit – or long-term customer?

The way you approach the plan will be governed by the objectives and expectations of the business and the market you are entering. It takes a far different strategy to enter a mature crowded market than it does to start up in a totally new niche. Equally, if the proprietor is in it for a quick buck, then customer acquisition strategies are poles apart from those required for a long-term project.

For the purposes of this Guide we shall look at the processes involved in developing a long-term business with real profits coming down the line from a retained customer base. We will, however, touch upon some of the techniques required for those with a shorter-term view.

The main catalogue success factors

Whether you are starting your catalogue from the beginning, or repositioning an existing business, the main factors in building your catalogue will always be:

- ✔ Product
- ✔ Target market
- ✔ Branding & positioning
- ✔ Format & design

We have deliberately put product first as this is the factor that will determine the market you enter. Defining the target audience will then form the basis for your product selection, pricing strategy and subsequently the overall positioning of your catalogue. In turn the positioning will guide you towards the best trading terms, eg the need for credit, etc. Finally comes the design and copy which should reflect all of these.

Towards the end of the chapter we shall look at three other factors vital to your success:

- ✔ Finding customers
- ✔ Developing customers
- ✔ Logistics & fulfilment

We now begin our closer look at each of the above, beginning with the product.

Finding the right product

A moment ago we highlighted the common denominator of all successful new catalogues. It's worth repeating here with some additional underlining:

The new catalogues

They are aimed at specific segments of the market. They are targeted at socio-economic groups qualified by interests, special needs or other identifying characteristics.

In the brave new world of direct response catalogues it is unlikely that you will be a generalist with no particular theme for your catalogue range. To really stand apart you need to differentiate your product range, or at least make your customers think your offering is different by treating it in a unique way.

Ideally your products should be selected around a theme, eg a room in the house, the source of the products, a time period, a fabric or a hobby. This approach is vital for positioning your catalogue and defining the target audience. Developing a golf catalogue, for instance, ostensibly makes targeting very easy – although even here there are new golfers and experienced club golfers with possibly different aspirations and different needs.

Branded or own label?

For your first catalogue it may be beneficial to include products with well-known brand names as this lends instant credibility. This is not essential. However, without well-known brands you will need to increase the branding of your catalogue and put more pressure on the promotion people to "get your catalogue across". Good examples are Racing Green and Scotts of Stow respectively. Racing Green launched to an unsuspecting market with a catalogue that contained only own-brand product (even though some of it was re-badged from the manufacturer's label). Scotts, on the other hand, contained a mix of well-known brands and unnamed products. This mix was strengthened by the inclusion of "exclusive" products with the added bonus of being very competitively priced.

Of course, if you are already blessed with a well-known corporate brand, eg Next, then your product should be truly representative of all the values normally associated with that brand. This applies whether your catalogue is another way of reaching your target audience, eg Harrods, or a new range diversification, eg Mini Boden.

We will return to the issue of branding in a moment.

The catalogue warning triangle

All right, so you have chosen the general theme for your products. Before you embark on your product scouring trips, there are three other issues and strategies that you need to address and finalise, each of which will directly impinge on your product selection. These are:

It is absolutely vital that these three elements are in congruency. If any one is out of line then product selection and subsequent marketing will become exceptionally difficult, if not impossible.

Who is your target customer?

Your next step, then, is to define the target audience. As with most direct marketing in the 1990s, simple age, gender and socio-economic groupings are not enough. To be really successful you need to get inside the minds of your typical prospects. You need to totally empathise with their needs, aspirations, expectations and circumstances.

Data analysis will help, but it cannot replace intimate knowledge of the product and the likely customer. This is one of the major reasons why retailers, even if they have only one outlet, start with a major advantage. They know what sells, having carried out intensive qualitative research through continuously seeing, and talking to, their customers.

Try and draw up a clear mental picture of your customer and carry it with you when you are looking at a product.

How about your pricing strategy?

Your pricing strategy will more or less be determined by the choice of target audience. Again Racing Green provides an excellent example:

"You pays your money ... "

In 1991 many cut-price or discount cataloguers were selling men's "Lacoste" style shirts for around £7. David Krantz knew intuitively that his customer would immediately perceive a product at this price as being of poor quality. He developed a product that was of near equal quality to well-known branded products and priced it at £16. The rest of his range was developed and priced in the same way.

But never try deliberately to mislead your audience by promising more than you can deliver. Everybody knows that a 20-piece towel bale is of modest quality and sizes are likely to err on the small side! Don't try to pretend that they are St Michael quality and the bath towel is the size of a door. You will get away with it only once and to think differently will lead to very high customer attrition.

Credit or cash-with-order?

Definition of your target audience and pricing strategy, combined with your product categories, will influence your terms of trade. If you are working with low value items, at almost any socio-economic level, then simply asking for payment by cheque or credit card will be sufficient.

If, however, you are selling products of higher value, say £50 and upwards, then it may be necessary to think about offering credit terms. This will be vital at the lower end of the market and good to have at the upper end. Even in the A and B socio-economic groups, credit (especially interest-free credit) will increase response levels and average order values.

If you do not wish to get involved with any kind of credit offer then choose your product, target audience, and pricing strategy with care.

Your catalogue starts to take shape

Back to our overall plan. Quite early on you will need some idea of how your catalogue will look and feel – it is, after all, an important aspect of your philosophy.

Now is the time to decide how many pages you will have in the catalogue, how many products will be on each page, how many ranges you will have, and how much space you will allocate to each range.

It may be only a start but if you do this now you will have taken one more important step on the road to success.

Product density, ie how many products per page, is a key issue. Here the best rule of thumb is to use the pricing guide. **The lower the prices of your products the more you should put on a page.** For higher priced items, lower the density.

Remember, though, that eye fatigue will set in if the pages are too busy, too densely packed – and you also have to fit in some copy! The technical term for this part of catalogue marketing is **pagination** which we return to shortly.

Shopping for products

Sooner or later it will be time to go shopping for products. And when you set off, remember **every** product must meet the stringent selection criteria laid down in your planning and positioning phase. Ideally try to find more products than you need, then let them fight it out for inclusion in your final range. Never select products that don't match your criteria just to fill up the space – reduce the number of pages in the catalogue instead.

Product scouring could be the subject of a book in its own right but for now we will stick to the basics. Here are three simple rules worth abiding by:

✔ Start by looking round the shops and at other catalogues to get a feel for the kind of products, designs, styles and colours that you think you want in your catalogue.

- ✔ Visit as many trade exhibitions as you can and meet as many suppliers as possible.
- ✔ Sample sparingly and don't try to make a supplier happy by sampling for the sake of it. It will only clutter your mind and build up the supplier's hopes.

Later on, when you're an established cataloguer, suppliers (some) will come to you. But there's still no substitute for getting out and about if you want to be first in the queue for innovative product.

Your catalogue needs a brand image

Branding a catalogue is no different from branding any other product – except that here the "product" is the catalogue in its entirety. There are no hard and fast rules but a number of elements, individually or in combination, help build a catalogue's image or personality. First, of course, comes the product selection, quality, and pricing which, as we have mentioned, help to define your target audience.

Close behind, in terms of importance, come the name, format, design, copy and illustrative style. We now look at each of these in terms of image. Later, we shall look at some of them again in terms of their persuasive effect.

The all-important name

Naming your catalogue goes a long way to creating your brand, and there are several routes you can follow. The three main ones are naming it after the owner or the location of the business, eg Boden (after Johnny Boden), Scotts of Stow, Kingshill Collection; using the range of products as a guide, eg Hold Everything, The Museum Collection, Past Times, Long Tall Sally; or choosing a generic or abstract title with appropriate connotations.

If you elect for a generic title, it is advisable to be evocative and to encapsulate one or two of the brand values in the name, eg Victoria's Secret (lingerie), Aspirations (housestyle), Racing Green (traditional casual clothing).

Your name may have the advantage of being unusual and memorable without describing your product or positioning it, in which case it may be useful to develop a strapline or positioning statement to support the brand, eg Divertimenti's "For people who love to cook."

Format

Before deciding on the format it is worth considering how the catalogue will be distributed. If inserting the whole catalogue in newspapers or magazines, your page size and number of pages will be critical. The same can be said of direct mail to cold lists. Here postage is a key element and therefore weight is very important. (See the advice given under inserts in Chapter 4.1.)

Another restriction is that many catalogues are based on economical print formats and become uniform in size. Nevertheless the paper can play a major role in differentiation and it may be worthwhile thinking about paper types, textures and colour.

Restrictions apart, it is as well to remember that **the format is probably the first thing recipients will notice about your catalogue**.

Good examples of format differentiation include Kingshill Collection's and Next Directory's hard-backed books, Rediscovered Original's brown paper stock, and the A3 page size favoured by Breck's Bulbs in the USA.

Format changes and unusual formats can be costly, even prohibitive. The best advice is to test. And before testing, rehearse your Profit & Loss calculations to see whether your ideas stand a chance of being viable. (See Chapter 2.5).

Design

The layout is the next opportunity to create individuality. But this too should follow as many of the golden rules as possible. The elements that can be mixed and matched for effect are photography versus illustrations, models versus still life, colour versus black and white; also typography and style of graphics.

Remember we're talking here about design as an image ingredient. Sometimes the requirements of a stylish design clash with the "rules" of selling, which calls for a delicate balancing act by the creative team!

Copy

Lands' End, still one of the finest examples of all that is good in cataloguing, has developed a copy style and tone which is the envy of many a writer. Not only does it sell the benefits of the product but it accomplishes the task in a way that creates its own unique positioning.

J Peterman, another fine catalogue out of the US, features the owner's idiosyncratic copywriting. A similar US catalogue was the late lamented Banana Republic. Our own Rediscovered Originals combines the best of both these books to stamp an indelible mark on the catalogue (which goes to show that you don't have to reinvent the wheel to be successful).

Models

Johnny Boden has used his friends (and pets!) as models in his catalogue to great effect, whilst Charles Tyrwhitt takes the opposite extreme using well-known professional sports personalities to model its Jermyn Street shirts.

Whatever tools you employ to differentiate your catalogue, be consistent, and make sure that each element plays a role in building the brand values that you want to communicate to your chosen target audience.

Examples of good catalogue design and pagination

Source: Graham Cundick, Viking Direct, 12.1.98

The more offer-driven the catalogue the busier the front cover should be

The lower the prices of your products the more you should put on a page.

Source: Graham Cundick, Viking Direct, 12.1.98

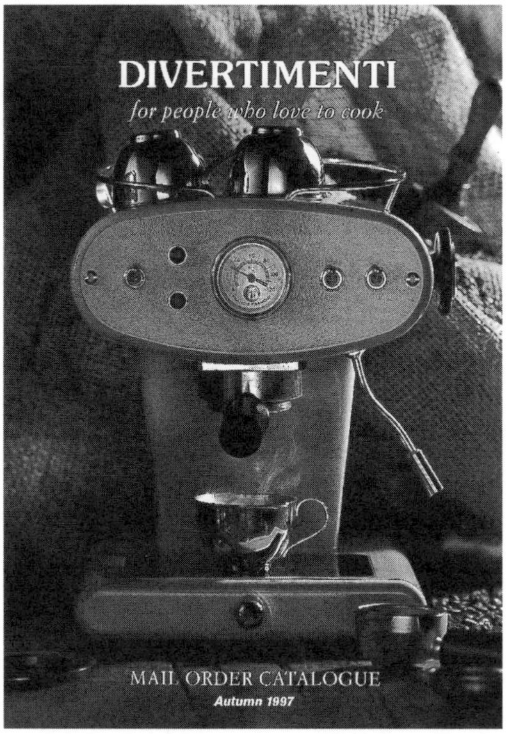

Source: Dean Lindell, Divertimenti (Mail Order) Ltd, 14.11.97

A strapline or positioning statement to support the brand

Source: Peter Higgins, Charles Tyrwhitt, 20.11.97

The more upmarket your positioning the more stylised the cover will be

Source: Karen Patterson, Racing Green, 3.11.97

For higher priced items lower the density

Source: Patti Millard, Historical Collections, 14.11.97

Naming the catalogue by using the range of products as a guide

Making your catalogue SELL

So far we have looked at aspects of your catalogue that will help it to develop a personality of its own – its brand character.

Now we must revisit some of those elements, only this time we are concerned with their influence on getting a response and increasing order values. What makes one catalogue sell and another fail?

Here the catalogue creator is engaged in a delicate and skilled balancing act. Not every design feature that lends distinction to a catalogue will be effective in terms of its selling power – in fact, "too much" design can be seriously detrimental. Before we go on to look at elements which induce customers to buy rather than just admire, look at the examples on the foregoing pages and see if you can deduce what it is that makes them all powerful sales channels.

Pagination – making every page work harder

Before you can start the creative process you must "construct" your catalogue page by page. We call this process "pagination" (although it is sometimes called merchandising). In effect we need a blueprint for the catalogue.

Pagination is the process of deciding several key factors that will affect the overall density, layout and pace of your catalogue, chiefly:

? Which product goes on which page?

? How much space should be allocated to each product?

? The sequence or position of each page in the catalogue.

The term pagination is obviously derived from "page" and we have used the word page in referring to each of the three main elements above. However, you are strongly advised to paginate in spreads (ie two facing pages). Pages are viewed as spreads by your customers and eye tracking research has proved categorically that the eye traverses the two pages as a single entity. It is even possible to view the front and back covers as a spread to get maximum consistency in the creative approach.

After product selection, pagination is the most important part of putting a successful catalogue together. Sadly it is also one of the least developed and most underrated of skills. The pagination will ultimately determine the overall performance of the catalogue especially with new or recently acquired customers.

Every catalogue has its "Hot spots"

One of the first and most important steps in the pagination is to decide which products are to occupy the HOT SPOTS. These are the most important parts of your catalogue. The hot spots are the same for all catalogues and are as follows:

- ✔ Outside front cover
- ✔ Outside back cover
- ✔ First inside spread
- ✔ Inside back spread
- ✔ The middle spread (if the catalogue is stapled)
- ✔ Opposite the order form

You should also consider the second and third spreads of larger catalogues, although their role is more educational in that they describe at a glance the range your catalogue contains.

The rule for hot spots is very simple. They **must** contain the products that are your best-sellers **and** match your brand and its positioning. A possible exception is the front cover which you may reserve for branding.

"Hot spots"

Products allocated to hot spots in your catalogue must be best-sellers and they must reflect and reinforce your brand and its positioning.

For established cataloguers following the above advice is easy: they can use their previous sales history as a guide to which products are the best-sellers.

But what about you, a new cataloguer? The best advice is again simple: be bold! Even if the products you allocate to hot spots don't turn out to be your best-sellers, hopefully you will have interested your readers and helped to establish your position in the market.

The only hot spot where the above rules may not apply is opposite the order form. The ideal use for this space is to include low value products that are relative impulse purchases, can be considered treats, or are "stock" items (eg batteries). These products will help build order values. (Take a look at the checkout of your local M&S or B&Q for good examples of how retailers use the same technique, ie placing low value treats close to the point of sale.)

How much space per product?

Again, deciding how much space to allocate to a product is easier if you have a detailed sales history. The simplest technique is to calculate the sales-to-space ratio for each product. This is a comparison of the percentage space a product has of the entire catalogue compared to its percentage of sales.

$$\frac{\%\text{ of sales}}{\%\text{ of catalogue space}} = \text{sales:space ratio}$$

For example, if a product attracts 7% of the revenue for a catalogue from only 3.5% of the space, the sales:space ratio is 2.

Any product where the result is "one" or greater has "taken its space". For products with a ratio of less than one the decision must be either to reduce the amount of space allocated to it or drop the product from the range altogether.

Of course, if you have no sales history, you will not be able to carry out this step. However, we have included it so that you will be in a position to calculate your own sales/space ratios at the first opportunity.

Q. If my product reaches the heady heights of a sales:space ratio of TWO or more, should I give it more space and prominence – because it is successful – or leave well alone because it is already doing more than its fair share?

A. On the surface leaving well alone is a sound argument, but it is wiser overall to exploit your successes to the full – possibly giving them even more space. This is especially effective if you are seeking new customers or trying to reactivate lapsed or dormant names.

In general, if you increase the space allocated to a successful product to match its previous sales, **the sales will grow at least in line with the increased space but, more often than not, will do even better**!

One factor that may modify your use of the sales:space formula in relation to hot spots is seasonality. You will naturally increase or reduce the space allocated to exceptionally seasonal products, eg lawnmowers, in line with the period in which the catalogue is issued. In such cases your sales:space calculations should refer to comparable seasons.

The need for a change of pace

Changing the space/product allocation helps to introduce a change of pace, and pace is synonymous with heightened interest. We use the term "pace" although we are literally trying to slow readers down.

Certain pages should be given the job of stopping the customer's eye flow and making him or her re-focus. Without these "stopper" pages it has been proved that a person can flip through an entire catalogue without the eye coming to rest.

One of the best ways to achieve pace is to dedicate entire pages to one product or photograph. Strong headlines, graphics or price points can achieve the same result. Your catalogue should contain a number of these pages spread evenly throughout.

Left- or right-hand pages? Despite some recommendations to the contrary, your stopper pages should be left- **and** right-hand pages. Many people, particularly those who are left-handed, start to browse from the back of the book and so see left-hand pages first. So use both sides of the spread for maximum effect.

"Heroes" are essential

Closely related to pace is the need for a "hero" on **every** spread. The hero is not a male model! – it is a dominant product that will provide a focal point for the eye, achieved by either the space given to it or its treatment. (See illustration of eye movements in Chapter 6.3.)

In this respect the design of a catalogue spread has much in common with that of, for example, a double-page advertisement. In fact, the early Scotcade catalogues were compiled by binding together dozens of full-page ads exactly as they had appeared in the Sunday supplements.

Make it easy!

While you are striving to achieve maximum impact and interest, don't overlook the need for the copy and order information to be accessible. Put obstacles in the way of prospective customers and you will reduce the overall response.

Remember, many people use catalogues for convenience, ie they save time. Do not reduce this power by making any part difficult to understand. **Make it easy to select and order from** – that's another golden rule.

Front cover: Sales counter or picture window?

Now, at last, we're ready to start the final design. We start, logically enough, with the front cover: Hot spot No 1.

There are endless arguments about the cover. Should you sell from it? Should it contain products? Should it reflect the season? etc, etc. Only one rule applies: **the cover must get your customer, or prospective customer, to look inside**. If your cover does not achieve this simple objective you don't have a chance.

Above all, the cover should reflect the overall positioning of your business. If you are in the discount market then perhaps a very strong offer backed by a graphic suggesting more savings inside. The Viking Direct office supplies catalogue often features the irrepressible Ian Helford pointing at some special offer, sometimes with an ink-jetted personalised message. Scotts of Stow, on the other hand, settles for a mood shot which encapsulates its brand positioning and aspirational range. Variations in set design and accessorising can set the seasonal tone.

The main point about the cover is that it should get your message across as quickly and as relevantly as possible, and not mislead your customer in any way. The more offer-driven the catalogue the busier the front cover should be. Alternatively, the more upmarket your positioning the more stylised the cover will be, with clear but understated messages. Good examples are Racing Green and Viking Direct, both successful despite their opposite styles.

And don't ignore the back cover. It's also a hot spot, remember. A good idea, as we have said, is to design it as if it were part of a spread along with the front cover.

The inside front cover – Hot spot No 2

Use the inside front cover to introduce yourself and your catalogue. Start the process of building a relationship with your customer by stating your principles, benefits and levels of service. Tell your customer how to order and, more importantly, how to return goods. Surprisingly, an open returns policy will have little effect on returns rates but it will help build confidence and generate more orders.

The rest of the first spread should provide a real guide of what the customer can expect from the remainder of the catalogue. Remember the rules for hot spots!

Is an index necessary?

If you have a large number of pages and a wide range of products then include at least one index. This can be an informal table of contents in the front of the book or a fully detailed index at the back.

There is no hard and fast rule but 64 pages and above would seem to be the point where you should consider this full indexing approach. Obviously, if your catalogue is also a reference work, as with many business-to-business catalogues, indexing and cross-referencing are vital.

Creating the body of your catalogue

Designing the pages and spreads of a catalogue obeys most of the principles of designing good direct response advertisements. One of the features of a modern catalogue is that every product is treated as a mini-ad in its own right.

It is not the purpose of this chapter to usurp the role of the creative chapters to come, but it is worth picking out some of the more important guidelines for designing and writing pages that sell.

It is also important to highlight any differences in the ways that ads and catalogues are prepared, so here we go.

How catalogues WORK

We start this section right away with a difference between advertisements and catalogues.

Whereas an advertisement is usually geared to persuading the prospect to agree to a single "Yes", success for a catalogue depends on obtaining a large number of smaller "yesses". Together these add up to the one big "Yes" – the order.

But in most other respects your reader is simply browsing through a series of ads – each with its own headline, illustration, proposition, benefits and price information.

And each entry works like an ad:

✔ The picture/headline stops the eye

✔ The headline/picture confirms the first interest

✔ The copy convinces with features and benefits

✔ The terms/offer close the sale

Of course, designing catalogue pages (and ads) is far more complex than that. Every product is a different problem. But there are some universal Do's and Don'ts as shown in the checklist opposite.

In general the following hierarchy exists in the way photographs are viewed:

Colour before black and white
Large before small
People before things
Children before adults
Portraits before figure shots

So a large colour portrait of a child will gain far more attention than a small black and white shot of a widget.

Make sure it's ENJOYABLE

Reading a catalogue should be an enjoyable and relaxing experience. Browsing in the comfort of the home is one of the real pleasures of catalogue shopping and the final product of your creative process should fulfil this expectation.

And when the customers have found themselves interested in a product, remember to make it **easy** for them to order.

Enjoyment plus ease are two more keys to successful catalogues.

Do's and don'ts of catalogue design

✔	Do vary the size of each shot and mix cut-outs with squared-ups; start the process when planning your pagination, then use this as your guide.
✘	Don't have all your shots the same size or your catalogue will quickly become boring – you will have failed to introduce "pace".
✔	Do use words to sell your product. The picture tells only half the story, make the copy do the rest.
✘	Don't assume that your customers know more than they do. Get across all the features and benefits as well as the technical details.
✔	Do use benefit headlines for either individual products or the range of products on a spread.
✔	Do start each copy block with the main benefit of the product.
✔	Do use an appropriate tone of voice for the target audience, from street cred for kids to plain English for adults. Correctly used, tone will add authority to your proposition.
✔	Do choose typefaces and sizes that are easy to read. Consider the age of your customer when making these decisions.
✔	Do make sure that copy is adjacent to the picture or use indexing to help your customer match pictures to copy.
✔	Do consider putting picture and copy in a self-contained box if you have a high product density.
✘	Don't skimp on photography. It is easy to look at photography as a commodity but the most successful cataloguers take every shot seriously. Use lighting and props to best advantage.
✔	Do use models liberally (even if they are just friends, relations or colleagues). People add interest to a book.
✔	Do keep restating and reinforcing your service benefits and calls to action, but vary the words and layout from spread to spread.

Finding customers for your new catalogue

Too many cataloguers put all their efforts into compiling their book and leave too little time, energy and resource for the vital step of finding the prospects who will read it.

Customer acquisition is the subject of many other chapters in this Guide, and so we shall not dwell on it here.

Instead we shall outline the essential building blocks of customer acquisition so that you can refer to them elsewhere.

One stage or 2?

There are three basic ways of recruiting new customers to your catalogue:

Two-stage cataloguing – The initial action required from your prospect is an enquiry for a catalogue or information pack.

One-stage cataloguing – Here you are looking for an order as the first transaction. One-stage cataloguing usually entails delivering your catalogue to prospects by mail or with a newspaper or magazine.

One-stage product ad – Here you are attempting to introduce a catalogue prospect by direct-selling a representative product, usually via a press ad or insert.

So how to decide between the above options?

The factors which will determine the most effective method for you include:

- ✔ Your business objectives
- ✔ The size of your catalogue
- ✔ The maturity of your brand
- ✔ The maturity of your product

Take business objectives. Recruiting good long-term customers costs money. If you are not in business for the long haul then one-stage is the only realistic option open to you. There's nothing wrong with that. But one-stage advertising rather than employing a catalogue is almost certainly a better option for immediate returns.

Be warned, however, all types of one-stage selling are fraught with difficulty. The chance of getting your product/offer (or mix) right first go could be as low as 20–1. But if you're sure you're not looking for long-term customers with high lifetime values, so be it.

One-stage cataloguing for immediate results

One-stage cataloguing describes the process whereby you put your catalogue direct into your prospect's hands without their having expressly requested you to do so.

One-stage catalogues are usually best inserted loose into selected media. This may be the whole catalogue (subject to size/weight limits set by the host media) or a condensed "prospecting" version – sometimes little more than a flyer.

Catalogues can also be distributed by direct mail as a recruitment method, but this practice is still in its infancy in the UK owing to the lack of good lists, the cost of list rental and postage, and the general scepticism of the target audience. Don't rule this route out, however, but keep it to a minimum in the overall mix – and compare your results closely with more established recruitment methods.

Evaluating a one-stage catalogue

You can easily develop a simplified model for one-stage cataloguing, often referred to as a cost per sale model, as the following example shows:

One-stage catalogue

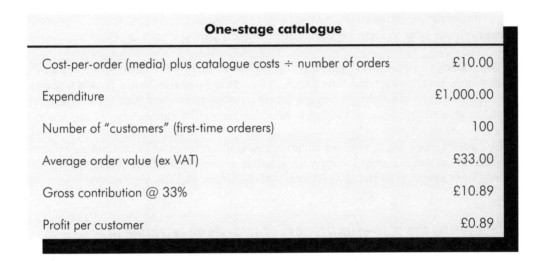

Cost-per-order (media) plus catalogue costs ÷ number of orders	£10.00
Expenditure	£1,000.00
Number of "customers" (first-time orderers)	100
Average order value (ex VAT)	£33.00
Gross contribution @ 33%	£10.89
Profit per customer	£0.89

Of course, if your bottom line figure shows a loss, then you will have invested in acquiring your first-time buyer, making the outcome similar to that described overleaf for two-stage cataloguing.

Unearthing prospects via direct advertising sales

Another way of building a list of prospects is via direct product offers, usually in the press, or with inserts, or increasingly using DRTV (off-the-screen).

The rules for the design and placement of one-stage sales ads have a lot in common with those for two-stage enquiry ads, and so mostly we shall leave these issues to other authors. Basically we are talking "mail order" advertising at this point.

One of the key rules for off-the-page, or any form of one-stage recruitment where you don't use your entire catalogue, is to **make sure that the products you offer are truly representative of your full range**. You may find a product that performs exceptionally well off-the-page, but if it sets up the wrong expectation of your range – or brings in the wrong target audience – the long-term benefits will be lost. The same goes for the pricing policy for your offer. The ideal is to use the price at which the product is offered in the catalogue.

You could go a stage further and use the same trannie and copy, as close to the original as possible. This will guarantee that you bring in the right customers and set the right expectation for your catalogue as a whole.

Whichever method you use, please make sure that you keep trying a mix of media. What is successful today may not work tomorrow as more and more cataloguers use the same methods, media and direct mail lists as you. This is cyclical business and the clever operator will have moved back into space advertising whilst the followers are still competing in a highly competitive insert environment, and vice versa.

Remember, if you think you'd prefer the one-stage option and **then** decide you'd like a longer-term relationship after all, your objectives may clash. Even though you may attract people to buy from your first catalogue, **ideally you should still treat them as prospects until they have placed subsequent orders**.

Two-stage cataloguing and the long-term customer

Avid users of this Guide will know by now that the future of direct marketing lies in customer development – and the catalogue business is one of the best possible examples of how to form relationships between yourself and the customer.

Two-stage recruitment is definitely the preferred option for companies launching a new book as the start of a long game. The newness of the brand plus the genuine inquisitiveness of catalogue buyers for new catalogues often leads to excellent results, although a word of caution follows the sample calculations below.

By two-stage, as explained, we mean starting the relationship by inviting customers to **actively** request or enquire for your catalogue – that's the first stage. They now become prospects in the true meaning of the word, but not yet customers.

Measuring the cost-effectiveness of two-stage recruitment

For your two-stage catalogue to be successful overall, it will need to be successful at a number of specific points during each transaction. These are as follows:

- ✔ Cost of enquiry
- ✔ Cost of conversion process (catalogue, literature, handling)
- ✔ Enquiry-to-order conversion percentage
- ✔ Average order value
- ✔ Gross profit/contribution

All five factors must work together and considerable care should be taken when planning your campaign. Higher than anticipated numbers of enquiries may lead to a lower cost-per-enquiry, but almost always to a lower conversion rate. If your catalogue packs are expensive, overall you may be out of pocket.

A reasonable objective should be to breakeven, the contribution from the first order covering all the recruitment costs including sending out the packs.

On the facing page is a simple calculation to demonstrate the principle, showing a shortfall or "loss" per prospect recruited.

However, although we may term the last figure the "loss" per customer, another way of looking at it is that we have paid a sum (in the first calculation opposite, £2.25) to make contact with a first-rate prospect; we have **invested** in that prospect.

Two-stage catalogue

Cost per enquiry	£2.20
Pack cost	£0.50
Cost per fulfilled enquiry	£2.70
Cost per 1,000 enquiries	£2,700.00
Conversion % = 10%	
No of customers @ 10%	100
Cost per customer	£27.00
Average first order value (ex VAT)	£75.00
Gross contribution @ 33% of sales	£24.75
Loss per customer	(£2.25)

Now let's look at the same model where enquiries come in at half the cost but with a resultant pro-rata fall in conversion (from 10% to 5%).

Two-stage catalogue (enquiries at half cost)

Cost per enquiry	£1.10
Pack cost	£0.50
Cost per fulfilled enquiry	£1.60
Cost per 1,000 enquiries	£1,600.00
Conversion % = 5%	
No of customers @ 5%	50
Cost per customer	£32.00
Average first order value (ex VAT)	£75.00
Gross contribution @ 33% of sales	£24.75
Loss per customer	(£7.25)

We cut the price of enquiries (eg possibly by offering a larger incentive to enquire) but because conversions fell, we are now spending £7.25 to acquire a customer instead of £2.25.

You can create models like the above, using this basic spreadsheet approach, to forecast the probable effect of changing any element in the mix – always a better option than trying to assess the outcome of every variation in an expensive and time-consuming test, as the profit and loss chapter explains (see Chapter 2.5).

What affects the costs of the various stages?

The most important cost in all the models above is almost certainly **the cost of an enquiry** (or first sale).

The speed with which this cost rises will depend on many factors, chiefly:

- ✔ **The overall size of your target market**, ie the number of prospects (also the activity of competitors) within the marketplace. This will depend to a great extent on your product type/range and your positioning.
- ✔ **How much you spend and how quickly.** Your objective may be to drip-feed your catalogue to your market over a long period – or you may go for maximum coverage early on, which means it will reach saturation sooner.
- ✔ **Your media plan.** The number and reach of your core media and the way media are planned and bought are fundamental elements in your cost structure.
- ✔ **Your creative prowess.** The direct response know-how employed in your ads and catalogue, including the use of incentives.

How and when to incentivise?

Incentivising the first order with progressively more valuable incentives (eg for order size), normally proves the best course of action. It is not recommended to incentivise the conversion pack as this usually means giving something away to people who would have ordered anyway.

The subject of incentives is dealt with elsewhere in this Guide (see Chapters 1.3 and 7.6).

However, regardless almost of how hard you try to combat its effects, **the law of diminishing returns will set in**. Then, in the time-honoured way direct marketers do, you must return to square one and rethink your plan for the season ahead.

A cataloguer's perspective on advertising media

Where possible, to announce your new consumer catalogue, use space advertising in daily and weekend national press, including colour supplements, and inserts in specialist press and periodicals of all kinds. You'll find plenty elsewhere in this Guide about the use of two-stage media (see especially Chapter 4.1).

Specialist interest (eg hobby) magazines are notoriously expensive for two-stage advertising, giving high cost-per-enquiry figures. One explanation is that people do not like to deform their favourite monthly mag by cutting out the coupon on your ad. So they wait until they have finished reading the magazine, by which time they have forgotten all about you! The telephone is certainly helping but we are not there yet for many product categories.

Direct mail is the other main method for two-stage recruitment but its success will be determined by the size of your prospective catalogue as the conversion figure required to breakeven will be quite high.

DRTV is also being used by many of the large catalogue houses for two-stage with national satellite coverage being the main media used.

Remember to follow up enquiries – soon!

You might think it surprising, but some would-be cataloguers store enquiries for months before doing anything with them. Wrong!

Once you have the names of your prospects it is vital that you have a follow-up programme in place. You have paid to get the name and address so you must now get as many prospects as possible to **order** from your catalogue.

The attrition rate on prospects is very high and you probably have a maximum of six months to convert them to buyers before they are no longer a cost-effective source and must be re-recruited.

And keep on mailing!

Customer development must be the most neglected area of the catalogue industry. Having paid good money to recruit new customers it is surprising how many companies do not make the most of their customers. They mail far too infrequently and do not employ tactical incentivisation to reactivate lapsing and dormant customers.

There is a real tendency for inexperienced cataloguers to mail their file only once with a new catalogue in the belief that people will not respond a second time to the same offer. Providing that you have a wide enough range and your product has a reasonable repeat purchase cycle, eg clothing, then you may be able to mail certain segments of your database up to three times with the same material before it is no longer cost-effective. This means that even if you produce only two catalogues per year you could mail the best performing segments up to six times a year or every eight weeks or so. This is the minimum for the best segments of your file.

Segmenting the best customers

How do you segment your file so that offers and messages can be accurately targeted to the customers most likely to buy?

There are many models, promotional scoring and statistical techniques, available to help segmentation and targeting, but the basic principle of recency, frequency and monetary value takes some beating and should be the starting point for selections.

Remember the golden rule: RFM (or RFV)
Recency, Frequency, (Monetary) Value.

Monetary value as an indicator of future custom

Let's take monetary value first. Monetary value can be looked at in two ways: total lifetime sales and lifetime average order values. Obviously a long-term customer will have had the opportunity to build high sales. **But new customers with the potential to become good customers can often be identified by the size of their first order.**

Typically, if the first order value is greater than the business average order value, then the customer is likely to go on to be a good customer. Similarly, if the first order is lower than the business average, then the newcomer is less likely to go on to be a high-worth customer.

Other factors can be used to refine this initial profile but you are recommended to get the simple things right before moving on.

Recency as an indicator of future custom

Recency must be overlaid with frequency to optimise selections and mailing frequency. Multi-buyers are more likely to buy again than single buyers who have gone six months without a repeat order. **In fact, it is quite likely that single buyers who have not purchased within nine to twelve months of their first order will not buy again.** (High-value multibuyers may still be worth mailing up to four years after their last order.)

Your primary objective, therefore, must be to convert single to multibuyers within six months using incentives and other tactics as necessary. This is absolutely vital if the customers were recruited by a one-stage strategy, eg off-the-page advertising.

As mentioned, off-the-page purchasers should be considered as very hot prospects, **and not as customers**, until you have received a second order from a mailing or catalogue. First-time buyers from a cold catalogue mailing are far more likely to buy again than off-the-page buyers and your communication programme should reflect this. One explanation must be that they have shown a liking for catalogue buying.

How often to mail a customer segment?

Once established, active buyers are the source of most, if not all, the profits of any mail order business, and it is therefore essential that they are mailed as frequently as possible to generate profit. It is not cost-effective to keep producing new catalogues, the same material can be mailed more than once. Another alternative is to change a small number of pages, eg the covers, and to change the sequence of the remainder to give the catalogue a fresh look.

The way to measure the profitability of each segment is to identify one factor that eliminates variables and gives an accurate, unweighted comparison. Typically, you can use a marketing cost-to-sales ratio. Or, ideally, use a return-on-investment index that reflects the marketing cost as a factor of the gross contribution from each segment. The latter gives you a guide to the actual profits being generated and the contribution to fixed overheads, etc (see Chapters 2.4 and 2.5).

The best way to assess the optimum mailing frequency is to identify cells where the actual performance of the mailing is at least twice as good as the "breakeven measure", eg an ROI index of 200 plus, or a marketing cost-to-sales ratio of less than 10%. **As a rule of thumb, a re-mail will only produce about 50% of the original mailing so any segment that did not achieve a better than twice the target will not be profitable if mailed again.** On the other hand, if the original mailing index was, say, over 400, then this group can be mailed twice more with the same material, allowing for a 50% drop-off with each mailing.

This simple methodology, plus constant testing of pack elements and offers, will ensure that you are mailing the file for optimum profits.

What about non-actives?

Non-active buyers, those who have not ordered for, say, twelve months, should be viewed as a recruitment source. Almost certainly you will be able to reactivate a large number of these at a far lower cost than recruiting totally new customers from outside. **Always mail as deeply as you can into the dormant part of your database before spending money on external recruitment.**

Compare your decision-making criteria, eg ROI, with that of outside sources to decide where best to deploy your recruitment budget.

Summing up

Catalogue marketing is complex and the outline above has given only a brief guide to the strategies and components that make up a successful operation.

The ten main guidelines, however, are these:

- ✔ Decide your target audience and product niche.
- ✔ Develop your strategic plan and stick to it.
- ✔ Do not select products to fill space, reduce the amount of space instead.
- ✔ Use every creative technique to develop your unique proposition and build a hard-working catalogue.
- ✔ Do not put any obstacle in the way of ordering.
- ✔ Recruit as cost-effectively as possible and use lapsed customers as much as possible.
- ✔ Set exactly the right expectation in your recruitment programme, one- or two-stage, or you will generate instant dormancy.
- ✔ Treat off-the-page buyers as prospects not customers.
- ✔ Mail your active buyer file as often as possible.
- ✔ Incentivise to achieve specific segment marketing objectives.

For advice on the physical production of catalogues, including resourcing and costing, refer to Chapter 7.5 in this Guide.

Chapter 4.7

Posters: Ready for a direct marketing role?

This chapter includes:

- ❑ **Traditional role of poster advertising**
- ❑ **Posters' unique advantages**
- ❑ **Outdoor advertising and direct marketing**
- ❑ **Can posters generate direct response?**
- ❑ **Available research data and sources**
- ❑ **How posters are bought and sold**
- ❑ **Main poster sizes and contractors**
- ❑ **Non-standard poster opportunities**

There are two major advertising media that have not so far earned a place in the hearts and minds of most direct marketers. They are posters (more precisely known in the industry as "outdoor" advertising) and the cinema. One of them, posters, may well be poised for a breakthrough any time soon.

In fact, posters have already been successfully used by direct marketers. There is the case of an environmental organisation which used posters to generate interest in its work. The content was a telephone number and a succinct one-line message – and therein lies the success of outdoor advertising in producing direct leads: simplicity.

In this brief résumé, Ian Prager sets out some basic data around which the alert direct marketer may wish to do a spot of lateral thinking.

New in this edition. The information in this chapter was not included in the first edition of this Guide.

Ian Prager, Managing Director, Prager & Partners

Ian is Managing Director of Prager & Partners, a media independent specialising in communication planning for direct marketing clients. The company was set up in December 1995 and has a client list which includes Eastern Electricity, COI, Legal & General, Thomson Holidays and Pizza Hut.

Before setting up Prager & Partners, Ian was at CIA for 16 years, the last 8 of which were as Managing Director of CIA Direct.

Ian sits on the Response Council of the DMA and regularly lectures for the IDM.

Ian Prager
Managing Director
Prager & Partners Limited
Thames Wharf
Rainville Road
London W6 9HT
Tel: 0171-610 1021

Chapter 4.7

Posters: Ready for a direct marketing role?

Outdoor advertising's traditional role

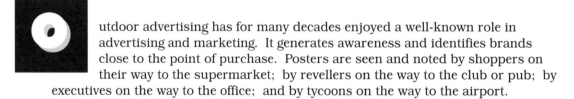

Outdoor advertising has for many decades enjoyed a well-known role in advertising and marketing. It generates awareness and identifies brands close to the point of purchase. Posters are seen and noted by shoppers on their way to the supermarket; by revellers on the way to the club or pub; by executives on the way to the office; and by tycoons on the way to the airport.

Their efficacy derives from their impact and simplicity, and from the fact that they are literally unavoidable.

The unique advantages of posters

Traditionally, posters are deployed by media planners to augment other media, chiefly press and television.

In brand advertising speak they offer:

- ✔ Opportunity to reach elusive audiences, eg light TV viewers, ABC1s and young people.

- ✔ Increased "share of voice", eg over advertisers who do not use or dominate the medium.
- ✔ A means of augmenting the cover and frequency of other forms of advertising.
- ✔ The media-multiplier effect, whereby prospects see more messages in more places, making the advertiser appear more familiar and more "accessible".
- ✔ Continuity: visibility is constant throughout the duration of a campaign.
- ✔ Regional flexibility – almost all sites (panels) are postcoded and many can be purchased individually.

Outdoor and the direct marketer

Posters offer direct marketers much the same benefits as they do other advertisers, and which modern direct marketer is not aware of the advantages of brand awareness in boosting responses to a specific direct marketing programme?

In this respect, posters can be, and are, used as support media (discussed elsewhere in this Guide), and their effects must be measured and costed in exactly the same way.

For example, the cost and response-enhancing effect of posters in a specific geographic area could easily be assessed in relation to, say, the boost they give to a door-to-door, radio or TV campaign confined to that area.

But what of response itself – can posters generate response? And should they ever be used for this purpose alone?

The answer is: yes, they can initiate response in their own right – as the Massachusetts case has ably demonstrated (see final paragraph of this chapter). In some situations (eg in reaching commuters) they can be an extremely effective method, although case studies are thin on the ground.

It is probable that if one could research responses generated by "Tube" posters, for example for such services as secretarial colleges, one would unearth numerous advertisers who are reliant on outdoor advertising to generate direct and measurable response. Unfortunately, this data is not currently available.

What research is available?

The outdoor advertising industry has historically researched its audiences and achievements much as do traditional awareness advertisers, ie in terms of "opportunities to see", noting scores, attitude surveys, and the like.

Needless to say, it would further the industry's growth among direct marketers were it to research and publish data on the measurable direct responses generated solely by outdoor advertising.

Research currently available hinges largely on that conducted by Postar Ltd, which covers roadside panels of varying size, chiefly 6-sheet, 48-sheet, and 96-sheet (see size data below).

Postar's research covers such factors as:

- ✔ **Visibility** – eye movements of drivers, passengers and pedestrians are analysed and reported on.
- ✔ **Coverage** – number of panels needed to achieve specific coverage and frequency targets, and how cover builds over time (80% of cover is built within 7 days).
- ✔ **Lighting** – effect of illumination and daylight hours on poster efficacy.
- ✔ **Socio-economics** – breakdown of people passing/exposed to poster sites, eg:

All adults	100
15–34-year-olds	111
All women	95
ABC1 adults	107

Postar Ltd can be contacted at Outdoor Advertising Association, Summit House, 27 Sale Place, London W2 1YR, Tel: 0171-298 8035

How posters are bought and sold

Posters are bought and sold according to size and location of sites. Individual sites can be purchased, known as "line-by-line" buying. Buying posters is best done through a specialist.

The most common method is to buy packages aimed at specific audiences, such as Family Pack (aimed at women with young children) costing £157,500 (approx £350 per 48-sheet site), or by region/city. The usual minimum period is four weeks. However, sites can be bought for a two-week period. Material is usually required two weeks prior to posting.

The main poster sizes

96-sheet	–	40' x 10'
64-sheet	–	26'8" x 10'
48-sheet	–	20' x 10'
32-sheet	–	13'4" x 10'
16-sheet	–	6'8" x 10'
12-sheet	–	10' x 5'
6-sheet	–	1.2m x 1.8m
4-sheet	–	3'4" x 5'

The contractors to contact

Three contractors own 60% of all 48-sheet and 96-sheet poster sites: More O'Ferral Adshel Ltd, Mills & Allen Ltd, and Maiden Outdoor Advertising Ltd, have equal shares of the 96-sheet sites.

Site inspection services

All campaigns should be inspected by an independent company to check that sites have been completely displayed. The main site inspection company is Site Reports, but also in the market are Site Seers, Checkers and Adcheck, the latter specialising in the inspection of transport advertising.

Site reports will produce a report grouping errors by their severity, as follows:

Group One errors are:

- ✗ not posted
- ✗ wrong design
- ✗ not in situ

Group Two errors include graffiti, fly posting, etc. These are not automatically creditable if the contractor rectifies within 3 working days.

Other outdoor advertising opportunities

The tables below and opposite briefly list other non-roadside types of poster site, any of which may have particular relevance to specific direct marketers.

For more information practitioners are advised to contact an outdoor advertising consultancy or widely versed advertising agency.

Non-standard outdoor opportunities
Special sites
Leisure centres – 4-sheet and 6-sheet
Pharmacists – 2,500 window sites
Supermarkets – trolleys at selected stores
Pub washrooms – 500 pubs in Granada area
Petrol stations – 6-sheet on BP garage forecourts
Petrol nozzles
Inside golf holes
Slide projections onto selected buildings

Transport advertising opportunities

Transport advertising excluding taxis

Interactive displays

Colour trains

Station floor media

Indicator boards

Taxi advertising

Two main contractors – Taxi Media
– Barnett Taxi Advertising

Range of sizes/opportunities available: liveried cars (whole car treatment); exterior door and double door panels; interior panels; tip-up seats; inserts in bulkheads.

Available in most UK cities, although the medium is at its strongest in London.

✔ Particularly good at covering London's West End and City
✔ Good at covering businessmen and decision-makers.

In recent years liveried cars have become popular. Current examples:

✔	United Airlines	170 taxis
✔	Capital Radio	100 taxis
✔	Yellow Pages	50 taxis
✔	Evening Standard	50 taxis

Cost of painted taxi: £6,000 per year.

The need for simplicity

The Massachusetts Department of Environmental Protection used its poster sites to display a bold telephone number with an invitation to the public to "Go ahead and report the scum" – ie anything (or anyone!) contravening its laws.

You can see how difficult it is to induce a response in so few words – but that is the challenge facing direct marketers who wish to break down yet another frontier. It's got to be worth a try.

Index

E

F

G

H

I

K

L

M

N

O

P

T

U

V

W

Tell us what you think of The Direct Marketing Guide

Feedback from readers of the first edition was a driving force in adapting and updating this Guide.

Please help us to continue to improve it by writing your comments in the space below. Then post the card to us – it's free!

Thank you.

____

____

____

____

Your details (optional)

Title: ________ First Name: ________________ Surname: ________________

Company Name : ________________________

Telephone No: ________________________

Complete NOW to order more Guides or to request information on The IDM ...

The Institute of Direct Marketing is Europe's No1 for direct marketing education, training and information. If you wish to purchase the Guide or learn more about any of our services, please tick the relevant box(es) and return this FREEPOST card.

- ☐ Order form for The Direct Marketing Guide
- ☐ Membership of The IDM
- ☐ Professional Training – Short Courses
- ☐ Tailored In-Company Training
- ☐ Qualifications: Diploma in Direct Marketing
- ☐ Qualifications: Call Centre Management Certificate
- ☐ Direct Marketing Books and Videos
- ☐ The MM Information Centre
- ☐ The IDM Education Programme

Title: (Mr/Mrs/Miss/Ms) First Name: ________________

Surname: ________________________

Job Title: ________________________

Are you a member of The IDM Yes/No

Company: ________________________

Address: ________________________

____

____

Postcode: ________________________

Tel: ________________ Fax: ________________

E-mail : ________________________

DMG39K

Complete NOW to order more Guides or to request information on The IDM ...

The Institute of Direct Marketing is Europe's No1 for direct marketing education, training and information. If you wish to purchase the Guide or learn more about any of our services, please tick the relevant box(es) and return this FREEPOST card.

- ☐ Order form for The Direct Marketing Guide
- ☐ Membership of The IDM
- ☐ Professional Training – Short Courses
- ☐ Tailored In-Company Training
- ☐ Qualifications: Diploma in Direct Marketing
- ☐ Qualifications: Call Centre Management Certificate
- ☐ Direct Marketing Books and Videos
- ☐ The MM Information Centre
- ☐ The IDM Education Programme

Title: (Mr/Mrs/Miss/Ms) First Name: ________________

Surname: ________________________

Job Title: ________________________

Are you a member of The IDM Yes/No

Company: ________________________

Address: ________________________

____

____

Postcode: ________________________

Tel: ________________ Fax: ________________

E-mail : ________________________

DMG39K

The institute of Direct Marketing

DIRECT MARKETING GUIDE – FEEDBACK
The Institute of Direct Marketing
FREEPOST
1 Park Road
TEDDINGTON
Middlesex
TW11 8BR

The institute of Direct Marketing

REQUEST FOR INFORMATION
The Institute of Direct Marketing
FREEPOST
1 Park Road
TEDDINGTON
Middlesex
TW11 8BR

The institute of Direct Marketing

REQUEST FOR INFORMATION
The Institute of Direct Marketing
FREEPOST
1 Park Road
TEDDINGTON
Middlesex
TW11 8BR